Analyzing Florida's Constitution

OTHER BOOKS BY THIS AUTHOR

Florida Elements of an Action

Florida Municipal Law and Practice

Florida Workers' Compensation

Florida Insurance Law (with co-authors)

Analyzing Florida's Constitution

Patrick John McGinley

OF THE FLORIDA BAR AND DISTRICT OF COLUMBIA BAR

CAROLINA ACADEMIC PRESS

Durham, North Carolina

ISBN   978-1-5310-1715-6
e-ISBN 978-1-5310-1716-3
LCCN   2020938274

Carolina Academic Press
700 Kent Street
Durham, NC 27701
Telephone (919) 489-7486
Fax (919) 493-5668
www.cap-press.com

Printed in the United States of America

To my wife Bernadette,
To our children Patrick and Madeleine,
To the Blessed Virgin Mary, Mother of God,
but above all,
To our Lord and Savior, Jesus Christ.

Contents

Table of Cases

Analyzing Florida's Constitution

Chapter 1

Federalism and State Constitutions

A. Why Do States Have Constitutions?

If you are familiar with the U.S. Constitution, then you know it to be the supreme law of the land. You know it to be applicable everywhere in the United States of America: throughout all 50 states, all sixteen territories, and the District of Columbia. You know it to be an adequate source of authority for striking down unconstitutional legislation or government action. With the U.S. Constitution being so broadly applicable and powerful, why do states have their own constitutions?

The historian could answer that states had constitutions before the enactment of the U.S. Constitution. Historians tell us that the similarities between some language in the U.S. Constitution and some language in the constitutions of the original thirteen colonies is because the federal constitution was inspired by the colonies' constitutions. The historian could also answer that before the U.S. Supreme Court's incorporation doctrine made the U.S. Constitution's Bill of Rights applicable to the states, state constitutions were the primary source of individual rights. The historian's answers tell us how state constitutions arose and what purpose they served in the past. The historian's answers do not tell us why state constitutions persist in the modern era.

The pragmatist could answer that states have constitutions as an organic source of law for establishing state and local governments. Indeed, the source and structure of any given state's legislative, executive, and judicial branches of state government is found in its state constitution. The pragmatist's answer describes a role that state constitutions play in our federal republic. The pragmatist's answer does not tell us why states desire a separate constitution to address issues that could be addressed uniformly in the federal constitution or in federal laws.

Perhaps the sincerest answer why state constitutions exist in the modern era is the human need for subsidiarity. Subsidiarity, as described by Saint Pope John Paul II's 1991 encyclical *Centesimus Annus*, means that "a community of a higher order should not interfere in the internal life of a community of a lower order, depriving the latter of its functions, but rather should support it in case of need and help to coordinate its activity with the activities of the rest of society, always with a view to the common good." Stated somewhat differently, subsidiarity means that local problems sometimes require local solutions. Subsidiarity rejects the notion that all problem-solving power should be vested only with the highest sovereign or federal authority. Subsidiarity respects the proper role in problem solving by states, counties, and cities, and where appropriate, by non-governmental organizations, private industry, religious institutions, corporations, charities, and families. Elements of subsidiarity may be present in governmental structures, such as its explicit reference in Article 5 of the Treaty on European Union. Although the word subsidiarity may not appear as explicitly in the text of any U.S. state's constitution, state constitutions serve the purposes of subsidiarity when they empower state and local governments to solve state and local problems. People of good will crave a voice in solving the issues facing their communities, and they deserve to be heard. Subsidiary brings government's problem-solving power closer to the people and increases their opportunity to be heard.

One benefit of subsidiarity in the context of subnational constitutional law is the ability to experiment on a regional level with new or expanded rights for the region's citizens. What if a given state wanted to experiment with granting its citizens not fewer but more rights than those provided by the U.S. Constitution? It is not difficult to imagine the benefits of allowing states to do so. "It is one of the happy incidents of the federal system that a single courageous state may, if its citizens choose, serve as a laboratory; and try novel social and economic experiments without risk to the rest of the country." *New State Ice Co. v. Liebmann*, 285 U.S. 262, 311 (1932) (Brandeis, J., dissenting). The existence of the national constitution would guarantee that the region's citizens do not have fewer rights than the nation, even while the subnational constitution experiments with granting greater rights to the citizens of that region. Commentators call this concept the "laboratory of democracy."

This concept of a "laboratory of democracy" contemplates that a state constitution can be a source for state-by-state expansion of fundamental rights and constitutional protection while federal law serves as a "floor" below which no state may sink. A given state's citizens continue to benefit from the full panoply of federal rights, while also benefitting from their own state's experiments in granting even greater rights.

Florida's supreme court fully embraced this concept in decisions such as *State v. Horwitz*, 191 So. 3d 429 (Fla. 2016). Donna Horowitz's silence was used against her by the prosecution, which the trial court agreed it could do under the U.S. Constitution as interpreted by *Miranda v. Arizona*, 384 U.S. 436 (1966) and its progeny. The U.S. Constitution was inadequate to protect Donna Horowitz. Could Florida's constitution provide greater protection?

State v. Horwitz

Supreme Court of Florida, 2016
191 So. 3d 429

. . . The issue before the Court is whether, under article I, section 9 of the Florida Constitution . . . the State is precluded from using a defendant's pre-arrest, pre-*Miranda* silence as substantive evidence of guilt when the defendant does not testify at trial. The State asserts that a defendant's silence occurring prior to his or her arrest is admissible [under the U.S. Constitution as interpreted by *Miranda v. Arizona*, 384 U.S. 436 (1966) and its progeny which holds that] the privilege against self-incrimination does not apply outside of the context of arrest or custodial interrogation, unless the defendant has expressly invoked the privilege against self-incrimination. . . . Horwitz counters that the Florida Constitution is more protective of the privilege against self-incrimination than its federal counterpart. . . .

In addressing the contours of the restrictions on the State's use of a defendant's pre-arrest, pre-*Miranda* silence, we begin with the Florida Constitution's more protective privilege against self-incrimination as compared to its federal counterpart. . . .

I. Florida's Constitutional Privilege Against Self-Incrimination

. . . The pertinent provision of the Florida Constitution provides that "No person shall . . . be compelled in any criminal matter to be a witness against oneself." Art. I, §9, Fla. Const. This constitutional right has been referred to interchangeably as the "right to remain silent" and the "privilege against self-incrimination."

Florida's privilege against self-incrimination is fundamental; it is part of the Florida Constitution's Declaration of Rights, "a series of rights so basic that the framers of our Constitution accorded them a place of special privilege." *Traylor v. State*, 596 So. 2d 957, 963 (Fla. 1992); art. I, Fla. Const. As this Court explained . . . :

> . . . These rights [enumerated in the Declaration of Rights] curtail and restrain the power of the State. It is more important to preserve them, even though at times a guilty man may go free, than it is to obtain a conviction by ignoring or violating them. The end does not justify the means. Might is not always right. Under our system of constitutional government, the State should not set the example of violating fundamental rights guaranteed by the Constitution to all citizens in order to obtain a conviction.

Bizzell v. State, 71 So. 2d 735, 738 (Fla. 1954). Thus, even here—especially here— where the rights of those suspected of wrongdoing are concerned, the framers drew a bright line and said to government, "Thus far shalt thou come, but no farther." . . .

. . . Unless the Florida Constitution specifies otherwise, this Court, as the ultimate arbiter of the meaning and extent of the safeguards and fundamental rights provided by the Florida Constitution, may interpret those rights as providing greater protections than those in the United States Constitution. *State v. Kelly*, 999 So. 2d 1029, 1042 (Fla. 2008). Put simply, the United States Constitution generally sets the "floor"—not the "ceiling"—of personal rights and freedoms that must be afforded to a defendant by Florida law. *Id.* As we explained in *Kelly*, "we have the duty to *independently* examine and determine questions of state law so long as we do not run afoul of federal constitutional protections or the provisions of the Florida Constitution that require us to apply federal law in state-law contexts." 999 So. 2d at 1043 (emphasis in original). Our Court reemphasized what we previously stated in *Traylor*: "[w]hen called upon to decide matters of fundamental rights, Florida's state courts are bound under federalist principles to give primacy to our state Constitution and to give independent legal import to every phrase and clause contained therein." *Id.* at 1044 (quoting *Traylor*, 596 So. 2d at 962–63).

As this Court held in *Traylor*, the privilege against self-incrimination, as one of our Constitution's fundamental rights, must be—and has long been—broadly construed. 596 So. 2d at 965 (citing *Ex parte Senior*, 37 Fla. 1, 19 So. 652, 654 (1896)). Indeed, as this Court has since reemphasized, the privilege against self-incrimination provided in the Florida Constitution offers *more* protection than the right provided in the Fifth Amendment to the United States Constitution. *Rigterink v. State*, 66 So. 3d 866, 888 (Fla. 2011).

This Court's interpretation of the state constitutional privilege against self-incrimination as providing more protection than its federal counterpart was applied to a defendant's post-arrest, pre-*Miranda* silence in *Hoggins*, 718 So. 2d 761. In that case, we held that the State's use of this post-arrest, pre-*Miranda* silence to impeach the defendant's trial testimony violated Florida's constitutional privilege against self-incrimination, even though such impeachment evidence is not barred by the Fifth Amendment. *Id.* at 765, 769–72. In other words, we interpreted the Florida constitutional right as providing more "rigorous constraints on the use of" a defendant's post-arrest, pre-*Miranda* silence than what is permissible under the federal Constitution. *Id.* at 768. In *Hoggins*, we expressly departed from the United States Supreme Court's decision in *Fletcher v. Weir*, 455 U.S. 603, 606, 102 S.Ct. 1309, 71 L.Ed.2d 490 (1982), which held that the federal Constitution did not preclude states from using a defendant's post-arrest, pre-*Miranda* silence for impeachment purposes. *Id.* at 769.

In *Hoggins*, after an armed robbery of a convenience store, the perpetrator "absconded with the cash register drawer and a cigar box containing lottery tickets." *Id.* at 762. The defendant was spotted riding a bicycle while carrying the missing items. *Id.* The defendant testified at trial, claiming that his bicycle had been stolen and that he had witnessed someone run into his apartment complex and hide something, which he later discovered was the drawer and cigar box. *Id.* at 763. The prosecutor cross-examined the defendant, asking whether the defendant had previously provided that explanation after his arrest, and the defendant admitted that he had not. *Id.* The prosecutor also relied on this "silence" in closing arguments, pointing out that the defendant did not tell the same version of events to the police on the night of his arrest that he provided in his testimony at trial. *Id.* at 764.

We reached a different conclusion in *Hoggins* than the Supreme Court on the issue of post-arrest, pre-*Miranda* silence for two reasons: (1) "unlike the United States Supreme Court, Florida courts have recognized that the defendant does not waive his or her right to silence at the time of arrest by taking the stand in his or her own defense," and (2) "[w]hile the absence of *Miranda* warnings may prevent a federal due process violation from occurring where the defendant's post-arrest silence is used for impeachment purposes, the same is not true of the defendant's right to remain silent. The absence of such warnings does not add to or detract from an individual's right to remain silent." *Id.* at 769–70. . . .

[So] in *Hoggins*, this Court concluded that "the use of a defendant's silence at the time of arrest violates article I, section 9 of Florida's Constitution regardless of whether *Miranda* warnings have been given," . . . .

The defendant should not be compelled to make the choice between testifying—with the possibility that his or her earlier silence might be used to impeach him or her—and not testifying—thereby, under the State's view, allowing the State to use the defendant's earlier silence as substantive evidence of the defendant's guilt. Our analysis is entirely consistent and directly flows from our decision in Hoggins, as well as our consistent commitment to providing greater protection to a defendant's privilege against self-incrimination guaranteed by the Florida Constitution. . . .

For all these reasons, we conclude that a defendant's privilege against self-incrimination guaranteed under article I, section 9 of the Florida Constitution is violated when his or her pre-arrest, pre-*Miranda* silence is used against the defendant at trial as substantive evidence of the defendant's consciousness of guilt. . . .

It is so ordered.

––––––––––

Notes and Questions to Consider:

1. What greater protection for Ms. Horwitz did Florida's Constitution provide that the federal constitution did not?

2. Is Florida's Supreme Court in *State v. Horwitz* attempting to overrule the Supreme Court of the United States' decision in *Miranda v. Arizona*, 384 U.S. 436 (1966)? Does *State v. Horwitz* hold that federal constitutional is wrong?

3. Explain how the concept of a "laboratory of democracy" is promoted by this sentence from *Miranda v. Arizona*: "Put simply, the United States Constitution generally sets the 'floor'—not the 'ceiling'—of personal rights and freedoms that must be afforded to a defendant by Florida law."

4. Must a Floridian exhaust her federal constitutional rights before turning to Florida's Constitution for protection? Consider this sentence from *State v. Horwitz*: "[w]hen called upon to decide matters of fundamental rights, Florida's state courts are bound under federalist principles to give primacy to our state Constitution. . . ."

5. How would you describe the relationship between the federal constitution and state constitutions? Is a state constitution a supplement to the federal? Are they co-equals? Is a state constitution a redundancy? Is a state constitutional a way for a state to reject federal law in whole or in part? Are none of these statements accurate?

B. Can Florida's Constitution Be Unconstitutional?

As precedent from Florida's supreme court such as *State v. Horwitz*, 191 So. 3d 429 (Fla. 2016), illustrates, states like Florida may become a "laboratory of democracy," and grant its citizens greater rights than under the federal constitution. To do so, Florida's constitutional case law precedent may diverge from federal constitutional case law precedent, but never in such a way as to deny Floridians the full panoply of rights provided by federal law.

Decisions of the U.S. Supreme Court are binding upon every lower court and cannot be overruled or overturned by any other court. Perhaps this famous quote from a U.S. Supreme Court justice says it best: "We are not final because we are infallible, but we are infallible only because we are final." *Brown v. Allen*, 344 U.S. 443 (1953) (Jackson, J., concurring).

A state's highest court, however, cannot make the same claim of finality. Surely a state's constitution can declare the decisions of the state's highest court binding upon that state's lower courts. But a state's constitution is not enough to prevent the U.S. Supreme Court from reviewing state court decisions over which the U.S. Supreme Court has jurisdiction. Federal supremacy is the reason.

Federal supremacy can interfere with the development of an independent body of state case law precedent interpreting the state constitution. Although this interferes with the development of state constitutional law jurisprudence, this is necessary, and this is good.

To see the good in it, imagine a state constitution that contradicts the federal constitution in a horribly offensive way, such as by discriminating against the state's citizens based on their race or religion. It is sad but true to say that Florida's constitution can serve as an example of this. From 1887 through 2018, the first page of Florida's constitution—specifically, Article I, Section 2—discriminated against Asian Americans. Until the 2018 amendment, Article I said that every natural person is equal before the law except for "aliens ineligible for citizenship," which is an archaic phrase intended to refer to Asians. Until that subsection was amended in 2018, the ownership, inheritance, disposition, and possession of Florida real estate by Asians could have been prohibited by Florida law. This was Florida's version of the Alien Land Law enacted in many U.S. states with the intent of discriminating against Asians. Does that mean that, until 2018, Florida courts could have developed a body of binding case law precedent approving of ways of discriminating against Asians because Florida's constitution permitted this? No. The U.S. Constitution forbids such discrimination, and so, the discriminatory language once appearing in Florida's constitution was unconstitutional. Any case law precedent enforcing it would have been unconstitutional also, despite the words that once existed in Florida's constitution.

Florida's constitution provides another example. Article I, Section 3 states: "No revenue of the state or any political subdivision or agency thereof shall ever be taken from the public treasury directly or indirectly in aid of any church, sect, or religious denomination or in aid of any sectarian institution." This was Florida's enactment of a Blaine Amendment, named after "Congressman James G. Blaine of Maine, who aspired to obtain the Republican party nomination to succeed [Ulysses S.] Grant as president and who fully appreciated the wide political appeal of the nativist and anti-Catholic rhetoric." Joseph P. Viteritti, *Blaine's Wake: School Choice, the First Amendment, and State Constitutional Law*, 21 Harv. J.L. & Pub. Pol'y 657, 670–71 (1998). Congressman Blaine supported a "movement that sought to amend several state constitutions (often successfully), and to amend the United States Constitution (unsuccessfully) to make certain that government would not help pay for 'sectarian' (i.e., Catholic) schooling for children." *Zelman v. Simmons-Harris*, 536 U.S. 639, 721 (2002).

Florida's constitution provides a third example. Article I, Section 27 of the Constitution of the State of Florida says: "Inasmuch as marriage is the legal union of only one man and one woman as husband and wife, no other legal union that is treated as marriage or the substantial equivalent thereof shall be valid or recognized." Does that mean two men or two women cannot purchase a marriage license from the state of Florida, or that their marriage license issued by a U.S. state other than Florida is not treated as valid by the state of Florida? No. The case law precedent interpreting the federal constitution holds that states must issue and honor same-sex marriage licenses, and this federal case law precedent applies in Florida even though Florida's constitution forbids it.

These examples illustrate an important point about subnational constitutional law jurisprudence: it may not contradict federal constitutional law. The text of Florida's constitution can be unconstitutional under the federal constitution. Likewise, state case law precedent that contradicts the federal constitution has no binding effect even if it is supported by the text of the state's constitution. One might envision federal constitutional rights as a floor below which state constitutional rights may not sink, just as Florida's Supreme Court held in *State v. Horwitz*. At a bare minimum, each state must recognize at least the rights granted to all Americans by the U.S. Constitution.

Obviously, a state constitution that contradicts a federal constitutional right is undesirable. So it is fitting that federal supremacy protects us. But what if a given state wanted to grant its citizens not fewer but more rights than those provided by the United States Constitution? How can a state like Florida be a "laboratory of democracy" without denying its citizens any of the full panoply of federally-protected rights and liberties?

The answer is twofold. First, state constitutional law jurisprudence may offer nothing less than the full panoply of federal rights. Second, within those federal boundaries, the state may develop particular areas of its state constitutional law jurisprudence that are either permitted by, or tolerated by, the limits of federal law.

Therefore, Florida's Constitution may provide additional rights for Floridians, so long as those additional rights do not contradict any federal rights, and so long as those additional rights are tolerated by federal laws such as the US Constitution.

C. Does Florida's Constitution Prevail Over Contrary Federal Laws?

As to the original thirteen states that created the United States of America, it may be said that first the states existed, and then, from their sovereignty, they created the United States. Seen from this perspective, one can view the states as the original sovereigns within our federal system. Yet only thirteen states can make such a claim. As to the remaining thirty-seven states, "[t]he very moment that a state is admitted to the Union is often also the moment of the creation of a state as a sovereign unit." Eric Biber, *The Price of Admission: Causes, Effects, and Patterns of Conditions Imposed on States Entering the Union*, 46 Am. J. Legal Hist. 119, 121–22 (2004). Regardless of when the state was created or when it acquired its sovereignty, a state surrenders its sovereign rights, in part, upon entering the Union. By ratifying the U.S. Constitution, each state agreed to the language of its Article VI that reads:

> This Constitution, and the laws of the United States which shall be made in pursuance thereof; and all treaties made, or which shall be made, under the authority of the United States, shall be the supreme law of the land; and the judges in every state shall be bound thereby, *anything in the Constitution* or laws *of any State to the contrary notwithstanding.* (emphasis added)

Note that this language, called the Supremacy Clause, creates a "supreme law of the land" notwithstanding even state constitutions. Note further that the Supremacy Clause does not limit supremacy to just the U.S. Constitution. Supremacy over state constitutions is also extended to "treaties" and to "the laws of the United States."

The United States Congress has not hesitated to use its authority to preempt state laws, including laws embodied in a state's constitution. Robert F. Williams, in his casebook STATE CONSTITUTIONAL LAW: CASES AND MATERIALS (Lexis Law Pub. 3d ed. 1999), provides this interesting example of federal congressmen representing Arkansas asking the U.S. Congress to pass a law that they know will overcome a contrary provision in the Constitution of the State of Arkansas.

125 Congressional Record — House, p. 993

Legislation to Bring Temporary Relief to Arkansas
vis-a-vis Interest Rates (Daily ed., Feb. 29, 1979)

[Statement of] Mr. Alexander:

> Mr. Speaker, I rise today to join my colleagues from Arkansas (Mr. Hammerschmidt, Mr. Anthony, and Mr. Bethune) in the introduction of legislation that will bring temporary relief to a situation existing in Arkansas.

> The legislation we are introducing today will allow . . . banks to charge interest on . . . loans in the amount of $25,000 or more, notwithstanding any State constitution or statute, at a rate of not more than 5 percent in excess of the discount rate. . . .

. . . Arkansas' Constitution sets the maximum interest rate which may be charged by business borrowers at 10 percent [as a usury limitation]. . . . Arkansas' lending institutions [are] paying up to 13 percent for money bought through the Federal Reserve System [but are not allowed to lend out that money at more than 10 percent due to the Arkansas Constitution's usury limitations, thereby making it unprofitable for Arkansas banks to write new loans at this time]. . . . Hardest hit by our usury limitations are construction, agricultural, and small business firms. . . .

Arkansas is presently rewriting its State constitution which will be presented to the voters in the 1980 general election. The usury issue will be one addressed in the document.

Given the credit crunch that our State's financial community finds itself in, it is the hope of the Arkansas delegation that Congress will approve this temporary legislation until such time as the Arkansas electorate has voted on a usury provision in the State constitution that will provide permanent relief.

[Statement of] Mr. Anthony:

Mr. Speaker, I, too, join my colleagues from the state of Arkansas in urgent support of this bill. It is with reservation that I do so, however, and that reservation should be explained. . . .

In 1874, the people of the state of Arkansas created our state constitution. At that period in our history, over 100 years ago, it was deemed by the people that 10% interest was the most any person should have to pay for money borrowed. The importance of that conclusion was such that it was inserted in the Constitution, not merely relegated to a rule of law passed by the State Legislature or forged by decisions of our state Supreme Court. It is also important to emphasize, Mr. Speaker, that the Supreme Court of Arkansas has through the years steadfastly guarded the mandate of our constitutional prohibition against interest in excess of 10%. Time and time again the [Arkansas Supreme C]ourt has found [that the Arkansas Constitution's usury provisions must be enforced whenever money is borrowed] . . .

. . . So, Mr. Speaker, the usury law [in the Constitution of] the State of Arkansas is not something to be casually pushed aside. . . .

We are asking this Congress to give [our state's] lending community temporary relief until once again, in a Constitutional Convention, the people of our state can decide what is and what is not usury.

Robert F. Williams, STATE CONSTITUTIONAL LAW: CASES AND MATERIALS (Lexis Law Pub. 3d ed. 1999) (reprinting the portion of the Congressional Record appearing above).

––––––––––

Notes and Questions to Consider:

1. Why Congress? Mr. Anthony noted that, time and time again, the Arkansas Supreme Court found that the Arkansas Constitution's usury provisions must be enforced whenever money is borrowed. So how can the US Congress help? Arkansas' credit crunch was caused by Arkansa's Constitution, and not by any act of the US Congress. What makes the US Congress the right solution for this urgent problem?

2. Despite the federal constitution's Supremacy Clause, does not the Bill of Rights to the US Constitution preserve the sovereignty of states so as to protect their constitutions from acts of the US Congress? Recall that in the Bill of Rights of the U.S. Constitution, the Tenth Amendment states: "The powers not delegated to the United States by the [federal] Constitution, nor prohibited by it to the States, are reserved to the States respectively, or to the people." Have we found this phrase to be an adequate federal authority to develop nearly any area of state constitutional law jurisprudence? Most often, the answer is no. Consider the observation in Erwin Chemerinsky, CONSTITUTIONAL LAW (3d ed. 2009):

> The issue has arisen throughout American history as to the extent to which concern for state governments and their prerogatives should matter. Between the late 19th century and 1937, and again in the past decade, concern for state governments has profoundly answered how the [U.S. Supreme] Court has dealt with both of these questions. The Court during these times limited [U.S.] Congressional power to leave areas of governance to state governments. During these times, the Court also directly protected state sovereignty, concluding that even valid exercises of legislative power are unconstitutional when they infringe [upon] state sovereignty. The [U.S. Supreme] Court has used the Tenth Amendment as the basis for this protection of state governments from federal encroachment.

> During other times of American history, however, the [U.S. Supreme] Court has refused to use concern over state governments either as a basis for narrowly interpreting the scope of [the United States] Congress' power or as a limit through the Tenth Amendment on the reach of federal legislation. From the 1930s until the 1990s, the Court broadly defined the scope of [the U.S.] Congress' authority under Article I of the [federal] Constitution and refused to use the Tenth Amendment as a limit on federal power.

Id. at 127–128. These words show that the Tenth Amendment is an historically tenuous basis for a strong, rigorous, and powerful state constitutional jurisprudence. From the 1930s to the 1990s—seven decades—the Supreme Court of the United States refused to use the Tenth Amendment as the basis for limiting federal power.

3. The hope of a Tenth Amendment source of strong state constitutional power seems just as grim under the correct analysis from Randy J. Holland, Stephen R. McAllister, Jeffrey M. Shaman, and Jeffrey S. Sutton, STATE CONSTITUTIONAL LAW: THE MODERN EXPERIENCE (Thomson Reuters 2010), where these authors opine:

> Article VI may contain the most important provision of all for the States with respect to the effect of federal law on the States. The Supremacy Clause [of Article VI of the U.S. Constitution] declares that: "This Constitution, and the Laws of the United States which shall be made in pursuance thereof; and all Treaties made, or which shall be made, under the Authority of the United States, shall be the supreme Law of the Land; and the Judges in every State shall be bound thereby, any Thing in the Constitution or Laws of any State to the Contrary notwithstanding." The Supremacy Clause is further bolstered by Article VI's provision that "the Members of the several State Legislatures, and all executive and judicial Officers, both of the United States and of the several States, shall be bound by Oath or Affirmation, to support this Constitution."
>
> These two clauses make clear—in explicit terms—that *federal law has primacy over state law, including state constitutions*, when there is a conflict between any federal law (constitutional, statutory, or even regulatory) and state law.

Id. at 91–92 (emphasis added).

4. The authors correctly note that "any federal law (constitutional, statutory, or even regulatory)" prevails over the state constitution. The federal law could be the language of the U.S. Constitution. Or the language of the United States Code. Or the language of the Code of Federal Regulations. Yes, even a mere federal regulation properly enacted by a bureaucrat from a low-budget federal agency takes precedence over the words of the people of the state of Florida as enacted in their highest law, their Constitution of the State of Florida. As the Supreme Court of the United States held in *Fidelity Federal Savings and Loan Association v. De La Cuesta*, 458 U.S. 141 (1982):

> Federal regulations have no less preemptive effect than federal statutes. Where Congress has directed an administrator to exercise his discretion, his judgments are subject to judicial review only to determine whether he has exceeded his statutory authority or acted arbitrarily. When the administrator promulgates regulations intended to preempt state law, the court's inquiry is similarly limited: if his choice represents a reasonable accommodation of conflicting policies that were committed to the agency's care by the statute, we should not disturb it unless it appears from the statute or its legislative history that the accommodation is not one that Congress would have sanctioned.

Id. at 153–54.

5. Are you surprised by the fact that a federal administrator's regulations may preempt a state constitution's provisions? Then you will be equally surprised that even "federal common law" may preempt a state constitution. Yes, the *Erie* doctrine eliminated most federal common law, but not all of it. When *Erie v. Thompkins*, 304 U.S. 64 (1938) overruled *Swift v. Tyson*, 41 U.S. 1 (1842) and held there is "no

federal general common law," the operative word was "general." As recently as 1981, the Supreme Court of the United States acknowledged that "federal common law exists only in such narrow areas as those concerned with the rights and obligations of the United States, interstate and international disputes implicating the conflicting rights of States or our relations with foreign nations, and admiralty cases." *Texas Indus., Inc. v. Radcliff Materials, Inc.*, 451 U.S. 630, 641 (1981). State constitutional rights may still be overcome by an uncodified "federal common law." That is exactly what happened in the case of *Hinderlider v. La Plata River & Cherry Creek Ditch Co.*, 304 U.S. 92 (1938). That case involved a fight over rights to water flowing in a river through Colorado and New Mexico. At the time, the Colorado Constitution, at Article 16, Section 5, provided that "The water of every natural stream within the state of Colorado, is hereby declared to be the property of the public, and the same is dedicated to the use of the people of the state." Likewise at that time, Article 16, Section 6, of the Colorado Constitution provided in part that "The right to divert the unappropriated waters of any natural stream to beneficial uses shall never be denied. Priority of appropriation shall give the better right as between those using the water for the same purpose." Regardless of these state constitutional rights, the Supreme Court of the United States decided the case based on "federal common law." Federal common law prevailed over state constitutional law.

6. One moral of all these proceeding pages is clear: the student of state constitutional law should not approach a state constitution the same way as the U.S. Constitution. If something is stated clearly in the U.S. Constitution, then that fact almost certainly means it is the prevailing law of the land. But with any state constitution, we must proceed with caution and check for federal preemption before assuming that provision is even an enforceable law.

1. The "Adequate and Independent State Ground" Doctrine of *Michigan v. Long*

In light of the federal constitution's Supremacy Clause and its resulting potential for federal preemption to overcome a state's constitution, how can a state develop its own, independent state constitutional law jurisprudence? The answer lies in the federal adoption of the Adequate and Independent State Ground Doctrine. To define that doctrine, we turn to the Supreme Court of the United States' 1983 decision in *Michigan v. Long*, 463 U.S. 1032 (1983).

Michigan v. Long

Supreme Court of the United States, 1983
463 U.S. 1032, 103 S. Ct. 3469, 77 L. Ed. 2d 1201

Justice O'Connor delivered the opinion of the Court.

In *Terry v. Ohio*, 392 U.S. 1 (1968), we upheld the validity of a protective search for weapons in the absence of probable cause to arrest because it is unreasonable to deny a police officer the right "to neutralize the threat of physical harm," *id.* at 24, when he possesses an articulable suspicion that an individual is armed and dangerous. We did not, however, expressly address whether such a protective search for weapons could extend to an area beyond the person in the absence of probable cause to arrest. In the present case, respondent David Long was convicted for possession of marijuana found by police in the passenger compartment and trunk of the automobile that he was driving. The police searched the passenger compartment because they had reason to believe that the vehicle contained weapons potentially dangerous to the officers. We hold that the protective search of the passenger compartment was reasonable under the principles articulated in *Terry* and other decisions of this Court. We also examine Long's argument that the decision below rests upon an adequate and independent state ground, and we decide in favor of our jurisdiction.

II

Before reaching the merits, we must consider Long's argument that we are without jurisdiction to decide this case because the decision below rests on an adequate and independent state ground. The court below referred twice to the state constitution in its opinion, but otherwise relied exclusively on federal law. Long argues that the Michigan courts have provided greater protection from searches and seizures under the state constitution than is afforded under the Fourth Amendment, and the references to the state constitution therefore establish an adequate and independent ground for the decision below.

It is, of course, incumbent upon this Court to ascertain for itself whether the asserted non-federal ground independently and adequately supports the judgment. Although we have announced a number of principles in order to help us determine whether various forms of references to state law constitute adequate and independent state grounds, we openly admit that we have thus far not developed a satisfying and consistent approach for resolving this vexing issue. In some instances, we have taken the strict view that if the ground of decision was at all unclear, we would dismiss the case. In other instances, we have vacated, or continued a case, in order to obtain clarification about the nature of a state court decision. In more recent cases, we have ourselves examined state law to determine whether state courts have used federal law to guide their application of state law or to provide the actual basis for the decision that was reached. In *Oregon v. Kennedy*, 456 U.S. 667, 670–71 (1982), we rejected an invitation to remand to the state court for clarification even when the decision rested in part on a case from the state court, because we determined that the state case itself rested upon federal grounds. We added that "[e]ven if the case admitted of more doubt as to whether federal and state grounds for decision were intermixed, the fact that the state court relied to the extent it did on federal grounds requires us to reach the merits." *Id.* at 671.

This *ad hoc* method of dealing with cases that involve possible adequate and independent state grounds is antithetical to the doctrinal consistency that is required when sensitive issues of federal-state relations are involved. Moreover, none of the various methods of disposition that we have employed thus far recommends itself as the preferred method that we should apply to the exclusion of others, and we therefore determine that it is appropriate to reexamine our treatment of this jurisdictional issue in order to achieve the consistency that is necessary.

The process of examining state law is unsatisfactory because it requires us to interpret state laws with which we are generally unfamiliar, and which often, as in this case, have not been discussed at length by the parties. Vacation and continuance for clarification have also been unsatisfactory both because of the delay and decrease in efficiency of judicial administration, and, more important, because these methods of disposition place significant burdens on state courts to demonstrate the presence or absence of our jurisdiction. Finally, outright dismissal of cases is clearly not a panacea because it cannot be doubted that there is an important need for uniformity in federal law, and that this need goes unsatisfied when we fail to review an opinion that rests primarily upon federal grounds and where the *independence* of an alleged state ground is not apparent from the four corners of the opinion. We have long recognized that dismissal is inappropriate where there is strong indication that the federal constitution as judicially construed controlled the decision below.

Respect for the independence of state courts, as well as avoidance of rendering advisory opinions, have been the cornerstones of this Court's refusal to decide cases where there is an adequate and independent state ground. It is precisely because of this respect for state courts, and this desire to avoid advisory opinions, that we do not wish to continue to decide issues of state law that go beyond the opinion that we review, or to require state courts to reconsider cases to clarify the grounds of their decisions. Accordingly, when, as in this case, a state court decision fairly appears to rest primarily on federal law, or to be interwoven with the federal law, and when the adequacy and independence of any possible state law ground is not clear from the face of the opinion, we will accept as the most reasonable explanation that the state court decided the case the way it did because it believed that federal law required it to do so. If a state court chooses merely to rely on federal precedents as it would on the precedents of all other jurisdictions, then it need only make clear by a plain statement in its judgment or opinion that the federal cases are being used only for the purpose of guidance, and do not themselves compel the result that the court has reached. In this way, both justice and judicial administration will be greatly improved. If the state court decision indicates clearly and expressly that it is alternatively based on bona fide separate, adequate, and independent grounds, we, of course, will not undertake to review the decision.

This approach obviates in most instances the need to examine state law in order to decide the nature of the state court decision, and will at the same time avoid the danger of our rendering advisory opinions. It also avoids the unsatisfactory and intrusive practice of requiring state courts to clarify their decisions to the satisfaction of this Court. We believe that such an approach will provide state judges with a clearer opportunity to develop state jurisprudence unimpeded by federal interference, and yet will preserve the integrity of federal law. It is fundamental that state courts be left free and unfettered by us in interpreting their state constitutions. But it is equally important that ambiguous or obscure adjudications by state courts do not stand as barriers to a determination by this Court of the validity under the federal constitution of state action.

The principle that we will not review judgments of state courts that rest on adequate and independent state grounds is based, in part, on "the limitations of our own jurisdiction." *Herb v. Pitcairn*, 324 U.S. 117, 125 (1945). The jurisdictional concern is that we not "render an advisory opinion, and if the same judgment would be rendered by the state court after we corrected its views of federal laws, our review could amount to nothing more than an advisory opinion." *Id.*, at 126. Our requirement of a "plain statement" that a decision rests upon adequate and independent state grounds does not in any way authorize the rendering of advisory opinions. Rather, in determining, as we must, whether we have jurisdiction to review a case that is alleged to rest on adequate and independent state grounds, we merely assume that there are no such grounds when it is not clear from the opinion itself that the state court relied upon an adequate and independent state ground and when it fairly appears that the state court rested its decision primarily on federal law.

Our review of the decision below under this framework leaves us unconvinced that it rests upon an independent state ground. Apart from its two citations to the state constitution, the court below relied *exclusively* on its understanding of *Terry* and other federal cases. Not a single state case was cited to support the state court's holding that the search of the passenger compartment was unconstitutional. Indeed, the court declared that the search in this case was unconstitutional because "[t]he Court of Appeals erroneously applied the principles of *Terry v. Ohio* . . . to the search of the interior of the vehicle in this case." 413 Mich., at 471, 320 N.W.2d, at 869. The references to the state constitution in no way indicate that the decision below rested on grounds in any way *independent* from the state court's interpretation of federal law. Even if we accept that the Michigan constitution has been interpreted to provide independent protection for certain rights also secured under the Fourth Amendment, it fairly appears in this case that the Michigan Supreme Court rested its decision primarily on federal law.

Rather than dismissing the case, or requiring that the state court reconsider its decision on our behalf solely because of a mere possibility that an adequate and independent ground supports the judgment, we find that we have jurisdiction in the absence of a plain statement that the decision below rested on an adequate and independent state ground. It appears to us that the state court "felt compelled by what it understood to be federal constitutional considerations to construe . . . its own law in the manner it did." *Zacchini v. Scripps-Howard Broadcasting Co.*, 433 U.S. 562, 568 (1977).

V

The decision of the Michigan Supreme Court is reversed, and the case is remanded for further proceedings not inconsistent with this opinion.

It is so ordered.

Justice Stevens, Dissenting:

The jurisprudential questions presented in this case are far more important than the question whether the Michigan police officer's search of respondent's car violated the Fourth Amendment. The case raises profoundly significant questions concerning the relationship between two sovereigns—the State of Michigan and the United States of America.

The Supreme Court of the State of Michigan expressly held "that the deputies' search of the vehicle was proscribed by the Fourth Amendment of the United States Constitution and *art. 1, § 11 of the Michigan Constitution.*" Pet. for Cert. 19 (emphasis added). The state law ground is clearly adequate to support the judgment, but the question whether it is independent of the Michigan Supreme Court's understanding of federal law is more difficult. Four possible ways of resolving that question present themselves: (1) asking the Michigan Supreme Court directly, (2) attempting to infer from all possible sources of state law what the Michigan Supreme Court meant, (3) presuming that adequate state grounds are independent unless it clearly appears otherwise, or (4) presuming that adequate state grounds are *not* independent unless it clearly appears otherwise. This Court has, on different occasions, employed each of the first three approaches; never until today has it even hinted at the fourth. In order to "achieve the consistency that is necessary," the Court today undertakes a reexamination of all the possibilities. *Ante,* at 3475. It rejects the first approach as inefficient and unduly burdensome for state courts, and rejects the second approach as an inappropriate expenditure of our resources. *Ibid.* Although I find both of those decisions defensible in themselves, I cannot accept the Court's decision to choose the fourth approach over the third—to presume that adequate state grounds are intended to be dependent on federal law unless the record plainly shows otherwise. I must therefore dissent.

If we reject the intermediate approaches, we are left with a choice between two presumptions: one in favor of our taking jurisdiction, and one against it. Historically, the latter presumption has always prevailed.

The Court today points out that in several cases we have weakened the traditional presumption by using the other two intermediate approaches identified above. Since those two approaches are now to be rejected, however, I would think that *stare decisis* would call for a return to historical principle. Instead, the Court seems to conclude that because some precedents are to be rejected, we must overrule them all.

Even if I agreed with the Court that we are free to consider as a fresh proposition whether we may take presumptive jurisdiction over the decisions of sovereign states, I could not agree that an expansive attitude makes good sense. It appears to be common ground that any rule we adopt should show "respect for state courts, and a desire to avoid advisory opinions." *Ante,* at 3475. And I am confident that all members of this Court agree that there is a vital interest in the sound management of scarce federal judicial resources. All of those policies counsel against the exercise of federal jurisdiction. They are fortified by my belief that a policy of judicial restraint—one that allows other decisional bodies to have the last word in legal interpretation until it is truly necessary for this Court to intervene—enables this Court to make its most effective contribution to our federal system of government.

The nature of the case before us hardly compels a departure from tradition. These are not cases in which an American citizen has been deprived of a right secured by the United States Constitution or a federal statute. Rather, they are cases in which a state court has upheld a citizen's assertion of a right, finding the citizen to be protected under both federal and state law. The complaining party is an officer of the state itself, who asks us to rule that the state court interpreted federal rights too broadly and "overprotected" the citizen.

Such cases should not be of inherent concern to this Court. The reason may be illuminated by assuming that the events underlying this case had arisen in another country, perhaps the Republic of Finland. If the Finnish police had arrested a Finnish citizen for possession of marijuana, and the Finnish courts had turned him loose, no American would have standing to object. If instead they had arrested an American citizen and acquitted him, we might have been concerned about the arrest but we surely could not have complained about the acquittal, even if the Finnish Court had based its decision on its understanding of the United States Constitution. That would be true even if we had a treaty with Finland requiring it to respect the rights of American citizens under the United States Constitution. We would only be motivated to intervene if an American citizen were unfairly arrested, tried, and convicted by the foreign tribunal.

In this case the State of Michigan has arrested one of its citizens and the Michigan Supreme Court has decided to turn him loose. The respondent is a United States citizen as well as a Michigan citizen, but since there is no claim that he has been mistreated by the State of Michigan, the final outcome of the state processes offended no federal interest whatever. Michigan simply provided greater protection to one of its citizens than some other State might provide or, indeed, than this Court might require throughout the country.

Until recently we had virtually no interest in cases of this type. Thirty years ago, this Court reviewed only one. *Nevada v. Stacher*, 358 U.S. 907 (1953). Indeed, that appears to have been the only case during the entire 1952 Term in which a state even sought review of a decision by its own judiciary. Fifteen years ago, we did not review any such cases, although the total number of requests had mounted to three. Some time during the past decade, perhaps about the time of the 5-to-4 decision in *Zacchini v. Scripps-Howard Broadcasting Co.*, 433 U.S. 562 (1977), our priorities shifted. The result is a docket swollen with requests by states to reverse judgments that their courts have rendered in favor of their citizens. I am confident that a future Court will recognize the error of this allocation of resources. When that day comes, I think it likely that the Court will also reconsider the propriety of today's expansion of our jurisdiction.

Finally, I am thoroughly baffled by the Court's suggestion that it must stretch its jurisdiction and reverse the judgment of the Michigan Supreme Court in order to show "[r]espect for the independence of state courts." *Ante,* at 3475. Would we show respect for the Republic of Finland by convening a special sitting for the sole purpose of declaring that its decision to release an American citizen was based upon a misunderstanding of American law?

I respectfully dissent.

Notes and Questions to Consider:

1. Is the state court opinion under review in *Michigan v. Long* an example of a state's high court successfully vesting its citizens with greater state constitutional rights than those granted by the federal constitution? Why or why not?

2. *Michigan v. Long* explains why the state court opinion under review did not satisfy the U.S. Supreme Court's criteria for having an adequate and independent state ground. In so holding, did the Court give us clear and actionable criteria that states can follow in seeking to draft opinions that have adequate and independent state grounds? If so, what are those criteria?

3. How does *Michigan v. Long* empower a state's high court to develop its own, independent state constitutional law jurisprudence? It does so by establishing the criteria that can allow the state's high court, instead of the U.S. Supreme Court, to be the final arbiter. Generally speaking, *Michigan v. Long* stands for the proposition that the Supreme Court of the United States may not take jurisdiction to review a state court decision that the U.S. Supreme Court finds upon its face to be based upon a plain statement of "adequate and independent state grounds." In this way, a state's highest court can make the same claim as the U.S. Supreme Court: "We are not final because we are infallible, but we are infallible only because we are final." *Brown v. Allen*, 344 U.S. 443 (1953) (Jackson, J., concurring).

4. *Michigan v. Long* shows how a single instance of a state high court's decision may avoid review by the U.S. Supreme Court. But can *Michigan v. Long* allow subsequent state court decisions to accumulate into an independent body of state constitutional law jurisprudence? Consider this example. The U.S. Supreme Court holds that a particular opinion of a state's high court meets the requirements of *Michigan v. Long*. Thereafter, the state's high court issues subsequent decisions that cite only to that prior decision. By this method, should not the subsequent opinions also avoid review under *Michigan v. Long*? If so, would not the state begin to accumulate its own, independent state constitutional law jurisprudence?

5. When, under *Michigan v. Long*, does a state court's decision rest on "adequate" and "independent" state grounds? The opinion is "adequate" if it does not deny or contradict the full panoply of federal rights. The opinion is "independent" if the face of the state court's decision either contains no reference to any federal law or federal case law decision because none were the basis of the decision, or if the face

of the decision makes a plain statement that federal cases are used only for the purpose of guidance. When the U.S. Supreme Court holds that both the conditions of
"adequate" and "independent" are met on the face of the state court's opinion, then
the U.S. Supreme Court lacks jurisdiction to review that opinion.

6. Where does the U.S. Supreme Court look to determine whether the state court's
decision rests on "adequate" and "independent" state grounds? The onus is on the
state court writing the opinion to meet these requirements on the face of the opinion. *Michigan v. Long* indicates that the U.S. Supreme Court will not remand to the
state court for clarification. If it is not clear from the face of the state court's decision
whether there are adequate and independent state grounds, then the U.S. Supreme
Court will presume it is not based on adequate and independent state grounds and
thus the U.S. Supreme Court has jurisdiction and may grant certiorari review. So in
a close case, the U.S. Supreme Court has jurisdiction.

7. If the state court's decision provides two or more explanations for its ruling,
must each explanation have "adequate" and "independent" state grounds in order
to avoid U.S. Supreme Court jurisdiction? Note that *Michigan v. Long* holds that a
state decision with two stated reasons for its ruling, one of which fails the tests of
"adequate" or "independent" may still deny the U.S. Supreme Court its jurisdiction
"[i]f the state court decision indicates clearly and expressly that it is alternatively
based upon bona fide separate, adequate, and independent grounds." This means
that if the opinion describes two reasons for its result, and at least one of the two
reasons is both "adequate" and "independent," then the U.S. Supreme Court "will
not undertake to review the decision." Only one of the many reasons needs to be
adequate and independent.

8. If you were the lawyer for a party whose case was just decided by Florida's
supreme court, and you were staring at the face of the court's opinion, how would
you make the argument for and against the U.S. Supreme Court taking certiorari
jurisdiction to review the Florida Supreme Court's opinion in light of *Michigan v.
Long*?

9. Does *Michigan v. Long* add uniformity to our national system of justice? Just
two years after the U.S. Supreme Court decided *Michigan v. Long*differences between
and among state high court opinions were already apparent, as illustrated by the
March/April 1985 issue of the Texas Law Review resulting from the University of
Texas School of Law's Symposium on the Emergence of State Constitutional Law.
That issue contained the article of Stewart G. Pollock, *Adequate and Independent
State Grounds as a Means of Balancing the Relationship between State and Federal
Courts,* 63 Tex. L. Rev. 977 (1985). It opined that:

> State constitutional law has evolved to the point where different meth-
> ods of analyzing constitutional claims have emerged. The Vermont and
> Washington Supreme Courts, for example, tie their decisions to both the
> state and federal constitutions. One problem with this approach is that
> dual reliance creates a body of unreviewable interpretations of the federal

constitution. The difficulty, however, is not so serious as may first appear. Diverse declarations of federal law by state courts necessarily must yield to interpretations of that law by the United States Supreme Court.

The two other methods are the primacy approach and the supplemental or interstitial approach. Under the primacy approach, a court looks first to its state constitution in cases involving such matters as fundamental liberties. Only if the alleged infringement is permissible under state constitutional standards would a court consult the federal constitution. This model avoids entanglement with federal law and also avoids United States Supreme Court review because of the failure to state an adequate and independent state ground.

10. Stewart G. Pollock's aforementioned *Texas Law Review* article provides the example of two states, Illinois and Washington, considering, under their own state constitutions, whether probable cause is established by confidential informers' tips. One state held yes, and the other, no. As a result, in prosecutions based on the state statutes, contraband seized as the fruit of such a tip was admissible in Illinois but inadmissible in Washington. Was this the intended result of *Michigan v. Long*'s adequate and independent state law doctrine? Is this a desirable result?

11. Have the effects of *Michigan v. Long* been positive or negative for our American federalism? Consider the opinions expressed in the following excerpt from a Summer 2015 article in the Duquesne Law Review by Lauren Gailey, *Thirty Years Too Long:Why the Michigan v. Long Presumption Should Be Rejected, and What Can Be Done to Replace It,* 53 Duq. L. Rev. 483 (2014–2015):.

When *Michigan v. Long* celebrated its thirtieth birthday in 2013, the occasion warranted little celebration. Over the course of the three decades since the United States Supreme Court . . . [decided *Michigan v. Long*] . . . , the *Long* framework has proven to be controversial at best, and unwieldy and ineffectual at worst. This article argues that the *Long* presumption should be rejected.

Several lines of reasoning support this conclusion. First, the vast majority of the long history of the Court's approach to reviewing the decisions of state high courts has been marked by deference to those courts; its current aggressive approach to reviewing the decisions of state high courts is a relatively recent development. Second, the Court itself has demonstrated some reservations as to the wisdom of *Long*. Members of the Court have, at times, expressed their doubts directly, as in the well-reasoned dissents of Justices John Paul Stevens and Ruth Bader Ginsburg [in *Florida v. Powell*, 559 U.S. 50, 64–76 (2010) (Stevens, J., dissenting); *Arizona v. Evans*, 514 U.S. 1, 23–34 (1995) (Ginsburg, J., dissenting); and *Delaware v. Van Arsdall*, 475 U.S. 673, 689–708 (1986) (Stevens, J., dissenting)]. The Court has also impliedly evinced a distrust of the *Long* presumption on a particularly consequential and high-profile occasion. In the first of the series of cases leading up to its

Bush v. Gore decision, which could arguably have determined the outcome of the 2000 presidential election, the Court quietly departed from the *Long* presumption, instead resuscitating an earlier approach to ambiguously grounded cases and remanding the case to the Florida Supreme Court for clarification as to the basis for its decision. Given the critical importance of the situation, the Court's decision not to rely on *Long* under the circumstances can be viewed as a symbolic "vote of no confidence."

D. Florida's Constitution as a Restriction upon Legislative Power

Many a course on state constitutional law, and many a book about Florida's constitution, begins with a bold proclamation akin to the following:

> The basic consideration in any course dealing with the constitutional law of a state is the fact that although the governmental power of the United States flows either directly or impliedly from its Constitution, the governmental power of a state does not flow from its constitution. The source of a state's governmental power is, rather, inherent. The state's constitution is, therefore, essentially a limitation on that inherent power.

The quotation above is from the excellent work of John F. Cooper, Tichia A. Dunham & Carlos L. Woody, Florida Constitutional Law: Cases and Materials (5th ed. Carolina Academic Press 2013). Words of similar import may be found in nearly every text regarding nearly any state's constitution. These words are not erroneous, but they are widely misunderstood. The misunderstanding arises from the fact that it is not the state, but the state's *legislature*, that can most accurately be described as having an inherent power. With that fact understood, the proper phrasing is that a state's constitution is a limitation upon *legislative* power.

Court are careful to include the word *legislative* when explaining this concept. For example, *Chiles v. Phelps*, 714 So. 2d 453 (Fla. 1998) holds:

> This decision is guided, in part, by the nature of our state constitution. We have noted that:

> > The Constitution of this state is not a grant of power to the Legislature, but a limitation only upon legislative power, and unless legislation be clearly contrary to some express or necessarily implied prohibition found in the Constitution, the courts are without authority to declare legislative Acts invalid. The Legislature may exercise any lawmaking power that is not forbidden by organic law.

> *Savage v. Board of Public Instruction*, 101 Fla. 1362, 1369, 133 So. 341, 344 (1931) (citing *State v. [Bryan]*, 50 Fla. 293, 39 So. 929 (1905); *Jordan v. Duval County*, 68 Fla. 48, 66 So. 298 (1914); and *Stone v. State*, 71 Fla. 514, 71 So.

634 (1916)). The legislature's power is inherent, though it may be limited by the constitution. Thus, the legislature "looks to the Constitution for limitations on its power and if not found to exist its discretion reasonably exercised is the sole brake on the enactment of legislation." *State v. Board of Pub. Instruction*, 126 Fla. 142, 151, 170 So. 602, 606 (1936).

Id. at 458.

The proposition that "[t]he Constitution of this state is not a grant of power to the Legislature, but a limitation only upon legislative power" means that the Legislature has general legislative or policy-making power except as those powers are specifically limited by the constitution. *Chiles v. Phelps*, 714 So. 2d 453, 458 (Fla. 1998). That is because "[t]he legislature's power is inherent, though it may be limited by the constitution." *Id.* For this reason, "[t]he legislative branch looks to the Constitution not for sources of power but for limitations upon power." *State ex rel. Green v. Pearson*, 153 Fla. 314, 14 So. 2d 565, 567 (1943).

Do not misinterpret these words to mean that state actors other than Florida's legislature have an inherent power to act. Despite this inherent power of Florida's legislature to enact laws in ways and on topics not forbidden by federal law or Florida's constitution, it and all other state actors still must obey the rule of law.

Consider your own personal experience with the state of Florida. Do its officers and officials have inherent power over you, or only that power given to them by the rule of law? What if you were to meet a Florida State Trooper who believes correctly that his government agency needs funding and that you have plenty of money. Surely that Trooper has the right to urge his state legislative representatives to pass a law providing additional funding to his agency. But does that Trooper have the inherent authority to take your money and give it to his agency? Of course not. The rule of law, and due process of law, exist to protect us from such invasions of our freedom and confiscations of our wealth. Likewise, if a county believes your home is the perfect location for a new ballpark, the county's legislative body may follow the rule of law and begin the procedures for eminent domain. But may the county simply bring its wrecking ball and start knocking down your house? Of course not. Laws exist granting counties the right of eminent domain, but due process of law requires that the stated formalities occur, and the rule of law requires appropriate burdens of proof to be met.

So if a Florida county wants to take away your land, or a Florida official wants to take away your money, such actions do not occur due to some kind of an inherent power vested with all parts of Florida's government. Instead, the rule of law applies and requires there must there be a legal basis for Florida's government to do such things, and due process of law requires certain minimum formalities.

———————

Notes and Questions to Consider:

1. Can Florida's inherent police power justify violating the U.S. Constitution?

2. Does Florida's inherent police power empower the government of the state of Florida to ignore or disobey federal laws?

3. Florida case law precedent identifies three "first principles" of state constitutional jurisprudence. First, the people are the ultimate sovereign. Second, unlike the federal constitution, our state constitution is a limitation upon the power of government rather than a grant of that power, which means that the state legislature has general and inherent legislative or policy-making power. Third, because general legislative or policy-making power is vested in the legislature, the power of judicial review over legislative enactments is strictly limited. To what extent do these "first principles" help you to understand better the concept that Florida's constitution is a restriction upon power, not a grant of power?

Chapter 2

Constitutional Construction

A. Judicial Ethics of Constitutional Interpretation

How must Florida's courts interpret Florida's constitution? Commentators note that:

> Over the years, scholars and courts have employed a wide range of methods for analyzing constitutions. Some principal methods include: deriving the meaning of the constitution from the pure and literal meaning of its text ("textualist"), finding meaning in the intent of the framers ("originalist"), and treating the constitution as a living document that must be interpreted to conform to the immediate needs of modern society ("interpretivist").

Daniel Webster & Donald L. Bell, *First Principles for Constitution Revision*, 22 Nova L. Rev. 391, 408 (1997). The gamut of preferences as to how to interpret a constitution includes "textualist," "originalist," "interpretivist," and others.

So does a constitution mean whatever the court interpreting it prefers it to mean? Those of us who are not lawyers might think so. If surveys are correct, Americans are divided in their beliefs about how a court does and should go about interpreting a constitution. A February 2014 survey by the Pew Research Center concludes that "[a]bout half of the public (49%) say the decisions of the [U.S.] Supreme Court should be based on its understanding of what the Constitution 'means in current times,' while roughly as many (46%) say decisions should be based on what the Constitution 'meant as it was originally written.'" Jocelyn Kiley, *Americans Divided on How the Supreme Court Should Interpret the Constitution* (July 31, 2014) (www .pewresearch.org/fact-tank/2014/07/31/americans-divided-on-how-the-supreme -court-should-interpret-the-constitution/).

Another survey suggests the public perceives constitutional interpretation as something done not according to rules but instead along partisan lines. A March 2017 survey by C-SPAN and Penn Schoen Berland (PSB) concludes that "62% of voters say that U.S. 'Supreme Court Justices are split on political grounds like Congress'" and concludes that just barely more than 1 out of 3 voters, or "38% of voters say that the 'U.S. Supreme Court acts in a serious and constitutionally sound manner.'" *C-SPAN/PSB Supreme Court Survey 2017* (Mar. 17, 2017) (www.c-span.org /SCOTUSsurvey2017/). "Robert Green, Principal at PSB, which has conducted 11 national public opinion studies on the high court, including six studies commissioned by C-SPAN[, opines that] 'The public's perception of the [U.S. Supreme] Court as a partisan, political entity did not form overnight. A direct line can be drawn between President Obama lecturing Justices during his State of the Union address and later President Trump openly criticizing decisions and judges by name. The high court's decision to remain literally out of sight has hurt rather than helped their reputation. . . ." Press Release, *New C-SPAN/PSB Survey: American Attitudes about U.S. Supreme Court* (Mar. 17, 2017) (http://static.c-spanvideo.org/files /pressCenter/C-SPAN+Poll+on+Supreme+Court+August+2018.pdf).

When it comes to the Supreme Court of the United States, we rely heavily upon the personal ethics of the lifetime appointees to this court to interpret the federal constitution free from partisan concerns and political influence. The U.S. Supreme Court has not imposed upon its justices any written or actionable code of judicial conduct. Federal law provides only incomplete protection. As explained in a Summer 2013 article in the Georgetown Journal of Legal Ethics by Amanda Frost, *Judicial Ethics and Supreme Court Exceptionalism*, 26 Geo. J. Legal Ethics 443 (2013):

> Today, three different statutes govern recusal of federal judges, of which only Title 28, Section 455 of the United States Code applies to the Supreme Court. That statute requires "[a]ny justice, judge, or magistrate judge of the United States" to "disqualify himself. . . ." The same is currently not true for the Justices on the U.S. Supreme Court. Although there are no written rules governing recusal procedures, the longstanding practice has been for each Justice to decide for him or herself whether to step aside, usually without issuing any explanation. . . .
>
> The [federal] Ethics in Government Act of 1978 requires most high-level federal officials in all three branches of the federal government to file annual reports in which they publicly disclose aspects of their finances. . . . The Act applies to all federal judges, including Supreme Court Justices. . . .
>
> The Ethics Reform Act of 1989 placed strict limits on outside earned income and gifts for all federal officials, including federal judges. Judges and Justices are prohibited from most outside employment with the exception of teaching. . . .
>
> The Judicial Councils Reform and Judicial Conduct and Disability Act of 1980 ("Judicial Conduct and Disability Act") authorizes anyone to file a complaint [against] a judge . . . The Act applies to circuit judges, district court judges, bankruptcy judges, and magistrate judges, but not Supreme Court Justices.
>
> The Code of Conduct for United States Judges . . . excludes the Supreme Court Justices. . . .

Id. at 445–455 (footnotes omitted). As this article indicates, the primary source of federal judicial ethics, the Code of Conduct for United States Judges, excludes the Justices of the United States Supreme Court.

The Supreme Court of the State of Florida, on the other hand, imposes the same Code of Judicial Conduct upon Florida Supreme Court justices as it does upon every other judge or person performing judicial functions under Article V of the Florida Constitution. *See In re Code of Judicial Conduct*, 643 So. 2d 1037, 1042 (Fla. 1994) (defining "Judge" under the Code of Judicial Conduct to include "Article V, Florida Constitution judges [of which Florida Supreme Court Justices are included] and, where applicable, those persons performing judicial functions under the direction or supervision of an Article V judge."). Perhaps in case the Code's definition of "Judge" leaves any doubt, a later provision of the Code adds: "This Code applies to justices of the Supreme Court and judges of the District Courts of Appeal, Circuit Courts, and County Courts." *Id.* at 1061. Yet does anything in this Code of Judicial Conduct subject a Florida Supreme Court justice to discipline or sanctions for failing to interpret properly the Constitution of the State of Florida? The answer: it depends.

Canon 2 of the Code requires a judge to "comply with the law" and "not allow family, social, political or other relationships to influence the judge's judicial conduct or judgment." *Id.* at 1043. Canon 3 requires a "judge shall be faithful to the law and . . . not be swayed by partisan interests, public clamor, or fear of criticism." *Id.* at 1045. "A judge shall disqualify himself or herself in a proceeding in which the judge's impartiality might reasonably be questioned" per Canon 3. *Id.* at 1047. Canons 4 and 5 prohibit certain judicial behavior and extrajudicial activities that might "cast reasonable doubt on the judge's capacity to act impartially as a judge . . . demean the judicial office; or . . . interfere with the proper performance of judicial duties." *Id.* at 1050. Canon 6 restricts judicial financial activities and creates reporting requirements. *Id.* at 1056.

But it is Canon 7 that addresses political activity most explicitly. It begins with the statement that "a judge or candidate for judicial office shall refrain from inappropriate political activity" in all caps and proceeds to enumerate examples of appropriate and inappropriate political activity. As would be expected in a state like Florida's where judges may be elected or retained via election, campaigning is permitted, but must "maintain the dignity appropriate to judicial office and act in a manner consistent with the integrity and independence of the judiciary. . . ." *Id.* at 1059. Case law precedent exists exploring the boundaries of Canon 7. But to date, no case law precedent disciplines or punishes a judge for interpreting the Constitution of the State of Florida in a partisan fashion.

So as to the question of whether anything in the Code of Judicial Conduct of the state of Florida subjects a Florida Supreme Court justice to discipline or sanctions for failing to interpret properly the Constitution of the State of Florida, we suggest the answer depends on whether that interpretation was reached in violation of the Code of Judicial Conduct. A particular philosophy, without more, would not appear to be actionable under the Code. It would seem that a Florida Supreme Court justice's underlying temperament could "lean left" or "lean right" without running afoul of the Florida Code of Judicial Conduct.

———————

Notes and Questions to Consider:

1. What benefits, if any, accrue from the fact that the Code of Conduct for United States Judges does not apply to the justices of the United States Supreme Court? Assuming there are benefits, why would the Florida Supreme Court subject its justices to the Florida Code of Judicial Conduct?

2. Generally speaking, when a judge or justice of a court other than the United States Supreme Court enters an order that makes a harmful legal error, and the aggrieved party preserved that error below and files a timely and sufficient Notice of Appeal, the appellate court could be convinced to reverse or quash the order containing the error. Would the fact that the lower court judge or judges signed such a legally erroneous order subject the judge or judges to discipline under the Florida Code of Judicial Conduct? Why or why not?

3. What would you call a decision of the Supreme Court of the State of Florida that misinterprets the plain language of the Constitution of the State of Florida, does so by citing only to the text of Florida's constitution and without any citation to any other authority, and contains a plain statement that the Supreme Court of the United States agrees is an adequate and independent basis for that decision under Florida state law? (Hint: Remember these words quoted in Chapter 1 of this text: "We are not final because we are infallible, but we are infallible only because we are final." *Brown v. Allen*, 344 U.S. 443 (1953) (Jackson, J., concurring)).

4. Florida's constitution will soon hold Florida judges to a higher ethical standard. Effective December 31, 2022, Article V, Section 13 of Florida's constitution will contain a new subsection b (and renumber the existing text as subsection a). As amended by Constitution Revision Commission, Revision No. 7 (2018), the new Article V will read:

SECTION 13. *Ethics in the judiciary.*—

(a) All justices and judges shall devote full time to their judicial duties. A justice or judge shall not engage in the practice of law or hold office in any political party.

(b) A former justice or former judge shall not lobby for compensation on issues of policy, appropriations, or procurement before the legislative or executive branches of state government for a period of six years after he or she vacates his or her judicial position. The legislature may enact legislation to implement this subsection, including, but not limited to, defining terms and providing penalties for violations. Any such law shall not contain provisions on any other subject.

B. Standards of Review and Levels of Scrutiny

When ruling on a state constitutional law claim, the Florida court must review the law or action at issue, and to the extent the Florida court is an appellate court, must also review the judgment or ruling made below. What rules apply to Florida courts in these activities, and do those rules restrain the judiciary or empower it? Consider the following.

1. Review of Findings of Fact and Conclusions of Law

Regarding the standard of appellate review, the Supreme Court of the State of Florida holds that when:

> the issues we consider are ones of constitutional or statutory interpretation, this Court's review is *de novo. See Zingale v. Powell*, 885 So. 2d 277, 280 (Fla. 2004) ("Although we take into consideration the district court's analysis on the issue, constitutional interpretation, like statutory interpretation, is performed *de novo*."). In *Zingale*, while recognizing the fundamental nature of a constitutional edict, we emphasized that the principles governing constitutional interpretation largely parallel those of statutory interpretation.

Florida Hosp. Waterman, Inc. v. Buster, 984 So. 2d 478, 485 (Fla. 2008). "The determination of a statute's constitutionality and the interpretation of a constitutional provision are both questions of law reviewed de novo by [the Florida Supreme] Court." *Florida Dep't of Revenue v. City of Gainesville*, 918 So. 2d 250, 256 (Fla. 2005). Because the appellate standard of review is *de novo*, the appellate court will read but will not give deference to the trial court's ultimate legal opinion as to whether the action or law is constitutional or unconstitutional:

> A *de novo* standard of review generally means that the trial court's findings are not binding on the appellate court. Courts have traditionally defined "*de novo* review" to mean that "the whole process before the reviewing court starts from scratch, as if the proceedings below had never occurred; by definition, *de novo* review entails consideration of an issue as if it had not been decided previously." *De novo* review requires the court to make a [legal] judgment independent of the lower court's judgment, and to do so without deference to that court's analysis and conclusions.

Patrick John McGinley, Florida Municipal Law and Practice § 10:9 (Thomson Reuters 2018 ed).

Although *de novo* is the standard of review of the lower Florida tribunal's conclusions of law, the standard of review of its findings of fact is whether competent, substantial evidence exists in support of the factual findings. A finding of fact is supported by competent and substantial evidence whenever the record on appeal contains admissible evidence supporting that fact, even if other evidence disputes that fact. The question of whether the evidence is competent and substantial is a question of sufficiency, not weight. The Florida Supreme Court holds that "the weight and sufficiency of evidence are two separate concepts. Specifically, sufficiency tests the adequacy and credibility of the evidence, whereas weight refers to the balance of the evidence." *Wiggins v. Florida Dep't of Highway Safety & Motor Vehicles*, 209

So. 3d 1165, 1173 (Fla. 2017). A competent, substantial evidence analysis only tests whether the evidence was sufficient and does not test its weight. In this way, the appellate courts defer to the trial courts and the finders of fact for their determination as to what evidence outweighs other evidence and what evidence is to be believed or disbelieved, credited or discredited. Granted, when considering whether the fact "findings were supported by competent, substantial evidence . . . [s]ome consideration of the evidence is inescapable in the competent, substantial evidence determination. But these are legal questions that call for an unbiased review" and not a review for weight, credibility, or persuasiveness. *Id.*

———

Notes and Questions to Consider:

1. Considering the greater deference given on appeal to findings of fact versus conclusions of law, just how important are the trial-level proceedings in a typical constitutional law claim? If, at the trial level, the judge or jury accepts disputed testimony that makes proving the constitutional violation more difficult, what effect will this have upon the constitutional law case as it proceeds upon appeal?

2. If a Florida state trial court misinterprets Florida's constitution or misinterprets the law that allegedly violates the constitution, what standard of review applies on appeal to a Florida appellate court? How onerous is that standard of review?

2. Levels of Scrutiny: Rational Basis, Intermediate, and Strict

In addition to the review of findings of fact for competent, substantial evidence, and the *de novo* review of conclusions of law, constitutional law litigation has evolved its own levels of scrutiny of the law under review, those typically being described as either strict scrutiny, intermediate scrutiny, or the rational relationship test. These levels of scrutiny evolved in federal courts interpreting the federal constitution and were adopted by Florida state courts interpreting Florida's constitution. A 2002 article from the University of Pennsylvania Journal of Constitutional Law opines why these different levels of scrutiny evolved. According to R. Randall Kelso, *Standards of Review under the Equal Protection Clause and Related Constitutional Doctrines Protecting Individual Rights: The "Base Plus Six" Model and Modern Supreme Court Practice*, 4 U. Pa. J. Const. L. 225 (2002):

> Whenever the [U.S.] Supreme Court reviews legislation, [it] considers whether the legislation represents a good enough fit to pass constitutional review. . . .
>
> The first inquiry is what governmental interests support a statute's constitutionality. Depending on the standard of review, the governmental interests must be legitimate or permissible; important, substantial, or significant; or compelling or overriding. . . . .

The second inquiry concerns the relationship between the statute's means and how it advances those governmental ends. Depending on the standard of review, the statute must have a rational relationship, a substantial relationship, or a direct relationship to its ends.

The third inquiry focuses on the burdens imposed by the statute's means. Depending on the standard of review, the statute's burden must not be irrational, substantially more burdensome than necessary, or it must be the least restrictive burden that would be effective in advancing the governmental interests.

The three main standards of review track the responses to these three questions. Thus, under minimum rationality review [also known as the rational relationship test], the legislation only has to be rationally related to [a] legitimate government interest[], and not impose irrational burdens on individuals. Under intermediate review, the legislation must be substantially related to advancing important or substantial governmental interests, and not be substantially more burdensome than necessary to advance these interests. Under strict scrutiny, the statute must directly advance compelling governmental interests and be the least restrictive effective means of doing so.

Id. at 227–29.

Although the article above refers to the decisions of the U.S. Supreme Court, the public policy concerns expressed in the article apply everywhere, including Florida. The Florida Supreme Court surely considered these same concerns when it adopted the same three main levels of scrutiny: strict scrutiny, intermediate scrutiny, and the rational relationship test.

In Florida, strict scrutiny is applied to review, for example, a law that severely burdens a Floridian's fundamental right. The Florida Supreme Court once held that:

a fundamental right[,] we believe[,] demands the compelling state interest standard. This test shifts the burden of proof to the state to justify an intrusion on privacy. The burden can be met by demonstrating that the challenged regulation serves a compelling state interest and accomplishes its goal through the use of the least intrusive means. . . . Although [strict scrutiny is] a strong standard to review a claim . . . , "this constitutional provision was not intended to provide an absolute guarantee against all governmental intrusion into the private life of an individual." [It] does not confer a complete immunity from governmental regulation and will yield to compelling governmental interests.

Winfield v. Div. of Pari-Mutuel Wagering, 477 So. 2d 544, 547 (Fla. 1985) (addressing Florida's enumerated right to privacy under its state constitution).

Intermediate scrutiny in Florida constitutional law, just as in the federal, examines whether the challenged law is:

"substantially related to an important governmental objective." *Clark v. Jeter*, 486 U.S. 456, 461 (1988). While the State still bears the burden under this standard, the relationship between the Legislature's ends and means need only be a "reasonable fit."

Norman v. State, 215 So. 3d 18, 36–37 (Fla. 2017), cert. denied, 138 S.Ct. 469 (2017).

The rational relationship test in Florida constitutional law, like in federal constitutional law, is as follows:

[First, the Florida court must] question [whether the legislation] is a legitimate goal within the scope of the state's police power. Having established that the legislative purpose is proper, [the court] must [then] determine whether the means chosen by the legislature bears a rational relationship to the concededly proper goal.

State v. Saiez, 489 So. 2d 1125 (Fla. 1986). When describing the lack of rigor of the rational relationship test, the Florida Supreme Court acknowledges that "[r]ational basis review is the most deferential to the State, as 'a relatively relaxed standard . . .'" *Norman v. State*, 215 So. 3d 18, 36 (Fla. 2017), cert. denied, 138 S.Ct. 469 (2017).

Recently, the Florida Supreme Court took the opportunity to elaborate on these three standards of scrutiny under the Florida Constitution in *Norman v. State*, 215 So. 3d 18 (Fla. 2017), cert. denied, 138 S.Ct. 469 (2017).

Norman v. State
Supreme Court of Florida, 2017
215 So. 3d 18

[T]here are three "traditionally expressed levels" of scrutiny: rational basis, intermediate scrutiny, and strict scrutiny. As this Court has clarified, each level has a concomitant presumption of validity or invalidity and standard of proof. Rational basis review is the most deferential to the State, as a relatively relaxed standard reflecting the Court's awareness that the drawing of lines that create distinctions is peculiarly a legislative task and an unavoidable one.

On the opposite end of the spectrum of constitutional analysis from rational basis review is strict scrutiny, the most rigorous level of review. If a law impairs the exercise of a fundamental right, it must pass strict scrutiny. The law is presumptively unconstitutional. Laws reviewed under strict scrutiny must further a compelling interest and be narrowly tailored to achieve that interest. *Citizens United v. Fed. Election Comm'n*, 558 U.S. 310, 340, 130 S.Ct. 876, 175 L.Ed.2d 753 (2010); see also *D.M.T. v. T.M.H.*, 129 So. 3d 320, 339 (Fla. 2013) ("Strict scrutiny . . . requires the State to prove that the legislation furthers a compelling governmental interest through the least intrusive means."). When a law is reviewed under strict scrutiny, the State bears the burden of proving its validity.

Somewhere between rational basis review and strict scrutiny is intermediate scrutiny. Under this less rigorous standard, the challenged law must be substantially related to an important governmental objective. While the State still bears the burden under this standard, the relationship between the Legislature's ends and means need only be a "reasonable fit."

———————

Notes and Questions to Consider:

1. Who bears the burden of proof under each level of scrutiny: the government defending the constitutionality of the statute, or the challenger?

2. In certain circumstances, would the outcome of a constitutional litigation turn on what level of scrutiny applies? Why or why not?

C. Canons of Construction for Interpreting Florida's Constitution

In addition to the Florida Code of Judicial Conduct, the Supreme Court of the State of Florida provides the state's lower courts with the following guidelines to the constitution's proper interpretation. We refer to them here as the "canons of construction."

1. Obey the Clear and Unambiguous Language in Florida's Constitution

The Supreme Court of the State of Florida holds that when "the issue presented in the case involves constitutional construction, we begin with the actual language of the constitutional provision." *Graham v. Haridopolos*, 108 So. 3d 597, 604 (Fla. 2013). This means that whenever a Florida court faces the issue of what Florida's constitution means, "any inquiry into the proper interpretation of a constitutional provision must begin with an examination of that provision's explicit language." *Caribbean Conservation Corp. v. Fla. Fish & Wildlife Conservation Comm'n*, 838 So. 2d 492, 501 (Fla. 2003).

In the words of the Supreme Court of Florida: "What is in the Constitution always must prevail over emotion. Our oaths as judges require that this principle is our polestar, and it alone." *Bush v. Schiavo*, 885 So. 2d 321, 336 (Fla. 2004).

Assuming the constitutional language is clear and unambiguous, then it answers the inquiry as to whether a constitutional infirmity exists. If Florida's constitution requires something to be done in a certain way, then doing it in a different way is unconstitutional. The Florida Supreme Court holds that:

> where the Constitution expressly provides the manner of doing a thing, it impliedly forbids its being done in a substantially different manner. Even though the Constitution does not in terms prohibit the doing of a thing in another manner, the fact that it has prescribed the manner in which

> the thing shall be done is itself a prohibition against a different manner of doing it. Therefore, when the Constitution prescribes the manner of doing an act, the manner prescribed is exclusive, and it is beyond the power of the Legislature to enact a statute that would defeat the purpose of the constitutional provision.

Bush v. Holmes, 919 So. 2d 392, 407 (Fla. 2006). Stated somewhat differently, "where one method or means of exercising a power is prescribed in a constitution it excludes its exercise in other ways." *S & J Transp., Inc. v. Gordon*, 176 So. 2d 69, 71 (Fla. 1965).

This requires, of course, that the language of Florida's constitution be clear and unambiguous. If the language is not clear and unambiguous, then Florida courts proceed to use the following canons of construction to overcome that ambiguity. In the words of the Florida Supreme Court: "It is precisely because [the particular language in the state constitution] is not clear and unambiguous regarding [the question at issue] that we look to accepted standards of construction applicable to constitutional provisions." *Bush v. Holmes*, 919 So. 2d 392, 408 (Fla. 2006).

We journey back in time to 1933 for *City of Jacksonville v. Continental Can Co.*, 113 Fla. 168 (1933), an excellent example as to how and why we obey the clear and unambiguous language we find in Florida's constitution:

City of Jacksonville v. Continental Can Co.
Supreme Court of Florida, Division A, 1933
113 Fla. 168

The provisions of a written Constitution are presumed to have been more carefully and deliberately framed than is the case with statutes; hence it would seem that less latitude should be taken by the courts in construing constitutions than in the construction of statutes, but it is a well-settled principle of construction that the construction should not be technical nor liberal, but the aim should be to give effect to the purpose indicated by a fair interpretation of the language, the natural signification of the words used in the order, and grammatical arrangement in which they have been placed. If the words thus regarded convey a definite meaning and involve no absurdity or contradiction between the parts of the same instrument, no construction is allowable.

The words and terms of a Constitution are to be interpreted in their most usual and obvious meaning, unless the text suggests that they have been used in a technical sense. The presumption is in favor of the natural and popular meaning in which the words are usually understood by the people who have adopted them.

The above principles are generally accepted as sound in the construction of State Constitutions.

It has been said that, as statutes are hastily and unskillfully drawn, they need construction to make them sensible, but Constitutions import the utmost discrimination in the use of language, that which the words declare is the meaning of the instrument. It must be very plain, nay absolutely certain, that the people did not intend what the language they had employed in its natural signification imports before a court should feel at liberty to depart from the plain meaning of a constitutional provision.

2. Presume the Law or Action Was Constitutional

When strict scrutiny does not apply, a duly enacted law is presumed to be constitutional and the Florida Supreme Court "recognize[s] that one asserting the unconstitutionality of an act has the burden of demonstrating clearly that the act is invalid." *Lasky v. State Farm Insurance*, 296 So. 2d 9 (Fla. 1974). A finding of unconstitutionality is disfavored. The Supreme Court of Florida holds that Florida courts "have the power to declare laws unconstitutional only as a matter of imperative and unavoidable necessity," *State ex rel. Crim v. Juvenal*, 118 Fla. 487, 159 So. 663, 664 (1935). For this reason, Florida courts are "bound 'to resolve all doubts as to the validity of [a] statute in favor of its constitutionality, provided the statute may be given a fair construction that is consistent with the federal and state constitutions as well as with the legislative intent.'" *Caple v. Tuttle's Design-Build, Inc.*, 753 So. 2d 49, 51 (Fla. 2000).

"When a legislative enactment is challenged the court should be liberal in its interpretation; every doubt should be resolved in favor of the constitutionality of the law, and the law should not be held invalid unless clearly unconstitutional beyond a reasonable doubt." *Taylor v. Dorsey*, 19 So. 2d 876, 882 (1944). "The Constitution of this state is not a grant of power to the Legislature, but a limitation only upon legislative power, and unless legislation be clearly contrary to some express or necessarily implied prohibition found in the Constitution, the courts are without authority to declare legislative Acts invalid." *Savage v. Board of Public Instruction*, 101 Fla. 1362, 133 So. 341, 344 (1931).

3. Consider Stare Decisis

To the extent that prior case law precedent might violate a current state constitutional right, that prior precedent cannot withstand a constitutional challenge because "[a]s is self-evident, even the common law must bend before the dictates of the Florida Constitution." *Haag v. State*, 591 So. 2d 614, 618 (Fla. 1992). But what about prior case law precedent that interprets the state constitution? Under the doctrine of stare decisis, such precedent might bind the hands of later courts who interpret those same constitutional provisions after the binding case law precedent is issued.

In Florida as elsewhere, stare decisis refers to the acknowledgement of precedent and the following of that precedent when the issues underlying that precedent arise again in later litigation. The Florida Supreme Court recognizes at least two forms of stare decisis:

"Rule stare decisis" involves the "Supreme Court's choice of [the applicable] legal standard or test" while "result stare decisis" is the result reached by applying that legal standard to the particular facts of the case.

Butterworth v. Nat'l League of Prof'l Baseball Clubs, 644 So. 2d 1021, 1024 n.7 (Fla. 1994).

"Critics argue that strict adherence to old decisions can result in grave injustices and cite as an example the repudiation of *Plessy v. Ferguson*, 163 U.S. 537 (1896) by *Brown v. Board of Education*, 347 U.S. 483 (1954)." *See* "Stare Decisis," BLACK'S LAW DICTIONARY (10th ed. 2014.)

As to Florida's exceptions to stare decisis, we present the Florida Supreme Court's 1992 decision in *Haag v. State*, 591 So. 2d 614 (Fla. 1992).

Haag v. State
Supreme Court of Florida, 1992
591 So. 2d 614

We have for review the . . . following question of great public importance:

Does the rule 3.850 provision which [sets a deadline for filing postconviction motions under that rule] prevent consideration of such a motion which was turned over to prison authorities for mailing within the prescribed time limit but was stamped in by the court clerk after that time period had run?

Id. at 1145. We have jurisdiction. Art. V, § 3(b)(4), Fla. Const. We answer the certified question in the negative and quash the decision below.

While incarcerated in Union Correctional facility, James J. Haag deposited in the outgoing prisoner mail a pro se motion for postconviction relief pursuant to Florida Rule of Criminal Procedure 3.850. He did so five days prior to the expiration of the two-year time limit imposed by the rule—a date reliably documented in the prison's mail log. Although there is no direct evidence of the date on which petitioner's motion was received at the court, it was not stamped "filed" by the clerk of court until four days after the time limit had run. Later, the trial court denied the motion as untimely. . . .

A basic guarantee of Florida law is that the right to relief through the writ of habeas corpus must be "grantable of right, freely and without cost." Art. I, § 13, Fla. Const. In the case of *State v. Bolyea*, 520 So. 2d 562, 563 (Fla. 1988), we recognized that Rule 3.850 is a "procedural vehicle for the collateral remedy otherwise available by writ of habeas corpus." Accordingly, in approaching the present case, we must be mindful that the right to habeas relief protected by article I, section 13 of the Florida Constitution is implicated here.

It is true that the right to habeas relief, like any other constitutional right, is subject to certain reasonable limitations consistent with the full and fair exercise of the right. For example, we have noted that the two-year time limitation imposed by Rule 3.850 serves to promote the fairness and finality required of our criminal justice system:

> It serves to reduce piecemeal litigation and the assertion of stale claims while at the same time preserves the right to unlimited access to the courts where there is newly discovered evidence or where there have been fundamental constitutional changes in the law with retroactive application.

Johnson v. State, 536 So. 2d 1009, 1011 (Fla. 1988). Accord art. I, § 21, Fla. Const. (right of access to courts). However, nothing in our law suggests that the two-year limitation must be applied harshly or contrary to fundamental principles of fairness. . . .

Finding this state of affairs fundamentally unfair, the United States Supreme Court held that a "mailbox rule" applies in this context. Under the mailbox rule, a petition or notice of appeal filed by a pro se inmate is deemed filed at the moment in time when the inmate loses control over the document by entrusting its further delivery or processing to agents of the state. Usually, this point occurs when the inmate places the document in the hands of prison officials. [*See Houston v. Lack*, 487 U.S. 266 (1988).] . . .

We find the approach taken by the [U.S. Supreme] Court in *Houston* to be most consistent with the simplicity and fairness demanded both by the Florida Rules of Criminal Procedure and article I, section 13 of the Florida Constitution. Rule 3.850 says that a person has two years to file the motion, and a full two years it must be. The state cannot subtract from that two-year period through the failure to deliver a pro se inmate's petition until after the period has expired, even if the delay is through honest oversight. Accordingly, we hold that the mailbox rule exists as a matter of Florida law. Art. I, § 13, Fla. Const.; Fla.R.Crim.P. 3.850. We caution, however, that this rule applies only to pro se petitioners who are incarcerated. Other litigants who have means of controlling the delivery of documents to the courthouse will continue to be subject to the traditional rules.

We also note that this mailbox rule will prevent yet another problem implicating constitutional rights. Under the Florida Constitution, all persons have a right to equal protection of the laws, particularly in matters affecting life and liberty. Art. I, § 2, Fla. Const. Obviously, this includes a right of equal access to the courts, which serve as the final arbiter of whether life or liberty may be forfeited lawfully. Compare id. with art. I, § 21, Fla. Const.

A rule other than the mailbox rule would interject a level of arbitrariness that could undermine equal protection and equal access to the courts. For example, two pro se inmates who delivered a document to prison officials at the same time, seeking the same relief, and facing the same court deadline, could be treated quite differently based entirely on happenstance. One inmate's petition might make it to the courthouse on time, while the other's might be delayed for unknown reasons. The first would obtain a full hearing, while the second would be denied relief. Such arbitrariness cannot fairly be characterized either as equal protection or equal access to the courts, and it therefore cannot be allowed. Art. I, §§ 2, 21, Fla. Const.

We recognize that our opinion today recedes from and overrules earlier precedent in this jurisdiction. The opinions of the district courts in *Lindsay v. State*, 579 So. 2d 350 (Fla. 1st DCA 1991), *Ruggirello v. State*, 566 So. 2d 30 (Fla. 4th DCA), review dismissed, 569 So. 2d 1280 (Fla. 1990), *Clifford v. State*, 513 So. 2d 772 (Fla. 2d DCA 1987), and *Tucker v. Wainwright*, 235 So. 2d 38 (Fla. 2d DCA 1970), contain results or analyses inconsistent with our views and accordingly are disapproved to the extent that they conflict with this opinion. We also are receding from *Walker v. Wainwright*, 303 So. 2d 321 (Fla. 1974), and *State ex rel. Ervin v. Smith*, 160 So. 2d 518 (Fla. 1964), to the extent they conflict with the views expressed above.

While the doctrine of stare decisis normally would require a greater deference to this prior precedent, we find that the demands of justice and the principles of constitutional law recited above require an alteration in the precedent. As is self-evident, even the common law must bend before the dictates of the Florida Constitution. Not even the hoariest precedent is permitted to violate the guarantees of habeas relief, equal protection, and equal access to the courts, or any of the other fundamental rights set forth in the Declaration of Rights. Art. I, Fla. Const.

Moreover, as we have said before, stare decisis is not an ironclad and unwavering rule that the present always must bend to the voice of the past, however outmoded or meaningless that voice may have become. It is a rule that precedent must be followed except when departure is necessary to vindicate other principles of law or to remedy continued injustice. *McGregor v. Provident Trust Co.*, 119 Fla. 718, 162 So. 323 (1935). We find that the guarantees embodied in Florida's Declaration of Rights are best vindicated by overruling the contrary precedent noted above.

For the foregoing reasons, the opinion below is quashed and this cause is remanded for further proceedings consistent with the views expressed above.

It is so ordered.

Notes and Questions to Consider:

1. What are Florida's exceptions to stare decisis as identified in *Haag v. State*?

2. To what extent was the departure from stare decisis in *Haag v. State* a result of prior precedent being unconstitutional? To what extent is it a result of a reinterpretation of the Florida Constitution's right of habeas corpus?

4. Determine the Intent of the Framers or Voters

For the U.S. Supreme Court, it is a political question as to whether to interpret the text of the U.S. Constitution by following the intent of the framers. Not so when Florida courts interpret Florida's constitution. Binding case law precedent of Florida's supreme court informs lower courts that, in construing provisions of Florida's constitution, the first step is to ascertain and effectuate the intent of the framers and the people. *Bailey v. Ponce de Leon Port Auth.*, 398 So. 2d 812, 814 (Fla. 1981). Stated somewhat differently, courts are to give the Florida Constitution's words the meaning suggested by the circumstances leading to the adoption of the constitutional provision the court is interpreting. *Gallant v. Stephens*, 358 So. 2d 536, 539 (Fla. 1978). In so doing, Florida courts have, with Florida Supreme Court approval, turned to sources such as the documents of the Florida Constitutional Revision Commission and the Florida Legislature. *See, e.g., Gallant v. Stephens*, 358 So. 2d 536, 539 (Fla. 1978).

When the provision being interpreted is within the Florida Constitution due to the passage by the people of an amendment to the Florida Constitution, the court must give effect to the intent of the voters who approved that amendment by their initiative. *Gallant v. Stephens*, 358 So. 2d 536, 540 (Fla. 1978).

Below are excerpts from three separate cases illustrating a Florida court's reliance on the intent of the framers or voters: *Department of Revenue v. Leon County*, 560 So. 2d 318 (Fla. 1st DCA 1990); *Gallant v. Stephens*, 358 So. 2d 536 (Fla. 1978), and *Graham v. Haridopolous*, 108 So. 3d 597 (Fla. 2013). When reviewing each case, please take note as to how and when the court considered the voters' or framers' intent.

Florida Department of Revenue v. Leon County

First District Court of Appeal of Florida, 1990
560 So. 2d 318

This appeal presents the question of whether the trial court correctly held that Chapter 83-339, Laws of Florida, is unconstitutional insofar as it provides for a deduction of a six percent service charge from the Gas Tax Collection Trust Fund. We agree with the trial court that the Florida Constitution prohibits this deduction.

Pursuant to Article IX, Section 16, 1885 Florida Constitution as amended, Article XII, Section 9, 1968 Florida Constitution as amended, and Section 206.41, Florida Statutes (1983), the state imposes upon the sale of motor fuel a two cent per gallon tax (the constitutional gas tax). The proceeds are placed in the Gas Tax Collection Trust Fund and administered by the State Board of Administration. Section 16 prescribes a formula for the allocation of the tax proceeds among the counties, and provides that the proceeds shall be used for the servicing of bonds and for the construction and maintenance of roads and bridges within the respective counties. Section 16(d) prohibits the use by the legislature of the proceeds for any other purpose. . . . Section 215.20(1), Florida Statutes (1983) provides in part:

> A service charge of 6 percent, representing the estimated pro rata share of the cost of general government paid from the General Revenue Fund, shall be deducted from the moneys and trust funds enumerated in s. 215.22.

The funds subject to this service charge are listed in Section 215.22, and Chapter 83-339 amends Section 215.22 to add the Gas Tax Collection Trust Fund to the list. . . . The parties agree that Section 16(d) of the 1885 Constitution prohibits deduction of such a charge. The issue is whether the 1968 Constitution authorizes the deduction.

The 1968 Constitution retains the constitutional gas tax but changes the formula for allocation to the counties. The old formula was retained for the purpose of securing preexisting obligations.

Section 9(c)(2) states:

> *Article IX, Section 16, of the Constitution of 1885, as amended, is adopted by this reference as a part of this revision as completely as though incorporated herein verbatim for the purpose of providing that after the effective date of this revision the proceeds of the "second gas tax" as referred to therein shall be allocated among the several counties in accordance with the formula stated therein to the extent necessary to comply with all obligations to or for the benefit of holders of bonds, revenue certificates and tax anticipation certificates or any refundings thereof secured by any portion of the "second gas tax."*

Section 9(c)(4) states:

> *Subject to the requirements of paragraph (2) of this subsection and after payment of administrative expenses, the "second gas tax" shall be allocated to the account of each of the several counties. . . .*

Appellant submits that the above reference to "administrative expenses" authorizes the deduction of the charge for the administrative expenses of general government. The trial court's final order held that "[t]he term administrative expenses . . . is intended to be specifically limited to the expenses of the State Board of Administration as set forth in Section 16(d) of Article IX, 1885 Florida Constitution." . . .

. . . [T]he 1968 Constitution as amended cannot be read as abolishing the prohibition expressed in the 1885 Constitution and incorporated into the more recent document. Provisions of the Florida Constitution are to be construed so as to effectuate the intent of the framers and the people. Gallant at 539. The framers of the 1968 Constitution incorporated Article IX, Section 16 of the 1885 Constitution and clearly stated that in certain respects, e.g., the method of allocation to the counties, the constitutional scheme was to be changed. There is no clear statement, however, that the long-standing limitation upon the use of constitutional gas tax revenue has been discarded. The general term "administrative expenses" cannot be read to override the specific language of prohibition found in the 1885 Constitution.

Rather, it is clear that Section 9(c)(4) is meant as a clarification of how gas tax funds are to be expended under the new formula. Section 9(c)(4), in conjunction with Section 9(c)(2), simply establishes that the new formula for allocation of gas tax proceeds to the counties is to be employed after payment of the Board's administrative expenses and subject to the directive in subsection (2) that the old formula is to be employed to the extent necessary. . . . It follows that the trial court correctly held that Ch. 83-339(1) is partially unconstitutional. AFFIRMED.

Gallant v. Stephens
Supreme Court of Florida, 1978
358 So. 2d 536

. . . The principal issue before us is whether the Legislature has the power to authorize a county to furnish municipal-type services funded by ad valorem taxes, solely in its unincorporated area, without referendum, by creating a taxing unit comprising that geographical area.

The overall scheme of Article VII, Section 9 [of Florida's constitution] provides the starting point for our analysis. Entitled "Local taxes", that section provides certain local governmental units—counties, municipalities and school districts—with the authority to levy ad valorem taxes on real . . . property for county, municipal and school purposes up to a maximum of ten mills for each. It also authorizes "special districts" to tax for their districts to the extent of millage limits prescribed by the Legislature, with the approval of voters within the district. In addition, the last sentence of Section 9(b) expressly provides that a "county furnishing municipal services may, to the extent authorized by law, levy additional taxes within the limits fixed for municipal purposes."

The major one is whether the last sentence of Section 9(b) enables a county, without referendum, to levy a municipal service tax in addition to other county taxes on county residents in unincorporated areas, or whether it restricts additional county levies for services furnished only to municipalities.

In construing provisions of the Florida Constitution, we are obliged to ascertain and effectuate the intent of the framers and the people. *State ex rel. Dade County v. Dickinson*, 230 So. 2d 130 (Fla. 1969); *Gray v. Bryant*, 125 So. 2d 846 (Fla. 1960). Where possible, we are guided by circumstances leading to the adoption of a provision. In this case we have attempted to discern the rationale which led to the adoption of the last sentence in Article VII, Section 9(b). Its history in the 1966 Constitution Revision Commission and in the Florida Legislature supports appellee's view of its import.

It is reasonably clear from the minutes and notes of the Commission, and from the reports of the Legislature, that the focus of the last sentence of Section 9(b) was the delivery of municipal-type services by counties to all county residents, rather than the more narrow delivery of services solely to residents of intra-county municipalities. In fact, a proposal to restrict the last sentence of Section 9(b) so that it would authorize additional taxation only to the extent a county furnished municipal services "in unincorporated areas" was defeated in the Legislature on the ground that it would prevent counties from offering municipal services as well within municipal boundaries. No historical material contradictory to these indicators has been called to our attention.

. . . For these reasons we conclude that the last sentence of Section 9(b) provides express authority for . . . sanctioning taxing units as a method by which counties may tax to provide municipal services, within the 10 mill limit for "municipal purposes", without voter approval. Wholly independent of this county taxing power is the authority provided for "special districts" to meet the need for special purpose services in any geographical area which may (but need not) be within one county, under legislatively-set and voter-approved millage limitations.

. . . We hold, therefore, that . . . the Pinellas County Commission's resolution establishing a municipal service taxing unit in the unincorporated area of the county without voter approval is valid. The order of the Pinellas County Circuit Court is AFFIRMED.

Graham v. Haridopolos

Supreme Court of Florida, 2013
108 So. 3d 597

The issue presented to the Court in this case is one of constitutional construction: whether the Legislature or the constitutionally created Board of Governors has the power to control the setting of and appropriating for the expenditure of tuition and fees for the Florida university system under article IX, section 7(d), of the Florida Constitution. In 2007, the Legislature passed several statutes and included a provision in the 2007–2008 General Appropriations Act that exerted control over the setting of and appropriating for the expenditure of tuition and fees. The Petitioners challenge these statutes as unconstitutional, contending that the 2002 constitutional amendment creating the Board of Governors transferred the authority over tuition and fees to the Board, divesting the Legislature of any power over these funds.

Although the question in this case is whether the challenged statutes are constitutional, the answer hinges on our interpretation of the Florida Constitution. . . .

"When interpreting constitutional provisions, this Court endeavors to ascertain the will of the people in passing the amendment." In re Senate Joint Resolution of Legislative Apportionment 1176, 83 So. 3d 597, 599 (Fla. 2012). "In accord with those tenets of constitutional construction, this Court 'endeavors to construe a constitutional provision consistent with the intent of the framers and the voters.'" Id. at 614 (quoting *Zingale v. Powell*, 885 So. 2d 277, 282 (Fla. 2004)) . . . .

Because the issue presented in this case involves constitutional construction, we begin with the actual language of the constitutional provision. . . . Simply put, the language of article IX, section 7, is not "clear" or "unambiguous" and does not expressly "address[ ] the matter in issue." FACDL, 978 So. 2d at 140. We therefore turn to principles of construction, always endeavoring to construe the constitutional provision "in a manner consistent with the intent of the framers and voters." *W. Fla. Reg'l Med. Ctr., Inc. v. See*, 79 So. 3d 1, 9 (Fla. 2012).

We also review the ballot summary, because it is indicative of voter intent. See *Benjamin v. Tandem Healthcare, Inc.*, 998 So. 2d 566, 570 n. 3 (Fla. 2008) ("[B]allot materials are one source from which the voters' intent and the purpose of the amendment can be ascertained."). Here, the ballot summary that accompanied the amendment and appeared on the ballot also indicated a grant of power that appears to be executive and administrative in nature. The ballot title and summary provided as follows:

> *Ballot title:* Local trustees and statewide *governing board to manage* Florida's university system
>
> *Ballot summary:* A local board of trustees shall administer each state university. Each board shall have thirteen members dedicated to excellence in teaching, research, and service to community. A statewide governing board of seventeen members shall be responsible for the *coordinated and accountable operation* of the whole university system. *Wasteful duplication of facilities or programs is to be avoided.* Provides procedures for selection and confirmation of board members, including one student and one faculty representative per board.

In re Advisory Op. to Atty. Gen. ex rel. Local Trs., 819 So. 2d at 727–28 (emphasis added). Nowhere in the ballot title or ballot summary does it indicate that the voters or framers intended for the Board of Governors to have authority over the setting of and appropriating for the expenditure of tuition and fees.

When this Court approved the amendment for placement on the ballot, we concluded that

> the sole purpose of the proposed amendment is to create a governance of the state university system. The enumeration of the duties and responsibilities of the statewide board of governors and the local university boards of trustees is a necessary component of a single dominant plan that complies with the single-subject requirement. While the proposed amendment may affect more than one branch of government, we cannot say it substantially alters or performs the functions of multiple branches of government. . . .

Id. at 730. This Court also concluded that the amendment did not "substantially affect or change" article IX, section 1, of the Florida Constitution, id., which provides that the Legislature must make adequate provision for the establishment, maintenance, and operation of Florida's universities. See art. IX, § 1(a), Fla. Const. ("Adequate provision shall be made by law . . . for the establishment, maintenance, and operation of institutions of higher learning and other public education programs that the needs of the people may require.") . . . .

For the foregoing reasons, we hold that the constitutional source of the Legislature's authority to set and appropriate for the expenditure of tuition and fees derives from its power to raise revenue and appropriate for the expenditure of state funds. Nothing within the language of article IX, section 7, of the Florida Constitution indicates an intent to transfer this quintessentially legislative power to the Board of Governors. Accordingly, we conclude that the challenged statutes by which the

Legislature has exercised control over these funds are facially constitutional and approve the First District's decision.

———————

Notes and Questions to Consider:

1. Compare and contrast the use of the "intent of the framers" in these three cases excerpted above. All three mention the intent but to different degrees of analysis. In which was it a mere mention but not part of a thorough analysis? In which did the court delve deeply into that intent?

2. Assume you are making an argument for or against the constitutionality of a Florida statute or ordinance. To where will you turn to do your research and to make an argument as to the "intent of the framers?" Will the answer be different for an amendment to Florida's constitution than it will for part of the original text?

5. Interpret Parts of Florida's Constitution to Yield a Consistent Whole

A court must consider Florida's constitution as a whole whenever a court interprets an individual part of the Constitution. *Hall v. State*, 136 Fla. 644, 187 So. 392 (Fla. 1939). This means that, when a particular interpretation "represents the only interpretation consistent with the whole [Florida] Constitution," then that particular interpretation is preferred. *Gallant v. Stephens*, 358 So. 2d 536, 541 (Fla. 1978).

The Supreme Court of Florida interpreted one part of Florida's constitution to yield a consistent whole with the rest of the state constitution in *Bailey v. Ponce de Leon Port Authority*, 398 So. 2d 812 (Fla. 1981). This complex tax law case is edited for simplicity here.

Bailey v. Ponce de Leon Port Authority
Supreme Court of Florida, 1981
398 So. 2d 812

This appeal is from a trial court's final judgment, which ruled that chapter 69-1705, Laws of Florida, the appellee port authority's enabling act, is constitutional. We have jurisdiction[under Art. V, § 3(b)(1), Fla. Const.] and affirm.

[A 1963 enabling act] created the Ponce de Leon Inlet and Port District [and in that enabling act the Port District is authorized to impose] an annual tax levy of three mills: two mills (subject to referendum) for accumulation of funds and for payment of principal and interest on any bonds issued and one mill (not subject to referendum) to finance the administration of the district. . . . In 1965 the legislature amended and revised the district's enabling act. The district operated under the 1965 act until 1969 when the legislature [amended it again].

The 1969 act revised the section regarding tax levies. It maintains the three-mill cap, but unlike the two previous acts, the 1969 act does not require a referendum for the accumulation of funds.

. . . [T]he appellants filed suit against the port authority, alleging that by removing the referendum requirement on accumulating funds the legislature had violated article VII, section 9(b) of the state constitution. . . . The trial court ruled that chapter 69-1705 does not violate article VII, section 9(b) and . . . declared all taxes collected by the district duly authorized and valid and denied the relief requested by appellants. This appeal ensued.

We can find nothing in the state constitution which prohibits the legislature from rearranging the port authority's power to tax in the instant manner. The 1964 referendum approved the three-mill levy. Article VII, section 9(a) provides that special districts may be authorized by law to levy ad valorem taxes. . . . We find that deleting the referendum requirement regarding the accumulation of funds was within the legislature's power.

. . . This Court has previously found article VII, section 9(b) to be a limit on ad valorem tax millages for county and municipal purposes. See *State ex rel. Dade County v. Dickinson*, 230 So. 2d 130 (Fla. 1969). Viewing section 9(b) as a limitation on the power to tax does not require reversal.

We disagree with appellants' contention that the 1968 constitution mandated a referendum. . . . [It] authorized a total tax levy of three mills, and chapter 69-1705 maintained that tax levy. . . . If section 9(b) is a millage cap, chapter 69-1705 does not run afoul of [the Florida Constitution] because the act maintains, but does not increase, the total millage rate. . . . [Therefore,] chapter 69-1705 does not violate article VII, section 9(b) and the accumulation of funds under the district's one-mill tax levy does not require a referendum. . . .

The final judgment is affirmed.

———————

Note and Question to Consider:

1. In *Bailey v. Ponce de Leon Port Authority*, a 1963 enabling act created the Ponce de Leon Inlet and Port District and required a referendum for part of its taxing power. A 1969 law expanded its powers by removing the referendum requirement. Why did the Supreme Court of Florida approve this expansion of the agency's power by the Florida Legislature?

6. Interpret Words in Florida's Constitution *In Pari Materia*

The Latin phrase *in pari materia*, roughly translated, means "of the same matter" or "on the same subject." As used in the jurisprudence of Florida's constitution and elsewhere, *in pari materia* is a canon of construction requiring two parts of a same subsection to be interpreted harmoniously as one. Separate clauses within the same section of Florida's constitution are interpreted *in pari materia*. In this way, *in pari materia* differs slightly from the previous rule that a court must consider the Constitution of the State of Florida as a whole because the previous rule requires the court to look at the entire document whereas *in pari materia* requires the court to look at the particular paragraphs of the document that surround the language at issue. *See Hall v. State*, 136 Fla. 644, 187 So. 392 (Fla. 1939). In this way, neighboring language serves a common purpose and achieves a common objective even if particular words or sentences within that language were enacted at different times.

7. Avoid Interpretations Resulting in Superfluous Language

One way to tie together most if not all of the canons of construction identified above is to keep in mind that nothing said in Florida's constitution is to be rendered meaningless in its interpretation. It is an oft-cited and fundamental rule of construction of the Florida Constitution that a construction of the constitution which renders superfluous, meaningless, or inoperative any of its provisions should not be adopted by the courts. *See, e.g., City of Tampa v. Birdsong Motors*, 261 So. 2d 1 (Fla. 1972).

Stated somewhat differently, when "a constitutional provision will bear two constructions, one of which is consistent and the other which is inconsistent with another section of the constitution, the former must be adopted so that both provisions may stand and have effect." *Burnsed v. Seaboard Coastline R. Co.*, 290 So. 2d 13, 16 (Fla. 1974). As the Supreme Court of the State of Florida explained in *Burnsed*:

> Construction of the constitution is favored which gives effect to every clause and every part thereof. Unless a different interest is clearly manifested, constitutional provisions are to be interpreted in reference to their relation to each other, that is *in pari materia*, since every provision was inserted with a definite purpose. This Court stated in *Amos v. Mathews*, 99 Fla. 1, 126 So. 308, 316:
>
>> The purpose of the people in adopting the Constitution should be deduced from the Constitution as an entirety. Therefore, in construing and applying provisions of the Constitution, such provisions should be considered, not separately, but in coordination with all other provisions.

———————

Note and Question to Consider:

1. In what way is this canon of construction of Florida's constitution a summary of the prior canons?

2. In what way is it different?

8. Defer to the Legislature's Choice among Permissible Meanings

"[W]here a constitutional provision may well have either of several meanings, it is a fundamental rule of constitutional construction that, if the Legislature has by statute adopted one, its action in this respect is well-nigh, if not completely, controlling." *Greater Loretta Improvement Ass'n v. State ex rel. Boone*, 234 So. 2d 665, 669 (Fla. 1969). This means that, "[i]n matters of constitutional interpretation, the Legislature's view of its authority is highly persuasive." *Gallant v. Stephens*, 358 So. 2d 536, 540 (Fla. 1978).

This does not mean that a law is constitutional simply because the legislature chose to enact it. It means that if by enacting that law, the Florida Legislature made a choice between or among equally permissible meanings to be given to the language in Florida's constitution, then Florida's courts should show deference to that choice. If the meaning was not permissible, then this canon does not apply.

This canon is particularly applicable to legislative enactments made contemporaneously, or in very close time, with the state constitutional provision at issue. "A relatively contemporaneous construction of the constitution by the Legislature is strongly presumed to be correct." *See, e.g., Brown v. Firestone*, 382 So. 2d 654 (Fla. 1980).

Chapter 3

Litigating Constitutional Issues

In a proper case, a member of The Florida Bar may argue that a law, action, or inaction violates the Constitution of the State of Florida. This chapter addresses some of the ethical, strategic, and technical concerns facing constitutional litigators in Florida.

A. Lawyer Ethics in Constitutional Litigation

Best practices require a lawyer to consider the question of whether the client's claim of unconstitutionality is one which a Florida lawyer is permitted to present under the code of ethics that governs all Florida lawyers. As relevant to this question, the *Rules Regulating The Florida Bar* contain the following permission and restriction upon Florida lawyers regarding claims and defenses:

Florida Bar Rule 4-3.1 Meritorious Claims and Contentions

A lawyer shall not bring or defend a proceeding, or assert or controvert an issue therein, unless there is a basis in law and fact for doing so that is not frivolous, which includes a good faith argument for an extension, modification, or reversal of existing law. A lawyer for the defendant in a criminal proceeding, or the respondent in a proceeding that could result in incarceration, may nevertheless so defend the proceeding as to require that every element of the case be established.

The Florida Bar's Official Comment to this particular Rule provides the following explanation for interpreting and understanding the scope and function of this Rule:

The advocate has a duty to use legal procedure for the fullest benefit of the client's cause, but also a duty not to abuse legal procedure. The law, both procedural and substantive, establishes the limits within which an advocate may proceed. However, the law is not always clear and never is static. Accordingly, in determining the proper scope of advocacy, account must be taken of the law's ambiguities and potential for change.

The filing of an action or defense or similar action taken for a client is not frivolous merely because the facts have not first been fully substantiated or because the lawyer expects to develop vital evidence only by discovery. What is required of lawyers, however, is that they inform themselves about the facts of their clients' cases and the applicable law and determine that they can make good faith arguments in support of their clients' positions. Such action is not frivolous even though the lawyer believes that the client's position ultimately will not prevail. The action is frivolous, however, if the lawyer is unable either to make a good faith argument on the merits of the action taken or to support the action taken by a good faith argument for an extension, modification, or reversal of existing law.

The lawyer's obligations under this rule are subordinate to federal or state constitutional law that entitles a defendant in a criminal matter to the assistance of counsel in presenting a claim or contention that otherwise would be prohibited by this rule.

See Comment to Rule 4-3.1 of the *Rules Regulating The Florida Bar.*

The Florida Bar, in its 1973 Continuing Legal Education book titled CONSTITUTIONAL LITIGATION IN FLORIDA, said the following about a Florida lawyer's professional responsibility regarding cases and controversies that give rise to questions under the Constitution of the State of Florida:

An attorney has a duty to advise his client when constitutional issues are present in an action. The duty is similar to his obligation to raise statutory or common law issues. Failure to prevent issues without obtaining the client's consent to waive that may raise a question of malpractice. Because of the expense of this litigation and the presumption in favor of constitutionality, the client should be fully informed of the nature and potential consequences before an action is filed in which constitutional issues are raised, and the decision should be the client's. Similar consideration must be given when the constitutional questions arise defensively.

Henry P. Trawick, Jr., Peter L. Nimkoff, Bruce S. Rogow, et al., *Presenting Constitutional Issues*, appearing as Chapter 8 in The Florida Bar, CONSTITUTIONAL LITIGATION IN FLORIDA 156 (1973). Note that even back in 1973, it was necessary to warn that an issue involving the allegation that an action or law of the state of Florida violates the Florida Constitution was an issue certain to increase the cost of the litigation.

———

Notes and Questions to Consider:

1. Do stronger ethics rules apply to lawyers who make constitutional law arguments than to the judges who adjudicate them?

2. In the instance of a Florida lawyer making a good faith argument for an extension, modification, or reversal of existing law, when should the lawyer inform the judge or tribunal that this is the lawyer's goal? Would that information be less convincing to a judge or tribunal if it is given *after* the opposing counsel makes an accusation of having raised a frivolous claim? Even less convincing if given *after*

the presiding judge adjudicates the lawyer as having made a frivolous claim? What about after The Florida Bar opens a grievance investigation about the alleged filing of a frivolous claim? Would it be best to raise such an issue before facing such an argument, and if so, when and how should the issue be raised?

3. The authors of the excerpt appearing above opine that "[b]ecause of the expense of this litigation and the presumption in favor of constitutionality, the client should be fully informed of the nature and potential consequences before an action is filed in which constitutional issues are raised. . . ." Do you agree? What if the lawyer is not being paid an hourly fee by his client, but instead, is being paid a contingency or flat fee?

———

As to whether a lawyer has an ethical duty to make a constitutional claim when one exists, consider the following excerpt from the 1983 decision of the Supreme Court of the United States in *Jones v. Barnes*, 463 U.S. 745 (1983).

Jones v. Barnes

Supreme Court of the United States, 1983
463 U.S. 745, 103 S.Ct. 3308, 77 L.Ed.2d 987

We granted certiorari to consider whether defense counsel assigned to prosecute an appeal from a criminal conviction has a constitutional duty to raise every nonfrivolous issue requested by the defendant.

I

In 1976, Richard Butts was robbed at knifepoint by four men in the lobby of an apartment building; he was badly beaten and his watch and money were taken. Butts informed a Housing Authority Detective that he recognized one of his assailants as a person known to him as "Froggy," and gave a physical description of the person to the detective. The following day the detective arrested respondent David Barnes, who is known as "Froggy."

Respondent was charged with first and second degree robbery, second degree assault, and third degree larceny. The prosecution rested primarily upon Butts' testimony and his identification of respondent. During cross-examination, defense counsel asked Butts whether he had ever undergone psychiatric treatment; however, no offer of proof was made on the substance or relevance of the question after the trial judge sua sponte instructed Butts not to answer. At the close of trial, the trial judge declined to give an instruction on accessorial liability requested by the defense. The jury convicted respondent of first and second degree robbery and second degree assault.

The Appellate Division of the Supreme Court of New York, Second Department, assigned Michael Melinger to represent respondent on appeal. Respondent sent Melinger a letter listing several claims that he felt should be raised. Included were claims that Butts' identification testimony should have been suppressed, that the trial judge improperly excluded psychiatric evidence, and that respondent's trial counsel was ineffective. Respondent also enclosed a copy of a pro se brief he had written.

In a return letter, Melinger accepted some but rejected most of the suggested claims, stating that they would not aid respondent in obtaining a new trial and that they could not be raised on appeal because they were not based on evidence in the record . . .

Melinger's brief to the Appellate Division concentrated on three of the seven points he had raised in his letter to respondent: improper exclusion of psychiatric evidence, failure to suppress Butts' identification testimony, and improper cross-examination of respondent by the trial judge. In addition, Melinger submitted respondent's own pro se brief. Thereafter, respondent filed two more pro se briefs, raising three more of the seven issues Melinger had identified.

At oral argument, Melinger argued the three points presented in his own brief, but not the arguments raised in the pro se briefs. On May 22, 1978, the Appellate Division affirmed by summary order. . . . The New York Court of Appeals [which is New York's highest state court] denied leave to appeal. . . .

On August 8, 1978, respondent filed a pro se petition for a writ of habeas corpus in the United States District Court for the Eastern District of New York. Respondent raised five claims of error, including ineffective assistance of trial counsel. The District Court held the claims to be without merit and dismissed the petition. . . . The Court of Appeals for the Second Circuit affirmed, 607 F.2d 994, and we denied a petition for a writ of certiorari. . . .

In 1980, respondent filed two more challenges in state court. On March 4, 1980, he filed a motion in the trial court for collateral review of his sentence. That motion was denied on April 28, and leave to appeal was denied on October 3. Meanwhile, on March 31, 1980, he filed a petition in the New York Court of Appeals for reconsideration of that court's denial of leave to appeal. In that petition, respondent for the first time claimed that his appellate counsel, Melinger, had provided ineffective assistance. The New York Court of Appeals denied the application on April 16, 1980. . . .

Respondent then returned to United States District Court for the second time, with a petition for habeas corpus based on the claim of ineffective assistance by appellate counsel. The District Court concluded that respondent had exhausted his state remedies, but dismissed the petition, holding that the record gave no support to the claim of ineffective assistance of appellate counsel on "any . . . standard which could reasonably be applied." . . . The District Court concluded:

> "It is not required that an attorney argue every conceivable issue on appeal, especially when some may be without merit. Indeed, it is his professional duty to choose among potential issues, according to his judgment as to their merit and his tactical approach." . . .

A divided panel of the Court of Appeals reversed. . . . Laying down a new standard, the majority held that when "the appellant requests that [his attorney] raise additional colorable points [on appeal], counsel must argue the additional points to the full extent of his professional ability." . . . In the view of the majority, this conclusion followed from *Anders v. California*, 386 U.S. 738 (1967). In *Anders*, this Court held that an appointed attorney must advocate his client's cause vigorously and may not withdraw from a nonfrivolous appeal. The Court of Appeals majority held that, since *Anders* bars counsel from abandoning a nonfrivolous appeal, it also bars counsel from abandoning a nonfrivolous issue on appeal.

. . . The court concluded that Melinger had not met the above standard in that he had failed to press at least two nonfrivolous claims: the trial judge's failure to instruct on accessory liability and ineffective assistance of trial counsel. The fact that these issues had been raised in respondent's own pro se briefs did not cure the error, since "[a] pro se brief is no substitute for the advocacy of experienced counsel." Ibid. The court reversed and remanded, with instructions to grant the writ of habeas corpus unless the State assigned new counsel and granted a new appeal. . . .

We granted certiorari . . . and we reverse.

II

. . . There is, of course, no constitutional right to an appeal. . . . [The client] has the ultimate authority to make certain fundamental decisions regarding the case, as to whether to plead guilty, waive a jury, testify in his or her own behalf, or take an appeal. . . . Neither *Anders* nor any other decision of this Court suggests, however, that the [client] has a constitutional right to compel appointed counsel to press nonfrivolous points requested by the client, if counsel, as a matter of professional judgment, decides not to present those points.

This Court . . . recognized the superior ability of trained counsel in the "examination into the record, research of the law, and marshalling of arguments on [the appellant's] behalf," *Douglas v. California*, 372 U.S., at 358, 83 S.Ct., at 817. Yet by promulgating a per se rule that the client, not the professional advocate, must be allowed to decide what issues are to be pressed, the Court of Appeals seriously undermines the ability of counsel to present the client's case in accord with counsel's professional evaluation.

Experienced advocates since time beyond memory have emphasized the importance of winnowing out weaker arguments on appeal and focusing on one central issue if possible, or at most on a few key issues. Justice Jackson, after observing appellate advocates for many years, stated:

> "One of the first tests of a discriminating advocate is to select the question, or questions, that he will present orally. Legal contentions, like the currency, depreciate through over-issue. The mind of an appellate judge is habitually receptive to the suggestion that a lower court committed an error. But receptiveness declines as the number of assigned errors increases. Multiplicity hints at lack of confidence in any one. . . . [E]xperience on the

bench convinces me that multiplying assignments of error will dilute and weaken a good case and will not save a bad one."

Jackson, *Advocacy Before the Supreme Court*, 25 Temple L.Q. 115, 119 (1951).

Justice Jackson's observation echoes the advice of countless advocates before him and since. An authoritative work on appellate practice observes:

> "Most cases present only one, two, or three significant questions. . . . Usually, . . . if you cannot win on a few major points, the others are not likely to help, and to attempt to deal with a great many in the limited number of pages allowed for briefs will mean that none may receive adequate attention. The effect of adding weak arguments will be to dilute the force of the stronger ones."

R. Stern, APPELLATE PRACTICE IN THE UNITED STATES 266 (1981).

There can hardly be any question about the importance of having the appellate advocate examine the record with a view to selecting the most promising issues for review. This has assumed a greater importance in an era when oral argument is strictly limited in most courts—often to as little as 15 minutes—and when page limits on briefs are widely imposed. . . . Even in a court that imposes no time or page limits, however, the new per se rule laid down by the Court of Appeals is contrary to all experience and logic. A brief that raises every colorable issue runs the risk of burying good arguments—those that, in the words of the great advocate John W. Davis, "go for the jugular," Davis, The Argument of an Appeal, 26 A.B.A.J. 895, 897 (1940)—in a verbal mound made up of strong and weak contentions. *See generally, e.g.,* Godbold, *Twenty Pages and Twenty Minutes: Effective Advocacy on Appeal*, 30 SW. L.J. 801 (1976).

This Court's decision in *Anders*, far from giving support to the new per se rule announced by the Court of Appeals, is to the contrary. *Anders* recognized that the role of the advocate "requires that he support his client's appeal to the best of his ability." 386 U.S., at 744. Here the appointed counsel did just that. For judges to second-guess reasonable professional judgments and impose on appointed counsel a duty to raise every "colorable" claim suggested by a client would disserve the very goal of vigorous and effective advocacy that underlies *Anders*. Nothing in the Constitution or our interpretation of that document requires such a standard. The judgment of the Court of Appeals is accordingly

Reversed.

Notes and Questions to Consider:

1. The U.S. Supreme Court quotes from several sources in *Jones v. Barnes* suggesting that good appellate advocacy may require abandoning some nonfrivolous and perhaps meritorious arguments in favor of stronger arguments. Do you agree? Or instead, can better legal writing allow for raising multiple legal issues without

diluting the strength of any of them? Perhaps not, suggests Justice Brennan's dissent in this very case, where he writes:

> the Court['s opinion] argues that good appellate advocacy demands selectivity among arguments. That is certainly true — the Court's advice is good. It ought to be taken to heart by every lawyer called upon to argue an appeal in this or any other court, and by his client. It should take little or no persuasion to get a wise client to understand that, if staying out of prison is what he values most, he should encourage his lawyer to raise only his two or three best arguments on appeal, and he should defer to his lawyer's advice as to which are the best arguments.

463 U.S. at 761 (Brennan, J., dissenting).

2. Were you surprised by the U.S. Supreme Court's holding at the beginning of part II of *Jones v. Barnes* that "[t]here is, of course, no constitutional right to an appeal"? A state can create such a right under stated circumstances, as the Florida Rules of Appellate Procedure often do. *See, e.g.*, Fla. R. App. P. 9.030 and 9.110.

3. Do the rules of professional conduct impose upon a lawyer the duty to obey his client's wishes as to what arguments to raise on appeal even though the U.S. Supreme Court says no such duty exists? No, say the American Bar Associations' *Model Rules of Professional Conduct*. ABA Model Rule 1.2 is titled "Scope of Representation and Allocation of Authority Between Client and Lawyer." It provides:

> a lawyer shall abide by a client's decisions concerning the objectives of representation and ... shall consult with the client as to the means by which they are to be pursued. A lawyer may take such action on behalf of the client as is impliedly authorized to carry out the representation. A lawyer shall abide by a client's decision whether to settle a matter. In a criminal case, the lawyer shall abide by the client's decision, after consultation with the lawyer, as to a plea to be entered, whether to waive jury trial and whether the client will testify.

Id. at sec. (a). Note that, although the lawyer is required to abide by the decisions of the client as to the objectives of the representation, the lawyer is not required to abide by the decisions of the client as to "the means by which they are to be pursued." All the lawyer must do is "consult with the client" as to those means and methods. So under the ABA Model Rules, the client decides whether to appeal, but the lawyer decides what arguments to raise in that appeal. The *Rules Regulating The Florida Bar* yield the same result in its Rule 4-1.2. It is titled "Objectives and Scope of Representation" and bears the same language quoted above from ABA Model Rule 1.2 except that the duty to consult about the means is reduced to a duty to "reasonably consult." The Official Comment to Florida Rule 4-1.2 explains that:

> a client also has a right to consult with the lawyer about the means to be used in pursuing those objectives. At the same time, a lawyer is not required to pursue objectives or employ means simply because a client may wish that

the lawyer do so. A clear distinction between objectives and means sometimes cannot be drawn, and in many cases the client-lawyer relationship
partakes of a joint undertaking. In questions of means, the lawyer should
assume responsibility for technical and legal tactical issues but should defer
to the client regarding such questions as the expense to be incurred and
concern for third persons who might be adversely affected. . . .

On occasion, however, a lawyer and a client may disagree about the
means to be used to accomplish the client's objectives. The lawyer should
consult with the client and seek a mutually acceptable resolution of the disagreement. If such efforts are unavailing and the lawyer has a fundamental
disagreement with the client, the lawyer may withdraw from the representation. . . . Conversely, the client may resolve the disagreement by discharg-
ing the lawyer. . . .

Id. Does this rule give greater rights to clients who can afford to pay for their lawyers
versus clients who need a pro bono attorney?

4. Do these same rules of professional conduct allow a lawyer to raise a state constitutional law issue that the client does not want to raise?

5. As is evident from the excerpt appearing above, *Jones v. Barnes* cites frequently
to the criminal law case of *Anders v. California*, 386 U.S. 738, 87 S.Ct. 1396, 18
L.Ed.2d 493 (1967) where the U.S. Supreme Court required attorneys defending
indigent appellants in a criminal law case who determine the client does not have
a meritorious argument on appeal to file with their Motion to Withdraw a brief
summarizing the record and identifying any potential errors that were preserved
for appeal: an *Anders* Brief as that has become known. But the requirement of an
Anders Brief is no longer imposed upon the states, as explained by Professor Paul T.
Hayden in Chapter 4 Section 3 of *Ethical Lawyering: Legal and Professional Responsibilities in the Practice of Law* (Thomson Reuters 3rd ed):

In *Anders v. California* . . . the [U.S. Supreme] court held that an appointed
counsel who sought permission to withdraw from representing a criminal
defendant on appeal must discuss in an appellate brief "anything in the record that might arguably support the appeal." The Court cut back on *Anders*
in *McCoy v. Court of Appeals of Wisconsin*, 488 U.S. 429, 108 S.Ct. 1895, 1000
L.Ed.2d 440 (1988), which approved of the constitutionality of a Wisconsin rule that required counsel to include in any *Anders* brief a discussion
of "why the issue lacks merit." In *Smith v. Robbins*, 58 U.S. 259, 120 S.Ct.
746, 145 L.Ed.2d 756 (2000), the Court largely abandoned this *Anders* brief
requirement. In a 5–4 decision, the *Smith* Court held that the *Anders* procedure was "not obligatory" on the states, and was just "one method" to
protect the right to counsel. The majority found constitutionally acceptable
California's procedure for handling "no merit" criminal appeals, as laid out
in *People v. Wende*, 25 Cal.2d 436, 600 P.2d 1071, 158 Cal.Rptr. 839 (1979),
in which counsel files a brief summarizing the factual and procedural

history of the case, with citations to the record, but makes no arguments at all. States are still free to require an *Anders* brief, and several do.

Id. at 244 n.2.

6. As to what a Florida lawyer must do when appointed to represent an indigent criminal appellant and the lawyer concludes the appellant does not have a non-frivolous, good faith argument to make in that appeal, consider the following from *N.H.S. v. Fla. Dept. of Child. & Fam. Svcs.*, 843 So. 2d 898 (Fla. 2003):

> In 1967, the United States Supreme Court decided *Anders*. . . . In 1971, this Court adopted the precise procedure set forth in the original Supreme Court opinion in *Anders* for criminal appeals in this state. See *State v. Wooden*, 246 So. 2d 755, 757–58 (Fla. 1971), abrogated on other grounds, *State v. District Court of Appeal*, 569 So. 2d 439, 442 (Fla. 1990); see also *In re Anders Briefs*, 581 So. 2d 149 (Fla. 1991). The Supreme Court has since clarified that the procedure set forth in *Anders* is "merely one method of satisfying the requirements of the Constitution for indigent criminal appeals." *Smith v. Robbins*, 528 U.S. 259, 276, 120 S.Ct. 746, 145 L.Ed.2d 756 (2000). . . . Although this Court has not yet reevaluated its current *Anders* procedures in light of *Smith*, this Court recently extended the use of the *Anders* procedure to appeals of involuntary civil commitment to a mental health facility where an individual's physical liberty is at stake. See *Pullen v. State*, 802 So. 2d 1113, 1120 (Fla. 2001).

Id. at 900–01. Therefore, Florida's appellate courts continue to require *Anders* Briefs. *See, e.g., Redmon v. State*, 211 So. 3d 306 (Fla. 1st DCA 2017).

B. Prerequisites and Presuit Requirements

Although an aggrieved litigant may want to rush to court on a challenge arising under Florida's constitution, for many such claims, presuit requirements must be met before the claim may proceed to a courthouse. The Florida Legislature has the authority to enact statutes creating presuit requirements for claims including constitutional claims. If a presuit requirement exists, but was not exhausted pre-suit, then the state constitutional law claim may be dismissed without granting relief even if the claim of a violation is true and meritorious.

For example, if a Florida Statute vests an agency with authority, the litigant must exhaust her administrative remedies before that agency when such remedies exist.

Another example is when a fundamental right from the Florida Constitution's Article I Declaration of Rights is actionable under the Florida Civil Rights Act. There, the Florida Commission on Human Relations has presuit jurisdiction. It may investigate, act on its own against the alleged perpetrator, or issue a "right to sue" letter allowing the alleged victim to proceed to court. The Florida Civil Rights Act, which is Chapter 760 of the Florida Statutes, provides in relevant part:

(1) Any person aggrieved by a violation of [the Florida Civil Rights Act] may file a complaint with the [Florida Commission on Human Relations] within 365 days of the alleged violation, naming the employer, employment agency, labor organization, or joint labor-management committee, or, ... the person responsible for the violation and describing the violation. Any person aggrieved by a [public lodging establishments or public food service establishment that refused accommodations or service to any person based upon race, creed, color, sex, pregnancy, physical disability, or national origin] may file a complaint with the commission within 365 days of the alleged violation naming the person responsible for the violation and describing the violation. The commission, a commissioner, or the Attorney General may in like manner file such a complaint. . . . In lieu of filing the complaint with the commission, a complaint under this section may be filed with the federal Equal Employment Opportunity Commission or with any unit of government of the state which is a fair-employment-practice agency under 29 C.F.R. ss. 1601.70-1601.80. . . . The complaint shall contain a short and plain statement of the facts describing the violation and the relief sought. The commission may require additional information to be in the complaint. The commission, within 5 days of the complaint being filed, shall by registered mail send a copy of the complaint to the person who allegedly committed the violation. The person who allegedly committed the violation may file an answer to the complaint within 25 days of the date the complaint was filed with the commission. Any answer filed shall be mailed to the aggrieved person by the person filing the answer. Both the complaint and the answer shall be verified.

(2) In the event that any other agency of the state or of any other unit of government of the state has jurisdiction of the subject matter of any complaint filed with the commission and has legal authority to investigate the complaint, the commission may refer such complaint to such agency for an investigation. . . . The referral of a complaint by the commission to a local agency does not divest the commission's jurisdiction over the complaint.

(3) Except as provided in subsection (2) [for referring the investigation to another agency that has jurisdiction], the commission shall investigate the allegations in the complaint. Within 180 days of the filing of the complaint, the commission shall determine if there is reasonable cause to believe that discriminatory practice has occurred in violation of the Florida Civil Rights Act of 1992. When the commission determines whether or not there is reasonable cause, the commission by registered mail shall promptly notify the aggrieved person and the respondent of the reasonable cause determination, the date of such determination, and the options available under this section.

(4) In the event that the commission determines that there is reasonable cause to believe that a discriminatory practice has occurred in violation of the Florida Civil Rights Act of 1992, the aggrieved person may either:

(a) Bring a civil action against the person named in the complaint in any court of competent jurisdiction; or

(b) Request an administrative hearing under ss. 120.569 and 120.57.

The election by the aggrieved person of filing a civil action or requesting an administrative hearing under this subsection is the exclusive procedure available to the aggrieved person pursuant to this act.

. . . (6) Any administrative hearing brought pursuant to paragraph (4)(b) shall be conducted under [the Florida Administrative Procedures Act as provided in chapter 120 of the Florida Statutes]. The commission may hear the case provided that the final order is issued by members of the commission who did not conduct the hearing or the commission may request that it be heard by an administrative law judge pursuant to s. 120.569(2)(a). If the commission elects to hear the case, it may be heard by a commissioner. If the commissioner, after the hearing, finds that a violation of the Florida Civil Rights Act of 1992 has occurred, the commissioner shall issue an appropriate proposed order in accordance with chapter 120 prohibiting the practice and providing affirmative relief from the effects of the practice, including back pay. If the administrative law judge, after the hearing, finds that a violation of the Florida Civil Rights Act of 1992 has occurred, the administrative law judge shall issue an appropriate recommended order in accordance with chapter 120 prohibiting the practice and providing affirmative relief from the effects of the practice, including back pay. Within 90 days of the date the recommended or proposed order is rendered, the commission shall issue a final order by adopting, rejecting, or modifying the recommended order as provided under ss. 120.569 and 120.57. The 90-day period may be extended with the consent of all the parties. An administrative hearing pursuant to paragraph (4)(b) must be requested no later than 35 days after the date of determination of reasonable cause by the commission. In any action or proceeding under this subsection, the commission, in its discretion, may allow the prevailing party a reasonable attorney's fee as part of the costs. It is the intent of the Legislature that this provision for attorney's fees be interpreted in a manner consistent with federal case law involving a Title VII action.

(7) If the commission determines that there is not reasonable cause to believe that a violation of the Florida Civil Rights Act of 1992 has occurred, the commission shall dismiss the complaint. The aggrieved person may request an administrative hearing under ss. 120.569 and 120.57, but any such request must be made within 35 days of the date of determination of

reasonable cause and any such hearing shall be heard by an administrative law judge and not by the commission or a commissioner. If the aggrieved person does not request an administrative hearing within the 35 days, the claim will be barred. If the administrative law judge finds that a violation of the Florida Civil Rights Act of 1992 has occurred, he or she shall issue an appropriate recommended order to the commission prohibiting the practice and recommending affirmative relief from the effects of the practice, including back pay. Within 90 days of the date the recommended order is rendered, the commission shall issue a final order by adopting, rejecting, or modifying the recommended order as provided under ss. 120.569 and 120.57. The 90-day period may be extended with the consent of all the parties. In any action or proceeding under this subsection, the commission, in its discretion, may allow the prevailing party a reasonable attorney's fee as part of the costs. It is the intent of the Legislature that this provision for attorney's fees be interpreted in a manner consistent with federal case law involving a Title VII action. In the event the final order issued by the commission determines that a violation of the Florida Civil Rights Act of 1992 has occurred, the aggrieved person may bring, within 1 year of the date of the final order, a civil action under subsection (5) as if there has been a reasonable cause determination or accept the affirmative relief offered by the commission, but not both.

(8) In the event that the commission fails to conciliate or determine whether there is reasonable cause on any complaint under this section within 180 days of the filing of the complaint, an aggrieved person may proceed under subsection (4), as if the commission determined that there was reasonable cause.

. . . (10) A judgment for the amount of damages and costs assessed pursuant to a final order by the commission may be entered in any court having jurisdiction thereof and may be enforced as any other judgment.

(11) If a complaint is within the jurisdiction of the commission, the commission shall simultaneously with its other statutory obligations attempt to eliminate or correct the alleged discrimination by informal methods of conference, conciliation, and persuasion. Nothing said or done in the course of such informal endeavors may be made public or used as evidence in a subsequent civil proceeding, trial, or hearing. The commission may initiate dispute resolution procedures, including voluntary arbitration, by special magistrates or mediators. The commission may adopt rules as to the qualifications of persons who may serve as special magistrates and mediators.

(12) All complaints filed with the commission and all records and documents in the custody of the commission, which relate to and identify a particular person, including, but not limited to, a complainant, employer, employment agency, labor organization, or joint labor-management

committee shall be confidential and shall not be disclosed by the commission, except to the parties or in the course of a hearing or proceeding under this section. The restriction of this subsection shall not apply to any record or document which is part of the record of any hearing or court proceeding.

(13) Final orders of the commission are subject to judicial review pursuant to s. 120.68. The commission's determination of reasonable cause is not final agency action that is subject to judicial review. Unless specifically ordered by the court, the commencement of an appeal does not suspend or stay the order of the commission, except as provided in the Rules of Appellate Procedure. In any action or proceeding under this subsection, the court, in its discretion, may allow the prevailing party a reasonable attorney's fee as part of the cost. It is the intent of the Legislature that this provision for attorney's fees be interpreted in a manner consistent with federal case law involving a Title VII action. In the event the order of the court determines that a violation of the Florida Civil Rights Act of 1992 has occurred, the court shall remand the matter to the commission for appropriate relief. The aggrieved party has the option to accept the relief offered by the commission or may bring, within 1 year of the date of the court order, a civil action under subsection (5) as if there has been a reasonable cause determination.

(14) The commission may adopt, promulgate, amend, and rescind rules to effectuate the purposes and policies of this section and to govern the proceedings of the commission under this section.

§ 760.11, Fla. Stat. (2017).

C. Standing

The right to challenge a law or government action as unconstitutional is not held universally and equally by everyone because it is limited to those who have "standing." A litigant has "standing" to make a claim under the Florida Constitution when the litigant has a direct, personal interest in the suit because her rights or duties are affected by its outcome. That direct, personal interest must be regarding the specific statute or state action at issue.

"Standing is a legal concept that requires a would-be litigant to demonstrate that he or she reasonably expects to be affected by the outcome of the proceedings, either directly or indirectly." *Hayes v. Guardianship of Thompson*, 952 So. 2d 498, 505 (Fla. 2006). The Florida Supreme Court holds that it "has long been committed to the rule that a party does not possess standing to sue unless he or she can demonstrate a direct and articulable stake in the outcome of a controversy." *Brown v. Firestone*, 382 So. 2d 654, 662 (Fla. 1980).

"Standing depends on whether a party has a sufficient stake in a justiciable controversy, with a legally cognizable interest which would be affected by the outcome of the litigation." *Weiss v. Johansen*, 898 So. 2d 1009, 1011 (Fla. 4th DCA 2005). Thus, standing to bring or participate in a particular legal proceeding often depends on the nature of the interest asserted. *Hayes v. Guardianship of Thompson*, 952 So. 2d 498, 505 (Fla. 2006).

Among the fundamental principles of standing is the "requirement that the claim be brought by or on behalf of one who is recognized in the law as a 'real party in interest.'" *Kumar Corp. v. Nopal Lines, Ltd.*, 462 So. 2d 1178, 1183 (Fla. 3d DCA 1985). The "real party in interest" is "the person in whom rests, by substantive law, the claim sought to be enforced." *Id.* (citation and quotation omitted). The purpose behind the real party in interest rule is "to protect a defendant from facing a subsequent similar action brought by one not a party to the present proceeding and to ensure that any action taken to judgment will have its proper effect as res judicata." *Id.* at 1178; see also Fla. R. Civ. P. 1.210.

Chapter 8 of CONSTITUTIONAL LITIGATION IN FLORIDA (1973) provides the following helpful summary of Florida decisions deciding who has standing to bring an action alleging a state law or state action to be in violation of the Constitution of the State of Florida. That summary has withstood the test of time and remains helpful today.

> Even though a statute is unconstitutional, only those who have a right to raise its unconstitutionality may invoke the aid of the courts to have it judicially set aside. "Standing to Sue" is an elementary doctrine of constitutional law. Thus, constitutionality of legislation is open to attack only by a person whose rights or duties are affected or prejudiced by it. The constitutionality of a statute may not be attacked by one who does not come within its purview, by an amicus curiae when the parties have not raised the question or by one who does not come within the class against which the statute is alleged to discriminate. . . . .
>
> Not only must a person be adversely affected by the statute in order to challenge its constitutionality, but he also must be affected by the part of the statute that he attacks.
>
> The interest of a public official as such does not entitle him to question the validity of a statute. As a prerequisite to raising the question, the official must show that his personal or property rights are adversely affected by the statute, or that his administration of it will require the expenditure of public funds. Officers of the executive department cannot attack the constitutionality of an act on the theory that it would be a violation of their oath of office. . . .
>
> The rule that a person may not attack the constitutionality of a statute whose rights it does not affect applies to private persons, but not to the attorney general. When sued, a state agency or department may question the constitutional validity of the statutory provision under which the action was filed by an appropriate pleading without violating the general principle

that officers may not refuse to perform a duty imposed by statute because they deem that it is unconstitutional. . . .

When declaratory relief is sought, a county or municipality must be joined as a party if a county or municipal charter, ordinance or franchise is asserted to be invalid. If a statute, charter, ordinance or franchise is alleged to be unconstitutional, the Attorney General or the state attorney of the circuit where the action is pending must be served with a copy of the complaint and be given an opportunity to be heard. This does not mean the attorney general or state attorney must be joined as parties. . . .

An individual seeking to raise a constitutional question must show a direct, personal interest in himself or the class he represents in defeating the law or preventing the action asserted to be unconstitutional. . . .

Henry P. Trawick, Jr., Peter L. Nimkoff, Bruce S. Rogow, et al., *Presenting Constitutional Issues*, appearing as Chapter 8 in The Florida Bar, CONSTITUTIONAL LITIGATION IN FLORIDA 157–158 (1973).

Note that Florida's attorney general has standing to *defend* a state statute or government action as constitutional. The same cannot be said for *challenging* a state statute or government action as unconstitutional. In *Citrus County Hosp. Bd. v. Citrus Mem'l Health Found., Inc.*, 150 So. 3d 1102 (Fla. 2014), Florida's supreme court held that:

Florida courts have precluded State agencies and local governments from challenging the constitutionality of certain legislation. For example, in *Department of Education v. Lewis*, this Court held that "State officers and agencies must presume legislation affecting their duties to be valid, and do not have standing to initiate litigation for the purpose of determining otherwise." 416 So. 2d 455, 458 (Fla. 1982) (addressing a challenge to an appropriations law under article III, section 12 of the Florida Constitution); see also *Fla. Dep't of Agric. & Consumer Servs. v. Miami-Dade Cnty.*, 790 So. 2d 555, 558 (Fla. 3d DCA 2001) (relying on *Lewis* to hold that county and city lacked standing under article I, section 12 of the Florida Constitution to challenge the constitutionality of the statutory citrus canker eradication program).

Id. at 1106.

Florida's requirements for standing for an individual to bring a claim alleging a violation of the Constitution of the State of Florida are illustrated in the First District Court of Appeal's decision in *Alachua Cty. v. Scharps*, 855 So. 2d 195 (Fla. 1st DCA 2003).

Alachua County v. Scharps

First District Court of Appeal of Florida, 2003
855 So. 2d 195

Appellant, Alachua County Board of County Commissioners (the County), was the defendant in an injunctive and declaratory action brought by appellee, Howard J. Scharps. The County challenges a final judgment invalidating a resolution passed by the County which directed that a referendum be placed on the general election ballot. Appellant raises a number of issues, including whether appellee had taxpayer standing to challenge the County's authorization of the referendum. We find that appellee lacks standing; therefore, we reverse the decision of the trial court on this basis and decline to address the other issues raised by the County.

On July 11, 2000, the County adopted Resolution 00–55 (the resolution), and directed that the following non-binding question be placed on the November 8, 2000, Alachua County general election ballot:

UNIVERSAL HEALTH CARE AND HEALTH INSURANCE TRUST FUND

Do you favor legislation to create a system of universal health care in Florida that provides all residents with comprehensive health care coverage (including the freedom to choose doctors and other health care professionals, facilities and services) and eliminates the role of health insurance companies in health care by creating a publicly administered health insurance trust fund? The trust fund would receive the funds presently going to the numerous health insurance companies throughout the state.

————   ————

Yes   No

On September 29, 2000, Scharps filed a second amended complaint (the complaint) for declaratory judgment and injunctive relief pursuant to Article V, Section 4 of the Florida Constitution and chapters 26 and 86 of the Florida Statutes. Regarding his standing, Scharps alleged the following:

> 3. Howard Scharps is resident, citizen and taxpayers [sic] of Alachua County, Florida and has been all times material hereto.
>
> . . .
>
> 46. Plaintiff Scharps opposes the substance of the matter stated in the non-binding referendum and objects on First Amendment and Florida Declaration of Rights grounds to Board's employment of the power and resources [sic] to the County and the State of Florida to promote one political point of view in the guise of a nonbinding referendum that does not pertain to the functions and powers of county government[.]

In count I of the complaint, Scharps sought a declaratory judgment that the resolution was invalid because the County had no power under section 125.01, Florida Statutes (2000), or Article III of the Florida Constitution, to conduct a referendum to determine elector sentiment on the issue of universal health care. In count II of the complaint, Scharps alleged violations of the First and Fourteenth Amendments to the United States Constitution and the Declaration of Rights in Article I of the Florida Constitution. Scharps sought injunctive relief to either keep the referendum off the November 2000 ballot or, alternatively, to seal the results of such a ballot.

The County asserted numerous defenses, including that Scharps did not have standing to bring the declaratory action against the County. On November 7, 2000, the eve of the election, the trial court rendered an order denying injunctive relief and reserving judgment on declaratory relief, finding that Scharps failed to meet the burden of persuasion that his own injury would outweigh the complications necessary to comply with any injunctive relief. Specifically, the court held,

> Plaintiff does not allege personal or financial injury as a result of the tabulating and releasing the votes on the non-binding referendum. Rather, Plaintiff alleges an inability on the part of the Board of County Commissioners to exercise any discretion as to potential future proposed referenda. . . . Apparently the referendum was held on November 8, 2000.

On March 12, 2002, the trial court entered the final judgment declaring the resolution invalid, finding that the County improperly placed a non-binding referendum regarding universal health care on the November 2000 election ballot. The judgment did not address or explicitly rule on the standing issue. The County filed a timely motion for rehearing, arguing in part that the issue of Scharps' standing was not addressed by the court. The trial court denied the motion for rehearing, and this appeal ensued.

Standard of Review

Determining whether a party has standing is a pure question of law to be reviewed de novo. The trial court failed to explicitly address the arguments as to Scharps' standing to bring this action. The trial court, however, implicitly found there was standing by addressing the merits of appellee's complaint. When standing is raised as an issue, the trial court must determine whether the plaintiff has a sufficient interest at stake in the controversy which will be affected by the outcome of the litigation. The trial court should have addressed the standing issue. See *Jones v. Dep't of Revenue*, 523 So. 2d 1211, 1214 (Fla. 1st DCA 1988) ("Before reaching the merits of appellant's challenge, however, it is first necessary to determine whether appellant had standing to challenge the constitutionality of the statute.").

Appellant admits he suffered no special injury, but he alleged in his complaint, asserted at the trial level, and argues on appeal that he is exempt from the special injury rule because he has "taxpayer standing" and constitutional standing. We find he has neither.

Taxpayer Standing

Generally, in order to have standing to bring an action the plaintiff must allege that he has suffered or will suffer a special injury. The special injury requirement, or the "Rickman rule," has an exception "[w]here there is an attack upon constitutional grounds based directly upon the Legislature's taxing and spending power." *N. Broward Hosp. Dist. v. Fornes*, 476 So. 2d 154, 155 (Fla. 1985). When such constitutional grounds exist "there is standing to sue without the Rickman requirement of special injury." *Id.* The supreme court refused to depart from this special injury rule or expand this exception. *Id.* at 155; see also *Sch. Bd. of Volusia County v. Clayton*, 691 So. 2d 1066 (Fla. 1997) (reaffirming long-established precedent that taxpayer standing requires special injury on constitutional challenge); *Dep't of Revenue v. Markham*, 396 So. 2d 1120 (Fla. 1981) (noting that absent a constitutional challenge, a taxpayer can only have standing upon a showing of special injury which is distinct from that suffered by other taxpayers in the taxing district).

Thus, taxpayer standing is available if the taxpayer can show that a government taxing measure or expenditure violates specific constitutional limitations on the taxing and spending power. See *Paul v. Blake*, 376 So. 2d 256, 259 (Fla. 3d DCA 1979) ("A taxpayer may institute such a suit without a showing of special injury if he attacks . . . taxing or spending authority on the ground that it exceeds specific limitations imposed on the . . . taxing or spending power by the . . . Florida Constitution."). Here, appellee generally asserts that the County employed the "powers and resources of the State of Florida or of Alachua County" outside the scope of section 125.01(1)(y), but he does not assert that the County violated a specific taxing and spending power under the state or federal constitution.

The case of *Martin v. Gainesville*, 800 So. 2d at 687, is instructive on this issue. The plaintiff in *Martin* filed a complaint for a declaratory judgment and injunctive relief as did Scharps in the instant case. There the plaintiff sought to prevent expenditures for a policy with which he disagreed, claiming that these expenditures were in violation of Article VIII, Section 2(b) of the Florida Constitution, which gives municipalities governmental, corporate, and proprietary powers for municipal purposes "except otherwise provided by law." *Id.* at 688. In *Martin* this court affirmed the trial court's dismissal for lack of standing, finding that the plaintiff had failed to show that the defendant "violated the specific limitations imposed upon a city in taxing or spending by the Florida Constitution. . . . [M]ere statutory violations did not constitute 'violations of specific provisions of the Florida Constitution.'" *Id.* at 688.

Similarly in *City of Atlantic Beach v. Bull*, 476 So. 2d 158 (Fla. 1985), the plaintiff relied on the same theory of standing which appellee argues here: he is a citizen, resident and taxpayer, and the local government's action was outside the general powers granted under the Florida Constitution. In *Bull*, however, the supreme court rejected that standing theory. See also *City of Sarasota v. Windom*, 736 So. 2d 741, 742 (Fla. 2d DCA 1999) (finding no standing where the plaintiffs challenged the city's authority to expend funds for the installation of a specific type of traffic control device); *Sch. Bd. of Volusia County v. Clayton*, 691 So. 2d at 1066 (Fla. 1997) (finding taxpayer did not have standing to challenge school board's purchase of real property pursuant to eminent domain proceeding on ground that school board did not obtain statutorily required extraordinary vote to approve purchase).

As in *Fornes*, *Martin*, and *Bull*, the appellee's general claims of expenditures beyond statutory authority fall short of the requirement that a taxpayer allege violations of specific constitutional limitations on taxing or spending powers in order to avoid the necessity of demonstrating special injury or as a prerequisite for taxpayer standing.

First Amendment Standing

Appellee relies on *Falzone v. State*, 500 So. 2d 1337 (Fla. 1987), to support his claim that he also has constitutional standing because he has alleged violations of free speech under the First and Fourteenth Amendments to the United States Constitution and Article I, Section 4 of the Florida Constitution. In *Falzone*, appellants had been indicted for allegedly failing to file a statement of organization as a political committee as required by certain sections of Florida's Campaign Finance Law. Unlike Scharps, the appellants there had made an explicit facial challenge alleging that the statutes were vague and overbroad. There, the court explained that there is a relaxed standing requirement in overbreadth cases because of the potential chilling effect on First Amendment freedoms. *Id.* at 1339. In this case, however, no potential chilling effect is implicated.

The exact nature of appellee's First Amendment challenge is unclear. However, it seems to be, "[The] board is left in a dilemma: it must either violate the First Amendment by picking and choosing among petitions, or it must grant all petitions and thereby abdicate its power as the constitutionally prescribed exclusive governing body for the county." There is nothing in the record reflecting that the County has picked among petitions or granted all petitions. There is also no indication that appellee was denied access to the referenda process or sought to have a referendum placed on the ballot. In *Florida National Organization for Women v. State*, 832 So. 2d 911 (Fla. 1st DCA 2002), the court held that appellants did not have standing to allege a violation of First Amendment rights where the facts alleged did not show that appellants' own First Amendment rights were violated:

> Appellants allege that their right to free speech has been violated by the mere existence of the Choose Life plate. As the trial court explained in dismissing Count II, "the facts alleged do not show that any of the plaintiffs have attempted any expression and been denied access to the alleged forum for speech, or that the statutes at issue have hindered or curtailed any plaintiff's speech in any way." Because Appellants have not applied for, and been denied, a pro-choice plate, and have stated their intention not to do so, they cannot amend the count to state a viable claim as they lack standing to do so.

Id. at 915. Because the appellee here is only claiming that there is potential for violating someone's (not even his own) freedom to speech, he does not have standing. *Id.*; see also *Sieniarecki v. State*, 756 So. 2d 68, 76 (Fla. 2000) (denying standing on the ground that a statute may "conceivably" be applied unconstitutionally). Furthermore, appellee has not established that his expression has been chilled or that he has been denied access to the referenda process as set forth by section 125.01. Thus, he has no First Amendment standing.

Equal Protection Standing

Appellee's equal protection argument is premised on the argument that "[b]ecause Board's discretion to pick and choose among petitions for referenda has not been circumscribed by adequate guidelines, general equal protection principles would render [section] 125.01(1)(y) unconstitutional in application." However, because Scharps did not attempt to get an alternative petition placed on the ballot or offer his own ballot for submission, he cannot show that he suffered any discrimination under section 125.01(1)(y). It is not enough that others may be discriminated against in the future.

In *Sancho v. Smith*, 830 So. 2d 856 (Fla. 1st DCA 2002), election supervisors brought a declaratory judgment and injunctive action attacking a statute limiting a ballot summary for a proposed constitutional amendment to 75 words, but exempting summaries submitted by joint resolution of legislature from the brevity requirement. As Scharps does here, the complaint brought an equal protection challenge under the Fourteenth Amendment of the United States Constitution, claiming the statute created an unconstitutional burden on those in the future who would submit a proposed amendment by citizen initiative. This court held that the election supervisors had no standing to bring the equal protection claim because "constitutional rights are personal":

> A party who is not adversely affected by a statute generally has no standing to argue that the statute is invalid. We acknowledge that courts have made an exception to this rule if the party asserting the claim is protecting the rights of non-parties who are unable to challenge the statute on their own. However, the exception does not apply here. Citizens who are adversely affected by the exemption in section 101.161(1), Florida Statutes (2000), can make the argument for themselves.

Id. at 864 (citations omitted); see also *Sieniarecki*, 756 So. 2d at 76 ("[C]onstitutional rights are personal in nature and generally may not be asserted vicariously.").

Similarly, in *Shands Teaching Hospital v. Smith*, 480 So. 2d 1366 (Fla. 1st DCA 1985), approved, 497 So. 2d 644 (Fla. 1986), this court held that a hospital lacked standing to assert an equal protection challenge to a statute that made a man liable for medical bills incurred by his wife, but did not also make a woman liable for medical bills incurred by her husband. Although the court agreed that the hospital had a general interest in collecting its debts, the court found that the hospital had no real interest in the argument that the statute unfairly discriminates against men. The equal protection problems at issue in *Smith* were best raised by men who were affected by the discrepancy or addressed by the legislature. *Smith*, 480 So. 2d at 1367 (Barfield, J., concurring). Because Scharps cannot assert that he personally has suffered discrimination, and citizens who are denied the right to place their non-binding referenda on ballots can make the argument for themselves, Scharps has no standing.

For the reasons expressed herein, we reverse the decision of the trial court and direct that appellee's complaint be dismissed.

Note and Question to Consider:

1. In *Alachua County v. Scharps*, the court notes that the rules regarding standing are relaxed in cases of statutes and rules that on their face allegedly violate the fundamental right of free speech and expression. The concern is that the legislation may have a "chilling effect" of preventing speech before spoken, and those who have not yet spoken might be hard pressed to argue that their speech was impeded. So why did the court find that the plaintiff did not meet this relaxed rule of standing as to his claims of a violation of his freedom of speech and expression?

2. Sometimes, in a lawsuit alleging a violation of Florida's constitution, the plaintiff is not an individual. Surely we have all seen news reports of groups such as the Becket Fund for Religious Liberty and American Civil Liberties Union (ACLU) bringing lawsuits challenging the constitutionality of a law, regulation, or government action. Some organizations appear to make such litigation one of their primary purposes. What gives them standing? This question was addressed in *Fraternal Order of Police, Miami Lodge No. 20 v. City of Miami*, 233 So. 3d 1240 (Fla. 3d DCA 2017).

Fraternal Order of Police, Miami Lodge Number 20 v. City of Miami

Third District Court of Appeal of Florida, 2017
233 So. 3d 1240

The Fraternal Order of Police, etc. ("the FOP") appeals from the trial court's entry of a final order determining that the FOP lacks standing to seek damages against the City of Miami ("the City") on behalf of some of the FOP's members. Based on our review of the record on appeal and the relevant case law, we agree with the trial court's determination that the FOP lacks standing to pursue damages on behalf of its members because the determination of damages will require the individual participation of the affected FOP members.

Background

This appeal concerns a promotional exam for the position of police sergeant. After conducting a bench trial on liability, the trial court entered a partial final declaratory judgment in 2007 in favor of the FOP, declaring the oral portion of the exam invalid.

Thereafter, the City sought clarification as to the FOP's associational standing to recover damages on behalf of its individually affected members. The trial court entered an order in 2008 finding that, although the FOP may possess associational standing to seek declaratory, injunctive, or other prospective relief for its members, it lacks associational standing to recover damages on behalf of the members affected by the flawed promotion examination. Specifically, the trial court found that because the determination of the damages sought by the FOP will require extensive and individualized discovery to determine whether and to what extent each individual member was damaged, the FOP does not have standing to recover damages on their behalf.

Analysis

At the outset, we note that this case appears to present an issue of first impression. Neither of the parties on appeal have cited to any Florida case that directly addresses whether and in what circumstances a union has standing to seek damages on behalf of its members, nor have we found such a case. However, based on our review of other union standing cases and related case law in the context of associational standing, we conclude that a union does not have standing to seek damages solely on behalf of its members where the union's claims for damages require individualized participation by and proof from its members.

1. The Federal Associational Standing Doctrine

Although the specific issue before us has not been resolved in Florida, it has been addressed in a number of cases before the federal courts. While we acknowledge that these federal authorities are not binding, we nevertheless find them to be persuasive. . . . Accordingly, our analysis begins with the development and application of associational standing in federal case law before turning to our analysis of Florida law.

The specific test that governs when an association has standing in its representational capacity to bring suit on behalf of its members can be traced to *Hunt v. Washington State Apple Advertising Commission*, 432 U.S. 333 (1977). In *Hunt*, the United States Supreme Court held that an association may have standing to bring a lawsuit on behalf of its members in its representational capacity, even if it has suffered no direct injury, so long as three requirements are met: "(a) its members would otherwise have standing to sue in their own right; (b) the interests it seeks to protect are germane to the organization's purpose; and (c) neither the claim asserted nor the relief requested requires the participation of individual members in the lawsuit." *Id.* at 343. As to the third prong of the *Hunt* test, which is the focus of our analysis in the present case, the Court elaborated:

> [W]hether an association has standing to invoke the court's remedial powers on behalf of its members depends in substantial measure on the nature of the relief sought. If in a proper case the association seeks a declaration, injunction, or some other form of prospective relief, it can reasonably be supposed that the remedy, if granted, will inure to the benefit of those members of the association actually injured. Indeed, in all cases in which we have expressly recognized standing in associations to represent their members, the relief sought has been of this kind.

Id. The Court concluded that the Washington State Apple Advertising Commission met each of the three associational standing requirements, and although the Washington State Apple Advertising Commission was a state agency, rather than a traditional voluntary membership organization, it was nevertheless permitted to seek declaratory and injunctive relief in its representational capacity on behalf of the apple growers and dealers who formed its constituency.

Since the United States Supreme Court's decision in *Hunt*, the apple has not fallen far from the tree. Nearly a decade later, the *Hunt* test was applied when a labor union sought to file suit in its representational capacity against the United States Department of Labor. *Int'l Union, United Auto., Aerospace & Agric. Implement Workers of Am. v. Brock*, 477 U.S. 274, 290, 106 S.Ct. 2523, 91 L.Ed.2d 228 (1986). Although it suffered no injury, the union sought injunctive and declaratory relief on behalf of its members, who were denied certain unemployment benefits. After carefully examining the type of relief the union sought, the Court found that the union had standing in its representational capacity because the lawsuit did not actually require the individual participation of union members. Instead, the case "raise[d] a pure question of law: whether the Secretary properly interpreted the Trade Act's [trade readjustment allowance] eligibility provisions." *Id*. at 287. In so holding, the Court reaffirmed the established limitation on associational standing: a labor union cannot seek damages on behalf of its members where the alleged injury "is peculiar to the individual member concerned, and both the fact and extent of injury would require individualized proof." *Id*. at 287.

One decade after *International Union*, the United States Supreme Court reiterated the general rule that associational standing is precluded when a union "seeks damages on behalf of its members." *United Food & Commercial Workers Union Local 751 v. Brown Grp., Inc.*, 517 U.S. 544, 554 (1996). The Court went on to find, however, that the third prong of the *Hunt* test is prudential, unlike the first two prongs of the *Hunt* test, which are constitutional. Thus, the Court concluded that Congress may abrogate the requirements of the third prong of the *Hunt* test by passing a statute that expressly provides unions with the authority to recover for its members' individualized claims. However, the United States Supreme Court specifically noted that the value of the third prong of the *Hunt* test is not somehow diminished by the fact that its requirements are not constitutional. Id. at 556 (stating, among other things, that the third prong may well "guard against the hazard of litigating a case to the damages stage only to find the plaintiff lacking detailed records or the evidence necessary to show the harm with sufficient specificity" and "hedge against any risk that the damages recovered by the association will fail to find their way into the pockets of the members on whose behalf injury is claimed").

Notwithstanding cases where Congress expressly permitted associations to pursue individualized claims on behalf of their members, several federal courts since *United Food* have honored the general prudential requirements of the third prong of the *Hunt* test. They have reaffirmed time and again that an association, (a word broadly construed to cover entities such as trade associations, non-profit associations, certain state agencies, and unions), cannot invoke the doctrine of associational standing in order to seek damages on behalf of its members, whose claims depend upon individualized proof.

Accordingly, based on these abundant federal authorities, we conclude that under federal law, generally, a union may not file suit solely in its representational capacity to seek damages on behalf of its members if individualized proof from the union's members would be required in the litigation.

2. A Union's Standing to Sue in Its Representational Capacity in Florida

Next, we consider the law in Florida. Florida has not adopted the *Hunt* test for associational standing. However, as demonstrated below, its "modified" associational standing doctrine contains requirements that closely resemble its federal counterpart, the *Hunt* test. Similarly, the few cases dealing with a union's standing to sue in its representational capacity have only permitted unions to seek declaratory or injunctive relief, and those claims did not require individualized participation from the unions' members.

Florida's "modified" associational standing doctrine applies primarily in the context of an association's rule challenges under section 120.56, Florida Statutes, where the association "is acting solely as the representative of its members." *Fla. Home Builders Ass'n v. Dep't of Labor & Emp't Sec.*, 412 So. 2d 351, 353 (Fla. 1982); see also *Palm Point Prop. Owners' Ass'n of Charlotte Cty., Inc. v. Pisarski*, 626 So. 2d 195, 197 (Fla. 1993) (stating that "our recognition of associational standing in the chapter 120 context was not a blanket adoption of the doctrine"). But see *Hillsborough Cty. v. Fla. Rest. Ass'n*, 603 So. 2d 587, 588 (Fla. 2d DCA 1992) (holding that an association has standing to seek injunctive and declaratory relief to challenge the enactment of a county ordinance on the ground that it is unconstitutional). In order to initiate a rule challenge in its representational capacity on behalf of its members, an association must meet the requirements of the following test enunciated in Florida Home Builders:

> [A]n association must demonstrate that a substantial number of its members, although not necessarily a majority, are "substantially affected" by the challenged rule. Further, the subject matter of the rule must be within the association's general scope of interest and activity, and *the relief requested must be of the type appropriate for a trade association to receive on behalf of its members.*

Fla. Home Builders, 412 So. 2d at 353–54 (emphasis added). Although we recognize that the modified associational standing doctrine relied on in *Florida Home Builders* does not apply in all contexts, we find that it is nevertheless instructive because its precepts mandate that an organization does not have associational standing in Florida if the relief requested is not "of the type appropriate for a trade association to receive on behalf of its members." *Id.* at 354. We specifically note that immediately after articulating the modified associational standing test in *Florida Home Builders*, the Florida Supreme Court clarified that "the only issue to be resolved in a section 120.56(1) proceeding is whether an agency rule is valid," and noted that a section 120.56(1) proceeding "*does not involve association or individual claims for money damages.*" *Id.* at 354 (emphasis added). This quote suggests that if the proceeding had involved individual claims for money damages, the Florida Supreme Court would have found that the organization lacked associational standing to pursue damages on behalf of its members.

The Florida Supreme Court's ruling in *Florida Home Builders* highlights the United States Supreme Court's comment in *United Food*, wherein the United States Supreme Court stated that one of the important purposes achieved by limiting associational standing to those circumstances where individualized participation of members in the litigation is not required is the protection such a limitation provides "against any risk that the damages recovered by the association will fail to find their way into the pockets of the members on whose behalf injury is claimed." *United Food*, 517 U.S. at 556. Accordingly, while not identical, it is apparent that the *Hunt* test and Florida's modified associational standing doctrine are closely aligned when it comes to the limitation of associational standing in cases where damages are sought.

Outside of the context of Florida's modified associational standing doctrine, there are only a few cases in Florida where a union attempted to file suit in its representational capacity. However, these cases have dealt only with injunctive or declaratory relief.

In the final analysis, we find that in both federal case law and Florida case law, the results are nearly uniform. In both contexts, if a union seeks and obtains injunctive or declaratory relief, it will often immediately "inure to the benefit of those members of the association actually injured," and individual participation will not be required of the union's members. See *Warth v. Seldin*, 422 U.S. 490, 515. However, when a union seeks damages on behalf of its members, rather than automatically inuring to the benefit of those members who suffer from an individualized injury, damages claims are often neither "common to the entire membership, nor shared by all in equal degree," and the injuries are often "peculiar to the individual member concerned," with "both the fact and extent of injury" requiring individualized proof. *Id*. at 515–516.

Thus, while an association may have standing to seek injunctive or declaratory relief on behalf of its members due to the automatic application of the relief to its injured members, an association does not have standing to seek damages on behalf of its members where individual participation from the association's injured members is "indispensable to proper resolution of the cause." *Id*. at 511. In short, disputes about claims for individualized damages are typically not "properly resolved in a group context." *Hunt*, 432 U.S. at 344, 97 S.Ct. 2434; see *Fla. Home Builders*, 412 So. 2d at 353–54. Accordingly, we find, consistent with both federal law and Florida law, that it is generally inappropriate for a union to seek damages solely in its representational capacity on behalf of its members when the calculation of those damages will depend on individualized participation from the union members.

3. The FOP Lacks Standing to Seek Damages on Behalf of Its Members

Our application of this principle to the instant case leads to a clear result. The trial court correctly found that the FOP cannot seek as a remedy damages for its members, as "[t]he determination of these damages will require extensive and individualized discovery to determine whether and to what extent each individual member was damaged" by the unlawful promotional exam. Some of its members were later promoted at different times, some were never promoted, and some might not have scored high enough to receive a promotion even if the oral examination portion of the test had not been flawed. Thus, the damages suffered by individuals who were not promoted according to the now invalid promotional exam are by no means uniform, and determining entitlement to such damages will be a fact-dependent process. Accordingly, we agree with the trial court that the FOP lacks standing to seek damages on behalf of these differently situated members, from whom individual participation in the damages portion of this litigation will be required.

Affirmed.

Note and Question to Consider:

1. In a footnote, the court in *Fraternal Order of Police v. Miami* noted that "the instant case does not involve a statutory right to recover damages on behalf of union members." Would the outcome have been different if it did?

2. The opinion cites to the U.S. Supreme Court's decision in *Hunt*, 432 U.S. at 344, where it opines that "disputes about claims for individualized damages are typically not properly resolved in a group context." If this is true, then why do both the Federal and Florida Rules of Civil Procedure allow for the filing of class-action lawsuits?

3. Some forms of litigation do not offer the opportunity for financial damage awards. Under the Florida Administrative Procedures Act, a law allows parties to engage in a type of administrative litigation called a "rule challenge" when, for example, the challenger believes the government has overstepped its authority in promulgating a rule that is "arbitrary" or "capricious." The relief available can include nullification of the rule but cannot include money damages. In the context of such litigation, Florida's supreme court adopted a three-prong test for "association standing" in *Florida Home Builders Ass'n v. Dep't of Labor & Employment Sec.*, 412 So. 2d 351 (Fla. 1982):

> In the instant case, Florida Home Builders Association instituted a challenge to the validity of a rule promulgated by the Bureau of Apprenticeship, Department of Labor and Employment Security of the State of Florida.

> The federal courts have consistently allowed standing for this type of association to represent the interests of its members in appropriate circumstances. In *Hunt v. Washington State Apple Advertising Commission*, 432 U.S. 333 (1977), the United States Supreme Court expressly set forth the requirements of associational standing:

>> [A]n association has standing to bring suit on behalf of its members when: (a) its members would otherwise have standing to sue in their own right; (b) the interests it seeks to protect are germane to

the organization's purpose; and (c) neither the claim asserted nor the relief requested requires the participation of individual members in the lawsuit.

432 U.S. at 343. An association must demonstrate that a substantial number of its members, although not necessarily a majority, are "substantially affected" by the challenged rule. Further, the subject matter of the rule must be within the association's general scope of interest and activity, and the relief requested must be of the type appropriate for a trade association to receive on behalf of its members.

The rule in issue concerns standards regarding apprenticeship programs in the building trades. Clearly, the content of the rule is such that the builders' association has a legitimate associational interest, on behalf of a substantial number of its members, in the rule's operation.

We conclude that the Florida Home Builders Association has standing.

Id. at 353–54. Compare the federal standard for "association standing" in federal administrative law actions that is quoted in the third paragraph above with Florida's rule for state administrative law actions promulgated in the fourth paragraph. Might Florida's three-prong test yield different results under the Florida Administrative Procedures Act than the federal three-prong test would yield under the federal Administrative Procedures Act?

4. In *Fraternal Order of Police v. Miami* above, first the court gives the holding of *Hunt v. Washington State Apple Advertising Commission*, then the court states: "Since the United States Supreme Court's decision in *Hunt*, the apple has not fallen far from the tree." Did you notice the pun? In your readings of case law precedent, what other examples do you recall of court opinions containing puns or jokes?

5. Historically, association standing was not always the norm. "Under traditional jus tertii jurisprudence, 'In the ordinary course, a litigant must assert his or her own legal rights and interests, and cannot rest a claim to relief on the legal rights or interests of third parties.'" *Alterra Healthcare Corp. v. Estate of Shelley*, 827 So. 2d 936, 941 (Fla. 2002) (citation omitted).

D. Indispensable Parties

A lawsuit must involve the correct participants. The Florida Rules of Civil Procedure allow a party to move to dismiss an action for the failure to join an indispensable party in a pre-answer motion, in the answer, in a reply, in a pre-trial motion, in a motion for judgment on the pleadings, or at the trial on the merits. Rule 1.140(2), Fla. R. Civ. P. Therefore, many opportunities exist for pleading and proving the failure to join an indispensable party.

An "indispensable party" is one whose interest in the subject matter of the action is such that if he is not joined, a complete and efficient determination of the equities, rights, and liabilities of the other parties is not possible. *Kephart v. Pickens*, 271 So. 2d 163 (Fla. 4th DCA 1972), cert. denied, 276 So. 2d 168 (Fla. 1973). As noted in the prior subsection above, a county or municipality is an indispensable party to an action challenging the constitutionality of its charter, ordinance, or franchise. § 86.091, Fla. Stat. Generally speaking, the Florida Supreme Court requires that "before any proceeding for declaratory relief is entertained all persons who have an 'actual, present, adverse, and antagonistic interest in the subject matter' should be before the court." *Florida Dep't of Educ. v. Glasser*, 622 So. 2d 944, 948 (Fla. 1993). The point is well-illustrated by that case, as seen in the following excerpt.

Florida Department of Education v. Glasser

Supreme Court of Florida, 1993
622 So. 2d 944

The school board filed its action for declaratory judgment against the tax collector of Sarasota County, without naming as a party the Department of Education or any other state agency. The board and tax collector stipulated to an expedited hearing to be held the next day, and at the same time notified the Attorney General of the next-day hearing by electronic facsimile transmission. The Attorney General's motion for dismissal, based on the board's failure to name the real party in interest, and his motion for postponement were denied. We hold that the Department of Education should have been named as a party to the trial court proceedings. "Trial by surprise" in cases of statewide importance is bad public policy and will not be condoned. We have said that before any proceeding for declaratory relief is entertained all persons who have an "actual, present, adverse, and antagonistic interest in the subject matter" should be before the court. *May v. Holley*, 59 So. 2d 636, 639 (Fla. 1952). The tax collector in the instant case had no interest antagonistic to the school district's interest and, in fact, made little or no attempt to defend the legislation at issue here.

Accordingly, we reverse the district court and remand for proceedings consistent with this opinion.

It is so ordered.

———————

Notes and Questions to Consider:

1. In the excerpt from *Florida Department of Education v. Glasser* appearing above, the court finds that "the tax collector stipulated to an expedited hearing to be held the next day" at which "[t]he tax collector . . . had no interest antagonistic to the school district's interest and, in fact, made little or no attempt to defend the legislation at issue here." Was this a genuine dispute? Or had both "opposing" sides had the same outcome in mind?

2. In what way is the rule requiring indispensable parties a safeguard against litigants manipulating the court system to obtain desired case law precedent and desirable holdings?

E. Give Notice to Florida's Attorney General Who May Intervene

Article IV of the Constitution of the State of Florida creates the executive branch of Florida's state government, the head officer of which is Florida's governor. The governor is given a cabinet, one member of which is a separately elected official called the attorney general. Because voters elect the governor and the attorney general separately, they may or may not share the same political party and ideals even though one is a member of the cabinet of the other.

Article IV, Section 4 of Florida's constitution provides that "[t]he attorney general shall be the chief state legal officer." Section 10 gives Florida's attorney general certain enumerated powers, including the authority to obtain certain advisory opinions from the Florida Supreme Court.

As a member of the Cabinet, Section 4 gives Florida's attorney general authority to "exercise such powers and perform such duties as may be prescribed by law." Florida Statutes § 86.091 implements that general grant of authority and requires that in any action for a declaratory judgment that a statute is unconstitutional the attorney general shall be served and is entitled to be heard. That statute was upheld in various cases such as *Brown v. Butterworth*, 831 So. 2d 683, 690 n.9 (Fla. 4th DCA 2002). The statute provides, in relevant part, that:

> When declaratory relief is sought, all persons may be made parties who have or claim any interest which would be affected by the declaration. No declaration shall prejudice the rights of persons not parties to the proceedings. In any proceeding concerning the validity of a county or municipal charter, ordinance, or franchise, such county or municipality shall be made a party and shall be entitled to be heard. If the statute, charter, ordinance, or franchise is alleged to be unconstitutional, the Attorney General or the state attorney of the judicial circuit in which the action is pending shall be served with a copy of the complaint and be entitled to be heard.

§ 86.091, Fla. Stat. (2017).

In 2010, the following rule was added to the Florida Rules of Civil Procedure implementing this statute. That rule, and the Committee Notes that were provided with that rule at its adoption, reads:

> *Rule 1.071 — Constitutional Challenge to State Statute or County or Municipal Charter, Ordinance, or Franchise; Notice by Party*
>
> A party that files a pleading, written motion, or other document drawing into question the constitutionality of a state statute or a county or municipal charter, ordinance, or franchise must promptly
>
>> (a) file a notice of constitutional question stating the question and identifying the document that raises it; and
>>
>> (b) serve the notice and the pleading, written motion, or other document drawing into question the constitutionality of a state statute or a

county or municipal charter, ordinance, or franchise on the Attorney General or the state attorney of the judicial circuit in which the action is pending, by either certified or registered mail.

Service of the notice and pleading, written motion, or other document does not require joinder of the Attorney General or the state attorney as a party to the action.

Committee Notes

This rule clarifies that, with respect to challenges to a state statute or municipal charter, ordinance, or franchise, service of the notice does not require joinder of the Attorney General or the state attorney as a party to the action; however, consistent with section 86.091, Florida Statutes, the Florida Attorney General or applicable state attorney has the discretion to participate and be heard on matters affecting the constitutionality of a statute. See, e.g., *State ex rel. Shevin v. Kerwin*, 279 So. 2d 836 (Fla. 1973) (Attorney General may choose to participate in appeal even though he was not required to be a party at the trial court). The rule imposes a new requirement that the party challenging the statute, charter, ordinance, or franchise file verification with the court of compliance with section 86.091, Florida Statutes. See form 1.975.

Rule 1.071, Fla. R. Civ. P.

The Committee Notes reference a form for providing the required notice. That form also appears in the Florida Rules of Civil Procedure as follows:

Notice of Compliance with Section 86.091, Florida Statutes

The undersigned hereby gives notice of compliance with Fla. R. Civ. P. 1.071, with respect to the constitutional challenge brought pursuant to . . . (Florida statute, charter, ordinance, or franchise challenged). . . . The undersigned complied by serving the . . . (Attorney General for the state of Florida or State Attorney for the . . . Judicial Circuit) . . . with a copy of the pleading or motion challenging . . . (Florida statute, charter, ordinance, or franchise challenged) . . . , by . . . (certified or registered mail) . . . on . . . (date). . . .

Committee Notes

This form is to be used to provide notice of a constitutional challenge as required by section 86.091, Florida Statutes. See rule 1.071. This form is to be used when the Attorney General or the State Attorney is not a named party to the action, but must be served solely in order to comply with the notice requirements set forth in section 86.091.

Rule 1.975, Fla. R. Civ. P.

The operation of section 86.091 is well described in the following excerpt from *Martin Mem'l Med. Ctr., Inc. v. Tenet Healthsystem Hosps., Inc.*, 875 So. 2d 797 (Fla. 1st DCA 2004) (footnotes omitted).

Martin Memorial Medical Center v. Tenet Healthsystem Hospitals

First District Court of Appeal of Florida, 2004
875 So. 2d 797

Appellees sued [the State of Florida Agency for Health Care Administration, hereinafter the] AHCA, seeking (among other things) a declaratory judgment that chapter 2003–289, Laws of Florida was unconstitutional as a special or local law which had not been adopted in compliance with article III, section 10, of the Florida Constitution, and an injunction permanently enjoining AHCA from issuing any exemptions pursuant to that law. AHCA was represented by the Attorney General's office. Appellants, who all alleged that they were hospitals qualified to receive certificate of need exemptions pursuant to chapter 2003–289, were granted leave to intervene, and aligned with AHCA.

We first address appellees' contention that the appeal must be dismissed. They point out that neither AHCA nor the Attorney General has elected to participate in the appeal. According to appellees, because the Attorney General is not a participant in the appeal, we are obliged to dismiss for lack of either a necessary or an indispensable party. We find appellees' argument unpersuasive.

In the first place, while AHCA has apparently elected not to participate actively in this appeal, by virtue of Florida Rule of Appellate Procedure 9.020(g)(2) it remains a party, as an appellee. Moreover, we can find no support in section 86.091 for the proposition that the Attorney General is either a necessary or an indispensable party to this appeal. To the extent pertinent, section 86.091 (which is a part of the chapter entitled "Declaratory Judgments") reads merely that, "[i]f [a] statute, charter, ordinance, or franchise is alleged to be unconstitutional, the Attorney General or the state attorney of the judicial circuit in which the action is pending shall be served with a copy of the complaint and be entitled to be heard." The purpose of this statute would appear from its language to be relatively clear—to ensure that the state (in the person of the Attorney General or appropriate state attorney) is aware of any litigation in which a plaintiff seeks a declaratory judgment that any of the enumerated forms of legislation is unconstitutional, and afforded an opportunity to present the state's position. There is nothing in the language of the statute which supports appellees' argument that, should the Attorney General or appropriate state attorney elect, after service, not to participate, such litigation may not proceed—i.e., that one of the two is an indispensable party. In fact, placing such a gloss on the words used would permit the Attorney General and state attorneys to prevent any such challenge merely by declining to participate in the litigation. Surely, such an absurd result could not have been intended. Rather, it seems to us relatively clear that, once the Attorney General or appropriate state attorney has been served, he or she may choose either to appear or not. However, in the latter event, non-participation has no effect on the litigation.

Appellees point to dicta in *Brown v. Butterworth*, 831 So. 2d 683 (Fla. 4th DCA 2002), to support their argument that the Attorney General is an indispensable party, without whom the litigation may not go forward. It is true that, in *Brown*, the court said that "[t]he only truly 'indispensable' party to an action attacking the constitutionality of Florida legislation . . . is the Attorney General," *id.* at 689–90, and that it defined an "indispensable party" as "a party without whom the action cannot proceed." *Id.* at 690 n. 9. However, the statement is pure dicta. Moreover, it is unsupported by any citation to authority other than section 86.091 which, as we have said, does not appear to support such a construction. In addition, the statement is directly contrary to positions taken in two prior decisions of our supreme court construing substantively identical versions of the statute.

In *Watson v. Claughton*, 160 Fla. 217, 34 So. 2d 243, 246 (1948), the court said that the statute "d[id] not prescribe that the Attorney General shall be a necessary party when the constitutionality of an act is assailed. It only provides that he shall be 'heard.'" *Id.* The court held that the trial court had not abused its discretion in denying the Attorney General's request for leave to intervene. *Id.*

Similarly, in *Mayo v. National Truck Brokers, Inc.*, 220 So. 2d 11 (Fla. 1969), the court denied relief to the appellants, who were challenging an adverse final declaratory judgment on the ground that the state attorney for the circuit in which the action had been filed had not been formally served, and did not participate. In doing so, the court said:

> that neither the Attorney General nor the State Attorney of the circuit in which the action is pending are necessary parties in the strict sense of that expression. . . . The State Attorney, after having received a copy of the complaint, advised the court that he had waived final service and did not desire to participate further in the hearing. This he had the right to do.

Id. at 13.

At least one federal court has reached a similar conclusion regarding the purpose of the statute. In *Mallory v. Harkness*, 923 F.Supp. 1546, 1553 (S.D.Fla. 1996), aff'd, 109 F.3d 771 (11th Cir. 1997) (table), the court said:

> The [Attorney General] intervened in this matter pursuant to Florida Statute § 86.091. . . . The [Attorney General] argues that § 86.091 imposes a statutory duty upon the state to defend all constitutionally challenged statutes. The Court, to the contrary, finds intervention by the [Attorney General] under § 86.091 to be discretionary. It has long been recognized that the [Attorney General] is not a necessary party each time the constitutionality of a statute is drawn into question. The [Attorney General] is thus not affirmatively required to intervene every time an entity challenges the constitutionality of a statute. Upon receipt of the complaint pursuant to § 86.091, the [Attorney General] could have filed with the Court a notice of acknowledgment declining to defend the statute as the [Attorney General] did in Rosenfeld.

Given the decisions in *Watson* and *Mayo*, we decline to follow the dicta from *Brown* upon which appellees rely. It is apparent that the Attorney General participated in the litigation at the trial level, as counsel for AHCA, and that he is aware of this appeal. Accordingly, it is equally apparent that the requirements of section 86.091 have been met, and that the presence of the Attorney General is not required in this appeal. Appellees' motion to dismiss the appeal is denied.

———————

Notes and Questions to Consider:

1. Perhaps most great pieces of drama or literature contain a powerful, motivated adversary. To what extent does the requirement to notify and allow the intervention of Florida's attorney general add such drama to state constitutional law litigation?

2. What if Florida's attorney general agrees that the law at issue violates Florida's constitution? Is her only proper response to decline the opportunity to intervene, or instead, may she intervene and attack the law?

F. Remedies

Even when the litigant's grievance is as important as an alleged violation of a state constitutional right, still the litigant bears the burden of starting his lawsuit by filing a sufficient pleading. "A complaint must allege ultimate facts which, if estab-lished by competent evidence, would support a decree granting the relief sought by the pleader." Patrick John McGinley, FLORIDA ELEMENTS OF AN ACTION § 101:1 (Thomson Reuters 2017-2018 ed.). When it comes to choosing the "relief sought by the pleader," or the "remedies," choices include a judgment for monetary damages, a judgment for declaratory relief, the entry of an injunction stopping current actions or preventing future actions, or some combination of these.

The action for declaratory judgment is the preferred route under the Florida Rules of Civil Procedure, as noted by the Florida Supreme Court when it held:

> Ordinarily, the constitutionality of a legislative act should be challenged by filing an action for declaratory judgment in circuit court. *Moreau v. Lewis*, 648 So. 2d 124, 126 (Fla. 1995). However, when a statute will adversely impact the functions of government to the extent that it requires an imme-diate determination of the constitutionality of the statute, we may consider a petition that challenges the constitutionality of that statute pursuant to our mandamus authority. See, e.g., *Allen v. Butterworth*, 756 So. 2d 52, 54–55 (Fla. 2000); *Moreau*, 648 So. 2d at 126; *Dickinson v. Stone*, 251 So. 2d 268, 271 (Fla. 1971).

Abdool v. Bondi, 141 So. 3d 529, 537 (Fla. 2014). The technical requirements for filing a sufficient pleading for an action for declaratory judgment under Florida law are identified in the following excerpt from Patrick John McGinley, FLORIDA ELEMENTS OF AN ACTION § 1101:1 (Thomson Reuters 2017-2018 ed.):

Elements of the Prima Facie Case of Declaratory Judgment in Florida Elements of an Action

by Patrick John McGinley
§ 1101:1 (2017–2018 ed.)
© 2017 by Thomson Reuters

[Florida Statutes] § 86.021 creates a right to a declaratory judgment when the elements of such a claim are pled and proven. The purpose of a declaratory judgment is to afford the parties relief from their insecurity and uncertainty with respect to their rights, status, and other equitable or legal relations.

The necessary minimum elements of the cause of action of declaratory judgment read as follows:

(1) there is a bona fide, actual, present practical need for the declaration;

AND

(2) the declaration deals with a present, ascertained or ascertainable state of facts or present controversy as to a state of facts;

AND

(3) some immunity, power, privilege or right of the complaining party is dependent upon the facts or the law applicable to the facts;

AND

(4) there is some person or persons who have, or reasonably may have an actual, present, adverse and antagonistic interest in the subject matter, either in fact or law;

AND

(5) the antagonistic and adverse interests are all before the court by proper process or class representation;

AND

(6) relief sought is not merely giving of legal advice by the courts or the answer to questions propounded from curiosity.

Regarding the first element, the plaintiff/petitioner must show need for the declaration that is bona fide, actual, present, and practical. For example, a tax collector's interest was sufficient to create a bona fide and a practical need for a declaration pursuant to Declaratory Judgment Act when the tax collector could not have performed her duties in compliance with state law if the school board attempted to levy taxes pursuant to its constitutional authority rather than seeking a declaration of the invalidity of the challenged statutes, and it was necessary for the trial court to order the tax collector to collect and remit certain amount based on the court's declaration in order to grant the relief requested by the school board.

Regarding the second element, the petition or complaint for a declaratory judgment must deal with "a present, ascertained or ascertainable state of facts or present controversy as to a state of facts." A typical example is whether a policy of insurance provides coverage.

Regarding the third element, the plaintiff/petitioner must show some immunity, power, privilege, or right of his is dependent upon the facts or the law applicable to the facts; or stated somewhat differently, that the plaintiff/petitioner has ascertainable rights. This is best achieved when a written instrument is shown to affect some immunity, power, privilege, or right of the plaintiff/petitioner, such as questions arising out of either the construction of, or the validity of, a written statute, contract, or instrument. In order for declaratory judgment action to lie, there must be some doubt as to existence or nonexistence of some right, status, immunity, power, or privilege, which may be at stake under a statute, deed, will, contract, or other article, memorandum, or instrument in writing. Florida's Declaratory Judgment Act is available also to determine the rights of parties under an oral contract. However, such an oral contract may not be the subject of a declaratory judgment when it cannot be shown that the plaintiff/petitioner has ascertainable rights under the oral agreement, such as when there was a material dispute as to terms, performance, breach, and general relief available pursuant to the alleged agreement.

Regarding the fourth element, the plaintiff/petitioner must show that he has standing to bring the suit, which means he must show that he is someone with an actual, present, adverse, and antagonistic interest in the subject matter.

Regarding the fifth element, the plaintiff/petitioner satisfies his burden of bringing the antagonistic and adverse interests before the court by proper process or class representation by bringing before the court a true adversary who will fight against the plaintiff/petitioner and against whom litigation is unavoidable. For example, in an action for a declaratory judgment regarding tax legislation funding education, the Sarasota County School Board did not meet its burden to bring all those with adverse interests before the court when it did not name the Florida Department of Education or any other state agency as a party, sued only the tax collector of Sarasota County, and stipulated with the tax collector for an expedited hearing to be held the next day where the tax collector made little or no attempt to defend the legislation at issue.

Regarding the sixth element, the plaintiff/petitioner satisfies this element by showing that the relief he seeks is not merely giving of legal advice by the courts or the answer to questions propounded from curiosity. The dispute must be actual, not theoretical. . . .

Id. at sec. 1101:1. As referenced above, these requirements arise out of Florida's declaratory judgment statute, which is currently codified in Florida Statutes section 86.11 and which reads in relevant part:

> The circuit and county courts have jurisdiction within their respective jurisdictional amounts to declare rights, status, and other equitable or legal relations whether or not further relief is or could be claimed. No action or procedure is open to objection on the ground that a declaratory judgment is demanded. The court's declaration may be either affirmative or negative in form and effect and such declaration has the force and effect of a final judgment. The court may render declaratory judgments on the existence, or nonexistence:
>
> (1) Of any immunity, power, privilege, or right; or
>
> (2) Of any fact upon which the existence or nonexistence of such immunity, power, privilege, or right does or may depend, whether such immunity, power, privilege, or right now exists or will arise in the future. Any person seeking a declaratory judgment may also demand additional, alternative, coercive, subsequent, or supplemental relief in the same action.

Id. at sec. 86.11, Fla. Stat. (2017).

Note, however, that an action for declaratory judgment offers as its relief a judgment declaring the rights of the parties. Thus, success in an action seeking only a declaratory judgment does not result in the award of a lump sum of money from which the plaintiff can mitigate its damages.

To obtain monetary relief, a complaint for damages is necessary. Under Florida law, that complaint must do more than just ask for money. It must also identify and properly plead entitlement to a particular cause of action for which money is an eligible form of relief. Such a "cause of action can arise under the common law or under a statute. In order to assert a statutory cause of action, the claimant must comply with all valid condition precedents; for an action cannot be properly commenced until all essential elements of the cause of action are present." Patrick John McGinley, FLORIDA ELEMENTS OF AN ACTION § 1101:1 (Thomson Reuters 2017-2018 ed.) (citing *Ferry-Morse Seed Co. v. Hitchcock*, 426 So. 2d 958 (Fla. 1983)). For example, a litigant might file a complaint for damages under the Florida Civil Rights Act, Chapter 760, Florida Statutes. It provides in relevant part that:

> In any civil action brought under this section, the court may issue an order prohibiting the discriminatory practice and providing affirmative relief from the effects of the practice, including back pay. The court may also award compensatory damages, including, but not limited to, damages for mental anguish, loss of dignity, and any other intangible injuries, and punitive damages. . . . The judgment for the total amount of punitive damages awarded under this section to an aggrieved person shall not exceed $100,000. In any action or proceeding under this subsection, the court, in its discretion, may allow the prevailing party a reasonable

attorney's fee as part of the costs. It is the intent of the Legislature that this provision for attorney's fees be interpreted in a manner consistent with federal case law involving a Title VII action. The right to trial by jury is preserved in any such private right of action in which the aggrieved person is seeking compensatory or punitive damages, and any party may demand a trial by jury.

§ 760.11, Fla. Stat. (2017).

As noted in the quotation from the Florida Civil Rights Act appearing above, one potential remedy on the list is the equitable relief of the entry of an injunction. A party may seek an injunction alone, or together with, a claim for monetary damages. The Florida Supreme Court holds that:

> To obtain a temporary injunction, the petitioner must satisfy a four-part test under Florida law: "a substantial likelihood of success on the merits; lack of an adequate remedy at law; irreparable harm absent the entry of an injunction; and that injunctive relief will serve the public interest." To obtain a permanent injunction, the petitioner must "establish a clear legal right, an inadequate remedy at law and that irreparable harm will arise absent injunctive relief."

Liberty Counsel v. Florida Bar Bd. of Governors, 12 So. 3d 183, 186 (Fla. 2009).

Another potential remedy on that list from the Florida Civil Rights Act is the potential for attorney fees and costs. This is the topic of the next section of this text.

G. Fee-Shifting Statutes and Awards of Attorney Fees

Regardless of whether the state constitutional law litigant chooses an action for declaratory judgment, a complaint for damages, a claim for injunctive relief, or some combination of those, the lawyer representing the constitutional litigant should consider pleading a claim for entitlement for attorney fees against the adversary if an applicable "fee shifting statute" like the one above exists. In Florida constitutional law cases, like most cases, the "American Rule" of attorney fees applies, and therefore, "[m]ost litigants involved in lawsuits in the United States are responsible for the cost of their own attorney's fees." Lawrence D. Rosenthal, *Adding Insult to No Injury: The Denial of Attorney's Fees to "Victorious" Employment Discrimination and Other Civil Rights Plaintiffs*, 37 Fla. St. U. L. Rev. 49 (2009).

Consider, for instance, a litigant whose state constitutional law claim arises under the Florida Civil Rights Act, Chapter 760, Florida Statutes. It states it is to be interpreted consistently with the federal Civil Rights Act, Chapter 42, United States Code. That law, and other anti-discrimination statutes, contain rights to monetary damages including "fee shifting" statutes varying from the "American Rule" and awarding attorney fees to successful plaintiffs under stated circumstances. :

Lawrence D. Rosenthal, *Adding Insult to No Injury: The Denial of Attorney's Fees to "Victorious" Employment Discrimination and Other Civil Rights Plaintiffs*, 37 FLA. ST. U. L. REV. 49, 49–52 (2009), , in its footnotes, identifies the following fee-shifting statutes applicable to federal constitutional law and civil rights claims such as those brought under 28 U.S.C. § 1983: the Americans with Disabilities Act, the fee-shifting provision for Title VII of the Civil Rights Act of 1964, the Age Discrimination in Employment Act's fee-shifting provision as found at 29 U.S.C. § 626(b), which incorporates the attorney's fees provision from the Fair Labor Standards Act, 29 U.S.C. § 216(b) (2006); and the Civil Rights Attorney's Fees Awards Act of 1976, 42 U.S.C. § 1988(b). *See* Rosenthal, *Adding Insult to No Injury*, 37 FLA. ST. U. L. REV. at 49–52 (quoted from footnotes 6 through 9).

The list above is not all-inclusive. Other fee-shifting statutes exist in state and federal law that might apply to a given claim depending on its factual basis. For example, both the Florida Statutes and the U.S. Code contain an Equal Access to Justice Act (EAJA) that may create fee entitlement in favor of a citizen who overcomes the act or omission of a government agency to which the law applies. The federal EAJA provides in relevant part:

Except as otherwise specifically provided by statute, a court shall award to a prevailing party other than the United States fees and other expenses, in addition to any costs awarded pursuant to subsection (a), incurred by that party in any civil action (other than cases sounding in tort), including proceedings for judicial review of agency action, brought by or against the United States in any court having jurisdiction of that action, unless the court finds that the position of the United States was substantially justified or that special circumstances make an award unjust.

28 U.S.C. § 2412(d)(1)(A). Thus, to be eligible for federal EAJA attorney fees:

(1) the claimant must be a "prevailing party";

(2) the government's position must not have been "substantially justified"; and

(3) no "special circumstances" must exist that make an award of attorney fees unjust.

Commissioner, Immigration and Naturalization Serv. v. Jean, 496 U.S. 154, 158 (1990).

Florida's EAJA operates as follows:

Unless otherwise provided by law, an award of attorney's fees and costs shall be made to a prevailing small business party in any adjudicatory proceeding or administrative proceeding pursuant to chapter 120 initiated by a state agency, unless the actions of the agency were substantially justified or special circumstances exist which would make the award unjust.

. . . To apply for an award under this section, the attorney for the prevailing small business party must submit an itemized affidavit . . . [It] must be made within 60 days after the date that the small business party becomes a prevailing small business party.

. . . The court, or the administrative law judge in the case of a proceeding under chapter 120, shall promptly conduct an evidentiary hearing on the application for an award of attorney's fees and shall issue a judgment, or a final order in the case of an administrative law judge. The final order of an administrative law judge is reviewable in accordance with the provisions of s. 120.68. If the court affirms the award of attorney's fees and costs in whole or in part, it may, in its discretion, award additional attorney's fees and costs for the appeal.

No award of attorney's fees and costs shall be made in any case in which the state agency was a nominal party.

No award of attorney's fees and costs for an action initiated by a state agency shall exceed $50,000.

§ 57.111, Fla. Stat. (2018).

H. Facial and As-Applied Challenges

When challenging whether a statute, regulation, governmental rule, or government policy is permissible under a constitution, the lawyer faces the strategic decision of attacking that law as unconstitutional on its face, or instead, as unconstitutional as applied to the lawyer's client and all those similarly situated to the lawyer's client—or both. That strategy affects the lawyer's burden of proof and affects the relief the reviewing court may grant.

"[A] determination that a statute is facially unconstitutional means that no set of circumstances exists under which the statute would be valid." *Florida Dep't of Revenue v. City of Gainesville*, 918 So. 2d 250, 256 (Fla. 2005). When a litigant argues that a Florida statute is unconstitutional on its face, "[i]f any state of facts, known or to be assumed, justify the law, the court's power of inquiry ends." *State v. Bales*, 343 So. 2d 9 (Fla. 1977). "A facial challenge to a statute is more difficult than an 'as applied' challenge, because the challenger must establish that no set of circumstances exists under which the statute would be valid." *Cashatt v. State*, 873 So. 2d 430, 434 (Fla. 1st DCA 2004). The Florida Supreme Court holds that:

In a facial challenge, we consider only the text of the statute, not its specific application to a particular set of circumstances. For a statute to be held facially unconstitutional, the challenger must demonstrate that no set of circumstances exists in which the statute can be constitutionally applied. As a result, the Act will not be invalidated as facially unconstitutional simply because it could operate unconstitutionally under some hypothetical circumstances.

Abdool v. Bondi, 141 So. 3d 529, 538 (Fla. 2014).

A finding that a statute is unconstitutional on its face yields a remedy making the statute unenforceable against anyone in any circumstance. A finding that a statute is not unconstitutional on its face does not foreclose a claim that the statute may still be unconstitutional as applied. *See generally Florida Dep't of Revenue v. City of Gainesville*, 918 So. 2d 250, 266 (Fla. 2005) (holding the statutes at issue "are not unconstitutional on their face. We do not determine the constitutionality of these provisions as applied.").

In an as-applied challenge, the litigant challenges the specific impact of the law or regulation upon that litigant and all those similarly situated to that litigant. An as-applied challenge requires a fact-intensive inquiry of the impact of the challenged law or regulation upon the litigant. The factfinder may be called upon to decide, and the court may then analyze, the permissible behaviors, actions, and uses by the litigant before and after enactment of the law or regulation being challenged. *See generally Shands v. City of Marathon*, 999 So. 2d 718, 723 (Fla. 3rd DCA 2008) (discussing an as-applied challenge to land use regulation as a taking).

Unlike a successful claim that a statute is unconstitutional on its face, a successful as-applied challenge to a statute does not result in the challenged statute being unenforceable against everyone in every circumstance. Instead, it yields the remedy specific to the challenger, and to all those who can prove they are similarly situated to the challenger in facing the same unconstitutional effects of the statute when applied to them.

So the relief available is different based upon whether the litigant alleges unconstitutionality on its face or as applied. Likewise, the defense of the statute is different. If the challenger alleges facial unconstitutionality, then the defense may prevail by proving a single instance where the statute operates constitutionally, whether under current facts or under reasonably foreseeable facts. But for as-applied, the defense's proof of instances of constitutionality are irrelevant if the statute is unconstitutional as applied to this litigant in his particular circumstances.

The WILLIAM & MARY BILL OF RIGHTS JOURNAL explains the difference in Alex Kreit, *Making Sense of Facial and As-Applied Challenges*, 18 WM. & MARY BILL RTS. J. 657 (2010):

> ... [The] law strongly favors as-applied challenges on the grounds that they are more consistent with the goals of resolving concrete disputes and deferring as much as possible to the legislative process. Facial challenges, on the other hand, should be used sparingly and only in exceptional circumstances. Perhaps the most well-known, succinct, and controversial formulation of this idea was the [United States] Supreme Court's statement in *United States v. Salerno* that a "facial challenge to a legislative Act is, of course, the most difficult challenge to mount successfully" and will only succeed if a litigant can "establish that no set of circumstances exists under which the Act would be valid."

Id. at 657–58.

Notes and Questions to Consider:

1. A new client of your law firm is affected by a Florida Statute that does not appear to be unconstitutional on its face. The way the statute affects most people is not in violation of their Florida constitutional rights. But the way the statute affects your client appears to be in violation of your client's Florida constitutional rights. Should you challenge the constitutionality of the statute "on its face" or "as applied?" How does your choice affect the legal burden to be carried by your new client and by the defendant? How does the choice affect the client's potential legal remedy?

2. The Florida Rules of Civil Procedure permit pleading in the alternative, and therefore, it is permissible in a single lawsuit challenging a single law to allege it is unconstitutional both on its face and as applied. Is this always the best strategy, or are there risks to this strategy?

I. Amicus Curiae

An *amicus curiae*, or "friend of the court" as that Latin phrase is loosely translated, is a person or group who is not a party to the appeal but wishes to be heard in it. Amicus are intervenors. Amicus are permissible under the following Florida Rule of Appellate Procedure:

(a) *When Permitted.* An amicus curiae may file a brief only by leave of court. A motion for leave to file must state the movant's interest, the particular issue to be addressed, how the movant can assist the court in the disposition of the case, and whether all parties consent to the filing of the brief. . . .

. . . (c) *Time for Service.* An amicus curiae must serve its brief no later than 10 days after the first brief, petition, or response of the party being supported is filed. An amicus curiae that does not support either party must serve its brief no later than 10 days after the initial brief or petition is filed. . . .

(d) *Notice of Intent to File Amicus Brief in Supreme Court.* When a party has invoked the discretionary jurisdiction of the supreme court, an amicus curiae may file a notice with the court indicating its intent to seek leave to file an amicus brief on the merits should the court accept jurisdiction. The notice shall state briefly why the case is of interest to the amicus curiae, but shall not contain argument. . . .

Rule 9.370, Fla. R. App. P.

It has been said that the "constitutionality of a statute may not be attacked by an amicus curiae when the parties have not raised the question." Henry P. Trawick et al., Constitutional Litigation in Florida 157–58 (Florida Bar 1973). "This does not mean, however, that an amicus curiae brief is restricted to the arguments made by the parties. An amicus brief may advance any reasonable theory or argument as long as it addresses an issue presented in the case." Philip J. Padovano, FLORIDA APPELLATE PRACTICE § 16:13 (Thomson Reuters 2017 ed.).

Further guidance as to the court's use of amicus briefs appears in the case of *Ciba-Geigy Limited v. The Fish Peddler*, 683 So. 2d 522 (Fla. 4th DCA 1996):

Ciba-Geigy Limited v. The Fish Peddler, Inc.
Fourth District Court of Appeal of Florida, 1996
683 So. 2d 522

Order on Motions to File Amicus Curiae Briefs

We have, to date, received motions to file two amicus briefs. Briefs from amicus curiae, which means "friend of the court," are generally for the purpose of assisting the court in cases which are of general public interest, or aiding in the presentation of difficult issues.

Although "by the nature of things an amicus is not normally impartial," amicus briefs should not argue the facts in issue. *Strasser v. Doorley*, 432 F.2d 567 (1st Cir. 1970). In the present case one of the amicus briefs appears to be nothing more than an attempt to present a fact specific argument of the same type as is contained in the appellants' 50 page brief. Since the parties are limited as to the number and length of briefs, amicus briefs should not be used to simply give one side more exposure than the rules contemplate. We therefore deny the motion to file an amicus brief on behalf of the Florida Chamber of Commerce.

Because our time for reading briefs is not unlimited, it would be helpful to the court if amicus would attempt to join together in one brief and cooperate with the parties so as not to be repetitious of the parties' briefs. In the interest of brevity, amicus briefs should not contain a statement of the case or facts, but rather should get right to the additional information which the amicus believes will assist the court. And, although Florida Rule of Appellate Procedure 9.370 does not require a motion for leave to file an amicus brief to state whether the parties have consented, it would be appropriate for the motion to contain that information. See Rule 9.300(a).

STONE, WARNER and KLEIN, JJ., concur.

––––––––––

Notes and Questions to Consider:

1. In the opinion quoted above, the court made the statement that amicus briefs are "generally for the purpose of assisting the court in cases which are of general public interest, or aiding in the presentation of difficult issues." Do you agree with this statement? At least one commentator disagreed with this statement when he wrote:

> This statement is one that was made by an appellate court and it necessarily reflects a judicial perspective. An advocate may have other good reasons for

filing an amicus brief. The association or individual submitting the brief typically has some interest in the precedent that will be set by the court's decision. Appearing in the case as amicus helps to ensure that a particular argument can be made before the decision is made. Amicus briefs are usually filed to support the position of a party, but that is not always the case. It would be proper to submit an amicus brief that addresses the issues, without supporting the view taken by either party.

Philip J. Padovano, FLORIDA APPELLATE PRACTICE §16:13 (Thomson Reuters 2017 ed.).

2. In your opinion, should appellate courts be more willing or more reluctant to allow amicus briefs in cases where the parties raise issues under Florida's constitution?

3. Assuming a case is not generating media attention, how would people or organizations know about it in order to file a motion for permission to submit an amicus brief?

4. If you were representing a litigant in a constitutional law case where an unexpected amicus filed a motion for permission to submit a brief in your case, what would you do? Would you object to their filing of a motion for permission to submit an amicus brief? Would you seek to "join together" or coordinate with them as the opinion quotation above suggests?

5. Should an amicus be liable for attorney fees payable to a prevailing party? Consider *Independent Federation of Flight Attendants v. Zipes*, 491 U.S. 754 (1989) (holding that section 706(k) of the Civil Rights Act of 1964, 42 U.S.C. §2000e-5(k), which provides that a "court, in its discretion, may allow the prevailing party, other than the [Equal Employment Opportunity] Commission or the United States, a reasonable attorney's fee as part of the costs" does not permit a court to award attorney's fees against intervenors who have not been found to have violated the Civil Rights Act or any other federal law).

6. Are the expense and delays of allowing amicus warranted by the benefits? Two law review commentators noted:

> [I]n *Rathkamp v. Department of Community Affairs* . . . Chief Judge Alan R. Schwartz based the Court's unanimous decision on the principles stated in Chief Judge Posner's opinion in *Ryan v. Commodities Trading Commission* [where] Chief Judge Posner declared, "After 16 years of reading amicus curiae briefs the vast majority of which have not assisted the judges, I have decided that it would be good to scrutinize these motions (to appear as amici) in a more careful, indeed a fish-eyed, fashion." Chief Judge Posner went on to acknowledge that American courts have moved beyond the original concept of amicus as a "friend of the court, not friend of a party," and "an adversary role of an amicus curiae has become accepted." . . . Emphasizing that courts are helped "by being pointed to considerations germane to our decision of the appeal that the parties for one reason or another have

not brought to our attention," Chief Judge Posner declared that the amicus briefs filed in the Seventh Circuit "rarely do that." He concluded by stating that "(i)n an era of heavy judicial caseloads and public impatience with the delays and expense of litigation, we judges should be assiduous to bar the gates to amicus curiae briefs that fail to present convincing reasons why the parties' briefs do not give us all the help we need for deciding the appeal." Despite Chief Judge Schwartz's enthusiastic adoption of Chief Judge Posner's dim view of the usefulness of amicus briefs, both the Florida Supreme Court and Florida district courts generally allow amicus briefs to be filed without the rigorous examination urged by Chief Judge Posner. Notably, no other Florida court has cited either Chief Judge Posner's decision in *Ryan* or Chief Judge Schwartz's opinion in *Rathkamp*. And, despite Chief Judge Schwartz's observation that amicus briefs "rarely" help that court, Florida courts—including the Third District—often have relied on amicus briefs in reaching their decisions.

Sylvia H. Walbolt & Joseph H. Lang, Jr., *Amicus Briefs: Friend or Foe of Florida Courts?*, 32 STETSON L. REV. 269, 297–98 (2003) (footnotes omitted).

Chapter 4

Florida's Declaration of Rights

A. Political Power

Just as the first ten amendments to the federal Constitution are known as the Bill of Rights, Article I of the Constitution of the State of Florida is known as the Declaration of Rights. This brief history of Florida's constitution from the Spring 1990 issue of the Nova Law Review alludes to how Article I and the rest of the document arose.

> Florida's constitutional history traces its lineage from 1838 when delegates from throughout the Territory of Florida assembled in a convention for the purpose of organizing a state government. Following the adoption of three intermediate constitutions, the state adopted its longest-lived constitution, the Constitution of 1885. During the 1960s, however, it had become apparent that the document reflected the imperatives of an age gone by and was "in dire need of revision." Under the Constitution of 1885, the legislature was empowered to propose by joint resolution an amendment to the document. Toward that end, the 1965 Legislature created the Florida Constitutional Revision Commission to carefully study the constitution. . . .
>
> With respect to article I, the 1968 revision substantially reasserts the personal rights contained in the Declaration of Rights of the Constitution of 1885 . . . . [B]y relocating personal rights from the Declaration to a numbered article, . . . the adopters preserved the primacy of position enjoyed by personal rights while assuring that those rights would be regarded with at least equal dignity as powers created elsewhere. . . .

David C. Hawkins, *Florida Constitutional Law: A Ten-Year Retrospective on the State Bill of Rights*, 14 Nova L. Rev. 693, 699–700 (1990).

It was by these means that Florida's Declaration of Rights acquired primacy in Florida's constitution. The first right of all reads: "All political power is inherent in the people. The enunciation herein of certain rights shall not be construed to deny or impair others retained by the people." Art. I, § 1, Fla. Const.

Thereafter, many of the rights in Article I of the Florida Constitution appear verbatim or in substantially the same form as in the U.S. Constitution. Article I of the Constitution of the State of Florida lists most of the civil liberties protected by the Florida Constitution, and it closely parallels the civil liberties protected by the

U.S. Constitution's Bill of Rights, as well as the Due Process, and Equal Protection Clauses. But as the concept of a "Laboratory of Democracy" illustrates, and as *Michigan v. Long* teaches us, an adequate and independent state ground clearly appearing within the state court opinion may result in evading U.S. Supreme Court review. Thus, examples exist of parallel rights from the Florida and U.S. Constitutions receiving disparate treatment at the state and federal court levels because the adequate and independent basis of the state court's opinion was Florida's constitution and Florida law only.

In addition, there are those rights in Article I of the Florida Constitution that do not have a counterpart in the U.S. Constitution. Subject to the requirements of *Michigan v. Long*, it is the Supreme Court of the State of Florida—and not the Supreme Court of the United States—that is the ultimate arbiter of those constitutional rights.

In the next three chapters, we examine each of these rights in turn.

———————

Notes and Questions to Consider:

1. Two rights in Florida's constitution's Article I Declaration of Rights require those rights to be interpreted consistently with their counterpart in the U.S. Constitution. Specifically, the right of protection from unlawful searches and seizures states: "This right shall be construed in conformity with the Fourth Amendment to the United States Constitution, as interpreted by the United States Supreme Court." Art. I, § 12, Fla. Const. The right of protection from excessive punishments states that it "shall be construed in conformity with decisions of the United States Supreme Court which interpret the prohibition against cruel and unusual punishment provided in the Eighth Amendment to the United States Constitution. Any method of execution shall be allowed, unless prohibited by the United States Constitution." Art. I, § 17, Fla. Const. Can Florida's courts interpret either of these rights differently than their federal counterparts?

2. What about the other rights appearing in Florida's constitution's Article I Declaration of Rights? May they be interpreted differently than their counterparts in the U.S. Constitution? What if there is no difference in the language of the Florida Constitution and the U.S. Constitution—would identical language mandate an identical interpretation?

3. Note that Section 27 of Florida's Declaration of Rights defines marriage to exclude same-sex couples. In *United States v. Windsor*, 133 S. Ct. 2675, 186 L. Ed. 2d 808 (2013), the Supreme Court of the United States found such an exclusion from the definition of marriage in the federal Defense of Marriage Act to be unconstitutional. Then in *Obergefell v. Hodges*, 135 S. Ct. 2584, 192 L. Ed. 2d 609 (2015), the U.S. Supreme Court held that states may not deprive same-sex couples of their fundamental right to marry. Yet Section 27 of Florida's Declaration of Rights remains unchanged and says that "marriage is the legal union of only one man and one

woman . . . [and] no other legal union that is treated as marriage . . . shall be valid or recognized." Why is this language still in the Constitution of the State of Florida? What is its legal effect in Florida?

B. Equal Protection

Article I, Section 2 of Florida's constitution provides:

Basic rights.—All natural persons, female and male alike, are equal before the law and have inalienable rights, among which are the right to enjoy and defend life and liberty, to pursue happiness, to be rewarded for industry, and to acquire, possess and protect property. No person shall be deprived of any right because of race, religion, national origin, or physical disability.

In so stating, Florida's constitution creates the same right of equal protection that is found in the U.S. Constitution. Florida's supreme court held, in *Shriners Hospitals v. Zrillic*, 563 So. 2d 64, 66–67 (Fla. 1990) and elsewhere, that in applying the equal protection guarantees from Florida's constitution, state courts must use the same equal protection analysis used by the Supreme Court of the United States in interpreting the federal Constitution.

It has been suggested (but, respectfully, this author is not quite convinced) that equal protection under the Florida Constitution may vary from that under the U.S. Constitution insofar as it was a U.S. Supreme Court decision finding corporations to be persons and not yet a Florida Supreme Court decision so finding, and thus, equal protection differs because corporations are not persons under the Florida Constitution. This author respectfully suggests that the U.S. Supreme Court's basis for corporate personhood was found under both the First Amendment and the Fourteenth Amendment to the U.S. Constitution, with the latter specifically making such applicable to the states, and thus, corporations should be considered people in every state including Florida. *See Citizens United v. Federal Elections Commission*, 558 U.S. 310 (2010). For this reason, your author suggests that equal protection under the Florida Constitution does not vary from that under the U.S. Constitution, even insofar as corporations are concerned.

Notes and Questions to Consider:

1. Regarding the right of corporations, do you agree or disagree with this author's conclusion that their right to equal protection under Florida's constitution does not vary from that under the U.S. Constitution?

2. Note that, until 2018, Section 2 of Florida's Declaration of Rights declared everyone to be equal before the law "except that the ownership, inheritance, disposition and possession of real property by aliens ineligible for citizenship may be

regulated or prohibited by law." The origin of this exception has a "strongly racialist basis—'aliens ineligible to citizenship' was a disingenuous euphemism designed to disguise the fact that the targets of such laws were first-generation Japanese immigrants." Keith Aoki, *No Right to Own?: The Early Twentieth-Century "Alien Land Laws" as a Prelude to Internment*, 40 B.C. L. Rev. 37, 38–39 (1998). As to why it was not purged from the Florida Constitution by the 1998 Constitutional Revision Commission, it is possible that the Commission "simply did not know what the term 'alien ineligible to citizenship' meant; this was the explanation of a reviser of the Florida Constitution for leaving that state's alien land provision in the constitution." Gabriel J. Chin, *Citizenship and Exclusion: Wyoming's Anti-Japanese Alien Land Law in Context*, 1 Wyo. L. Rev. 497, 506 (2001). In November 2008, Floridians voted on the proposed Amendment 1 to the Constitution of the State of Florida, which attempted to repeal Florida's Alien Land Law. "Ultimately, Amendment 1 failed by a vote of 47.9% (3,369,894 votes) to 52.1% (3,669,812 votes)." Christine M. Ho, *Florida's Alien Land Law: The Last Vestige of Discrimination*, Greater Orlando Asian American Bar Ass'n, http://goaaba.org/floridas-alien-land-law-the-last-vestige-of-discrimination/. In 2018, another Constitutional Revision Commission completed its work, proposed an amendment to Florida's constitution deleting the language of Florida's Alien Land Law, and bundling this issue with others, required voters to vote yes or no as part of the bundle. The voters voted yes in favor of the bundle, the amendment passed, and Florida's Alien Land Law was repealed from Florida's constitution.

C. Freedoms Akin to First Amendment Rights

The freedoms secured by the First Amendment to the Constitution of the United States also appear within the Declaration of Rights of the Constitution of the State of Florida. *See* Talbot D'Alemberte, The Florida State Constitution 29 (Oxford University Press 2011). *See also Henderson v. Antonacci*, 62 So. 2d 5 (Fla. 1953); *Nohrr v. Brevard County Educational Facilities Authority*, 247 So. 2d 304 (Fla. 1971); and *Hermanson v. State*, 604 So. 2d 775 (Fla. 1992). So as to this group of rights, the question is not whether Florida's constitution grants greater rights and freedoms to Floridians. Instead, as seen below, the question becomes whether the language of Florida's constitution attempts to provide fewer rights and freedoms than the federal minimum.

1. Freedom of Religion

Like the federal Constitution, Florida's constitution seeks to safeguard religious freedom, and does so by imposing religious neutrality upon the state. "The dominant idea in the current judicial interpretation of the Religion Clauses is the concept of neutrality." Richard S. Myers, *Church and State*, in Ronald J. Rychlak, American Law from a Catholic Perspective 95 (2015).

Article I, Section 3 of Florida's constitution states:

Section 3. Religious freedom.—There shall be no law respecting the establishment of religion or prohibiting or penalizing the free exercise thereof. Religious freedom shall not justify practices inconsistent with public morals, peace or safety. No revenue of the state or any political subdivision or agency thereof shall ever be taken from the public treasury directly or indirectly in aid of any church, sect, or religious denomination or in aid of any sectarian institution.

Analyzing Section 3, we find that the first part of the first sentence prohibits Florida from creating a state religion or recognizing a religion as the state's official religion. The second part of the first sentence restricts Florida from prohibiting the practice of a particular religion, penalizing those who practice, or controlling the practice. The third and fourth sentences purport to limit religious freedom. In the subsections below, we address each in turn.

a. Establishment Clause

The first part of the first sentence of Article I, Section 3 is akin to the federal Establishment Clause that prohibits Congress from establishing a national religion. "The Florida Establishment Clause and the federal Establishment Clause have nearly identical wording and are interpreted in the same manner by courts." *Williamson v. Brevard County*, 276 F. Supp. 3d 1260, 1297 (M.D. Fla. 2017) (citing, inter alia, *Todd v. State*, 643 So. 2d 625, 628 & n.3 (Fla. 1st DCA 1994).

Prior to 2019, some courts interpreting Florida's Establishment Clause held that it required a statute or ordinance must pass the three-part test set forth by the United States Supreme Court in *Lemon v. Kurtzman*, 403 U.S. 602 (1971) ("the *Lemon* test"): "[f]irst, the statute must have a secular legislative purpose; second, its principal or primary effect must be one that neither advances nor inhibits religion; finally, the statute must not foster 'an excessive government entanglement with religion.'" *Id.* at 612–13. Such holdings may have misinterpreted the scope of *Lemon*. In 2019, the U.S. Supreme Court noted: "While the *Lemon* Court ambitiously attempted to find a grand unified theory of the Establishment Clause, in later cases, [the U.S. Supreme Court has] taken a more modest approach that focuses on the particular issue at hand and looks to history for guidance." *Am. Legion v. Am. Humanist Ass'n*, 17-1717, 2019 WL 2527471, at *16 (U.S. June 20, 2019). For example, "[i]n *Marsh v. Chambers*, 463 U.S. 783, (1983), the Court upheld the Nebraska Legislature's practice of beginning each session with a prayer by an official chaplain, and in so holding, the Court conspicuously ignored *Lemon* and did not respond to Justice Brennan's argument in dissent that the legislature's practice could not satisfy the *Lemon* test." *Id.* at *16.

b. Free Exercise Clause

Florida's constitution, like the federal, contains a Free Exercise right. The result is that "[b]oth the Federal and the Florida Constitutions guarantee an individual's right to freely exercise his religion. When considering assertions that these provisions exempt a person from regulatory mandates when compliance would contravene his religious beliefs, courts avoid questioning the rationality of those beliefs." *Toca v. State*, 834 So. 2d 204, 207 (Fla. 2d DCA 2002), rev. denied, 846 So. 2d 1150 (Fla. 2003). "State power is no more to be used so as to handicap religions, than it is to favor them." *Koerner v. Borck*, 100 So. 2d 398, 401 (Fla. 1958) (quoting *Everson v. Board of Education*, 330 U.S 1 (1947)).

The Free Exercise Clause requires the government to remain neutral on matters of faith and religion. "[T]he government, if it is to respect the Constitution's guarantee of free exercise, cannot impose regulations that are hostile to the religious beliefs of affected citizens and cannot act in a manner that passes judgment upon or presupposes the illegitimacy of religious beliefs and practices." *Masterpiece Cakeshop, Ltd. v. Colorado Civil Rights Com'n*, 138 S. Ct. 1719, 1731 (2018). The Free Exercise Clause bars even "subtle departures from neutrality" on matters of religion. *Id.* (quoting *Church of Lukumi Babalu Aye, Inc. v. Hialeah*, 508 U.S. 520, 540–542 (1993)). This means the "government has no role in deciding or even suggesting whether the religious ground for [a] conscience-based objection is legitimate or illegitimate." *Id.* "Factors relevant to the assessment of governmental neutrality include 'the historical background of the decision under challenge, the specific series of events leading to the enactment or official policy in question, and the legislative or administrative history, including contemporaneous statements made by members of the decision-making body.'" *Id.* (citing *Lukumi Babalu Aye*, 508 U.S. at 540).

c. Religious Discrimination and the Blaine Amendment (No-Aid Clause)

Under Florida's constitution, "[t]he statute must not authorize the use of public moneys, directly or indirectly, in aid of any sectarian institution." *Rice v. State*, 754 So. 2d 881, 883 (Fla. 5th DCA 2000) (quoting *Silver Rose Entm't, Inc. v. Clay County*, 646 So. 2d 246, 251 (Fla. 1st DCA 1994), rev. denied, 658 So. 2d 992 (Fla. 1995)). This is because the third sentence of Article I, Section 3 of Florida's constitution was added to state that "[n]o revenue ... shall ever be taken from the public treasury directly or indirectly ... in aid of any sectarian institution." Recall from Chapter 1 of this text that the intent of this sentence — a Blaine Amendment — was to discriminate against Catholics and Catholic schools. Florida's Blaine Amendment is sometimes called Florida's No-Aid Clause.

To interpret the Blaine Amendment, we know from our cannons of construction that, in construing provisions of Florida's constitution, the first step is to ascertain and effectuate the intent of the framers and the people. *Bailey v. Ponce de Leon Port Auth.*, 398 So. 2d 812, 814 (Fla. 1981). The intent of Congressman James G. Blaine and his supporters who lobbied states to enact Blaine Amendments was to capitalize "on the wide political appeal of the nativist and anti-Catholic rhetoric." Joseph P. Viteritti, *Blaine's Wake: School Choice, the First Amendment, and State Constitutional Law*, 21 HARV. J.L. & PUB. POL'Y 657, 670–71 (1998). Congressman Blaine and his supporters led a "movement that sought to amend several state constitutions (often successfully), and to amend the United States Constitution (unsuccessfully) to make certain that government would not help pay for 'sectarian' (i.e., Catholic) schooling for children." *Zelman v. Simmons-Harris*, 536 U.S. 639, 721 (2002).

Florida's constitution, like any state constitution, is unconstitutional under the U.S. Constitution to the extent that the state constitution fails to guarantee the full panoply of federal rights and liberties. It would be proper to find Florida's Blaine Amendment unenforceable for this reason. However, an opinion has yet to do so.

d. Church Autonomy

The two Religion Clauses—the Establishment Clause and the Free Exercise Clause—"guarantee religious organizations autonomy in matters of internal governance." *Hosanna-Tabor Evangelical Lutheran Church & Sch. v. E.E.O.C.*, 565 U.S. 171, 196–97 (2012) (Justice Thomas, concurring). In 2012, the U.S. Supreme Court affirmed the holdings of many federal Courts of Appeal in holding that the Free Exercise Clause "protects a religious group's right to shape its own faith. . . ." *Id.* at 188. Specifically, the Court affirmed that the "Establishment Clause prevents the Government from appointing ministers, and the Free Exercise Clause prevents it from interfering with the freedom of religious groups to select their own." *Id.* at 184. The Court holds "that the ministerial exception is not limited to the head of a religious congregation. . . . We are reluctant, however, to adopt a rigid formula for deciding when an employee qualifies as a minister." *Id.* at 190. Consider Florida's use of the Church Autonomy Doctrine in *Malichi v. Archdiocese of Miami*, 945 So. 2d 526 (Fla. 1st DCA 2006), review denied, 965 So. 2d 122 (Fla. 2007).

Malichi v. Archdiocese of Miami

First District Court of Appeal of Florida, 2006
945 So. 2d 526

The issue before this court is one of first impression: whether the Free Exercise Clause of the First Amendment to the United States Constitution precludes judicial review of a Catholic priest's workers' compensation claim.

Appellant, a Catholic priest, appeals the Judge of Compensation Claims' (JCC) summary final order dismissing his workers' compensation claim filed against Appellee, the Archdiocese of Miami, because the JCC lacked subject-matter jurisdiction under the First Amendment to the United States Constitution to consider Appellant's claim. We now affirm.

We hold that civil courts lack subject-matter jurisdiction, as a matter of law, to consider Appellant's claim because it constitutes an internal employment dispute between a priest and his church. The church autonomy doctrine, also known as the ecclesiastical abstention doctrine, protects the Archdiocese from state interference in its internal employment disputes. To allow Appellant to litigate his claim as a purported "employee" would violate the Free Exercise Clause of the First

Amendment to the United States Constitution by entangling the civil courts in the Catholic Church's internal governance.

Facts and Procedural History

Appellant filed a petition seeking workers' compensation benefits. He asserted that while serving as an associate pastor with the Archdiocese, he suffered an injury lifting a television and assisting another priest. The Archdiocese ultimately filed a motion for summary final order seeking dismissal based solely on lack of subject-matter jurisdiction. The Archdiocese asserted that the First Amendment precluded Appellant's workers' compensation claim and filed a monsignor's affidavit stating that Appellant was an incardinated cleric under canon law. . . .

The Archdiocese further explained that because Appellant's employment relationship is governed by canonical law, his workers' compensation claim necessarily raises issues of ecclesiastical law, faith, religious doctrine and internal church organization. According to the Archdiocese, applying the workers' compensation law to Appellant would preclude his ability to maintain confidences, thus violating church law. Therefore, the Archdiocese argued, the church autonomy doctrine bars Appellant's claim. . . .

Analysis

The church autonomy doctrine is based on the Free Exercise Clause of the First Amendment. The doctrine prevents secular courts from reviewing disputes requiring an analysis of "theological controversy, church discipline, *ecclesiastical government*, or the conformity of the members of the church to the standard of morals required," and under the doctrine, secular courts must accept the decision by the highest ecclesiastical authority on such matters. *Watson v. Jones*, 80 U.S. (13 Wall.) 679, 733 (1871) (emphasis added). . . .

Once the Archdiocese asserts that the Appellant is an incardinated cleric and not an employee, we must respect the relationship between the Church and its priest because "[t]he relationship between an organized church and its ministers is its lifeblood. . . . Matters touching this relationship must necessarily be recognized as of prime ecclesiastical concern." *McClure v. Salvation Army*, 460 F.2d 553, 558–59 (5th Cir. 1972) (holding that the "ministerial exception" doctrine precludes judicial review of a minister's Title VII claim). . . .

Because the Archdiocese maintains an absolute ecclesiastical right to control and direct Appellant's duties and functions, any inquiry into this subject required the JCC to inquire into internal matters of church governance. This is constitutionally impermissible. See *Kedroff v. St. Nicholas Cathedral of Russian Orthodox Church*, 344 U.S. 94, 116 (1952), (stating that the Supreme Court's decision in *Watson* allows churches the "power to decide for themselves, free from state interference, matters of church government *as well as faith and doctrine*.") (emphasis added). In *Southeastern Conference Association of Seventh-Day Adventists, Inc. v. Dennis*, 862 So.2d 842 (Fla. 4th DCA 2003), the Fourth District correctly explained that "[c]ourts may not consider employment disputes between a religious organization and its clergy because such matters necessarily involve questions of internal church discipline, faith, and organization that are governed by ecclesiastical rule, custom and law." *Id.* at 844 (citations omitted). Therefore, the Fourth District held that the circuit court did not have jurisdiction over a minister's negligence claim filed against his church for its response to a parishioner's allegations against the minister. We think the same rationale and analysis apply here. Thus, the church autonomy doctrine similarly precludes this court from considering Appellant's claim.

As the Fourth District explained in *Dennis*, civil courts are bound to accept the Archdiocese's absolute ecclesiastical authority under the church autonomy doctrine. Id.; see also *Serbian E. Orthodox Diocese for the U.S. & Can. v. Milivojevich*, 426 U.S. 696, 709 (1976) . . . ; *Dennis*, 862 So.2d at 844. Because this court must accept the Archdiocese's authority, Appellant must accept its authority as well and cannot seek review of his claim in this court. As the United States Supreme Court has explained,

> The right to organize voluntary religious associations to assist in the expression and dissemination of any religious doctrine, and to create tribunals for the decision of controverted questions of faith within the association, and for the ecclesiastical government of all the individual members, congregations, and officers within the general association, is unquestioned. *All who unite themselves to such a body do so with an implied consent to this government, and are bound to submit to it.* But it would be a vain consent and would lead to the total subversion of such religious bodies, if any one aggrieved by one of their decisions could appeal to the secular courts and have them reversed. It is of the essence of these religious unions, and of their right to establish tribunals for the decision of questions arising among themselves, that those decisions should be binding in all cases of ecclesiastical cognizance, subject only to such appeals as the organism itself provides for.

Watson, 80 U.S. at 728–29 (emphasis supplied).

A controverted workers' compensation claim places an employer . . . in an adversarial legal relationship with an employee. See, e.g., *Brown v. Justin C. Johnson & Assoc., P.A.*, 937 So. 2d 780 (Fla. 1st DCA 2006) (determining whether the claimant's activity was within the "course and scope of his employment"); *Chapman v. Nationsbank*, 937 So. 2d 788 (Fla. 1st DCA 2006) (considering whether the claimant knowingly made a false statement to obtain benefits); *Dollar Gen. Corp. v. MacDonald*, 928 So. 2d 464, 466 (Fla. 1st DCA 2006) (holding that the claimant's work activity was not the "major contributing cause" of the injury); *European Marble Co. v. Robinson*, 885 So. 2d 502, 503 (Fla. 1st DCA 2004) (defending claim on the ground that the claimant was intoxicated or under the influence of drugs which caused the injury). All of these examples of workers' compensation claims would place the Archdiocese and its priest in an adversarial legal relationship. Therefore, judicial consideration of Appellant's claim violates the Archdiocese's Free Exercise rights under the First Amendment.

Although [Florida's Workers' Compensation Law codified at Florida Statutes] chapter 440 was enacted, in part, to minimize this adversarial relationship by providing a quick and efficient recovery to injured workers, adversarial litigation occurs quite regularly. Resolving an adversarial workers' compensation dispute would invariably interfere in the critical and constitutionally protected relationship between a church and its minister. This explains why a state might choose to exempt ministers from the definition of "employee" for purposes of workers' compensation laws. In *South Ridge Baptist Church v. Industrial Commission of Ohio*, 676 F.Supp. 799 (S.D.Ohio 1987), the court noted that the exemption provided in Ohio law "seeks to obviate excessive interference with the religious ministry of churches." *Id*. at 806.

Although Florida law provides no such exemption, application of chapter 440 to priests' claims would excessively interfere with the Archdiocese's ministry because the Archdiocese would necessarily have to defend itself regarding these claims. This would require civil courts to determine the good faith or credibility of the Archdiocese, or its priests, which we find is barred by the church autonomy doctrine. While Appellant correctly asserts that Florida law does not specifically exempt clergy from its workers' compensation statutes, this argument would only be significant absent the requirements of the First Amendment because the statute must yield to the United States Constitution. See *Bollard v. Ca. Province of the Soc'y of Jesus*, 196 F.3d 940, 945 (9th Cir. 1999) (determining that the source of the ministerial exception, a subpart of the church autonomy doctrine, is "the Constitution rather than the statute."). Thus, the church autonomy doctrine precludes application of chapter 440 to Appellant regardless of whether a ministerial exemption exists in Florida law.

An inquiry about whether a priest was properly engaged in his assigned duties and injured as a result of his employment could inevitably lead to disputes regarding whether the church exercised its ecclesiastical authority in assigning those duties. Determination of a priest's duties is a matter of the church's internal administration and government. See *McClure*, 460 F.2d at 559. As the Archdiocese argues, similar questions could affect the special relationship between a priest and his church or the ability of a priest to receive and maintain church confidences.

Another impermissible infringement upon a priest's employment relationship and the church's internal governance could arise pursuant to section 440.205, Florida Statutes (2006), which protects an employee from a retaliatory discharge in response to the employee's filing of a valid workers' compensation claim. Claims brought under anti-retaliation statutes may be barred by the Free Exercise Clause. See *Starkman v. Evans*, 198 F.3d 173, 175 (5th Cir. 1999) (explaining that a claim brought under a Louisiana retaliatory discharge statute was barred by the Free Exercise Clause). Because resolving any of these issues in the judicial branch would necessarily infringe on the Archdiocese's constitutional right of free exercise, this court cannot consider Appellant's workers' compensation claim.

Although we find that this court lacks jurisdiction to consider Appellant's claim, we acknowledge our supreme court's holdings that permit third parties to file negligent-hiring and negligent-supervision claims against hierarchical churches.

See *Doe v. Evans*, 814 So. 2d 370, 376 (Fla. 2002); *Malicki*, 814 So.2d at 347 (holding that due to the neutral principles inherent in tort law, such claims do not implicate the Free Exercise Clause). We find Appellant's claim distinguishable from both *Evans* and *Malicki* because Appellant's claim would excessively entangle civil courts in the resolution of a completely internal church matter involving no third parties.

Conclusion

We hold that a priest's workers' compensation claim is barred by the church autonomy doctrine of the First Amendment. The JCC, therefore, correctly dismissed Appellant's workers' compensation claim for lack of subject matter jurisdiction. . . .

AFFIRMED.

Notes and Questions to Consider:

1. *Malichi v. Archdiocese of Miami* interprets the Religion Clauses to mean that Florida lacks jurisdiction as to whether a priest is entitled to benefits under Florida's workers' compensation law. Why?

2. Just as Florida in *Malichi v. Archdiocese of Miami* holds that Florida lacks jurisdiction over a priest's workers' compensation claim, the U.S. Supreme Court in *Hosanna-Tabor Evangelical Lutheran Church & Sch. v. E.E.O.C.* held that courts lack jurisdiction over a minister's employment discrimination claim. Toward the end of *Malichi v. Archdiocese of Miami*, the First District Court of Appeal acknowledges the Florida Supreme Court's "holdings that permit third parties to file negligent-hiring and negligent-supervision claims against hierarchical churches. See *Doe v. Evans*, 814 So. 2d 370, 376 (Fla. 2002); *Malicki*, 814 So.2d at 347 (holding that due to the neutral principles inherent in tort law, such claims do not implicate the Free Exercise Clause)." Note that the U.S. Supreme Court has not done the same. In *Hosanna-Tabor*, the Court held:

> The case before us is an employment discrimination suit brought on behalf of a minister, challenging her church's decision to fire her. Today we hold only that the ministerial exception bars such a suit. We express no view on whether the exception bars other types of suits, including actions by employees alleging breach of contract or tortious conduct by their religious employers. There will be time enough to address the applicability of the exception to other circumstances if and when they arise.

Id. at 196. When the time comes for the U.S. Supreme Court to address such claims, how do you believe they will rule?

e. Florida Religious Freedom Restoration Act

In the 1990s, Florida's legislature supplemented Florida's Establishment Clause by enacting the Florida Religious Freedom Restoration Act of 1998 (FRFRA), codified at Florida Statutes §§ 761.01–.05. An example of Florida's supreme court's application of Florida's Establishment Clause and FRFRA is *Warner v. City of Boca Raton*, 887 So. 2d 1023 (Fla. 2004).

Warner v. City of Boca Raton

Supreme Court of Florida, 2004
887 So. 2d 1023

We have for review . . . two questions concerning Florida law . . . [and] the Florida Religious Freedom Restoration Act (FRFRA). . . .

Material Facts and Proceedings

The City of Boca Raton (the City) owns, operates, and maintains a 21.5 acre cemetery for its residents. In November 1982, the City passed a regulation prohibiting vertical grave markers, memorials, monuments, and structures on cemetery plots. The regulation allows individuals to place stone or bronze markers on plots provided that they are level with the ground surface. Richard Warner is a member of a class of city residents (appellants) who purchased burial plots in the City's cemetery. Despite the prohibition, between 1984 and 1996 appellants decorated family graves with vertical grave decorations.

In 1991, the City sent notices to plot owners who had placed vertical grave decorations at their plots, informing them that if they did not remove the noncomplying structures within thirty days, the structures would be removed. A small group of plot owners failed to comply with the City's request to remove the vertical grave decorations. A second notice was sent in 1992, requesting compliance, and again not all plot owners complied with the City's request. However, in response to objections from plot owners, the City agreed to postpone removal of the noncomplying structures pending further study. In 1996, the City amended the regulation to permit some vertical grave decorations up to sixty days from the date of burial and on certain holidays.

During this time, the City commissioned a survey of plot owners to identify their desires concerning vertical grave decorations in the cemetery. The study, conducted by researchers at Florida Atlantic University in 1997, concluded that most plot owners approved of the City's amended regulation. Subsequently, on June 10, 1997, at the regular meeting of the City Council, the City announced that it would begin enforcing the regulations as amended in 1996. All plot owners were notified that if they did not comply with the regulations by January 15, 1998, the City would remove all the noncomplying structures.

Thereafter, appellants filed suit alleging that the prohibition on vertical grave decorations violated their state and federal rights to freedom of expression, freedom of speech, and due process of law. Specifically, appellants argued that the City's prohibition violates the Florida Religious Freedom Restoration Act of 1998 (FRFRA). . . . After a bench trial, the United States District Court for the Southern

District of Florida held that the right to place vertical grave structures was not protected under the FRFRA. . . .

The Southern District rejected appellants' argument that the City's regulation violated their right to the free exercise of religion because the FRFRA protected any act substantially motivated by a sincerely held religious belief. Instead, the Southern District concluded that the FRFRA was "intended to protect conduct that, while not necessarily compulsory or central to a larger system of religious beliefs, nevertheless reflects some tenet, practice or custom of a religious tradition." . . .

After determining the scope of the FRFRA, the Southern District determined whether the placement of vertical decorations on grave sites reflected a tenet, custom or practice of appellants' religious traditions or merely represented a personal preference regarding religious exercise. The Southern District adopted the framework used by Dr. Daniel Pals to determine the place appellants' practices hold within a religious tradition. The court said:

> Under Dr. Pals' framework, a court should consider four criteria in order to determine the place of a particular practice within a religious tradition. In particular, a court should consider whether the practice: 1) is asserted or implied in relatively unambiguous terms by an authoritative sacred text; 2) is clearly and consistently affirmed in classic formulations of doctrine and practice; 3) has been observed continuously, or nearly so, throughout the history of the tradition; and 4) is consistently observed in the tradition as we meet it in recent times. If a practice meets all four of these criteria, it can be considered central to the religious tradition. If the practice meets one or more of these criteria, it can be considered a tenet, custom or practice of the religious tradition. If the practice meets none of these criteria, it can be considered a matter of purely personal preference regarding religious exercise.

. . . Using this test, the Southern District found that marking graves with religious symbols constituted a practice of appellants' religious traditions. However, it found that the particular manner in which such markers and religious symbols are displayed—vertically or horizontally—amounted to a matter of purely personal preference. The Southern District also found that the City's prohibition on vertical grave structures did not substantially burden appellants' practice of religion. The court reasoned that the City's regulation did not prohibit appellants from decorating the graves with religious symbols. The Southern District pointed out that the regulations permitted horizontal grave markers which "may be engraved with any type of religious symbol. Moreover, out of consideration for mourners, vertical grave decorations are permitted for sixty days after the date of burial and for a few days around certain holidays." . . . Accordingly, the court found that the City's regulation did not violate appellants' rights under the FRFRA. Appellants appealed the Southern District's decision to the Eleventh Circuit, which certified the aforementioned questions. . . .

Law and Analysis

I. Certified Question I

The Eleventh Circuit has certified two questions to this Court. The first question reads:

> Does the Florida Religious Freedom Restoration Act broaden, and to what extent does it broaden, the definition of what constitutes religiously motivated conduct protected by law beyond the conduct considered protected by the decisions of the United States Supreme Court?

... Before we define the parameters of our state law, we will first examine the applicable federal law.

Federal Law

Over the past hundred plus years, the United States Supreme Court has vacillated on the standard applicable to laws which in some way infringe on an individual's right to the free exercise of religion. Initially, the Supreme Court held that the Free Exercise Clause did not excuse an individual from the obligation to comply with neutral laws of general applicability. *See, e.g., Minersville Sch. Dist. v. Gobitis*, 310 U.S. 586, 594 (1940), *overruled by West Va. State Bd. of Educ. v. Barnette*, 319 U.S. 624 (1943); *Reynolds v. United States*, 98 U.S. 145, 166–67 (1878). Thus, it appeared that if a neutral law of general applicability was rationally related to a matter of governmental interest, it would not violate the Free Exercise Clause.

However, in 1963 the Supreme Court expanded the protection given to religious freedom. In *Sherbert v. Verner*, 374 U.S. 398, 406 (1963), the Supreme Court expressly rejected the use of the rational basis standard when evaluating religious freedom claims when it said, "It is basic that no showing merely of a rational relationship to some colorable state interest would suffice; in this highly sensitive constitutional area, 'only the gravest abuses, endangering paramount [compelling] interests, give occasion for permissible limitation.'" ...

Later, the Supreme Court modified the *Sherbert* "compelling interest" test by creating exceptions to its application. The Supreme Court found that the compelling interest test was inapplicable to Free Exercise claims in military and prison situations. *See Goldman v. Weinberger*, 475 U.S. 503, 508 (1986) (holding that the First Amendment did not prevent the Air Force from passing regulations which prohibited the wearing of headgear required by a person's religion). *See also Turner v. Safley*, 482 U.S. 78, 87 (1987) (holding that a court examining prison regulations must only inquire as whether the regulation is "reasonably related" to legitimate penological objectives, or whether it represents an "exaggerated response" to those concerns). The Supreme Court also began to retreat from the compelling interest test in cases involving Free Exercise challenges to a neutral law of general application. *See Bowen v. Roy*, 476 U.S. 693, 707–08 (1986) ("Absent proof of an intent to discriminate against particular religious beliefs or against religion in general, the Government meets its burden when it demonstrates that a challenged requirement for governmental benefits, neutral and uniform in its application, is a reasonable means of promoting a legitimate public interest.") (plurality opinion); *Lyng v. Northwest Indian Cemetery Prot. Ass'n*, 485 U.S. 439, 450 (1988) ("[I]ncidental effects of government programs, which may make it more difficult to practice certain religions but which have no tendency to coerce individuals into acting contrary to their religious beliefs, [do not] require government to bring forward a compelling justification.").

The Supreme Court further receded from *Sherbert* and the compelling interest test in *Employment Division, Department of Human Resources v. Smith*, 494 U.S. 872 (1990), which involved:

> [W]hether the Free Exercise Clause of the First Amendment permits the State of Oregon to include religiously inspired peyote use within the reach of its general criminal prohibition on use of that drug, and thus permits the State to deny unemployment benefits to persons dismissed from their jobs because of such religiously inspired use.

Id. at 874. The Supreme Court held that the Free Exercise Clause analysis articulated in *Sherbert* was inapplicable because the law was not aimed at promoting or restricting religious beliefs. Noting that it had never invalidated any governmental action on the basis of the *Sherbert* test except for the denial of unemployment compensation, the Supreme Court stated its reasons for refusing to apply the test in the context of the *Smith* case:

> We conclude today that the sounder approach, and the approach in accord with the vast majority of our precedents, is to hold the [compelling state interest] test inapplicable to such challenges. The government's ability to enforce generally applicable prohibitions of socially harmful conduct, like its ability to carry out other aspects of public policy, "cannot depend on measuring the effects of a governmental action on a religious objector's spiritual development." To make an individual's obligation to obey such a law contingent upon the law's coincidence with his religious beliefs, except where the State's interest is "compelling" — permitting him, by virtue of his beliefs, "to become a law unto himself" — contradicts both constitutional tradition and common sense.

Id. at 885 (citations omitted). The Supreme Court rejected the argument advanced by the respondents in *Smith* that the compelling interest test should be used when the conduct prohibited by the State is central to the individual's religion. The Supreme Court opined: "What principle of law or logic can be brought to bear to contradict a believer's assertion that a particular act is 'central' to his personal faith? Judging the centrality of different religious practices is akin to the unacceptable 'business of evaluating the relative merits of differing religious claims.'" *Id.* at 887 (quoting *United States v. Lee*, 455 U.S. 252, 263 n. 2 (1982) (Stevens, J., concurring in the judgment)). The Court stated that an inquiry into the centrality of particular beliefs to a faith was not within the "judicial ken" and thus, improper. *Id.* at 887 (quoting *Hernandez v. Commissioner*, 490 U.S. 680, 699 (1989)).

Thereafter, in 1993, the United States Congress passed the Religious Freedom Restoration Act (RFRA). RFRA was intended to essentially overrule the Supreme Court's decision in *Smith* and restore the compelling state interest test set forth in *Sherbert* as the standard for free exercise challenges to laws of general applicability. *See* 42 U.S.C. § 2000bb (2000). Accordingly, RFRA prohibited the government from substantially burdening a person's free exercise of religion unless the government showed that the burden: "(1) is in furtherance of a compelling governmental interest; and (2) is the least restrictive means of furthering that compelling governmental interest." 42 U.S.C. § 2000bb–1(b) (2000). Prior to 2000, RFRA defined the "exercise of religion" as "the exercise of religion under the First Amendment to the Constitution." Religious Freedom Restoration Act, P.L. 103–141, § 5(4), 107 Stat. 1488, 1489 (1993). Now, RFRA defines the "exercise of religion" as "any exercise of religion, whether or not compelled by, or central to, a system of religious belief." *Id.* (adopting definition in 42 U.S.C. § 2000cc–5(7)(A) (2000)).

Initially, RFRA applied to any governmental entity, whether state or federal. . . . The constitutionality of RFRA as applied to the states was challenged in *City of Boerne v. Flores*, 521 U.S. 507 (1997). In arguing that RFRA could be constitutionally applied to the states, the respondent argued that RFRA was a proper exercise of Congress's remedial and enforcement power under the Fourteenth Amendment. *Id.* at 517, 529. According to the respondent in *Flores*, RFRA was a reasonable means of protecting the free exercise of religion as defined by *Smith*. *Id.* at 529.

The Supreme Court rejected this argument, concluding that the scope and reach of RFRA distinguished it from other remedial and enforcement measures passed by Congress. Rather, the Court determined that RFRA was substantive in nature because it imposed a more stringent test for determining the constitutionality of laws burdening religion than that demanded by the United States Constitution as interpreted by the Supreme Court in *Smith*. According to the Court, state "[l]aws valid under *Smith* would fall under RFRA." *Id.* at 534. Noting that under the Fourteenth Amendment the federal government did not have the power to substantively alter constitutional rights, *id.* at 529, the Supreme Court invalided RFRA as applied to the states. *Id.* at 536. Therefore, the standard articulated by the Supreme Court in *Smith* remains the threshold of protection for religiously based activities afforded by the Free Exercise Clause contained in the United States Constitution.

Florida Law

Florida's Free Exercise Clause is found in the Florida Constitution's Declaration of Rights and provides:

> There shall be no law respecting the establishment of religion or prohibiting or penalizing the free exercise thereof. Religious freedom shall not justify practices inconsistent with public morals, peace or safety. No revenue

of the state or any political subdivision or agency thereof shall ever be taken from the public treasury directly or indirectly in aid of any church, sect, or religious denomination or in aid of any sectarian institution.

Art. I, § 3, Fla. Const. In interpreting the scope of constitutional rights, this Court has stated that in any state issue, the federal constitution represents the "floor" for basic freedoms, and the state constitution represents the "ceiling." *See Traylor v. State*, 596 So. 2d 957, 962 (Fla. 1992). This Court has not squarely addressed the parameters of Florida's free exercise clause, but other Florida courts have "treated the protection afforded under the state constitutional provision as coequal to the federal [provision], and have measured government regulations against it accordingly." *Toca v. State*, 834 So. 2d 204, 208 (Fla. 2d DCA 2002) (applying *Smith* to conclude that rule of judicial administration requiring the signing of pleadings did not violate petitioner's rights under article I, section 3 of the Florida Constitution); *see also Allen v. Allen*, 622 So. 2d 1369 (Fla. 1st DCA 1993) (finding that post-dissolution order prohibiting wife from attending church attended by husband was prohibited under free exercise clause of both the Florida Constitution and the First Amendment). Indeed, a commentary on the 1968 revision of this provision explains that the language of the Florida section "parallels the First Amendment of the U.S. Constitution" and that "cases under the First Amendment of the United States Constitution are of great value in evaluating the status of religious freedoms." Talbot "Sandy" D'Alemberte, Commentary to 1968 Revision, Art. I, § 3, Fla. Const., 25A Fla. Stat. Ann. 106–07 (West 2004).

Prior to the Supreme Court's decision in *Smith*, this Court applied the compelling interest test to free exercise claims. For example, in *Town v. State ex rel. Reno*, 377 So. 2d 648 (Fla. 1979), we applied the Supreme Court's decisions in *Sherbert* and *Yoder* to the question of whether the State had a compelling interest in restricting the use of cannabis as a religious practice. Testimony before the trial court showed that the church permitted children and individuals who had no interest in learning the religion to use the drug. In light of these facts, we found that the State's compelling interest in protecting society from a dangerous drug outweighed the petitioner's free exercise interest. *Id.* at 651.

In 1998, in response to the United States Supreme Court's decision in *Flores*, the Florida Legislature enacted a state version of the federal Religious Freedom Restoration Act, which was modeled after the federal RFRA. The preamble to the Florida Religious Freedom Restoration Act (FRFRA) provides:

> WHEREAS, it is the finding of the Legislature of the State of Florida that the framers of the Florida Constitution, recognizing free exercise of religion as an unalienable right, secured its protection in s. 3, Art. I of the State Constitution, and

> WHEREAS, laws which are "neutral" toward religion may burden the free exercise of religion as surely as laws intended to interfere with the free exercise of religion, and

WHEREAS, governments should not substantially burden the free exercise of religion without compelling justification, and

WHEREAS, the compelling interest test as set forth in certain federal court rulings is a workable test for striking sensible balances between religious liberty and competing prior governmental interests, and

WHEREAS, it is the intent of the Legislature of the State of Florida to establish the compelling interest test as set forth in *Sherbert v. Verner*, 374 U.S. 398 (1963), and *Wisconsin v. Yoder*, 406 U.S. 205 (1972), to guarantee its application in all cases where free exercise of religion is substantially burdened, and to provide a claim or defense to persons whose religious exercise is substantially burdened by government....

Ch. 98–412, at 3296–97, Laws of Fla. The FRFRA ... also details the protections afforded to religious freedom:

(1) The government shall not substantially burden a person's exercise of religion, even if the burden results from a rule of general applicability, except that government may substantially burden a person's exercise of religion only if it demonstrates that application of the burden to the person:

(a) Is in furtherance of a compelling governmental interest; and

(b) Is the least restrictive means of furthering that compelling governmental interest.

(2) A person whose religious exercise has been burdened in violation of this section may assert that violation as a claim or defense in a judicial proceeding and obtain appropriate relief.

§ 761.03, Fla. Stat. (2003). Another provision of the FRFRA provides attorney's fees to the prevailing plaintiff from the government. *See* § 761.04, Fla. Stat. (2003). Lastly, the FRFRA states that nothing in the act will be construed to interpret or address the portion of article I, section 3 of the Florida Constitution or the First Amendment to United States Constitution which deals with the establishment of religion. *See* § 761.05, Fla. Stat. (2003). Thus, the FRFRA has made the compelling state interest test applicable to state cases involving questions of the free exercise of religion.

Based on the foregoing, we answer the first certified question in the affirmative. The protection afforded to the free exercise of religiously motivated activity under the FRFRA is broader than that afforded by the decisions of the United States Supreme Court for two interrelated reasons. First, the FRFRA expands the free exercise right as construed by the Supreme Court in *Smith* because it reinstates the Court's pre-*Smith* holdings by applying the compelling interest test to neutral laws of general application. Second, under the FRFRA the definition of protected "exercise of religion" subject to the compelling state interest test includes any act or refusal to act *whether or not compelled by or central to a system of religious belief.* The legislative history of the FRFRA suggests that in order to state a claim that the government has infringed upon the free exercise of religion, a plaintiff must only establish that the government has placed a substantial burden on a practice motivated by a sincere religious belief. Thus, the FRFRA is necessarily broader than United States Supreme Court precedent, which holds that the "right of free exercise does not relieve an individual of the obligation to comply with a valid and neutral law of general applicability on the ground that the law proscribes (or prescribes) conduct that his religion prescribes (or proscribes)." *Smith*, 494 U.S. at 879 (internal quotation marks omitted).

Although we conclude that the FRFRA is broader than United States Supreme Court precedent, our analysis of this issue does not end here. Appellants and amici curiae argue that under the FRFRA any act by an individual motivated by religion is subject to the compelling state interest test, or strict scrutiny standard. However, we find that appellants' interpretation of the FRFRA is too broad. According to the FRFRA, only government regulations which "substantially burden" a person's exercise of religion are subject to strict scrutiny. *See* § 761.03, Fla. Stat. (2003).

As discussed in *Mack v. O'Leary*, 80 F.3d 1175, 1178 (7th Cir. 1996), there are three main definitions of substantial burden adopted at the federal level with regard to RFRA.

> The Fourth, Ninth, and Eleventh Circuits define "substantial burden" as one that either compels the religious adherent to engage in conduct that his religion forbids (such as eating pork, for a Muslim or Jew) or forbids him to engage in conduct that his religion requires (such as prayer). *Goodall by Goodall v. Stafford County School Board*, 60 F.3d 168, 172–73 (4th Cir. 1995); *Cheffer v. Reno*, 55 F.3d 1517, 1522 (11th Cir. 1995); *Bryant v. Gomez*, 46 F.3d 948 (9th Cir. 1995) (per curiam). The Eighth and Tenth Circuits use a broader definition-action that forces religious adherents "to refrain from religiously motivated conduct," *Brown-El v. Harris*, 26 F.3d 68, 70 (8th Cir. 1994), or that "significantly inhibit[s] or constrain[s] conduct or expression that manifests some central tenet of a [person's] individual beliefs," *Werner v. McCotter*, 49 F.3d 1476, 1480 (10th Cir. 1995), imposes a substantial burden on the exercise of the individual's religion. The Sixth Circuit seems to straddle this divide, asking whether the burdened practice is "essential" or "fundamental."

Id. at 1178. After considering these differing views, we reject the middle and broad definitions of "substantial burden" as inconsistent with the language and intent of the FRFRA. The middle definition employed by the Sixth Circuit is contrary to the definition of "exercise of religion" contained in the FRFRA in that it is dependent on whether an action is essential or fundamental to a person's religious belief system. If this Court were to make religious motivation the key for analysis of a claim, that would "read out of [FRFRA] the condition that only substantial burdens on the exercise of religion trigger the compelling interest requirement." *Henderson v. Kennedy*, 253 F.3d 12, 17 (D.C.Cir. 2001).

Accordingly, we conclude that the narrow definition of substantial burden adopted by the Fourth, Ninth, and Eleventh Circuits is most consistent with the language and intent of the FRFRA. Thus, we hold that a substantial burden on the free exercise of religion is one that either compels the religious adherent to engage in conduct that his religion forbids or forbids him to engage in conduct that his religion requires. *See Mack*, 80 F.3d at 1178. We acknowledge that our adoption of this definition may occasionally place courts in the position of having to determine whether a particular religious practice is obligatory or forbidden. However, we conclude that this inquiry is preferable to one that requires the Court to question the centrality of a particular religious belief or negates the legislative requirement that only conduct that is substantially burdened be protected by strict scrutiny.

II. Certified Question II

We now address the second question certified by the Eleventh Circuit, which asks:

> If the Act does broaden the parameters of protected religiously motivated conduct, will a city's neutral, generally-applicable ordinance be subjected to strict scrutiny by the courts when the ordinance prevents persons from acting in conformity with their sincerely held religious beliefs, but the acts the persons wish to take are not 1) asserted or implied in relatively unambiguous terms by an authoritative sacred test, or 2) clearly and consistently affirmed in classic formulations of doctrine and practice, or 3) observed continuously, or nearly so, throughout the history of the religion, or 4) consistently observed in the tradition in recent times?

... Appellants and amici curiae object to the phrasing of the second certified question because the question is taken from the test used by Dr. Daniel L. Pals. Appellants argue that Dr. Pals' test adds requirements to the FRFRA because the test reads into the statute a requirement that the practice must have a basis in a larger system of beliefs. The focus under the FRFRA, however, is whether the appellants' action is substantially motivated by a religious belief and whether the governmental action enacted substantially burdens the free exercise of that religious belief. *See* §§ 761.02(3), 761.03(1), Fla. Stat. (2003).

Therefore, we have chosen to rephrase the second certified question as follows:

> Whether the City of Boca Raton Ordinance at issue in this case violates the Florida Religious Freedom Restoration Act (FRFRA)?

We answer the second certified question in the negative. As noted above, the Act specifically mandates that the strict-scrutiny standard be applied irrespective of whether or not the burden results from a rule of general applicability. *See* § 761.03, Fla. Stat. (2003). Under the test articulated by the FRFRA, the plaintiff bears the initial burden of showing that a regulation constitutes a substantial burden on his or her free exercise of religion. *See* § 761.03(1), Fla. Stat. (2003). Once that threshold determination has been made, the government bears the burden of establishing that the regulation furthers a compelling governmental interest and is the least restrictive means of furthering that interest. *See* § 761.03(1)(a)-(b), Fla. Stat. (2003). Thus, the plaintiffs must demonstrate that the government has placed a substantial burden on a practice motivated by a sincere religious belief. *See, e.g., Weir v. Nix,* 890 F.Supp. 769, 783 (S.D.Iowa 1995). The Southern District specifically noted: "It is undisputed that the plaintiffs placed vertical decorations on their [c]emetery plots in observance of sincerely held religious beliefs." *Warner,* 64 F.Supp.2d at 1277. Since appellants have demonstrated that their religious beliefs are sincere, the next issue is whether the government's regulation constitutes a substantial burden on the free exercise of religion.

A plaintiff who claims that a governmental regulation constitutes a substantial burden must "prove that a governmental regulatory mechanism burdens the adherent's practice of his or her religion by pressuring him or her to commit an act forbidden by the religion or by preventing him or her from engaging in conduct or having a religious experience which the faith mandates." *Graham v. Comm'r,* 822 F.2d 844, 850–51 (9th Cir. 1987), *aff'd sub nom. Hernandez v. Comm'r,* 490 U.S. 680, 699 (1989) . . . . In the instant case, the Southern District found that the City's regulation did not substantially burden appellants' free exercise of religion. . . . We agree with the Southern District's reasoning:

> The City's Regulations do not prohibit the plaintiffs from marking graves and decorating them with religious symbols. Rather, the Regulations permit only horizontal grave markers. These markers may be engraved with any type of religious symbol. Moreover, out of consideration for mourners vertical grave decorations are permitted for sixty days after the date of burial and for a few days around certain holidays. Aside from these times, however, vertical grave decorations are not permitted in the Cemetery. The Court finds that these restrictions on the manner in which religious decorations may be displayed merely inconvenience the plaintiffs' practices of marking graves and decorating them with religious symbols. Accordingly, the Court finds that the prohibition on vertical grave decorations does not substantially burden the plaintiffs' exercise of religion within the meaning of the Florida RFRA.

Id. Since the City's regulation does not substantially burden appellants' religious beliefs, no further analysis is required under the FRFRA. . . .

Conclusion

We hold that the FRFRA expands the scope of religious protection beyond the conduct considered protected by cases from the United States Supreme Court. We also hold that under the Act, any law, even a neutral law of general applicability, is subject to the strict scrutiny standard where the law substantially burdens the free exercise of religion. For the foregoing reasons, we answer the first certified question in the affirmative and the rephrased certified question in the negative and return this case to the United States Court of Appeals for the Eleventh Circuit.

It is so ordered.

Notes and Questions to Consider:

1. Does the Florida Religious Freedom Restoration Act of 1998 (FRFRA) provide greater rights to religious Floridians than is provided by Florida's constitution? Does it provide greater rights than is provided by the U.S. Constitution?

2. When does strict scrutiny apply, according to *Warner v. City of Boca Raton*, 887 So. 2d 1023 (Fla. 2004)?

3. When does a Florida law substantially burden a religious belief, according to *Warner v. City of Boca Raton*, 887 So. 2d 1023 (Fla. 2004)?

2. Freedom of Speech and the Press

Article I, Section 4 of Florida's constitution provides:

> *Section 4. Freedom of speech and press.* —Every person may speak, write and publish sentiments on all subjects but shall be responsible for the abuse of that right. No law shall be passed to restrain or abridge the liberty of speech or of the press. In all criminal prosecutions and civil actions for defamation the truth may be given in evidence. If the matter charged as defamatory is true and was published with good motives, the party shall be acquitted or exonerated.

It has been suggested (but, respectfully, this author is not quite convinced) that freedom of speech under Florida's constitution may vary from that under the U.S. Constitution insofar as it was a U.S. Supreme Court decision finding corporations to be persons and not yet a Florida Supreme Court decision so finding, and thus, it is suggested by some that the right differs because corporations are not persons under Florida's constitution. This author respectfully suggests that the U.S. Supreme Court's basis for corporate personhood was found under both the First Amendment and the Fourteenth Amendment to the U.S. Constitution, with the latter specifically making such applicable to the states, and thus, corporations are considered people in every state including Florida when it comes to freedom of speech. *See Citizens United v. Federal Elections Commission*, 558 U.S. 310 (2010). For this reason, your author suggests that freedom of speech under Florida's constitution does not vary from that under the U.S. Constitution, even insofar as corporations are concerned.

Notes and Questions to Consider:

1. Regarding the right of corporations, do you agree or disagree with this author's conclusion that their right to equal protection under Florida's constitution does not vary from that under the U.S. Constitution?

3. Freedom of Assembly and to Petition for Grievances

Article I, Section 5 of Florida's constitution states:

Section 5. Right to assemble. — The people shall have the right peaceably to assemble, to instruct their representatives, and to petition for redress of grievances.

D. Freedom from Ex Post Facto Laws and from Bills of Attainder

Article I, Section 10 of Florida's constitution references three separate rights when it states:

Prohibited laws. — No bill of attainder, ex post facto law or law impairing the obligation of contracts shall be passed.

Addressing first the "bill of attainder," Florida's supreme court defines it as follows:

A bill of attainder is a law that legislatively determines guilt for prior conduct and inflicts punishment upon an identifiable individual without the protections of a judicial trial. See *Cassady v. Moore*, 737 So. 2d 1174, 1178 (Fla. 1st DCA 1999). By prohibiting bills of attainder, the framers of the Constitution intended to protect the concept of separation of powers and due process by limiting legislatures to the task of lawmaking, leaving "the application of those rules to individuals in society . . . [to the] other departments." *Fletcher v. Peck*, 6 Cranch 87, 10 U.S. 87, 136, 3 L.Ed. 162 (1810).

Mayes v. Moore, 827 So. 2d 967, 972 (Fla. 2002).

Regarding "ex post facto" laws, Florida's supreme court provides the following definition:

An ex post facto law is 'one which, in its operation, makes that criminal which was not so at the time the action was performed, or which increases the punishment, or, in short, which in relation to the offense or its consequences alters the situation of a party to his disadvantage.' *Higginbotham v. State*, (Fla. 1924) 88 Fla. 26, 101 So. 233.

Wilensky v. Fields, 267 So. 2d 1, 5 (Fla. 1972).

The U.S. Constitution prohibits bills of attainder and ex post facto laws also. Florida's interpretation of its state constitutional requirements for bills of attainder and ex post facto laws are the same as the requirements of the U.S. Constitution. Talbot D'Alemberte, THE FLORIDA STATE CONSTITUTION 33 (Oxford University Press 2011) opines correctly that, in Florida case law, "[t]here are no significant departures from the decisions of the federal courts construing similar provisions of the U.S. Constitution."

E. Contracts Clause and Protection from Impairment of Contracts

Returning to Article I, Section 10 of Florida's constitution, it also contains a "contracts clause" as follows:

Prohibited laws.—No . . . law impairing the obligation of contracts shall be passed.

The U.S. Constitution, at Article I, Section 10, clause 1, prohibits the states from passing any law impairing the obligation of contract. Comparing and contrasting this federal right with the contracts clause of the Florida Constitution, the Florida Supreme Court held in *Pomponio v. Claridge of Pompano Condo., Inc.*, 378 So. 2d 774 (Fla. 1979):

> We recognize that this Court, when construing a provision of the Florida Constitution, is not bound to accept as controlling the United States Supreme Court's interpretation of a parallel provision of the federal Constitution. Yet such rulings have long been considered helpful and persuasive, and are obviously entitled to great weight. With this in mind, we now choose to adopt an approach to contract clause analysis similar to that of the United States Supreme Court. That Court's decisions in this area of law convince us that such an approach is the one most likely to yield results consonant with the basic purpose of the constitutional prohibition.

Id. at 779–80.

To better understand the operation of the contracts clause, consider the following opinion in *Citrus County Hosp. Bd. v. Citrus Mem'l Health Found., Inc.*, 150 So. 3d 1102 (Fla. 2014).

Citrus County Hospital Board v. Citrus Memorial Health Foundation., Inc.

Supreme Court of Florida, 2014
150 So. 3d 1102

This case is before the Court on appeal from the First District Court of Appeal's decision which held that the special law enacted at chapter 2011–256, Laws of Florida, impairs the Foundation's contracts in violation of article I, section 10 of the Florida Constitution. For the reasons below, we affirm the First District's decision.

I. Background

In 1949, the Florida Legislature created the Citrus County Hospital Board, an independent special district charged with operating a public hospital in Citrus

County, Florida. Through two contracts—a lease and an agreement for hospital care—the Hospital Board turned the hospital's operation and management over to the Citrus Memorial Health Foundation, Inc., a Florida not-for-profit. Transferring control of the hospital to the Foundation through these agreements, which are effective until 2033, allows the hospital to avoid participating in the State retirement program and to engage in joint ventures previously not available to it because of the Hospital Board's public status. The Foundation has likewise benefited from its relationship with the Hospital Board, by for example, using its status as the operator of a public hospital and its accountability to the Hospital Board to obtain sovereign immunity and recalculate its Medicaid rates.

Disputes arose between the parties. In 2011, the Legislature became involved and enacted chapter 2011–256, Laws of Florida. In pertinent part, section 3 of the special law reenacts the Hospital Board's charter. Section 16 of the charter includes fifteen subsections that, for the first time, specifically address the Hospital Board's relationship with the Foundation (or any future lessee) and that are "in addition to the requirements for any [ ] lease set forth in section 155.40." Ch.2011–256, § 3(16), at 59–60, Laws of Fla. For example, these provisions (i) require the Hospital Board to approve the Foundation's articles of incorporation and bylaws (including those currently in effect)—section 16(2); (ii) require the Foundation to amend its articles of incorporation so that the Hospital Board's trustees constitute a majority of its voting directors—section 16(5); (iii) require the Hospital Board to approve all Foundation directors, including current directors—section 16(6); (iv) require the Hospital Board to approve certain borrowing, indebtedness, policies, budgets, capital projects, and expenditures—sections 16(8) and (10); (v) require the Hospital Board to approve the Foundation's annual and operating capital budget—section 16(9); (vi) allow the Hospital Board to order, at the Foundation's expense, an independent audit of the Foundation's fiscal management of the hospital—section 16(11); and (vii) require that any dispute between the Foundation and the Hospital Board be subject to the statutory procedures applicable to governmental disputes—section 16(15).

The Foundation filed suit against the Hospital Board and the State in circuit court challenging the special law and seeking, among other things, a declaratory judgment that section 16 of the Hospital Board's charter as enacted in section 3 of the special law applies to impair its articles of incorporation, lease, and agreement for hospital care in violation of article I, section 10 of the Florida Constitution.

On appeal, the First District held that, as applied to the Foundation, the special law "significantly alters the parties' contractual rights and is an unconstitutional impairment of their contracts so as to be prohibited by [a]rticle I, [s]ection 10" of Florida's Constitution.

II. Analysis

The dispositive issue before this Court [is] whether the contract clause of the Florida Constitution applies and, if so, whether, as applied, the special law unconstitutionally impairs the Foundation's contracts.

A. The Contract Clause Applies to the Foundation's Contracts

Article I, section 10 of the Florida Constitution provides that "[n]o . . . law impairing the obligation of contracts shall be passed." As part of the Florida Constitution's Declaration of Rights, this right belongs to the people, including corporations, as against the government. See *Traylor v. State*, 596 So. 2d 957, 963 (Fla. 1992) (explaining that "[e]ach right" in the Declaration of Rights is "a distinct freedom guaranteed to each Floridian against government intrusion" and "operates in favor of the individual, against [the] government"); see also *State Farm Mut. Auto. Ins. Co. v. Gant*, 478 So. 2d 25, 26 (Fla. 1985) (applying the contract clause to a corporation).

Florida law is clear that corporations, like individuals, are entitled to protection under the contract clause.

Accordingly, we hold that the contract clause applies to the Foundation's contracts.

B. The Special Law Unconstitutionally Impairs the Foundation's Contracts

The Hospital Board and the State next argue that, even if the contract clause applies, the First District erred by concluding that the special law unconstitutionally impairs the Foundation's articles of incorporation, lease, and agreement for hospital care. We disagree and hold that, as applied to these contracts, section 16 of the Hospital Board's charter as enacted in section 3 of the special law is unconstitutional.

The contract clause prohibits any "law impairing the obligation of contracts." Art. I, § 10, Fla. Const. We have defined impairment

> as meaning to make worse; to diminish in quantity, value, excellency, or strength; to lessen in power; to weaken. Whatever legislation lessens the efficacy of the means of enforcement of the obligation is an impairment. Also if it tends to postpone or retard the enforcement of the contract, it is an impairment.

State ex rel. Woman's Benefit Ass'n v. Port of Palm Beach Dist., 121 Fla. 746, 164 So. 851, 856 (1935) (emphasis omitted). And we have "generally prohibited all forms of contract impairment." *State, Dep't of Transp. v. Edward M. Chadbourne, Inc.*, 382 So. 2d 293, 297 (Fla. 1980); see also *Dewberry v. Auto-Owners Ins. Co.*, 363 So. 2d 1077, 1080 (Fla. 1978) ("Any conduct on the part of the [L]egislature that detracts in any way from the value of the contract is inhibited by the Constitution." (quoting *Pinellas Cnty. v. Banks*, 154 Fla. 582, 19 So. 2d 1, 3 (1944)).

Section 16 of the Hospital Board's charter as enacted in section 3 of the special law meets our definition of impairment. It eliminates the Foundation's ability to operate and manage the hospital as it has contracted to do by turning the Foundation's governance over to the Hospital Board in disregard of the Foundation's status as a separate legal entity. And it also obligates the Foundation to comply with public accountability and financial responsibility measures that are mentioned nowhere in the parties' agreements and that are "in addition to the requirements for any [ ] lease set forth in section 155.40." In other words, as the First District cogently stated, the special law "is a rewrite of the parties' contractual agreements and the imposition of further obligations on the Foundation, while permitting the [Hospital] Board's privatization of hospital management functions as [authorized by section 155.40]."

In light of this impairment, we hold that section 16 of the Hospital Board's charter as enacted in section 3 of the special law is unconstitutional as applied to the Foundation's contracts. See *Cohn v. Grand Condo. Ass'n, Inc.*, 62 So. 3d 1120, 1122 (Fla. 2011) (affirming the district court's decision that a state statute was unconstitutional "because [it] impairs the obligation of contract as applied to [the plaintiff]"); see also *Dewberry*, 363 So. 2d at 1080 ("It is axiomatic that subsequent legislation which diminishes the value of a contract is repugnant to our Constitution.").

III. Conclusion

For the foregoing reasons, we affirm the First District's decision.

F. Protection from Searches and Seizures

As discussed in further detail in Chapter 8 of this book, Article I, Section 12 of Florida's constitution protects its citizens against searches and seizures using different language than how that protection is phrased in the Fourth Amendment to the U.S. Constitution. This section 12 of Florida's constitution was amended in 1982. Prior to its amendment, Florida's supreme court interpreted this section 12 differently than the Fourth Amendment. But as can be seen when quoted in relevant part, the 1982 amendment to this section 12 added the requirement that it be interpreted consistently with the Supreme Court of the United States' interpretations of the Fourth Amendment:

> *Section 12. Searches and seizures.* — The right of the people to be secure in their persons, houses, papers and effects against unreasonable searches and seizures, and against the unreasonable interception of private communications by any means, shall not be violated. No warrant shall be issued except upon probable cause, supported by affidavit, particularly describing the place or places to be searched, the person or persons, thing or things to be seized, the communication to be intercepted, and the nature of evidence to be obtained. This right shall be construed in conformity with the 4th Amendment to the United States Constitution, as interpreted by the United States Supreme Court. Articles or information obtained in violation of this right shall not be admissible in evidence if such articles or information would be inadmissible under decisions of the United States Supreme Court construing the 4th Amendment to the United States Constitution.

Perhaps a perfect illustration of how Florida's law of search and seizure may not vary from federal law can be seen in the following U.S. Supreme Court decision of *Florida v. Casal*, 462 U.S. 637 (1983):

Florida v. Casal

Supreme Court of the United States, 1983
462 U.S. 637, 103 S. Ct. 3100, 77 L. Ed. 2d 277

Per Curiam.

The writ is dismissed as improvidently granted, it appearing that the judgment of the court below rested on independent and adequate state grounds.

Chief Justice Burger, Concurring:

The Court today concludes that the Florida Supreme Court relied on independent and adequate state grounds when it affirmed the suppression of over 100 pounds of marijuana discovered aboard a fishing vessel — the evidence upon which respondents' convictions for possession and importation of marijuana were based. The Florida Supreme Court did not expressly declare that its holding rested on state grounds, and the principal state case cited for the probable cause standard, *Florida v. Smith*, 233 So. 2d 396 (Fla. 1970), is based entirely upon this Court's interpretation of the Fourth Amendment of the Federal Constitution. I write not to challenge today's determination that the State Court relied on independent and adequate state grounds, however, but rather to emphasize that this Court has decided that Florida law, and not federal law or any decision of this Court, is responsible for the untoward result in this case.

The two bases of state law upon which the Florida Supreme Court appears to have relied are Art. 1, § 12 of the State Constitution and Florida Statute § 371.58 (1977), *currently codified at* Florida Statute § 327.56 (1983 Supp.). Article I, § 12 of Florida's Constitution is similar to the Fourth Amendment of the Federal Constitution. I question that anything in the language of either the Fourth Amendment of the United States Constitution or Art. 1, § 12 of the Florida Constitution required suppression of the drugs as evidence. However, the Florida Supreme Court apparently concluded that state law required suppression of the evidence, independent of the Fourth Amendment of the United States Constitution.

The people of Florida have since shown acute awareness of the means to prevent such inconsistent interpretations of the two constitutional provisions. In the general election of November 2, 1982, the people of Florida amended Art. 1, § 12 of the State Constitution. That section now provides:

"This right shall be construed in conformity with the 4th Amendment to the United States Constitution, as interpreted by the United States Supreme Court. . . . Articles or information obtained in violation of this right shall not be admissible in evidence if such articles or information would be inadmissible under decisions of the United States Supreme Court construing the 4th Amendment to the United States Constitution."

As amended, that section ensures that the Florida courts will no longer be able to rely on the State Constitution to suppress evidence that would be admissible under the decisions of the Supreme Court of the United States.

In requiring suppression of the evidence, the Florida Supreme Court also may have been relying upon Florida Statute § 371.58 (1977), currently codified at Florida Statute § 327.56 (1983 Supp.). That statute permits a state marine patrol officer to board a vessel for a safety inspection only if there is consent or probable cause to believe a crime is being committed. The Florida Legislature enacted that statute, and the people of Florida and their representatives have full responsibility for the burden it places on the State's law enforcement officers.

With our dual system of state and federal laws, administered by parallel state and federal courts, different standards may arise in various areas. But when state courts interpret state law to require *more* than the Federal Constitution requires, the citizens of the state must be aware that they have the power to amend state law to ensure rational law enforcement. The people of Florida have now done so with respect to Art. 1, § 12 of the State Constitution; they have it within their power to do so with respect to Florida Statute § 327.56.

Notes and Questions to Consider:

1. Note that the opinion of the court, appearing just before Chief Justice Burger's concurring opinion, has not been edited and has been reprinted in its entirety. Yet it is only one sentence long. Why is it so short?

2. Can and should a state constitution, like the Constitution of the State of Florida, contain a requirement that it must be interpreted consistently with the U.S. Constitution? If so, why have a state constitution?

G. Basic Rights of a Criminal Defendant

Article I, Section 16(a) of Florida's constitution provides, in relevant part, that:

> In all criminal prosecutions the accused shall, upon demand, be informed of the nature and cause of the accusation, and shall be furnished a copy of the charges, and shall have the right to have compulsory process for witnesses, to confront at trial adverse witnesses, to be heard in person, by counsel or both, and to have a speedy and public trial by impartial jury in the county where the crime was committed. If the county is not known, the indictment or information may charge venue in two or more counties conjunctively and proof that the crime was committed in that area shall be sufficient; but before pleading the accused may elect in which of those counties the trial will take place. Venue for prosecution of crimes committed beyond the boundaries of the state shall be fixed by law.

As Talbot D'Alemberte, THE FLORIDA STATE CONSTITUTION 36 (Oxford University Press 2011) correctly notes: "This extensive list parallels rights guaranteed in the federal Constitution, and there is no major departure from the decisions that construe the federal Constitution."

H. Freedom from Imprisonment for Debt

Case law precedent finds that this right arises both under the Constitution of the United States and also appears in the text of the Constitution of the State of Florida. *Del Valle v. State*, 80 So. 3d 999 (Fla. 2011) holds:

> The Equal Protection and Due Process Clauses of the United States Constitution ensure that an indigent probationer is not incarcerated based solely upon inability to pay a monetary obligation. *See Bearden v. Georgia*, 461 U.S. 660, 664 (1983); U.S. Const. amends. V, XIV. Further, the Florida Constitution contains its own due process clause that parallels the language of the Fourteenth Amendment and states that "[n]o person shall be deprived of life, liberty or property without due process of law." Art. I, § 9, Fla. Const. The Florida Constitution contains a separate and specific provision that ensures that "[n]o person shall be imprisoned for debt, except in cases of fraud." Art. I, § 11, Fla. Const.

Id. at 1005. It is noteworthy, however, that *Del Valle v. State* finds imprisonment for an unpaid debt could be proper under certain facts involving restitution for crimes. Specifically, it holds that a probationer can be imprisoned for failing to pay a financial obligation such as a court-ordered restitution but only after a trial court enquires into the probationer's ability to pay and finds by the greater weight of the evidence that the ability exists but the probationer is willfully disobeying the requirement to pay. Any requirement that a probationer prove his inability to pay by the heightened standard of clear and convincing evidence is unconstitutional per *Del Valle v. State*, 80 So. 3d 999 (Fla. 2011).

Although *Del Valle v. State* disapproves of *Gonzales v. State*, *Guardado v. State*, and *Martin v. State*, it is also consistent with prior case law precedent of both the Supreme Court of Florida and the Supreme Court of the United States. For example, *State ex rel. Lanz v. Dowling*, 110 So. 522 (1926), holds that Article I Section 11 of the Florida Constitution's "prohibition against imprisonment for debt protects against imprisonment of a person found in contempt for failure to pay a money judgment but does not prohibit imprisonment for failure to pay fines or penalties. . . ." Talbot D'Alemberte, THE FLORIDA STATE CONSTITUTION 33 (Oxford University Press 2011).

I. Right to Work

Florida's constitution at Article I Section 6 provides the following protections and restrictions upon the rights of Florida's workers:

> SECTION 6. *Right to work.*—The right of persons to work shall not be denied or abridged on account of membership or non-membership in any labor union or labor organization. The right of employees, by and through a labor organization, to bargain collectively shall not be denied or abridged. Public employees shall not have the right to strike.

Although this section of Florida's constitution addresses the rights of workers and labor unions, Florida courts observe correctly that the majority of such issues are to be answered under federal law. The U.S. Supreme Court holds that federal laws "safeguard the right of employees to self-organization and to select representatives of their own choosing for collective bargaining or other mutual protection without restraint or coercion by their employer. That is a fundamental right. Employees have as clear a right to organize and select their representatives for lawful purposes. . . ." *N.L.R.B. v. Jones & Laughlin Steel Corp.*, 301 U.S. 1, 33 (1937). Florida's Third District Court of Appeal summarized an important part of federal law when it held that:

> the Supreme Court of the United States has generally construed the Labor Management Relations Act [codified at 29 U.S.C. § 141 et seq.] as pre-empting the field in labor matters where the conduct complained of affects interstate commerce and, though the state power has not been exclusively absorbed, the states have been left a very narrow field of operation. Basically, as outlined in *United Auto Aircraft & Agr. Implement Workers of America v. Wisconsin Employment Relations Board*, 351 U.S. 266 (1985), the state's power in labor relations matters is confined to a prevention of mass picketing, acts of violence and threats of violence. See *Allen-Bradley Local, etc. v. Wisconsin Board*, 315 U.S. 740 (1942); *United Construction Workers, etc. v. Labernum Corp.*, 347 U.S. 656 (1954); *Algoma Plywood & Veneer Co. v. Wisconsin Board*, 336 U.S. 301 (1949). It would appear now to be an established rule that a state court may not enjoin peaceful picketing where it is arguable that the activities complained of are within the purview of the Labor Management Relations Act. *San Diego Building Trades Council v. Garmon*, 359 U.S. 236 (1959).

Wood, Wire & Metal Lathers Intern. Union, Local No. 345 v. Babcock Co., 132 So. 2d 16, 18 (Fla. 3d DCA 1961). In addition to the federal Labor Management Relations Act mentioned above, Congress enacted many laws designed to address collective bargaining and labor unions: the federal National Labor Relations Act (codified at 29 U.S.C. § 151 et seq.), the Norris-LaGuardia Act (codified at 29 U.S.C. § 101 et seq.), and the Fair Labor Standards Act (29 U.S.C. § 201 et seq.), to name a few. See generally *Janus v. American Federation of State, County, and Municipal Employees, Council 31*, 138 S.Ct. 2448 (2018).

Within this myriad of federal laws, the Taft-Hartley Act empowers states to enact Right to Work laws like the one found in Florida's constitution at Article I, Section 6 when the federal law states: "Nothing in this subchapter shall be construed as authorizing the execution or application of agreements requiring membership in a labor organization as a condition of employment in any State or Territory in which such execution or application is prohibited by State or Territorial law." 29 U.S.C. § 164(b).

Right to Work laws, like Florida's, mean that workers may not be compelled to join, to refrain from joining, or to pay dues to a labor union as a condition of employment. Along with Florida, 26 other states enacted Right to Work laws.

Despite the Florida Constitution's right to work, Florida is an "employment at will" state, as described in FLORIDA ELEMENTS OF AN ACTION:

> It is clear that "there is no action in Florida for the common law tort of wrongful termination." The State of Florida provides state employees with civil service remedies for disagreeing with their terminations and adverse employment actions. Under Florida law, a private employer has a right to discharge an at-will employee for any reason, or no reason at all, so long as the reason is not prohibited by law. The only other exception is an employee who works under an employment contract, who also can be terminated, but who has rights under the contract for either breach or for the damages stated in the contract.

> If the wrongful termination action is upon a breach of a contract action, then the elements of an action for breach of contract should be alleged and proven. . . . Care should be taken to allege an employment contract for a definite term, because without a definite term, the employment is at-will and no action for wrongful termination may lie. . . . ["]No action may be maintained for the breach of an employment contract terminable at will." . . . Ordinarily, the equitable remedy of specific performance is not available to enforce an employment contract. The rationale for this rule is that such agreements lack the mutuality of remedy and obligation which would make specific performance an appropriate form of relief.

> If the allegation of a wrongful employment action is based upon a retaliation, then a statute outlawing such retaliation must be identified and its elements met because "no clearly established right exists under the equal protection clause to be free from retaliation." One statute provides that no employer may discharge, threaten to discharge, intimidate, or coerce any employee by reason of the employee's valid claim for compensation or attempt to claim compensation under the Workers' Compensation Law. Other statutes provide protection for whistleblowers in both the public and the private sector. A civil statute protects against retaliation for labor union activity. A criminal statute prohibits the discharge of an employee for trading or dealing with any particular merchant or other person or class of persons in any business calling and provides a criminal remedy. Retaliation based on race, sex, religion, national ancestry, age, marital status, and HIV status are illegal in Florida under the Florida Civil Rights Act of 1992 (FCRA), which is codified at Fla. Stat. §§ 760.01 through 760.11.

> Similarly, if the wrongful termination is based upon alleged discrimination, a Floridian may find protection under the FCRA.

Patrick John McGinley, FLORIDA ELEMENTS OF AN ACTION § 901:1 (2018-2019 ed.).

J. Right to Bear Arms

This right from the Constitution of the United States also appears in substantial form within the Constitution of the State of Florida as well as within the state constitutions of most U.S. states. This particular right is fodder for most law school textbooks on the general topic of state constitutional law because it serves as an easy example of a right that is parallel to that in the federal constitution but that is subject to various interpretations when appearing in a state constitution. *See, e.g.,* Robert F. Williams, STATE CONSTITUTIONAL LAW: CASES AND MATERIALS (3d ed. 1999 Lexis Law Publishing); Randy J. Holland, Stephen R. McAllister, Jeffrey M. Shaman, and Jeffrey S. Sutton, STATE CONSTITUTIONAL LAW: THE MODERN EXPERIENCE (Thomson Reuters 2010).

Article I, Section 8 of the Constitution of the State of Florida reads as follows:

Section 8. Right to bear arms. —

(a) The right of the people to keep and bear arms in defense of themselves and of the lawful authority of the state shall not be infringed, except that the manner of bearing arms may be regulated by law.

(b) There shall be a mandatory period of three days, excluding weekends and legal holidays, between the purchase and delivery at retail of any handgun. For the purposes of this section, "purchase" means the transfer of money or other valuable consideration to the retailer, and "handgun" means a firearm capable of being carried and used by one hand, such as a pistol or revolver. Holders of a concealed weapon permit as prescribed in Florida law shall not be subject to the provisions of this paragraph.

(c) The legislature shall enact legislation implementing subsection (b) of this section, effective no later than December 31, 1991, which shall provide that anyone violating the provisions of subsection (b) shall be guilty of a felony.

(d) This restriction shall not apply to a trade in of another handgun.

As for the interpretation of this provision of the Florida Constitution, Talbot D'Alemberte, THE FLORIDA STATE CONSTITUTION 31 (Oxford University Press 2011) writes: "the Florida language specifically recognizes the right to bear arms as a right to self-defense. This language explicitly states that the matter of bearing arms may be regulated by law. Thus, the legislature may make it unlawful to possess machine guns."

Professor D'Alemberte's analysis quoted above falls short of stating whether Florida's Section 8 Right to Bear Arms is interpreted differently than the Right to Bear Arms found in the Second Amendment to the U.S. Constitution. But perhaps the case law he cites, *Rinzler v. Carson*, 262 So. 2d 661 (Fla. 1972) yields the answer when it holds that:

the right to keep and bear arms is not an absolute right, but is one which is subject to the right of the people through their legislature to enact valid police regulations to promote the health, morals, safety and general welfare of the people. It seems to us to be significant that the type of firearms, the possession of which is outlawed by Section 790.221, Florida Statutes, is that weapon which is too dangerous to be kept in a settled community by individuals, and one which, in times of peace, finds its use by a criminal. The Supreme Court of Michigan in *People v. Brown*, 253 Mich. 537, 235 N.W. 245, upheld a statute very similar to the one under attack. The Court noted that the list of weapons outlawed by the statute including machine guns was a partial inventory of the arsenal of the public enemy and the gangster, and included weapons with which the gangster wars on the State, and were not such weapons which by common opinion and usage by law-abiding people are proper and legitimate to be kept upon private premises for the protection of persons and property. To like effect is the holding of the Court of Criminal Appeals of Texas in *Morrison v. State*, 170 Tex.Cr.R. 218, 339 S.W.2d 529.

We hold that the Legislature may prohibit the possession of weapons which are ordinarily used for criminal and improper purposes and which are not among those which are legitimate weapons of defense and protection and protected by Section 8 of the Florida Declaration of Rights. A machine gun, particularly a hand-barreled one, which is, or which may readily be made, operable, is peculiarly adaptable to use by criminals in the pursuit of their criminal activities. The Legislature may in the exercise of the police power of the State make its possession or ownership unlawful.

The definition of the term 'machine gun' used in the statute as being 'any firearm, as defined herein, which shoots or is designed to shoot, automatically or semi-automatically, more than one shot, without manually reloading, by a single function of the trigger,' could be construed to prohibit any person owning or possessing any semi-automatic hand gun. But such a construction might run counter to the historic constitutional right of the people to keep and bear arms. We cannot believe that it was the intention of the Legislature in enacting this statute to attempt to deny such right, and it is our duty in construing the statute to preserve its constitutionality, if reasonably possible. We, therefore, hold that the statute does not prohibit the ownership, custody and possession of weapons not concealed upon the person, which, although designed to shoot more than one shot semi-automatically, are commonly kept and used by law-abiding people for hunting purposes or for the protection of their persons and property, such as semi-automatic shotguns, semi-automatic pistols and rifles.

We reject as without merit the contention of appellant that the adding of the word 'keep' to the phrase concerning the right of the people to bear arms as now contained in Section 8 of the Declaration of Rights has specific significance such as to make inapplicable the decisions of this Court concerning the power of the Legislature to regulate the manner of bearing arms. It is evident that the purpose of adding this word to the phrase is to bring the protection in line with the phraseology used in the Second Amendment to the Constitution of the United States. The Supreme Court of the United States has held, in construing that amendment, that the right of the people to keep and bear arms is not infringed by the prohibition of state statutes which make it unlawful to possess certain kinds of firearms. *Presser v. Illinois*, 116 U.S. 252 (1886). The statute is not per se unconstitutional.

Id. at 666–67.

A more recent case from the Florida Supreme Court, *Norman v. State*, 215 So. 3d 18 (Fla. 2017), cert. denied, 138 S.Ct. 469 (2017), provides the following detailed analysis of the federal and Florida constitutional rights to bear arms.

Norman v. State

Supreme Court of Florida, 2017
215 So. 3d 18

In this case, we determine the constitutionality of section 790.053, Florida Statutes (2012) ("Florida's Open Carry Law"), first passed by the Legislature in 1987 and challenged by Norman as a violation of his right to bear arms for self-defense outside the home under both the United States and Florida Constitutions. The Fourth District Court of Appeal concluded that Florida's Open Carry Law does not violate the Second Amendment to the United States Constitution or article I, section 8, of the Florida Constitution. *Norman v. State*, 159 So. 3d 205 (Fla. 4th DCA 2015). We accepted jurisdiction on the basis that the Fourth District expressly construed the United States and Florida Constitutions and expressly declared valid a state statute. See art. V, § 3(b)(3), Fla. Const.

Florida's Open Carry Law is a provision within Florida's overall scheme regulating the use of firearms (codified in chapter 790, Florida Statutes), but still allowing the possession of firearms in most instances. See § 790.06, Fla. Stat. (2012). Chapter 790 permits individuals to carry firearms in public, so long as the firearm is carried in a concealed manner. Pursuant to section 790.06, Florida employs a "shall issue" scheme for issuing licenses to carry concealed firearms in public. See id. Under this licensing scheme, which leaves no discretion to the licensing authority, the licensing authority must issue an applicant a concealed carry license, provided the applicant meets objective, statutory criteria. Id. Accordingly, as the Fourth District observed in explaining the breadth of Florida's "shall issue" licensing scheme, the right of Floridians to bear arms for self-defense outside of the home is not illusory:

> Florida's licensing statute does not effectively act as an exclusionary bar to the right to bear arms in lawful self-defense outside the home. . . . [In] over two decades from 1987 to 2014, Florida issued concealed weapons permits to more than 2.7 million people. As of December 2014 there were 1,535,030 active permits issued in a population of over 19 million. No empirical evidence suggests in any way that Florida concealed carry permits are unduly

restricted to only a few people, such that a citizen's right to lawfully carry a firearm is illusory.

Norman, 159 So. 3d at 219 (footnotes omitted). Further, pursuant to chapter 790, Florida law provides sixteen exceptions to Florida's Open Carry Law, including a broad exception that applies to persons "engaged in fishing, camping, or lawful hunting or *going to or returning* from a fishing, camping, or lawful hunting expedition." §790.25(3)(h), Fla. Stat. (2012) (emphasis added); see also §790.25(3), Fla. Stat. (2012) (providing a list of sixteen statutory exceptions to the Open Carry Law). Because of the comprehensive nature of Florida's regulatory scheme of firearms, we review the constitutionality of Florida's Open Carry Law within the context of chapter 790.

As we explain more fully below, we agree with the Fourth District that the State has an important interest in regulating firearms as a matter of public safety, and that Florida's Open Carry Law is substantially related to this interest. Norman, 159 So. 3d at 222–23. We conclude that Florida's Open Carry Law violates neither the Second Amendment to the United States Constitution, nor article I, section 8, of the Florida Constitution. Accordingly, we affirm the Fourth District's well-reasoned opinion upholding Florida's Open Carry Law under intermediate scrutiny. See id. at 209. . . .

Florida's right provides explicitly to Floridians what the United States Supreme Court has interpreted the federal right to guarantee—an individual right to bear arms for self-defense, subject to legislative regulation.

A. History and Scope of the Right Provided by the Second Amendment to the United States Constitution

The Second Amendment to the United States Constitution states, in full:

> A well regulated Militia, being necessary to the security of a free State, the right of the people to keep and bear Arms, shall not be infringed.

In 2008, in *District of Columbia v. Heller*, the United States Supreme Court thoroughly analyzed the history of this constitutional guarantee in reviewing the constitutionality of a District of Columbia law that entirely banned the possession of handguns in the home and required that firearms otherwise lawfully allowed to be kept in the home be rendered inoperable. In a 5–4 decision, the Court invalidated the District of Columbia law and concluded that the Second Amendment provides an individual right to bear arms that is grounded in self-defense. *Id.* at 599 (noting that the "central component" of the Second Amendment was and remains self-defense). One basis for the Court's conclusion that the Second Amendment guarantees an individual right, not connected to service in a militia, was a review of post-Civil War legislation that concerned "how to secure constitutional rights for newly freed slaves." *Id.* at 614, 128 S.Ct. 2783. As the *Heller* Court explained, "[b]lacks were routinely disarmed by Southern States after the Civil War." *Id.*

After determining that the Second Amendment guarantees an individual right, the Court explicitly noted that the Second Amendment's individual right is not unlimited, and, historically, the right has been subject to laws prohibiting how fire-arms are carried, including antebellum laws prohibiting the concealed carrying of weapons. *Id.* at 626–27. Indeed, as one scholar has explained, "[e]ven in Dodge City, that epitome of the Wild West, gun carrying was prohibited." Saul Cornell, *The Right to Carry Firearms Outside of the Home: Separating Historical Myths from Historical Realities*, 39 Fordham Urb. L.J. 1695, 1724 (2012).

Two years after *Heller*, in *McDonald v. City of Chicago*, 561 U.S. 742 (2010), the United States Supreme Court considered a broad-sweeping handgun ban in Chicago, which was "similar to the District of Columbia's" that was at issue in *Heller* because it prevented possession of "any firearm unless such person is the holder of a valid registration certificate for such firearm." Relying on *Heller*, the *McDonald* Court struck down the handgun ban at issue. In reviewing the handgun ban, the Court noted that its previous decision in *Heller* "protects the right to possess a handgun in the home for the purpose of self-defense," *id.*, and the plurality opinion "recognized that the right to keep and bear arms is not 'a right to keep and carry any weapon whatsoever in any manner whatsoever and for whatever purpose.'" Significantly, after an exhaustive review of its selective incorporation jurisprudence, the Court applied the Second Amendment to the States via the Due Process Clause of the Fourteenth Amendment. *Id.* at 791.

Recently, the United States Supreme Court shed further light on the scope of the Second Amendment in *Caetano v. Massachusetts*, 136 S.Ct. 1027, 194 L.Ed.2d 99 (2016). In *Caetano*, the Court reviewed a judgment of the Supreme Judicial Court of Massachusetts upholding a Massachusetts law prohibiting the possession of stun guns, reasoning "stun gun[s] [were not] the type of weapon contemplated by Congress in 1789 as being protected by the Second Amendment." 136 S.Ct. at 1027. On review, the Supreme Court vacated the judgment, finding that this explanation contradicted *Heller*'s "statement that the Second Amendment 'extends to arms that were not in existence at the time of the founding." Thus, the *Caetano* Court confirmed that the Second Amendment is a right evolving with advances in technology. See *id.*

The Court also recently considered "whether a misdemeanor conviction for recklessly assaulting a domestic relation disqualifies an individual from possessing a gun under [a federal law prohibiting possession of firearms by persons previously convicted of a misdemeanor crime of domestic violence]." *Voisine v. United States*, 136 S.Ct. 2272, 2277–78 (2016). Importantly, in holding that the federal law applied to reckless assaults in addition to knowing or intentional ones, the Court chose not to address Voisine's claim that the law violated the Second Amendment and, instead, resolved the issue on statutory interpretation grounds. See *id.* at 2278–80. But see *id.* at 2290 (Thomas, J., dissenting) (noting that the majority's statutory construction of the statute at issue improperly extended the "statute into . . . constitutionally problematic territory").

While the Supreme Court in *Heller* and *McDonald* struck down laws that, by design and effect, totally prohibited the use of operable firearms in the home, the Court has not further defined the scope of the Second Amendment to preclude laws regulating the manner of how arms are borne. Indeed, the Court acknowledged that its decision in *Heller* left "many applications of the right to keep and bear arms in doubt," . . . and clarified in *Caetano* that the right evolves with advances in technology. See 136 S.Ct. at 1028.

In the eight years since *Heller*, federal circuit courts have considered an array of Second Amendment challenges to laws regulating the manner and use of firearms. For instance, the Second, Third, Fourth, Ninth, and Tenth Circuits have all considered and upheld state laws either prohibiting entirely the concealed carrying of firearms or requiring a demonstration of "good cause" or a "justifiable need" before a person is licensed to carry concealed firearms. Some federal circuit courts have held that laws prohibiting the concealed carrying of firearms without first demonstrating a subjective "good cause," did not even implicate the Second Amendment. For instance, the Ninth Circuit in *Peruta v. County of San Diego*, 824 F.3d 919 (9th Cir. 2016), conducted a historical examination of the Second Amendment and, based on this historical analysis, held "that the Second Amendment right to keep and bear arms does not include, in any degree, the right of a member of the general public to carry concealed firearms in public." Id. at 939. The Tenth Circuit has also held "that the concealed carrying of firearms falls outside the scope of the Second Amendment's guarantee," but did not conduct a historical examination of the Second Amendment right as the Ninth Circuit conducted in *Peruta*. *Peterson v. Martinez*, 707 F.3d 1197, 1212 (10th Cir. 2013). In *Peterson*, the petitioner challenged a residency requirement of Colorado's "shall issue" permitting scheme for the concealed carrying of firearms as violating the Second Amendment, even though Colorado law permitted nonresidents to openly carry firearms in the state. Id. at 1209. Importantly, the Tenth Circuit did not premise its holding on the fact that residents and nonresidents of Colorado may openly carry. See *id.*

Similarly, the Fourth Circuit considered a Maryland law requiring that handgun permits be issued only to individuals with "good-and-substantial-reason" to wear, carry (open or concealed), or transport a handgun. *Woollard v. Gallagher*, 712 F.3d 865, 868 (4th Cir. 2013). Unlike the Ninth and Tenth Circuits, however, the Fourth Circuit "refrain[ed] from any assessment of whether Maryland's good and substantial reason requirement for obtaining a handgun permit implicate[d] Second Amendment protections," but concluded that the law nevertheless passed constitutional muster under intermediate scrutiny. Id. at 876.

In holding that the law passed intermediate scrutiny, the Fourth Circuit noted that "intermediate scrutiny applies to laws burdening any right to carry firearms outside the home, where 'firearm rights have always been more limited, because public safety interests often outweigh individual interests in self-defense.'"

The Third Circuit considered a similar, subjective "justifiable need" restriction on carrying handguns in public (without distinguishing between open and concealed carrying) in *Drake v. Filko*, 724 F.3d 426 (3d Cir. 2013), and concluded that the law did "not burden conduct within the scope of the Second Amendment's guarantee." Id. at 429. Regardless, the Third Circuit held that even if the "justifiable need" restriction was not presumptively lawful, it would still pass intermediate scrutiny. Id. at 430. The Third Circuit noted that the law "fits comfortably within the long-standing tradition of regulating the public carrying of weapons for self-defense. In fact, it does not go as far as some of the historical bans on public carrying; rather, it limits the opportunity for public carrying to those who can demonstrate a justifiable need to do so." Id. at 433.

In contrast, the Second Circuit concluded that New York's "proper cause" restriction to obtain a license to carry a concealed firearm implicated the Second Amendment in *Kachalsky v. County of Westchester*, 701 F.3d 81, 93 (2d Cir. 2012). However, like its sister courts that have subjected laws regulating the carrying of firearms in public to some level of scrutiny, the Second Circuit held that the "proper cause" restriction passed intermediate scrutiny. Id. at 96, 100. Explaining that the law passed intermediate scrutiny, the Second Circuit noted that "extensive state regulation of handguns has never been considered incompatible with the Second Amendment or, for that matter, the common-law right to self-defense. This includes significant restrictions on how handguns are carried, complete prohibitions on carrying the weapon in public, and even in some instances, prohibitions on purchasing handguns." Id. at 100. Therefore, federal circuit courts have found restrictions on the public carrying of firearms as not only surviving intermediate scrutiny, but, in some instances, not even implicating the Second Amendment right at all. See *Drake*, 724 F.3d at 429–30.14.

B. History and Scope of the Right Provided by Article I, Section 8, of the Florida Constitution

Not only is the Federal right to bear arms applicable to the states under *McDonald* by selective incorporation through the Due Process Clause of the Fourteenth Amendment, but the Florida Constitution includes a separate constitutional right to bear arms in article I, section 8. Specifically, the Florida Constitution provides:

> The right of the people to keep and bear arms in defense of themselves and of the lawful authority of the state shall not be infringed, *except that the manner of bearing arms may be regulated by law.*

Art. I, § 8(a), Fla. Const. (emphasis added). In contrast to the federal right, Florida's Constitution explicitly states that the purpose of the constitutional right is self-defense while simultaneously expressly limiting that right by providing the Legislature the authority to regulate the manner of bearing arms.

This constitutional right has endured in Florida—with only a small gap—since 1838 when Florida's Constitution was adopted by the then Territory of Florida. *Fla. Carry v. Univ. of N. Fla.*, 133 So. 3d 966, 983–84 (Fla. 1st DCA 2013) (Makar, J., concurring). When Florida's current Constitution was adopted in 1968, the explicit right of the Legislature to regulate the manner in which arms are borne first announced in the 1885 Constitution remained.

Near the turn of the twentieth century, in one of this Court's earliest decisions interpreting Florida's constitutional right to keep and bear arms for self-defense, this Court recognized in *Carlton v. State*, 63 Fla. 1, 58 So. 486 (1912), that article

I, section 20, the precursor to today's constitutional right, which was contained in the 1885 Constitution's Declaration of Rights, was "intended to give the people the means of protecting themselves against oppression and public outrage, and was not designed as a shield for the individual man, who is prone to load his stomach with liquor and his pockets with revolvers or dynamite, and make of himself a dangerous nuisance to society." Id. at 488.

A former member of this Court also echoed the *Heller* Court's statement that some early gun laws were enacted with a racial motivation in mind. As Justice Buford explained in *Watson v. Stone*, 148 Fla. 516, 4 So. 2d 700 (1941), when concurring specially in a decision of this Court, which applied the rule of lenity to strictly construe the predecessor of section 790.05 in favor of the defendant:

> *The original Act of 1893 was passed when there was a great influx of [African-American] laborers in this State drawn here for the purpose of working in turpentine and lumber camps. The same condition existed when the Act was amended in 1901 and the Act was passed for the purpose of disarming the [African-American] laborers and to thereby reduce the unlawful homicides that were prevalent in turpentine and saw-mill camps and to give the white citizens in sparsely settled areas a better feeling of security.* The statute was never intended to be applied to the white population and in practice has never been so applied. We have no statistics available, but it is a safe guess to assume that more than 80% of the white men living in the rural sections of Florida have violated this statute. It is also a safe guess to say that not more than 5% of the men in Florida who own pistols and repeating rifles have ever applied to the Board of County Commissioners for a permit to have the same in their possession and there had never been, within my knowledge, any effort to enforce the provisions of this statute as to white people, because it has been generally conceded to be in contravention of the Constitution and non-enforceable if contested.

Id. at 703 (Buford, J., concurring specially) (emphasis added).

Consistent with the plain language of article I, section 8, and its predecessor providing that the Legislature may regulate the manner and use of firearms, as well as the Heller Court's interpretation of the federal right as not unlimited, the Legislature has enacted various laws regulating the manner in which arms are carried. This Court has upheld these various regulations of this constitutional right upon challenge. For instance, in *Nelson v. State*, 195 So. 2d 853 (Fla. 1967), this Court concluded that the "statutory prohibition of possession of a pistol by one convicted of a felony, civil rights not restored, [was] a reasonable public safeguard." Id. at 855–56. Then, in *Rinzler v. Carson*, 262 So. 2d 661 (Fla. 1972), this Court upheld a statute that barred the usage of an entire class of firearms, explaining that "[a]lthough the Legislature may not entirely prohibit the right of the people to keep and bear arms," pursuant to article I, section 8, "it can determine that certain arms or weapons may not be kept or borne by the citizen." *Id*. at 665. In doing so, the Court did not apply any level of scrutiny and noted that it had previously upheld other regulations enacted by the Legislature that regulated the use and manner of bearing specific weapons:

> In *Nelson v. State*, 195 So. 2d 853 (1967) we held constitutional Section 790.23, Florida Statutes, which makes it unlawful for a convicted felon to have in his possession a pistol, sawed-off rifle, or sawed-off shotgun. In *Davis v. State*, 146 So. 2d 892 (1962) we held valid Section 790.05, Florida Statutes of 1961, which made it a criminal offense for any person to carry around with him or to have in his manual possession a pistol, Winchester rifle or other repeating rifle in a county without a license from the county commissioners. In *Carlton v. State*, 63 Fla. 1, 58 So. 486 (1912) we upheld as valid against the contention that it unlawfully infringed upon the right of the citizen to bear arms a statute of this State which made it unlawful to carry concealed weapons.

Rinzler, 262 So. 2d at 665–66.

As we recognized in *Rinzler*, inherent in the holdings of these cases is the acknowledgment that under the Florida Constitution, "*the right to keep and bear arms is not an absolute right*, but is one which is subject to the right of the people through their legislature to enact valid police regulations to promote the health, morals, safety and general welfare of the people." *Id.* at 666 (emphasis added). In light of *Heller*'s clarification that the federal right under the Second Amendment is not unlimited, the Florida right is, thus, consistent with the federal right.

Note with Questions to Consider:

1. At the beginning of *Norman v. State*, when comparing and contrasting the right to bear arms under the state and federal constitutions, the Florida Supreme Court observes that "Florida's right provides explicitly to Floridians what the United States Supreme Court has interpreted the federal right to guarantee." Does not this statement imply that the right under the Florida Constitution may be different than that found in the federal constitution? Yet by the end of this excerpt from this opinion, the court holds that the "Florida right is, thus, consistent with the federal right." Does not this imply that there is no difference between the two rights?

2. We have now examined several fundamental rights in the Declaration of Rights of Florida's constitution that also appear in the Bill of Rights of the federal Constitution, including equal protection, freedom of religion, freedom of speech and of the press, the right to assemble, protection from searches and seizures, the right to bear arms, and others. We know that a state's high court has the power to interpret its own state constitution to provide greater protection than that of the federal Constitution even when the language is parallel. But for the most part, have state courts taken the opportunity to do so? Consider the following commentary from Lawrence Friedman, *Path Dependence and the External Constraints on Independent State Constitutionalism*, 115 PENN ST. L. REV. 783 (2011):

The promise of "the New Judicial Federalism"—of the independent interpretation by state courts of state constitutional corollaries to the federal Bill of Rights—has gone largely unfulfilled. In terms of doctrinal development, the project of independent state constitutionalism . . . is today more an aspiration than a practice. State courts often do not engage in the difficult task of trying to establish doctrinal tests that do not flow from federal precedent. . . . .

I am not the first commentator to suggest the promise of the New Judicial Federalism has not been met. In an article published nearly twenty years ago, as well as a more recent book on the subject, James Gardner identified issues with independent state constitutional interpretation that persist. He argues that state courts, for example, "often appropriate and adopt federal constitutional doctrine as the rule of decision for state constitutional provisions not only when the state constitutional text is identical to its federal counterpart, but even when it differs in potentially significant ways."

Id. at 783–84 (internal footnotes omitted).

3. If state court interpretations of their own state constitutions have not resulted in greater protections than are found in the federal constitution, is one of the reasons the state's lack of an adoption of clear state constitutional doctrinal standards independent of federal constitutional standards? Consider the following from James A. Gardner, *The Failed Discourse of State Constitutionalism*, 90 MICH. L. REV. 761 (1992).

When you undertake [state constitutional law] research, here is what you are likely to find. After reading dozens of state constitutional decisions, you have absolutely no sense of the history of the state constitution. You do not know the identity of the founders, their purposes in creating the constitution, or the specific events that may have shaped their thinking. You find nothing in the decisions indicating how the various provisions of the document fit together into a coherent whole. . . . You are able to form no conception of the character or fundamental values of the people of the state, and no idea how to mount an argument that certain things are more important to the people than others. . . . [N]othing in these state opinions gives you any idea of what you, as an advocate, could say to convince the state courts once again to reject the federal approach as a matter of state constitutional law.

This story illustrates what I call the poverty of state constitutional discourse, by which I mean the lack of a language in which participants in the legal system can debate the meaning of the state constitution. Further, to the extent that such a state constitutional discourse exists, its terms and conventions are often borrowed wholesale from federal constitutional discourse, as though the language of federal constitutional law were some sort of *lingua franca* of constitutional argument generally.

Id. at 764–66 (footnotes omitted). Granted, James Garner's description of "the poverty of state constitutional discourse" appearing above was written in 1992. Much has changed in the world since the early 1990s. But has much changed in constitutional discourse? *See* James Gardner, Interpreting State Constitutions: A Jurisprudence of Function in a Federal System (University of Chicago Press 2005) (levying many of the same criticisms in 2005 that he made in 1992).

K. Enforcement of Florida Constitutional Rights via the Florida Civil Rights Act

In a proper case, one means of enforcement of Florida constitutional rights may be via the Florida Civil Rights Act. Discrimination based on race, sex, religion, national ancestry, age, marital status, and HIV status is illegal in Florida under the Florida Civil Rights Act of 1992, which is codified at Fla. Stat. §§ 760.01 through 760.11.

The general purpose of the Florida Civil Rights Act is to secure for all individuals within the state of Florida freedom from discrimination because of race, color, religion, sex, national origin, age, handicap, or marital status. To that end, the Florida Civil Rights Act provides a cause of action for a person who suffers discrimination from an employer. As defined in the Florida Civil Rights Act, "person" includes "an individual, association, corporation, joint apprenticeship committee, joint-stock company, labor union, legal representative, mutual company, partnership, receiver, trust, trustee in bankruptcy, or unincorporated organization; any other legal or commercial entity; the state; or any governmental entity or agency." Under the Florida Civil Rights Act, "employer" means "any person employing 15 or more employees for each working day in each of 20 or more calendar weeks in the current or preceding calendar year, and any agent of such a person."

In addition to race, sex, religion, and national ancestry, the Florida Civil Rights Act protects Floridians from employment discrimination based upon a physical disability. As Florida's Fifth District Court of Appeal stated in *Smith v. Avatar Properties*, 714 So. 2d 1103 (Fla. 5th DCA 1998):

> We note that our legislature still uses the term 'handicap.' Many people with disabilities, however, prefer the term 'disabled' as they view the term 'handicap' as having a derogatory connotation, since literally translated it means 'hand in cap,' implying the need for handouts or charity. Dolatly, *The Future of the Reasonable Accommodation Duty in Employment Practices*, 26 Colum. J.L. & Soc. Prob. 523, n.7 (1993). In recognition of this preference, at least six states have amended their respective statutes to substitute the term 'disability' for 'handicap.'

The Florida Civil Rights Act protects against discriminatory job termination as well as all other forms of on-the-job discrimination that do not involve the termination of the employment. The necessary minimum elements for any such cause of action under the Florida Civil Rights Act are:

(1) The employee is a member of a protected class or has a "disability";

AND

(2) is a "qualified" individual;

AND

(3) was discriminated against because of being a member of the protected class or because of the disability.

Patrick John McGinley, FLORIDA ELEMENTS OF AN ACTION. § 903:1 (2017-2018 ed.). These three elements are interpreted in conformity with Title VII of the federal Civil Rights Act of 1964, 42 U.S.C. §§ 2000e et seq., in conformity with the federal Americans with Disabilities Act, 42 U.S.C. §§ 12101 et seq., (ADA) and in conformity with the federal Rehabilitation Act, 29 U.S.C. §§ 701 et seq.

The Florida Civil Rights Act applies to all Florida employers who have 15 or more employees. Assuming the Florida Civil Rights act applies, the potential plaintiff must meet its presuit requirement of filing a Charge of Discrimination with the Florida Commission on Human Relations (FCHR), which is the state law equivalent of the federal Equal Employment Opportunity Commission (EEOC). One permissible alternative to filing with FCHR is filing with the EEOC, or dual-filing with both agencies. In counties where Florida law permits the creation of a fair-employment-practice agency under 29 C.F.R. sections 1601.70 to 1601.80, this agency becomes another permissible alternative to filing with FCHR.

However, filing directly with a court of law before filing with FCHR or an alternative agency is not a permissible option. This is because the potential plaintiff must exhaust all administrative remedies available to those who file a Charge of Discrimination before the potential plaintiff has the right to sue.

A lawsuit cannot be filed unless the potential plaintiff satisfies all statutory time limits and deadlines. The deadline to file a Charge of Discrimination with the FCHR is within 365 days of the last violation. The deadline for filing with the EEOC is within 300 days. If FCHR's "Notice of Determination" finds "no reasonable cause," then the deadline to request an agency hearing is within 35 days. If instead the agency issues a "Right to Sue Letter," then the plaintiff must file a complaint in state Circuit Court within 1 year of FCHR's letter or within 90 days if either "dual filed" with EEOC or the Right to Sue Letter was issued by the EEOC instead of the FCHR. Overall, a four-year statute of limitations applies to filing suit under Fla. Stat. chap. 760, with the four-year deadline commencing upon the day of the last violation. Therefore, the four-year Statute of Limitation's clock is ticking throughout the administrative process.

When a suit is filed, the civil suit allegations are limited to those raised in the Charge of Discrimination and for which all administrative remedies were exhausted. The Charge of Discrimination is admissible into evidence only to prove the plaintiff's compliance with its requirements, and neither it nor any other agency finding is admissible to prove the guilt of the employer. In the lawsuit, the plaintiff bears the burden to prove a prima facie case of discrimination by direct or indirect ("circumstantial") evidence. If the plaintiff meets this burden, then the burden shifts temporarily to the defendant to show a legitimate, non-discriminatory reason for the act that the plaintiff alleged was discriminatory. If the defendant meets that burden, then the burden of proof shifts back to the plaintiff to prove that the reason given by the defendant was pretextual. Any party may request a trial by jury.

Damages available for a violation of the Florida Civil Right Act include the following. The court may issue an order prohibiting the discriminatory practice and providing affirmative relief from the effects of the practice, including back pay. The court may also award compensatory damages, including, but not limited to, damages for mental anguish, loss of dignity, and any other intangible injuries, and punitive damages. The punitive damages may not exceed $100,000.

If the court finds a party to be a prevailing party, it may recover its taxable costs. The court, in its discretion, may allow the prevailing party a reasonable attorney's fee as part of the costs, but Florida law states "[i]t is the intent of the Legislature that this provision for attorney's fees be interpreted in a manner consistent with federal case law involving a Title VII action." *See* Florida Statutes section 760.11(5). The result, therefore, is just like under 28 U.S.C. § 1988 where the court awards reasonable attorney fees to a prevailing plaintiff unless the defendant overcomes a strong presumption of entitlement, but a prevailing defendant wins fees only if the defendant proves that the plaintiff's claim was frivolous.

———————

Notes and Questions to Consider:

1. Noting that the Florida Civil Rights Act is to be interpreted in conformity with the federal Civil Rights Act, of what value is the Florida act?

2. Imagine you are a Florida attorney representing Mr. Ben Wronged. He was fired by Bullseye, a privately owned supermarket in Orlando, Florida. He believes he was fired because of his race. In light of the Florida Civil Rights Act, how would you answer these questions asked by Mr. Wronged?

   (a) What lawsuit, writ, claim, or administrative action can you file for me?

   (b) What is the full, proper name of the specific court, tribunal, entity, or agency where we should file my case?

   (c) What are the legal issues and things we will need to prove in my case, or stated somewhat differently, what are the elements of the action we are filing?

3. Perhaps nothing in law is more cherished, nor more protected, than our constitutional rights. Does that mean that the victim whose constitutional rights were violated is entitled to free legal services? What about a victim who cannot afford a lawyer? The criminally accused get a free public defender, so do constitutional law victims get one, too?

L. Enumerated Rights

In addition to those rights mentioned above, Florida's constitution enumerates other rights in its Declaration of Rights. Those involving criminal justice are discussed in Chapter 16 of this text. The right of access to public records and meetings, which is part of Florida's Sunshine Laws, is discussed in Chapter 14 of this text. The right of privacy, and the right of due process of law, are discussed in Chapters 5 and 6, respectively. The Taxpayers Bill of Rights is covered in Chapter 15.

Other enumerated rights from Florida's Declaration of Rights, Article I of Florida's constitution, include:

SECTION 7. Military power.—The military power shall be subordinate to the civil.

SECTION 18. Administrative penalties.—No administrative agency, except the Department of Military Affairs in an appropriately convened court-martial action as provided by law, shall impose a sentence of imprisonment, nor shall it impose any other penalty except as provided by law.

SECTION 20. Treason.—Treason against the state shall consist only in levying war against it, adhering to its enemies, or giving them aid and comfort, and no person shall be convicted of treason except on the testimony of two witnesses to the same overt act or on confession in open court.

SECTION 26. Claimant's right to fair compensation.—

(a) Article I, Section 26 is created to read "Claimant's right to fair compensation." In any medical liability claim involving a contingency fee, the claimant is entitled to receive no less than 70% of the first $250,000.00 in all damages received by the claimant, exclusive of reasonable and customary costs, whether received by judgment, settlement, or otherwise, and regardless of the number of defendants. The claimant is entitled to 90% of all damages in excess of $250,000.00, exclusive of reasonable and customary costs and regardless of the number of defendants. This provision is self-executing and does not require implementing legislation.

(b) This Amendment shall take effect on the day following approval by the voters.

————

Note and Question to Consider:

1. Is a claimant's right to fair compensation something a claimant's lawyer can allow a claimant to waive? Florida's supreme court enacted a form as part of the Florida Rules of Civil Procedure for Florida attorneys to use when a client wishes to waive his or her right to fair compensation under Article I, Section 26 of Florida's constitution.

Chapter 5

Due Process of Law and Access to Courts

A. Rights in the Florida Constitution That May Not Parallel or May Exceed the Rights Appearing in the U.S. Constitution

The rights mentioned in the previous chapters of this book appear in Florida's constitution and have a counterpart in the text of the U.S. Constitution. But Florida's constitution also contains rights for its citizens that either do not appear in the text of the U.S. Constitution or that expand upon those rights.

With this as our background, we analyze the following representative examples of rights enumerated under the Constitution of the State of Florida that do not have an exact parallel to the rights enumerated in the U.S. Constitution. These examples highlight how a right that is similar to that in the federal Constitution may be interpreted differently in a state constitution.

B. Applying Due Process of Law to Conclusive Presumptions (or "Irrebuttable" Presumptions)

Like the federal Constitution, the Constitution of the State of Florida provides for both substantive due process and procedural due process. "The Florida case law in these areas is generally similar to that developed by the federal courts in interpreting similar language of the U.S. Constitution." Talbot D'Alemberte, THE FLORIDA STATE CONSTITUTION 32 (Oxford University Press 2011). This excerpt from the 1991 decision of the Supreme Court of the State of Florida in *Department of Law Enforcement v. Real Property*, 588 So. 2d 957 (Fla. 1991) reminds us of what we learned in our studies of the U.S. Constitution:

The Due Process Requirement

The basic due process guarantee of the Florida Constitution provides that: "[n]o person shall be deprived of life, liberty or property without due process of law." Article I, section 9, Florida Constitution. Substantive due process under the Florida Constitution protects the full panoply of individual rights from unwarranted encroachment by the government. To ascertain whether the encroachment can be justified, courts have considered the propriety of the state's purpose, the nature of the party being subjected to state action, the substance of that individual's right being infringed upon, the nexus between the means chosen by the state and the goal it intended to achieve, whether less restrictive alternatives were available, and whether individuals are ultimately being treated in a fundamentally unfair manner in derogation of their substitute rights. . . .

Procedural due process serves as a vehicle to ensure fair treatment through the proper administration of justice where substantive rights are at issue. Procedural due process under the Florida Constitution:

> guarantees to every citizen the right to have that course of legal procedure which has been established in our judicial system for the protection and enforcement of private rights. It contemplates that the defendant shall be given fair notice . . . and afforded a real opportunity to be heard . . . before judgment is rendered against him.

> While the doctrines of substantive and procedural due process play distinct roles in the judicial process, they frequently overlap. Hence, many cases do not expressly state the distinction between procedural and substitute of due process.

Id. at 980; *see* also John F. Cooper, Tichia A. Dunham & Carlos L. Woody, FLORIDA CONSTITUTIONAL LAW: CASES AND MATERIALS (5th ed. Carolina Academic Press 2013)(citing this precedent).

So, as summarized above, substantive due process and procedural due process as provided by the Florida Constitution are the same rights as provided by the U.S. Constitution.

But with that truth having been acknowledged, perhaps the argument could be made that the right of due process of law under the Florida Constitution slightly exceeds that granted by the U.S. Constitution at least insofar as Florida constitutional jurisprudence makes much ado about rejecting as unconstitutional any civil law of the Florida Legislature that establishes a factual presumption that may not be rebutted by contrary factual evidence. "An irrebuttable presumption removes an element that must be proved once the State has proved the predicate fact or facts giving rise to the presumption. The fact finder, however, is not free to reject the presumption. Thus, once it is presented, the defendant may not attempt to rebut the connection between the proven and the presumed facts." *Ibarrondo v. State*, 1 So. 3d 226, 233 (Fla. 5th DCA 2008).

It is important to understand the difference between a presumption and an inference. As former Chief Judge and current Judge of Florida's Fifth District Court of Appeal, Thomas D. Sawaya explains:

> An inference is a deduction of fact that the factfinder may logically draw from another group of facts that are found to exist from the evidence or are

otherwise established in the proceedings. The most important difference between a presumption and an inference relates to how each is considered by the jury. When the basic fact giving rise to a presumption is established and there is no evidence to contradict the presumption, the presumed fact must be found to exist by the jury. When an inference is established, the jury may, in its discretion, completely disregard it even though there is no evidence to contradict or rebut it. Thus an inference is always permissive while a presumption is mandatory.

Thomas D. Sawaya, FLORIDA PERSONAL INJURY LAW AND PRACTICE § 24:7 (Thomson Reuters 2019-2020 ed.).

Once a statute is properly identified as a presumption, it may be tested as to whether it is unconstitutional under the Florida Constitution. "The test for the constitutionality of statutory presumptions is twofold. First, there must be a rational connection between the fact proved and the ultimate fact presumed. . . . Second, there must be a right to rebut in a fair manner." *Straughn v. K & K Land Management, Inc.*, 326 So. 2d 421, 424 (Fla. 1976).

When the second element is not met, then Florida case law refers to that presumption as either a "conclusive presumption" or an "irrebuttable presumption." Such a presumption is invalid as violating the right to due process of law as enshrined in the Constitution of the State of Florida, even when that presumption applies solely to civil actions.

"Presumptions in criminal proceedings are treated much differently than in civil proceedings primarily because of the constitutional guarantees that are afforded an individual accused of a crime that do not apply to litigants in civil proceedings." Thomas D. Sawaya, FLORIDA PERSONAL INJURY LAW AND PRACTICE § 24:7 (2019-2020 ed.). Perhaps for this reason, conclusive or irrebuttable presumptions in **criminal** law statutes routinely are found to violate the federal Constitution. *See Tot v. United States*, 319 U.S. 463, 466 (1943); *United States v. Gainey*, 380 U.S. 63, 66 (1965). On rare occasions, conclusive or irrebuttable presumptions in **civil** law statutes can be found to violate the federal Constitution. *See Lindsley v. Natural Carbonic Gas Co.*, 220 U.S. 61 (1911); *Mobile, Jackson & Kansas City R. Co. v. Turnipseed*, 219 U.S. 35 (1910).

Where Florida constitutional law jurisprudence arguably expands upon that federal constitutional right is in *always* finding conclusive or irrebuttable presumptions in *civil* law statutes to violate the due process rights enshrined in the Florida Constitution. As explained by Professor Charles W. Ehrhardt:

> Frequently judges and lawyers refer to a presumption as a conclusive or irrebuttable presumption. If facts X and Y are proven, fact A must be found to be true. Most of these so-called conclusive presumptions are not true presumptions but are rules of law. . . .
>
> The [Florida Evidence] Code does not make any provision for conclusive presumptions since most are not valid in Florida. Although some rules of law are called conclusive presumptions from time to time, they are not

properly included in a codification of the law of evidence since they are rules of substantive law in the particular area in which they exist.

Charles W. Ehrhardt, EHRHARDT'S FLORIDA EVIDENCE § 301.3 (Thomson Reuters 2019 ed.).

Regarding case law precedent striking civil law statutory presumptions as violating the Florida Constitution's due process clause, examples exist in the decisions of the Supreme Court of the State of Florida. *See, e.g., Straughn v. K & K Land Management, Inc.*, 326 So. 2d 421 (Fla. 1976); *Bass v. General Development Corp.*, 374 So. 2d 479 (Fla. 1979). For our purposes, we turn first to this 1996 decision of the First District Court of Appeal of Florida in *Hall v. Recchi America, Inc.*, 671 So. 2d 197 (Fla. 1st DCA 1996), aff'd, 692 So. 2d 153 (Fla. 1997).

Hall v. Recchi America Inc.

First District Court of Appeal of Florida, 1996
671 So. 2d 197

Davis, Judge.

Appellant, Astley Hall, appeals an order of the judge of compensation claims (JCC) denying his workers' compensation claim solely on the basis that he had a positive drug test shortly after his accident at the employer's drug-free workplace. The JCC based the denial of benefits upon the conclusive presumption of section 440.09(3), Florida Statutes (1991), that an injury in a drug-free workplace to an employee who has positive confirmation of a drug shall be presumed to have been occasioned primarily by the intoxication of the employee. The JCC did not find, however, that marijuana ingestion by appellant primarily caused the injury. Because section 440.09(3), Florida Statutes (1991), establishes an irrebuttable or conclusive presumption which violates the constitutional right to due process, we reverse. . . .

On the morning of Thursday, June 13, 1991, three weeks after commencing work, the claimant and a co-worker were doing concrete form work. . . . [T]he claimant's co-worker tripped over a steel form work and jabbed the screed into the back of the claimant's head. . . . After his supervisor appeared on the scene, the claimant was taken to the Workers' Compensation Medical Center. The claimant provided a urine sample for drug testing within 30 minutes of arriving at the Workers' Compensation Medical Center. . . . The test result was two percent above the 100 nanogram per milliliter positive cut-off for marijuana metabolites. A confirmatory gas chromatography/mass spectrography analysis showed [this first test result was accurate]. . . . The claimant admitted he had smoked marijuana five days earlier. . . . Dr. Jay Poupko, who holds a Ph.D. in pharmacology and is a member of the University of Miami School of Medicine, . . . testified that the 78 nanograms per milliliter of inactive metabolite found in the claimant's urine was entirely consistent with the claimant having smoked marijuana five days before the accident as the claimant claimed. He explained that a person who smokes marijuana remains impaired for only four to six hours after ingestion of the drug. Based upon Dr. Poupko's testimony, the JCC found it probable that the claimant was not, at the time of the injury, impaired from marijuana ingestion.

In denying all benefits, the JCC concluded, "the Legislature intended to deny workers' compensation benefits to any employee who chooses to engage in drug use where their employer has implemented a drug-free workplace." In this appeal, the claimant maintains that the workers' compensation drug-free workplace statutes facially violate the Federal and Florida Constitutions by encouraging indiscriminate, suspicionless searches. He further argues that the irrebuttable presumption of causation provided in section 440.09(3), which results in forfeiture of workers' compensation benefits, violates due process and equal protection.

We hold that section 440.09(3), Florida Statutes (1991), establishes an irrebuttable or conclusive presumption which violates the constitutional right to due process. Section 440.09(3), provides, in pertinent part:

> No compensation shall be payable if the injury was occasioned primarily by the intoxication of the employee.... If there was at the time of the injury 0.10 percent or more by weight of alcohol in the employee's blood, or if the employee has a positive confirmation of a drug as defined in this act, it shall be presumed that the injury was occasioned primarily by the intoxication of, or by the influence of the drug upon, the employee. In the absence of a drug-free workplace program, this presumption may be rebutted by clear and convincing evidence that the intoxication or influence of the drug did not contribute to the injury....

Under the plain language of this statute, the presumption that the injury was occasioned primarily by the intoxication or influence of drugs is rebuttable when there is no drug-free workplace program in place, and is irrebuttable when such a program has been properly instituted. A presumption is conclusive if a party is not given a reasonable opportunity to disprove either the predicate fact or the ultimate fact presumed. *City of Coral Gables v. Brasher*, 120 So. 2d 5, 9 (Fla. 1960); *Chandler v. Department of Health & Rehabilitative Servs.*, 593 So. 2d 1183 (Fla. 1st DCA 1992). In this instance it is the ultimate fact, that the injury was primarily occasioned by intoxication or the influence of drugs, that the claimant is being foreclosed from disproving.

The constitutionality of a conclusive presumption under the due process clause is measured by determining (1) whether the concern of the legislature was reasonably aroused by the possibility of an abuse which it legitimately desired to avoid; (2) whether there was a reasonable basis for a conclusion that the statute would protect against its occurrence; and (3) whether the expense and other difficulties of individual determinations justify the inherent imprecision of a conclusive presumption. *Markham v. Fogg*, 458 So. 2d 1122, 1125 (Fla. 1984); *Bass v. General Dev. Corp.*, 374 So. 2d 479, 484 (Fla. 1979).

As to the first prong of the due process test, the concern of the legislature regarding drug use in the workplace is reasonable. Section 440.101, Florida Statutes (1991), provides that "[i]t is the intent of the Legislature to promote drug-free workplaces in order that employers in the state be afforded the opportunity to maximize their levels of productivity, enhance their competitive positions in the marketplace, and reach their desired levels of success without experiencing the costs, delays, and tragedies associated with work-related accidents resulting from drug abuse by employees." As to the second prong of the due process test, there is a reasonable basis to conclude that the statute would deter drug use in the workplace. Section 440.101 provides that it is "the intent of the Legislature that drug abuse be discouraged and that employees who choose to engage in drug abuse face the risk of unemployment and the forfeiture of workers' compensation benefits."

The conclusive presumption contained in section 440.09(3) fails, however, to satisfy the third prong of the due process test. Because of the high potential for inaccuracy of the conclusive presumption set forth in section 440.09(3), and the feasibility of individualized determinations, fact finding on an individualized basis must be required to afford the employee due process. The conclusive presumption that "it shall be presumed that the injury was occasioned primarily by the intoxication of, or by the influence of the drug upon, the employee" if the employee has a positive confirmation of a drug as defined in section 440.102, may be erroneous. A positive confirmation of a drug at the time of the industrial injury does not conclusively establish that the industrial accident was causally related to the intoxication of, or the influence of the drug upon, the employee. The lack of a causal relationship between a positive drug test and the industrial accident is readily apparent in the present case because the uncontradicted testimony established that the industrial accident was not the fault of the claimant, but rather resulted from a co-worker tripping and jabbing him in the back of the head with a screed that he and the co-worker were carrying.

Additionally, the imprecision of the presumption of intoxication or influence of a drug upon the employee when urine testing is employed was established in the present case through the testimony of Dr. Poupko, a pharmacologist. Dr. Poupko testified that urine testing is inherently incapable of determining whether the active drug was present in an individual at the precise time of the injury. Rather, urine testing measures drug metabolites, which implies nothing about the presence of the active drug in the blood at the relevant time. In the case of marijuana, the drug used by the claimant, Dr. Poupko testified that urine testing measures an inactive metabolite, which has no effect on the nervous system. Dr. Poupko testified that the concentration of inactive metabolite found in the claimant's urine was entirely consistent with his having smoked marijuana five days before the industrial accident, as contended by the claimant. Dr. Poupko explained that an individual who smokes marijuana remains impaired for only four to six hours following ingestion of the marijuana. The JCC relied upon Dr. Poupko's testimony in concluding that it was probable that the claimant was *not* impaired from the ingestion of marijuana at the time of the industrial accident. Nevertheless, because section 440.09(3) creates an irrebuttable presumption that the industrial injury was occasioned primarily by the intoxication of, or by the influence of the drug upon, the employee when the employee has a positive confirmation of a drug as defined in section 440.102, the JCC concluded that the claimant's claim was not compensable. These findings and conclusions clearly support our conclusion that the presumption contained in section 440.09(3) must be rebuttable to survive due process analysis.

Because section 440.09(3) fails to allow rebuttal of the presumption that the industrial accident was causally related to the intoxication or influence of a drug upon the employee if the employer has a drug-free workplace program in effect, the conclusive presumption set forth in section 440.09(3) results in a denial of due process. The unconstitutionality of that one presumption, however, does not render all of the workers' compensation drug-free workplace provisions defective. In determining whether parts of a statute are severable from the remainder of the law, the court must look to the relationship between the unconstitutional provisions and the overall legislative intent. The court must then evaluate whether the remaining provisions of the statute continue to accomplish that intent. *See Eastern Air Lines, Inc. v. Department of Revenue*, 455 So. 2d 311, 317 (Fla. 1984), *appeal dismissed mem.*, 474 U.S. 892 (1985). The workers' compensation drug-free workplace statutes are designed to accomplish twin goals: discouraging drug abuse and maximizing industrial productivity by eliminating "the costs, delays, and tragedies associated with work-related accidents resulting from drug abuse by employees." § 440.101, Fla. Stat. (1991). The remaining provisions of this statute will serve those goals even if the irrebuttable presumption is excised. For example, an employer instituting a drug-free workplace must provide education and notice which should discourage drug abuse. It is also clear that requiring a causal nexus between the drug abuse and the work-related accident will do nothing to detract from the legislative goal of eliminating such accidents attributable to such cause. We therefore hold that section 440.09(3) is severable from the remainder of the law.

Accordingly, the order of the JCC is reversed and remanded for further proceedings using the constitutionally legitimate rebuttable presumption.

Kahn, Judge, concurring.

I agree completely with the analysis and conclusion reached by Judge Davis. I would also note that the result in this case is completely consistent with my understanding of Florida's workers' compensation system.

A basic premise of workers' compensation law in Florida, as in other places, has always been to release society of the expenses of injuries caused by industry in favor of a program under which industry would bear such costs. *Whitehead v. Keene Roofing Co.*, 43 So. 2d 464 (Fla. 1949). The purpose of our [Florida Workers' Compensation] Act is "to provide for employers a liability that is limited and determinative, and to employees a remedy that is both expeditious and independent of proof of fault." *Florida Erection Services, Inc. v. McDonald*, 395 So. 2d 203, 209 (Fla. 1st DCA 1981). The legislation now at hand abrogates these long-accepted understandings, at least in a class of cases, including Mr. Hall's. Despite the apparent fact that

Hall's injury was caused completely by risks normally attendant to the construction industry, he would be left without any remedy under the Workers' Compensation Act. Thus, the limited statutory provision we invalidate today was itself at odds with a central premise of compensation law. Moreover, it directly contravenes the intent of our legislature recently set out in the 1993 revisions to the workers' compensation law: "[W]orkers' compensation cases shall be decided on their merits." § 440.015, Florida Statutes (1994 Supp.).

Notes and Questions to Consider:

1. It appears the Florida Legislature may have pursued two permissible goals with the legislation at issue in *Hall v. Recchi America*: to provide an expeditious remedy for those injured at work, and to discourage drug use at the workplace. So why was the statutory presumption arising from a positive drug test a violation of the Constitution of the State of Florida?

2. What was the remedy for this violation of state constitutional law? When else would that remedy apply?

3. Did the court apply procedural due process, or substantive due process, in striking down the presumption at issue in *Hall v. Recchi America*? Does it matter?

4. How could the statute at issue have advanced the goal of a drug free workplace, and created consequences for a positive drug test showing controlled substances, without running afoul of the constitutional prohibition against conclusive or "irrebuttable" presumptions?

5. How persuasive is Judge Kahn's concurring opinion? To what extent does Judge Kahn do a better job of applying the canons of construction in reaching his interpretation of the statute?

The issue of conclusive or "irrebuttable" presumptions as addressed in *Hall v. Recchi America* was also one of the topics of the Florida's supreme court holding in *Castellanos v. Next Door Co.*, 192 So. 3d 431 (Fla. 2016) where the court struck down a mandatory fee schedule in a fee-shifting statute.

Castellanos v. Next Door Co.

Supreme Court of Florida, 2016
192 So. 3d 431

Justice Pariente wrote the opinion for the court.

This case asks us to evaluate the constitutionality of the mandatory fee schedule in section 440.34, Florida Statutes (2009), which eliminates the requirement of a reasonable attorney's fee to the successful claimant.... [W]e conclude that the mandatory fee schedule in section 440.34, which creates an irrebuttable presumption that precludes any consideration of whether the fee award is reasonable to compensate the attorney, is unconstitutional under both the Florida and United States Constitutions as a violation of due process. *See* art. I, §9, Fla. Const.; U.S. Const. amend. XIV, §1.1 . . . .

The Petitioner, Marvin Castellanos, was injured during the course of his employment with the Respondent, Next Door Company. Through the assistance of an attorney, Castellanos prevailed in his workers' compensation claim, after the attorney successfully refuted numerous defenses raised by the employer and its insurance carrier. However, because section 440.34 limits a claimant's ability to recover attorney's fees to a sliding scale based on the amount of workers' compensation benefits obtained, the fee awarded to Castellanos' attorney amounted to only $1.53 per hour for 107.2 hours of work determined by the Judge of Compensation Claims (JCC) to be "reasonable and necessary" in litigating this complex case.

Castellanos had no ability to challenge the reasonableness of the $1.53 hourly rate, and both the JCC and the First District were precluded by section 440.34 from assessing whether the fee award—calculated in strict compliance with the statutory fee schedule—was reasonable. Instead, the statute presumes that the ultimate fee will always be reasonable to compensate the attorney, without providing any mechanism for refutation. . . .

We reject the assertion of Justice Polston's dissenting opinion that our holding "turns this Court's well-established precedent regarding facial challenges on its head." Dissenting op. at 53 (Polston, J.). It is immaterial to our holding whether, as Justice Polston points out, the statutory fee schedule could, in some cases, result in a constitutionally adequate fee. It certainly could.

But the facial constitutional due process issue, based on our well-established precedent regarding conclusive irrebuttable presumptions, is that the statute precludes *every* injured worker from challenging the reasonableness of the fee award. *See Recchi Am. Inc. v. Hall*, 692 So. 2d 153, 154 (Fla. 1997) (clarifying that its holding "invalidates the irrebuttable presumption altogether," including as applied to certain situations). It is the irrebuttable statutory presumption—not the ultimate statutory fee awarded in a given case—that we hold unconstitutional.

The contrary approach embraced by Justice Polston's dissenting opinion, which leaves open the possibility of an as applied challenge to the statute on a case-by-case basis, would be both unworkable and without any standards for determining when the fee schedule produces a constitutionally inadequate fee. Simply put, the statute is not susceptible to an as applied challenge, but instead fits into our precedent governing the constitutionality of irrebuttable presumptions, which is a distinct body of case law that differs from the typical "facial" versus "as applied" cases cited by Justice Polston's dissent. . . .

The statute prevents every injured worker from challenging the reasonableness of the fee award in his or her individual case. . . . Accordingly, we answer the rephrased certified question in the affirmative, quash the First District's decision upholding the patently unreasonable $1.53 hourly fee award, and direct that this case be remanded to the JCC for entry of a reasonable attorney's fee.

I. Facts and Procedural History

... Castellanos was diagnosed with multiple contusions to his head, neck, and right shoulder. ... Next Door, as the employer, and Amerisure, as Next Door's insurance carrier (collectively, the "E/C"), failed to authorize its own doctor's recommendations, and Castellanos subsequently filed a petition for benefits, seeking a compensability determination for temporary total or partial disability benefits, along with costs and attorney's fees. The E/C filed a response to the petition, denying the claim based on sections 440.09(4) (intentional acts) and 440.105(4)(b)9 (fraud), Florida Statutes (2009), ultimately asserting that Castellanos was responsible for his own injuries.

The parties subsequently filed a stipulation, in which the E/C raised twelve defenses. A final hearing was then held before the JCC, in which numerous depositions, exhibits, and live testimony were submitted for consideration.

In its Final Compensation Order, the JCC determined that Castellanos was entitled to be compensated by the E/C for his injuries and was therefore entitled to recover attorney's fees and costs from the E/C. The JCC explicitly found that Castellanos' attorney was successful in securing compensability and defeating all of the E/C's defenses, and retained jurisdiction to determine the amount of the attorney's fee award.

Based on the JCC's finding of compensability, Castellanos filed a motion for attorney's fees, seeking an hourly fee of $350 for the services of his attorney. Section 440.34, however, strictly constrains an award of attorney's fees to the claimant's attorney, requiring the fee to be calculated in conformance with the amount of benefits obtained.

Specifically, subsection (3) of section 440.34 was amended in 2009 to remove the longstanding requirement that the fee be "reasonable" and instead to provide, except for disputed medical-only claims, that the fee equal the amount provided for in subsection (1), which sets forth the following sliding scale fee schedule:

> ... 20 percent of the first $5,000 of the amount of the benefits secured, 15 percent of the next $5,000 of the amount of the benefits secured, 10 percent of the remaining amount of the benefits secured to be provided during the first 10 years after the date the claim is filed, and 5 percent of the benefits secured after 10 years.

§ 440.34(1), Fla. Stat. (emphasis added). Application of the fee schedule in this case resulted in a statutory fee of $1.53 per hour.

In support of his motion for attorney's fees, which argued that an award limited to the statutory fee would be unreasonable and manifestly unjust, Castellanos presented expert testimony from attorneys James Fee and Brian Sutter. Fee testified that there is "no way on this planet" that Castellanos could have prevailed in obtaining benefits "without the skilled and tenacious representation" of an attorney, based on "the onslaught of defenses that were asserted." He agreed that the 107.2 hours claimed by Castellanos' attorney were reasonable and necessary and an "exceedingly efficient use of time" given that "this was a very difficult case."

Sutter testified that it is "absolutely illusory to think" that a claimant could present his case without counsel "because of all the dangers and pitfalls" of the workers' compensation law. He further stated that fees under $2.00 an hour, such as the statutory fee in this case, are "absurd" and "manifestly unjust," and "would provide an extreme chilling effect" that would "prevent any attorney from handling a similar case in the future."

[A]n expert witness on behalf of the E/C . . . [was] asked what percentage of workers' compensation cases showed claimants to be successful in prosecuting their claims without an attorney, [and] responded that, although he regularly reviewed JCC orders, "I can't say that I've seen one that's been entirely successful," and, "as far as litigating a complicated case throughout, I honestly haven't seen it." He agreed that a statutory fee as low as the one in this case was "an unreasonably low hourly rate" and "an absurd result."

After hearing the testimony and considering the evidence and the law, the JCC issued an order awarding fees, finding that Castellanos "ultimately prevailed in obtaining a finding of compensability, a necessary precursor to obtaining benefits." According to the JCC, in order to obtain this result, Castellanos "had to overcome between 13 and 16 different defenses raised by the E/C throughout the course of litigation." The JCC further found that it was "highly unlikely that [Castellanos] could have succeeded and obtained the favorable result he did without the assistance of capable counsel."

Constrained to the statutory fee schedule, however, the JCC found that Castellanos was limited to an attorney's fee of $164.54, based on the application of the conclusive fee schedule to the actual value of benefits secured of $822.70. Nevertheless, in its order, the JCC "fully accept[ed] the notion that 'Lawyers can't work for $1.30 an hour,'" and stated that Castellanos' attorney "is an exceptionally skilled, highly respected practitioner who has been awarded as much as $350 to $400 an hour for his success in workers' compensation cases." The JCC, in addition, found that "[t]here is no question . . . that the 107.2 hours expended by his firm . . . were reasonable and necessary," and that these hours constituted an "exceedingly efficient use of time," which was "wholly consistent with the 115.20 defense hours documented" by counsel for the E/C.

But as an executive branch official, the JCC had no authority to address Castellanos' claim that section 440.34, and the resulting $1.53 hourly fee, was unconstitutional. *See Ariston v. Allied Bldg. Crafts*, 825 So. 2d 435, 438 (Fla. 1st DCA 2002) ("A JCC clearly does not have jurisdiction to declare a state statute unconstitutional or violative of federal law."). Castellanos thus appealed the JCC's order to the First District, raising the constitutional claim.

The First District affirmed the JCC's decision to award "only $164.54 for 107.2 hours of legal work reasonably necessary to secure the claimant's workers' compensation benefits," holding that "the statute required this result" and that the court was "bound by precedent to uphold the award, however inadequate it may be as a practical matter." . . .

II. Analysis

Our review of the constitutionality of section 440.34 is de novo. *See Graham v. Haridopolos*, 108 So. 3d 597, 603 (Fla. 2013). We begin our analysis by tracing the history of awarding attorney's fees to the claimant under our state's workers' compensation law. . . . Then, we consider whether the statute, as amended in 2009, creates an unconstitutional, irrebuttable presumption in violation of due process of law. Finally, concluding that the statute is unconstitutional, we address the remedy.

A. The History of Awarding Attorney's Fees to the Claimant under Florida's Workers' Compensation Law

In 1935, the Legislature adopted the workers' compensation law to provide "simple, expeditious" relief to the injured worker. *Lee Eng'g & Constr. Co. v. Fellows*, 209 So. 2d 454, 456 (Fla. 1968). As an integral part of that goal from 1941 until 2009, the Legislature provided for an award of a reasonable attorney's fee to an injured worker who was successful in obtaining workers' compensation benefits. . . .

This Court has long recognized the factors to be considered in determining the reasonableness of an attorney's fee award under the statute. . . . [T]his Court concluded that Canon 12 of the Canons of Professional Ethics, the predecessor to rule 4–1.5 of the *Rules Regulating The Florida Bar*—the ethical rule governing attorneys' fees—was a "safe guide in fixing the amount of [E/C-paid] fees" awarded to the claimant. . . . In addition to the minimum schedule, this Court explained that "it appears to us that supplemental evidence should be presented." *Id.* This Court specifically noted the principle that, "especially in this type of matter [,] fees should be carefully considered so that on the one hand they will not be so low as to lack attraction for capable and experienced lawyers to represent workmen's compensation claimants" while, "[o]n the other hand, they should not be so high as to reflect adversely on the profession or in actuality to enter disproportionately into the cost of maintaining the workmen's compensation program." *Id.* at 4.

Then, in *Lee Engineering*, this Court rejected the strict application of a contingent percentage of the benefit award based on a schedule of minimum fees, holding that a "schedule of fees . . . was helpful but unreliable". . . . "Thus, to determine a reasonable fee, the JCC applied the formula and then increased or decreased the amount after consideration of the factors in order to determine a reasonable fee." *Murray*, 994 So. 2d at 1059. As the First District noted, the sliding fee schedule "embodies a legislative intent to standardize fees." *Fiesta Fashions, Inc. v. Capin*, 450 So. 2d 1128, 1129 (Fla. 1st DCA 1984). . . .

In 1993, the Legislature again revised the statute, this time to reduce the percentage amounts for attorney's fees in the sliding schedule:

[A]ny attorney's fee approved by a judge of compensation claims <u>for services rendered to a claimant</u> ~~shall~~ <u>must</u> be equal to ~~25~~ <u>20</u> percent of the first $5,000 of the amount of the benefits secured, ~~20~~ <u>15</u> percent of the next $5,000 of the amount of the benefits secured, and ~~15~~ <u>10</u> percent of the remaining amount of the benefits secured <u>to be provided during the first 10 years after the date the claim is filed, and 5 percent of the benefits secured after 10 years.</u>

Ch. 93–415, § 34, at 154 Laws of Fla. (statutory additions underlined; statutory deletions struck-through). . . .

. . . [The Florida] Legislature in 2009 removed any ambiguity as to its intent [as to why it revised the statute downward]. Deleting the word "reasonable" in relation to attorney's fees, the Legislature provided that a claimant is entitled to recover only "<u>an</u> ~~a reasonable~~ attorney's fee <u>in an amount equal to the amount provided for in subsection (1) or subsection (7)</u> from a carrier or employer." Ch.2009–94, § 1, Laws of Fla. (statutory additions underlined; statutory deletions struck-through). Subsection (1) requires the fee to be calculated in strict conformance with the fee schedule. . . .

The Legislature has, thus, eliminated any consideration of reasonableness and removed any discretion from the JCC, or the judiciary on review, to alter the fee award in cases where the sliding scale based on benefits obtained results in either a clearly inadequate or a clearly excessive fee. . . .

B. Violation of Due Process

Section 440.34 . . . does not allow for any consideration of whether the fee is reasonable or any way for the JCC or the judiciary on review to alter the fee, even if the resulting fee is grossly inadequate—or grossly excessive—in comparison to the amount of time reasonably and necessarily expended to obtain the benefits.

Stated another way, the statute establishes a conclusive irrebuttable presumption that the formula will produce an adequate fee in every case. This is clearly not true, and the inability of any injured worker to challenge the reasonableness of the fee award in his or her individual case is a facial constitutional due process issue. . . .

. . . This Court has set forth the following three-part test for determining the constitutionality of a conclusive statutory presumption, such as the fee schedule provided in section 440.34: (1) whether the concern of the Legislature was "reasonably aroused by the possibility of an abuse which it legitimately desired to avoid"; (2) whether there was a "reasonable basis for a conclusion that the statute would protect against its occurrence"; and (3) whether "the expense and other difficulties of individual determinations justify the inherent imprecision of a conclusive presumption." *Recchi*, 692 So. 2d at 154 (citing *Markham v. Fogg*, 458 So. 2d 1122, 1125 (Fla. 1984)).

In *Recchi*, this Court fully adopted the reasoning of the First District, which concluded that a statute violated the constitutional right to due process where it provided no opportunity for an employee working in a drug-free workplace program to rebut the presumption that the intoxication or influence of drugs contributed to his or her injury. *Id.* "According to the district court of appeal, the irrebuttable presumption failed the three-pronged test because the expense and other difficulties of individual determinations did not justify the inherent imprecision of the conclusive presumption." *Id.* (citing *Hall v. Recchi Am. Inc.*, 671 So. 2d 197, 201 (Fla. 1st DCA 1996)).

The same, and more, can be said of the conclusive presumption in section 440.34. We address each prong of the due process test to explain why.

1. Whether the Concern of the Legislature Was Reasonably Aroused by the Possibility of an Abuse Which It Legitimately Desired to Avoid

As to the first prong, one of the Legislature's asserted justifications for the fee schedule is to standardize fees. . . . [A] a fee schedule has typically been considered merely a starting point in determining an appropriate fee award. . . . To the extent the Legislature was also concerned about the excessiveness of attorney's fee awards, however, this is not a reasonable basis for the unyielding formulaic fee schedule. Other factors, such as Rule Regulating The Florida Bar 4–1.5, already prevent against excessive fees. That Rule provides a number of factors to be considered as a guide to determining a reasonable fee, including, among many others, "the time and labor required, the novelty, complexity, and difficulty of the questions involved, and the skill requisite to perform the legal service properly." R. Reg. Fla. Bar 4–1.5(b)(1)(A). In fact, since *Lee Engineering*, this Court has made clear that it does not condone excessive fee awards. . . .

. . . Further, claimants' attorneys are prohibited by statute from negotiating a different fee with the claimant, and the JCC is precluded from approving a different fee — even if the negotiated rate would actually produce a more reasonable fee than the statutory fee schedule. *See* §440.34(1), Fla. Stat. ("The judge of compensation claims shall not approve a compensation order, a joint stipulation for lump-sum settlement, a stipulation or agreement between a claimant and his or her attorney, or any other agreement related to benefits under this chapter which provides for an attorney's fee in excess of the amount permitted by this section."). In fact, it is a *crime* for an attorney to accept any fee not approved by the JCC, which is of course constrained to award a fee only pursuant to the statutory fee schedule. *See* §440.105(3)(c), Fla. Stat. ("It is unlawful for any attorney or other person, in his or her individual capacity or in his or her capacity as a public or private employee, or for any firm, corporation, partnership, or association to receive any fee or other consideration or any gratuity from a person on account of services rendered for a person in connection with any proceedings arising under this chapter, unless such fee, consideration, or gratuity is approved by a judge of compensation claims or by the Deputy Chief Judge of Compensation Claims.").

2. Whether There Was a Reasonable Basis for a Conclusion That the Statute Would Protect Against Its Occurrence

Even assuming, however, that the first prong of the due process test is satisfied because the Legislature desired to avoid excessive fees, there is no reasonable basis to assume that the conclusive fee schedule actually serves this function—as required by the second prong of the test. Excessive fees can still result under the fee schedule, just as inadequate ones can—for instance, in a simple and straightforward case where the claimant obtains a substantial amount of benefits.... The fee schedule does nothing to adjust fees downward when the recovery is high, even if the time required to obtain significant benefits was relatively minor and the resulting fee is actually excessive....

... [A] customary fee based on an hourly rate is likely to be more significant in a case in which the value of the attorney's services greatly exceeds the financial benefit obtained on behalf of the client.... For example, the work necessary to establish a connection between chemical exposure and respiratory illness might not bear a reasonable relationship to the benefit obtained, and to apply the statutory formula in such a case might result in a fee that is inadequate and unfair.... In other words, the elimination of any authority for the JCC or the judiciary on review to alter the fee award completely frustrates the purpose of the workers' compensation scheme.

3. Whether the Expense and Other Difficulties of Individual Determinations Justify the Inherent Imprecision of a Conclusive Presumption

But even if none of that were true, the third prong of the test for evaluating a conclusive presumption—that the feasibility of individual assessments of what constitutes a reasonable fee in a given case must justify the inherent imprecision of the conclusive presumption—certainly weighs heavily against the constitutionality of the fee schedule. Indeed, the JCC in this case actually made these individual determinations, but the inherent imprecision of the conclusive presumption prevented both the JCC and the First District from doing anything about the unreasonableness of the resulting fee.

Courts have, in fact, long operated under the view that the fee schedule was merely a starting point, and judges of compensation claims have determined, awarded, and approved attorney's fees without undue expense or difficulty to avoid unfairness and arbitrariness since the reasonable attorney's fee provision was adopted in 1941. Under prior versions of the statutory scheme, the JCC considered legislatively enumerated factors, and, after the deletion of these factors, continued to consider whether the fee was reasonable and not excessive.... This type of review to control abuse, limit excessive fees, and award reasonable fees provides no basis for concern about abuse.

The cases cited in opposition are readily distinguishable. Although the United States Supreme Court held that the unreasonably low fee provisions at issue in those cases passed constitutional muster despite the existence of a fee schedule, the judiciary still had discretionary authority to raise or lower the final fee according to articulated standards—unlike the conclusive presumption established by section 440.34.

For example, the Longshore and Harbor Workers' Compensation Act (LHWCA), the federal statutory workers' compensation scheme, which provides benefits to maritime workers, prohibits an attorney from receiving a fee unless approved by the appropriate agency or court. This provision has been upheld by the United States Supreme Court. *See U.S. Dep't of Labor v. Triplett*, 494 U.S. 715, 721–26, 110 S.Ct. 1428, 108 L.Ed.2d 701 (1990) (upholding the LHWCA provision, as incorporated into the Black Lung Benefits Act of 1972, against Fifth Amendment Due Process challenge).

Unlike the conclusive fee schedule in section 440.34, however, the Code of Federal Regulations creates factors to guide the adjudicator in awarding a fee "reasonably commensurate with the necessary work done." *Triplett*, 494 U.S. at 718. In other words, the fee provision in the LHWCA does not establish a conclusive irrebuttable presumption without consideration of whether the fee is "reasonable," but actually allows for the award of a "reasonable attorney's fee"—the precise constitutional problem with section 440.34.

In addition, in the federal cases cited in *Triplett*, the fees were intentionally set low due to the simple and non-adversarial nature of the services required—a far cry from the complex nature of Florida's current workers' compensation system. Indeed, Florida's workers' compensation law has become increasingly complex over the years. As a result of the complexity of the statutory scheme, the JCC specifically concluded in this case that it was "highly unlikely that [Castellanos] could have succeeded and obtained the favorable results he did without the assistance of capable counsel."

The stated goal of the workers' compensation system remains to this date the "quick and efficient delivery of disability and medical benefits to an injured worker" so as "to facilitate the worker's return to gainful reemployment at a reasonable cost to the employer." §440.015, Fla. Stat. This case, and many others like it, demonstrate that despite the stated goal, oftentimes the worker experiences delay and resistance either by the employer or the carrier. Without the likelihood of an adequate attorney's fee award, there is little disincentive for a carrier to deny benefits or to raise multiple defenses, as was done here....

While the E/C's attorney is adequately compensated for the hours reasonably expended to unsuccessfully defend the claim, as here, the claimant's attorney's fee may be reduced to an absurdly low amount, such as the $1.53 hourly rate awarded to the attorney for Castellanos. In effect, the elimination of any requirement that the fee be "reasonable" completely eviscerates the purpose of the attorney's fee provision and fails to provide any penalty to the E/C for wrongfully denying or delaying benefits in contravention to the stated purpose of the statutory scheme....

... Without the ability of the attorney to present, and the JCC to determine, the reasonableness of the fee award and to deviate where necessary, the risk is too great that the fee award will be entirely arbitrary, unjust, and grossly inadequate. We therefore conclude that the statute violates the state and federal constitutional guarantees of due process.

C. Statutory Revival

Having concluded that the statute is unconstitutional, we must consider the remedy until the Legislature acts to cure the constitutional infirmity. "Florida law has long held that, when the legislature approves unconstitutional statutory language and simultaneously repeals its predecessor, then the judicial act of striking the new statutory language automatically revives the predecessor unless it, too, would be unconstitutional." *B.H. v. State*, 645 So. 2d 987, 995 (Fla. 1994).

Accordingly, our holding that the conclusive fee schedule in section 440.34 is unconstitutional operates to revive the statute's immediate predecessor. This is the statute . . . where we construed the statute to provide for a "reasonable" award of attorney's fees.

[Therefore, from today forward,] a JCC must allow for a claimant to present evidence to show that application of the statutory fee schedule will result in an unreasonable fee. We emphasize, however, that the fee schedule remains the starting point, and that the revival of the predecessor statute does not mean that claimants' attorneys will receive a windfall. Only where the claimant can demonstrate, based on the standard this Court articulated long ago in *Lee Engineering*, that the fee schedule results in an unreasonable fee—such as in a case like this—will the claimant's attorney be entitled to a fee that deviates from the fee schedule. . . .

It is so ordered.

Lewis, J., concurring:

. . . [C]ircumstances such as this case result in providing counsel attorney fees in an amount of $1.53 per hour, which is clearly unreasonable and insufficient to afford workers the ability to secure competent counsel, and the irrebuttable or conclusive presumption with regard to attorney fees violates the three-pronged analysis applicable to determine constitutionality here. This irrebuttable or conclusive presumption violates the constitutional right to due process. *See Recchi America Inc. v. Hall*, 692 So. 2d 153 (Fla. 1997); *Markham v. Fogg*, 458 So. 2d 1122 (Fla. 1984).

Additionally, where workers face the exclusive remedy under Florida's workers' compensation statutes, but are then denied the ability to secure competent counsel due to the totally unreasonable attorney fees provision, the legislation operates to unconstitutionally deny Florida workers access to our courts. As stated in *Kluger v. White*, 281 So. 2d 1, 4 (Fla. 1973):

> [W]here a right of access to the courts for redress for a particular injury has been provided by statutory law predating the adoption of the Declaration of Rights of the Constitution of the State of Florida, or where such right has become a part of the common law of the State pursuant to Fla. Stat. § 2.01, the Legislature is without power to abolish such a right without providing a reasonable alternative to protect the rights of the people of the State to redress for injuries.

Canady, Justice, dissenting:

The fee schedule in section 440.34, Florida Statutes, embodies a policy determination by the Legislature that there should be a reasonable relationship between the value of the benefits obtained in litigating a workers' compensation claim and the amount of attorney's fees the employer or carrier is required to pay to the claimant. This policy violates none of the constitutional provisions on which the petitioner relies. Accordingly, I dissent from the majority's invalidation of this statutory provision.

In reaching the conclusion that the statute violates due process, the majority fails to directly address the actual policy of the statute. Instead, the majority assumes — without any reasoned explanation — that due process requires a particular definition of "reasonableness" in the award of statutory attorney's fees. The definition assumed by the majority categorically precludes the legislative policy requiring a reasonable relationship between the amount of a fee award and the amount of the recovery obtained by the efforts of the attorney. Certainly, this legislative policy may be subject to criticism. But there is no basis in our precedents or federal law for declaring it unconstitutional.

. . . [W]e have never held that it is unreasonable to require that an award of attorney's fees be commensurate with the benefits obtained. The policy adopted by the Legislature in section 440.34 may be subject to criticism, but it unquestionably has a rational basis.

This case illustrates the rationale for the legislative policy requiring that a fee award be commensurate with the recovery obtained. Here, the value of the claim was $822.70, and the claimant sought attorney's fees in the amount of $36,817.50 — a fee nearly 45 times the amount of the recovery. Of course, an argument can be made that an award of fees in an amount so disproportionate to the recovery is necessary and appropriate to allow the effective litigation of a complex low-value claim. And a counter argument can be made that such disproportionate fee awards impose an unwarranted social cost. But the question for this Court is not which side of this policy debate has the best argument, but whether the policy adopted by the Legislature violates some constitutional requirement.

Our precedents and federal law provide no authority to support the proposition that due process — or any other constitutional requirement relied on by the petitioner — requires that statutory fee awards fully compensate for the effective litigation of all claims. Under the American Rule, parties must ordinarily bear the expense of obtaining their own legal representation. Inevitably, under the American Rule, obtaining the assistance of an attorney for the litigation of low-value claims — whether simple or complex — often is not feasible. Given the undisputed constitutionality of the American Rule, there is no impediment to a legislative policy requiring that the amount of statutory fee awards be reasonably related to the amount of the recovery obtained. *See Florida Patient's Comp. Fund v. Rowe*, 472 So. 2d 1145, 1149 (Fla. 1985) ("We find that an award of attorney fees to the prevailing party is 'a matter of substantive law properly under the aegis of the legislature,' in accordance with the long-standing American Rule adopted by this Court.")

The majority's reliance on the "three-part test for determining the constitutionality of a conclusive statutory presumption" . . . to invalidate the statute is unjustified because the majority misunderstands the test and misapplies it in the context presented by this case. The majority's decision ignores the background of the three-part test. When that background is considered, it becomes abundantly clear that the majority has misapplied the test in this case.

The three-part test . . . was derived from *Weinberger v. Salfi*, 422 U.S. 749, 752–53, 95 S.Ct. 2457, 45 L.Ed.2d 522 (1975), which reversed a lower court's decision "invalidating [9-month] duration-of-relationship Social Security eligibility requirements for surviving wives and stepchildren of deceased wage earners." The lower court had held the statutory requirements invalid on the ground that they constituted an irrebuttable presumption that violated due process.

In *Salfi*, the three parts of the test utilized by the majority here were simply elements considered by the Court in determining whether the challenged statutory provisions comported with "standards of legislative reasonableness." 422 U.S. at 776–77. *Salfi* relied on "[t]he standard for testing the validity of Congress' Social Security classification" set forth in *Flemming v. Nestor*, 363 U.S. 603, 611, 80 S.Ct. 1367, 4 L.Ed.2d 1435 (1960): "'Particularly when we deal with a withholding of a noncontractual benefit under a social welfare program such as [Social Security], we must recognize that the Due Process Clause can be thought to interpose a bar only if the statute manifests a patently arbitrary classification, utterly lacking in rational justification.'" *Salfi*, 422 U.S. at 768. *Salfi* also cited *Richardson v. Belcher*, 404 U.S. 78, 84, 92 S.Ct. 254, 30 L.Ed.2d 231 (1971), which, in rejecting a due process challenge to a provision of the Social Security Act, said: "'If the goals sought are legitimate, and the classification adopted is rationally related to the achievement of those goals, then the action of Congress is not so arbitrary as to violate the Due Process Clause of the Fifth Amendment.'" *Salfi*, 422 U.S. at 768–69.

Accordingly, the *Salfi* Court's reasoning was—unlike the majority's reasoning here—highly deferential to the legislative judgment underlying the challenged statutory provision:

> Under those standards [of legislative reasonableness], the question raised is not whether a statutory provision precisely filters out those, and only those, who are in the factual position which generated the congressional concern reflected in the statute. Such a rule would ban all prophylactic provisions. . . . Nor is the question whether the provision filters out a substantial part of the class which caused congressional concern, or whether it filters out more members of the class than nonmembers. The question is [1] whether Congress, its concern having been reasonably aroused by the possibility of an abuse which it legitimately desired to avoid, [2] could rationally have concluded both that a particular limitation or qualification

would protect against its occurrence, and [3] that the expense and other difficulties of individual determinations justified the inherent imprecision of a prophylactic rule. We conclude that the duration-of-relationship test meets this constitutional standard.

Salfi, 422 U.S. at 777.

The particular elements of the rational basis analysis in *Salfi* were based on the particular justification advanced by the Social Security Administration for the duration-of-relationship requirement—that is, as a "general precaution against the payment of benefits where the marriage was undertaken to secure benefit rights." 422 U.S. at 780. The Court concluded that this concern was undoubtedly "legitimate," that it was "undoubtedly true that the duration-of-relationship requirement operates to lessen the likelihood of abuse through sham relationships entered in contemplation of imminent death" and that "Congress could rationally have concluded that any imprecision from which [the requirement] might suffer was justified by its ease and certainty of operation." *Id.*

It is readily apparent that the framework of the three-part analysis does not fit the context presented by the case on review here. Section 440.34 does not embody a prophylactic requirement akin to the eligibility requirement in *Salfi*. Section 440.34 thus does not present any question of "inherent imprecision." *Id.* at 777. By definition, the rule of proportionality embodied in the statute precisely and comprehensively protects against fee awards disproportionate to the recovery obtained. The award of such disproportionate fees is the very evil that the Legislature sought to eliminate. In its application of the inapposite three-part test, the majority simply ignores this fundamental point. Beyond that, the majority applies the elements of the test in a manner totally contrary to the manner in which *Salfi* applied them and totally at odds with the general rule "that the Due Process Clause can be thought to interpose a bar only if the statute manifests a patently arbitrary classification, utterly lacking in rational justification." *Id.* at 768 (citing *Nestor*, 363 U.S. at 611).

It should not be ignored that *Salfi* reversed the lower court's application of the irrebuttable presumption doctrine and took pains to distinguish and limit earlier cases that had relied on that doctrine to invalidate legislation. 422 U.S. at 771–72. In doing so, the Court expressed its strong concern that an expansive application of the irrebuttable presumption doctrine—like the application by the lower court— would turn that doctrine "into a virtual engine of destruction for countless legislative judgments which have heretofore been thought wholly consistent with the Fifth and Fourteenth Amendments to the Constitution." *Id.* at 772. Underlying this concern is the reality that any legislative classification can be characterized as an irrebuttable presumption. The majority here has applied a test extracted from *Salfi* in a manner that flies in the face of the central concern expressed by the Court in *Salfi* justifying its reversal of the lower court. The line of reasoning adopted by the majority unquestionably has the potential to become a "virtual engine of destruction for countless legislative judgments" previously understood to be constitutional.

Although some of our prior cases have relied on the three-part test derived from *Salfi*, we have never applied that test to find a statutory provision unconstitutional in circumstances that have any similarity to the circumstances presented here. In *Recchi America Inc. v. Hall*, which is briefly discussed by the majority, the underlying legislative policy—as expressly stated in the statute—was that no workers' compensation would be payable for an injury occasioned primarily by the employee's intoxication. With that legislative policy in view, we upheld the invalidation of a statutory irrebuttable presumption that an employee's injury was caused primarily by intoxication if the employee was working in a workplace with a drug-free workplace program and tested positive for alcohol or drugs at the time of injury. We concluded that "the conclusive presumption created a high potential for inaccuracy" and emphasized that the injured worker in the case "was injured when a coworker tripped and jabbed a long steel apparatus into the back of his head." *Recchi*, 692 So. 2d at 154–55.

Leaving aside the question of whether our analysis in *Recchi* is consistent with Salfi—which we did not mention—*Recchi* is readily distinguishable from the case now on review. Here, there is no expressly stated legislative policy regarding attorney's fees that might be implemented through a process of individualized determinations analogous to the expressly stated legislative policy regarding causation that was addressed in *Recchi*. No process of individualized factual determinations could better serve the legislative purpose of establishing proportionality between fee awards and recoveries obtained than does the statutory fee schedule.

Finally, I agree with Justice Polston that the majority "turns this Court's well-established precedent regarding facial challenges on its head [.]" Dissenting op. at 53 (Polston, J.)

I would answer the rephrased certified question in the negative and approve the decision of the First District.

Polston, Justice, dissenting:

There is no conclusive presumption. The majority has rewritten the statute to avoid the standard governing facial challenges. I respectfully dissent.

In 2008, this Court issued an opinion interpreting the attorney's fees provision of Florida's workers' compensation law as amended in 2003 to include a reasonableness requirement. *See Murray v. Mariner Health*, 994 So. 2d 1051 (Fla. 2008) (interpreting section 440.34, Florida Statutes (2003)). This Court in *Murray* determined that the plain language of the statute was ambiguous regarding reasonableness because subsection (1) did not include the term reasonable when providing for a mandatory fee schedule but subsection (3) did employ the term. *Id.* at 1061. Such ambiguity necessitated a judicial interpretation utilizing the rules of statutory construction. *Id.* In response to this Court's decision in *Murray*, the Legislature amended the statute to eliminate any ambiguity, which the Legislature is constitutionally authorized to do. Specifically, in 2009, the Legislature eliminated all references to reasonableness, rendering moot this Court's 2008 interpretation of the provision as including a reasonableness requirement. *See* ch.2009–94, § 1, Laws of Fla. However, with today's decision, the majority reinstates its prior 2008 holding by turning facial constitutional review completely on its head and rewriting the 2009 statute.

To be clear, I am not saying that a constitutional challenge to section 440.34, Florida Statutes (2009), could never succeed. In fact, I would not foreclose the possibility of a successful as-applied constitutional challenge to the attorney's fees provision based upon access to courts, depending upon the particular facts of the case involved. However, as acknowledged during oral argument, the petitioner did not raise any as-applied challenge to the statute in this Court, even given what would certainly seem to be the rather egregious facts of his case. Instead, the petitioner raised a facial challenge that lacks any merit under our precedent.

In a facial challenge, this Court has emphasized that "our review is limited." *Abdool v. Bondi*, 141 So. 3d 529, 538 (Fla. 2014). Specifically, "we consider only the text of the statute." *Id.* "For a statute to be held facially unconstitutional, the challenger must demonstrate that no set of circumstances exists in which the statute can be constitutionally applied." *Id.*; *see also Cashatt v. State*, 873 So. 2d 430, 434 (Fla. 1st DCA 2004) ("A facial challenge to a statute is more difficult than an 'as applied' challenge, because the challenger must establish that no set of circumstances exists under which the statute would be valid."); *cf. Accelerated Benefits Corp. v. Dep't of Ins.*, 813 So. 2d 117, 120 (Fla. 1st DCA 2002) ("In considering an 'as applied' challenge, the court is to consider the facts of the case at hand."). Moreover, "when we review the constitutionality of a statute, we accord legislative acts a presumption of constitutionality and construe the challenged legislation to effect a constitutional outcome when possible." *Abdool*, 141 So. 3d at 538 (citing *Fla. Dep't of Revenue v. Howard*, 916 So. 2d 640, 642 (Fla. 2005)). "As a result, [an] Act will not be invalidated as facially unconstitutional simply because it could operate unconstitutionally under some [ ] circumstances." *Id.*

Applying this well-established precedent, the facial challenge at issue here fails, even assuming that adequate and reasonable attorney's fees are constitutionally required. There are some workers' compensation cases where "the amount of benefits is substantial, but the legal issues are simple and direct, and do not require exceptional skill, knowledge, and experience." *Murray*, 994 So. 2d at 1057 n. 4. In these high pay-off, low-effort cases, the statutory fee schedule could provide reasonable compensation for a prevailing claimant's attorney. After all, section 440.34(1), Florida Statutes (2009), provides that the attorney's fee must equal 20 percent of the first $5,000 in benefits, 15 percent of the next $5,000, 10 percent of the remaining during the first 10 years of the claim, and 5 percent after 10 years. Therefore, because there are a set of circumstances under which the attorney's fees provision could be constitutionally applied, the provision is facially constitutional under our precedent. See *Fla. Dep't of Revenue v. City of Gainesville*, 918 So. 2d 250, 265 (Fla. 2005) ("[I]n a facial constitutional challenge, we determine only whether there is any set of circumstances under which the challenged enactment might be upheld.").

The majority reaches a contrary holding, not by applying our precedent regarding facial challenges, but by ignoring it altogether and never even citing the well-established standard. The majority just declares that the attorney's fees provision in Florida's workers' compensation law includes an irrebuttable presumption of reasonableness, and then it holds that this presumption is a violation of procedural due process under both the United States and Florida constitutions. But the 2009 provision does not mention reasonableness at all and, therefore, does not include any such presumption, irrebuttable or otherwise. Cf. *Recchi America Inc. v. Hall*, 692 So. 2d 153 (Fla. 1997) (declaring an irrebuttable presumption invalid as a violation of due process where the statute plainly and *expressly included* a presumption that an accident was primarily caused by the worker's intoxication if that worker's urine test revealed the presence of alcohol or drugs). Section 440.34 as plainly written prescribes a mandatory schedule for prevailing party attorney's fees. It never states that those attorney's fees have to be or should be considered reasonable. In fact, it was specifically amended post-*Murray* to eliminate the term reasonable, which eliminates the ability of this Court to say that the statute includes anything about reasonableness. And because the statute does not include any presumption of reasonableness (let alone a conclusive presumption), the majority's analysis of the constitutionality of that non-existent presumption is erroneous.

The majority's decision turns this Court's well-established precedent regarding facial challenges on its head and accomplishes by the backdoor what it could not do by the front door. The majority is really deciding that reasonable attorney's fees are constitutionally required. But by rewriting the 2009 statute to include a conclusive presumption, the majority avoids the fact that the state and federal due process clauses do not require Florida's workers' compensation scheme to include reasonable prevailing party attorney's fees. The majority also invalidates a statute that might sometimes, but not all the time, be applied in a manner that denies reasonable attorney's fees. However, this Court's precedent regarding facial challenges requires that such a statute be upheld. *See State v. Ecker*, 311 So. 2d 104, 110 (Fla. 1975) ("While the statute might be unconstitutionally applied in certain situations, this is no ground for finding the statute itself [facially] unconstitutional.").

C. Right of Access to Courts: Creating a Right to a Remedy

Article I, Section 21, of the Constitution of the State of Florida provides in its Declaration of Rights that:

> The courts shall be open to every person for redress of any injury, and justice shall be administered without sale, denial or delay.

Like in our analysis of previous rights from Florida's Declaration of Rights, it could be said that this may be an example of Florida constitutional law jurisprudence expanding upon the rights embodied in the federal Constitution insofar as it affords Floridians rights in civil cases that the federal Constitution typically restricts in whole or in part to criminal cases. Of course, be it via a writ of habeas corpus or via the right to a prison law library, those facing punishment under a criminal statute have a right to access to the courts under the First, Fifth, and Fifteenth Amendments to the United States Constitution. *See, e.g., Lewis v. Casey*, 518 U.S. 343 (1996); *Bounds v. Smith*, 430 U.S. 817 (1977); *Johnson v. Avery*, 383 U.S. 483 (1969); *Ex parte Hull*, 312 U.S. 546 (1941).

Yet Article I, Section 21 of Florida's constitution enshrines a right to access to courts that is fully applicable to civil cases.

Stated somewhat differently, Article I, Section 21 of the Florida Constitution provides a limitation upon the Florida Legislature's power to abolish causes of action that existed prior to the enactment of the 1968 Constitution of the State of Florida. That limitation is that the Legislature must provide a "reasonable alternative" to the abolished cause of action unless there is an "overpowering public necessity" not to do so. Such is the holding of *Kluger v. White*, 281 So. 2d 1 (Fla. 1973), which despite its age remains the leading Florida opinion on the topic, and which has frequently appeared on the Florida Bar Exam.

Kluger v. White

Supreme Court of Florida, 1973
281 So. 2d 1

Adkins, Justice.

This is an appeal from an order of dismissal entered for defendants and against plaintiff in this property damage action by the Dade County Circuit Court, specifically passing upon the constitutionality of Fla. Stat. section 627.738. We have jurisdiction pursuant to Fla. Const., art. V, s 3(b)(1).

The cause of action arose from an automobile collision between a car owned by appellant, and driven by her son, and one owned by appellee, and driven by another person. The amended complaint filed by appellant alleged that the driver of appellee's car was negligent and had been formally charged with failure to yield the right of way; that there were no personal injuries; that there were damages to appellant's car to the extent of $774.95; and that the fair market value of the car was $250.00.

Appellant was insured with appellee, Manchester Insurance and Indemnity Company, but the policy did not provide for 'basic or full' property damage coverage. Appellant alleged that the Manchester agent had not specifically explained to her the possible results of failing to include property damage coverage.

Fla. Stat. section 627.738 provides, in effect, that the traditional right of action in tort for property damage arising from an automobile accident is abolished, and one must look to property damage with one's own insurer, unless the plaintiff is one who (1) has chosen not to purchase property damage insurance, and (2) has suffered property damage in excess of $550.00.

The appellant falls into that class of accident victims with no recourse against any person or insurer for loss caused by the fault of another, taking her allegations as true. She did not choose to purchase either 'full or basic coverage for accidental property damage' to her automobile, and her damages were the fair market value of her automobile since repair costs cannot be recovered where they exceed the fair market value of the automobile before the collision.

Appellant has raised numerous constitutional challenges to Fla. Stat. section 627.738. We find, as explained below, that Florida Statutes section 627.738 fails to comply with a reasonable interpretation of Fla. Const., art. I, sec. 21, which reads as follows:

> The courts shall be open to every person for redress of any injury, and justice shall be administered without sale, denial or delay.'

This Court has never before specifically spoken to the issue of whether or not the constitutional guarantee of a 'redress of any injury' (Fla. Const., art. I, sec. 21) bars the statutory abolition of an existing remedy without providing an alternative protection to the injured party.

Corpus Juris Secundum provides:

> A constitutional provision insuring a certain remedy for all injuries or wrongs does not command continuation of a specific statutory remedy. However, in a jurisdiction wherein the constitutional guaranty applies to the legislature as well as to the judiciary, . . . it has been held that the guaranty precludes the repeal of a statute allowing a remedy where the statute was in force at the time of the adoption of the Constitution. Furthermore, . . . the guaranty also prevents, in some jurisdictions, the total abolition of a common-law remedy.'

16A C.J.S. Constitutional Law sec. 710, pp. 1218-1219.

This Court has held that the Declaration of Rights of the Constitution of the State of Florida does apply to State government and to the Legislature. *Spafford v. Brevard County*, 92 Fla. 617, 110 So. 451 (1926). The right to a cause of action in tort for negligent causation of damage to an automobile in a collision was recognized by statute prior to the adoption of the 1968 Constitution of the State of Florida, as evidenced by the fact that Fla. Stat. section 627.738, the statute under attack, specifically exempts owners and drivers of automobiles from tort liability for such damages. In addition, the cause of action for damage to property by force or violence—*trespass Vi et armis*—was one of the earliest causes of action recognized at English Common Law.

It is essential, therefore, that this Court consider whether or not the Legislature is, in fact, empowered to abolish a common law and statutory right of action without providing an adequate alternative.

Upon careful consideration of the requirements of society, and the ever-evolving character of the law, we cannot adopt a complete prohibition against such legislative change. Nor can we adopt a view which would allow the Legislature to destroy a traditional and long-standing cause of action upon mere legislative whim, or when an alternative approach is available.

We hold, therefore, that where a right of access to the courts for redress for a particular injury has been provided by statutory law predating the adoption of the Declaration of Rights of the Constitution of the State of Florida, or where such right has become a part of the common law of the State . . . the Legislature is without power to abolish such a right without providing a reasonable alternative to protect the rights of the people of the State to redress for injuries, unless the Legislature can show an overpowering public necessity for the abolishment of such right, and no alternative method of meeting such public necessity can be shown.

It is urged that this Court has previously approved action by the Legislature which violated the rule which we have laid down. We disagree.

In *McMillan v. Nelson*, 149 Fla. 334, 5 So. 2d 867 (1942), this Court approved the so-called 'Guest Statute' which merely changed the degree of negligence necessary for a passenger in an automobile to maintain a tort action against the driver. It did not abolish the right to sue, and does not come under the rule which we have promulgated.

Workmen's compensation abolished the right to sue one's employer in tort for a job-related injury, but provided adequate, sufficient, and even preferable safeguards for an employee who is injured on the job, thus satisfying one of the exceptions to the rule against abolition of the right to redress for an injury.

The Legislature in 1945 enacted Fla. Stat. Chapter 771, which abolishes the rights of action to sue for damages for alienation of affections, criminal conversation, seduction or breach of promise. This Court upheld the validity of the chapter in *Rotwein v. Gersten*, 160 Fla. 736, 36 So. 2d 419 (1948). The Court opined:

> The causes of action proscribed by the act under review were a part of the common law and have long been a part of the law of the country. They have no doubt served a good purpose, but *when they become an instrument of extortion and blackmail, the legislature has the power to, and may, limit or abolish them.* (Emphasis supplied)

Id. at 421.

Thus, in abolishing the right of action for alienation of affections, etc., the Legislature showed the public necessity required for the total abolition of a right to sue.

The Legislature has not presented such a case in relation to the abolition of the right to sue an automotive tortfeasor for property damage. Nor has alternative protection for the victim of the accident been provided, as evidenced by the facts here before the Court.

Had the Legislature chosen to require that appellant be insured against property damage loss — as is, in effect, required by Fla. Stat. section 627.733 with respect to other possible damages — the issues would be different. A reasonable alternative to an action in tort would have been provided and the issue would have been whether or not the requirement of insurance for all motorists was reasonable. That issue is not before us.

Retaining the right of action for damages over $550.00 (Fla. Stat. section 627.738(5)) does not correct the constitutional infirmity. . . .

Accordingly, the decision of the trial court holding Fla. Stat. section 627.738 to be constitutional and denying appellant a cause of action against appellee is reversed, and the cause is remanded for further proceedings not inconsistent herewith.

It is so ordered.

D. Right of Access to Courts: Allowing for the Creation of an Alternative but Adequate Remedy

Article I, Section 21 of the Constitution of the State of Florida provides a right of access to courts, but that right is not absolute. *Kluger v. White*, 281 So. 2d 1 (Fla. 1973) is the seminal Florida case interpreting Article I, Section 21 of the Florida Constitution and its limitation upon the Florida Legislature's power to abolish causes of action that existed prior to the enactment of the 1968 Constitution of the State of Florida. Identical language does not appear in the federal Constitution. But many other U.S. state constitutions contain language similar to Florida's Article I Section 21.

Thirty-nine states have such "open courts" or "remedies" clauses in their state constitutions. David Schuman, *The Right to a Remedy*, 65 Temp. L. Rev. 1197, 1201 & n.25 (1992). A commentator notes the following:

> Historically, these provisions were intended as constitutional safeguards of an individual's right to a legal remedy [and as more] than state equivalents of the federal Due Process Clause. . . .Plaintiffs generally use state remedy provisions to challenge statutes restricting or eliminating previously established causes of action. In the last few decades, for example, injured parties have used state remedy provisions to challenge tort reform legislation, such as workers' compensation acts and statutory caps on medical malpractice damages.

Shannon M. Roesler, *The Kansas Remedy by Due Course of Law Provision: Defining a Right to a Remedy*, 47 U. Kan. L. Rev. 655 (1999).

Other commentators agree that a state constitution's "access to courts" clause "is often at the epicenter of the current battle between businesses and the plaintiffs' bar over legislative tort reform, as well as the historic power struggle between legislatures and courts." Jonathan M. Hoffman, *Questions before Answers: The Ongoing Search to Understand the Origins of the Open Courts Clause*, 32 Rutgers L.J. 1005 (2001).

Indeed, here in Florida, the seemingly unceasing accusation that the Florida Workers' Compensation Law is unconstitutional is often a battle fought under Florida's Article I, Section 21 "Access to Courts" Clause, as I once wrote in an earlier edition of my book FLORIDA WORKERS' COMPENSATION. *See* Patrick John McGinley, FLORIDA WORKERS' COMPENSATION § 28:3 (Thomson Reuters 2015 ed.).

One might fairly conclude that it is a high burden to prove a law to be unconstitutional under Florida's Article I Section 21 "Access to Courts" Clause. Consider, for example, the Supreme Court of Florida's decision in *Anderson v. Gannett Co.*, 994 So. 2d 1048 (Fla. 2008) and its rationale as to why the Florida Supreme Court's apparent abrogation of a previously used common law cause of action did not violate Florida's right of access to courts:

Anderson v. Gannett Company
Supreme Court of Florida, 2008.
994 So. 2d 1048

This case is before the Court for review of the decision of the First District Court of Appeal in *Gannett Co. v. Anderson*, 947 So. 2d 1 (Fla. 1st DCA 2006). In its decision, the district court ruled upon the following question, which the court certified to be of great public importance:

> Is an action for invasion of privacy based on the false light theory governed by the two-year statute of limitations that applies to defamation claims or by the four-year statute that applies to unspecified tort claims?

Id. at 11. The First District concluded that the two-year statute of limitations for defamation applied to false light, reversed the judgment for the plaintiff on the false light cause of action, and certified conflict with *Heekin v. CBS Broadcasting, Inc.*, 789 So. 2d 355 (Fla. 2d DCA 2001), which held that false light invasion of privacy was governed by the four-year statute of limitations for unspecified torts. We have jurisdiction. *See* art. V, § 3(b)(4), Fla. Const.

Although the First District questioned the validity of false light, the certified question is predicated upon the existence of such a cause of action. At the time of its decision, the First District did not have benefit of our decision in *Jews for Jesus v. Rapp*, 997 So. 2d 1098 (Fla. 2008), in which we addressed the following question certified by the Fourth District:

> Does Florida recognize the tort of false light invasion of privacy, and if so, are the elements of the tort set forth in section 652E of Restatement (Second) of Torts?

Id. at 1100. We answered the question in the negative, concluding that Florida does not recognize the tort of false light "because the benefit of recognizing the tort, which only offers a distinct remedy in relatively few unique situations, is outweighed by the danger in unreasonably impeding constitutionally protected speech." *Id.* at 1114.

Because we declined to recognize the tort of false light, our analysis of the applicable statute of limitations in this case is unnecessary and moot. However, Anderson received a jury verdict based on false light and asserted in his amicus brief in *Rapp* that we cannot retroactively abolish the cause of action. *Cf. Warren v. State Farm Mut. Auto. Ins. Co.*, 899 So. 2d 1090, 1097 (Fla. 2005) (stating that a statute is unconstitutional if it abolishes a cause of action that was provided for at common law without providing a reasonable alternative, absent an "overpowering public necessity," quoting *Kluger v. White*, 281 So. 2d 1, 4 (Fla. 1973)); *Village of El Portal v. City of Miami Shores*, 362 So. 2d 275, 277 (Fla. 1978) (holding that retrospective statutes are unconstitutional "in those cases wherein *vested rights* are adversely affected or destroyed or when a new obligation or duty is created or imposed") (quoting *McCord v. Smith*, 43 So. 2d 704, 709 (Fla. 1950)). Although we acknowledged in *Rapp* that this Court had previously referred to false light as one of the four common law invasion of privacy torts, we also stated that "none of these cases actually involved a claim of false light and we have never discussed any of the competing policy concerns." *Rapp*, 997 So. 2d at 1103.

We therefore determined in *Rapp* that the issue of whether false light actually existed in Florida was one of first impression because the tort never existed at common law and any of our statements concerning false light in previous cases were dicta. Unlike cases where a previously recognized common law cause of action was abolished by the Legislature, see *Kluger* and its progeny, *Rapp* involved the refusal to recognize a cause of action that never existed at common law. Accordingly, our decision in *Rapp* did not retroactively abolish a cause of action for false light, but rather concluded that false light should not be recognized as a common law tort.

Because we decided false light was not a viable cause of action in this state, it is not necessary for us to resolve the issue of what would be the applicable statute of limitations and whether any exceptions would apply if the defamation and false light causes of action arose from the same set of facts. We thus decline to answer the certified question. We approve the result of the First District's decision in *Anderson*, but not the reasoning to the extent it recognized that a cause of action for false light existed. Because *Heekin* also assumed the existence of a cause of action and discussed the elements, we disapprove of the Second District's decision in *Heekin* on that basis.

It is so ordered.

E. Right of Access to Courts: When One Party's Access Impedes Another's

The following case provides an example of yet another limitation upon the Right of Access to Courts as found in Constitution of the State of Florida. After the case, I reprint a portion from another one of my books that is relevant to this point.

Sibley v. Sibley

Florida's Third District Court of Appeal, 2004
885 So. 2d 980

Montgomery Blair Sibley (the former husband) appeals two post-judgment orders entered after dissolution of marriage. Final judgment in the dissolution action was entered in 1994 and there have been numerous post-judgment proceedings since that time. In this proceeding, the former husband appeals orders compelling payment of attorney's fees and tuition. We affirm those orders.

The former wife requests an order precluding the former husband, an attorney, from representing himself in further appeals in this court. We grant the request.

I.

On this appeal, the former husband argues that one of the underlying attorney's fee orders was entered in error and that the trial court erred in enforcing it. This argument is without merit.

The underlying attorney's fee order which the former husband is trying to attack was entered on March 4, 2003 ("the March 4 order"). The former husband appealed the March 4 order to this court, arguing procedural error. This court affirmed without opinion. *Sibley v. Sibley*, 866 So. 2d 1223 (Fla. 3d DCA 2003) (table), *cert. denied*, 542 U.S. 937, 124 S.Ct. 2909, 159 L.Ed.2d 813 (2004). Since the former husband already appealed the March 4 order and this court already affirmed it, common sense and principles of res judicata dictate that the former husband cannot now mount a second appeal of the March 4 order. This court has explained that res judicata applies where, as here, there have been multiple final orders in post-dissolution proceedings.

The former husband argues that it would be a manifest injustice to enforce the March 4 order because the prior panel which affirmed the March 4 order did not write an opinion explaining the panel's reasoning. In the former husband's view, the prior panel was mistaken and should have written an opinion to explain the ruling. This is not a legally sufficient showing of manifest injustice. The district courts of appeal are allowed to issue affirmances without opinion.

II.

The former husband next appeals a July 17, 2003, order compelling him to reimburse tuition expenses for two of the parties' children.

Under the parties' marital settlement agreement, the former husband is responsible for payment of educational expenses through college. See *Sibley v. Sibley*, 816 So. 2d 136 (Fla. 3d DCA 2002). The former husband has failed to pay tuition. In February 2003 the former wife filed the Emergency Motion and the trial court granted the tuition-related requests.

The former husband argues that the trial court should not have heard the motion because at that time of the hearing the former husband's seventh motion to disqualify the trial judge was pending. We reject the former husband's argument, as the point has been waived. The former husband and his counsel personally attended the hearing on the Emergency Motion. Nowhere in the transcript did they object that the hearing could not proceed until the court ruled on the pending motion for disqualification.

A party cannot go to a hearing knowing that he has filed a motion for disqualification, make no mention of the pending motion, participate in the hearing, and then after receiving an unfavorable ruling, argue that the court must start over because there was a pending motion for disqualification. [The trial court was correct to deny] the husband's seventh motion for disqualification.

III.

The former husband next argues that the July 17 order erroneously holds him in contempt when no motion for contempt was made. The former husband is incorrect. He was not held in contempt.

The former wife filed the Emergency Motion described previously. The court reserved jurisdiction on the issues of contempt and attorney's fees for a subsequent hearing.

IV.

The former husband argues that the trial court erred by refusing to approve a statement of proceedings under Florida Rule of Appellate Procedure 9.200(b)(4). During the pendency of this appeal, the former husband prepared a proposed statement of the proceedings for the hearing which took place on August 27, 2002. This is the hearing which resulted in the order of March 4, 2003, awarding attorney's fees to the former wife.

As explained earlier in this opinion, the March 4, 2003, order has become final and is not subject to collateral attack in this appeal. The time to have submitted a statement of proceedings for the August 27, 2002, hearing would have been in connection with the earlier appeal of the March 4, 2003, order, not the present appeal.

V.

The former wife has filed a Motion for Sanctions in which she seeks to preclude the husband from any further self-representation in this court without being represented by counsel. The former wife contends that the husband's appeals have repeatedly been shown to be without merit and have constituted an abuse of the legal process. Upon consideration of the motion, the former husband's response filed January 5, 2004, and after review of this court's files, we agree.

The Florida Supreme Court has said:

> Abuse of the legal system is a serious matter, one that requires this Court to exercise its inherent authority to prevent. As we held in *Rivera v. State*, 728 So. 2d 1165, 1166 (Fla. 1998): "This Court has a responsibility to ensure every citizen's access to courts. To further that end, this Court has prevented abusive litigants from continuously filing frivolous petitions, thus

enabling the Court to devote its finite resources to those who have not abused the system."

Although rare, we have not hesitated to sanction petitioners who abuse the legal process by requiring them to be represented by counsel in future actions. In *Jackson v. Florida Department of Corrections*, 790 So. 2d 398 (Fla. 2001), the sanction of requiring a member of The Florida Bar to sign all of petitioner's filings with this Court and dismissing all other pending cases was imposed on a litigious inmate who repeatedly filed frivolous lawsuits that disrupted the Court's proceedings. In *Martin v. State*, 747 So. 2d 386, 389 (Fla. 2000), the sanction was imposed against a petitioner who, like Lussy, repeatedly filed lawsuits that included personal attacks on judges, were "abusive," "malicious," "insulting," and demeaning to the judiciary. In *Attwood v. Singletary*, 661 So. 2d 1216 (Fla. 1995), the petitioner was sanctioned for filing numerous frivolous petitions, including one that was filed shortly after the Court's order to show cause was issued.

Like the individual in *Attwood*, Lussy has abused the processes of this Court with his constant filings. Accordingly, a limitation on Lussy's ability to file would further the constitutional right of access because it would permit this Court to devote its finite resources to the consideration of legitimate claims filed by others. *See generally In re McDonald*, 489 U.S. 180, 184, 109 S.Ct. 993, 103 L.Ed.2d 158 (1989) (finding that "[e]very paper filed with the Clerk of this Court, no matter how repetitious or frivolous, requires some portion of the institution's limited resources") .... *see also Safir v. United States Lines, Inc.*, 792 F.2d 19 (2d Cir. 1986).

In *Safir*, the court stated:

> [I]n determining whether or not to restrict a litigant's future access to the courts, [a court] should consider the following factors: (1) the litigant's history of litigation and in particular whether it entailed vexatious, harassing or duplicative lawsuits; (2) the litigant's motive in pursuing the litigation, e.g., does the litigant have an objective good faith expectation of prevailing?; (3) whether the litigant is represented by counsel; (4) whether the litigant has caused needless expense to other parties or has posed an unnecessary burden on the courts and their personnel; and (5) whether other sanctions would be adequate to protect the courts and other parties.

792 F.2d at 24.

The fact that the former husband is an attorney does not insulate him from this analysis. On a proper showing, an attorney may be barred from self-representation. . . .

The parties were divorced in 1994. Several years later, post judgment disputes arose, leading to litigation of increasing intensity. The former husband was eventually incarcerated for civil contempt for failing to pay child support. . . . In correspondence between the former husband and the former wife, the former husband stated, "And if you want to attempt to squeeze me until I am dry, we will litigate until I am disbarred and bankrupt if necessary for you leave me no other choice."

The former husband, an attorney, has initiated twenty-five appellate proceedings in this court in which he has represented himself, and has filed two more in which he was represented by counsel. These are listed in the Appendix to this opinion. The former husband prevailed in an early appeal to this court. *See Sibley v. Sibley*, 710 So. 2d 1017 (Fla. 3d DCA 1998). However, the former husband's subsequent pro se proceedings in this court have been found to have no merit. As is shown by this appeal, the former husband has repeatedly tried to re-litigate matters decided in earlier proceedings, without any legitimate basis to do so.

In addition, the former husband has filed at least twelve actions in federal court against judges who have been assigned to his cases, the court system, and the former wife. In *Sibley v. Wilson*, No. 04-21000-CIV-MORENO, the federal court catalogued the former husband's federal litigation history as follows: . . .

1. Sibley v. Judge Maxine Cohen Lando

United States District Court, Southern District of Florida

Case No. 01-2940-CIV-UNGARO-BENAGES

Summary: allegations of constitutional violations by judge

Outcome: dismissed on basis of *Younger* abstention [*aff'd*, 37 Fed. Appx. 979 (11th Cir. 2002)].

2. Sibley v. Judges David Gersten, Juan Ramirez, and Joseph Nesbitt

United States District Court, Southern District of Florida

Case No. 00-3665-CIV-MORENO

Summary: allegations of constitutional violations by judges

Outcome: dismissed on basis of judicial immunity, lack of subject-matter jurisdiction [*aff'd*, 252 F.3d 443 (11th Cir.), *cert. denied*, 534 U.S. 827, 122 S.Ct. 67, 151 L.Ed.2d 34 (2001)].

3. Sibley v. Mark Martinez

United States District Court, Southern District of Florida

Case No. 02-22931-CIV-HIGHSMITH

Summary: allegations of constitutional violations by clerk's filing process

Outcome: dismissed for lack of constitutional violation.

4. Sibley v. Judges Alan Schwartz, David Gersten, Mario Goderich, Gerald Cope, Robert Shevin, Maxine Cohen Lando, Victoria Platzer, and Barbara Sibley

United States District Court, Southern District of Florida

Case No. 01-3746-CIV-KING

Summary: allegations of constitutional violations by judges

Outcome: dismissed on basis of *Younger* abstention, lack of subject-matter jurisdiction. Rule 11 sanctions imposed against Plaintiff [*aff'd*, 45 Fed. Appx. 878 (11th Cir. 2002)].

5. Sibley v. Sibley

United States District Court, Southern District of Florida

Case No. 01-2770-CIV-HUCK

Summary: allegations of interference with parent-child relationship by ex-wife

Outcome: dismissed on basis of lack of subject-matter jurisdiction [*aff'd*, 34 Fed. Appx. 969 (11th Cir. 2002)].

6. Sibley v. Sibley

United States District Court, Southern District of Florida

Case No. 01-1349-CIV-GOLD

Summary: removal of divorce action from Judge Lando's court

Outcome: remanded on basis of lack of subject-matter jurisdiction.

7. Sibley v. Spears

United States District Court, Southern District of Florida

Case No. 02-22106-CIV-JORDAN

Summary: petition for habeas corpus regarding contempt orders

Outcome: dismissed for lack of subject-matter jurisdiction.

8. Sibley v. Judge Maxine Cohen Lando

United States District Court, Southern District of Florida

Case No. 03-20942-CIV-HUCK

Summary: allegations of violations of right of access to the courts

Outcome: dismissed on basis of *Rooker-Feldman* and *Younger* abstentions [*aff'd*, 99 Fed. Appx. 886 (11th Cir. 2004)].

9. Sibley v. Florida Supreme Court, Harry Lee Anstead, Third District Court of Appeal, and Eleventh Judicial Circuit Court of Dade County

United States District Court, Southern District of Florida

Case No. 03-21199-CIV-LENARD

Summary: allegations of equal protection violations in decisions by Florida courts

Outcome: dismissed *sua sponte* for lack of subject-matter jurisdiction.

10. Sibley v. Maxine Cohen Lando

United States District Court, Southern District of Florida

Case No. 03-21885-CIV-HUCK

Summary: allegations of equal protection violations in divorce proceedings

Outcome: dismissed on basis of *Rooker-Feldman* and *Younger* abstentions [*aff'd*, 97 Fed. Appx. 907 (11th Cir.), *cert. denied*, 542 U.S. 921, 124 S.Ct. 2885, 159 L.Ed.2d 779 (2004)].

The Plaintiff has also filed a lawsuit against his wife in federal court in Delaware which was dismissed for lack of subject matter jurisdiction (Case No. 8:00-cv-02997-JFM), and has filed a number of appeals and/or petitions before Florida state courts as well.

Sibley v. Wilson, No. 04-21000-CIV-MORENO, slip op. at 2–3 (S.D.Fla. July 7, 2004).

In dismissing *Sibley v. Wilson*, Judge Moreno said that it is "the court's recognized right and duty, in both Federal and Florida state courts, to protect their jurisdiction from vexatious litigants and abuse of the judicial system." *Id.* at 6 (citations omitted). We agree.

The former husband has served as an unending source of vexatious and meritless litigation. This has caused needless consumption of resources by the court system and needless expense to the former wife. Awards of attorney's fees have not served as a deterrent, as the former husband has not paid them.

We conclude that the standards of *Lussy* are met. We have considered the criteria set forth in the *Safir* decision and conclude that those are met as well. We therefore prohibit the former husband from further self-representation in this court.

We direct the clerk of this court to reject any further filings in this court on the former husband's behalf unless signed by a member of the Florida Bar (other than the former husband). Any other cases that are pending in this court in which the former husband is representing himself will be dismissed unless a notice of appearance signed by a member in good standing of the Florida Bar (other than the former husband) is filed in each case within thirty days of this opinion becoming final. *See Lussy*, 828 So. 2d at 1028.

VI.

For the stated reasons, the orders now under review are affirmed. The former wife's motion for sanctions is granted. The former husband is precluded from further self-representation in this court.

Affirmed; sanctions granted.

Appendix
(*Sibley v. Sibley*, Case No. 3D03-2083)

A. Completed proceedings in which the former husband has represented himself:

1) *Sibley v. Sibley*, 866 So. 2d 1223 (Fla. 3d DCA 2003) *cert. denied*, 542 U.S. 937, 124 S.Ct. 2909, 159 L.Ed.2d 813 (2004);

2) *Sibley v. Sibley*, No. 03-1392 (Fla. 3d DCA Aug. 6, 2003);

3) *Law Offices of Rodriguez & Sibley v. Sibley*, No. 03-3090 (Fla. 3d DCA Dec. 12, 2003);

4) *Sibley v. Sibley*, 835 So. 2d 1140 (Fla. 3d DCA 2002) (01-3496);

5) *Sibley v. Sibley*, 833 So. 2d 143 (Fla. 3d DCA 2002), *reh'g denied,* 835 So. 2d 1140 (Fla. 3d DCA 2002);

6) *Sibley v. Sibley*, 831 So. 2d 193 (Fla. 3d DCA 2002) (02-2764);

7) *Sibley v. Sibley*, 831 So. 2d 193 (Fla. 3d DCA 2002) (02-2190), *reh'g denied*, 835 So. 2d 1141 (Fla. 3d DCA 2002);

8) *Sibley v. Sibley*, 831 So. 2d 192 (Fla. 3d DCA 2002) (02-412);

9) *Sibley v. Sibley*, 823 So. 2d 785 (Fla. 3d DCA 2002);

10) *Sibley v. Sibley*, 816 So. 2d 136 (Fla. 3d DCA 2002);

11) *Sibley v. Sibley*, 815 So. 2d 673 (Fla. 3d DCA 2002), *rev. denied*, 833 So. 2d 774 (Fla. 2002);

12) *Sibley v. Sibley*, 814 So. 2d 1054 (Fla. 3d DCA 2002);

13) *Sibley v. Sibley*, 803 So. 2d 738 (Fla. 3d DCA 2001);

14) *Sibley v. Sibley*, 795 So. 2d 71 (Fla. 3d DCA 2001);

15) *Sibley v. Sibley*, 793 So. 2d 959 (Fla. 3d DCA 2001);

16) *Sibley v. Sibley*, 791 So. 2d 481 (Fla. 3d DCA 2001);

17) *Sibley v. Sibley*, 771 So. 2d 1175 (Fla. 3d DCA 2000);

18) *Sibley v. Sibley*, 751 So. 2d 586 (Fla. 3d DCA 2000);

19) *Sibley v. Sibley*, 733 So. 2d 529 (Fla. 3d DCA 1999);

20) *Sibley v. Sibley*, 732 So. 2d 1079 (Fla. 3d DCA 1999);

21) *Sibley v. Sibley*, 725 So. 2d 1273 (Fla. 3d DCA 1999);

22) *Sibley v. Sibley*, 710 So. 2d 1017 (Fla. 3d DCA 1998).

B. Pending appellate proceedings in which the former husband represents himself:

23) *Sibley v. Sibley*, Case No. 3D04-294;

24) *Sibley v. Sibley*, Consolidated Case No. 3D04-1260/3D04-803;

25) *Sibley v. Sibley*, Case No. 3D04-1466.

C. Completed appellate proceedings in which the former husband was represented by counsel:

26) *Sibley v. Spears*, 837 So. 2d 988 (Fla. 3d DCA 2002) *cert denied*, 540 U.S. 1016, 124 S.Ct. 567, 157 L.Ed.2d 429 (2003);

27) *Sibley v. Sibley*, 833 So. 2d 847 (Fla. 3d DCA 2002), *review dismissed*, 854 So. 2d 660 (Fla. 2003), *cert. denied*, 542 U.S. 937, 124 S.Ct. 2909, 159 L.Ed.2d 813 (2004). . . .

On Motion for Rehearing

Per Curiam.

We grant the motion for rehearing in one respect, and deny the remainder of the motion.

The former husband argues that under the terms of this court's opinion dated November 3, he is precluded from filing a pro se motion to invoke the discretionary review jurisdiction of the Florida Supreme Court. That is so because this court's opinion directs "the clerk of this court to reject any further filings in this court on the former husband's behalf unless signed by a member of the Florida Bar (other than the former husband)." Opinion at 988.

This court has permitted the former husband to file a pro se motion for rehearing and rehearing en banc in this case. Consistent with that procedure, we modify our opinion of November 3, 2004, to permit the filing of a pro se notice to invoke discretionary jurisdiction of the Florida Supreme Court, should the former husband choose to do so.

The former husband maintains that this court should not have quoted his correspondence to his former wife, arguing that the quoted correspondence is not in the record of this appeal. That point is without merit. We clearly stated in our opinion of November 3 that for purposes of part V of the opinion, this court reviewed its files in all of the former husband's prior appellate proceedings. The quoted letter is found in *Sibley v. Sibley*, No. 3D02-3171, 833 So. 2d 847 (Fla. 3d DCA 2002), Appendix to Appellee's Answer Brief.

We deny rehearing on the remaining points without further discussion.

Rehearing granted in part, denied in part.

———

One of the results of behavior like that seen in *Sibley v. Sibley* is Florida's Vexatious Litigant Law. *See* Patrick John McGinley, FLORIDA ELEMENTS OF AN ACTION § 1801:1 (2015-2016 ed.):

> Due in part to the fact that the Constitution of the State of Florida guarantees access to courts, the Florida Legislature and Florida's "courts generally do not have the authority to restrict a litigant's access to the courts, unless the litigant is abusing the legal process." One permissible restriction is the court's authority to require a frivolous litigant to be represented by counsel in future actions. Another permissible restriction is Florida's Vexatious Litigation Law.

The statutory basis for the cause of action under Florida's Vexatious Litigant Law reads as follows:

Section 68.093. Florida Statutes: Florida Vexatious Litigant Law

(1) This section may be cited as the "Florida Vexatious Litigant Law."

(2) As used in section, the term:

(a) "Action" means a civil action governed by the Florida Rules of Civil Procedure and proceedings governed by the Florida Probate Rules, but does not include actions concerning family law matters governed by the Florida

Family Law Rules of Procedure or any action in which the Florida Small Claims Rules apply.

(b) "Defendant" means any person or entity, including a corporation, association, partnership, firm, or governmental entity, against whom an action is or was commenced or is sought to be commenced.

(c) "Security" means an undertaking by a vexatious litigant to ensure payment to a defendant in an amount reasonably sufficient to cover the defendant's anticipated, reasonable expenses of litigation, including attorney's fees and taxable costs.

(d) "Vexatious litigant" means:

1. A person as defined in Fla. Stat. s. 1.01(3) who, in the immediately preceding five-year period, has commenced, prosecuted, or maintained, pro se, five or more civil actions in any court in this state, except an action governed by the Florida Small Claims Rules, which actions have been finally and adversely determined against such person or entity; or

2. Any person or entity previously found to be a vexatious litigant pursuant to this section.

An action is not deemed to be "finally and adversely determined" if an appeal in that action is pending. If an action has been commenced on behalf of a party by an attorney licensed to practice law in this state, that action is not deemed to be pro se even if the attorney later withdraws from the representation and the party does not retain new counsel.

(3)

(a) In any action pending in any court of this state, including actions governed by the Florida Small Claims Rules, any defendant may move the court, upon notice and hearing, for an order requiring the plaintiff to furnish security. The motion shall be based on the grounds, and supported by a showing, that the plaintiff is a vexatious litigant and is not reasonably likely to prevail on the merits of the action against the moving defendant.

(b) At the hearing upon any defendant's motion for an order to post security, the court shall consider any evidence, written or oral, by witness or affidavit, which may be relevant to the consideration of the motion. No determination made by the court in such a hearing shall be admissible on the merits of the action or deemed to be a determination of any issue in the action. If, after hearing the evidence, the court determines that the plaintiff is a vexatious litigant and is not reasonably likely to prevail on the merits of the action against the moving defendant, the court shall order the plaintiff to furnish security to the moving defendant in an amount and within such time as the court deems appropriate.

(c) If the plaintiff fails to post security required by an order of the court under this section, the court shall immediately issue an order dismissing the action with prejudice as to the defendant for whose benefit the security was ordered.

(d) If a motion for an order to post security is filed prior to the trial in an action, the action shall be automatically stayed and the moving defendant need not plead or otherwise respond to the complaint until 10 days after the motion is denied. If the motion is granted, the moving defendant shall respond or plead no later than 10 days after the required security has been furnished.

(4) In addition to any other relief provided in this section, the court in any judicial circuit may, on its own motion or on the motion of any party, enter a pre-filing order prohibiting a vexatious litigant from commencing, pro se, any new action in the courts of that circuit without first obtaining leave of the administrative judge of that circuit. Disobedience of such an order may be punished as contempt of court by the administrative judge of that circuit. Leave of court shall be granted by the administrative judge only upon a showing that the proposed action is meritorious and is not being filed for the purpose of delay or harassment. The administrative judge may condition the filing of the proposed action upon the furnishing of security as provided in this section.

(5) The clerk of the court shall not file any new action by a vexatious litigant pro se unless the vexatious litigant has obtained an order from the administrative judge permitting such filing. If the clerk of the court mistakenly permits a vexatious litigant to file an action pro se in contravention of a pre-filing order, any party to that action may file with the clerk and serve on the plaintiff and all other defendants a notice stating that the plaintiff is a pro se vexatious litigant subject to a pre-filing order. The filing of such a notice shall automatically stay the litigation against all defendants to the action. The administrative judge shall automatically dismiss the action with prejudice within 10 days after the filing of such notice unless the plaintiff files a motion for leave to file the action. If the administrative judge issues an order permitting the action to be filed, the defendants need not plead or otherwise respond to the complaint until 10 days after the date of service by the plaintiff, by United States mail, of a copy of the order granting leave to file the action.

(6) The clerk of a court shall provide copies of all prefiling orders to the Clerk of the Florida Supreme Court, who shall maintain a registry of all vexatious litigants.

(7) The relief provided under this section shall be cumulative to any other relief or remedy available to a defendant under the laws of this state and the Florida Rules of Civil Procedure, including, but not limited to, the relief provided under s. 57.105.

F. Right of Access to Courts: Can an Amendment to a "Reasonable Alternative" Become a "Tipping Point" That Transforms a Previously "Reasonable Alternative" into an Unreasonable One?

In *Kluger v. White*, the Supreme Court of Florida cited Florida's Workers' Compensation Law as its example of an "adequate alternative" to the access to court. But in 2016, a new generation of Florida Supreme Court justices applied the holding of *Kluger v. White* to find an amendment to Florida's Workers' Compensation Law to be a violation of the access to courts under the Florida Constitution.

A potential cessation of payments of temporary "indemnity" (a type of wage-substitution benefits), combined with a potential delay on the start of permanent "indemnity," created a potential "gap" where injured workers were unpaid for a potentially indefinite period. This prompted the Florida Supreme Court to hold that "there must eventually come a 'tipping point,' where the diminution of benefits becomes so significant as to constitute a *denial* of benefits—thus creating a constitutional violation." *Westphal v. City of St. Petersburg*, 194 So. 3d 311 (Fla. 2016). That opinion appears below.

Westphal v. City of St. Petersburg
Supreme Court of Florida, 2016
194 So. 3d 311

In this case, we consider the constitutionality of section 440.15(2)(a), Florida Statutes (2009)—part of the state's workers' compensation law—which cuts off disability benefits after 104 weeks to a worker who is totally disabled and incapable of working but who has not yet reached maximum medical improvement. We conclude that this portion of the worker's compensation statute is unconstitutional under article I, section 21, of the Florida Constitution, as a denial of the right of access to courts, because it deprives an injured worker of disability benefits under these circumstances for an indefinite amount of time—thereby creating a system of redress that no longer functions as a reasonable alternative to tort litigation.

... [W]e conclude that section 440.15(2)(a) of the workers' compensation law is plainly written and therefore does not permit this Court to resort to rules of statutory construction. *See Knowles v. Beverly Enters.-Fla., Inc.*, 898 So. 2d 1, 5 (Fla. 2004). Instead, we must give the statute its plain and obvious meaning, which provides that "[o]nce the employee reaches the maximum number of weeks allowed [104 weeks], or the employee reaches the date of maximum medical improvement, whichever occurs earlier, temporary disability benefits shall cease . . .".

... Applying the statute's plain meaning, we conclude that the 104-week limitation on temporary total disability benefits results in a statutory gap in benefits, in violation of the constitutional right of access to courts. ...

. . . [F]or injured workers like Westphal who are not yet legally entitled to assert a claim for permanent total disability benefits at the conclusion of 104 weeks of temporary total disability benefits, the workers' compensation law lacks adequate and sufficient safeguards and cannot be said to continue functioning as a "system of compensation without contest" that stands as a reasonable alternative to tort litigation. . . . [T]he seminal case on the meaning of the Florida Constitution's access to courts provision, *Kluger v. White*, 281 So. 2d 1 (Fla. 1973), specifically discussed the test for determining the constitutionality of the workers' compensation statutory scheme under the access to courts provision, article I, section 21, of the Florida Constitution. The constitutional yardstick . . . determining whether an access-to-courts violation occurred as a result of changes made to the workers' compensation statutory scheme, is whether the scheme continues to provide "adequate, sufficient, and even preferable safeguards for an employee who is injured on the job." *Kluger*, 281 So. 2d at 4.

Accordingly, we hold that the statute as written by the Legislature is unconstitutional. However, we conclude that this unconstitutional limitation on temporary total disability benefits does not render the entire workers' compensation system invalid. Rather, we employ the remedy of statutory revival and direct that the limitation in the workers' compensation law preceding the 1994 amendments to section 440.15(2)(a) is revived, which provides for temporary total disability benefits not to exceed 260 weeks—five years of eligibility rather than only two years, a limitation we previously held "passes constitutional muster." *Martinez*, 582 So. 2d at 1172.

I. Facts and Procedural History

In December 2009, Bradley Westphal, then a fifty-three-year-old firefighter in St. Petersburg, Florida, suffered a severe lower back injury caused by lifting heavy furniture in the course of fighting a fire. As a result of the lower back injury, Westphal experienced extreme pain and loss of feeling in his left leg below the knee and required multiple surgical procedures, including an eventual spinal fusion. . . .

At the expiration of temporary total disability benefits, Westphal was still incapable of working or obtaining employment, based on the advice of his doctors and the vocational experts that examined him. In an attempt to replace his pre-injury wages of approximately $1,500 per week that he was losing because of his injuries, Westphal filed a petition for benefits, claiming either further temporary disability or permanent total disability pursuant to section 440.15(1), Florida Statutes (2009).

A. Judge of Compensation Claims Decision

The Judge of Compensation Claims (JCC) . . . denied Westphal's claim. . . . Thus, Westphal fell into the statutory gap—still totally disabled at the cessation of temporary total disability benefits, but not yet entitled to permanent total disability benefits. . . . He was, in essence, completely cut off from disability benefits for an indefinite amount of time, unless and until he could claim entitlement to permanent total disability benefits at some future date and, even then, without any ability to recover disability benefits for his time in the statutory gap.

B. First District Panel Decision

. . . [R]elying on *Kluger*, 281 So. 2d 1, the First District panel concluded that the 104-week limitation on temporary total disability benefits was an inadequate remedy as compared to the 350 weeks available when voters adopted the access to courts provision in the 1968 Florida Constitution. The First District panel also observed that the 104-week limitation on temporary total disability benefits was the lowest in the United States. The First District panel applied its decision prospectively and instructed the JCC to grant Westphal additional temporary total disability benefits, not to exceed 260 weeks, as would have been provided under the relevant statutory provisions in effect before the 1994 amendment of section 440.15(2)(a). . . .

C. First District En Banc Decision

Subsequent to the panel decision, the First District granted motions for rehearing en banc . . . then issued an en banc decision withdrawing the panel opinion that had declared the statute unconstitutional [by s]etting forth a new interpretation of the statute to avoid a holding of unconstitutionality. . . .

As a result of this new interpretation of the statute, which eliminated the statutory gap, the First District found it unnecessary to consider whether . . . the gap . . . rendered the statute unconstitutional as a denial of the right of access to courts. *Id.* at 447. The First District then certified the question it passed upon as one of great public importance. *Id.* at 448. We granted review and now quash the First District's en banc decision and hold the statute unconstitutional as applied, in accordance with the prior panel opinion.

II. Analysis

. . . We thus begin our analysis by interpreting section 440.15 to determine if the First District's en banc opinion — eliminating the statutory gap — provides a permissible statutory construction. . . . After concluding that the First District's en banc opinion is an impermissible judicial rewrite of the Legislature's plainly written statute, we are forced to confront the constitutional issue of whether the statute, as applied to Westphal and other similarly situated severely injured workers, is unconstitutional. Concluding that the statute, as applied, violates the access to courts provision of the Florida Constitution, we conclude by considering the appropriate remedy.

A. Section 440.15, Florida Statutes

Section 440.15, Florida Statutes (2009), governs the payment of disability benefits to injured workers. As of the 1968 adoption of the Florida Constitution, . . . section 440.15(2) provided for the payment of temporary total disability benefits for a duration not to exceed 350 weeks. § 440.15(2), Fla. Stat. (1968). . . .

In 1990, the Legislature reduced the duration of temporary total disability benefits from 350 weeks to 260 weeks. § 440.15(2), Fla. Stat. (1990). Then, just four years later, and as part of an extensive statutory overhaul, the Legislature further reduced the duration of temporary total disability benefits from 260 weeks to 104 weeks. § 440.15(2)(a), Fla. Stat. (1994). . . .

As the First District recognized . . . "[t]he statutory scheme in section 440.15 works seamlessly when the injured employee reaches [maximum medical improvement] prior to the expiration of the 104 weeks of temporary disability benefits." *Id.* But where "the employee is not at [maximum medical improvement] at the expiration of the 104 weeks, there is the potential for a 'gap' in disability benefits because [temporary total disability] benefits cease by operation of law after 104 weeks and entitlement to [permanent total disability] benefits is generally not ripe until the employee reaches [maximum medical improvement]." *Id.*

. . . It is clear from the statute that the Legislature intended to limit the duration of temporary total disability benefits to a maximum of 104 weeks. It is further clear that the Legislature intended to limit the class of individuals who are entitled to permanent total disability benefits to those with catastrophic injuries and those who are able to demonstrate a permanent inability to engage in even sedentary employment within a fifty-mile radius of their home. In other words, these provisions "create a gap in disability benefits for those injured workers who are totally disabled upon the expiration of temporary disability benefits but fail to prove prospectively that total disability will exist after the date of [maximum medical improvement]."

Because we hold that the statute is clear in creating a statutory gap in benefits, and thus not susceptible to the rules of statutory construction, we turn to Westphal's constitutional challenge—that the statute as plainly written results in a denial of access to courts.

B. Denial of Access to Courts

Article I, section 21, of the Florida Constitution, part of our state constitutional "Declaration of Rights" since 1968, guarantees every person access to the courts and ensures the administration of justice without denial or delay: "The courts shall be open to every person for redress of any injury, and *justice shall be administered without sale, denial or delay.*" Art. I, § 21, Fla. Const. (emphasis added). This important state constitutional right has been construed liberally in order to "guarantee broad accessibility to the courts for resolving disputes." . . . In *Kluger,* this Court explained the meaning of the access to courts provision and the necessary showing for demonstrating a constitutional violation based on access to courts:

> [W]here a right of access to the courts for redress for a particular injury has been provided by statutory law predating the adoption of the Declaration of Rights of the Constitution of the State of Florida, or where such right has become a part of the common law of the State pursuant to Fla. Stat. § 2.01, F.S.A., the Legislature is without power to abolish such a right without providing a reasonable alternative to protect the rights of the people of the State to redress for injuries, unless the Legislature can show an overpowering public necessity for the abolishment of such right, and no alternative method of meeting such public necessity can be shown.

281 So. 2d at 4.

Prior to 1968, when the access to courts provision was adopted, the Legislature had already abolished the common-law tort remedy for injured workers and enacted a workers' compensation law "as administrative legislation to be simple, expeditious, and inexpensive so that the injured employee, his family, or society generally, would be relieved of the economic stress resulting from work-connected injuries, and place the burden on the industry which caused the injury." *Lee Eng'g & Constr. Co. v. Fellows*, 209 So. 2d 454, 456 (Fla. 1968). The workers' compensation law "abolishes the right to sue one's employer and substitutes the right to receive benefits under the compensation scheme." *Sasso v. Ram Prop. Mgmt.*, 452 So. 2d 932, 933 (Fla. 1984).

Nevertheless, the fact that workers' compensation was created prior to 1968 as a non-judicial statutory scheme of no fault benefits intended to provide full medical care and wage-loss payments does not mean that changes to the workers' compensation law to reduce or eliminate benefits are immune from a constitutional attack based on access to courts. In fact, this Court in *Kluger* specifically discussed the alternative remedy of workers' compensation, explaining that "[w]orkmen's compensation abolished the right to sue one's employer in tort for a job-related injury, *but provided adequate, sufficient, and even preferable safeguards for an employee who is injured on the job*, thus satisfying one of the exceptions to the rule against abolition of the right to redress for an injury." *Kluger*, 281 So. 2d at 4 (emphasis added). In other words, as *Kluger* held, workers' compensation constitutes a "reasonable alternative" to tort litigation—and therefore does not violate the access to courts provision—so long as it provides adequate and sufficient safeguards for the injured employee. *Id.* . . .

Therefore, although this Court has rejected constitutional challenges to the workers' compensation law in the past, our precedent clearly establishes that, when confronted with a constitutional challenge based on access to courts, we must determine whether the law "remains a reasonable alternative to tort litigation." *Acton v. Fort Lauderdale Hosp.*, 440 So. 2d 1282, 1284 (Fla. 1983). . . .

The 104-week limitation on temporary total disability benefits and the statutory gap must therefore be viewed through the analytical paradigm of *Kluger*, asking whether the workers' compensation law continues to provide adequate and sufficient safeguards for the injured worker and thus constitutes a constitutional, reasonable alternative to tort litigation. *Kluger*, 281 So. 2d at 4. The "reasonable alternative" test is then the linchpin and measuring stick, and this Court has undoubtedly upheld as constitutional many limitations on workers' compensation benefits as benefits have progressively been reduced over the years and the statutory scheme changed to the detriment of the injured worker.

But, there must eventually come a "tipping point," where the diminution of benefits becomes so significant as to constitute a denial of benefits—thus creating a constitutional violation. [Emphasis added.] We accordingly must review what has occurred to the workers' compensation system . . . in order to determine whether we have now reached that constitutional "tipping point."

As applied to Westphal, the current workers' compensation statutory scheme does not just reduce the amount of benefits he would receive . . . but in fact completely cuts off his ability to receive any disability benefits at all. It does so even though there is no dispute that Westphal remained a severely injured and disabled firefighter under active treatment by doctors the City selected for him. . . . In other words, even though doctors chosen by the City had performed multiple surgical procedures culminating in a five-level spinal fusion, because those same doctors did not render an opinion that Westphal had reached [his Maximum Medical Improvement,] leaving Westphal without disability benefits for an indefinite amount of time while he was still totally disabled and incapable of working.

In comparing the rights of a worker such as Westphal injured on the job today with those of a worker injured in 1968, the extent of the changes in the workers' compensation system is dramatic. A worker injured in 1968 was entitled to receive temporary total disability benefits for up to 350 weeks. *See* § 440.15(2), Fla. Stat. (1968). In 1990, the Legislature reduced the availability of temporary total disability benefits from 350 to 260 weeks — a 25.7% reduction of two years. *See* ch. 90–201, § 20, Laws of Fla. Then, in 1993, the Legislature again reduced the availability of temporary total disability benefits, this time from 260 weeks to 104 weeks — a 60% reduction. *See* ch. 93–415, § 20, Laws of Fla. This means that an injured worker such as Westphal is now eligible to receive only 104 weeks of temporary total disability benefits — a massive 70% reduction when compared to the temporary total disability benefits available in 1968.

It is uncontroverted that decreasing substantially the period of payments from 350 weeks to 104 weeks, standing alone, results in a dramatic reduction from almost seven years of disability benefits down to two years. Whereas almost seven years or even five years post-accident should be a reasonable period for an injured worker to achieve maximum medical improvement, clearly two years is not for the most severely injured of workers, like Westphal, who might be in need of multiple surgical interventions.

Currently, at the conclusion of the 104-week limit, temporary total disability benefits cease, regardless of the condition of the injured worker. Therefore, rather than receive "full medical care and wage-loss payments" for a continuing disability, as the workers' compensation law was intended, an injured worker's full medical care and wage-loss payments are eliminated after 104 weeks if the worker falls into the statutory gap. This is true even if the worker remains incapable of working for an indefinite period of time, based on the advice of the employer-selected doctors.

. . . We have now reached that point at which "the claimant's cause of action has been effectively eliminated"—the constitutional "tipping point" of which [prior case law precedent] forewarned. [emphasis added]

We conclude that the 104-week limitation on temporary total disability benefits, as applied to a worker like Westphal, who falls into the statutory gap at the conclusion of those benefits, does not provide a "reasonable alternative" to tort litigation. Under the current statute, workers such as Westphal are denied their constitutional right of access to the courts. . . .

Thus, under the access to courts analysis articulated in *Kluger*, the only way to avoid a holding of unconstitutionality under these circumstances would be to demonstrate an overwhelming public necessity to justify the Legislature's elimination of temporary total disability benefits after 104 weeks for our most injured workers. *See Kluger*, 281 So. 2d at 4. We conclude that this showing has not been made. The statute is unconstitutional as applied.

Accordingly, the question becomes one of remedy. "Florida law has long held that, when the legislature approves unconstitutional statutory language and simultaneously repeals its predecessor, then the judicial act of striking the new statutory language automatically revives the predecessor unless it, too, would be unconstitutional." *B.H. v. State*, 645 So. 2d 987, 995 (Fla. 1994). We therefore conclude that the proper remedy is the revival of the pre-1994 statute that provided for a limitation of 260 weeks of temporary total disability benefits. *See* § 440.15(2)(a), Fla. Stat. (1991). The provision of 260 weeks of temporary total disability benefits amounts to two and a half times more benefits — five years of eligibility for benefits rather than only two — and thus avoids the constitutional infirmity created by the current statutory gap as applied to Westphal.

In this regard, we respectfully disagree with the assertion in Justice Lewis's concurring in result opinion that this remedy is insufficient because it still allows for the possibility of a statutory gap, and would therefore unconstitutionally deprive claimants of access to courts. Concurring in result op. of Lewis, J., at 35. In fact, as we have indicated throughout this opinion, we previously held that the pre-1994 statute's limitation of 260 weeks "passes constitutional muster" because it "remains a reasonable alternative to tort litigation," where a worker "is not without a remedy." *Martinez*, 582 So. 2d at 1171–72. Although the length of time available for the administration of temporary total disability benefits to a worker before the worker reaches maximum medical improvement does involve line drawing, the difference between a period of only two years (104 weeks) and five years (260 weeks) is significant as it relates to the time it takes a worker to attain maximum medical improvement.

III. Conclusion

For all the reasons explained in this opinion, we hold section 440.15(2)(a), Florida Statutes (2009), unconstitutional as applied to Westphal and all others similarly situated, as a denial of access to courts under article I, section 21, of the Florida Constitution. . . . Accordingly, we quash the First District's en banc decision in *Westphal* and remand this case to the First District for further proceedings consistent with this opinion.

LaBarga, Chief Justice, and Quince, and Perry, Justices, concur.

Justice Lewis concurs in result with an opinion:

I agree with the conclusion reached by the majority that section 440.15(2)(a) is unconstitutional as applied to Bradley Westphal.... However, at this point in time, I conclude that the remedy relied upon by the majority is insufficient. Statutory revival of the 1994 limitation, which provides for the administration of temporary total disability for 260 weeks, may provide relief for those individuals who remain totally disabled but have not been deemed permanently disabled at the end of 104 weeks. However, this remedy simply moves the goalposts without eliminating the unconstitutional statutory gap that will still persist for those who remain totally—but not permanently—disabled after 260 weeks. Therefore, I do not believe that this is a situation in which statutory revival is appropriate. *Cf. B.H. v. State*, 645 So. 2d 987, 995 (Fla. 1994) ("[T]he judicial act of striking the new statutory language automatically revives the predecessor *unless it, too, would be unconstitutional.*" (emphasis added)). In my opinion, the only appropriate remedy would be to require the Legislature to provide a comprehensive, *constitutional* Workers' Compensation scheme, rather than rely on the courts to rewrite existing law or revive prior law. I believe that the remedy provided today fails to fully address the problems with the Workers' Compensation scheme because it will still leave some injured Florida workers without access to benefits to which they are entitled. Thus, the majority decision leaves Florida workers in an only marginally better position than they were in prior to this matter by failing to address and remove the inadequate alternative remedy, thereby leaving the Workers' Compensation scheme unconstitutional and in need of major reform. As I see it, such a system is fundamentally unconstitutional and in need of legislative—not judicial—reform.

Over time, the Florida judiciary has repeatedly rewritten provisions of the Workers' Compensation Law to avoid a declaration of unconstitutionality. No fair-minded individual who reads these decisions can reasonably conclude that they involve simple statutory interpretation.... I have a full appreciation for the judicial attempts to save the Workers' Compensation statute from total disaster. Florida needs a valid Workers' Compensation program, but the charade is over. Enough is enough, and Florida workers deserve better....

The truth of the matter is that section 440.15 is hopelessly broken and cannot be constitutionally salvaged. The judicial branch must terminate the practice of rewriting the statute....

Accordingly, I concur in the result.

Justice Canady, dissenting:

...I would reject Westphal's argument that the statutory limitation on the period of eligibility for temporary total disability benefits violates the right of access to courts provided for in article I, section 21 of the Florida Constitution.

In the foundational case of *Kluger v. White*, 281 So. 2d 1, 4 (Fla. 1973) (emphasis added), we set forth the test for determining whether an access-to-courts violation has occurred:

> [W]here a right of access to the courts for redress for a particular injury has been provided by statutory law predating the adoption of the Declaration of Rights of the [1968] Constitution of the State of Florida, or where such right has become a part of the common law of the State pursuant to [section 2.01, Florida Statutes], the Legislature is without power to *abolish such a right* without providing a reasonable alternative to protect the rights of the people of the State to redress for injuries, unless the Legislature can show an overpowering public necessity for the abolishment of such right, and no alternative method of meeting such public necessity can be shown.

The threshold question in evaluating an access-to-courts claim therefore is whether the Legislature has abolished a right of redress that was in existence when the access to courts provision was incorporated into the 1968 Constitution.

Here, the challenged statutory provision restructures an existing right of redress. It does not abolish that right. The State argues persuasively that "today's workers' compensation system allowed Westphal substantially greater temporary total disability benefits than any 1968 statutory right provided" and that "[t]he amendment limiting temporary total disability benefits to 104 weeks, therefore, did not 'abolish' any pre-existing right." State's Answer Brief at 14. Westphal does not dispute the State's assertion that the aggregate compensation paid to him for temporary total disability benefits substantially exceeded the aggregate compensation for such benefits that would have been available under the pre-1968 law, even when the pre-1968 benefits are adjusted for inflation. Instead, he contends that "[t]his case is about weeks, not about dollars." Petitioner's Reply Brief at 9. But the decision to substantially increase weekly compensation for temporary total disability and to reduce the number of weeks that such benefits are paid is a trade-off that is a matter of policy within the province of the Legislature. The Legislature — rather than this Court — has the institutional competence and authority to make such policy judgments.

We have long recognized that the Legislature should be afforded latitude in the structuring of remedies both outside the worker's compensation context . . . and within the workers compensation context. . . . We should do likewise here and reject Westphal's access-to-courts challenge.

Justice Polston Concurs.

Chapter 6

Privacy

In previous chapters of this book, we reviewed representative examples of rights secured by the Constitution of the State of Florida that do not appear to be interpreted in quite the same way as similar rights that appear in the federal Constitution.

In this chapter of this book, we change our focus to analyze rights that do not appear in the text of the federal Constitution but that appear in the text of the Florida Constitution.

A. Different Origins of the Federal and Florida's Constitutional Right of Privacy

The text of the U.S. Constitution does not enumerate a right of privacy. But of course, case law precedent of the Supreme Court of the United States found one. The World War I-era case of *Meyer v. Nebraska*, 262 U.S. 390 (1923), overturned school teacher Robert T. Meyer's criminal conviction for teaching the German language to his students. In so doing, the Supreme Court of the United States cited the Fourteenth Amendment to the U.S. Constitution and held:

> While this court has not attempted to define with exactness the liberty thus guaranteed, the term has received much consideration and some of the included things have been definitely stated. Without doubt, it denotes not merely freedom from bodily restraint but also the right of the individual to contract, to engage in any of the common occupations of life, to acquire useful knowledge, to marry, establish a home and bring up children, to worship God according to the dictates of his own conscience, and generally to enjoy those privileges long recognized at common law as essential to the orderly pursuit of happiness by free men. . . . The established doctrine is that this liberty may not be interfered with, under the guise of protecting the public interest, by legislative action which is arbitrary or without reasonable relation to some purpose within the competency of the state to effect. Determination by the Legislature of what constitutes proper exercise of police power is not final or conclusive but is subject to supervision by the courts.

262 U.S. at 399.

This 1923 decision implies but does not find a right to privacy, and does so under the right of "substantive due process" arising from the Fourteenth Amendment to the U.S. Constitution. But contemporaneously with this opinion, justices of the U.S. Supreme Court were citing to parts of the U.S. Constitution other than the Fourteenth Amendment as the source of a right to privacy. For example, in the 1928 decision of *Olmstead v. United States*, 277 U.S. 438 (1928), Justice Brandeis, dissenting, wrote:

> The protection guaranteed by the amendments [to the U.S. Constitution] is much broader in scope. The makers of our Constitution undertook to secure conditions favorable to the pursuit of happiness. They recognized the significance of man's spiritual nature, of his feelings and of his intellect. They knew that only a part of the pain, pleasure and satisfactions of life are to be found in material things. They sought to protect Americans in their beliefs, their thoughts, their emotions and their sensations. They conferred, as against the government, the right to be let alone — the most comprehensive of rights and the right most valued by civilized men. To protect, that right, every unjustifiable intrusion by the government upon the privacy of the individual, whatever the means employed, must be deemed a violation of the Fourth Amendment. And the use, as evidence in a criminal proceeding, of facts ascertained by such intrusion must be deemed a violation of the Fifth.

277 U.S. at 478 (Brandeis, J., dissenting).

But as time progressed, the U.S. Supreme Court did not confine itself to the Fourth, Fifth, or Fifteenth Amendment as the alleged source of a federal constitutional right to privacy. In the 1960s, the implication of a right of privacy arising from the First Amendment to the U.S. Constitution "reemerged under the Warren Court to protect personal liberties of speech, association, religion, and privacy." Kathleen M. Sullivan, *Unconstitutional Conditions*, 102 Harv. L. Rev. 1417 (1989). From this era came the U.S. Supreme Court's decision regarding a right to privacy called *Griswold v. Connecticut*, 381 U.S. 479 (1965). Two members of the Connecticut branch of Planned Parenthood opened a clinic with the goal of getting themselves arrested and convicted of violating Connecticut's law against birth control. In overturning the conviction, the Supreme Court of the United States held:

> In *NAACP v. State of Alabama*, 357 U.S. 449, 462, 78 S.Ct. 1163, 1172, we protected the 'freedom to associate and privacy in one's associations,' noting that freedom of association was a peripheral First Amendment right. Disclosure of membership lists of a constitutionally valid association, we held, was invalid 'as entailing the likelihood of a substantial restraint upon the exercise by petitioner's members of their right to freedom of association.' *Ibid*. In other words, the First Amendment has a penumbra where privacy is protected from governmental intrusion. . . .
>
> The right of 'association,' like the right of belief (*West Virginia State Board of Education v. Barnette*, 319 U.S. 624, 63 S.Ct. 1178), is more than

the right to attend a meeting; it includes the right to express one's attitudes or philosophies by membership in a group or by affiliation with it or by other lawful means. Association in that context is a form of expression of opinion; and while it is not expressly included in the First Amendment its existence is necessary in making the express guarantees fully meaningful.

The foregoing cases suggest that specific guarantees in the Bill of Rights have penumbras, formed by emanations from those guarantees that help give them life and substance. See *Poe v. Ullman*, 367 U.S. 497, 516–522, 81 S.Ct. 1752, 6 L.Ed.2d 989 (1961) (dissenting opinion). Various guarantees create zones of privacy. The right of association contained in the penumbra of the First Amendment is one, as we have seen. The Third Amendment in its prohibition against the quartering of soldiers 'in any house' in time of peace without the consent of the owner is another facet of that privacy. The Fourth Amendment explicitly affirms the 'right of the people to be secure in their persons, houses, papers, and effects, against unreasonable searches and seizures.' The Fifth Amendment in its Self-Incrimination Clause enables the citizen to create a zone of privacy which government may not force him to surrender to his detriment. The Ninth Amendment provides: 'The enumeration in the Constitution, of certain rights, shall not be construed to deny or disparage others retained by the people.'

The Fourth and Fifth Amendments were described in *Boyd v. United States*, 116 U.S. 616, 630, 6 S.Ct. 524, 532, 29 L.Ed. 746, as protection against all governmental invasions 'of the sanctity of a man's home and the privacies of life.' We recently referred in *Mapp v. Ohio*, 367 U.S. 643, 656, 81 S.Ct. 1684, 1692, 6 L.Ed.2d 1081, to the Fourth Amendment as creating a 'right to privacy, no less important than any other right carefully and particularly reserved to the people.' See Beaney, *The Constitutional Right to Privacy*, 1962 Sup.Ct.Rev. 212; Griswold, *The Right to Be Let Alone*, 55 Nw. U. L. Rev. 216 (1960).

We have had many controversies over these penumbral rights of 'privacy and repose.' . . . These cases bear witness that the right of privacy which presses for recognition here is a legitimate one.

381 U.S. at 483–84.

This quoted rationale from *Griswold v. Connecticut* shows that, unlike *Meyer v. Nebraska*, which implied a right to privacy arising from the Fourteenth Amendment to the U.S. Constitution, *Griswold v. Connecticut* found a right to privacy in "penumbras, formed by emanations" from the First Amendment (per the majority opinion) and Ninth Amendment (per a concurring opinion) to the U.S. Constitution.

Yet by 1973, the majority of the justices of the Supreme Court of the United States cited the Fourteenth Amendment, and not the First Amendment, as the source of this unwritten Right to Privacy that U.S. Supreme Court case law developed out of the penumbras and emanations of the Bill of Rights of the U.S. Constitution.

Specifically, in *Roe v. Wade*, 410 U.S. 113 (1973), the appellant argued to the Supreme Court of the United States:

> that the Texas statutes were unconstitutionally vague and that they abridged her right of personal privacy, protected by the First, Fourth, Fifth, Ninth, and Fourteenth Amendments. . . . The principal thrust of appellant's attack on the Texas statutes is that they improperly invade a right, said to be possessed by the pregnant woman, to choose to terminate her pregnancy. Appellant would discover this right in the concept of personal 'liberty' embodied in the Fourteenth Amendment's Due Process Clause; or in personal marital, familial, and sexual privacy said to be protected by the Bill of Rights or its penumbras, see *Griswold v. Connecticut*, 381 U.S. 479 (1965); . . . or among those rights reserved to the people by the Ninth Amendment, *Griswold v. Connecticut*, 381 U.S. at 486 (Goldberg, J., concurring).

410 U.S. at 120 & 129. In response, the U.S. Supreme Court held:

> The Constitution [of the United States] does not explicitly mention any right of privacy. In a line of decisions, however, going back perhaps as far as [1891] . . . the Court has recognized that a right of personal privacy, or a guarantee of certain areas or zones of privacy, does exist under the Constitution. In varying contexts, the Court or individual Justices have, indeed, found at least the roots of that right in the First Amendment, . . . in the Fourth and Fifth Amendments, . . . in the penumbras of the Bill of Rights, *Griswold v. Connecticut*, 381 U.S., at 484–485; in the Ninth Amendment, *id*. at 486 (Goldberg, J., concurring); or in the concept of liberty guaranteed by the first section of the Fourteenth Amendment, see *Meyer v. Nebraska*, 262 U.S. 390, 399 (1923). These decisions make it clear that only personal rights that can be deemed 'fundamental' or 'implicit in the concept of ordered liberty,' . . . are included in this guarantee of personal privacy. They also make it clear that the right has some extension to activities relating to marriage, . . . procreation, . . . contraception, . . . family relationships, . . . and child rearing and education. . . .
>
> This right of privacy, whether it be founded in the Fourteenth Amendment's concept of personal liberty and restrictions upon state action, as we feel it is, or, as the District Court determined, in the Ninth Amendment's reservation of rights to the people, is broad enough to encompass a woman's decision whether or not to terminate her pregnancy.

410 U.S. at 153. Thus, the Supreme Court of the United States both acknowledged that the U.S. "Constitution does not explicitly mention any right of privacy" but that nevertheless a federal right to privacy exists and is "founded in the Fourteenth Amendment's concept of personal liberty and restrictions upon state action." *Id*.

By comparison, the Constitution of the State of Florida contains language enumerating an explicit right to privacy. Specifically, Article I, Section 23, of Florida's constitution states:

Every natural person has the right to be let alone and free from governmental intrusion into the person's private life except as otherwise provided herein. This section shall not be construed to limit the public's right of access to public records and meetings as provided by law.

Professor D'Alemberte analyzes this section as it was enacted in 1980 and before it was amended in 1998 and notes that "the language originated with the 1978 Constitution Revision Commission. When the wide-ranging proposals of that commission met defeat in 1978, this provision was taken up separately by the legislature in 1980 and passed by the electorate [even though] it was opposed by most media organizations . . .". Talbot D'Alemberte, THE FLORIDA STATE CONSTITUTION 39–40 (Oxford University Press 2011).

B. Applying Florida's Right of Privacy

Note that Professor D'Alemberte opines in 2011 that "it is conceivable that a person would have a cause of action under this section to prevent the collection of private information by the government." *Id.* at 39. Time has proven this opinion correct. As explained in FLORIDA ELEMENTS OF AN ACTION:

Section 23, Article I of the Constitution of the State of Florida [and its] right to privacy . . . "embraces more privacy interests, and extends more protection to the individual in those interests, than does the federal Constitution." The elements of an action in Florida for a violation of this right to privacy are:

(1) State action;

and

(2) A legitimate expectation of privacy;

and

(3) Infringement upon that expectation of privacy by the state action;

and

(4) Such infringement cannot be shown [by the government] to both:

(a) protect a compelling state interest and

(b) achieve that protection in the least-intrusive manner possible.

The right of privacy "was not intended to provide an absolute guarantee against all governmental intrusion into the private life of an individual." However, Florida's supreme court has held that "although there is no catalogue in our constitutional provision as to those matters encompassed by the term privacy, it seems apparent to us that personal finances are among those private matters kept secret by most people." . . .

The Florida right to privacy has been found to protect the privacy rights of citizens from the unreasonable interception of communications.

Similarly, "the constitutional right of privacy undoubtedly expresses a policy that compelled disclosure through discovery be limited to that which is necessary for a court to determine contested issues. . . ."

Patrick John McGinley, FLORIDA ELEMENTS OF AN ACTION § 1502:1 (2017 ed.) (footnotes omitted).

In the following case of *Winfield v. Division of Pari-Mutual Wagering*, 477 So. 2d 544 (Fla. 1985)—a case that from time to time appears on the Florida Bar Exam—the Supreme Court of the State of Florida identified the right of privacy as a fundamental right entitled to heightened protection under Florida's constitution.

Winfield v. Division of Pari-Mutuel Wagering, Department of Business Regulation

Supreme Court of Florida, 1985
477 So. 2d 544

This cause is before us for review of two questions certified by the Fourth District Court of Appeal to be of great public importance. . . . We have jurisdiction. Art. V, § 3(b)(4), Fla. Const.

The Department of Business Regulation and the Division of Pari-Mutuel Wagering, respondents, issued subpoenas duces tecum to various banking institutions to obtain banking records of the accounts of Nigel Winfield and Malcolm Winfield, petitioners. Respondents gave no notice of the subpoenas to petitioners and asked the banks not to inform petitioners of the investigation.

Petitioners filed for declaratory and injunctive relief against the subpoenas duces tecum alleging that the subpoenas were facially invalid, that they violated petitioners' constitutional right to privacy and due process, and that maintenance of the records as public records in the respondent's files constituted an additional violation of their constitutional right to privacy. The circuit court found that respondents had probable cause to institute the investigation, and that it had acted within its authority. The court nevertheless granted petitioners relief on the grounds that their constitutional privacy rights would be violated if the subpoenaed records became public records in the hands of respondents pursuant to chapter 119, Florida Statutes. The court thereupon confirmed a previous interlocutory order in effect restraining respondents from inspecting, copying or using the records or the information contained in them, and directing that the records be maintained under court seal. Appeal was taken to the district court which ruled in favor of respondents and certified the following questions to this Court as being of great public importance:

I. Does article I, section 23 of the Florida Constitution prevent the Division of Pari-Mutuel Wagering from subpoenaing a Florida citizen's bank records without notice?

II. Does the subpoenaing of *all* of a citizen's bank records under the facts of this case constitute an impermissible and unbridled exercise of legislative power?

443 So. 2d at 457. We answer both questions in the negative and approve the decision of the district court.

The concept of privacy or right to be let alone is deeply rooted in our heritage and is founded upon historical notions and federal constitutional expressions of ordered liberty. Justice Brandeis, sometimes called the father of the idea of privacy, recognized this fundamental right of privacy when he wrote:

> The makers of our Constitution undertook to secure conditions favorable to the pursuit of happiness. They recognized the significance of man's spiritual nature, of his feelings and of his intellect. . . . They sought to protect Americans in their beliefs, their thoughts, their emotions and their sensations. They conferred, as against the Government, the right to be let alone—the most comprehensive of rights and the right most valued by civilized men.

Olmstead v. United States, 277 U.S. 438, 478 (1928) (Brandeis, J., dissenting).

The United States Supreme Court has fashioned a right of privacy which protects the decision-making or autonomy zone of privacy interests of the individual. The Court's decisions include matters concerning marriage, procreation, contraception, family relationships and child rearing, and education. *Roe v. Wade*, 410 U.S. 113, 152–53 (1973). Other privacy interests enunciated by the Court in *Nixon v. Administrator of General Services*, 433 U.S. 425 (1977), and *Whalen v. Roe*, 429 U.S. 589 (1976), involve one's interest in avoiding the public disclosure of personal matters. However, *Nixon*, *Whalen*, and those cases involving the autonomy zone of privacy are not directly applicable to the case at bar.

In formulating privacy interests, the Supreme Court has given much of the responsibility to the individual states. *Katz v. United States*, 389 U.S. 347, 350–51, 88 S.Ct. 507, 511, 19 L.Ed.2d 576 (1967). Thus, on November 4, 1980, the voters of Florida approved article I, section 23, thereby adding a new privacy provision to the Florida Constitution. Article I, section 23 provides:

> *Right of privacy.* - Every natural person has the right to be let alone and free from governmental intrusion into his private life except as otherwise provided herein. This section shall not be construed to limit the public's right of access to public records and meetings as provided by law.

Heretofore, we have not enunciated the appropriate standard of review in assessing a claim of unconstitutional governmental intrusion into one's privacy rights under article I, section 23. Since the privacy section as adopted contains no textual standard of review, it is important for us to identify an explicit standard to be applied in order to give proper force and effect to the amendment. The right of privacy is a fundamental right which we believe demands the compelling state interest standard. This test shifts the burden of proof to the state to justify an intrusion on privacy. The burden can be met by demonstrating that the challenged regulation serves a compelling state interest and accomplishes its goal using the least intrusive means.

Although we choose a strong standard to review a claim under article I, section 23, "this constitutional provision was not intended to provide an absolute guarantee against all governmental intrusion into the private life of an individual." *Florida Board of Bar Examiners Re: Applicant*, 443 So. 2d 71, 74 (Fla. 1983). The right of privacy does not confer a complete immunity from governmental regulation and will yield to compelling governmental interests.

However, before the right of privacy is attached and the delineated standard applied, a reasonable expectation of privacy must exist. Thus, implicit within the question of whether article I, section 23 of the Florida Constitution prevents the Division of Pari-Mutuel Wagering from subpoenaing a Florida citizen's bank records without notice, is the threshold question of whether the law recognizes an individual's legitimate expectation of privacy in financial institution records.

The United States Supreme Court addressed the threshold question in *United States v. Miller*, 425 U.S. 435 (1976), where it held that bank records, subpoenaed by the government without notice to a depositor under investigation, did not fall within a protected zone of privacy and were not "private papers" protected by the Fourth Amendment. *Id.* at 440. In reaching its conclusion, the Court further noted that there is no legitimate "expectation of privacy" in the contents of original checks and deposit slips in the possession of a bank. *Id.* at 442. However, as previously noted, the United States Supreme Court has also made it absolutely clear that the states, not the federal government, are responsible for the protection of personal privacy: "the protection of a person's general right to privacy—his right to be let alone by other people—is, like the protection of his property and of his very life, left largely to the law of the individual States." *Katz v. United States*, 389 U.S. 347, 350–51 (1967). This Court accepted that responsibility of protecting the privacy interests of Florida citizens when we stated that "the citizens of Florida, through their state constitution, may provide themselves with more protection from governmental intrusion than that afforded by the United States Constitution." *State v. Sarmiento*, 397 So. 2d 643, 645 (1981).

The citizens of Florida opted for more protection from governmental intrusion when they approved article I, section 23, of the Florida Constitution. This amendment is an independent, freestanding constitutional provision which declares the fundamental right to privacy. Article I, section 23, was intentionally phrased in strong terms. The drafters of the amendment rejected the use of the words "unreasonable" or "unwarranted" before the phrase "governmental intrusion" in order to make the privacy right as strong as possible. Since the people of this state exercised their prerogative and enacted an amendment to the Florida Constitution which expressly and succinctly provides for a strong right of privacy not found in the United States Constitution, it can only be concluded that the right is much broader in scope than that of the Federal Constitution.

This is a case of first impression in the state of Florida; therefore, it is within the discretion of this Court to decide the limitations and latitude afforded article I, section 23. We believe that the amendment should be interpreted in accordance with the intent of its drafters. Thus, we find that the law in the state of Florida recognizes an individual's legitimate expectation of privacy in financial institution records. However, we further find that the state's interest in conducting effective investigations in the pari-mutuel industry is a compelling state interest and that the least intrusive means was employed to achieve that interest. We also note that pre-disclosure notification by a bank to its customers should not be and is not mandated by article I, section 23. Thus, we hold that article I, section 23, of the Florida Constitution does not prevent the Division of Pari-Mutuel wagering from subpoenaing a Florida citizen's bank records without notice.

Concerning the second certified question, we believe that the information sought by the government was essential to its inquiry. To ensure that it has all of the information necessary for a complete investigation, the agency rather than the bank or depositor must calculate what is and what is not relevant. The subpoenas in question were reasonably calculated to obtain information relevant to a state investigation. There is nothing in the record to support a contrary finding. Thus, we hold that the subpoenaing of all of a citizen's bank records under the facts of this case does not constitute an impermissible and unbridled exercise of legislative power.

It is so ordered. . . .

C. Limits upon Florida's Right of Privacy

The following case of *City of North Miami v. Kurtz*, 653 So. 2d 1025 (Fla. 1995) is an illustration of the limits that the Supreme Court of the State of Florida places upon the right of privacy enumerated in Florida's constitution.

City of North Miami v. Kurtz
Supreme Court of Florida, 1995.
653 So. 2d 1025

Overton, Justice.

We have for review . . . the following question as one of great public importance:

Does Article I, Section 23 of the Florida Constitution Prohibit a Municipality from Requiring Job Applicants to Refrain from Using Tobacco or Tobacco Products for One Year before Applying for, and as a Condition for Being Considered for Employment, Even Where the Use of Tobacco Is Not Related to the Job Function in the Position Sought by the Applicant?

This question involves the issue of whether applicants seeking government employment have a reasonable expectation of privacy under article I, section 23, as to their smoking habits. . . . We have jurisdiction. Art. I, § 3(b)(4), Fla. Const. For the reasons expressed, we answer the certified question in the negative, finding that Florida's constitutional privacy provision does not afford Arlene Kurtz, the job applicant in this case, protection under the circumstances presented.

The record establishes the following unrefuted facts. To reduce costs and to increase productivity, the City of North Miami adopted an employment policy designed to reduce the number of employees who smoke tobacco. In accordance with that policy decision, the City issued Administrative Regulation 1–46, which requires all job applicants to sign an affidavit stating that they have not used tobacco or tobacco products for at least one year immediately preceding their application for employment. The intent of the regulation is to gradually reduce the number of smokers in the City's work force by means of natural attrition. Consequently, the regulation only applies to job applicants and does not affect current employees. Once an applicant has been hired, the applicant is free to start or resume smoking at any time. Evidence in the record, however, reflects that a high percentage of smokers who have adhered to the one year cessation requirement are unlikely to resume smoking.

Additional evidence submitted by the City indicates that each smoking employee costs the City as much as $4,611 per year in 1981 dollars over what it incurs for non-smoking employees. The City is a self-insurer and its taxpayers pay for 100% of its employees' medical expenses. In enacting the regulation, the City made a policy decision to reduce costs and increase productivity by eventually eliminating a substantial number of smokers from its work force. Evidence presented to the trial court indicated that the regulation would accomplish these goals.

The respondent in this case, Arlene Kurtz, applied for a clerk-typist position with the City. When she was interviewed for the position, she was informed of Regulation 1–46. She told the interviewer that she was a smoker and could not truthfully sign an affidavit to comply with the regulation. The interviewer then informed Kurtz that she would not be considered for employment until she was smoke-free for one year. Thereafter, Kurtz filed this action seeking to enjoin enforcement of the regulation and asking for a declaratory judgment finding the regulation to be unconstitutional.

In ruling on a motion for summary judgment, the trial judge recognized that Kurtz has a fundamental right of privacy under article I, section 23, of the Florida Constitution. The trial judge noted that Kurtz had presented the issue in the narrow context of whether she has a right to smoke in her own home. While he agreed that such a right existed, he concluded that the true issue to be decided was whether the City, as a governmental entity, could regulate smoking through employment. Because he found that there is no expectation of privacy in employment and that the regulation did not violate any provision of either the Florida or the federal constitutions, summary judgment was granted in favor of the City.

The Third District Court of Appeal reversed. The district court first determined that Kurtz' privacy rights are involved when the City requires her to refrain from smoking for a year prior to being considered to employment. The district court then found that, although the City does have an interest in saving taxpayers money by decreasing insurance costs and increasing productivity, such interest is insufficient to outweigh the intrusion into Kurtz' right of privacy and has no relevance to the performance of the duties involved with a clerk-typist. Consequently, the district court concluded that the regulation violated Kurtz's privacy rights under article I, section 23, of the Florida Constitution. We disagree.

Florida's constitutional privacy provision, which is contained in article I, section 23, provides as follows:

> *Right of privacy.*—Every natural person has the right to be let alone and free from governmental intrusion into his private life except as otherwise provided herein. This section shall not be construed to limit the public's right of access to public records and meetings as provided by law.

This right to privacy protects Florida's citizens from the government's uninvited observation of or interference in those areas that fall within the ambit of the zone of privacy afforded under this provision. *Shaktman v. State*, 553 So. 2d 148 (Fla. 1989). Unlike the implicit privacy right of the federal constitution, Florida's privacy provision is, in and of itself, a fundamental one that, once implicated, demands evaluation under a compelling state interest standard. *Winfield v. Division of Pari-Mutuel Wagering*, 477 So. 2d 544 (Fla. 1985). The federal privacy provision, on the other hand, extends only to such fundamental interests as marriage, procreation, contraception, family relationships, and the rearing and educating of children. *Carey v. Population Serv. Int'l*, 431 U.S. 678 (1977).

Although Florida's privacy right provides greater protection than the federal constitution, it was not intended to be a guarantee against all intrusion into the life of an individual. *Florida Bd. of Bar Examiners re Applicant*, 443 So. 2d 71 (Fla. 1983). First, the privacy provision applies only to government action, and the right provided under that provision is circumscribed and limited by the circumstances in which it is asserted. *Id.* Further, "[d]etermining 'whether an *individual* has a legitimate expectation of privacy in any given case must be made by considering all the circumstances, especially objective manifestations of that expectation.'" *Stall v. State*, 570 So. 2d 257, 260 (Fla. 1990) (alteration in original). Thus, to determine whether Kurtz, as a job applicant, is entitled to protection under article I, section 23, we must first determine whether a governmental entity is intruding into an aspect of Kurtz's life in which she as a "legitimate expectation of privacy." If we find in the affirmative, we must then look to whether a compelling interest exists to justify that intrusion and, if so, whether the least intrusive means is being used to accomplish the goal.

In this case, we find that the City's action does not intrude into an aspect of Kurtz' life in which she has a legitimate expectation of privacy. In today's society, smokers are constantly required to reveal whether they smoke. When individuals are seated in a restaurant, they are asked whether they want a table in a smoking or non-smoking section. When individuals rent hotel or motel rooms, they are asked if they smoke so that management may ensure that certain rooms remain free from the smell of smoke odors. Likewise, when individuals rent cars, they are asked if they smoke so that rental agencies can make proper accommodations to maintain vehicles for non-smokers. Further, employers generally provide smoke-free areas for non-smokers, and employees are often prohibited from smoking in certain areas. Given that individuals must reveal whether they smoke in almost every aspect of life in today's society, we conclude that individuals have no reasonable expectation of privacy in the disclosure of that information when applying for a government job and, consequently, that Florida's right of privacy is not implicated under these unique circumstances.

In reaching the conclusion that the right to privacy is not implicated in this case, however, we emphasize that our holding is limited to the narrow issue presented. Notably, we are not addressing the issue of whether an applicant, once hired, could be compelled by a government agency to stop smoking. Equally as important, neither are we holding today that a governmental entity can ask any type of information it chooses of prospective job applicants.

Having determined that Kurtz has no legitimate expectation of privacy in revealing that she is a smoker under the Florida constitution, we turn now to her claim that the regulation violates her rights under the federal constitution. As noted, the federal constitution's implicit privacy provision extends only to such fundamental interests as marriage, procreation, contraception, family relationships, and the rearing and educating of children. *Carey.* Clearly, the "right to smoke" is not included within the penumbra of fundamental rights protected under that provision. *Grusendorf v. City of Oklahoma City*, 816 F.2d 539 (10th Cir. 1987) (the act of smoking a cigarette does not rise to the level of a fundamental right). Moreover, even if we were to find that some protected interest under the federal constitution were implicated so as to require a rational basis for the regulation we would still find the regulation to be constitutional. *Kelley v. Johnson*, 425 U.S. 238 (1976) (when assuming a liberty interest exists in an employment regulation, regulation must be reviewed under a rational basis test). As acknowledged by the district court, the City has a legitimate interest in attempting to reduce health insurance costs and to increase productivity. On these facts, the City's policy cannot be deemed so irrational that it may be branded arbitrary. *Kelley.* In fact, under the special circumstances supported by the record in this case, we would find that the City has established a compelling interest to support implementation of the regulation. As previously indicated, the record reflects that each smoking employee costs the City as much as $4,611 per year in 1981 dollars over what it incurs for non-smoking employees; that, of smokers who have adhered to the one year cessation requirement, a high percentage are unlikely to resume smoking; and that the City is a self-insurer who pays 100% of its employees' medical expenses. We find that the elimination of these costs, when considered in combination with the other special circumstances of this case, validates a compelling interest in the City's policy of gradually eliminating smokers from its work force. We also find that the City is using the least intrusive means in accomplishing this compelling interest because the regulation does not prevent current employees from smoking, it does not affect the present health care benefits of employees, and it gradually reduces the number of smokers through attrition. Thus, we find the regulation to be constitutional under both the federal and Florida constitutions.

For the reasons expressed, we answer the question in the negative, finding that Florida's constitutional privacy provision does not afford the applicant, Arlene Kurtz, protection because she has no reasonable expectation of privacy under the circumstances of this case. Accordingly, we quash the district court's decision, and we remand this case with directions that the district court of appeal affirm the trial court judgment.

It is so ordered.

Justice Kogan, dissenting:

As the majority itself notes, job applicants are free to return to tobacco use once hired. I believe this concession reveals the anti-smoking policy to be rather more of a speculative pretense than a rational governmental policy. Therefore, I would find it unconstitutional under the right of due process. See *Department of Law Enforcement v. Real Property*, 588 So. 2d 957 (Fla. 1991).

The privacy issue is more troublesome, to my mind. There is a "slippery-slope" problem here because, if governmental employers can inquire too extensively into off-job-site behavior, a point eventually will be reached at which the right of privacy under article I, section 23 clearly will be breached. An obvious example would be an inquiry into the lawful sexual behavior of job applicants in an effort to identify those with the "most desirable" lifestyles. Such an effort easily could become the pretext for a constitutional violation. The time has not yet fully passed, for example, when women job applicants have been questioned about their plans for procreation in an effort to eliminate those who may be absent on family leave. I cannot conceive that such an act is anything other than a violation of the right of privacy when done by a governmental unit.

Health-based concerns like those expressed by the City also present a definite slippery slope to the courts. The time is fast approaching, for example, when human beings can be genetically tested so thoroughly that susceptibility to particular diseases can be identified years in advance. To my mind, any governmental effort to identify those who might eventually suffer from cancer or heart disease, for instance, itself is a violation of bodily integrity guaranteed by article I, section 23. Moreover, I cannot help but note that any such effort comes perilously close to the discredited practice of eugenics.

The use of tobacco products is more troubling, however. While legal, tobacco use nevertheless is an activity increasingly regulated by the law. If the federal government, for instance, chose to regulate tobacco as a controlled substance, I have no trouble saying that this act alone does not undermine anyone's privacy right. However, regulation is not the issue here because tobacco use today remains legal. The sole question is whether the government may inquire into off-job-site behavior that is legal, however unhealthy it might be. In light of the inherently poor fit between the governmental objective and the ends actually achieved, I am more inclined to agree with the district court that the right of privacy has been violated here. I might reach a different result if the objective were better served by the means chosen.

———————

Note and Question to Consider:

1. To what extent does *City of North Miami v. Kurtz* acknowledge a greater right to privacy than found under the federal constitution?

2. If the Supreme Court of the United States issued a new decision, disagreeing with its own prior precedent, and finding that there never was a right to privacy under the federal Constitution, then would a right to privacy still exist in Florida? If so, to what extent would its existence change?

3. A FLORIDA LAW REVIEW article concludes that "the state constitutional right of privacy in Florida extends protection no greater in scope than the minimum federal guarantee." *See* Joseph Beatty, *Is the Expectation of Privacy under the Florida Constitution Broader in Scope Than It is under the Federal Constitution?* City of North Miami v. Kurtz, *653 So. 2d 1025 (Fla. 1995).* 47 FLA. L. REV. 287 (April 1995). Do you agree? If so, where do you find a right to financial privacy under the U.S. Constitution? Was not such a right found under Florida's constitution in *Winfield v. Div. of Pari-Mutuel Wagering,* 477 So. 2d 544 (Fla. 1983)?

D. Florida's Right of Privacy and Technology

As technology advances, courts consider how Florida's right of privacy applies to various forms of technology. For example, consider the phone in your pocket. It allows for communication in many ways other than voice calls, including live video chat, trading emojis, posting to social media, and for many of us, sexting.

> *"We shouldn't be labeling our children as sexual predators for this type of behavior."*
>
> — Florida State Representative Joseph Abruzzo (D—Wellington), on prosecuting children under child pornography laws for sexting one another.

The quotation above appears in Lawrence G. Walters, *How to Fix the Sexting Problem: An Analysis of the Legal and Policy Considerations for Sexting Legislation,* 9 FIRST AMEND. L. REV. 98, 99 (2010). In that article, "sexting" is defined as follows:

> Sexting, a combination of the words "sex" and "texting," is the term coined to describe the activity of sending nude, semi-nude, or sexually explicit depictions in electronic messages, most commonly through cellular phones. While this behavior is perfectly legal and accepted among consenting adults, ... juveniles prosecuted for this behavior end up being included

on the public sex offender registry alongside the worst child molesters and pedophiles.

Id. at 99.

A.H. v. State, 949 So. 2d 234 (Fla. 2007) illustrates the Florida Supreme Court's application of the Florida right of privacy in the technological context of sexting.

A.H., a child v. State of Florida

First District Court of Appeal of Florida, 2007
949 So. 2d 234

Wolf, Justice.

A.H. challenges her adjudication of delinquency for producing, directing or promoting a photograph or representation that she knew included sexual conduct of a child in violation of section 827.071(3), Florida Statutes. She filed a motion to dismiss the charges alleging that the statute was [unconstitutional] as applied to her. She contended that, because the photographs were not actually distributed to a third party and the other participant in the sexual act was an older minor, her right to privacy was implicated and that criminal prosecution was not the least intrusive means of furthering a compelling state interest. The trial court ruled that there was a compelling state interest in preventing the production of these photographs and criminal prosecution was the least intrusive means of furthering the State's compelling interest. We agree with this analysis and further determine that the privacy provision of the state constitution does not protect the behavior of appellant. We, thus, affirm.

By Amended Petition of Delinquency, 16-year-old appellant, A.H., and her 17-year-old boyfriend, J.G.W., were charged as juveniles under the child pornography laws. The charges were based on digital photos A.H. and J.G.W. took on March 25, 2004, of themselves naked and engaged in sexual behavior. The State alleged that, while the photos were never shown to a third party, A.H. and J.G.W. emailed the photos to another computer from A.H.'s home. A.H. and J.G.W. were each charged with one count of producing, directing or promoting a photograph or representation that they knew to include the sexual conduct of a child, in violation of section 827.071(3), Florida Statutes.

A.H. filed a motion to dismiss on October 24, 2005, arguing that section 827.071(3), Florida Statutes, was unconstitutional as applied to her. She contended that her privacy interests were implicated in the charges, that she was actually younger than her alleged victim, J.G.W., and that criminal prosecution was not the least intrusive means of furthering a compelling state interest. A hearing was held on the motion to dismiss on November 30, 2005, after which the trial court issued an order denying the motion. The order included the following conclusions:

> Assuming that the child's right to privacy is implicated, the standard for evaluating whether the State may regulate the sexual conduct of minors,

articulated in *B.B. v. State*, 659 So. 2d 256, 258–59 (Fla. 1995), requires the State to show both that it has a compelling interest and that it is furthering this interest in the least intrusive manner.

As to the first prong of the test, whether the State has a compelling interest in regulating the sexual behavior of minors, this Court recognizes a compelling state interest in protecting children from sexual exploitation, particularly the form of sexual exploitation involved in this case. This compelling interest exists whether the person sexually exploiting the child is an adult or a minor and is certainly triggered by the production of 117 photographs of minors engaging in graphic sexual acts. *State v. A.R.S.*, 684 So. 2d 1383, 1387 (Fla. 1st DCA 1996).

The Court further finds that prosecuting the child under the statute in question is the least intrusive means of furthering the State's compelling interest. Not prosecuting the child would do nothing to further the State's interest. Prosecution enables the State to prevent future illegal, exploitative acts by supervising and providing any necessary counseling to the child. The Court finds that the State has shown that Section 827.071(3), Florida Statutes, as applied to the child, is the least intrusive means of furthering the State's compelling interest in preventing the sexual exploitation of children, rendering the statute constitutional.

Three weeks later, A.H. entered a nolo contendere plea to the charge and was placed on probation. Based on the supplemental record that has been filed, we find appellant specifically reserved her right to appeal the issue raised on the motion to dismiss.

A.H. argues that the trial court erred in denying her motion to dismiss below because the statute is unconstitutional as applied to her. She relies, in part, on the 1995 Florida Supreme Court decision in *B.B. v. State*, 659 So. 2d 256 (Fla. 1995), in which she alleges the court held that a child's privacy interests under article I, section 23 of the Florida Constitution are triggered by engaging in sexual conduct.

According to A.H., given the lack of a significant age difference or of any allegation that the pictures were shown to a third party, the only compelling state interest that could be involved here was the protection of the co-defendants from engaging in sexual behavior until their minds and bodies had matured. A.H. argues that prosecuting her for the second-degree felony of promoting a sexual performance by a child was not the least intrusive means of furthering this interest. Therefore, she maintains that section 827.071(3), Florida Statutes, is unconstitutional as applied to her, and the trial court's ruling to the contrary must be reversed.

Implicit in A.H.'s argument is that article I, section 23 protects a minor's right to have sexual intercourse and that this right of privacy extends to situations where the minor memorializes the act through pictures or video. We cannot accept this argument.

In *State v. A.R.S.*, 684 So. 2d 1383 (Fla. 1st DCA 1996), we addressed the constitutionality of section 827.071(3), Florida Statutes, the same statute at issue in this case. In that case, the court assumed "that a minor's privacy interests were implicated." *Id.* The court went on to hold that the State had a compelling interest "to protect minors from exploitation by anyone who induces them to appear in a sexual performance and shows that performance to other people." *Id.* at 1387.

As Judge Allen noted in his concurrence in *A.R.S.,* the law relating to a minor's right of privacy to have sex with another minor is anything but clear. *See also State v. Raleigh*, 686 So. 2d 621 (Fla. 5th DCA 1996). It is unnecessary, however, for us to enter that quagmire. The question before us is, even assuming that the privacy provision of article I, section 23 of the Florida Constitution extends to minors having sexual intercourse, whether that right extends to them memorializing that activity through photographs.

"Florida's right to privacy is a fundamental right that requires evaluation under a compelling state interest standard. However, before the right to privacy attaches and the standard is applied, a reasonable expectation of privacy must exist." *Bd. of County Comm'rs of Palm Beach County v. D.B.*, 784 So. 2d 585, 588 (Fla. 4th DCA 2001). Whether an individual has a legitimate expectation of privacy is determined by considering all the circumstances, especially objective manifestations of that expectation. *City of N. Miami v. Kurtz*, 653 So. 2d 1025, 1028 (Fla. 1995).

A number of factors lead us to conclude that there is no reasonable expectation of privacy under these circumstances.

First, the decision to take photographs and to keep a record that may be shown to people in the future weighs against a reasonable expectation of privacy. See *Four Navy Seals v. Associated Press*, 413 F.Supp.2d 1136 (S.D.Cal. 2005) (holding active duty military members who allowed photographs to be taken of prisoner abuse did not have reasonable expectation of privacy under state constitution).

Second, the photographs which were taken were shared by the two minors who were involved in the sexual activities. Neither had a reasonable expectation that the other would not show the photos to a third party. Minors who are involved in a sexual relationship, unlike adults who may be involved in a mature committed relationship, have no reasonable expectation that their relationship will continue and that the photographs will not be shared with others intentionally or unintentionally. One motive for revealing the photos is profit. Unfortunately, the market for child pornography in this country, according to news reports, appears to be flourishing. *See, e.g.,* "Child porn ring busted, 27 face charges," March 15, 2006, http://www .msnbc.msn.com /id/11839832; Jeremy W. Peters, *Another Arrest in Webcam Pornography Case*, N.Y. Times, May 16, 2006, available at http://www.nytimes.com (search the NYT Archive since 1981 for "Webcam Pornography Case," then click on title). These 117 sexually explicit photographs would undoubtedly have market value.

In addition, a number of teenagers want to let their friends know of their sexual prowess. Pictures are excellent evidence of an individual's exploits. A reasonably prudent person would believe that if you put this type of material in a teenager's hands that, at some point either for profit or bragging rights, the material will be disseminated to other members of the public.

Distribution of these types of photos is likely, especially after the relationship has ended. It is not unreasonable to assume that the immature relationship between the co-defendants would eventually end. The relationship has neither the sanctity of law nor the stability of maturity or length. The subjective belief of these co-defendants that the photos might not be shared is not dispositive. In fact, the defendant in this case expressed her concern to law enforcement that her co-defendant might do something disagreeable with the photographs.

The mere fact that the defendant may have subjectively believed that the pictures would remain private does not control; it is whether society is willing to recognize an objective expectation.

> As this court previously stated in *State v. Conforti*, 688 So. 2d 350, 358–59 (Fla. 4th DCA 1997):
>
> Although a person's subjective expectation of privacy is one consideration in deciding whether a constitutional right attaches, the final determination of an expectation's legitimacy takes a more global view, placing the individual in the context of a society and the values that the society seeks to foster. The right to privacy has not made each person a solipsistic island of self-determination.

Bd. of County Comm'rs of Palm Beach County v. D.B., 784 So. 2d 585, 590 (Fla. 4th DCA 2001).

The fact that these photographs may have or may not have been shown in no way affects the minor's reasonable expectation that there was a distinct and real possibility that the other teenager involved would at some point make these photos public.

Even assuming, arguendo, that a reasonable expectation of privacy existed, the statute in the instant case serves a compelling state interest. In *A.R.S.*, 684 So. 2d at 1387, this court addressed the statute in question where a minor had videotaped himself involved in sexual conduct with a female minor and played the videotape for a third party.

Assuming that a minor's privacy interests are implicated in the instant case, we recognize that the state's compelling interest in section 827.071 is different. The statute is not limited to protecting children only from sexual exploitation by adults, nor is it intended to protect minors from engaging in sexual intercourse. The state's purpose in this statute is to protect minors from exploitation by anyone who induces them to appear in a sexual performance and shows that performance to other people. See *Schmitt v. State*, 590 So. 2d 404, 412 (Fla. 1991) (stating that the "obvious purpose" of section 827.071 "is to prohibit certain forms of child exploitation"), *cert. denied*, 503 U.S. 964 (1992). The State's interest in protecting children from exploitation in this statute is the same regardless of whether the person inducing the child to appear in a sexual performance and then promoting that performance is an adult or a minor. *Id.*

Appellant asserts that the State only has a compelling interest when the photograph or video is shown to a third party. The Legislature has, however, recognized a compelling interest in seeing that the videotape or picture including "sexual conduct by a child of less than 18 years of age" is never produced. § 827.071(3), Fla. Stat.

As previously stated, the reasonable expectation that the material will ultimately be disseminated is by itself a compelling state interest for preventing the production of this material. In addition, the statute was intended to protect minors like appellant and her co-defendant from their own lack of judgment.

Without either foresight or maturity, appellant engaged in the conduct at issue, then expressed concern to law enforcement personnel that her co-defendant may do something inappropriate, i.e., disseminate sexually explicit photos that were lodged on his computer. Appellant was simply too young to make an intelligent decision about engaging in sexual conduct and memorializing it. Mere production of these videos or pictures may also result in psychological trauma to the teenagers involved.

Further, if these pictures are ultimately released, future damage may be done to these minors' careers or personal lives. These children are not mature enough to make rational decisions concerning all the possible negative implications of producing these videos.

In addition, the two defendants placed the photos on a computer and then, using the internet, transferred them to another computer. Not only can the two computers be hacked, but by transferring the photos using the net, the photos may have been and perhaps still are accessible to the provider and/or other individuals. Computers also allow for long-term storage of information which may then be disseminated at some later date. The State has a compelling interest in seeing that material which will have such negative consequences is never produced.

The decision of the trial court is affirmed.

Judge Padovano, dissenting:

Section 827.071(3) Florida Statutes was designed to protect children from abuse by others, but it was used in this case to punish a child for her own mistake. In my view, the application of this criminal statute to the conduct at issue violates the child's right to privacy under Article I, Section 23 of the Florida Constitution. For this reason, I would reverse.

The supreme court held in *B.B. v. State*, 659 So. 2d 256 (Fla. 1995), that a statute prohibiting unlawful carnal intercourse is unconstitutional as applied to a minor. In support of this holding, the court reasoned that the citizens of Florida had issued a "clear constitutional mandate in favor of privacy" by adopting Article I, Section 23 of the Florida Constitution. *B.B.* 659 So. 2d at 259. The court went on to say that the right of privacy is not limited to adults, but that it applies to children, as well.

I am not able to reconcile the supreme court's holding in *B.B.* with the court's decision in this case. The majority points out that the child in *B.B.* was charged with unlawful sexual intercourse while the child in this case was charged with photographing an act of sexual intercourse, but I think this a distinction without a difference. As in *B.B.*, the child in this case had sex with another minor. The only additional fact is that, in this case, the two took photographs of themselves and shared the photos with each other. There is no indication that the photos were intended to be any less private than the act itself. Consequently, I am unable to conclude that Article I, Section 23 is inapplicable or that it somehow offers the child in this case less protection.

The majority is correct to say that *B.B.* involved a prosecution under a different statute. However, the principle of constitutional law articulated in the opinion is not one that applies only to a particular statute. To the contrary, it is a principle that would apply to any statute that is used in a way that violates the right of privacy. If a minor cannot be criminally prosecuted for having sex with another minor, as the court held in *B.B.*, it follows that a minor cannot be criminally prosecuted for taking a picture of herself having sex with another minor. Although I do not condone the child's conduct in this case, I cannot deny that it is private conduct. Because there is no evidence that the child intended to show the photographs to third parties, they are as private as the act they depict.

The majority relies on the decision of this court in *State v. A.R.S.*, 684 So. 2d 1383 (Fla. 1st DCA 1996), but that case does not support the decision the court has made here. In *A.R.S.*, the child made a videotape of himself and a younger female child engaging in a sexual activity and then played the videotape to a third person at a time when the female was not present. The act of displaying the videotape was the main reason the court gave for its decision. As the court explained, "The state's purpose in [section 827.071] is to protect minors from exploitation by anyone who induces them to appear in a sexual performance *and shows that performance to other people.*" *A.R.S.*, 684 So. 2d at 1387. In contrast, the child in this case did not show the photographs to anyone. Nor has she been charged with doing so. She stands accused of nothing more than taking photographs of herself and her boyfriend.

The fact that the delinquent child in *A.R.S.* showed the videotape to a third party is significant for the reasons given by the court and for another reason not mentioned in the opinion. The voluntary publication of the videotape to a third party completely undermined the delinquent child's claim of privacy. Unlike the accused child in this case, A.R.S. was not in a good position to claim that his actions were protected by the constitutional right of privacy. Whatever privacy rights he had in the videotape he made of himself and another child engaging in an intimate act, he gave up entirely when she showed the tape to another person.

The majority concludes that the child in this case did not have a reasonable expectation that the photographs would remain private. To support this conclusion, the majority speculates about the many ways in which the photographs might have been revealed to others. The e-mail transmission might have been intercepted. The relationship might have ended badly. The boyfriend might have wanted to show the photo to someone else to brag about his sexual conquest. With all due respect, I think these arguments are beside the point. Certainly there are circumstances in which the photos might have been revealed unintentionally to third parties, but that would always be the case.

That the Internet is easily hacked, as the majority says, is not material. The issue is whether the child intended to keep the photos private, not whether it would be possible for someone to obtain the photos against her will and thereby to invade her privacy. The majority states that the child "placed the photos on a computer and then, using the internet, transferred them to another computer," as if to suggest that she left them out carelessly for anyone to find. That is not what happened. She sent the photos to her boyfriend at his personal e-mail address, intending to share them only with him.

The method the child used to transmit the photos to her boyfriend carries some danger of disclosure, but so do others. If the child had taken a printed photograph and placed it in her purse, it might have been disclosed to third parties if her purse had been lost or stolen. If she had mailed it to her boyfriend in an envelope, it might have been revealed if the envelope had been delivered to the wrong address and mistakenly opened. As these examples illustrate, there is always a possibility that something a person intends to keep private will eventually be disclosed to others. But we cannot gauge the reasonableness of a person's expectation of privacy merely by speculating about the many ways in which it might be violated.

The critical point in this case is that the child intended to keep the photographs private. She did not attempt to exploit anyone or to embarrass anyone. I think her expectation of privacy in the photographs was reasonable. Certainly, an argument could be made that she was foolish to expect that, but the expectation of a sixteen year old cannot be measured by the collective wisdom of appellate judges who have no emotional connection to the event. Perhaps if the child had as much time to reflect on these events, she would have eventually concluded, as the majority did, that there were ways in which these photos might have been unintentionally disclosed. That does not make her expectation of privacy unreasonable.

For these reasons, I believe the court has committed a serious error. The statute at issue was designed to protect children, but in this case the court has allowed the state to use it against a child in a way that criminalizes conduct that is protected by constitutional right of privacy. In the process, the court has rendered a decision that expressly and directly conflicts with the decision of the Florida Supreme Court in *B.B.* on the same point of law. The child in that case was prosecuted under a different statute, but the constitutional principles are the same and they should be applied in the same way in this case.

Notes and Questions to Consider:

1. Prosecutors in the state of Florida have discretion as to whether to bring criminal charges, even in cases where a criminal offense has occurred. Would the prosecutor in this case have been wise to exercise his or her discretion to decline to bring charges? If charges had not been brought, what harm to the public would have occurred?

2. Did the punishment fit the crime?

3. Judge Padovano's dissenting opinion compares and contrasts this case with *B.B. v. State*, 659 So. 2d 256 (Fla. 1995), where the Supreme Court of Florida held that minors have a right to privacy under the Florida Constitution when it comes to premarital sexual intercourse. Why would such a right to privacy extend to having sex, yet not extend to photographing it?

4. Note the following criticism of Judge Wolf's majority opinion that appears in Judge Padovano's dissent: "That the Internet is easily hacked, as the majority says, is not material. The issue is whether the child intended to keep the photos private, not whether it would be possible for someone to obtain the photos against her will and thereby to invade her privacy. The majority states that the child "placed the photos on a computer and then, using the internet, transferred them to another computer," as if to suggest that she left them out carelessly for anyone to find. That is not what happened." Judge Wolf's opinion was written in 2007. It was several years later than whistleblowers such as Edward Snowden alleged that our federal government often requires computer and laptop manufacturers who sell their products to install "back door access" into these devices. Allegedly the "back door" allows our federal government to monitor what we do. *See, e.g.,* T.C. Sottek, *NSA Reportedly Intercepting Laptops Purchased Online to Install Spy Malware*, The Verge (Dec. 29, 2013) www.theverge.com/2013/12/29/5253226/nsa-cia-fbi-laptop-usb-plant-spy. If these allegations are true, then under the logic of Judge Wolf's majority decision, would that mean that a Floridian has no right to privacy regarding anything that can be stored or accessed on a computer or laptop?

5. Similarly, technology has advanced after this 2007 decision to include an "Internet of Things" or "IoT" involving things like internet-connected lights, doorbell and doorbell cameras, music speakers, and appliances for the home. Many are run by devices such as Amazon Echo or Google Home or Microsoft Xbox, which have internet connected microphones listening at all times to the sounds and talk occurring in our homes. Perhaps some or all of these "connected home" or IoT devices can be hacked. Under the logic of Judge Wolf's majority decision, does a Floridian still a right to privacy in such a "connected home?"

6. Can the goal of eliminating sexting by children be achieved by the concerted efforts of families, educators and technology providers? Joseph Paravecchia, in his 2011 Ave Maria Law Review Article titled *Sexting and Subsidiarity: How Increased Participation and Education from Private Entities May Deter the Production, Distribution, and Possession of Child Pornography Among Minors:*

provides a unique approach to the problem of minors engaged in the production and distribution of child pornography. . . . [D]ue to the problems associated with the prosecution of minors engaged in the act, non-governmental entities may be both in a better position to prevent minors from sexting, and do so more efficiently.

At the core of the notion of permitting the private sector to address the problem of sexting is the concept of "subsidiarity." Pursuant to the theological component of that principle, when a decentralized entity—such as the family or a private institution—can effectively address a social concern, the sovereign State should allow it to proceed. . . . [N]o other entity can better communicate values and moral human development than the family, particularly, the parents.

10 Ave Maria L. Rev. 235 at 238. What is your opinion of the potential for parents, educators and technology companies to work together to minimize or eliminate sexting by minors?

E. Florida's Right of Privacy and Refusing Medical Treatment

The Supreme Court of Florida addresses the issue of Florida's right of privacy, the right to refuse medical treatment, and the protection of the unborn in *Burton v. State*, 49 So. 2d 264 (Fla. 1st DCA 2010). After the case, we present an excerpt from a law review article discussing that case.

Burton v. State of Florida

First District Court of Appeal of Florida, 2010
49 So. 3d 263

Clark, Justice.

This is an appeal of a circuit court order compelling a pregnant woman to submit to any medical treatment deemed necessary by the attending obstetrician, including detention in the hospital for enforcement of bed rest, administration of intravenous medications, and anticipated surgical delivery of the fetus. The action was initiated in the circuit court by the State Attorney under the procedure described in *In re Dubreuil*, 629 So. 2d 819 (Fla. 1994). As provided in *Dubreuil*, after the State Attorney received notification from a health care provider that a patient refused medical treatment, the State Attorney exercised his discretion to determine that a sufficient state interest was at stake to justify legal action.

This appeal is moot with regard to Appellant because, as ordered, she submitted to the hospital confinement, medical treatment and surgical delivery. Two days after entry of the order, Appellant's deceased fetus was delivered by Cesarean section. Thus, the justiciable controversy between these parties has expired. However, mootness does not preclude appellate jurisdiction if the issue is "capable of repetition yet evading review," as in the case of medical issues which require immediate resolution.

The situation presented to the trial court in this case is capable of repetition yet evading review. Florida case precedent has addressed the right to privacy where a patient seeks to discontinue life-sustaining medical treatment, refuse a life-saving medical procedure, and as applied to statutory regulation of a minor's decision whether or not to continue her pregnancy. *In re Guardianship of Browning*, 568 So. 2d 4 (Fla. 1990); *In re Dubreuil*, 629 So. 2d 819 (Fla. 1994); *In re T.W.*, 551 So. 2d 1186 (Fla. 1989). However, case precedent governing the use of a *Dubreuil* proceeding to compel a pregnant woman to undergo medical confinement, treatment and procedures against her wishes for the benefit of her unborn fetus is not found in Florida's jurisprudence. In an effort to assist trial courts and counsel involved in these expedited, if not emergency proceedings, we exercise our discretionary authority to address this appeal.

The trial court found that the appellant had failed to follow the doctor's instructions and recommendations, rendering her pregnancy "high-risk," and found a "substantial and unacceptable" risk of severe injury or death to the unborn child if the appellant continued to fail to follow the recommended course of treatment. The trial court stated the rule that "as between parent and child, the ultimate welfare of the child is the controlling factor," and concluded that the State's interests in the matter "override Ms. Burton's privacy interests at this time." The court ordered Samantha Burton to comply with the physician's orders "including, but not limited to" bed rest, medication to postpone labor and prevent or treat infection, and eventual performance of a cesarean section delivery.

The law in Florida is clear: Every person has the right "to be let alone and free from government intrusion into the person's private life." Art. I, sec. 23, Fla. Const. This fundamental right to privacy encompasses a person's "right to the sole control of his or her person" and the "right to determine what shall be done with his own body." *In re Guardianship of Browning*, 568 So. 2d 4, 10 (Fla. 1990). The Florida Supreme Court has specifically recognized that "a competent person has the constitutional right to choose or refuse medical treatment, and that right extends to all relevant decisions concerning one's health." *Browning*, 568 So. 2d at 11.

A patient's fundamental constitutional right to refuse medical intervention "can only be overcome if the state has a compelling state interest great enough to override this constitutional right." *Singletary v. Costello*, 665 So. 2d 1099, 1105 (Fla. 4th DCA 1996). Thus, the threshold issue in this situation is whether the state established a compelling state interest sufficient to trigger the court's consideration and balance of that interest against the appellant's right to refuse to submit to the medical intervention the obstetrician prescribed. The state's interest in the potentiality of life of an unborn fetus becomes compelling "at the point in time when the fetus becomes viable," defined as "the time at which the fetus becomes capable of meaningful life outside the womb, albeit with artificial aid." *Roe v. Wade*, 410 U.S. 113, 163, 93 S.Ct.

705, 35 L.Ed.2d 147 (1973); *In re T.W.*, 551 So. 2d 1186, 1193 (Fla. 1989). The Legislature has defined "viability" as "that stage of fetal development when the life of the unborn child may with a reasonable degree of medical probability be continued indefinitely outside the womb." § 390.0111(4), Fla. Stat. No presumption of viability is provided in the statute.

Because there is no statutory or precedential presumption of viability, in terms of the stage of pregnancy or otherwise, there must be some evidence of viability via testimony or otherwise. Only after the threshold determination of viability has been made may the court weigh the state's compelling interest to preserve the life of the fetus against the patient's fundamental constitutional right to refuse medical treatment.

Even if the State had made the threshold showing of viability and the court had made the requisite determination, the legal test recited in the order on appeal was a misapplication of the law. The holding in *M.N. v. Southern Baptist Hosp. of Florida*, 648 So. 2d 769 (Fla. 1st DCA 1994), "that as between parent and child, the ultimate welfare of the child is the controlling factor," does not apply to this case. Unlike this case, in *M.N.*, the parents refused consent for a blood transfusion and chemotherapy for their 8-month-old infant. No privacy rights of a pregnant woman were involved.

The test to overcome a woman's right to refuse medical intervention in her pregnancy is whether the state's compelling state interest is sufficient to override the pregnant woman's constitutional right to the control of her person, including her right to refuse medical treatment. *Dubreuil*, 629 So. 2d 819; *Browning*, 568 So. 2d 4; *Public Health Trust of Dade County v. Wons*, 541 So. 2d 96 (Fla. 1989). In addition, where the state does establish a compelling state interest and the court has found the state's interest sufficient to override a pregnant patient's right to determine her course of medical treatment, the state must then show that the method for pursuing that compelling state interest is "narrowly tailored in the least intrusive manner possible to safeguard the rights of the individual." *Browning*, 568 So. 2d at 14.

REVERSED.

VAN NORTWICK, J., concurring.

I concur completely with Judge Clark's opinion. I write because, given the deprivation of her physical liberty and violation of her privacy interests, the proceeding below violated Samantha Burton's constitutional right to appointed counsel in this case. Accordingly, I would reverse on these constitutional grounds as well.

The constitutional right to appointed counsel in criminal proceedings is well-established under the Sixth Amendment. *Gideon v. Wainwright*, 372 U.S. 335 (1963). In civil proceedings, however, there is no corollary to the Sixth Amendment right to counsel. The Supreme Court has held that, under the Due Process Clause, "an indigent litigant has a right to appointed counsel only when, if he loses, he may be deprived of his physical liberty." *Lassiter v. Department of Social Services*, 452 U.S. 18, 26–27 (1981). For example, in *In Re Gault*, 387 U.S. 1 (1967), the Court held that the Due Process Clause of the Fourteenth Amendment requires appointment of counsel to represent a child in state civil delinquency proceedings "which may result in commitment to an institution in which the juvenile's freedom is curtailed." *Id.* at 36.

In the context of a case involving the termination of parental rights, the Court in *Lassiter* examined the limited nature of the right to counsel in civil proceedings. There, the Court applied the case-by-case due process analysis established in *Mathews v. Eldridge*, 424 U.S. 319 (1976), to the question of whether indigent parents are entitled to counsel in proceedings to terminate their parental rights. *Lassiter*, 452 U.S. at 27. As the *Lassiter* court explained, courts must first evaluate the three *Eldridge* elements: "the private interests at stake, the government's interest, and the risk that the procedures used will lead to erroneous decisions." *Id.* Courts then "must balance these elements against each other, and then set their net weight in the scales against the presumption that there is a right to appointed counsel only where the indigent, if he is unsuccessful, may lose his personal freedom." *Id.*

The Florida Supreme Court has recognized the right to appointed counsel in certain civil proceedings under Florida's Due Process Clause. *See* Art. I § 9, Fla. Const. Thus, "[t]he subject of an involuntary civil commitment proceeding has the right to the effective assistance of counsel at all significant stages of the commitment process." *In Re Beverly*, 342 So. 2d 481, 489 (Fla. 1977); *see also Pullen v. State*, 802 So. 2d 1113, 1116 (Fla. 2001). Similarly, there is a right to appointed counsel in proceedings which can result in the permanent loss of parental custody. *In Interest of D.B.*, 385 So. 2d 83, 90–91 (Fla. 1980).

An individual who faces involuntary hospitalization and mandated invasive medical treatment under the procedure established in *In Re Dubreuil*, 629 So. 2d 819 (Fla. 1994), has serious liberty and privacy interests at stake. Here, Ms. Burton was involuntarily admitted to the hospital and, ultimately, required to undergo a caesarian section against her will. She suffered a significant deprivation of her physical liberty and personal freedom at least the equivalent of the interests at stake in *D.B.* and *Beverly*. Although in the order under review the trial court directed the special assistant state attorney appointed for this proceeding to contact North Florida Legal Services, Inc., to request that office to provide Ms. Burton representation, no counsel appeared on her behalf until after the caesarian section was performed. Appointment of counsel after the fact does not satisfy the due process requirements under the Federal and Florida Constitutions. Here, the State had the time to appoint a special assistant state attorney to institute this proceeding. I see no reason why there was not also the opportunity to appoint counsel for Ms. Burton prior to the hearing.

BERGER, W., Associate Judge, dissenting.

I agree with the majority that the trial judge applied the wrong legal standard. If this case were not moot, I would reverse and remand for consideration using the correct, compelling state interest standard. However, because I disagree with the majority view that this is a case capable of repetition yet evading review, I would dismiss the appeal as moot. Accordingly, I dissent.

This court was not presented with a case of first impression warranting an opinion to assist trial courts and counsel in similar future expedited cases. It matters not that the case before us involves a hospital's desire to compel medical treatment over the objection of a pregnant woman. *See Pemberton v. Tallahassee Mem'l Reg'l Med. Ctr., Inc.*, 66 F.Supp.2d 1247 (N.D.Fla. 1999) (State's interest in preserving the life of the unborn child outweighed the pregnant mother's constitutional right to refuse medical treatment.). The law to be followed is clear and unambiguous. The proper test to be applied when a trial court is presented with a request to override a competent adult's constitutional right to refuse medical treatment was decided in *In re Guardianship of Browning*, 568 So. 2d 4 (Fla. 1990) (State has a duty to assure that a person's wishes regarding medical treatment are respected unless the State has a compelling interest great enough to override this constitutional right.). The proper procedure to be followed when a healthcare provider wishes to override a patient's decision to refuse medical treatment was outlined in *In re Matter of Dubreuil*, 629 So. 2d 819 (Fla. 1994) (Health care provider must immediately provide notice to both the state attorney, who is responsible for deciding whether to engage in legal action, and to interested third parties known to the provider.). Additionally, it is well settled that the State's interest in preserving the life of an unborn child becomes compelling upon viability. *Roe v. Wade*, 410 U.S. 113, 163, 93 S.Ct. 705 (1973); *In re T.W.*, 551 So. 2d 1186, 1194 (Fla. 1989) (Viability under Florida law occurs at that point in time when the fetus becomes capable of meaningful life outside the womb through standard medical measures. Under current standards, this point generally occurs upon completion of the second trimester.). Here the trial judge followed the correct procedure but applied the wrong legal standard. Instead of determining whether the State had a compelling interest in overriding the appellant's right to refuse medical treatment, the judge determined forced treatment was in the best interest of the child.

The trial court specifically found that the risk of severe injury or death to the unborn child was substantial and unacceptable and that the interests of the State in this matter overrode appellant's privacy interests. While I believe the balancing of interests employed by the trial judge would have been appropriate under [*In re Guardianship of*] *Browning*, it was the trial court's application of the State's *parens patriae* authority to override the appellant's right to refuse medical treatment for an existing child that was in error. However, since the principles of law to be applied in this case are not new and the case is now moot, I would dismiss the appeal.

Notes and Question to Consider:

1. How may the state of Florida respond when a pregnant mother exercises her right to refuse medical care? Consider the following excerpt from the Spring 2013 issue of the WILLIAM AND MARY JOURNAL OF WOMEN AND THE LAW in Mark H.

Bonner and Jennifer A. Sheriff, *A Child Needs a Champion: Guardian Ad Litem Representation for Prenatal Children*, 19 Wm. & Mary J. Women & L. 511 (2013):

> ... When should the legal status of a prenatal child be recognized as being the same as that of a newborn infant? ... Many courts have compelled pregnant women to submit to medical care, such as blood transfusions and caesarean sections, to protect the health of their prenatal children.
>
> In the case of *Pemberton v. Tallahassee Memorial Regional Medical Center, Inc.*, a pregnant woman was ultimately forced to have a cesarean section after multiple physicians concluded that vaginal birth posed "a substantial and unacceptable risk of death" to her child. Notably, Ms. Pemberton had delivered her previous baby by cesarean section in 1995. When Ms. Pemberton became pregnant again in 1996, she was unable to find a physician who would allow her to deliver vaginally; consequently, she attempted to deliver her baby at home, unattended by any physician and "without any backup arrangement with a hospital." After more than a day of grueling labor, Ms. Pemberton decided to go to the emergency room to request intravenous fluids. A board-certified physician advised Ms. Pemberton that she needed to have a cesarean section, but she adamantly refused and "left the hospital against medical advice, apparently surreptitiously." The hospital called an attorney, who in turn contacted the State Attorney, at which time a special assistant was deputized to handle the legal controversy.
>
> Shortly thereafter, a judge visited the hospital to conduct an emergency hearing and multiple doctors testified "that vaginal birth would pose a substantial risk of uterine rupture and resulting death of the baby." After ordering Ms. Pemberton to return to the hospital, the judge continued the hearing in her room and afforded both Ms. Pemberton and her husband an opportunity to express their personal views. At the conclusion of the proceeding, the judge ordered that an emergency cesarean section be performed and Ms. Pemberton delivered a healthy baby boy with no complications.

2. Both the *Burton* case whose opinion is reprinted above, and the *Pemberton* case whose facts are described in the law review article excerpted above, were an "action [that] was initiated in the circuit court by the state attorney under the procedure described in *In re Dubreuil*, 629 So. 2d 819 (Fla. 1994). As provided in *Dubreuil*, after the state attorney received notification from a health care provider that a patient refused medical treatment, the state attorney exercised his discretion to determine that a sufficient state interest was at stake to justify legal action. Perhaps the intent was to afford procedural due process protection to the pregnant mother's fundamental right to privacy in her decision to decline medical treatment. But would the typical pregnant mother subjected to such procedures be in any condition to defend herself in an unannounced, unanticipated court proceeding? What do you think of the dissent in *Burton*, and its argument for a right to counsel for the pregnant mother?

3. Perhaps another intent of these *Dubreil* procedures was to give a measure of protection to the needs of the unborn yet viable child? If so, does the child have a sufficient advocate in such proceedings, or would a guardian ad litem be appropriate? On that point, consider by analogy the 1989 holding of the Supreme Court of Florida in an abortion parental notification case called *In re T.W.*, 551 So. 2d 1186 (Fla. 1989) (holding the lower tribunal erred in appointing a guardian ad litem for the pregnant minor's unborn child).

4. What is the proper test for determining when and whether a Floridian has the right to refuse medical treatment under the Floridian's right to privacy under the Florida Constitution?

F. Florida's Right of Privacy and Suicide

Does Florida's right of privacy, and its right to refuse medical treatment, create a constitutional right to assisted suicide? The Supreme Court of the State of Florida answered this question in *Krischer v. McIver*, 697 So. 2d 97 (Fla. 1997):

Krischer v. Mciver

Supreme Court of Florida, 1997
697 So. 2d 97

Grimes, Justice.

We have on appeal a judgment of the trial court certified by the Fourth District Court of Appeal to be of great public importance and to require immediate resolution by this Court. We have jurisdiction under article V, section 3(b)(5) of the Florida Constitution.

Charles E. Hall and his physician, Cecil McIver, M.D., filed suit for a declaratory judgment that section 782.08, Florida Statutes (1995), which prohibits assisted suicide, violated the Privacy Clause of the Florida Constitution and the Due Process and Equal Protection Clauses of the Fourteenth Amendment to the United States Constitution. They sought an injunction against the state attorney from prosecuting the physician for giving deliberate assistance to Mr. Hall in committing suicide. After a six-day bench trial, the trial court issued a final declaratory judgment and injunctive decree responding to the "question of whether a competent adult, who is terminally ill, immediately dying and acting under no undue influence, has a constitutional right to hasten his own death by seeking and obtaining from his physician a fatal dose of prescription drugs and then subsequently administering such drugs to himself." The court concluded that section 782.08 could not be constitutionally enforced against the appellees and enjoined the state attorney from enforcing it against Dr. McIver should he assist Mr. Hall in committing suicide. The court based its conclusion on Florida's privacy provision and the federal Equal Protection Clause but held that there was no federal liberty interest in assisted suicide guaranteed by the federal Due Process Clause.

Mr. Hall is thirty-five years old and suffers from acquired immune deficiency syndrome (AIDS) which he contracted from a blood transfusion. The court found that Mr. Hall was mentally competent and that he was in obviously deteriorating health, clearly suffering, and terminally ill. The court also found that it was Dr. McIver's professional judgment that it was medically appropriate and ethical to provide Mr. Hall with the assistance he requests at some time in the future.

The state attorney appealed. The trial court then set aside the automatic stay imposed by Florida Rule of Appellate Procedure 9.310(b)(2). When this Court assumed jurisdiction of the case, we reinstated the stay and provided for expedited review.

At the outset, we note that the United States Supreme Court recently issued two decisions on the subject of whether there is a right to assisted suicide under the United States Constitution. In *Washington v. Glucksberg*, 521 U.S. 702 (1997), the Court reversed a decision of the Ninth Circuit Court of Appeals which had held that the State of Washington's prohibition against assisted suicide violated the Due Process Clause. Like the trial court's decision in the instant case, the Court reasoned that the asserted "right" to assistance in committing suicide was not a fundamental liberty interest protected by the Due Process Clause.

In the second decision, the [U.S. Supreme] Court upheld New York's prohibition on assisted suicide against the claim that it violated the Equal Protection Clause. *Vacco v. Quill*, 521 U.S. 793 (1997). In reversing the Second Circuit Court of Appeals, the Court held that there was a logical and recognized distinction between the right to refuse medical treatment and assisted suicide and concluded that there were valid and important public interests which easily satisfied the requirement that a legislative classification bear a rational relation to some legitimate end. Thus, the Court's decision in *Vacco* rejected one of the two bases for the trial court's ruling in the instant case.

The remaining issue is whether Mr. Hall has the right to have Dr. McIver assist him in committing suicide under Florida's guarantee of privacy contained in our constitution's declaration of rights. Art. I, § 23, Fla. Const. Florida has no law against committing suicide. However, Florida imposes criminal responsibility on those who assist others in committing suicide. Section 782.08, Florida Statutes (1995), which was first enacted in 1868, provides in pertinent part that "every person deliberately assisting another in the commission of self murder shall be guilty of manslaughter." *See also* §§ 765.309, 458.326(4), Fla. Stat. (1995) (disapproving mercy killing and euthanasia). Thus, it is clear that the public policy of this state as expressed by the legislature is opposed to assisted suicide.

Florida's position is not unique. Forty-five states that recognize the right to refuse treatment or unwanted life support have expressed disapproval of assisted suicide. Edward R. Grant & Paul Benjamin Linton, *Relief or Reproach?: Euthanasia Rights in the Wake of Measure 16*, 74 OR. L. REV. 449, 462–63 (1995). As of 1994, thirty-four jurisdictions had statutes which criminalized such conduct. *People v. Kevorkian*, 447 Mich. 436, 527 N.W.2d 714 (1994). Since that date, at least seventeen state legislatures have rejected proposals to legalize assisted suicide. . . .

The only case in the nation in which a court has considered whether assisted suicide is a protected right under the privacy provision of its state's constitution is *Donaldson v. Lungren*, 2 Cal.App. 4th 1614, 4 Cal.Rptr. 2d 59, 63 (1992), which held: "We cannot expand the nature of Donaldson's right of privacy to provide a protective shield for third persons who end his life." The court reasoned:

> In such a case, the state has a legitimate competing interest in protecting society against abuses. This interest is more significant than merely the abstract interest in preserving life no matter what the quality of that life is. Instead, it is the interest of the state to maintain social order through enforcement of the criminal law and to protect the lives of those who wish to live no matter what their circumstances. This interest overrides any interest Donaldson possesses in ending his life through the assistance of a third person in violation of the state's penal laws.

Id. See *Kevorkian v. Arnett*, 939 F.Supp. 725 (C.D.Cal.1996) (there is no persuasive authority to believe that the California Supreme Court would hold contrary to *Donaldson* when directly presented with the issue).

In 1984, Governor Mario Cuomo convened the New York State Task Force on Life and the Law . . . with a mandate to develop public policy on a number of issues arising from medical advances. With respect to assisted suicide and euthanasia, the task force concluded . . . that New York laws prohibiting assisted suicide and euthanasia should not be changed. In essence, [the New York task force found that d]ecisions to forgo treatment are an integral part of medical practice; [but":]

> Assisted suicide and euthanasia would carry us into new terrain. American society has never sanctioned assisted suicide or mercy killing. We believe that the practices would be profoundly dangerous for large segments of the population, especially in light of the widespread failure of American medicine to treat pain adequately or to diagnose and treat depression in many cases.

When Death Is Sought: Assisted Suicide and Euthanasia in the Medical Context, vi-vii (May 1994).

The task force addressed the issue again in a supplement to the report dated April 1997 and reaffirmed this position.

The Advocacy Center for Persons with Disabilities, Inc., is a Florida nonprofit corporation organized pursuant to Executive Order of the Governor which is charged with the responsibility of carrying out the federally mandated and funded protection and advocacy system for persons with disabilities in the State of Florida. In its amicus brief filed herein, the Center states:

To give someone, including a physician, the right to assist a person with a severe disability in killing himself or herself is discrimination based on a disability. It lessens the value of a person's life based on health status and subjects persons with severe physical and mental disabilities to undue pressure to which they may be especially vulnerable.

We have previously refused to allow the state to prohibit affirmative medical intervention, such as the case with the right to an abortion before viability of the fetus, only because the state's interests in preventing the intervention were not compelling. *In re T.W.*, 551 So. 2d 1186 (Fla. 1989) (state's interest in prohibiting abortion is compelling after fetus reaches viability). This is because, under our privacy provision, once a privacy right has been implicated, the state must establish a compelling interest to justify intruding into the privacy rights of an individual. *Winfield v. Division of Pari-Mutuel Wagering*, 477 So. 2d 544 (Fla. 1985).

This Court has also rendered several prior decisions declaring in various contexts that there is a constitutional privacy right to refuse medical treatment. Those cases recognized the state's legitimate interest in (1) the preservation of life, (2) the protection of innocent third parties, (3) the prevention of suicide, and (4) the maintenance of the ethical integrity of the medical profession. However, we held that these interests were not sufficiently compelling to override the patient's right of self-determination to forego life-sustaining medical treatment.

... We cannot agree that there is no distinction between the right to refuse medical treatment and the right to commit physician-assisted suicide through self-administration of a lethal dose of medication. The assistance sought here is not treatment in the traditional sense of that term. It is an affirmative act designed to cause death—no matter how well-grounded the reasoning behind it. Each of our earlier decisions involved the decision to refuse medical treatment and thus allow the natural course of events to occur. *In re Dubreuil*, 629 So. 2d 819 (Fla. 1993) (due to religious beliefs, individual wanted to refuse blood transfusion); *In re Guardianship of Browning*, 568 So. 2d 4 (Fla. 1990) (surrogate asserted right of woman who was vegetative but not terminally ill to remove nasogastric feeding tube); *Public Health Trust v. Wons*, 541 So. 2d 96 (Fla. 1989) (same facts as *Dubreuil*); *Satz v. Perlmutter*, 379 So. 2d 359 (Fla. 1980) (individual suffering from Lou Gehrig's disease sought to remove artificial respirator needed to keep him alive).

In the instant case, Mr. Hall seeks affirmative medical intervention that will end his life on his timetable and not in the natural course of events. There is a significant difference between these two situations. As explained by the American Medical Association:

When a life-sustaining treatment is declined, the patient dies primarily because of an underlying disease. The illness is simply allowed to take its natural course. With assisted suicide, however, death is hastened by the taking of a lethal drug or other agent. Although a physician cannot force a patient to accept a treatment against the patient's will, even if the treatment is life-sustaining, it does not follow that a physician ought to provide a lethal agent to the patient. The inability of physicians to prevent death does not imply that physicians are free to help cause death.

AMA Council on Ethical and Judicial Affairs, Report I–93–8, at 2.

Measured by the criteria employed in our cases addressing the right to refuse medical treatment, three of the four recognized state interests are so compelling as to clearly outweigh Mr. Hall's desire for assistance in committing suicide. First, the state has an unqualified interest in the preservation of life. *Cruzan v. Director, Missouri Department of Health*, 497 U.S. 261 (1990). The opinion we adopted in Perlmutter included the caveat that suicide was not at issue because the discontinuation of life support would "merely result in [the patient's] death, if at all, from natural causes." *Satz v. Perlmutter*, 362 So. 2d 160, 162 (Fla. 4th DCA 1978); *accord Browning*, 568 So. 2d at 14. Although the constitutional privacy provision was not involved, in Mr. Perlmutter's case a sharp distinction was drawn between disconnecting a respirator that would result in his death from "natural causes" (i.e., the inability to breathe on his own) and an "unnatural death by means of a 'death producing agent.'" *Perlmutter*, 362 So. 2d at 162. It is the second scenario that we encounter in the instant case. Mr. Hall will not die from the complications of his illness. Rather, a physician will assist him in administering a "death producing agent" with the intent of causing certain death. The state has a compelling interest in preventing such affirmative destructive act and in preserving Mr. Hall's life.

The state also has a compelling interest in preventing suicide. . . . Those who attempt suicide—terminally ill or not—often suffer from depression or other mental disorders. See New York Task Force 13–22, 126–128 (more than 95% of those who commit suicide had a major psychiatric illness at the time of death; among the terminally ill, uncontrolled pain is a "risk factor" because it contributes to depression); *Physician-Assisted Suicide and Euthanasia in the Netherlands: A Report of Chairman Charles T. Canady to the Subcommittee on the Constitution of the House Committee on the Judiciary*, 104th Cong., 2d Sess., 10–11 (Comm. Print 1996); cf. Back, Wallace, Starts, & Pearlman, *Physician-Assisted Suicide and Euthanasia in Washington State*, 275 JAMA 919, 924 (1996) ("[I]ntolerable physical symptoms are not the reason most patients request physician-assisted suicide or euthanasia"). Research indicates, however, that many people who request physician-assisted suicide withdraw that request if their depression and pain are treated. H. Hendin, SEDUCED BY DEATH: DOCTORS, PATIENTS AND THE DUTCH CURE 24–25 (1997) (suicidal, terminally ill patients "usually respond well to treatment for depressive illness and pain medication and are then grateful to be alive"); New York Task Force 177–178. The New York Task Force, however, expressed its concern that, because depression is difficult to diagnose, physicians and medical professionals often fail to respond adequately to seriously ill patients' needs. *Id.*, at 175. Thus, legal physician-assisted suicide could make it more difficult for the State to protect depressed or mentally ill persons, or those who are suffering from untreated pain, from suicidal impulses.

Finally, the state also has a compelling interest in maintaining the integrity of the medical profession.... [T]he *Code of Medical Ethics*, § 2.211, states that physician-assisted suicide is "fundamentally incompatible with the physician's role as healer, would be difficult or impossible to control, and would pose serious societal risks." Even the Hippocratic Oath itself states that a physician "will neither give a deadly drug to anybody if asked for it, nor ... make a suggestion to this effect." Physician-assisted suicide directly contradicts these ethical standards and compromises the integrity of the medical profession and the role of hospitals in caring for patients.

We do not hold that a carefully crafted statute authorizing assisted suicide would be unconstitutional. Nor do we discount the sincerity and strength of the respondents' convictions. However, we have concluded that this case should not be decided on the basis of this Court's own assessment of the weight of the competing moral arguments. By broadly construing the privacy amendment to include the right to assisted suicide, we would run the risk of arrogating to ourselves those powers to make social policy that as a constitutional matter belong only to the legislature. *See* art. II, § 3, Fla. Const. (separation of powers).

We reverse the judgment of the trial court and uphold the constitutionality of section 782.08.

It is so ordered.

Notes and Questions to Consider:

1. After holding that Florida "has a compelling interest in preventing suicide," the Florida Supreme Court in *Krischer v. McIver* went to great lengths to identify the competing public policy concerns. But was *Krischer v. McIver* decided based on public policy or based upon judicial restraint?

2. *Krischer v. McIver* turned to the case law of various states in interpreting Florida's constitution. Is turning to the language of another state's constitution an appropriate means of interpretation?

3. Does the holding in *Krischer v. McIver* strengthen, weaken, or not affect the strength of a Floridian's right to privacy under Florida's constitution? Consider the opinion of one commentator in Eryn R. Ace, *Krischer v. McIver: Avoiding the Dangers of Assisted Suicide*, 32 AKRON L. REV. 723 (1999):

> In *Krischer v. McIver*, the Florida Supreme Court upheld the constitutionality of Florida's statute prohibiting assisted suicide under both the Florida privacy amendment and the U.S. Constitution. After *Krischer*, Florida residents cannot rely on their privacy rights to protect from prosecution a person who assists them in committing suicide. While this decision promotes

the policy arguments against assisted suicide, it also limits the previously broad construction of Florida's right of privacy. However, while denying constitutional protection, the court stated that the legislature could enact laws allowing assisted suicide. With this, the court effectively and purposefully left this question open for continued public debate.

Id. at 724–25 (internal footnotes omitted).

Chapter 7

Homestead

A. Introduction to Homestead

"Florida has been a popular choice to take up residency for many individuals because of the expansive creditor protection afforded by the homestead laws in this state. This expansive protection stems from the purpose of homestead: to preserve the family home." Joseph M. Percopo, *The Impact of Co-Ownership on Florida Homestead*, FLA. B.J., at 32, 34–35 (May 2012).

Florida's constitution protects homestead property from a forced sale by most creditors under Article X, § 4, which states in relevant part:

> (a) There shall be exempt from forced sale under process of any court, and no judgment, decree or execution shall be a lien thereon except for the payment of taxes and assessments thereon, obligations contracted for the purchase, improvement or repair thereof, or obligations contracted for house, filed or other labor performed on the realty, the following property owned by a natural person:

> (1) a homestead, if located outside the municipality, to the extent of one hundred sixty acres of contiguous land and improvements thereon, which shall not be reduced without the owner's consent by reason of subsequent inclusion in a municipality; or if located within a municipality, to the extent of one-half acre of contiguous land, upon which the exemption shall be limited to the residence of the owner or the owner's family.

But protection from creditors is not the only right provided for homesteads. The Constitution of the State of Florida protects a Floridian's homestead in three distinct ways:

> First, a clause ... provides homesteads with [a partial] exemption from taxes. Second, the homestead provision protects the homestead from forced sale by [most] creditors. Third, the homestead provision delineates the restrictions a homestead owner faces when attempting to alienate or devise the homestead property. . . . As a matter of public policy, the purpose of the homestead exemption is to promote the stability and welfare of the state by securing to the householder a home, so that the homeowner and his or her heirs may live beyond the reach of financial misfortune and the demands of creditors who have given credit under such law.

Snyder v. Davis, 699 So. 2d 999, 1002 (Fla. 1997).

Any "natural person" may benefit from Florida's Homestead protection from creditors. Even if, perhaps, the original intent of the homestead protection might have been to protect those dependents living in the homestead after the bread-winner's death, the current scope of Florida's homestead protection is far broader due to a constitutional amendment making it available to more than just the head of household. "The [1985] change in the constitutional language from 'a head of household' to 'a natural person' expanded the class of persons afforded constitutional homestead protections to include individuals who are single and those with no dependents." Alex Cuello, *The Long-Standing Concept of "Abandonment" of the Homestead Did Not Survive the 1985 Amendments to the Florida Constitution*, Fla. B.J., December 2012, at 37, 38.

B. Common Homestead Protection from Full Taxation

The common homestead tax exemptions in Florida's constitution should not be confused with similarly named homestead protection rights embodied in Florida's constitution that protect the homestead from loss to creditor and restrict the home-steader's power of devise. Although these two sets of laws bear similar names, most similarities end there. Florida Jurisprudence 2d explains:

> There are three contexts in which the homestead has significance in Florida law: (1) taxation, (2) exemption from forced sale, and (3) descent and devise. The type of homestead for ad valorem tax exemption is sometimes called "common homestead" to distinguish it from the less well-known, but important, life-time and death-time exemptions from creditor's claims, limitations on devise, and restrictions on alienation of separately defined homestead property appearing in the Florida Constitution. The definition of "homestead" in the context of property taxation is distinct from its definition in the context of the other exemptions. Moreover, unlike the ad valorem homestead exemption, the "forced sale" provision is to be liberally construed for the benefit of those whom it was designed to protect.

51A Fla. Jur 2d Taxation § 1231 (June 2019 update). Stated somewhat differently, "[i]t is well settled that homestead decisions for tax purposes are based upon a completely different statutory provision (§ 196.041, Florida Statutes) and may have no relevancy to decisions for forced sale purposes." *In re Duque*, 33 B.R. 201, 202 (Bankr. S.D. Fla. 1983).

Back in 1951, Florida's supreme court observed that it "appears that Mississippi and Florida are practically alone in their policy of withdrawing homesteads as a source of revenue for the support of local government." *Overstreet v. Tubin*, 53 So. 2d 913, 914 (Fla. 1951). The same could not be said today, because the majority of states place some degree of limitation or exemption upon the taxes levied upon some homesteads for some groups of citizens.

Florida's homestead tax exemption provides, in relevant part:

SECTION 6. Homestead exemptions. —

(a) Every person who has the legal or equitable title to real estate and maintains thereon the permanent residence of the owner, or another legally or naturally dependent upon the owner, shall be exempt from taxation thereon, except assessments for special benefits, up to the assessed valuation of twenty-five thousand dollars and, for all levies other than school district levies, on the assessed valuation greater than fifty thousand dollars and up to seventy-five thousand dollars, upon establishment of right thereto in the manner prescribed by law. The real estate may be held by legal or equitable title, by the entireties, jointly, in common, as a condominium, or indirectly by stock ownership or membership representing the owner's or member's proprietary interest in a corporation owning a fee or a leasehold initially in excess of ninety-eight years. The exemption shall not apply with respect to any assessment roll until such roll is first determined to be in compliance with the provisions of section 4 by a state agency designated by general law. This exemption is repealed on the effective date of any amendment to this Article which provides for the assessment of homestead property at less than just value.

(b) Not more than one exemption shall be allowed any individual or family unit or with respect to any residential unit. No exemption shall exceed the value of the real estate assessable to the owner or, in case of ownership through stock or membership in a corporation, the value of the proportion which the interest in the corporation bears to the assessed value of the property.

(c) By general law and subject to conditions specified therein, the Legislature may provide to renters, who are permanent residents, ad valorem tax relief on all ad valorem tax levies. Such ad valorem tax relief shall be in the form and amount established by general law.

(d) The legislature may, by general law, allow counties or municipalities, for the purpose of their respective tax levies and subject to the provisions of general law, to grant either or both of the following additional homestead tax exemptions:

(1) An exemption not exceeding fifty thousand dollars to a person who has the legal or equitable title to real estate and maintains thereon the permanent residence of the owner, who has attained age sixty-five, and whose household income, as defined by general law, does not exceed twenty thousand dollars; or

(2) An exemption equal to the assessed value of the property to a person who has the legal or equitable title to real estate with a just value less than two hundred and fifty thousand dollars, as determined in the first tax year that the owner applies and is eligible for the exemption, and who

has maintained thereon the permanent residence of the owner for not less than twenty-five years, who has attained age sixty-five, and whose household income does not exceed the income limitation prescribed in paragraph (1).

The general law must allow counties and municipalities to grant these additional exemptions, within the limits prescribed in this subsection, by ordinance adopted in the manner prescribed by general law, and must provide for the periodic adjustment of the income limitation prescribed in this subsection for changes in the cost of living.

Florida's common homestead tax exemption appearing above is one that evolved over time as new amendments were made to Florida's constitution, some as a result of Florida's legislature, but often as a result of the initiative process started directly by Floridians. This may explain its complexity.

I summarized Florida's common homestead tax exemption in my book FLORIDA ELEMENTS OF AN ACTION as follows:

The plain language of article VII, section 6(a) provides that an owner of residential real estate in Florida is constitutionally entitled to an exemption from ad valorem taxation — more accurately, a reduction in the assessed value — under either of the following two separate and independent scenarios:

1. Where the owner of the property is a permanent resident on the property,

OR

2. Where someone legally or naturally dependent on the owner is a permanent resident on the subject property.

Florida Statutes Section 196.012 defines "permanent residence" for purposes of this provision as follows:

"Permanent residence" means that place where a person has his or her true, fixed, and permanent home and principal establishment to which, whenever absent, he or she has the intention of returning. A person may have only one permanent residence at a time; and, once a permanent residence is established in a foreign state or country, it is presumed to continue until the person shows that a change has occurred.

Patrick John McGinley, *Elements of a Prima Facie Case for a Property Tax Exemption for a Common Homestead*, in FLORIDA ELEMENTS OF AN ACTION § 1901:1 (2017-2018 ed.) (footnotes omitted).

In summarizing Florida's common homestead tax exemption, one internet commentator said:

The state of Florida has a generous homestead law compared to other states; it's also one of the most complicated systems in the country. The current exemption is $50,000, of which the first $25,000 applies to all property taxes including school district taxes, and the second $25,000 applies to assessed values between $50,000 and $75,000 and only to nonschool taxes. If you owned a home with an assessed value of $85,000, for example, the first $25,000 would be exempt from all property taxes, the next $25,000 of value would be taxable, the third $25,000 would be exempt from non-school taxes, and the final $10,000 would be taxable. Did we mention it was complicated?

https://finance.zacks.com/states-homestead-tax-exemption-3925.html.

Florida's homestead tax exemption is not self-executing. Instead, Florida home-steaders must apply for the homestead tax exemption in a timely and proper manner. Florida's supreme court holds that "[r]equiring a timely filing for a homestead exemption imposes only a slight burden on the taxpayer in comparison to the tax benefit received. At the same time, this requirement prevents substantial uncertainty in taxing authorities' annual taxing and budgeting process." *Zingale v. Powell*, 885 So. 2d 277, 285 (Fla. 2004).

C. Right of Heirs to the Homestead Exemption from Forced Sale

Turning next to the protection of homestead beyond issues of state government taxation, we turn to the seminal case of *Snyder v. Davis*, 699 So. 2d 999 (Fla. 1997) (with its footnotes omitted).

Snyder v. Davis
Supreme Court of the State of Florida, 1997
699 So. 2d 999

We have for review the decision of the Second District Court of Appeal [where the] district court held that the testator could not both devise her homestead property to her granddaughter and preserve its exemption from creditors. The court found that while the homestead could be devised, the constitutional exemption from creditors would follow the homestead only if it were devised to the person or persons who would have actually taken the homestead had the testator died intestate. In this case the granddaughter would not have taken the homestead under the intestacy statutes because the testator's natural son was still alive at the death of the testator. See § 732.103, Fla. Stat. (1995). The court then certified the following question to be of great public importance:

> whether Article X, Section 4, of the Florida Constitution exempts from forced sale a devise of a homestead by a decedent not survived by a spouse or minor child to a lineal descendant who is not an heir under the definition in section 731.201(18), Florida Statutes (1993).

Id. at 1193. We have jurisdiction. Art. V, § 3(b)(4), Fla. Const.

For the reasons expressed, we answer the certified question in the affirmative and quash the district court's decision. We find that in these circumstances the word "heirs," when determining entitlement to the homestead protections against creditors, is not limited to only the person or persons who would actually take the homestead by law in intestacy on the death of the decedent. Instead, we hold that the constitution must be construed to mean that a testator, when drafting a will prior to death, may devise the homestead (if there is no surviving spouse or minor children) to any of that class of persons categorized in section 732.103 (the intestacy statute). To hold otherwise would mean that a testator, when making an effort to avoid intestacy by drafting a will, would have to guess who his or her actual heirs would be on the date of death in order to maintain the homestead's constitutional protections against creditors.

Facts

Betty Snyder died testate on February 15, 1995. In her will, she made the following dispositions:

> First, the expenses of my funeral, burial, or other disposition of my remains I may have directed, my just debts, and the costs of administering my estate shall be paid out of the residue of my estate.
>
> Second, I give, devise and make special provisions as follows:
>
> a. The sum of $3,000 to my son, MILO SNYDER, provided he survives me.
>
> b. The sum of $2,000 to my friends, JOE BEDRIN and BARBARA BEDRIN, or to the survivor of them.
>
> Third, I give and devise all the rest, residue, and remainder of my property of every kind and wherever situated, as follows: All to my granddaughter, KELLI SNYDER.
>
> Betty Snyder was not survived by a spouse. She was, however, survived by her only son, Milo Snyder and his only daughter, Kelli Snyder. Both Milo and Kelli are adults.

Kent W. Davis, the personal representative of Betty Snyder's estate, sought to sell the homestead property to satisfy creditors' claims, to fund specific bequests, and to pay the costs of administration. Kelli Snyder, the residuary beneficiary, asserted that the testator's homestead passed to her free of claims because she was protected by article X, section 4, of the Florida Constitution (the homestead provision). The homestead provision reads, in relevant part, as follows:

> (a) There shall be exempt from forced sale under process of any court, and no judgment, decree, or execution shall be a lien thereon, except for the payment of taxes and assessments thereon, obligations contracted for the purchase, improvement or repair thereof, or obligations contracted for house, field or other labor performed on the realty, the following property owned by a natural person:

(1) a homestead. . . .

. . .

(b) These exemptions shall inure to the surviving spouse or *heirs of the owner.*

Art. X, §4, Fla. Const. (emphasis added).

There is no dispute in this case that Betty Snyder's home was homestead property for the purpose of distribution or that said property was properly devised in the residuary clause of her will. The sole issue is whether Kelli Snyder, as the granddaughter, may be properly considered an heir under the homestead provision, qualifying her for protection from the forced sale of the homestead property when her father, the next-in-line heir under statutory intestate succession, is still living.

The personal representative argues that, had Betty Snyder died intestate, Kelli Snyder would not have qualified as an heir under the intestacy statute. He asserts that Milo Snyder, as the testator's son, would have been the sole taker of the homestead under the intestacy statute and, consequently, the homestead was not devised to an heir by Betty Snyder's will. Accordingly, he argues that the homestead property is not protected by the homestead provision and is subject to creditors' claims.

The trial judge disagreed with these assertions and found that the homestead provision protected the homestead from creditors in this case. The district court reversed, finding that because Milo Snyder would have been the sole heir had there been intestacy, Kelli Snyder is precluded from benefitting from the homestead provision's protections against creditors. In so finding, the district court explained its position as follows:

> Section 731.201(18) defines "heirs" as "those persons, including the surviving spouse, who are entitled under the statutes of intestate succession to the property of a decedent." While Kelli Snyder is a lineal descendant of her grandmother, the decedent's adult son, Milo Snyder, is the only member of the next generation of "lineal descendant." A reference to "heirs" is generally considered as referring to those who inherit under the laws of intestate succession. See, e.g., *Arnold v. Wells*, 100 Fla. 1470, 131 So. 400 (1930). If Betty Snyder had died intestate, Milo Snyder would have inherited everything as her "heir," i.e., next lineal descendant in line, and Kelli Snyder, under any construction of section 732.103, would have inherited nothing. This would be so because inheritance in Florida is "per stirpes." §732.104, Fla. Stat. (1993). Because Milo Snyder survived, Kelli Snyder is not an intestate "heir" of her grandmother. Therefore, for purposes of the homestead exemption inuring to "the heir of the decedent," as defined by intestate succession, the exemption cannot inure to Kelli Snyder.

681 So. 2d at 1193. We granted review in order to answer the certified question. . . .

The circumstances under which a homestead may be devised while still retaining its protections against creditors present a significant issue for both the legal profession and the public in general. All Floridians need to fully understand how their homestead property might be properly devised while still maintaining its protections against creditors (when there are no surviving spouses or minor children).

The Homestead Provision

The homestead provision has been characterized as "our legal chameleon." Our constitution protects Florida homesteads in three distinct ways.

First, a clause, separate and apart from the homestead provision applicable in this case, provides homesteads with an exemption from taxes. Second, the homestead provision protects the homestead from forced sale by creditors. Third, the homestead provision delineates the restrictions a homestead owner faces when attempting to alienate or devise the homestead property. This case involves the second and third protections described above.

Homestead law in the United States has evolved over time, and it is strictly an American innovation. In Florida, moreover, our case law surrounding the homestead provision has its own contours and legal principles. As a result, it is not susceptible to comparisons with similar provisions in other jurisdictions. Importantly, our courts have emphasized that, in Florida, the homestead provision is in place to protect and preserve the interest of the family in the family home. We recently reaffirmed that general policy by stating:

> As a matter of public policy, the purpose of the homestead exemption is to promote the stability and welfare of the state by securing to the householder a home, so that the homeowner and his or her heirs may live beyond the reach of financial misfortune and the demands of creditors who have given credit under such law.

Public Health Trust v. Lopez, 531 So. 2d 946, 948 (Fla. 1988). Further, it is clear that the homestead provision is to be liberally construed in favor of maintaining the homestead property. . . . As a matter of policy as well as construction, our homestead protections have been interpreted broadly.

In addition, in 1984, the people further expanded homestead provision to substantially broaden the class of people eligible to take advantage of our homestead protections. While those protections had been previously limited to the "head of a family," they are now available to any "natural person." Compare art. X, § 4(a), Fla. Const.(1972) ("There shall be exempt from forced sale under process of any court . . . the following property owned by the head of a family") with art. X, § 4(a), Fla. Const. ("There shall be exempt from forced sale under process of any court . . . the following property owned by a natural person").

Finally, it is important to note that creditors are aware of the homestead provision and its inherent protections. As we discussed in *Public Health Trust*, we will not narrowly interpret the homestead provision simply because "financially independent heirs" may receive a windfall. 531 So. 2d at 950. There we wrote:

The homestead protection has never been based on principles of equity . . . but always has been extended to the homesteader and, after his or her death, to the heirs whether the homestead was a twenty-two room mansion or a two-room hut and whether the heirs were rich or poor.

Id. Creditors have been on notice for many years that the plain language of the constitution protects homestead property from most creditors.

It is with these policy considerations in mind that we address the two major issues in this case.

Devisees of a Homestead May Be Entitled to the Homestead Provision's Protections against Creditors

The first question we must resolve is whether the protection against creditors found in the homestead provision can be transferred, with a will, to a devisee. This Court has never addressed whether the term "heirs" in the homestead provision includes devisees.

Under the common law, an heir was a person designated to inherit in the event of intestacy at the death of the decedent. Now, however, "the term is frequently used in a popular sense to designate a successor to property either by will or by law." BLACK'S LAW DICTIONARY 724 (6th ed. 1990) ("Word 'heirs' is no longer limited to designated character of estate as at common law.") If we define the term "heirs" in the homestead provision by its strict common-law definition, the very act of devising the homestead would abolish the homestead protections against creditors. We refuse to construe the homestead provision in such a narrow way. In reaching this conclusion, we are persuaded by the reasoning of the Third District Court of Appeal, sitting en banc, in *Bartelt v. Bartelt*, 579 So. 2d 282 (Fla. 3d DCA 1991). That court addressed the situation in which the decedent, who died without a surviving spouse but with two surviving adult children, a son and a daughter, devised his homestead only to his son. There, the district court held that the homestead exemption passed to the devisee through the will even though the omitted child would have been entitled to an equal share of the homestead had the decedent died intestate. In so holding, the *Bartelt* court stated:

When the decedent's homestead is devised to his son—a member of the class of persons who are the decedent's "heirs"—the constitutional exemption from forced sale by the decedent's creditors found in Article X, Section 4(b) of the Florida Constitution, inures to that son. The test is not how title was devolved, but rather to whom it passed. . . .

The personal representative argues that, although "heirs" may avail themselves of the constitutional protection from creditors, "devisees" may not. Section 731.201(18), Florida Statutes (1989), defines heirs or heirs at law as "those persons . . . who are entitled under the statutes of intestate succession to the property of a decedent." Devisees are defined in section 731.201(9) as persons "designated in a will to receive a devise." According to the personal representative, a devisee cannot be an heir because a devisee takes by will and an heir takes only where there is no will. We disagree. Heirs, as defined in section 731.201(18), are simply those persons entitled to receive property under the laws of intestacy; the decedent's son, as his lineal descendant, is a member of that class. § 732.103(1), Fla. Stat. (1989). The class designated as "heirs" does not exclude those who, but for the decedent's foresight in executing a will, would have taken by the laws of intestate succession. . . . Article X, section 4 of the Florida Constitution defines the class of persons to whom the decedent's exemption from forced sale of homestead property inures; it does not mandate the technique by which the qualified person must receive title.

Id. at 283–84. An academic commentator on this subject writes approvingly of the result reached by that district court:

This author supports the *Bartelt* decision. The constitutional exemption from forced sale by creditors, as found in article X, § 4(b) of the Florida Constitution, inures to the surviving spouse or heirs of the owner. *Bartelt* includes within the term "heirs" devisees who but for the will would have been heirs. It properly takes a broad gauged approach to the constitutional terminology. It places substance over form. The persons involved as takers are the same whether there is a will or there is not a will. The court points out that without such a determination, with respect to homestead, Florida residents would be discouraged from making wills and would be encouraged to let the property in issue pass by intestate succession. Such a result would be an anathema.

David T. Smith, FLORIDA PROBATE CODE MANUAL § 4.05, at 29–30 (1995).

We agree that, in cases in which there is no surviving spouse or minor children, the protections against creditors found in the homestead provision may inure to the benefit of the person to whom the homestead property is devised by will. As explained below, though, the class of persons to which such protections may be devised is limited.

The Class of Devisees to Which the Protections against Creditors Found in the Homestead Provision May Be Devised

Having found that the protections against creditors found in the homestead provision may be devised by will, we now must define the scope of the class of persons to which those protections may be so devised. The *Davis* court and the *Walker* court present us with two alternatives. First, the *Davis* court defined the word "heirs" narrowly and found that, in order to preserve the protection against creditors, a devisee had to be entitled to inherit the homestead property under the intestacy statute. The *Walker* court applied a broader definition of the term "heirs." It held that the protections against creditors could be devised to any of the class of potential heirs under the intestacy statute. It found no occasion to require that a testator leave the homestead property to the actual person or persons who would have actually inherited under the intestacy statute. These two views of the term "heirs" can be characterized as the "entitlement definition" and the "class definition," respectively.

We are persuaded by the *Walker* court's view. In a situation almost identical to that in this Davis case, the First District Court held that a decedent's grandson was entitled to the homestead protection even though the grandson was not the closest consanguine heir. In doing so, the court found that any person categorized in the intestacy statute was an heir for the purpose of the homestead provision. In particular, it wrote:

> Article X, section 4(b) of the Florida Constitution provides that the exemptions and protections established for homestead property under article X, section 4(a) "shall inure to the surviving spouse or heirs of the owner." As this court explained in *State Department of Health and Rehabilitative Services v. Trammell*, 508 So. 2d 422 (Fla. 1st DCA 1987), the term "heir" under article X, section 4(b) means "those who may under the laws of the state inherit from the owner of the homestead." *Id*. at 423. Because Bavle, as the decedent's grandson, was a lineal descendent of the decedent, he is a member of the class of persons entitled to receive property under the laws of intestacy, see sections 732.103(1) and 732.401(1), Florida Statutes (1993), and accordingly, is an "heir" for the purposes of article X, section 4(b). A remainderman is entitled to claim a homestead exemption.

687 So. 2d at 1329.

The *Walker* court expressly rejected the holding of the *Davis* court. It wrote:

> We find the *Davis* opinion contrary to the purpose of the homestead exemption from forced sale. We start with the well-established principle that the laws regarding homestead exemption are to be liberally construed. *Jetton Lumber Co. v. Hall*, 67 Fla. 61, 64 So. 440 (1914); and *In re Estate of Skuro*, 467 So. 2d 1098 (Fla. 4th DCA 1985), aff'd, 487 So. 2d 1065 (Fla. 1986). Although the constitution is silent as to the intent of the drafters with respect to the rights of creditors of estates, we conclude that, as amended in 1984, article V, section 4(b), however, does reflect the intent that the exemption is to inure to whomever the homestead property passes.

Id. at 1330. The *Walker* court grounded its conclusion on the following policy consideration:

> It seems clear to us that the intent of the homestead exemption is to protect the decedent's homestead from the decedent's creditors for the benefit of the decedent's heirs. To deny the exemption for a homestead property simply because the person chosen by the decedent to receive the property under the will, even though that person is within the class of persons entitled to take under the laws of intestate succession, is not the closest consanguine heir, is contrary to that constitutional intent.

Id. at 1331.

The *Walker* court, it seems to us, announces the correct view of our homestead provision. Indeed, the approach used by the *Davis* court would force a testator to guess as to his or her survivors in order to successfully devise, by will, the homestead property with the protections against creditors intact. That reading of our constitution is, in our view, unreasonable. If a severe limitation is to be placed on the ability of Floridians to keep the homestead within the family, it should not be done by a narrow judicial construction of the homestead provision.

We are reinforced in our view when the ramifications of the alternative position are considered. Under the *Davis* court's reasoning, an attorney would be faced with giving the following illogical advice to a potential testator with no surviving spouse or minor children:

> You have two bad choices. You can devise your homestead to any person you choose. If you do, though, the homestead provision's protections against creditors will be inapplicable and your homestead may be subject to forced sale. On the other hand, you can guess as to which family members will survive you. After we have established the list of your guesses, I can tell you which of those family members would inherit under our intestacy statute. If you leave your homestead to those family members and they really do survive you, the homestead provision's protections against creditors will remain intact. If you guess incorrectly, though, the protections against creditors will be inapplicable. The point is this: If you want to ensure protection of the homestead property against creditors under our constitution, you have no choice as to which family member might best maintain your homestead property. The law requires that in order to utilize the homestead provision's protections against creditors, the homestead property must pass to the person or persons dictated by the intestacy statute.

Creating a system, by engaging a narrow judicial construction of the homestead provision, in which this type of advice must be given is unreasonable. Will-making, in these circumstances, becomes an act of prophecy. Clearly, as a policy matter, we should not be encouraging intestacy as a means of distributing one's property. In many instances where there is no surviving spouse or minor children, the homestead property is the most significant part of a testator's estate. If a testator loses control over the disposition of his or her homestead property, the need for a will is effectively eliminated. Such an approach takes away from the testator any ability to make a choice as to which family member will best preserve and maintain the family homestead. Instead, it promotes absolute adherence to the strict priorities found in the intestacy statute without paying any respect to the needs of individual testators and their families.

The whole purpose of the homestead provision is to protect and maintain the family homestead. The testator is likely in the best position to know which family member is most likely to need or to properly maintain the homestead. A plain reading of the homestead provision establishes that it only prohibits devising the homestead property when the testator is survived by a spouse or minor children. There is no prohibition against devising the homestead property to any of that class of persons who could potentially receive the homestead property under the intestacy statute. We must emphasize, however, that today's ruling does not authorize a testator to devise homestead property to any person not categorized by our intestacy statute with any expectation that the protections against creditors will survive such a devise. See *State Dep't of Health & Rehabilitative Servs. v. Trammell*, 508 So. 2d 422 (Fla. 1st DCA 1987) (holding that a devise of homestead to a good friend does not qualify for the homestead exemption).

Conclusion

We have consistently made it clear that the homestead provision must be given a broad and liberal construction. In the context of this case, we reject the narrow entitlement definition of the term "heirs" that includes only those people who would inherit under the intestacy statute at the death of the decedent. Instead, we hold that the homestead provision allows a testator with no surviving spouse or minor children to choose to devise, in a will, the homestead property, with its accompanying protection from creditors, to any family member within the class of persons categorized in our intestacy statute.

Accordingly, we answer the certified question in the affirmative, quash the decision of the district court in *Davis*, and approve the district court's opinion in *Walker*.

It is so ordered.

Notes and Questions to Consider:

1. Under the facts of *Snyder v. Davis*, Florida's supreme court notes that "[t]here is no dispute in this case that Betty Snyder's home was homestead property . . .". But what about cases where this is in dispute? For a homestead to exist, "[t]here are four basic requirements that must be satisfied: (1) The real property must be owned by a 'natural person;' (2) The person claiming the exemption must be a Florida resident who established that he or she made, or intended to make, the real property his or her 'permanent residence;' (3) The person claiming the exemption must establish that he or she is the 'owner' of the property; [and] (4) The property claimed as the homestead must satisfy the 'size and contiguity' requirements of [Florida's C]onstitution." John F. Cooper, Tishia A. Dunham & Carlos L. Woody, FLORIDA CONSTITUTIONAL LAW: CASES AND MATERIALS 696 (Carolina Academic Press 5th edition 2013).

2. The size and contiguity requirements are in Article X, §4(a)(1) of Florida's constitution: "if located outside the municipality, to the extent of one hundred sixty acres of contiguous land and improvements thereon, which shall not be reduced without the owner's consent by reason of subsequent inclusion in a municipality; or if located within a municipality, to the extent of one-half acre of contiguous land, upon which the exemption shall be limited to the residence of the owner or the owner's family."

3. As seen above, *Snyder v. Davis* holds that homestead protection is lost after the death of the homesteader unless his or her estate plan devises the homestead solely to one or more of his or her family members who fall within the class of persons categorized in § 732.103, Fla. Stat. (which is Florida's intestacy statute). Yet the intestacy statute lists a long and deep line of consanguinity. *Synder v. Davis* cites to *State Dep't of Health & Rehabilitative Servs. v. Trammell*, 508 So. 2d 422 (Fla. 1st DCA 1987) for the example "that a devise of homestead to a good friend does not qualify for the homestead exemption." In light of the depth and breadth of Florida's Intestacy Statutes, are there any other examples?

D. Right of Co-Owners to Homestead Exemption from Forced Sale

Although "ownership" is required before homestead rights attach, "[a]n individual need not hold legal or fee simple title to the property to meet this requirement. . . . Homestead status may be derived from any equitable or beneficiary interest in real property." John F. Cooper, Tishia A. Dunham & Carlos L. Woody, FLORIDA CONSTITUTIONAL LAW: CASES AND MATERIALS 697 (Carolina Academic Press 5th edition 2013) (citing *Bessemer Props., Inc. v. Gamble*, 27 So. 2d 832 (Fla. 1946) and *Heiman v. Capital Bank*, 438 So. 2d 932 (Fla. 3d DCA 1983)).

What exactly does this mean? Consider the following excerpt from Joseph Percopo's famous article *The Impact of Co-Ownership on Florida Homestead*, FLA. B.J., May 2012, at 32, 35–38:

The Impact of Co-Ownership on Florida Homestead
By Joseph M. Percopo
THE FLORIDA BAR JOURNAL, May 2012
© 2012 by The Florida Bar and Joseph M. Percopo

Creditor Protection

[I]n order to qualify for the homestead creditor exemption, three conditions must be satisfied: 1) acreage limitations, 2) residency requirements, and 3) ownership requirements. Provided all three of these conditions are satisfied, creditors of the person claiming the homestead creditor exemption will not be able to force sale of or place a lien on the homestead property. This article now examines how co-ownership of property affects the homestead creditor protection.

• Tenants by the Entirety — Only married couples can own property as tenants by the entirety, and there is a presumption that real property acquired during marriage is owned as such. . . . Provided either spouse qualifies for the homestead creditor exemption, the property will be afforded protection from either spouse's creditors. However, upon dissolution of marriage, unless the divorce decree makes one spouse a complete owner or provides terms granting one spouse exclusive possession of the home, the spouses become tenants in common subject to the rules discussed below.

• Tenants in Common and Joint Tenants with Right of Survivorship — . . . Unless specific language is used indicating "survivorship rights," tenants in common is the default form of co-owned property in Florida. . . . Co-ownership of property will not prevent an owner from claiming the homestead creditor exemption; however, the status of each co-owner impacts the level of creditor protection retained by the property. When all co-owners qualify for the homestead creditor exemption, the home will be exempt from forced sale and liens. . . . When at least one co-owner does not qualify for the homestead creditor exemption, a potential problem exists. In *Tullis v. Tullis*, 360 So. 2d 375 (Fla. 1978), the Florida Supreme Court held that the Florida "constitutional provisions allow the partition and forced sale of homestead property upon suit by one of the owners of that property" provided it is to protect the owner's beneficial enjoyment. Thus, any of the co-owners of real property can force the property to be partitioned and sold. Therefore, if a co-owner does not qualify for the homestead creditor exemption, a creditor of that co-owner can acquire that interest and then force a sale. . . . A chain is only as strong as its weakest link, and this holds true for property owned as tenants in common or as joint tenants with right of survivorship. Property will be completely shielded from creditors when all co-owners qualify for the homestead creditor exemption. However, if at least one co-owner does not qualify for the homestead creditor exemption, the property becomes subject to that co-owner's creditors. This is extremely important to understand when acquiring property with others. It is common to see family, especially parents and children, purchase property together or add each other to the title of property. Parents need to know that if they place a child's name on the deed and that property is not the child's homestead for creditor protection purposes, then that property is subject to the child's creditors. Additionally, children need to be aware that if their parents are on the title to their homestead (maybe they helped purchase the property many years ago), that property is subject to their parents' creditors (unless, of course, the parents are now living there, and it is their homestead for creditor protection purposes).

• Life Estates and Remainder Interests — Individuals may also take title to property in a manner that divides ownership into present and future interests. Under this type of ownership, a person may take a life estate, which means he or she has a present possessory interest in the property and is entitled to all ordinary uses of the property until death. However, ordinary use does not permit a life tenant to do anything that injures the future interest in the property. Therefore, a life tenant cannot neglect the property allowing it to fall into disrepair or commit waste, such as consuming or exploiting the resources upon the property. The remainder (future) interest holder must approve any improvements to the property, and has the right to inspect the property for waste or damage. Upon the death of the life tenant, the life estate ends and the remainderman (person with the remainder interest) becomes the owner by operation of law.

To determine if and how the homestead creditor exemption applies to life estates and remainder interests, the following questions must be addressed: 1) whether individuals with fractional ownership in time can claim the homestead creditor exemption, and if so 2) which of the co-owners qualify for the homestead creditor exemption. . . . The Florida Supreme Court in *Aetna Ins. Co. v. Lagasse*, 223 So. 2d 727 (Fla. 1969), held that remainder interests, including vested remainders, were not able to qualify for the homestead creditor exemption, even if he or she lived on the property, because there was no "present right to possession." Thus, a life tenant can qualify for the homestead creditor exemption with a life estate, but the Florida Supreme Court has determined that a remainderman cannot qualify with a remainder interest.

When the life tenant qualifies for the homestead creditor exemption, the property is still protected from the life tenant's creditors, but it is not safe from the remainderman's creditors. . . . Co-owners who share interests in time (life tenants and remainderman), unlike co-owners who share present interests, may not partition life estates. Therefore, a life tenant . . . could continue to reside on the property without worrying about the remaindermans' creditors being able to force sale of the property.

However, it is important to note that recently, two Florida bankruptcy cases held that a person with a vested remainder who lived on and made the property his or her residence could qualify for the homestead creditor exemption. Therefore, if a remainderman finds himself or herself in a Florida bankruptcy court, he or she has precedent to argue for the homestead creditor exemption. Of course, for Florida courts, the bankruptcy court decisions are merely persuasive and not binding; nevertheless, it does leave room for discussion on the subject.

Id. at 35–38 (footnotes omitted).

———————

Notes and Questions to Consider:

1. Florida Statutes § 732.401 provides that a homestead jointly owned via "tenancy by the entireties" or via "joint tenancy with rights of survivorship" becomes solely owned by the surviving owner upon the co-owner's death, and does so free and clear of the deceased's debts and financial obligations. *See also* Fla. Stat. § 731.201.

2. The excerpt above ends with a discussion of bankruptcy court interpretations of these portions of the homestead law but states this caveat: "the bankruptcy court decisions are merely persuasive and not binding." How persuasive do you find the logic of the cited bankruptcy court decisions?

E. Homestead Restrictions upon Devise and Inheritance

What is meant by Florida's constitution's restriction upon the inheritance and devise of homestead property? It means three things.

First, it means that the deceased's will or revocable living trust or other estate planning documents do *not* void or avoid homestead protection when there is a surviving child or spouse of the deceased because it does not control the devise of the homestead when there are such survivors. §732.4015, Fla. Stat. (2017).

Second, it means the decedent's surviving spouse inherits—despite any will, trust, or estate plan to the contrary—the surviving spouse's choice of a life estate or undivided ½ interest if the deceased's child or children survive the deceased (and they, per stirpes, hold a vested remainder), or, if the deceased's child or children did not survive the deceased, then the surviving spouse inherits the homestead in fee simple unless the surviving spouse waived that right.

Third, it means that if the decedent does not have a surviving spouse, but has one or more surviving children, then the surviving child or children inherit—despite any will/trust to the contrary—the homestead in fee simple as tenants in common. §732.103(1), Fla. Stat. (2015).

For a more detailed understanding of these rules, let us again consider another excerpt from Joseph Percopo's famous article *The Impact of Co-Ownership on Florida Homestead*, Fla. B.J., May 2012, at 32, 35–38:

The Impact of Co-Ownership on Florida Homestead

By Joseph M. Percopo

The Florida Bar Journal, May 2012

© 2012 by The Florida Bar and Joseph M. Percopo

Alienation, Devise, and Descent

Florida has certain restrictions on how homestead property may be alienated and devised, as well as rules dealing with improperly devised homestead upon the owner's death. Fla. Const. art. X, §4(c) provides that:

> (c) The homestead shall not be subject to devise if the owner is survived by spouse or minor child, except the homestead may be devised to the owner's spouse if there be no minor child. The owner of homestead real estate, joined by the spouse if married, may alienate the homestead by mortgage, sale or gift and, if married, may by deed transfer the title to an estate by the entirety with the spouse.

This provision is codified in [Florida Statutes] §732.4015(1), where it is similarly states that "the homestead shall not be subject to devise if the owner is survived by a spouse or a minor child or minor children, except that the homestead may be devised to the owner's spouse if there is no minor child or children." [Florida Statutes] §732.401(1) further states that "[i]f not devised as authorized by law and the constitution, the homestead shall descend in the same manner as other intestate property; but if the decedent is survived by a spouse and one or more descendants, the surviving spouse shall take a life estate in the homestead, with a vested remainder to the lineal descendants in being at the time of the decedent's death per stirpes." However, the spouse may also make an election "to take an undivided one-half interest in the homestead as tenants in common, with the remaining one-half interest vesting in the decedent's descendants in being at the time of the decedent's death, per stirpes," instead of taking the life estate.

When an individual has no spouse or minor children, he or she is free to devise the homestead property anyway he or she pleases. Conversely, when an individual is survived either by a spouse or minor child(ren), then the property is not subject to devise and will pass as intestate property (meaning that the sole surviving spouse will become the sole owner if there are no descendants, or the surviving minor child(ren) will become the sole owner if there is no surviving spouse).

The rules concerning alienation, devise, and descent only apply to a co-owner if the property is the co-owners' homestead pursuant to Fla. Const. art. X, § 4 ("transfer restricted homestead"); thus, any of the other co-owners who do not reside on the property are free to dispose of their property as they see fit. The article now examines how these rules apply to a co-owner of property where he or she owns transfer restricted homestead property.

• Alienation: With regard to alienation of property, the Florida Constitution does not place any restrictions on alienation except that a married owner must have spousal consent to do so (despite whether the spouse has an ownership interest of his or her own in the property).

• Devise and Descent, Tenants by the Entirety: The rules regarding devise and descent of transfer restricted homestead property do not apply to property owned as tenants by the entirety. This is because at the death of one spouse, property owned as tenants by the entirety passes to the surviving spouse automatically, outside of probate — therefore, there is no devise or descent of the homestead property.

• Devise and Descent, Joint Tenants with Right of Survivorship: The rules regarding devise and descent do not apply to transfer restricted homestead owned as joint tenants with right of survivorship, because, similar to property owned as tenants by the entirety, at death the property passes automatically to the other joint owners. Therefore, co-owners who want to preserve the transfer restricted homestead for their spouse or children should be cautious about owning property as joint tenants with right of survivorship. . . .

• Devise and Descent, Tenants in Common: When property is owned as tenants in common, the constitutional and statutory rules of devise and descent apply to transfer restricted homestead. Therefore, a co-owner is not free to devise his or her transfer restricted homestead when he or she has a surviving spouse or minor child. Instead, the co-owner's interest in the transfer restricted homestead property must pass to his or her surviving spouse and/or minor child(ren) as designated by law.

• Devise and Descent, Life Estates and Remainders: The rules regarding devise and descent of transfer restricted homestead do not apply to life estates because life estates end at the death of the life tenant; thus, there is no interest for the life tenant to devise or pass along. Like tenants by the entirety and joint tenants with right of survivorship, at death the interest passes automatically, and in the case of a life estate, to the remainderman. As for the remainderman, the devise and descent rules do not apply because the remainderman, under current Florida law, do not have a present possessory interest necessary to receive the homestead protections.

Id. at 35–38 (footnotes omitted).

———————

Notes and Questions to Consider:

1. The excerpt above opines that "co-owners who want to preserve the transfer restricted homestead for their spouse or children should be cautious about owning property as joint tenants with right of survivorship." Do you agree? Why or why not?

2. The excerpt reminds us that "the rules concerning alienation, devise, and descent only apply to a co-owner if the property is the co-owners' homestead pursuant to Fla. Const. art. X, §4 ('transfer restricted homestead')." Is the author referring to Florida Statutes §732.401? It provides that a homestead jointly owned via "tenancy by the entireties" or via "joint tenancy with rights of survivorship" becomes solely owned by the surviving owner upon the co-owner's death, and does so free and clear of the deceased's debts and financial obligations. Or is the author referring to Florida Statutes §731.201? It provides, in subsection 33, that "real property owned in tenancy by the entireties or in joint tenancy with rights of survivorship is not protected homestead."

F. Homestead Protection from Creditors for Proceeds from Home's Sale or Its Insurance Recovery

A Floridian may sell his homestead, and buy another, without losing his homestead protections. The proceeds from the sale are protected from levy or confiscation by creditors for a reasonable period of time. Likewise, the homesteader might suffer damage to her homestead for which she might receive an insurance recovery, and if so, those proceeds are protected from creditors. *See Orange Brevard Plumbing & Heating Co. v. La Croix*, 137 So. 2d 201, 203–04 (Fla. 1962). But what if the very creditor from whom the homesteader seeks protection is the person whose labor won the insurance recovery for the homesteader? Consider the holding of *Quiroga v. Citizens Prop. Ins. Corp.*, 34 So. 3d 101 (Fla. 3rd DCA 2010) (with the text that is omitted from the footnote now added to the opinion in brackets):

Quiroga v. Citizens Property Insurance
Third District Court of Appeal of Florida, 2010
34 So. 3d 101

This is an appeal from an order denying the law firm of Katzman Garfinkel and Rosenbaum's motion to impress a charging lien on the homeowner's insurance proceeds for damages caused by two hurricanes. The Katzman law firm secured the proceeds for the benefit of its client and policy insured, Jesse Quiroga, in appreciation for which Quiroga not only terminated the law firm's contingent fee representation of him, but also sought to shield himself from any responsibility to compensate his counsel by claiming the insurance proceeds are exempt homestead property, not subject to attachment by means of a charging lien. See Art. X, § 4(a), Fla. Const. [Article X, Section 4(a) reads as follows insofar as pertinent here:

> There shall be exempt from forced sale under process of any court, and no judgment, decree or execution shall be a lien thereon, except for the payment of taxes and assessments thereon, obligations contracted for the purchase, improvement or repair thereof, or obligations contracted for house, field or other labor performed on the realty, the following property owned by a natural person:
>
> (1) a homestead . . .]

The parties do not dispute the hurricane-damaged property is constitutionally exempt homestead property. See *Cutler v. Cutler*, 994 So. 2d 341, 343 (Fla. 3d DCA 2008) ("To qualify for protection under Article X, section 4 of the Florida Constitution, a parcel of property must meet constitutionally defined size limitations and must be owned by a natural person who is a Florida resident who either makes or intends to make the property that person's residence."). In the event a homestead is damaged through fire, wind or flood, the proceeds of any insurance recovery are imbued with the same privilege. *Orange Brevard Plumbing & Heating Co. v. La Croix*, 137 So. 2d 201, 203–04 (Fla. 1962). Because Quiroga did not and, as a matter of public policy in this State, cannot through an unsecured agreement, such as the contingent fee agreement in this case, enter into an enforceable contract to divest himself from the exemptions afforded him through Article X, section 4(a), see *Chames v. DeMayo*, 972 So. 2d 850, 853 (Fla. 2007), this Court is compelled to affirm the order under review, the equities of the matter notwithstanding. See *Pub. Health Trust of Dade County v. Lopez*, 531 So. 2d 946, 951 (Fla. 1988) ("The homestead protection has never been based upon principles of equity.") (citing *Bigelow v. Dunphe*, 143 Fla. 603, 197 So. 328, 330 (1940)); *Pierrepont v. Humphreys (In re Newman's Estate)*, 413 So. 2d 140, 142 (Fla. 5th DCA 1982) ("The homestead character of a piece of property . . . arises and attaches from the mere existence of certain facts in combination in place and time.").

Affirmed.

Notes and Questions to Consider:

1. The facts of *Quiroga v. Citizens Property Insurance* involve a charging lien. As I wrote in my book FLORIDA ELEMENTS OF AN ACTION, "[a] charging lien is an equitable remedy by which an attorney can have his fee for his litigation services secured to him in his client's judgment that was awarded in the litigation where his services were rendered." Patrick John McGinley, *Elements of the Prima Facie Case of a*

Charging Lien, in Florida Elements of an Action § 1601:1 (2017-2018 ed.). Noting that a charging lien is an equitable remedy, why did not the equities of the situation control the outcome of *Quiroga v. Citizens Property*?

2. Did you sense a hint of sarcasm in the *Quiroga* court noting that "[t]he Katzman law firm secured the proceeds for the benefit of its client and policy insured, Jesse Quiroga, in appreciation for which Quiroga not only terminated the law firm's contingent fee representation of him, but also sought to shield himself from any responsibility to compensate his counsel by claiming the insurance proceeds are exempt homestead property . . ."?

3. Would the outcome of *Quiroga* been different if the money to which the law firm was attempting to impose a charging lien had instead been the proceeds from the sale of the homestead? Consider this holding from *Orange Brevard Plumbing & Heating Co. v. La Croix*, 137 So. 2d 201 (Fla. 1962):

> [I]n recognition of the liberal interpretation of the homestead exemption to which this court is committed, we hold the proceeds of a voluntary sale of a homestead to be exempt from the claims of creditors just as the homestead itself is exempt if, and only if, the vendor shows, by a preponderance of the evidence an abiding good faith intention prior to and at the time of the sale of the homestead to reinvest the proceeds thereof in another homestead within a reasonable time. Moreover, only so much of the proceeds of the sale as are intended to be reinvested in another homestead may be exempt under this holding. Any surplus over and above that amount should be treated as general assets of the debtor. We further hold that in order to satisfy the requirements of the exemption the funds must not be commingled with other monies of the vendor but must be kept separate and apart and held for the sole purpose of acquiring another home. The proceeds of the sale are not exempt if they are not reinvested in another homestead in a reasonable time or if they are held for the general purposes of the vendor.

> The homestead exemption provision was not placed in our Constitution for the purpose of tying the owner thereof and his family to a particular home, once established, for the remaining period of their natural lives. . . .

Id. at 206.

Chapter 8

Amending Florida's Constitution

A. Different than Amending the U.S. Constitution

"Unlike the Federal Constitution, Florida's Constitution is constantly being amended." *Amending the Constitution*, 18 Nova L. Rev. 1487 (1994). "The Florida Constitution has more methods of amendment than any other state constitution." P. K. Jameson & Marsha Hoscak, *Citizen Initiatives in Florida: An Analysis of Florida's Constitutional Initiative Process, Issues, and Alternatives*, 23 Fla. St. U. L. Rev. 417, 424 (1995).

To learn how to amend a constitution, we look to the plain language of the constitution itself. Like the federal Constitution, the Constitution of the State of Florida may be amended by following the terms and conditions that are stated in the text of the constitution. But the terms and conditions of amending the federal and the Florida Constitution are quite different.

To amend the U.S. Constitution, Article V of that document states:

> The Congress, whenever two thirds of both houses shall deem it necessary, shall propose amendments to this Constitution, or, on the application of the legislatures of two thirds of the several states, shall call a convention for proposing amendments, which, in either case, shall be valid to all intents and purposes, as part of this Constitution, when ratified by the legislatures of three fourths of the several states, or by conventions in three fourths thereof, as the one or the other mode of ratification may be proposed by the Congress; provided that no amendment which may be made prior to the year one thousand eight hundred and eight shall in any manner affect the first and fourth clauses in the ninth section of the first article; and that no state, without its consent, shall be deprived of its equal suffrage in the Senate.

Art. V, U.S. Const. By comparison, the terms and conditions for amending Florida's constitution appear in Article XI, where it is not Florida's counties but Florida's citizenry who decide the fate of amendments to Florida's constitution. As you will see in this chapter, Article XI of Florida's constitution offers five sources of proposed constitutional amendments. The success or failure of any proposal, regardless of its source, depends upon a vote of the people of the state of Florida.

Article V of the U.S. Constitution provides citizens with a relatively smaller and more indirect role in amending the federal constitution. The January 1996 edition of Columbia Law Review, in Henry Paul Monaghan, *We the People(s), Original Understanding, and Constitutional Amendment*, 96 Colum. L. Rev. 121 (1996), opined that:

Article V clearly demonstrates that, in requiring supermajorities to amend the Constitution and in entrenching state equality in the Senate, the original Constitution not only envisaged the continued existence of the states as vital parts of the new constitutional order, but also excluded the people from any direct role in constitution-making. . . .

Federalist No. 39 has long been understood to provide the canonical explanation for Article V's strongly state-centered (and counter-majoritarian) process. In a famous passage, Madison states that:

> [The Constitution] is neither wholly national nor wholly federal. Were it wholly national, the supreme and ultimate authority would reside in the majority of the people of the Union; and this authority would be competent at all times, like that of a majority of every national society to alter or abolish its established government. . . . In requiring more than a majority, and particularly in computing the proportion by States, not by citizens, it departs from the national and advances towards the federal character.

In Federalist No. 43, Madison adds that Article V's amendment mechanism "guards . . . against that extreme facility, which would render the Constitution too mutable."

Id. at 125–27.

Putting aside the issue of why Article V of the federal Constitution reads as it does, history suggests that Article V's language has not "render[ed] the Constitution too mutable." In the more than 230 years since the U.S. Constitution was approved on September 17, 1787, by the majority of the delegates to the Constitutional Convention, the Constitution had only 27 amendments.

State constitutions do not share the characteristic of a lack of mutability. Nor do state constitutions further a goal, if any, of excluding the people from amending the constitution. To the contrary, state constitutions have been criticized for the ease and frequency of amendments.

Notes and Questions to Consider:

1. You represent a client who does not like a part of Florida's constitution. What can you do about that?

2. Would society benefit from allowing the U.S. Constitution to be amended with the relative ease and frequency of Florida's constitution?

B. Five Methods of Proposing Amendments

Five methods exist for proposing amendments to Florida's constitution. In the next five subsections of this chapter, we discuss each in turn. Each method results in a proposal. Each proposal is put before Florida's electorate. So regardless of the origin of the proposal, all amendments are made by a vote of the people of the state of Florida—if Florida's courts allow such a vote. The penultimate section of this chapter discusses the requirements for the vote, and as discussed in the final subsection of this chapter, grounds exist for Florida courts to strike a proposal from the ballot.

1. Proposal by Florida's Legislature

"State legislatures typically have a role in amending state constitutions, and Florida is no exception. According to Article XI Section 1 of the Florida Constitution, the Florida Legislature may propose an amendment to the Florida Constitution via a joint resolution agreed to by three-fifths of the membership of each house of the legislature." Patrick John McGinley, FLORIDA MUNICIPAL LAW AND PRACTICE § 1:4 (2017-2018 ed.). The relevant language appears in Florida's constitution in its Article XI, where is says:

> SECTION 1. Proposal by legislature.—Amendment of a section or revision of one or more articles, or the whole, of this constitution may be proposed by joint resolution agreed to by three-fifths of the membership of each house of the legislature. The full text of the joint resolution and the vote of each member voting shall be entered on the journal of each house.

2. Constitutional Revision Commission

Florida's Constitutional Revision Commission, or CRC, is a:

> means by which a proposed amendment may arise [that] is rather unique to Florida. . . . Once every 20 years, a 37-member revision commission is created as required by Florida's Constitution for the purpose of reviewing Florida's Constitution and proposing changes for voter consideration. The 37 members consist of the Florida Attorney General, three members appointed by the Chief Judge of the Supreme Court of Florida, nine members each appointed by the Florida Senate President and Speaker of the House of Representatives, and the remaining 15 members (including the chairman) by Florida's governor. The Commission typically meets for approximately one year to perform its research and possibly recommend changes. The commission's final recommendations are transmitted to the Florida Secretary of State to be included in the November ballot for voting by the franchised citizens of Florida. The last comprehensive review of Florida's Constitution occurred in 2017.

Patrick John McGinley, FLORIDA MUNICIPAL LAW AND PRACTICE § 1:4 (2017-2018 ed.). The CRC's operative language appears in Florida's constitution in Article XI, which reads:

SECTION 2. Revision commission. —

(a) Within thirty days before the convening of the 2017 regular session of the legislature, and each twentieth year thereafter, there shall be established a constitution revision commission composed of the following thirty-seven members:

(1) the attorney general of the state;

(2) fifteen members selected by the governor;

(3) nine members selected by the speaker of the house of representatives and nine members selected by the president of the senate; and

(4) three members selected by the chief justice of the supreme court of Florida with the advice of the justices.

(b) The governor shall designate one member of the commission as its chair. Vacancies in the membership of the commission shall be filled in the same manner as the original appointments.

(c) Each constitution revision commission shall convene at the call of its chair, adopt its rules of procedure, examine the constitution of the state, hold public hearings, and, not later than one hundred eighty days prior to the next general election, file with the custodian of state records its proposal, if any, of a revision of this constitution or any part of it.

3. Initiative by the People

The 1968 enactment of Florida's constitution provided citizens with the right to propose amendments to the constitution by initiative. This means that "[r]esidents of Florida have a specific right that citizens of many other states do not have. They have the power to amend their state constitution by gathering a set number of signatures on petitions calling for an amendment to be placed on a statewide ballot for ratification." Jim Smith, *So You Want to Amend the Florida Constitution? A Guide to Initiative Petitions*, 18 Nova L. Rev. 1509. 1510 (1994).

Note that Floridians are the direct origin of these proposed constitutional amendments, and no involvement is required of Florida's executive, legislative, or judicial branches, by any state agency or administrative law entity, or by any county, city, town, village lawmaking body. This makes a citizen initiative different from a referendum. "Earlier Florida Constitutions provided for a referendum to amend or revise the constitution. A referendum is first proposed by the Legislature and then decided by the voters at a general election. Initiatives, by contrast, originate with the people and do not require legislative approval." *Id.*

The operative language appears in Article XI of Florida's constitution and reads:

SECTION 3. Initiative. — The power to propose the revision or amendment of any portion or portions of this constitution by initiative is reserved to the people, provided that, any such revision or amendment, except for those limiting the power of government to raise revenue, shall embrace but one subject and matter directly connected therewith. It may be invoked by filing with the custodian of state records a petition containing a copy of the proposed revision or amendment, signed by a number of electors in each of one half of the congressional districts of the state, and of the state as a whole, equal to eight percent of the votes cast in each of such districts respectively and in the state as a whole in the last preceding election in which presidential electors were chosen.

The *Nova Law Review* published the following step-by-step guide to amending Florida's constitution by initiative. It was written by a former Florida attorney general and secretary of state:

1. Contact the Department of State's Division of Elections and request a free packet of information. You will receive a packet which includes the 1994 initiative petition information, a handbook for committees, all pertinent laws and rules, and necessary forms for filing as a political committee. [Also, this information is available on the Division's website.]

2. Sponsors must register as a political committee with the Division of Elections, before circulating a petition. The division will furnish the sponsors with all necessary information on how to form a committee and the duties of a committee. Committees are advised to begin work at least four years before the election in order to have sufficient time to gather the necessary signatures and deal with any legal challenges that might arise. However, some committees have made ballot position in less than two years.

3. Sponsors must submit the text of the proposed amendment to the Secretary of State for review. The Secretary approves the form of the petition, but not its legal sufficiency. The form will be checked for completeness, for the correct number of words in the ballot title (fifteen or less) and in the summary (seventy-five or less), and for correct size and format of the petition. Once approved, the petition can be circulated to obtain signatures of registered voters.

4. When at least ten percent of the required number of signatures from one-quarter of the congressional districts is collected, the Secretary of State shall submit the petition language to the attorney general, who will then forward the petition to the Supreme Court of Florida for an advisory opinion on whether the text conforms to the requirements of article XI, section 3 of the Florida Constitution. The court will also determine if the ballot title and summary of the amendment comply with section 101.161 of the Florida Statutes.

5. Sponsors must deliver the petitions to the supervisors of elections in order for the signatures to be verified, a process that can take several weeks or longer if the supervisor's staff is extremely busy. Verification will usually take less time if signature cards are submitted as they are collected and the final group is submitted several months before the deadline. Once certified

as having obtained the necessary number and distribution of signatures of registered voters, certification is sent to the Division of Elections by the supervisor of elections. The actual petitions are retained by the supervisor of elections. Any initiative which receives the required number of signatures no later than ninety-one days prior to the general election will appear on the ballot, unless successfully challenged in court.

Id. at 1512–13.

Notes and Questions to Consider:

1. What are the advantages and disadvantage to amending state constitutions by citizen initiatives? Consider this comment from FLORIDA MUNICIPAL LAW AND PRACTICE:

> From one point a view, this is the purest form of direct democracy in state lawmaking. From another point of view, this is the reason why state constitutions are so long and mundane. For example, thanks to a voter initiative, the Constitution of the State of Florida grants constitutional rights to pregnant pigs in Article X, Section 21.

Patrick John McGinley, FLORIDA MUNICIPAL LAW AND PRACTICE § 1:4 (2017-2018 ed.).

2. FLORIDA MUNICIPAL LAW AND PRACTICE summarizes the voter initiative process as follows:

> Voter initiatives occur in Florida when the custodian of state records receives a petition containing a copy of the proposed revision or amendment, signed by a number of electors in each of one half of the congressional districts of the state, and of the state as a whole, equal to 8% of the votes cast in each of such districts respectively and in the state as a whole in the last preceding election in which presidential electors were chosen. These specific numbers and percentages are mandated by Article XI, Section 3 of the Florida Constitution.

Id. Are these requirements unduly burdensome?

4. Constitutional Convention

One way of "amending a state's constitution is to do away with the existing constitution and start over. Like most states, Florida refers to this as the calling of a constitutional convention." Patrick John McGinley, FLORIDA MUNICIPAL LAW AND PRACTICE § 1:4 (2017-2018 ed.). The procedure may be summarized as follows:

> Article XI Section 3 of the Florida Constitution requires the following actions and deadlines. A Constitutional Convention convenes if Florida's voters file, with the custodian of the state records, a petition containing a declaration that a constitutional convention is desired, signed by a number

of electors in each of one half of the congressional districts of the state, and of the state as a whole, equal to fifteen per cent of the votes cast in each such district respectively and in the state as a whole in the last preceding election of presidential electors. At the next general election held more than ninety days after the filing of such petition there shall be submitted to the electors of the state the question: "Shall a constitutional convention be held?" If a majority voting on the question votes in the affirmative, at the next succeeding general election there shall be elected from each representative district a member of a constitutional convention. On the twenty-first day following that election, the convention shall sit at the capital, elect officers, adopt rules of procedure, judge the election of its membership, and fix a time and place for its future meetings. Not later than ninety days before the next succeeding general election, the convention shall cause to be filed with the custodian of state records any revision of this constitution proposed by it.

Id. at § 1:4. The full text of the relevant section of Florida's constitution provides:

SECTION 4. Constitutional convention. —

(a) The power to call a convention to consider a revision of the entire constitution is reserved to the people. It may be invoked by filing with the custodian of state records a petition, containing a declaration that a constitutional convention is desired, signed by a number of electors in each of one half of the congressional districts of the state, and of the state as a whole, equal to fifteen per cent of the votes cast in each such district respectively and in the state as a whole in the last preceding election of presidential electors.

(b) At the next general election held more than ninety days after the filing of such petition there shall be submitted to the electors of the state the question: "Shall a constitutional convention be held?" If a majority voting on the question votes in the affirmative, at the next succeeding general election there shall be elected from each representative district a member of a constitutional convention. On the twenty-first day following that election, the convention shall sit at the capital, elect officers, adopt rules of procedure, judge the election of its membership, and fix a time and place for its future meetings. Not later than ninety days before the next succeeding general election, the convention shall cause to be filed with the custodian of state records any revision of this constitution proposed by it.

5. Taxation and Budget Reform Commission

Article VII of Florida's constitution creates a Taxation and Budget Reform Commission that is scheduled to convene once every twenty years to consider making proposals for amending Florida's constitution. The operative language reads:

SECTION 6. Taxation and budget reform commission. —

(a) Beginning in 2007 and each twentieth year thereafter, there shall be established a taxation and budget reform commission composed of the following members:

(1) eleven members selected by the governor, none of whom shall be a member of the legislature at the time of appointment.

(2) seven members selected by the speaker of the house of representatives and seven members selected by the president of the senate, none of whom shall be a member of the legislature at the time of appointment.

(3) four non-voting ex officio members, all of whom shall be members of the legislature at the time of appointment. Two of these members, one of whom shall be a member of the minority party in the house of representatives, shall be selected by the speaker of the house of representatives, and two of these members, one of whom shall be a member of the minority party in the senate, shall be selected by the president of the senate.

(b) Vacancies in the membership of the commission shall be filled in the same manner as the original appointments.

(c) At its initial meeting, the members of the commission shall elect a member who is not a member of the legislature to serve as chair and the commission shall adopt its rules of procedure. Thereafter, the commission shall convene at the call of the chair. An affirmative vote of two thirds of the full commission shall be necessary for any revision of this constitution or any part of it to be proposed by the commission.

(d) The commission shall examine the state budgetary process, the revenue needs and expenditure processes of the state, the appropriateness of the tax structure of the state, and governmental productivity and efficiency; review policy as it relates to the ability of state and local government to tax and adequately fund governmental operations and capital facilities required to meet the state's needs during the next twenty year period; determine methods favored by the citizens of the state to fund the needs of the state, including alternative methods for raising sufficient revenues for the needs of the state; determine measures that could be instituted to effectively gather funds from existing tax sources; examine constitutional limitations on taxation and expenditures at the state and local level; and review the state's comprehensive planning, budgeting and needs assessment processes to determine whether the resulting information adequately supports a strategic decisionmaking process.

(e) The commission shall hold public hearings as it deems necessary to carry out its responsibilities under this section. The commission shall issue a report of the results of the review carried out, and propose to the legislature any recommended statutory changes related to the taxation or budgetary laws of the state. Not later than one hundred eighty days prior to the general election in the second year following the year in which the commission is established, the commission shall file with the custodian of state records its proposal, if any, of a revision of this constitution or any part of it dealing with taxation or the state budgetary process.

C. Voting on Proposed Amendments

Although proposals for amendments can arise using any of the five methods, proposals become amendments only from one source: the people. Ultimately, the decision as to whether the proposal will become an amendment to Florida's constitution is a decision made directly by the Floridians who vote on that amendment. As Florida's supreme court acknowledged:

> A[] thing we should keep in mind is that we are dealing with a constitutional democracy in which sovereignty resides in the people. It is their Constitution that we are construing. They have a right to change, abrogate or modify it in any manner they see fit so long as they keep within the confines of the Federal Constitution.

Gray v. Golden, 89 So. 2d 785, 790 (Fla. 1956).

Article VI of Florida's constitution contains two sections relevant to the vote of the people:

SECTION 5. Amendment or revision election. —

(a) A proposed amendment to or revision of this constitution, or any part of it, shall be submitted to the electors at the next general election held more than ninety days after the joint resolution or report of revision commission, constitutional convention or taxation and budget reform commission proposing it is filed with the custodian of state records, unless, pursuant to law enacted by the affirmative vote of three-fourths of the membership of each house of the legislature and limited to a single amendment or revision, it is submitted at an earlier special election held more than ninety days after such filing.

(b) A proposed amendment or revision of this constitution, or any part of it, by initiative shall be submitted to the electors at the general election provided the initiative petition is filed with the custodian of state records no later than February 1 of the year in which the general election is held.

(c) The legislature shall provide by general law, prior to the holding of an election pursuant to this section, for the provision of a statement to the public regarding the probable financial impact of any amendment proposed by initiative pursuant to section 3.

(d) Once in the tenth week, and once in the sixth week immediately preceding the week in which the election is held, the proposed amendment or revision, with notice of the date of election at which it will be submitted to the electors, shall be published in one newspaper of general circulation in each county in which a newspaper is published.

(e) Unless otherwise specifically provided for elsewhere in this constitution, if the proposed amendment or revision is approved by vote of at least sixty percent of the electors voting on the measure, it shall be effective as an amendment to or revision of the constitution of the state on the first Tuesday after the first Monday in January following the election, or on such other date as may be specified in the amendment or revision.

. . .

SECTION 7. Tax or fee limitation. — Notwithstanding Article X, Section 12(d) of this constitution, no new State tax or fee shall be imposed on or after November 8, 1994, by any amendment to this constitution unless the proposed amendment is approved by not fewer than two-thirds of the voters voting in the election in which such proposed amendment is considered. For purposes of this section, the phrase "new State tax or fee" shall mean any tax or fee which would produce revenue subject to lump sum or other appropriation by the Legislature, either for the State general revenue fund or any trust fund, which tax or fee is not in effect on November 7, 1994, including without limitation such taxes and fees as are the subject of proposed constitutional amendments appearing on the ballot on November 8, 1994. This section shall apply to proposed constitutional amendments relating to State taxes or fees which appear on the November 8, 1994, ballot, or later ballots, and any such proposed amendment which fails to gain the two-thirds vote required hereby shall be null, void and without effect.

D. Judicial Review of Proposed Amendments and Ballot Summaries

Florida Statutes chapter 101 contains the enabling acts for the voting requirements in Article V Sections 5 and 7 of Florida's constitution. These enabling acts contain various requirements for the amendments that appear on the ballot. The enabling acts state that the full text of the amendment does not appear. Instead, a ballot summary appears, and it is restricted to a maximum length. The summary is preceded by a ballot title, which also has a maximum length. The summary is followed by a question that the voter can answer with "yes" or "no." The question must be phrased so that a "yes" vote indicates approval of the proposal.

One means by which Florida's supreme court can review such ballots prior to election day is as follows. Article IV, Section 4 of Florida's constitution provides that Florida's "attorney general shall, as directed by general law, request the opinion of the justices of the supreme court as to the validity of any initiative petition circulated pursuant to Section 3 of Article XI." Section 4 also provides that Florida's supreme court "[J]ustices shall, subject to their rules of procedure, permit interested persons to be heard on the questions presented and shall render their written opinion no later than April 1 of the year in which the initiative is to be submitted to the voters pursuant to Section 5 of Article XI."

A recent example of such judicial review is *Detzner v. Anstead*, 256 So. 3d 820 (Fla. 2018):

Detzner v. Anstead

Supreme Court of Florida, 2018
256 So. 3d 820

PER CURIAM.

Secretary of State Ken Detzner seeks review of the judgment of the Circuit Court for the Second Judicial Circuit . . . which . . . ordered that ballot titles and summaries of three proposed amendments to the Florida Constitution ("Amendment 7," "Amendment 9," and "Amendment 11") be stricken from the November 2018 general election ballot. The First District Court of Appeal certified the order as presenting a question of great public importance requiring immediate resolution by this Court. We have jurisdiction. *See* art. V, § 3(b)(5), Fla. Const. As explained below, we reverse the judgment of the circuit court. . . .

. . . [T]he circuit court was incorrect in finding any deficiency in the proposals or ballot summaries on the merits.

The circuit court found the ballot language of Amendments 7, 9, and 11 to be defective because each of those amendments bundled together separate and unrelated proposals. The court held that such bundling violates section 101.161(1), Florida Statutes, and potentially deprives voters of their First Amendment right to vote on independent proposals. We rejected similar arguments regarding "bundling" in *County of Volusia v. Detzner*, 253 So. 3d 507 (Fla. 2018), and reject the circuit court's contrary conclusions in this case. Unlike proposed amendments that originate through initiative petitions, amendments proposed by the CRC are not bound by the single-subject rule limiting amendments to one subject. *Charter Review Comm'n of Orange Cty. v. Scott*, 647 So. 2d 835, 836–37 (Fla. 1994). The CRC's proposed amendments, may, and often do, combine several subjects "because [the CRC's] process embodies adequate safeguards to protect against logrolling and deception." *Id.* at 837. CRC revisions containing bundled proposals have previously been placed on the ballot by the Secretary. Moreover, the Florida Constitution expressly authorizes bundling, as it gives the CRC authority to revise the entire constitution or any part of it. *See* art. XI, § 2(c), Fla. Const. The power to amend the whole constitution in one proposal necessarily includes the lesser power to amend parts of the constitution in one proposal. . . .

The circuit court also addressed Appellees' First Amendment argument and determined that the bundling of proposals prevents voters from voting yes or no "without potentially being deprived of their First Amendment constitutional right to cast a meaningful vote on each independent and unrelated proposal." *Anstead*, No. 2018-CA-1925, slip op. at 5. However, neither Appellees nor the circuit court supply any analysis in support of the bald assertion of a potential constitutional violation. Appellees merely assert that they have a right to vote for a proposition without voting against an unrelated proposition, a novel theory with no apparent support in the law. Because Appellees have not demonstrated the violation of any First Amendment right, we conclude that the circuit court erred to the extent that it found that the bundling of amendments implicates the First Amendment.

Finally, the circuit court also concluded that Amendment 11's ballot language was defective because it would mislead voters by failing to inform them of the effect and consequences of their vote. We disagree with this conclusion as well. The summary accurately describes the effect of Amendment 11's approval—the removal of discriminatory language in the constitution regarding real property rights. The amendment would delete the state's alien land law, a short provision authorizing the Legislature to regulate or prohibit the ownership, inheritance, disposition, or possession of real property by aliens ineligible for citizenship as an exception to constitutional language providing that all "natural persons" have "inalienable rights" to "acquire, possess and protect property." The summary states that the amendment would "[r]emove[ ] discriminatory language related to real property rights." This is an accurate description of what the proposed amendment will do, consistent with the requirement that ballot language accurately represent the main legal effect and ramifications of a proposed amendment. *See Armstrong*, 773 So. 2d at 12; *Wadhams v. Bd. of Cty. Comm'rs*, 567 So. 2d 414, 417–18 (Fla. 1990). In other words, the summary clearly communicates what it is that voters are being asked to approve or reject, and Florida law does not require that it do more than that. *See Evans v. Firestone*, 457 So. 2d 1351, 1355 (Fla. 1984) (explaining that the ballot summary should tell the voter "the legal effect of the amendment, and no more"); *see also Askew v. Firestone*, 421 So. 2d 151, 155 (Fla. 1982) (stating that the ballot summary must "advise the voter sufficiently to enable him intelligently to cast his ballot" . . .)); *cf. Fla. Educ. Ass'n v. Fla. Dep't of State*, 48 So. 3d 694, 702 (Fla. 2010) (upholding proposed amendment and concluding that it was not misleading where the ballot summary did not disclose the amendment's specific financial impact on class size funding).

For the foregoing reasons, we hold that the circuit court erred in granting the petition for writ of quo warranto because the standard for obtaining relief was not met. We further hold the proposed amendments are not defective for bundling independent and unrelated measures. Finally, we hold the ballot language of Amendment 11 does not mislead voters with respect to the amendment's legal effect. Accordingly, we reverse the decision of the circuit court and order that Amendments 7, 9, and 11 appear on the ballot for the November 2018 general election. No motion for rehearing will be allowed, and the mandate shall issue immediately.

It is so ordered.

CANADY, C.J., and POLSTON, LABARGA, and LAWSON, JJ., concur.

PARIENTE, J., concurs in result with an opinion, in which LEWIS and QUINCE, JJ., concur.

PARIENTE, J., concurring in result.

Voters beware! When amending our Florida Constitution, voters should not be forced to vote "yes" on a proposal they disfavor in order to also vote "yes" on a proposal they support because of how the Constitution Revision Commission (CRC) has unilaterally decided to bundle multiple, independent and unrelated proposals. . . . I write separately to emphasize the obvious dangers of logrolling—combining popular and unpopular proposals into a single proposal—even by the CRC.

I also respectfully disagree that the process that occurred with this CRC provided "adequate safeguards to protect against logrolling." Majority op. at 823. . . . Logrolling occurs when proposals that are attractive to one group of voters are intentionally combined with proposals that may be unpopular to the same group of voters in order to secure approval of the unpopular proposal. *Advisory Op. to the Att'y Gen.—Save Our Everglades*, 636 So. 2d 1336, 1339 (Fla. 1994). Logrolling can also be used to mask a controversial or unpopular proposal because it is more difficult to accurately explain multiple, independent and unrelated proposals in a single ballot title and 75-word summary. *Advisory Op. to the Att'y Gen. re Right of Citizens to Choose Health Care Providers*, 705 So. 2d 563, 566 (Fla. 1998). For these reasons, I would conclude that the CRC improperly bundled multiple, independent and unrelated proposals.

The per curiam opinion's justification for allowing the CRC to employ this type of bundling is that the CRC's process embodies "adequate safeguards to protect against logrolling and deception." Majority op. at 823. . . . However, as CRC Commissioner Roberto Martinez, one of this Court's three appointees, explained, the safeguards envisioned by the per curiam opinion do not exist. First, the CRC's legal staff provided no guidance with respect to the bundling. . . .

Second, the CRC's public hearings also provide no additional safeguards with respect to the bundling because the Style and Drafting Committee bundled the proposals after the CRC concluded its public hearings. . . .

The more complex an amendment is and the more independent and unrelated the proposals are, the more difficult it will be for voters to ascertain its true purpose and effect on Election Day. Rather than being able to vote up or down on each individual proposal based on its merits, voters will be forced to weigh the costs and benefits of each group of proposals.

For example, the ballot summary for Amendment 7 states:

> *Grants mandatory payment of death benefits and waiver of certain educational expenses to qualifying survivors of certain first responders and military members who die performing official duties. Requires supermajority votes by university trustees and state university system board of governors to raise or impose all legislatively authorized fees if law requires approval by those bodies. Establishes existing state college system as constitutional entity; provides governance structure.*

This amendment bundles together (1) a proposal to require university boards of trustees and the university board of governors to approve any proposal or action to raise, impose, or authorize any fee by a designated minimum number of members; (2) a proposal to create a single state college system comprised of all public community and state colleges; and (3) a proposal to provide death benefits for survivors of first responders and military members. It would seem self-evident that death benefits for survivors of first responders and military members, however laudable, is completely unrelated to amendments dealing with the university system, which may be controversial.

Additionally, Amendment 9 bundles together a proposal to prohibit drilling for exploration or extraction of oil or natural gas in certain lands beneath all state waters with a proposal to prohibit the use of vapor-generating electronic devices in enclosed indoor workspaces—two independent and unrelated subjects about which voters may feel strongly. However, the bundled amendment requires voters to either agree with both proposals or reject both. While both proposals deal in an attenuated manner with improving the environment, they do so in totally different and unrelated ways.

Bundling multiple, independent and unrelated proposals in this way makes the task of voting significantly more difficult for Florida's citizens, requiring them to decide—in addition to weighing the independent merits of each proposal— whether voting in favor of one proposal they approve of is worth also approving a proposal they do not favor. Voters should not be required to exercise their all-important authority to amend the constitution under these restrictions.

As I explained in relation to another CRC proposed amendment challenged before this Court:

> [T]he manner in which Revision 8 was bundled . . . added to the misleading nature of the amendment by explaining term limits and civic literacy before the ambiguous and cursory explanation of the change to the operation and establishment of free public schools. . . . [V]oters would have been presented with "two . . . proposals that are popular and easily understood" before getting to the "vague but significant proposal" [about public schools]. [A]s a result of the bundling, voters who really wanted term limits and civic literacy would be forced "to give up control of [their] local schools."

Detzner v. League of Women Voters, 256 So. 3d 803 (Fla. 2018) (Pariente, J., concurring) . . . .

The bottom line is that the ultimate authority to amend the constitution rests with the voters in this State. By bundling multiple, independent and unrelated proposals, combining "popular" amendments with controversial amendments on the ballot, the CRC makes it more difficult for voters to intelligently exercise their right to vote. Indeed, in some cases, bundling prohibits voters from exercising this right altogether because it forces them to reject proposals they would otherwise approve because they disapprove of another unrelated controversial proposal. . . .

LEWIS and QUINCE, JJ., concur.

———————

Notes and Questions to Consider:

1. The dissent laments the majority's decision because, in the dissent's opinion, the majority does not honor the fact that "the ultimate authority to amend the constitution rests with the voters in this State." But is the dissent correct? If the voters can overcome the burdens imposed in getting a proposed amendment into the hands of the Secretary of State, only to have that amendment removed from the ballot by Florida's supreme court, then is it not more accurate to say that Florida's supreme court is the ultimate authority?

2. Does Florida's supreme court have sufficient safeguards and rules to follow to assure that it is not arbitrary or subjective in its decision as to what proposals make the ballot?

Chapter 9

Local Government

A. Why Local Governments Exist

Floridians have more than just a federal and state government. Florida Munici-pal Law and Practice describes the situation as follows:

> A Floridian may fall under the jurisdiction of more sovereigns than just the United States and Florida. Inside Florida's 1,350 miles of coast-line lies 65,755 square miles of counties, cities, municipalities, and unin-corporated areas. There are 67 counties in Florida, but some reports show only 66 because of Duval County, which is consolidated with the City of Jacksonville. There are 379 cities in Florida (out of 411) that report regu-larly to the Florida Department of Revenue. There are other incorporated municipalities.
>
> The authority of the state of Florida geographically overlaps the author-ity of Florida's counties, cities, municipalities, and unincorporated areas. The authority of other municipal governments also overlaps. All of Florida's potable water resources, and designated activities of persons and companies that affect those resources, are regulated by five regional water authorities that geographically overlap with and cross the borders of Florida's counties, cities, and municipalities. Various utility commissions regulate various per-sons, counties, cities, and municipalities within the concern of the commis-sions' activities in providing utilities. The Florida Legislature, from time to time, has created various compacts and empowered the agencies governing those compacts to impose fees and otherwise exercise jurisdiction over Flo-ridians and their counties, cities, municipalities, and unincorporated areas.

Patrick John McGinley, Florida Municipal Law and Practice § 10:2 (2017-18 ed.).

Is there an advantage to having local governments? Proponents of local govern-ments argue:

> Neighborhood-level governments can tailor their policies and allocate resources more efficiently than can larger governments. They also provide increased opportunities for political participation and thus offer venues for individual engagement in collective governance, which is a positive good for the individual and for the wider political community. Indeed, neighbor-hoods may be our most central and resilient sites for civic involvement [in] an increasingly globalized society.

Richard C. Schragger, *The Limits of Localism*, 100 MICH. L. REV. 371, 381–82 (2001).

Proponents suggest that the "idea that localization of government begets more responsive and effective government is deeply ingrained in the American ethos. This idea stems from a Jeffersonian notion that local government is an effective way to ensure citizen participation in government." Russel M. Lazega & Charles R. Fletcher, *The Politics of Municipal Incorporation in South Florida*, 12 J. LAND USE & ENVTL. L. 215, 225–27 (1997). The theory is that "citizens are more apt to participate in smaller, more localized government because they are more likely to believe that their participation counts. This . . . restores decision-making power to the community." *Id.*

In addition to efficiency and greater civic involvement, proponents suggest that "[l]ocalization of government also provides more basic benefits. Citizens are closer to their local officials. . . . [L]ocalization restores control of government to people who are both familiar to and familiar with the community." *Id.*

Localization might even help thwart partisanship. "There's no Democratic or Republican way to fix a pothole, pick up garbage, respond to a 911 call or build parks for our children." Florida League of Cities, *Home Rule Handbook* (2018).

Notes and Questions to Consider:

1. Do you agree with these arguments in favor of localism? How would you make the argument against localism?

2. Imagine a Floridian, living in the Orange County city of Winter Park, who has a concern about a problem occurring in her own backyard. Would it be easier for her voice to be heard if the decisionmaker was in Washington, D.C.? In Tallahassee? In Orange County? In Winter Park?

B. State's Power to Create Local Governments

Considering the supremacy of the federal Constitution, what rights do states hold to create and regulate local governments such as counties, cities, towns, and similar municipal corporations? The U.S. Constitution is silent about the powers related to local governments. As can be seen in the following excerpt from the 1907 decision of the U.S. Supreme Court in *Hunter v. City of Pittsburgh*, 207 U.S. 161 (1907), the creation and regulation of local government is a matter of state, not federal, law.

HUNTER V. CITY OF PITTSBURGH
Supreme Court of the United States, 1907
207 U.S. 161, 28 S. Ct. 40, 52 L. Ed. 151

The plaintiffs in error seek a reversal of the judgment of the Supreme Court of Pennsylvania, which affirmed a decree of a lower court, directing the consolidation of the cities of Pittsburgh and Allegheny. This decree was entered by authority of an act of the General Assembly of that State. The act authorized the consolidation of two cities.

We have nothing to do with the policy, wisdom, justice or fairness of the act under consideration; those questions are for the consideration of those to whom the State has entrusted its legislative power, and their determination of them is not subject to review or criticism by this court. We have nothing to do with the interpretation of the constitution of the State and the conformity of the enactment of the Assembly to that constitution; those questions are for the consideration of the courts of the State, and their decision of them is final.

This court has many times had occasion to consider and decide the nature of municipal corporations, their rights and duties, and the rights of their citizens and creditors. It would be unnecessary and unprofitable to analyze these decisions or quote from the opinions rendered. We think the following principles have been established by them and have become settled doctrines of this court, to be acted upon wherever they are applicable. Municipal corporations are political subdivisions of the State, created as convenient agencies for exercising such of the governmental powers of the State as may be entrusted to them. For the purpose of executing these powers properly and efficiently they usually are given the power to acquire, hold, and manage personal and real property. The number, nature and duration of the powers conferred upon these corporations and the territory over which they shall be exercised rests in the absolute discretion of the State. Neither their charters, nor any law conferring governmental powers, or vesting in them property to be used for governmental purposes, or authorizing them to hold or manage such property, or exempting them from taxation upon it, constitutes a contract with the State within the meaning of the Federal Constitution.

The State, therefore, at its pleasure may modify or withdraw all such powers, may take without compensation such property, hold it itself, or vest it in other agencies, expand or contract the territorial area, unite the whole or a part of it with another municipality, repeal the charter and destroy the corporation. All this may be done, conditionally or unconditionally, with or without the consent of the citizens, or even against their protest. In all these respects the State is supreme, and its legislative body, conforming its action to the state constitution, may do as it will, unrestrained by any provision of the Constitution of the United States.

Although the inhabitants and property owners may by such changes suffer inconvenience, and their property may be lessened in value by the burden of increased taxation, or for any other reason, they have no right by contract or otherwise in the unaltered or continued existence of the corporation or its powers, and there is nothing in the Federal Constitution which protects them from these injurious consequences. The power is in the State and those who legislate for the State are alone responsible for any unjust or oppressive exercise of it.

For these reasons we are without jurisdiction to consider it, and neither express nor intimate any opinion upon it.

The judgment is: Affirmed.

———————

Notes and Questions to Consider:

1. *Hunter* discusses "municipal corporations." What are they? Florida's supreme court once held that:

> a municipal corporation is an instrumentality of the state established for the more convenient administration of local government. It is possessed of certain governmental powers which it may exercise only in the manner prescribed in the law by which it is created. These powers are generally vested in a city council or other such governing body chosen by the electors who act for the municipality.

Turk v. Richard, 47 So. 2d 543, 543–44 (Fla. 1950). Under Article VIII of Florida's constitution, Florida's municipal corporations take one of two forms: counties or municipalities. The sole exception is Miami-Dade County, which takes both forms because Article VIII Sections 6(e) and 6(f) of Florida's constitution provides that "the Metropolitan Government of Dade County" may exercise "all the powers conferred now or hereafter by general law upon municipalities" and Miami-Dade's charter does so.

2. How do counties differ from municipalities in Florida? Article VIII of Florida's constitution provides that counties include charter counties and non-charter counties, the difference being whether the county operates under a county charter. All land in Florida falls within one and just one county. Within a county's borders, various municipalities may exist. Municipalities include cities, towns, and villages. Not all land falls within a municipality. Land that does not is called an unincorporated area. All of the geography of a municipality must exist within the borders of a single county, and a municipality's borders may not exceed the borders of that county. For this reason, all of Florida's municipalities are geographically smaller than their county of residence with one exception. The City of Jacksonville's borders are coterminous with the borders of Duval County, making that city and county the same size.

3. What powers can local governments wield? In *Hunter v. Douglas*, the U.S. Supreme Court holds that "[m]unicipal corporations are ... given the power to acquire, hold, and manage personal and real property. The powers conferred upon these corporations ... rests in the absolute discretion of the state. ... Neither their charters, nor any law conferring [their] governmental powers ... [is controlled by] the Federal Constitution." *Id.* at 178. For this reason, a state "at its pleasure, may modify or withdraw all such powers. ... In all these respects the state is supreme, and its legislative body, conforming its action to the state Constitution, may do as it will, unrestrained by any provision of the Constitution of the United States." *Id.* at 178. This means that states like Florida can determine the rules under which local

governments are created, the powers they exercise, and their relationships to the other local governments in the state. Is this a good result?

4. Imagine the people of the state of Florida amend Florida's constitution, and pursuant to that amendment, the Legislature of the State of Florida passes a law dissolving Florida's current counties, dividing the state into new counties, and distributing the assets of the former counties to the new counties. What rights would the old counties hold under *Hunter v. City of Pittsburg* to challenge this as a violation of federal constitutional rights?

5. Imagine a group of neighbors would like their neighborhood to be its own city, but the state of Florida will not allow it. What federal constitutional rights, if any, might be violated?

C. Home Rule

"Home Rule" describes the concept that Florida's charter counties, cities, towns, and villages have governmental, corporate, and proprietary powers unless expressly prohibited by federal law, Florida's constitution, or the Florida Legislature. Home Rule is the source of authority to provide municipal services, perform municipal functions, own municipal property, and enact municipal laws unless provided otherwise by law. *See, e.g.*, Judge James R. Wolf and Sarah Harley Bolinder, *The Effectiveness of Home Rule: A Preemption and Conflict Analysis*, FLORIDA BAR JOURNAL 92-94 (June 2009).

Commentators suggest that "[t]here is perhaps no term in the literature of political science or law which is more susceptible to misconception and a variety of meaning than 'home rule.'" Hugh Spitzer, *"Home Rule" vs. "Dillon's Rule" for Washington Cities*, 38 SEATTLE U. L. REV. 809, 820 (2015). The Florida League of Cities, in their *Home Rule Handbook*, acknowledges that the public does not always fully understand the meaning of Home Rule and appears to try to simplify its meaning as follows:

> The people of Florida overwhelmingly support Home Rule. The term, however, is not recognized by all. It is our job to explain it in a simple way. . . . *Home Rule is the flexibility to address unique local needs with local solutions.* . . .

> When it comes to local issues like tree trimming, vacation rentals, neighborhood safety, road improvements or even urban chickens, we turn to our city leaders. Why? Because Miami is not Mount Dora. Tampa is not Titusville. Local leaders are more connected to our needs and better reflect our values than state politicians.

Florida League of Cities, *Home Rule Handbook* (2018) (emphasis in original).

Home Rule delegates sufficient police powers to local governments to allow them to pass local laws (which, in Florida and elsewhere, are called ordinances and resolutions). Without Home Rule or some other form of delegation of the state's police power, a Florida county or municipality would need the Florida Legislature to pass a special law applicable to the county or municipality. Home Rule empowers the county or municipality to make that law itself.

1. Home Rule versus Dillon's Rule

Historically, Florida and the majority of U.S. states did not provide their municipal corporations with Home Rule power. The prevailing rule was Dillon's Rule, where "powers not granted a municipality by the legislature were deemed to be reserved to the legislature. This reservation of authority was known as 'Dillon's Rule' [because it refers to the works of law professor and Iowa Judge] John F. Dillon, THE LAW OF MUNICIPAL CORPORATIONS § 55 (1st ed. 1872)." *City of Boca Raton v. State*, 595 So. 2d 25, 27 (Fla. 1992).

The difference between Home Rule and Dillon's Rule is that the former means a municipal corporation can enact a local law unless forbidden, and the latter means a municipal corporation cannot enact a local law unless permitted. The result is that Dillon's Rule defines the powers of local governments more narrowly than Home Rule:

> Municipal home rule provisions provide more autonomy to local governments, which was not traditionally granted under "Dillon's Rule." In *City of Clinton v. Cedar Rapids & M.R.R. Co.*, [24 Iowa 455 (1868), overruled by *Berent v. City of Iowa City*, 738 N.W.2d 193 (Iowa 2007),] Judge John Dillon created what would be known as "Dillon's Rule" by recognizing state control over municipal government, except as limited by the state or federal constitution. According to Dillon's Rule, a municipality may only act in accordance with the powers granted to it by the state. . . .
>
> Dillon's Rule ultimately created undue state interference and left local governments without power in municipal affairs. As a result, many municipalities sought to reclaim their autonomy from the states. Municipalities did so by lobbying for the enactment of home rule provisions, which would allow them greater self-governance.

Jarit C. Polley, *Uncertainty for the Energy Industry: A Fractured Look at Home Rule*, 34 ENERGY L.J. 261, 267–68 (2013).

Today, there are as many as forty-eight states that grant Home Rule powers to their municipal corporations. Richard Briffault & Laurie Reynolds, STATE AND LOCAL GOVERNMENT LAW 268 (6th ed. 2004). Florida is among them, having added Home Rule to Florida's 1968 Constitution and to various Florida statutes thereafter.

2. Limits upon Home Rule

Florida's Home Rule does not include fiscal home rule. Florida's constitution reserves all taxing authority for the Florida Legislature. Home Rule contains the power to enact a valid special assessment or fee, but not a tax.

Florida's Home Rule does not preempt the U.S. Constitution or Florida's constitution. Stated somewhat differently, Florida's Home Rule is an insufficient basis to uphold an unconstitutional local law or unconstitutional local government action. "A Florida municipality may not make any law on a matter preempted to the state or county government by the Florida Constitution, by general law, or pursuant to a county charter." Patrick John McGinley, FLORIDA MUNICIPAL LAW AND PRACTICE § 10:3 (2017-18 ed.).

Home Rule power does not preempt general or special laws of the Florida Legislature. "A municipal corporation derives not only its existence but its power from the Legislature." *Brooks v. Watchtower Bible & Tract Soc. of Florida, Inc.*, 706 So. 2d 85, 87 (Fla. 4th DCA 1998). The Legislature has not given Florida's municipal corporations the power to contradict the Legislature. Home Rule gives Florida's counties broad power to govern "to the extent not inconsistent with general or special law." *See* Fla. Stat. § 125.01(1). Home Rule gives Florida's municipalities broad power to govern "except when expressly prohibited by law." *See* Fla. Stat. § 125.01(1). So regardless of whether the Florida municipal corporation is a county, city, town, or village, its laws may not be inconsistent with the Florida Statutes. "Generally speaking, local ordinances are consistent with general or special law unless state preemption precludes a local government from exercising authority in a particular area or unless state legislation may override local action because that action expressly conflicts with the state legislation." Patrick John McGinley, FLORIDA MUNICIPAL LAW AND PRACTICE § 10:3 (2017-18 ed.).

3. "Constitutional Home Rule" and "Statutory Home Rule"

Home Rule power is extended to all of Florida's counties, and to all of its incorporated cities, towns, and villages. But what is the source of that home rule power? Does it flow directly from a self-executing provision in Florida's constitution, which is what scholars call a "Constitutional Home Rule?" Does it flow from a state statute, which is what scholars call a "Statutory Home Rule?" Scholars explain that:

> Municipal home rule states can be divided into three varieties: two types of constitutional home rule states, and statutory home rule states. The two types of constitutional home rule states are the following: states that follow the *imperium in imperio* model, which grants full police power over municipal issues and immunity from state legislative interference; and states that follow the legislative model, which grants municipalities power to legislate, subject to restriction by state legislation.

Jarit C. Polley, *Uncertainty for the Energy Industry: A Fractured Look at Home Rule*, 34 ENERGY L.J. 261, 268 (2013). Florida's counties benefit from what scholars call a "Statutory Home Rule." Florida's incorporated cities, towns, and villages benefit from it also, but in addition, benefit from a "Constitutional Home Rule." The following paragraphs explain why.

The Home Rule power of cities, towns, and villages appears in the plain language of the text of Florida's constitution. Article VIII, Section 2 is titled "Municipalities" and has a subsection labeled "powers" that reads: "Municipalities shall have governmental, corporate and proprietary powers to enable them to conduct municipal government, perform municipal functions and render municipal services, and may exercise any power for municipal purposes except as otherwise provided by law." This phrase provides incorporated cities, towns, and villages with Home Rule, but omits counties.

The Home Rule power of counties is not so plain in the text of Florida's constitution. Article VIII, Section 1 is titled "Counties." But section 1 does not have a subsection labeled "powers." Article VIII, Section 6(e) preserves the Home Rule status of four Florida counties that were granted Home Rule by the Constitution of 1885, but does not provide a means of Home Rule for Florida's other 63 counties. Also, Florida's constitution does not contain a sentence for counties similar to the one empowering municipalities to "exercise any power for municipal purposes except as otherwise provided by law." It seems one must look beyond the plain text of Florida's constitution to find a source of Home Rule power for at least 63 of Florida's 67 counties.

For these counties, one source of Home Rule power is the Municipal Home Rule Powers Act. It contains, at Florida Statutes section 166.021, a subsection labeled "powers." It says that "[t]he provisions of this section shall be so construed as to secure for municipalities the broad exercise of home rule powers granted by the constitution." It adds virtually the same sentence found in Article VIII's section on Municipalities when it says, "municipalities shall have the governmental, corporate, and proprietary powers to enable them to conduct municipal government, perform municipal functions, and render municipal services, and may exercise any power for municipal purposes, except when expressly prohibited by law." Oddly, it does not define the word "municipalities." But it contains this important definition: "'municipal purpose' means any activity or power which may be exercised by the state or its political subdivisions." With this expansive definition of "municipal purpose," Home Rule power exists.

Another source of Home Rule for counties is the enactment of a charter that imbues the county with Home Rule power. This assumes that the county charter can be interpreted properly to say that the county has Home Rule power. It also assumes that the county has a charter. Florida's constitution in Article VIII, Section 1 contemplates the continued existence of non-charter counties.

Perhaps the most direct source of Home Rule power is Florida Statutes section 125.01. This statute grants counties "the power to carry on county government[] ... [t]o the extent not inconsistent with general or special law." This statute enumerates a long list of county powers, and then states that the "power to carry on county government ... is not restricted to" the enumerated subjects. This statute provides that the "provisions of this section shall be liberally construed in order to effectively carry out the purpose of this section and to secure for the counties the broad exercise of home rule powers authorized by the State Constitution." Most importantly for non-charter counties, this statute is interpreted to grant Home Rule power to all counties with or without a charter. As Florida's First District Court of Appeal held:

> The Florida Supreme Court has commented on the broad scope of home-rule authority conferred upon non-charter counties in no less than three opinions: *Taylor v. Lee County*, 498 So. 2d 424 (Fla. 1986); *Speer v. Olson*, 367 So. 2d 207 (Fla. 1979); and *State v. Orange County*, 281 So. 2d 310 (Fla. 1973). As the court recognized in *Speer*, 367 So. 2d at 211:

>> The first sentence of Section 125.01(1), Florida Statutes, (1975), grants to the governing body of a county the full power to carry on county government. Unless the Legislature has pre-empted a particular subject relating to county government by either general or special law, the county governing body, by reason of this sentence, has full authority to act through the exercise of home rule power.

>> Thus, the specific powers enumerated under section 125.01 are not all-inclusive, and a non-charter county's authority comprises that which is reasonably implied or incidental to carrying out its enumerated powers. The only limitation on a county's implied power to act occurs if there is a general or special law clearly inconsistent with the powers delegated.

Santa Rosa County v. Gulf Power Co., 635 So. 2d 96, 99 (Fla. 1st DCA 1994), cause dismissed sub nom. *Escambia River Elec. Co-op., Inc. v. Santa Rosa County*, 641 So. 2d 1345 (Fla. 1994).

In conclusion, Florida's counties, as well as its incorporated cities, towns, and villages, derive their Home Rule power from Florida's constitution, from the Municipal Home Rule Powers Act codified at Florida Statutes chapter 166, from the laws empowering county governments codified at Florida Statutes section 125.01, and from the laws empowering municipalities codified at Florida Statutes section 166.012. For cities, towns, and villages, the statutes serve to strengthen an existing Home Rule power found in the text of Florida's constitution. For counties, and for non-charter counties in particular, the statutes serve as the source of their Home Rule power.

D. Charter Counties

Article VIII of Florida's constitution provides for the creation of counties, county charters, and county governance when it states, in relevant part:

Section 1. Counties.

(a) POLITICAL SUBDIVISIONS. The state shall be divided by law into political subdivisions called counties. Counties may be created, abolished or changed by law, with provision for payment or apportionment of the public debt.

(b) COUNTY FUNDS. The care, custody and method of disbursing county funds shall be provided by general law.

(c) GOVERNMENT. Pursuant to general or special law, a county government may be established by charter which shall be adopted, amended or repealed only upon vote of the electors of the county in a special election called for that purpose.

(d) COUNTY OFFICERS. There shall be elected by the electors of each county, for terms of four years, a sheriff, a tax collector, a property appraiser, a supervisor of elections, and a clerk of the circuit court; except, when provided by county charter or special law approved by vote of the electors of the county, any county officer may be chosen in another manner therein specified, or any county office may be abolished when all the duties of the office prescribed by general law are transferred to another office. When not otherwise provided by county charter or special law approved by vote of the electors, the clerk of the circuit court shall be ex officio clerk of the board of county commissioners, auditor, recorder and custodian of all county fund.

(e) COMMISSIONERS. Except when otherwise provided by county charter, the governing body of each county shall be a board of county commissioners composed of five or seven members serving staggered terms of four years. After each decennial census the board of county commissioners shall divide the county into districts of contiguous territory as nearly equal in population as practicable. One commissioner residing in each district shall be elected as provided by law.

(f) NON-CHARTER GOVERNMENT. Counties not operating under county charters shall have such power of self-government as is provided by general or special law. The board of county commissioners of a county not operating under a charter may enact, in a manner prescribed by general law, county ordinances not inconsistent with general or special law, but an ordinance in conflict with a municipal ordinance shall not be effective within the municipality to the extent of such conflict.

(g) CHARTER GOVERNMENT. Counties operating under county charters shall have all powers of local self-government not inconsistent with general law, or with special law approved by vote of the electors. The governing body of a county operating under a charter may enact county ordinances not inconsistent with general law. The charter shall provide which shall prevail in the event of conflict between county and municipal ordinances.

Technically, a county's charter is not the county's "constitution." But it is helpful to note the similarities between a constitution and a county charter so as to better understand the workings of a charter. Like a constitution, a county charter may possess a unique set of laws different from neighboring territories. The county charter, like a constitution, forms the legal foundation of the county's local system of government. Florida's supreme court once held that "the word 'charter,' when used in connection with a municipal corporation, is defined as follows: 'The charter, as it is called, consists of the creative act and all laws in force relating to the [municipal] corporation, whether in defining its powers or regulating their mode of exercise." *City of St. Petersburg v. English*, 45 So. 483, 487 (Fla. 1907). This definition from Florida's supreme court has much in common with a constitution.

A county may, but is not required, to have a charter. As of June 2019, the website of the Florida Association of Counties reports that, "[t]o date, there are 20 charter counties in Florida. Collectively these counties are home to more than 75 percent of Fl'orida's residents." https://www.fl-counties.com/charter-county-information.

Article VIII, Section 1 of Florida's constitution provides that "[c]ounties not operating under county charters shall have such power of self-government as is provided by [the applicable law]" and that "[c]ounties operating under county charters shall have all powers of local self-government not inconsistent with [the applicable law]. . . ."

One advantage of a charter is that it structures the county's government as specified in that county's charter. This is an advantage because representatives of that county's electorate draft the charter and a majority of that county's electorate must vote affirmatively as part of enacting the charter. This may result in a unique charter for that county, whereas non-charter county governments are all uniform. This may also result in a charter handcrafted by the residents to meet the specific local needs of those residents. Perhaps most advantageously, it empowers the electorate of the county to change the structure of county government more flexibly because the county's electorate remains free to enact changes and amendments to the county's charter. In a non-charter county, the structure of the county government is specified in Florida's constitution and the Municipal Home Rule Powers Act. So the structure of a non-charter county can only be changed by amending Florida's constitution or the Florida Statutes, and thus, by amending every non-charter county's charter in the same way.

The website of the Florida Association of Counties summarizes more differences between Florida's charter and non-charter counties as follows. In non-charter counties, state Statutes do not provide for initiative or referendum, or recall of county officers. But a county charter may provide for initiative, referendum, and recall at the county level. In non-charter counties, the Florida Statutes do not require an Administrative Code. But a county charter can require an Administrative Code detailing all regulations, policies and procedures. A non-charter county cannot levy a utility tax in the unincorporated area. But a county charter can provide that a "municipal utility tax" is levied in the unincorporated area.

Yet perhaps the most critical difference between charter and non-charter counties is the charter county's greater ability to preempt municipalities when passing local laws. In a non-charter county, in the event of a conflict between a county ordinance and a municipal ordinance, the non-charter county's ordinance shall not be effective within the municipality to the extent of such conflict. *Santa Rosa County v. Gulf Power Corp.*, 635 So. 2d 96 (Fla. 1st DCA 1994). This topic is the subject of further discussion in this text in Chapter 10, titled "Legislative Power" and its sub-section titled "Lawmaking and Its Limits."

What are the limits of a non-charter county's power that a charter might fix? Consider, for example, the following case of *Gretna Racing, LLC v. Florida Department of Business and Professional Regulation*, 225 So. 3d 759 (Fla. 2017).

Gretna Racing, LLC v. Florida Department of Business and Professional Regulation

Supreme Court of Florida, 2017
225 So. 3d 759

"Shall slot machines be approved for use at the pari-mutuel [horse track] facility in Gretna, F[lorida]?" This is the question presented by the Gadsden County Commission to the county's voters in a ballot question. And it is the question we now must decide. A majority of the voters answered the question in the affirmative, but the Division of Pari-Mutuel Wagering subsequently denied a slot machine permit to Gretna Racing, LLC. The First District upheld the Division's denial of the permit and certified a question of great public importance, which establishes our jurisdiction. *See* art. V, § 3(b)(4), Fla. Const. Gretna Racing contends that the Division was required to issue the permit once the voters had answered the ballot question in the affirmative. Based on the provisions of chapter 551, Florida Statutes (2013), governing slot machines and the law establishing the powers of non-charter counties, we conclude that the Division's denial of the slot machine permit sought by Gretna Racing was correct because submission of the ballot question to the voters was not legally authorized. . . .

To explain our decision on this point, we turn first to the text of the constitutional provision and the general statutory provisions relied on by Gretna Racing.

Article VIII, section 1(f) of the Florida Constitution provides:

> NON-CHARTER GOVERNMENT. Counties not operating under county charters shall have such power of self-government as is provided by general or special law. The board of county commissioners of a county not operating under a charter may enact, in a manner prescribed by general law, county ordinances not inconsistent with general or special law. . . .

Art. VIII, § 1(f), Fla. Const.

As the text specifies, the powers granted to non-charter counties are "such power[s] of self-government as [are] provided by general or special law." *Id.* The general law relied on by Gretna Racing is section 125.01(1), Florida Statutes (2013), which provides broadly that "[t]he legislative and governing body of a county shall have the power to carry on county government." The statute goes on to provide that the power to carry on county government, "[t]o the extent not inconsistent with general or special law, . . . includes, but is not restricted to, the power to" do

certain enumerated things. § 125.01(1), Fla. Stat. (2013). Among those enumerated things is the power specified in subsection (1)(y) to conduct a "straw ballot."
§ 125.01(1)(y), Fla. Stat. (2013). But none of the enumerated powers relate to slot
machine gaming. Nor is a general power to conduct binding referenda among the
enumerated powers.

Of course, the absence of a relevant enumerated power is not dispositive. In
addition to the provision in section 125.01(1) that the "power to carry on county
government . . . is not restricted to" the enumerated subjects, section 125.01(3)(a)
provides that the enumeration of powers will "not be deemed exclusive or restrictive, but shall be deemed to incorporate all implied powers necessary or incident to
carrying out such powers enumerated, including, specifically, authority to employ
personnel, expend funds, enter into contractual obligations, and purchase or lease
and sell or exchange real or personal property." Further, section 125.01(3)(b) contains a rule of liberal construction: "The provisions of this section shall be liberally
construed in order to effectively carry out the purpose of this section and to secure
for the counties the broad exercise of home rule powers authorized by the State
Constitution." Which brings us back to the constitutional specification of "such
power of self-government as is provided by general or special law," art. VIII, § 1(f),
Fla. Const., and the general law provision of the "power to carry on county government" in a way that is "not inconsistent with general or special law," § 125.01(1),
Fla. Stat. (2013).

Based on the analysis we employ to resolve this case, we reframe the certified
question as follows:

> Is a referendum conducted by a non-charter county concerning approval
> of slot machine licenses at pari-mutuel facilities authorized by the general
> powers conferred on non-charter counties by article VIII, section 1(f) of
> the Florida Constitution and section 125.01(1), Florida Statutes (2013)?

An affirmative answer to this question could only be given if we conclude that
conducting such a referendum regarding the issuance of slot machine licenses by
the Division is inherent in the "power to conduct county government." . . .

In support of its position on this point, Gretna Racing relies on two decisions
upholding the authority of a county to conduct a referendum—*Speer v. Olson*, 367
So. 2d 207 (Fla. 1978), which approved the issuance of bonds authorized by a referendum for the expansion of sewer and water systems, and *Watt v. Firestone*, 491
So. 2d 592 (Fla. 1st DCA 1986), which rejected a challenge to a ballot initiative for a
constitutional amendment authorizing casino gambling in certain areas if approved
in an initiative referendum by county voters. An examination of these cases shows
that they do not support Gretna Racing's argument. In both cases, the authorization
to conduct a referendum did not stem from the general home rule power conferred
by section 125.01(1). Instead, the authority to conduct the referendum in each of
the two cases was based on specific constitutional or statutory authority to act on a
subject that required approval by referendum. Here, in contrast, there is no specific

constitutional or statutory authority for Gadsden County to act on the subject of slot machine gaming.

In *Speer*, Pasco County had "enacted an ordinance creating a Municipal Service Taxing Unit . . . composed of the entire unincorporated area of the county." *Speer*, 367 So. 2d at 208. The county had "called a special election by the residents of the Unit for the purpose of securing their approval for the issuance of . . . general obligation bonds by the Unit." *Id.* The purpose of the issuance of the bonds was "for the expansion of sewer and water systems." *Id.* In rejecting the claim that the referendum was unauthorized, we referred to the enumerated power provided in section 125.01(1)(k), Florida Statutes, to "[p]rovide and regulate waste and sewage collection and disposal, water supply, and conservation programs." *Speer*, 367 So. 2d at 208–09. We also referred to the power in section 125.01(1)(q) to create municipal service taxing units for various purposes including "water" and "waste and sewage collection and disposal," which includes "the authorization for all counties to levy additional taxes, within the limits fixed for municipal purposes, within such municipal service taxing units under the authority of the second sentence of Article VII, Section 9(b) of the State Constitution." *Speer*, 367 So. 2d at 209. . . .

Watt addressed removal from the ballot of a proposed constitutional amendment providing for casino gambling if approved by initiative referendum of county voters. Removal was sought on the ground that the proposed amendment violated due process because of "the alleged lack of authority, by statute or ordinance, for many of Florida's counties to conduct initiative referenda." *Watt*, 491 So. 2d at 593. The challengers thus contended that "many Floridians would be unable to implement casino gambling in their own counties because an initiative referendum on the subject could not be held." *Id.*

The First District in *Watt* rejected this argument, reasoning as follows:

> Charter counties have the authority to conduct such referenda under Article VIII, section 1(g) of the Florida Constitution and non-charter counties have similar power under Article VIII, section 1(f) of the state constitution and section 125.01 of the Florida Statutes. Even if some counties do not have currently valid ordinances to spell out the specifics of holding a referendum, we hardly find this to be grounds for invalidating a proposed constitutional amendment. If the proposal is approved and the governing body of a county fails to provide for referenda, an aggrieved citizen could seek redress in the courts.

Id.

We reject the suggestion that *Watt* supports a broad home rule authority to conduct binding referenda on any and every subject. *Watt*'s discussion of the legal powers of counties cannot be divorced from the authorization of initiative referenda in the proposed constitutional amendment. *Watt* simply holds that if a constitutional provision authorizes initiative referenda in certain counties then those counties will — under the general authority to exercise the power of self-government — have the power to establish the mechanism necessary to implement the constitutional provision. As in *Speer*, the authority to conduct a binding referendum was predicated on a constitutional provision empowering counties to conduct referenda on a particular subject.

Here, no relevant analogous constitutional authority exists regarding the subject of slot machine gaming. As the Division points out, in Florida gambling is generally illegal. Section 849.08, Florida Statutes (2013), provides that "game[s] of chance" are illegal. But certain forms of gambling are legal. *See, e.g.*, ch. 550, Fla. Stat. (2013) (the "Florida Pari-mutuel Wagering Act"). And although slot machines and slot machine gaming are specifically outlawed under section 849.15(1), Florida Statutes (2013), in sweeping terms, slot machine gaming is permitted under tight restrictions as laid out by the Legislature in chapter 551. Nothing in chapter 551, however, grants any authority to regulate slot machine gaming to any county. The only role that counties play regarding slot machine gaming is conducting referenda when authorized by law. . . .

. . . The First District thus was correct in upholding the Division's decision to deny the license sought by Gretna Racing. So we approve the result reached by the First District. . . .

It is so ordered.

———————

Notes and Questions to Consider:

1. The local option at issue in *Gretna Racing v. DBPR* is no longer available due to an amendment to Florida's constitution enacted in 2018.

2. What power did the non-charter county lack that resulted in its inability to hold a valid referendum?

E. Local Government as Provider of Utilities and Services

Of course, one role of local government is to provide services to Floridians. Is this the local government's right, or is it a privilege? Consider the case of *City of Winter Park v. S. States Utilities, Inc.*, 540 So. 2d 178 (Fla. 5th DCA 1989):

City of Winter Park v. Southern States Utilities, Inc.

Fifth District Court of Appeal of Florida, 1989
540 So. 2d 178

Appellant, City of Winter Park, enacted, pursuant to section 180.02(3), Florida Statutes, an ordinance extending its corporate power over its municipal sewer service zone outside its corporate limits so as to require property owners outside the city but within such service zone to connect to the city's sewer system when it became available. Appellee Southern States Utility, Inc., a non-governmental utility company (public service corporation) with a certificate issued by the Florida Public Service Commission (PSC) pursuant to section 367.031, Florida Statutes, authorizing it to provide sewer service, entered into a contract with appellee landowners to supply sewer service to a tract of land lying within a portion of the area embraced within the city's ordinance where the city does not presently have sewer service capability.

The city filed this action against the utility company and the landowners alleging that the utility company was providing sewer service to the landowners within the city's exclusive sewer service zone and that the city would have capacity to serve the land owners' property by a date about 17 months in the future from the date the action was originally filed. The complaint prayed for a declaratory judgment to the effect that the landowners would be required to disconnect from the utility company's sewer system and connect with the city's sewer system when the city could provide sewer service.

The trial court held that the city under its ordinance could compel the landowners to connect with its sewer system only if the city sewer treatment capacity was available at the time it was needed by the landowners and found that there was no material issue as to the fact that the city did not have the present ability to provide sewer service to the landowners' property and that, accordingly, the utility company was free to contract to provide sewer service to the landowners' property without intervention [interference] from the city. Although not affirmatively expressed, the effect of the trial court's denial of the city's prayer for a declaratory judgment that the landowners would be required to disconnect from the utility company's sewer system and connect with the city's sewer system when it became available and entry of summary judgment against the city was that the landowners would not be required to terminate their sewer service contract with the utility company and connect to the city's sewer system if and when it became available to the landowners' property. The city appeals.

Interestingly, this litigation is somewhat of a shadow of a prior litigation as to the same issue between the same parties that came about as follows: earlier, the utility company applied to the Public Service Commission to amend its certificate of public necessity to provide sewer service to the property now in question and other property. The city objected. The PSC, by order numbered 18525, and dated December 9, 1987 (87 FPSC 12:125), found that the city had more demand for sewer service than it had capacity and that while the city expected to be able to provide sewer service at some time in the future, the city would not execute a commitment to provide sewer service and desired to place those needing service on a list to wait until the city could provide service while the utility company had existing unused sewer treatment capacity and was willing and able to serve the public. As to the city's claim to the exclusive right to serve the property in question under its municipal service zone, the commission noted that it is not bound by the city's ordinance extending its corporate power beyond its city limits, nor by a local comprehensive plan enacted under section 163.3161, Florida Statutes, stating that the test was who was in the best position to provide the needed sewer service which the commission found to be the utility company rather than the city. The commission expressly declined the city's request that the utility company's certificate for authority to serve this area be issued subject to the condition requiring disconnection when the city became able to supply sewer service, noting that the commission had no jurisdiction over the city sewer system. The city appealed the Public Service Commission's order to the First District Court of Appeal which affirmed. *See City of Winter Park v. Southern States Utilities*, 530 So. 2d 310 (Fla. 1st DCA 1988).

We agree with the Public Service Commission and the trial court. All corporations which voluntarily undertake to engage in performing a service of a public nature whether a governmental agency, such as a municipality, or a private corporation, assume an obligation implied by law to render, for reasonable compensation and without discrimination and to all of the public in the area sought to be served, a service reasonably adequate to meet the just requirements of those sought to be served.

A city cannot undertake to extend its service franchise beyond an area it is able to serve and thereby prevent the public from being served by anyone else. The public is entitled to be served and served by the entity best able to serve it. In this case, the utility company is able to provide the public with the service that the city is unable to provide. The city has no legal right to prevent the utility company from serving the consuming public and no right to require the public to disconnect from the utility company that can now serve it and connect with the city's sewer system if and when the city gets around to meeting its duty to provide the service that it has undertaken to provide.

AFFIRMED.

Note and Question to Consider:

1. Was the City of Winter Park's desire to be the utilities provider unreasonable in your opinion? Consider McQuillin's summary of the majority rule in other jurisdictions:

> In most jurisdictions a municipality may contract to furnish a supply from its plant, for use outside the city, where not prohibited by statute or charter provision, and where the supply is sufficient to furnish the residents all that is necessary for their use. This may include the power to furnish a supply to another municipality or to a state institution, or to customers in a housing development, or to residents within the service area of an incorporated water and sewer authority contiguous to but lying outside the municipal limits. . . . Further, a municipality may extend its own services to municipal-owned facilities located outside its territorial limits, even

though these facilities may have already been supplied through a private company.

12 McQUILLIN MUN. CORP. § 35:36 (3d ed.).

———————

Can a local government use its position as the provider of services to gain concessions from those who wish to receive services? This was the main issue Florida's supreme court addressed in *Allen's Creek Properties, Inc. v. City of Clearwater*, 679 So. 2d 1172 (Fla. 1996).

Allen's Creek Properties, Inc. v. City of Clearwater
Supreme Court of Florida, 1996
679 So. 2d 1172

We have for review *City of Clearwater v. Allen's Creek Properties, Inc.*, 658 So. 2d 539 (Fla. 2d DCA 1995), wherein the district court, by separate order, certified the following question to be of great public importance:

> *May a municipality refuse to provide sewer service, or condition the provision of sewer service on annexation, as to nonresidents located within its exclusive sewer service territory established pursuant to inter-local agreements with neighboring municipal sewer service providers?*

Id. at 543. We have jurisdiction. Art. V, § 3(b)(4), Fla. Const. We answer the question in the affirmative based upon the general rule that a municipality has no duty to supply services to areas outside its boundaries. *See Allstate Insurance Co. v. City of Boca Raton*, 387 So. 2d 478 (Fla. 4th DCA 1980); C.C. Marvel, Annotation, *Right to Compel Municipality to Extend Its Water System*, 48 A.L.R. 1222, 1230 (1956). Allen's Creek Properties (Allen's Creek) contends that the facts in this case establish an exception to this general rule and that consequently, Clearwater's refusal to provide services to unincorporated property located within its service area was improper. For the reasons expressed below, we disagree.

Allen's Creek owns a parcel of land located in the unincorporated area of Pinellas County immediately adjacent to Clearwater's city limits. In September 1990, Allen's Creek submitted to Pinellas County a site plan for the development of this parcel. Pinellas County officials directed Allen's Creek to apply to Clearwater for sewer services because the parcel was located within Clearwater's sanitary sewer service district.

Upon receiving the request for sewer services, Clearwater officials informed Allen's Creek that, pursuant to City of Clearwater, Florida, Ordinance 68–97 (August 5, 1968), the developer would have to consent to annexation before receiving sewer services. Allen's Creek refused to allow the City to annex the property and filed suit for declaratory and other relief.

The trial court held that Clearwater, through the Central Pinellas County 201 Facilities Plan (the 201 Plan) and its interlocal agreement with the City of Largo, had assumed an obligation to provide sewer service in its designated service area. That service area included the land owned by Allen's Creek. Further, the trial court concluded that the record did not present a rational basis to require annexation as a condition to service.

Clearwater appealed the trial court's decision, and the district court reversed. *Allen's Creek*, 658 So. 2d at 542. The district court examined each of the documents on which the trial court based its decision. The first document, the 201 Plan, was devised pursuant to the Federal Water Pollution Control Act of 1972, Pub.L. No. 92–500, § 2, 86 Stat. 816. . . .

Clearwater, along with the several other entities, participated in the development of a 201 Plan for its geographic area. The Plan delineated service areas for Clearwater as well as the other local entities involved in developing the Plan. . . .

The district court also examined the interlocal agreement that the City of Clearwater and the City of Largo entered pursuant to section 163.01, Florida Statutes (1983). The agreement designated service areas for the City of Clearwater and the City of Largo consistent with the service areas designated for those cities in the 201 Plan. With respect to these service areas the agreement provides: "The parties shall have the exclusive right to provide wholesale and retail sanitary sewer service within the area allocated to such part and further agree not to compete with each other as to the provision of such sewer service outside their designated area."

. . . Allen's Creek maintains that this case establishes an exception to the general rule that a municipality cannot be compelled to supply services to areas outside its municipal boundaries. We recognize that exceptions to this general rule do exist. For example, a municipality may be required to extend its services if it has agreed to do so by contract. A contract may require the municipality to serve only a particular entity outside its municipal boundaries. Such a contract does not necessarily require the municipality to serve other similarly situated entities. On the other hand, a contract may require the municipality to service an entire area outside its limits. In such cases the municipality will be required to serve all the public in that area at the lowest possible cost with the most efficiency as demonstrated by the decision in *City of Clearwater v. Metco Development Corp.*, 519 So. 2d 23 (Fla. 2d DCA 1987), *review denied*, 525 So. 2d 876 (Fla. 1988).

In *Metco*, the developer owned unincorporated property located in Clearwater's water service area. 519 So. 2d at 24. The City was already serving the northern portion of the developer's property but refused to serve the southern portion unless the developer agreed to annexation. *Id.* The court determined that the City by contractually agreeing to serve the entire water service area, which included the developer's land, became obligated to do so. *Id.* at 24–25. A contract like that relied on by the court in *Metco* does not exist in the instant case. This exception is therefore inapplicable.

Some jurisdictions recognize another exception to the general rule for those municipalities that through their conduct hold themselves out as public utilities.

According to the jurisdictions that recognize this exception, a municipality that holds itself out as a public utility for a particular area outside its city limits has a duty to supply everyone in that area. Allen's Creek contends that Clearwater held itself out as a public utility by entering an interlocal agreement that designated certain unincorporated areas as a part of its service area and by supplying sewer services to certain nonresidents. Accordingly, Allen's Creek contends that Clearwater has a legal obligation to provide sewer service to nonresidents located within its service area.

We agree that through its conduct a municipality may assume the legal duty to provide reasonably adequate services for reasonable compensation to all of the public in an unincorporated area. See *City of Winter Park v. Southern States Utilities, Inc.*, 540 So. 2d 178, 180 (Fla. 5th DCA 1989) (city's passage of ordinance requiring property owners outside the city but within a zone designated by the ordinance to connect to the city's sewer service when available was conduct sufficient to bring into effect law applicable to public utilities). We add however that the conduct must expressly manifest the municipality's desire or intent to assume that duty. A municipality's decision to provide service without restriction in an area outside its boundaries would meet this requirement. The 201 Plan and interlocal agreement relied on here do not. Like the plan in *Allstate*, nothing in either the Plan or agreement affirmatively states that Clearwater will provide services to the unincorporated area. . . . Providing service outside its boundaries in only limited situations, as Clearwater has done here, does not amount to an affirmative expression of intent to serve all in the area. Clearwater therefore has not accepted a duty to provide services to the unincorporated land located in its service area.

Because Clearwater has no duty to provide services to the unincorporated land within its service area, we conclude that the City may condition upon annexation the landowner's receipt of sewer services. That condition however must be applied consistently, and a reasonable justification for the condition must exist. See *Sebring Utilities Comm'n. v. Home Savings Ass'n. of Florida*, 508 So. 2d 26, 28 (Fla. 2d DCA) ("Courts will not interfere with a municipal utility's exercise of its authority as long as the municipality does not arbitrarily discriminate between its customers and can present reasonable justifications for its actions."), *review denied*, 515 So. 2d 230 (Fla. 1987). We find that Clearwater's condition of annexation meets both these requirements. The annexation policy is applied to the entire unincorporated area with only specific limited exceptions. . . .

Accordingly, we approve the decision of the district court. We find that the agreements entered by Clearwater in this case did not affirmatively express the City's intent to supply sewer service to the unincorporated portion of its sewer service area. Nor did Clearwater engage in any other conduct that expressed the intent to serve this area. The general rule thus still applies to this case and requires us to answer the certified question in the affirmative.

It is so ordered.

Notes and Questions to Consider:

1. The slang phrase "up a creek without a paddle" (and its four-letter variants) describes being in an awkward or unpleasant predicament without a ready means of resolution. In a FLORIDA BAR JOURNAL article titled *Up* Allen's Creek *without a Paddle: Can Cities Leverage Utility Service for Annexation?*, the author describes *Allen's Creek* as follows:

> Cities should beware because even 20 years after it was decided, *Allen's Creek Properties, Inc. v. City of Clearwater*, 679 So. 2d 1172 (Fla. 1996), continues to raise questions about the legality of municipalities compelling county property owners to annex into a city to obtain that city's utilities. Hailed as a victory for cities, the Florida Supreme Court decision held that cities can require landowners in unincorporated areas to execute "voluntary" annexation petitions in return for access to city utilities. But the decision brings up many troubling issues familiar to those in local government, such as judicial interference in the operation of local government, cities' ability to control growth on their borders through annexation, and the right to leverage annexation for utilities.

Catherine D. Reischmann, *Up* Allen's Creek *without A Paddle: Can Cities Leverage Utility Service for Annexation?*, FLA. B.J., July/August 2016, at 60 (footnotes omitted). Do you agree that *Allen's Creek* creates an appropriate solution to these problems?

2. So the rule of *Allen's* Creek is that a Florida local government is not obliged to provide utility services, even within its exclusive area. But what are the exceptions to the rule? Consider the case of *Corrections Corp. of Am., Inc. v. City of Pembroke Pines*, 230 So. 3d 477 (Fla. 4th DCA 2017), *review denied*, SC17-2117, 2018 WL 1057372 (Fla. Feb. 27, 2018).

Corrections Corporation of America, Inc. v. City of Pembroke Pines

Fourth District Court of Appeal of Florida, 2017
230 So. 3d 477

Corrections Corporation of America ("CCA") appeals a trial court order—sounding in declaratory relief—holding that the City of Pembroke Pines did not have a duty to provide water and sewer services to CCA's property site, as well as a final order dismissing CCA's counterclaims. Because we find that Pembroke Pines affirmatively expressed its intention to assume such a duty, we reverse the order. . . .

Background

CCA sought sewer and water services from Pembroke Pines for its property located in the Town of Southwest Ranches but adjacent to Pembroke Pines ("the CCA site"). Pembroke Pines operates potable water and sewer systems that service properties within its boundaries, as well as some properties outside of those boundaries. Those services provided outside of the boundaries extend to a limited number of residential and commercial properties. Southwest Ranches does not have potable water or sewer systems to service its residents, and Pembroke Pines is the only provider in the area. The CCA site is surrounded by four other properties, all of which are, or were at one time, serviced by Pembroke Pines' water or sewer systems (or both). Only one of these properties is actually located within the boundaries of Pembroke Pines. At all times relevant to this dispute, Pembroke Pines admitted that it had the capacity and infrastructure in place to provide water and sewer services to the CCA site through its systems that abut the site.

In 2005, CCA and Southwest Ranches entered into an agreement concerning the development of a correctional facility on the CCA site. The agreement provided that "all required water, sewer and other utility services are available" at the CCA site. CCA was advised that while a water and sewer agreement with Pembroke Pines would be required, it was unclear whether the Pembroke Pines City Commission would grant those services. However, later in 2005, Southwest Ranches entered into an interlocal agreement with Pembroke Pines regarding local roadways and other matters ("Roadways ILA"), in which Pembroke Pines agreed not to interfere with the development or operation of CCA's jail facility:

> *Jail Facility:* [Pembroke Pines] shall not interfere with [CCA's], or its successors or assigns, development and/or operation of the jail facility, or with [Southwest Ranches]'s Agreement with [CCA] concerning development of same.

In 2011, Immigration and Customs Enforcement ("ICE") tentatively selected the CCA site to build a new detention facility. A few days later, Pembroke Pines and Southwest Ranches entered into another interlocal agreement concerning emergency medical and fire services (the "EMS ILA") that provided in pertinent part:

> *Jail Facility:* [Pembroke Pines] acknowledges that it has sufficient capacity to deliver emergency medical protection and fire prevention services to [Southwest Ranches]'s future 2,500 bed detention/corrections facility, located on property currently owned by [CCA]. [Pembroke Pines] agrees to timely provide Broward County, upon request, any documentation that Broward County may require to acknowledge that Pembroke Pines has the capacity, ability, and the willingness to service this facility under the terms and conditions contained herein. . . . Further, [Pembroke Pines] agrees that it has sufficient capacity to provide water and sewer service to [Southwest Ranches]'s future 2,500 bed detention/corrections facility (approximately 500,000 gross square feet of floor area), *and that it will expeditiously approve a water/waste water utility agreement to provide such service, at [Pembroke Pines]'s then prevailing rate, in accordance with state law* ([Pembroke Pines]'s rate + surcharge).

(Emphasis added). In a special meeting on June 27, 2011, the Pembroke Pines City Commission voted on and approved the EMS ILA in Resolution No. 3312.

Some five months later, in December 2011, the City Commission passed yet another affirmative motion, that one being "to approve direction that, should CCA come forward with a request for Pembroke Pines to provide them water and sewer service, that the water and sewer agreement stipulate that it would be for not more than 1,500 beds based on the Engineer's report" (the "December 2011 Motion"). CCA then submitted to Pembroke Pines a proposed Water and Sewer Installation and Service Agreement (the "W & S Agreement") for a 1,500-bed facility. . . .

. . . In an abrupt departure from the numerous manifestations of intent expressed by the Pembroke Pines City Commission over the previous six years, the City Commission did not vote on the W & S Agreement and quite to the contrary, formally adopted a resolution *expressing its opposition* to erecting the ICE detention center on the CCA site. In a later meeting, the City Commission voted to both terminate the EMS ILA and, because it was "in doubt as to its rights and obligations," and to direct the city attorney to seek declaratory relief.

In its action for declaratory judgment, Pembroke Pines sought a ruling that it was not required to provide CCA with water and sewer services. . . . Following trial, the court entered an order determining that Pembroke Pines did not, in fact, have a duty to provide water and sewer services to CCA.

Analysis

On appeal, CCA argues that Pembroke Pines assumed a legally enforceable duty to provide the CCA site with those services by expressly manifesting a desire or intent to provide the services. CCA maintains the evidence at trial established that the ongoing conduct of Pembroke Pines created a duty to provide utilities. As such, the trial court's rulings concerned a question of fact that "must be sustained if supported by competent substantial evidence." *Bellino v. W & W Lumber & Bldg. Supplies, Inc.*, 902 So. 2d 829, 832 (Fla. 4th DCA 2005) (quoting *State v. Glatzmayer*, 789 So. 2d 297, 301 n.7 (Fla. 2001)). We agree with CCA.

As a general rule, "a municipality has no duty to supply services to areas outside its boundaries." *Allen's Creek Props., Inc. v. City of Clearwater*, 679 So. 2d 1172, 1174 (Fla. 1996). In *Allen's Creek*, the Florida Supreme Court recognized exceptions to this general rule where (1) a municipality has agreed to extend its services by contract, and (2) where a municipality has assumed a duty to provide such services through its conduct. *Id.* at 1175–76. With regard to the conduct exception, the court explained:

> According to the jurisdictions that recognize this exception, a municipality that holds itself out as a public utility for a particular area outside its city limits has a duty to supply everyone in that area. . . .

> We agree that through its conduct a municipality may assume the legal duty to provide reasonably adequate services for reasonable compensation to all of the public in an unincorporated area. *See City of Winter Park v. Southern States Utilities, Inc.*, 540 So. 2d 178, 180 (Fla. 5th DCA 1989) (city's

passage of ordinance requiring property owners outside the city but within a zone designated by the ordinance to connect to the city's sewer service when available was conduct sufficient to bring into effect law applicable to public utilities). We add however that *the conduct must expressly manifest the municipality's desire or intent to assume that duty.* A municipality's decision to provide service without restriction in an area outside its boundaries would meet this requirement.

Id. at 1176 (emphasis added).

Allen's Creek presents a scenario somewhat similar to the one at hand. There, Allen's Creek owned a parcel of land located in the unincorporated area of Pinellas County, but adjacent to Clearwater. *Id.* at 1174. When Allen's Creek submitted a site development plan to Pinellas County, Pinellas officials directed Allen's Creek to Clearwater for sewer services because the parcel was located within Clearwater's sanitary sewer service district. *Id.* Clearwater informed Allen's Creek that it would have to consent to annexation before receiving sewer services. *Id.* Allen's Creek declined and filed suit for declaratory judgment. *Id.*

On appeal to the Florida Supreme Court, Allen's Creek argued that the conduct exception to the general rule applied, as Clearwater had assumed an obligation to provide sewer service in its designated service area through the Central Pinellas County 201 Facilities Plan ("201 Plan") and its interlocal agreement with the City of Largo. *Id.* at 1175–76. The interlocal agreement between Clearwater and the City of Largo designated service areas and stated, "The parties shall have the exclusive right to provide wholesale and retail sanitary sewer service within the area allocated to such part and further agree not to compete with each other as to the provision of such sewer service outside their designated area." *Id.* at 1175.

The 201 Plan was created in connection with the Federal Water Pollution Control Act of 1972, the goal of which was "to eliminate the discharge of pollutants into navigable waters by 1985," and a provision of which was federal "funding for the research and development of wastewater treatment management plans." *Id.* at 1174. Within the 201 Plan, "service areas" were designated "to determine the scope of facilities needed in the future." *Id.* Allen's Creek's property was within Clearwater's service area as designated by the plan. *Id.* Clearwater approved the 201 Plan by local resolution in 1978, but the EPA rejected it, so the plan was never implemented and Clearwater proceeded with development of alternative methods for wastewater disposal. *Id.*

The supreme court declined to extend the conduct exception to Allen's Creek, reasoning:

> [N]othing in either the Plan or agreement affirmatively states that Clearwater will provide services to the unincorporated area. Nor do these agreements preclude those located outside Clearwater's city limits but within its service area from seeking services from an alternative source....
>
> ... We find that the agreements entered by Clearwater in this case did not affirmatively express the City's intent to supply sewer service to the

> unincorporated portion of its sewer service area. Nor did Clearwater engage
> in any other conduct that expressed the intent to serve this area.

Id. at 1176–77 (emphasis added). The court concluded that Clearwater's annexation requirements were therefore permissible, so long as the requirements were reasonably justified and consistently applied. *Id.*

While similar to the facts of the instant case, *Allen's Creek* is somewhat distinguishable. There, the 201 Plan and interlocal agreement on which Allen's Creek relied were in place before it requested service from the city. As an apparent consequence, the court looked to the agreements at issue for "affirmative[ ] state[ments] that Clearwater will provide services to the unincorporated area." *Id.* at 1176. In other words, the court reviewed the documents for expressions of Clearwater's intent to provide utility services to anyone located within the specific, unincorporated service area. *Id.*

Here, on the other hand, CCA relies on documents *specifically addressing* the CCA site. Applying *Allen's Creek* to the agreements at hand, we find direct expressions of intent to provide services to the area at issue in the EMS ILA:

> *Jail Facility:* . . . [Pembroke Pines] agrees to timely provide Broward County, upon request, any documentation that Broward County may require to acknowledge that Pembroke Pines has the capacity, ability, and the willingness to service this facility. . . . Further, [Pembroke Pines] agrees that it has sufficient capacity to provide water and sewer service to [Southwest Ranches]'s future 2,500 bed detention/corrections facility (approximately 500,000 gross square feet of floor area), *and that it will expeditiously approve a water/waste water utility agreement to provide such service, at* [*Pembroke Pines*]*'s then prevailing rate, in accordance with state law* ([Pembroke Pines]'s rate + surcharge).

(Emphasis added). By including a statement that it would "approve a water/waste water agreement to provide such service," Pembroke Pines affirmatively and expressly manifested its desire and intent to assume that duty.

Further, although they may not constitute *affirmative* expressions of intent to provide water and sewer service, other actions of the City of Pembroke Pines indicated its willingness to provide services to the CCA site. Pembroke Pines provided these services to all surrounding sites. Also, knowing that it was the only water and sewer service provider in the area, Pembroke Pines agreed in the Roadways ILA that it "shall not interfere with [CCA's] . . . development and/or *operation* of the jail facility." Finally, Pembroke Pines indicated its willingness to provide these services by the City Commission's passage of the December 2011 motion to direct CCA to limit its request for water and sewer services to a 1,500-bed facility. . . .

Consequently, we find that the conduct exception to the general rule that a municipality has no duty to supply services to areas outside its boundaries applies in the instant case. We reverse the trial court's determination to the contrary.

Reversed and remanded for further proceedings.

———————

Notes and Questions to Consider:

1. What are the exceptions to the rule of *Allen's Creek* as identified in this case?

2. Are these exceptions enough to provide justice when equity requires it?

Chapter 10

Legislative Power

A. Purpose of a Legislature

What is the purpose of Florida's legislature? Consider this excerpt from Daniel Webster & Donald L. Bell, *First Principles for Constitution Revision*, 22 Nova L. Rev. 391 (1997):

The Legislative Branch

John Locke saw the establishment of legislative power as the first and foremost of all positive laws. He called the law-making function the "supreme power of the commonwealth" because it is the responsibility of the legislative branch to make laws that will govern all, including the executive and the judiciary. . . . In Florida, the constitution divides the Legislature between two separate houses—the House of Representatives, with one-hundred and twenty members, and the Senate, with forty members. . . . .

One would also hope that in making legislative decisions, the Legislature would avoid creating laws that are sharply opposed to natural human interests or behaviors. . . . Adam Smith once said:

> [Man] seems to imagine that he can arrange the different members of the great society with as much ease as the hand arranges the pieces upon a chessboard; he does not consider that the pieces upon the chessboard have no other principle of motion than that which the hand impresses upon them; but that, in the great chessboard of human society, every single piece has a principle of motion of its own, altogether different from that which the Legislature may wish to impress upon it. If those two principles coincide and act in the same direction, the game of human society will go on easily and harmoniously, and is very likely to be happy and successful. If they are opposite or different, the game will go on miserably, and the society must be at all times in the highest degree of disorder.

Notes and Questions to Consider:

1. In the discussion of Florida's legislative branch in the article quoted above, the authors opine that "our foundational legal document should be applied to limit the exercise of legislative power by executive branch officials." Years after this article

appeared, Florida's supreme court did as the article suggested. In *Bush v. Schiavo*, 885 So. 2d 321 (Fla. 2004), Florida's supreme court held:

> In addition to concluding that the Act is unconstitutional as applied in this case because it encroaches on the power of the judicial branch, we further conclude that the Act is unconstitutional on its face because it delegates legislative power to the Governor. The Legislature is permitted to transfer subordinate functions "to permit administration of legislative policy by an agency with the expertise and flexibility to deal with complex and fluid conditions." *Microtel, Inc. v. Fla. Public Serv. Comm'n*, 464 So. 2d 1189, 1191 (Fla. 1985). However, under article II, section 3 of the constitution the Legislature "may not delegate the power to enact a law or the right to exercise unrestricted discretion in applying the law." *Sims v. State*, 754 So. 2d 657, 668 (Fla. 2000). This prohibition, known as the nondelegation doctrine, requires that "fundamental and primary policy decisions . . . be made by members of the legislature who are elected to perform those tasks, and [that the] administration of legislative programs must be pursuant to some minimal standards and guidelines ascertainable by reference to the enactment establishing the program." *Askew v. Cross Key Waterways*, 372 So. 2d 913, 925 (Fla. 1978); see also *Avatar Dev. Corp. v. State*, 723 So. 2d 199, 202 (Fla. 1998) (citing *Askew* with approval). In other words, statutes granting power to the executive branch "must clearly announce adequate standards to guide . . . in the execution of the powers delegated. The statute must so clearly define the power delegated that the [executive] is precluded from acting through whim, showing favoritism, or exercising unbridled discretion." *Lewis v. Bank of Pasco County*, 346 So. 2d 53, 55–56 (Fla. 1976). The requirement that the Legislature provide sufficient guidelines also ensures the availability of meaningful judicial review:
>
> > In the final analysis it is the courts, upon a challenge to the exercise or nonexercise of administrative action, which must determine whether the administrative agency has performed consistently with the mandate of the legislature. When legislation is so lacking in guidelines that neither the agency nor the courts can determine whether the agency is carrying out the intent of the legislature in its conduct, then, in fact, the agency becomes the lawgiver rather than the administrator of the law.
>
> *Askew*, 372 So. 2d at 918–19.
>
> We have recognized that the "specificity of the guidelines [set forth in the legislation] will depend on the complexity of the subject and the 'degree of difficulty involved in articulating finite standards.'" *Brown v. Apalachee Regional Planning Council*, 560 So. 2d 782, 784 (Fla. 1990) (quoting *Askew*, 372 So. 2d at 918). However, we have also made clear that "[e]ven where a general approach would be more practical than a detailed scheme of legislation, enactments may not be drafted in terms so general and unrestrictive that administrators are left without standards for the

guidance of their official acts." *State Dep't of Citrus v. Griffin*, 239 So. 2d
577, 581 (Fla. 1970).

Id. at 332–33 (Fla. 2004).

2. Florida's supreme court once held: "Generally speaking, legislative action
results in the formulation of a general rule of policy, whereas judicial action results in
the application of a general rule of policy." *Bd. of County Com'rs of Brevard County v.
Snyder*, 627 So. 2d 469, 474 (Fla. 1993). Can you think of some instances where government action might blur the lines between legislative action and judicial action?

B. Entities Authorized to Make Florida Law

As seen in previous chapters, Florida's sovereignty gives it an inherent power
called the police power. Florida's constitution is not a grant of the police power, but
may be a limitation upon it. The police power enables Florida to pass laws. Florida's constitution limits the state's lawmaking power to the Florida Legislature and,
through constitutional Home Rule, to Florida's incorporated cities, towns, and villages. The Florida Legislature, through Statutory Home Rule, delegates its Constitutional Home Rule to non-charter counties as well as to charter counties, cities,
towns, and villages.

Therefore, Florida's lawmaking power is not limited to Florida's legislature.
Instead, Florida's constitution limits the power to make Florida laws to the Florida
Legislature and Florida's municipal corporations (charter counties, non-charter
counties, cities, towns, and villages).

The Florida Legislature's lawmaking authority is the result of Florida's constitution vesting the state's sovereign police power directly in its legislature. Specifically,
Florida's constitution provides at Article III, Section 1: "The legislative power of
the state shall be vested in a legislature of the State of Florida, consisting of a senate
composed of one senator elected from each senatorial district and a house of representatives composed of one member elected from each representative district." A
law made by the Florida Legislature is called an "act." Collectively, acts are called
the Florida Statutes or the Laws of Florida.

Local laws made by municipal corporations, typically, are named either ordinances
or resolutions. Regarding counties, Florida's charter counties and non-charter counties have the same lawmaking authority but obtain it differently. Florida's constitution contemplates a county having a governing body, enacting ordinances, legislating
on topics that might also be addressed by the Florida Legislature or a municipality,
recording such laws, and naming punishments applicable to those who violate the
law. This is because Article VIII of Florida's constitution provides:

> (f) NON-CHARTER GOVERNMENT. Counties not operating under
> county charters shall have such power of self-government *as is provided by
> [the applicable law]*. . . .

> (g) CHARTER GOVERNMENT. Counties operating under county charters shall have all powers of local self-government *not inconsistent with [the applicable law]*. . . .

Id. at subsections (f) and (g) (emphasis added). The emphasized language illustrates that charter counties can enact an ordinance or resolution unless a law forbids it, whereas non-charter counties can enact an ordinance or resolution if a law permits it. This would be a meaningful difference but for Florida's Municipal Home Rule Powers Act codified at Florida Statutes chapter 166 and the Florida Supreme Court's expansive reading of that statutory Home Rule power. Because binding precedent of Florida's supreme court interprets the Municipal Home Rule Powers Act to give non-charter counties the same, broad Home Rule power as charter counties, the relevant inquiry as to any county becomes whether the exercised power of local self-government is "not inconsistent with" the applicable law.

Regarding municipalities, Florida's constitution provides: "Municipalities shall have governmental, corporate and proprietary powers to enable them to conduct municipal government, perform municipal functions and render municipal services, and may exercise any power for municipal purposes *except as otherwise provided by law*." Art. VIII, § 2, Fla. Const. (emphasis added). The emphasized language means that the relevant inquiry as to any city's, town's, or village's law becomes whether the exercised power is "not inconsistent with" the applicable law. This makes the inquiry the same as counties.

C. How a Bill Becomes a Law in Florida's Legislature

During a session of the Florida Legislature, new Florida laws may be enacted. The process begins with the drafting of the proposed law, which is called a bill. Anyone can draft a bill, and it if it not drafted by the House or Senate's Bill Drafting Service, then the service will review it for style. All bills contain, at a minimum, a short one-paragraph description of the bill called its "title," an enacting clause, and an effective date.

A bill can originate in either chamber: Florida's Senate or Florida's House of Representatives. Under House rules, each House member is given six bill slots. Senate rules do not impose such a limit on the number of bills that a senator may file.

Bills are filed with the Secretary of the Florida Senate or the Clerk of the House of Representatives. Preferably, when a bill is filed with one chamber (the chamber of origination), a companion bill is filed with the other. A bill is considered a companion bill if it is similar to, and addresses the same issues as, a bill on file with the other chamber. The secretary or clerk files the bill, prints it, and numbers it. Florida Senate bill numbers begin with the letters SB and are even numbers. House bills begin with HB and are odd numbers.

At any time after a bill is filed, it may "die" for that legislative session, which means it will no longer be considered. In a typical legislative session, many bills die at various stages during the following process.

Before a bill can be passed by a chamber, it must be "read" by that chamber three times, unless this rule is waived by a two-thirds vote. On each reading, it shall be read by title only, unless one-third of the members present desire it to be read in full. The first reading is by publication in the chamber's journal of the bill's title, the bill's number, and the name of the senator or representative that is the bill's sponsor.

After the bill's first reading, it either dies or is assigned to one or more committees or subcommittees by the Speaker of the House or the President of the Senate. The membership of these committees and subcommittees consists of representatives in the House or senators in the Senate. Committees are named for and focused upon particular topics such as appropriations, commerce, education, finance and tax, government accountability, health and human services, rules, ways and means, and judiciary. The committee's role is to analyze bills, to conduct hearings to obtain information about the subject of the bill, and if desired, to vote on the bill. All committee and subcommittee meetings must be open and noticed to the public.

After the committee or committees of reference receive(s) the referral of the bill, it will die if the committees' chairpersons do not include it on their committee's agenda. After a bill is debated and possibly amended at these committees, the chairs may call it up for a vote if the bill did not die during debate. Bills voted favorably are placed on the chamber's calendar, making the bill available for a second reading.

The Rules and Calendar Committee decides which bills from the calendar die and which get heard "on the floor" (meaning read by and possibly debated by the full chamber). Rules and Calendar does so by creating a recommended Special Order Calendar of bills, and the chamber votes on each Special Order Calendar prior to the chamber hearing those bills on the floor. After a bill has been introduced and read on the Special Order Calendar, then the chamber considers debating the bill, amending the bill, or allowing the bill to die. Bills that do not die are reported by the committee to the chamber with the result of the committee's vote. This constitutes the second reading of the bill.

The third reading occurs on a subsequent legislative day. Amendments are still permitted at this stage, but only on a two-thirds vote. Debate may occur. The bill's sponsor makes a closing statement. Then the chamber votes, and the bill either passes or dies.

Bills that pass the chamber of origin go to the other chamber with a "message." The process differs slightly depending on whether the other chamber is the House or the Senate, but generally speaking, the other chamber can kill the bill or refer it to one or more committees where it might be debated or amended or killed. Bills making it out of committee may be defeated or passed on the floor of the chamber with or without amendments. If passed, the bill returns to its chamber of origin.

If the passed bill returns to its chamber of origin without amendments, it is enrolled and then sent to the governor for consideration. If there were amendments, the chamber of origin must consider passage of those amendments because amendments require approval by both chambers. Both the House and Senate must pass identical bills for the bill to become a law. Therefore, amendments can kill the bill if rejected by the chamber of origin. Back-and-forth negotiations between the House and Senate occur, usually informally, but sometimes via a Conference Committee comprised of Representatives and Senators that is open and noticed to the public. If successful, the amended bill is enrolled and sent to the governor.

The governor can sign the bill into law, allow the bill to become law without signing it, or veto the bill. A two-thirds vote of the Legislature is required to override a veto. A bill becomes law if too much time passes without the governor's signature or veto. The governor has seven days to sign if the Legislature remains in session, or 15 days if the Legislature adjourns "sine die."

A bill that the Florida Legislature enacts into law is called an act. It is printed in the Laws of Florida and codified in the Florida Statutes. If the legislature overrode a governor's veto to make the bill a law, then it takes effect on the 60th day after adjournment sine die of the session in which the veto is overridden, on a later date stated in the law, or on a date fixed by a resolution passed by both the Florida House of Representatives and the Florida Senate. If the law passed without a veto, then the law takes effect on the date stated in the law, or if not stated, then on the 60th day after adjournment sine die of the session of the legislature in which the law was enacted.

Notes and Questions to Consider:

1. Although much of the legislative lawmaking procedures of Florida's legislature as summarized above are the result of a requirement found in Florida's constitution, some are the result of rulemaking by Florida's legislature. In your opinion, would Floridians be better served by a more simplified procedure?

2. Back in 1970, a proposal to amend Florida's constitution to create a unicameral legislature existed, but that proposal failed to qualify to appear on the ballot. *See Adams v. Gunter*, 238 So. 2d 824 (Fla. 1970). If ever such a proposal were on the ballot, how would you vote, and why?

D. Lawmaking and Its Limits

Now we identify limitations upon the power of lawmaking in Florida. Past Florida constitutional law questions on the Florida Bar Exam raised one or more issues about lawmaking and its limits.

In making any list of the limits upon state lawmaking, we would be remiss not to reiterate that a Florida law may not violate the U.S. Constitution or Florida's constitution. A statute that is inconsistent with either constitution is invalid and legally ineffective. These constitutions provide substantive matters that make a law invalid, such as a violation of one of the rights in the Declaration of Rights in Florida's constitution or the Bill of Rights in the U.S. Constitution. These were the topics of prior chapters of this text.

Here, we examine technical or procedural flaws in Florida lawmaking that render laws invalid. These flaws are fatal, and result in the law being facially unconstitutional, regardless of the substantive matter addressed in that lawmaking. For the lawmaker, these are pitfalls to be avoided. For the litigant fighting to strike down a law as unconstitutional on its face, the following are the arrows in the quiver.

1. Valid Exercise of the State's Police Power

For the Florida Legislature, Florida's counties, and Florida's incorporated cities, towns, and villages, their power to make laws is a result of the state's police power. So any law, to be valid, must be a valid exercise of the state's police power.

To be a valid exercise of the state's police power, a Florida law must be for a public purpose and it must be enacted to protect the health, safety, and welfare of the people. This is the most basic test of the constitutionality of any Florida law. Any law that is not for a public purpose, or was not enacted to protect the health, safety, and welfare of the people, is void and unconstitutional as an improper exercise of the state's police power.

As to whether a law serves a public purpose, Florida's courts grant broad discretion to the decision of the lawmaking body. "The Legislature is vested with wide discretion to determine the public interest and the measures necessary for its achievement." *Fraternal Order of Police, Metro. Dade County, Lodge No. 6 v. Dep't of State*, 392 So. 2d 1296, 1302 (Fla. 1980). Florida's supreme court holds:

> The fact that the legislature may not have chosen the best possible means to eradicate the evils perceived is of no consequence to the courts provided that the means selected are not wholly unrelated to achievement of the legislative purpose. A more rigorous inquiry would amount to a determination of the wisdom of the legislation . . . would usurp the legislative prerogative to establish policy.

Id. at 1302. So the test for whether a law serves a "public purpose" is not a rigorous inquiry but instead is a deferential one.

As a special application of the requirement of a "public purpose," as applied to lawmaking by Florida's counties, cities, towns, and villages, the law is invalid if not done for a "municipal purpose." In most instances, this is a requirement without bite, because Florida's Municipal Home Rule Powers Act as codified in Florida Statutes chapter 166 defines "municipal purpose" so broadly. There, a municipal purpose "means any activity or power which may be exercised by the state or its political subdivisions." This broad definition of "municipal purpose" is a full delegation and extension of the state's sovereign police power to municipalities because the Municipal Home Rule Powers Act states that:

> The provisions of this section shall be so construed as to secure for municipalities the broad exercise of home rule powers granted by the constitution. It is the further intent of the Legislature to extend to municipalities the exercise of powers for municipal governmental, corporate, or proprietary purposes not expressly prohibited by the constitution, general or special law, or county charter and to remove any limitations, judicially imposed or otherwise, on the exercise of home rule powers other than those so expressly prohibited.

Id. at section 166.021(4), Fla. Stat.

Why does the law establish that a state has an inherent police power, and why does that police power have its limits? The answer lies in the freedom of the individual, and in society's limited need for the subordination of individual freedom to the common welfare. As noted by the United States Supreme Court in its 1905 decision in *Jacobson v. Massachusetts*, 197 U.S. 11 (1905) the state's limited right to subordinate individual freedom is known as its "police power." As noted by the Florida Supreme Court in its 1986 case of *State v. Saiez*, 489 So. 2d 1125 (Fla. 1986), the Florida Legislature implements the state's "police power" when it enacts statutes for the protection of the public health, safety, welfare, or morals. Relevant portions of both cases appear below.

Jacobson v. Massachusetts

Supreme Court of the United States, 1905
197 U.S. 11, 25 S. Ct. 358, 49 L. Ed. 643

. . . The authority of the state to enact [a] statute is to be referred to what is commonly called the police power—a power which the state did not surrender when becoming a member of the Union under the Constitution. Although this court has refrained from any attempt to define the limits of that power, yet it has distinctly recognized the authority of a state to enact quarantine laws and 'health laws of every description;' indeed, all laws that relate to matters completely within its territory and which do not by their necessary operation affect the people of other states. According to settled principles, the police power of a state must be held to embrace, at least, such reasonable regulations established directly by legislative enactment as will protect the public health and the public safety. . . . It is equally true that the state may invest local bodies called into existence for purposes of local administration with authority in some appropriate way to safeguard the public health and the public safety. The mode or manner in which those results are to be accomplished is within the discretion of the state, subject, of course, so far as Federal power is concerned, only to the condition that no rule prescribed by a state, nor any regulation adopted by a local governmental agency acting under the sanction of state legislation, shall contravene the Constitution of the United States, nor infringe any right granted or secured by that instrument. A local enactment or regulation, even if based on the acknowledged police powers of a state, must always yield in case of conflict with the exercise by the general government of any power it possesses under the Constitution, or with any right which that instrument gives or secures. . . .

. . . But the liberty secured by the Constitution of the United States to every person within its jurisdiction does not import an absolute right in each person to be, at all times and in all circumstances, wholly freed from restraint. There are manifold restraints to which every person is necessarily subject for the common good. On any other basis organized society could not exist with safety to its members. Society based on the rule that each one is a law unto himself would soon be confronted with disorder and anarchy. Real liberty for all could not exist under the operation of a principle which recognizes the right of each individual person to use his own, whether in respect of his person or his property, regardless of the injury that may be done to others. This court has more than once recognized it as a fundamental principle that 'persons and property are subjected to all kinds of restraints and burdens in order to secure the general comfort, health, and prosperity of the state; of the perfect right of the legislature to do which no question ever was, or upon acknowledged general principles ever can be, made, so far as natural persons are concerned.' . . . The possession and enjoyment of all rights are subject to such reasonable conditions as may be deemed by the governing authority of the country essential to the safety, health, peace, good order, and morals of the community. Even liberty itself, the greatest of all rights, is not unrestricted license to act according to one's own will. It is only freedom from restraint under conditions essential to the equal enjoyment of the same right by others. It is, then, liberty regulated by law. . . .

State v. Saiez

Supreme Court of Florida, 1986
489 So. 2d 1125

. . . The [Florida L]egislature enacts penal statutes . . . under the state's "police power" which derives from the state's sovereign right to enact laws for the protection of its citizens. See *Carroll v. State*, 361 So. 2d 144, 146 (Fla. 1978). Such power, however, is not boundless and is confined to those acts which may be reasonably construed as expedient for protection of the public health, safety, welfare, or morals. *Hamilton v. State*, 366 So. 2d 8, 10 (Fla. 1978); *Newman v. Carson*, 280 So. 2d 426, 428 (Fla. 1973). The due process clauses of our federal and state constitutions do not prevent the legitimate interference with individual rights under the police power, but do place limits on such interference. *State v. Leone*, 118 So. 2d 781, 784 (Fla. 1960). See also *Coca-Cola Co., Food Division v. State, Department of Citrus*, 406 So. 2d 1079, 1084–85 (Fla. 1981), appeal dismissed sub nom. *Kraft, Inc. v. Florida Department of Citrus*, 456 U.S. 1002 (1982). . . . See also *Foster v. State*, 286 So. 2d

549, 551 (Fla. 1973) ("[i]t would be an unconstitutional act—in excess of the State's police power—to criminalize the simple possession of a screwdriver").…

So long as the legislative activity does not encroach upon constitutional guarantees, or run afoul of federal statutory law, a state has a broad scope of discretion in which to regulate the conduct of its citizens.… It need only be shown that the challenged legislative activity is not arbitrary or unreasonable.… Courts will not be concerned with whether the particular legislation in question is the most prudent choice, or is a perfect panacea, to cure the ill or achieve the interest intended.… If there is a legitimate state interest which the legislation aims to effect, and if the legislation is a reasonably related means to achieve the intended end, it will be upheld.… Nevertheless, despite a state's wide discretion, and the cautious restraint of the courts, there remain basic restrictions and limits on a state's legislative power to intrude upon individual rights, liberties, and conduct. To exceed those bounds without rational justification is to collide with the Due Process Clause.… Such an exercise of the police power is unwarranted under the circumstances and violates the due process clauses of our federal and state constitutions.

Notes and Questions to Consider:

1. In the context of state constitutional law, what is the definition of a state's "police power?" When may a state exercise it?

2. What are the limits of a sovereign state's police power? In addressing this question near the height of the U.S. Supreme Court's use (or some might say, abuse) of that power, author Ray A. Brown, in his 1927 article "Due Process of Law, Police Power, and the Supreme Court" appearing in the HARVARD LAW REVIEW at 40 HARV. L. REV. 943, cites us to these opinions of the Supreme Court of the United States: *Otis v. Parker*, 187 U.S. 606, 608 (1903) ("It is true, no doubt, that neither a state legislature nor a state constitution can interfere arbitrarily with private business or transactions, and the mere fact that an enactment purports to be for the protection of public safety, health or morals, is not conclusive upon the courts."); *Eubank v. City of Richmond*, 226 U.S. 137, 143 (1912) (holding that the police power necessarily "has its limits and must stop when it encounters the prohibitions of the [U.S.] Constitution."); *Atlantic Coast Line R. R. v. City of Goldsboro*, 232 U.S. 548, 559 (1914) ("If… there is wanton or arbitrary interference with private rights, the question arises whether the lawmaking body has exceeded the legitimate bounds of the police power."); *Buchanan v. Warley*, 245 U.S. 60, 74 (1917) ("It is equally well established that the police power, broad as it is, cannot justify the passage of a law or ordinance which runs counter to the limitations of the Federal Constitution.") *Truax v. Corrigan*, 257 U.S. 312, 329 (1921) ("… the legislative power of a State can only be exerted in subordination to the fundamental principles of right and justice which the guaranty of due process in the Fourteenth Amendment is intended to preserve.") For an egregious example of a misapplication of the federal police power, and its use as an excuse for a lack of judicial restraint, see the infamous case

of *Lochner v. New York*, 198 U.S. 45, 25 S. Ct. 539, 49 L. Ed. 937 (1905), overruled in part by *Day-Brite Lighting Inc. v. State of Mo.*, 342 U.S. 421, 72 S. Ct. 405, 96 L. Ed. 469 (1952), and overruled in part by *Ferguson v. Skrupa*, 372 U.S. 726, 83 S. Ct. 1028, 10 L. Ed. 2d 93 (1963), and abrogated by *W. Coast Hotel Co. v. Parrish*, 300 U.S. 379, 57 S. Ct. 578, 81 L. Ed. 703 (1937).

2. Proper Subject Matter

Despite the state's inherent police power, lawmaking is limited to a proper subject matter. For the Florida Legislature, lawmaking is proper on any subject matter that is not preempted by federal law and not forbidden by the U.S. Constitution or Florida's constitution. A bill on any topic may originate in either chamber: the Florida Senate or the Florida House of Representatives. This differs from the U.S. Congress, where tax and appropriations bills must originate in the U.S. House of Representatives.

Florida's counties, cities, towns, and villages may enact legislation on any subject matter on which the Florida Legislature may act, if done for a municipal purpose, except (1) annexation, merger, or exercise of extraterritorial power; (2) any subject expressly preempted by the U.S. Constitution, Florida's constitution, or general law; (3) any subject expressly prohibited by Florida's constitution; and (4) any subject preempted to a county pursuant to a Supremacy Clause enacted in a county charter.

The first restriction is because the language of Florida's constitution, such as Article VIII, Section 2, where it restricts such action to the Florida Legislature by stating: "Municipal annexation of unincorporated territory, merger of municipalities, and exercise of extra-territorial powers by municipalities shall be as provided by general or special law." Note that an exception exists regarding the lack of extra-territorial power of a local government: the Florida Legislature can pass a general or special law granting extraterritorial power. For example, Florida Statutes section 180.02 empowers a municipality to enact "an ordinance extending its corporate power over its municipal sewer service zone outside its corporate limits so as to require property owners outside the city but within such service zone to connect to the city's sewer system when it became available." *City of Winter Park v. S. States Utilities, Inc.*, 540 So. 2d 178, 179 (Fla. 5th DCA 1989).

The second and third restrictions are because Home Rule is a lesser power than a constitution or a statute. Stated somewhat differently, a local government, even with its Home Rule power, cannot make legal what a constitution or a statute has made illegal.

The fourth restriction is because Article VIII, Section 1 provides: "The governing body of a county operating under a charter may enact county ordinances not inconsistent with general law. The charter shall provide which shall prevail in the event of conflict between county and municipal ordinances."

Note that the result of these restrictions upon counties, cities, towns, and villages is that they can enact ordinances on the exact same topics as one another and as the Florida Legislature. The mere fact that the Florida Legislature or a local government enact a law on a particular topic does not preclude another county, city, town, or village from legislating on that same topic. This is true even if one is within the territorial jurisdiction of another.

With all these legislating bodies free to enact laws on many of the same topics at the same time and over the same territory, it is possible that a law of the Florida Legislature might preempt, either expressly or impliedly, a local government law on that same subject. It is possible that a Supremacy Clause in a county's charter might preempt a law of a city, town, or village located within that county. These and other topics of preemption are discussed later in this chapter.

3. "Be It Enacted" or "Be It Resolved"

Article III of Florida's constitution, which discusses the Florida Legislature, states:

SECTION 6. Laws. — . . . The enacting clause of every law shall read: "Be It Enacted by the Legislature of the State of Florida:".

Therefore, in order to be validly enacted, all laws of the Florida Legislature must begin with this phrase: "Be It Enacted by the Legislature of the State of Florida." A law is invalid, and unconstitutional on its face, if the bill passed into law by the Florida Legislature did not begin with this phrase.

A resolution does not begin with the phrase "Be It Enacted" but instead begins with this phrase: "Be It Resolved." Not just the Florida Legislature, but also Florida's local governments, are empowered to enact a resolution.

4. Resolution Made When Ordinance or Statute Was Required

A resolution is not always enough. If Florida's legislature enacts a resolution when an act (a statute) was required — or if a Florida city, town, or village enacts a resolution when an ordinance is required — then the resolution is ineffective, facially unconstitutional, and unenforceable.

The difference between the two depends on administration and permanency. Resolutions are sufficient for ceremonial or nonbinding purposes. Likewise, resolutions are sufficient for a matter that is purely administrative in nature, or if not permanent.

To be valid, any local law intended to be permanent must be passed as an ordinance, not a resolution, unless it is a matter of administration or administrative business. Florida Statutes chapter 166 defines "ordinance" to be "an official legislative action of a governing body, which action is a regulation of a general and permanent nature and enforceable as a local law." It defines "resolution" to be "an expression of a governing body concerning matters of administration, an expression of a temporary character, or a provision for the disposition of a particular item of the administrative business of the governing body."

This point is well illustrated by *White v. Town of Inglis*, 988 So. 2d 163 (Fla. 2008).

White v. Town of Inglis
First District Court of Appeal of Florida, 2008
988 So. 2d 163

Michael A. White appeals a final summary judgment entered in favor of the Town of Inglis, Florida, appellee, in his action challenging the Town's adoption of Resolution Number R14–05 (R14–05) which prohibits White's access to a street from his commercial property adjoining that street. We hold that R14–05 constitutes an "ordinance" as defined in [Florida's Municipal Home Rule Powers Act] and, because the Town adopted this ordinance without complying with the ten-day notice requirement in [Florida's Municipal Home Rule Powers Act], we hold the ordinance void. Accordingly, we reverse and remand for further proceedings.

White owns two contiguous lots in the Town of Inglis which front on Highway U.S. 19 and operates a used car business on the lots. Palm Point Drive is a residential street located immediately to the north of and adjacent to White's commercial property. On October 20, 2005, the Inglis Town Commission held a workshop meeting at which the subject of closing off commercial access to Palm Point Drive was discussed. White was present at the meeting. He states in his affidavit included in the record that he "had informally heard that the Town, was considering the construction of a fence along the road which might affect my access." According to the affidavit of Town Clerk Sally McCranie, those at the meeting were advised that a special meeting would be held on October 31, 2005, to consider a resolution to close commercial access to Palm Point Drive.

On October 31, 2005, the Town enacted R14–05 as a "resolution." R14–05 makes it unlawful for a person to drive from commercial properties onto Palm Point Drive. A fence has now been constructed along the drive blocking view of White's property and any access to Palm Point Drive from the property.

[Florida's Municipal Home Rule Powers Act] defines "ordinance" as "an official legislative action of a governing body, which action is a regulation of a general and permanent nature and enforceable as a local law." [Florida's Municipal Home Rule Powers Act] defines "resolution" to mean "an expression of a governing body concerning matters of administration, an expression of a temporary character, or a provision for the disposition of a particular item of the administrative business of the governing body." "A resolution cannot be substituted for and have the force and effect of an ordinance, nor can a resolution supply initial authority which is required to be vested by ordinance." *Wallace v. Leahy*, 496 So. 2d 970, 971 (Fla. 3d DCA 1986) (citing *Brown v. City of St. Petersburg*, 111 Fla. 718, 153 So. 140 (1933); and *Carlton v. Jones*, 117 Fla. 622, 158 So. 170 (1934) ("An act which is required to be accomplished by ordinance may not be accomplished by resolution.")).

It is clear that the action by the Town is . . . neither a matter of administration for the Town nor an expression of a temporary character. Because the Town enacted R14–05 without following the requirements of [Florida's Municipal Home Rule Powers Act], the ordinance is void. *Ellison v. City of Fort Lauderdale*, 183 So. 2d 193 (Fla. 1966); *Healthsouth Doctors' Hosp. v. Hartnett*, 622 So. 2d 146 (Fla. 3d DCA 1993); *see also Carlton v. Jones*, 158 So. at 171 (recognizing that when an ordinance is not published according to law it is "invalid and of no effect"); *Webb v. Town Council of Town of Hilliard*, 766 So. 2d 1241 (Fla. 1st DCA 2000). Because we hold the ordinance void, it is not necessary to reach the other issues raised on appeal.

REVERSED and REMANDED for proceedings consistent with this opinion.

5. Procedural Requirements

Florida's constitution at Article III provides certain procedural requirements the Florida Legislature must use when enacting laws. Different procedures apply to the Florida Legislature than apply to Florida's counties, cities, towns, and villages.

Generally speaking, due to the doctrine of the separation of powers, issues unaddressed by Florida's constitution as to how the Florida Legislature conducts its business and fulfills its legislative function are issues to be decided solely by the Florida Legislature itself. For this reason, the Florida Legislature's procedural requirements are governed by the rules of the House and Senate.

As to local lawmaking bodies, Florida Statutes section 125.66 provides the minimum procedural requirements for counties to enact, and Florida's Home Rule Powers Act at Florida Statutes section 166.041 provides nearly identical minimum requirements for cities, towns, and villages. The following minimum requirements may be strengthened but not reduced by an ordinance or a county charter. A notice of intent to enact the ordinance must be published in a newspaper of general circulation at least 10 days prior to enactment. The required format of, and statements in, the notice appears as a form in the Florida Statutes. An exception to the 10-day notice requirement may be made in an emergency. But a four-fifths vote of the legislating body must find that such an emergency exists warranting short notice. An emergency is not sufficient grounds for short notice when enacting a change to a zoning map. A five-year statute of limitations applies to an action or defense arising out of the failure to meet these procedural requirements. *See* Patrick John McGinley, Florida Municipal Law and Practice § 3:4 (2017-2018 edition).

6. Single Subject Rule

Together, Florida's constitution and Florida's Municipal Home Rule Powers Act require that each statute, ordinance, or resolution "shall embrace but one subject and matters properly connected therewith." For example, Article III of Florida's constitution contains these two clauses:

SECTION 6. Laws. — Every law shall embrace but one subject and matter properly connected therewith,

SECTION 12. Appropriation bills. — Laws making appropriations for salaries of public officers and other current expenses of the state shall contain provisions on no other subject.

Therefore, every law enacted by the Legislature, a county, a city, a town, or a village may cover only one subject. This "Single Subject Rule" is interpreted by Florida's supreme court to contain three requirements. First, each law must embrace only one subject. Second, the law may include any matter that is properly connected with the subject. The third requirement, related to the first, is that the subject shall be briefly expressed in the title. The three requirements are given a liberal not strict interpretation because any doubt is resolved in favor of finding that the Single Subject Rule is not violated.

Florida Municipal Law and Practice identifies the following public policy reasons behind the Single Subject Rule:

> Two major considerations underlie the Single Subject Rule. The first is the need to prevent a legislative practice sometimes called "logrolling." Logrolling is when a legislature or lawmaking body includes in a single act some desirable or important matters together with some undesirable or unimportant matters. The result is that, order to enact into law the desirable matter, the bill must be passed in its entirely including the unwanted portion. Logrolling may have adverse affects upon the legislative process. Good bills can be held hostage by those who add undesirable or unimportant matters to the bill. The relative negotiating strengths of the proponents and opponents of a bill can be affected. Logrolling also severely limits if not destroys the veto power of the Governor or chief executive, and thereby negates one of the intended checks on the authority of the legislature.

> The second consideration behind the Single Subject Rule is to ensure the integrity of the legislative process in substantive lawmaking. The Florida Constitution demands that each bill dealing with substantive matters be scrutinized separately. Putting provisions on different substantive topics into a single bill could hinder the ability to fully debate some of the topics. Bills should not be cluttered with extraneous matters which might cloud the legislative mind when it should be focused solely upon the one substantive matter addressed in the bill. Legislatures and lawmaking bodies include, by necessity, large numbers of elected members representing even larger numbers of individuals from diverse locations and backgrounds with diverse concerns. All want their ideas considered and their concerns heard. Under these conditions, debating a single subject is difficult enough.

Commentators suggest that the general disposition of Florida's courts is to avoid interpreting the Single Subject Rule in such a way so as to strike down otherwise valid laws as unconstitutional by use of a construction whose strictness is unnecessary to the accomplishment of the beneficial purposes for which the law has been adopted. Sometimes a broadly phrased title for the act will justify covering various subjects in that act. A statute will not be unconstitutional for embracing more than one subject if the title is sufficiently broad to connect it with the general subject matter of the enactment.

Likewise, laws containing provisions that are corollaries to the act's main purpose do not violate the Single Subject Rule. For example, a statute designed to confer exclusive jurisdiction on a court of record does not violate the Single Subject Rule when it contains a provision abolishing the court previously holding that jurisdiction.

Patrick John McGinley, Florida Municipal Law and Practice (2017-2018 edition). A fine illustration of Florida's use of its Single Subject Rule appears in *Franklin v. State*, 887 So. 2d 1063 (Fla. 2004).

Franklin v. State
Supreme Court of Florida, 2004
887 So. 2d 1063

The issue in this case is the constitutionality of . . . the "Three-Strike Violent Felony Offender Act." The specific constitutional question presented is whether the fourteen provisions of the Act "embrace but one subject and matter properly connected therewith" as mandated by article III, section 6 of the Florida Constitution, the single subject clause. We . . . conclude that the Act does not violate the single subject clause of the Florida Constitution.

I. Summary of [the "Three Strikes Act"]

. . . [The "Three Strikes Act"] is identified at the beginning of its full title as "an act relating to sentencing." The remainder of the full title sets forth the statutory provisions. . . . A lengthy preamble, consisting of twenty-one "Whereas" clauses, follows the full title. The Act contains fourteen separate sections, twelve of which are substantive. . . . [O]nly two of the Act's twelve substantive sections relate specifically to the "Three-Strike" violent felony provisions. . . . However, three of the other sections, sections 2, 4, and 5, establish harsher sentences for violent and repeat offenders.

Four of the remaining sections involve substantive criminal offenses. . . .

Finally, [the "Three Strikes Act"] contains two administrative provisions. Section 11 requires the clerk of the court to transmit to the appropriate United States immigration officer records pertaining to aliens who are convicted of or who enter a plea to any crime. Section 12 requires the Governor to publish the penalties contained in the Act.

II. Facts and Procedural Background

Franklin was convicted of armed robbery and resisting arrest based on acts that occurred after the effective date of [the "Three Strikes Act"]. He received a sentence of forty years in prison as a habitual felony offender, pursuant to [a law that] had been amended by [the "Three Strikes Act"]. Franklin's prior criminal history consisted of one felony conviction (possession of cocaine) and one felony for which adjudication of guilt was withheld (burglary of a dwelling). Prior to [the "Three Strikes Act"], an offense for which adjudication of guilt had been withheld would not have qualified as a predicate for habitual offender. . . .

Franklin appealed [to Florida's Third District Court of Appeal]. While his appeal was pending, [Florida's] Second District held in *Taylor v. State*, 818 So. 2d 544 (Fla. 2d DCA 2002), that [the "Three Strikes Act"] violated the single subject requirement of article III, section 6. In [Franklin's appeal] the Third District held that [the "Three Strikes Act"] did not violate the constitutional requirement of a single subject. The Third District also certified conflict with *Taylor*. . . .

. . . As the [conflicting] cases from the district courts illustrate, the methods for determining both the single subject of an act and those matters that are properly connected to that subject vary. We take this opportunity to review our jurisprudence in this area of the law and clarify the single subject analysis.

IV. Single Subject Rule Analysis

A. Applicable Law

1. The Purpose of the Single Subject Clause

Currently, forty-three states have some form of single subject clause applicable to legislation contained in their state constitutions. In Florida, the single subject clause has been part of our state constitution since 1868 . . . and is presently set forth [as follows]:

> Every law shall embrace but one subject and matter properly connected therewith, and the subject shall be briefly expressed in the title.

Art. III, §6, Fla. Const.

Thus, the single subject clause contains three requirements. First, each law shall "embrace" only "one subject." Second, the law may include any matter that is "properly connected" with the subject. The third requirement, related to the first, is that the subject shall be "briefly expressed in the title." . . . [T]he purposes of the single subject provision [are]: (1) to prevent hodgepodge or "log rolling" legislation, i.e., putting two unrelated matters in one act; (2) to prevent surprise or fraud by means of provisions in bills of which the title gave no intimation, and which might therefore be overlooked and carelessly and unintentionally adopted; and (3) to fairly apprise the people of the subjects of legislation that are being considered, in order that they may have opportunity of being heard thereon.

In *Colonial Inv. Co. v. Nolan*, 100 Fla. 1349, 131 So. 178 (1930), this Court explained the historical backdrop for the constitutional mandate:

> It had become quite common for legislative bodies to embrace in the same bill incongruous matters having no relation to each other, or to the subject

specified in the title[. B]y [these] means, measures were often adopted without attracting attention. And frequently such distinct subjects, affecting diverse interests, were combined in order to unite members who favored either in support of all. And the failure to indicate in the title the object of the bill often resulted in members voting ignorantly for measures which they would not knowingly have approved. And not only were the members thus misled, but the public also; and legislative provisions were sometimes pushed through which would have been made odious by popular discussion and remonstrance if their pendency had been seasonably demonstrated by the title of the bill.

Id. at 179. In fact, as we observed in *State v. Bryan*, 50 Fla. 293, 39 So. 929 (1905),

[n]early all the states having Constitutions of recent adoption have incorporated therein provisions in nearly identical language, and their courts agree as to the purpose of such provisions. They also agree that the provision refers to the subject-matter of the legislation, and not to a single purpose or end sought to be accomplished. Its purpose was to avoid the confusion incident to the evil which had grown out of 'omnibus' legislation.

Id. at 961 (quoting *Gibson v. State*, 16 Fla. 291, 299, 1877 WL 2625 (1877)).

Extant in our constitution since 1868, the single subject clause is a direct expression of the people's intent to provide a limitation on the Legislature's power to enact laws. The judiciary's obligation is to apply the constitutional limitation to legislation that violates the constitution. See generally *Sebring Airport Authority v. McIntyre*, 783 So. 2d 238, 244 n.5 (Fla. 2001) ("To the judges belongs the power of expounding the laws; and although in the discharge of that duty they may render a law inoperative by declaring it unconstitutional, it does not arise from any supremacy which the judiciary possesses over the Legislature, but from the supremacy of the Constitution over both.") . . .

2. Standard of Review

When courts are called upon to assess legislation for compliance with article III, section 6, the standard of review is highly deferential. "[T]he general disposition of the courts [is] to construe the constitutional provision liberally, rather than to embarrass legislation by a construction whose strictness is unnecessary to the accomplishment of the beneficial purposes for which it has been adopted." . . . [T]o overcome the presumption in favor of constitutionality, the single subject violation must occur beyond a reasonable doubt. . . .

3. Defining the Single Subject

The key to determining whether a legislative enactment violates the single subject clause of the Florida Constitution is the method by which the court defines the "single subject" of the legislation and the analysis employed to determine matters "properly connected therewith." . . .

In determining the single subject, we start with the basic principle that "the subject is the one that is expressed in the title of the act." . . . Indeed, the constitutional provision requires that the subject be briefly expressed in the title.

For purposes of single subject analysis, every law published in the Laws of Florida has both a short title, i.e., "An act relating to . . . ," and a full title, which begins with the chapter law number and ends with "providing an effective date," and encompasses the short title. . . .

This Court has adhered to the presumption that an act complies with article III, section 6, even when the full title of an act is lengthy. . . . [T]he precise language of the constitution itself mandates that the single subject be "briefly expressed in the title." Although the full title may be as lengthy as the Legislature chooses, the actual expression of the single subject within the full title must be briefly stated. Therefore . . . the single subject of an act is derived from the short title, i.e., the language immediately following the customary phrase "an act relating to" and preceding the indexing of the act's provisions. In so doing, we specifically note that although many acts may contain a citation name by which either the entire act or portions of it may be identified, the citation name is not synonymous with the single subject.

This relatively simple method for defining the one subject of an act is supported by our precedent. Indeed, we have consistently stated that only the subject, not matters connected to the subject, must be expressed in the title. . . . In order to comply with the requirement that the subject of a law be briefly expressed in the title, the title need not be an index of all the features of the legislation. In other words, it is not constitutionally necessary to index the provisions contained in the body of the act in the title. . . . However, the full title nonetheless must be "so worded as not to mislead a person of average intelligence as to the scope of the enactment and [be] sufficient to put that person on notice and cause him to inquire into the body of the statute itself."

Our determination that the single subject of an act can be found in the short title is subject to the following caveat: the title of an act may be general, "so long as it is not made a cover to legislation incongruous in itself." In other words, the short title of the legislation cannot be so broad as to purportedly cover unrelated topics, and thus provide no real guidance as to what the body of the act contains. Indeed, allowing an overly broad short title to become the single subject runs the risk of permitting logrolling and hodgepodge or omnibus legislation. . . . [I]f the Legislature's short title is suspect for being overly broad, a court should look to the remainder of the act and the history of the legislative process to determine if the act actually contains a single subject or violates the constitution by encompassing more than one subject.

Ordinarily, determining the single subject of an act by reference to the short title will be a straightforward process. The more difficult analysis is whether the various provisions are "properly connected" to the single subject. We now turn to the analysis to be used when evaluating the "properly connected" question.

4. Properly Connected

As stated above, the second requirement of the single subject clause in article III, section 6 mandates that all provisions in the body of the act be "properly connected" to the single subject. . . .

A review of our jurisprudence reveals that we have defined a "proper" connection in various ways. We have described a proper connection as one that is "natural or logical.". . . . We have stated that whether a connection is proper will depend on "common sense." . . . We have also stated that if the provision is "necessary" to the subject, "fairly and naturally germane" to the subject, or promotes the purposes of the legislation as set forth in the subject, the provision may be regarded as properly connected. As we explained in surveying the law to date as of 1957,

> if a matter is germane to or reasonably connected with the expressed title of the act, it may be incorporated within the act without being in violation of [the single subject provision] of our constitution. Provisions which are necessary incidents to, or tend to make effective or promote the object and purpose of the legislation included in the subject expressed in the title of the act may be regarded as matters properly connected with the subject thereof. . . . In determining if matters are properly connected with the subject, the test is whether such provisions are fairly and naturally germane to the subject of the act, or are such as are necessary incidents to or tend to make effective or promote the objects and purposes of legislation included in the subject.

Canova, 94 So. 2d at 184 (citations omitted).

More recently, we explained that a connection between the subject and the provision is proper if a "reasonable explanation" exists as to why the Legislature chose to join the provision to the legislative act. . . .

After reviewing these various methods of defining a "proper connection," we take this opportunity to set forth the correct test to be applied when determining whether a connection between a provision in the act and the act's subject is "proper" within the meaning of the single subject clause: A connection between a provision and the subject is proper (1) if the connection is natural or logical, or (2) if there is a reasonable explanation for how the provision is (a) necessary to the subject or (b) tends to make effective or promote the objects and purposes of legislation included in the subject.

In setting forth this test, we clarify that there is a difference between the subject of the act that is briefly stated in the title and the object of the act. Simply stated, "The subject is the matter to which an act relates; the object, the purpose to be accomplished." . . . In this regard, we caution that the "accomplishment of several 'purposes' may be logically embraced in one 'subject' so long as all such purposes are germane to . . . the expressed general subject." . . . The term 'subject' is broader than the word 'object,' as one subject may contain many objects." . . . The purposes of an act may be instructive in determining whether there is a reasonable explanation for the inclusion of a specific provision in the chapter law. However, the purposes of an act cannot be used to either define or expand the single subject. The single subject clause contained in article III, section 6 "refers to the subject-matter of the legislation, and not to a single purpose or end sought to be accomplished." . . .

. . . [I]n determining whether a reasonable explanation exists for the connection between a specific provision and the single subject, the court may consider the citation name, the full title, the preamble, and the provisions in the body of the act. . . . However, if, after examining the act in its entirety, we cannot discern a "reasonable explanation" for the inclusion of a seemingly disparate provision, we will look to the history of the legislative process to determine how the challenged provision was added to the act. In other words, this Court has looked to the legislative history of the enactment to buttress our conclusion that the provision is not properly connected. . . .

. . . [P]articular combinations of various statutory provisions may not be properly connected. To date, this Court has regarded two such combinations with caution: substantive changes to the criminal law that are contained in acts that do not predominately address the substantive criminal law, and chapter laws that combine civil and criminal provisions. However, other improperly combined provisions may run afoul of the single subject clause as well. For example, we recently found that a provision concerning the assignment of bad check debts to a private debt collector had "no natural or logical connection" to an act's subject, which was driver's licenses, operation of motor vehicles, and vehicle registrations.

There is no bright line rule this Court can create to determine whether a connection is proper — that is, whether the connection is natural or logical, or if a reasonable explanation exists for how the provision is necessary to the subject or tends to make effective or promote the objects and purposes of legislation included in the subject. Nonetheless, we examine [the "Three Strikes Act"] against the backdrop of this jurisprudence.

B. [The "Three Strikes Act"]

. . . [O]ur resolution of this case flows from our highly deferential standard of review in this area of the law — that every reasonable doubt should be resolved in favor of a law's constitutionality. . . .

The short title of [the "Three Strikes Act"] is "An act relating to sentencing." The citation name is the "Three-Strike Violent Felony Offender Act." The full title is lengthy, running two pages and almost one thousand words. As we have explained, the constitution requires that the subject be briefly expressly in the title and we give considerable deference to the Legislature's selection of the title. Based on our determination that ordinarily the subject will be found in the short title, we conclude that the subject [the "Three Strikes Act"] is sentencing. . . .

We now turn to the controverted issue of whether sections 11 and 13 [of the "Three Strikes Act"] are properly connected to sentencing. The Second District in *Taylor* determined that sections 11 and 13 lack a proper connection. The test we utilize is whether there is a natural or logical connection to sentencing, or whether a reasonable explanation exists for how these provisions are either necessary to sentencing or tend to make effective or promote the purposes of the sentencing legislation. . . .

We first address section 11, which provides that the clerk of the court shall furnish to the INS officers the charging document, judgment, and sentence "in every case in which an alien is convicted of a felony or misdemeanor or enters a plea of guilty or nolo contendre to any felony or misdemeanor charge." Under the language of the provision, this shall be done after the alien offender's sentencing proceeding.

We conclude that there is a natural or logical and thus proper connection between the requirements of section 11 that sentences of non-citizen offenders be provided to INS and the Act's subject of sentencing, in that section 11 is a post-sentencing measure. Our conclusion that the connection is proper is buttressed by the fact that in requiring the transmission of sentences to the INS, section 11 also promotes the Act's purpose of protecting the public from persons sentenced as serious or repeat violent offenders. . . . [S]ection 11 aids in the removal of violent alien offenders from the country after sentence completion. . . . Thus, there is also a reasonable explanation why the Legislature would include a provision that facilitates the removal of non-citizens who are serious or repeat violent offenders after sentence completion in an Act whose subject is sentencing and whose purposes include the use of sentencing to protect the public from this class of criminals.

In reaching this conclusion, we are not persuaded by Franklin's argument that the fact that the section applies to all persons who receive a criminal sentence, whether felony or misdemeanor, violent or nonviolent, first offense or fiftieth, renders this provision in violation of article III, section 6. The inquiry is not whether the section solely relates to the purpose of protecting the public from violent and repeat offenders, but rather whether the section is properly connected to the single subject of sentencing. Accordingly, the inclusion of section 11 does not result in a violation of the single subject clause of article III, section 6.

We next turn to section 13, which expands the substantive crime of burglary to specifically add "railroad vehicle" to the definition of conveyance. The Second District found the relationship between the substantive crime of burglary and sentencing too "tenuous, so dependent on the happenstance of individual cases, that it simply cannot be characterized as natural or logical." *Taylor*, 818 So. 2d at 549. In contrast, the Third and Fourth Districts determined that including section 13 does not violate the single subject clause because the section expands the definition of the crime of armed burglary, which is an offense included in section 775.084, the habitual offender sentencing statute. See *Franklin*, 836 So. 2d at 1113–1114; *Hernandez-Molina*, 860 So. 2d at 490.

We agree with the Third and Fourth Districts. The proper connection between the expanded definition of burglary and sentencing is found in the fact that armed burglary is one of the qualifying offenses for a harsher sentence in the Act. In broadening the definition of conveyance in section 810.11, Florida Statutes, which previously encompassed a "railroad car" but not a "railroad vehicle," the Legislature ensured that a serious crime against a person inside a railroad vehicle (to wit, a locomotive) will be punished accordingly. See *Hernandez-Molina*, 860 So. 2d at 490.28 Thus, there is a proper connection to sentencing in that section 13 makes effective one of the purposes included within the subject — imposing harsher sentences on violent offenders. Considering that the purpose of the Act is to protect the public from serious and repeat violent offenders, a reasonable explanation exists for including this substantive section within an Act whose subject is sentencing.

In determining that section 13 did not relate to sentencing and therefore violates article III, section 6, the Second District in *Taylor* and Judge Cope in his dissenting opinion in *Franklin* relied, in part, on the fact that section 13 substantively amended the criminal law. See *Taylor*, 818 So. 2d at 549; *Franklin*, 836 So. 2d at 1120 (Cope, J., dissenting). However, we do not consider this fact to be determinative in this case.

In contrast to other acts that we found in violation of the single subject rule because they combined the creation of new crimes with other disparate provisions, in this case, section 13 is one of four sections of the Act that relate to and amend the substantive criminal law. We note that section 7 creates a new category of offender, a repeat sexual batterer; section 8 adds references to the new statute defining "repeat sexual batterer" to the sexual battery statute, section 794.011, wherein "sexual battery" is defined; and section 9 modifies the drug trafficking statute to allow prosecution on the basis of the number of cannabis plants which a person possesses, sells, or delivers, and modifies the weight benchmarks for prosecution. Therefore, similar to section 13, sections 7 and 9 amend substantive crimes. We note that both the *Taylor* court and Judge Cope in his dissent determined that section 9 was logically related to sentencing because the modified crime was punishable by a mandatory minimum term created by the Act. See *Taylor*, 818 So. 2d at 549; *Franklin*, 836 So. 2d at 1120 (Cope, J., dissenting). The same is true of the new "repeat sexual batterer" offense classification created in section 7.

This reasoning is equally applicable to section 13. Although not every person charged under the modification to the burglary statute contained in section 13 will be subject to a mandatory minimum sentence, the fact remains that armed burglary, which is an aggravated form of the crime modified by section 13, is subject to an enhanced sentence under this Act. Therefore, as with sections 7 and 9, there is a proper connection between section 13 and the single subject of sentencing.

For the reasons stated above, we conclude that sections 11 and 13 are properly connected to the single subject of sentencing. [The "Three Strikes Act"] does not violate the single subject clause of article III, section 6 of the Florida Constitution. Accordingly, we approve the Third District's decision in *Franklin*, which is before us for review. We also approve the Fourth District's decision in *Hernandez-Molina* and disapprove the Second District's decision in *Taylor*.

It is so ordered.

Notes and Questions to Consider:

1. Two considerations addressed by the Single Subject Rule are "logrolling" and legislative integrity. Is this a difference between Florida's legislature and the U.S. Congress? As a famous example, consider Congress's 2010 passage of the Patient Protection and Affordable Care Act, colloquially known as Obamacare. The U.S. Supreme Court noted that the Affordable Care Act contained many topics unrelated to the subject of affordable health care:

> The ACA is over 900 pages long. Its regulations include requirements ranging from a break time and secluded place at work for nursing mothers, . . . to displays of nutritional content at chain restaurants. . . . The Act raises billions of dollars in taxes and fees, including exactions imposed on high-income taxpayers . . . and tanning booths. . . . It spends government money on, among other things, the study of how to spend less government money. . . . And it includes a number of provisions that provide benefits to the State of a particular legislator. . . .

> Such provisions validate the Senate Majority Leader's statement, "I don't know if there is a senator that doesn't have something in this bill that was important to them. . . . [And] if they don't have something in it important to them, then it doesn't speak well of them.["] . . . (quoting Sen. Reid). Often, a minor provision will be the price paid for support of a major provision. . . .

> . . . [T]he ACA . . . includes not only many provisions that are ancillary to its central provisions but also many that are entirely unrelated—hitched on because it was a quick way to get them passed despite opposition, or because their proponents could exact their enactment as the quid pro quo for their needed support. . . . [W]e are confronted with . . . a so-called "Christmas tree," a law to which many nongermane ornaments have been attached. . . . We have no reliable basis for knowing which pieces of the Act would have passed on their own.

Nat'l Fed'n of Indep. Bus. v. Sebelius, 567 U.S. 519, 704 (2012). If the U.S. Constitution had a Single Subject Rule like Florida's constitution, would federal laws like Obamacare have the characteristics described by the U.S. Supreme Court? Is that good or bad?

2. Exceptions to the Single Subject Rule include corollaries and a well-drafted title. To what extent do the exceptions eliminate the rule?

3. Are there "suspect classes," so-to-speak, in the jurisprudence of the Single Subject Rule? Consider this statement from the *Taylor* opinion above: "Particular combinations of various statutory provisions may not be properly connected. To date, this Court has regarded two such combinations with caution: substantive changes to the criminal law that are contained in acts that do not predominately address the substantive criminal law, and chapter[s] that combine civil and criminal provisions."

7. Amending Existing Laws

Once the Florida Legislature or the legislative body of a county, city, town, or village enact a law, can that law be changed later? Yes, but special requirements apply, such as this one from Article III of Florida's constitution:

SECTION 6. Laws.— ... No law shall be revised or amended by reference to its title only. Laws to revise or amend shall set out in full the revised or amended act, section, subsection or paragraph of a subsection.

Although this requirement appears in the article of Florida's constitution discussing Florida's legislature, it also applies to lawmaking by Florida's counties, cities, towns, and villages as explained in FLORIDA MUNICIPAL LAW AND PRACTICE:

The Florida Constitution says that a law may not be amended solely by reference to its title. This requires that any law amending an existing law must set out in full the complete text of the newly amended law as it will read after amendment. It is not enough to simply state what is amended. Instead, the old law with its new amendments incorporated into it must be printed out in its entirety. If a statutory enactment is complete and intelligible in itself, without the necessity of referring to the books to relate it to an amended statute in order to ascertain the meaning of an amendment, then the section of the Constitution concerning the amendment of a law is satisfied; but if the amendatory enactment is not a complete, coherent, and intelligible act, or if it necessitates separate research and analysis of the statute which is being amended, it does not meet the requirements of the constitutional provision.

Because of this state constitutional requirement, neither a state statute nor a local ordinance is effectively amended or revised simply by reference to its title. Instead, laws or ordinances intended to revise or amend are only effective when they set out in full the revised or amended act, section, subsection, or paragraph of a subsection.

For this reason, it is invalid to reenact a law simply by passing an amendment that does nothing more than state that the soon-to-expire law's expiration clause is stricken. For example, an amendment to reenact a law is invalid where a section of an original act provided for the expiration of the act by a certain date ... and an amendatory act simply stated that such section "is amended to read: 'The provisions of this act shall be in full force and effect until terminated by law.'"

This applies to all laws or ordinances that assume, in terms, to revise, alter, or amend some prior act or section thereof.

Patrick John McGinley, FLORIDA MUNICIPAL LAW AND PRACTICE § 3:6 (2017-2018 ed.). What if a bill is intended to create a new law that does not amend an old law but instead replaces it in its entirety? That was the question addressed in the following century-old Florida lawyer applicant case called *In re: De Woody*, 113 So. 677,

678–80 (Fla. 1927). At this point in Florida's history, Florida's constitution was not an impediment to the legislative branch enacting laws regulating the admission of lawyers to the Florida Bar. We examine this case today for the procedure, not the substance of the lawmaking. Putting aside the substance of the law at issue in *In re De Woody*, this case remains instructive on the issue of what procedure is required when a new law replaces an old law.

In re: De Woody

Supreme Court of Florida, 1927
113 So. 677

Charles F. De Woody moves for his admission to the bar. [He was denied admission by] the State Board of Law Examiners, [which] provides, amongst other things, for the method of examination and admission to the bar of applicants.

The movant contends that [the statute creating the Board of Law Examiners is] inoperative, because it violates . . . article 3, section 16, of [Florida's] Constitution, that 'no law shall be amended or revised by reference to its title only, but in such case the act, as revised, or section, as amended, shall be reenacted and published at length,' was not observed in the passage of [the statute creating the Board of Law Examiners.]

. . . [The movant is correct that the statute creating the Board of Law Examiners] contains no express repealing clause, nor does it in terms undertake to amend any other statute, though its provisions may be in conflict with certain prior statutes, thereby, and to the extent of the manifest inconsistency or repugnancy, effecting the repeal by implication of such prior statutes.

This court has previously held that:

> It was never intended by the Constitution that every law which would affect some previous statute of varied provisions on the same subject should set out the statute, or statutes, so affected at full length.

> The constitutional provision forbidding the amendment or revision of a law by reference to its title only, and requiring the act as revised, or section as amended, to be re-enacted and published at length, does not apply to amendments or repeals of statutes that are affected by implication, but applies only to laws that assume in terms to revise, alter, or amend some particular prior act or section of an act.

Van Pelt v. Hilliard, 78 So. 693 (1918).

. . . The Legislature is presumed to have known what the existing law was when [the statute creating the Board of Law Examiners] was enacted. It is also presumed to have known what the effect of the enactment . . . would be upon the existing statutes on the subject. The journals of the House and Senate disclose that [the statute creating the Board of Law Examiners] was carefully considered by committees composed of members of the bar. . . .

None of the objections here urged by the movant to the constitutional validity of [the statute creating the Board of Law Examiners] are well taken. The motion must be and is hereby denied.

———————

Notes and Questions to Consider:

1. Does *In re: De Woody* mean that a Florida lawmaking body need not <u>underline</u> the text in a bill that is new language, and need not ~~strike through~~ the text that is to be deleted from an existing law? Consider the following from Sutherland Statutory Construction:

> To enforce the constitutional limitation that no act shall be amended by reference to its title only, but the act as amended shall be set out and published at length, courts have upheld legislation and avoided classifying an act as an amendment wherever possible. In litigation, the issue of compliance with the constitutional provision generally arises where a statute does not purport to amend any prior act, since the legislature usually complies with the limitation when a statute purports to amend a prior statute. To sustain legislation, courts have tested the amendatory character of an act by its form. Thus, if an act does not purport to amend a prior act, either directly or by inserting or striking words, it is not an amendatory act within the constitutional limitation. . . .

> Also as a result of this policy to uphold legislation, several classes of statutes that do not purport to amend but which in fact change the law are recognized by courts and held not to be amendments within the constitutional limitations. An implied amendment, an act complete within itself, an implied repeal, an express repeal, a supplementary act, and an act adopting the provisions of another statute by reference are not treated as amendments within the constitutional limitations.

Amendment of an Act by Reference to Its Title — Acts Amendatory in Form, 1A Sutherland Statutory Construction § 22:17 (7th ed.).

2. Are "reference statutes" permitted under Florida's constitution? Stated somewhat differently, can a new Florida law adopt by reference the terms or procedures of an existing law without copying-and-pasting the existing law into the text of the new law? Consider the following from Florida Jurisprudence:

> Enactments that refer to other statutes and make them applicable to the subject of the new legislation are called "reference statutes." . . . A statute incorporating the provisions of other statutes by reference and adoption thereby avoids encumbering the statute books with unnecessary repetition. Such a procedure is not improper. A code or compilation of laws need not be set out in the statute adopting it. . . .

Where a statute adopts a part of, or all of, another statute by a specific and descriptive reference thereto, the effect is the same as if the provisions adopted were written into the adopting statute.

Reference Statutes, 48A Fla. Jur 2d Statutes § 11 (Mar. 2019 update).

8. Title Requirements

Florida's constitution, at Article III, requires the following:

SECTION 6. Laws.—[For e]very law . . . the subject shall be briefly expressed in the title.

In addition to this phrase in Florida's constitution, Florida's Municipal Home Rule Powers Act contain identical requirements for Florida's counties, cities, towns, and villages. *See* Florida Statutes section 166.041. Together, these requirements mean that "for each and every law—including every local ordinance or resolution—Art. III, § 6, Fla. Const. requires that the subject of the law, ordinance, or resolution must be clearly stated in the title." Patrick John McGinley, Florida Municipal Law and Practice § 3:7 (2017-2018 ed.). Stated somewhat differently, the act, "ordinance or resolution may include every matter germane, incidental, or subsidiary to, and not inconsistent with or foreign to, the general subject of the law as expressed in its title." *Id.*

What is the "title" of a law? It is not the "citation name," which is the short name given by a law for use in citing to that law. For example, Florida Statutes chapter 166 tells us that "[t]his chapter shall be known and may be cited as the 'Municipal Home Rule Powers Act'" but that phrase is its citation name and is not its title. Florida's supreme court, in *Franklin v. State*, 887 So. 2d 1063 (Fla. 2004), tells us exactly what is meant by the "title" and makes the following observations regarding the Florida Legislature's use of titles:

[E]very law published in the Laws of Florida has both a short title, i.e., "An act relating to . . . ," and a full title, which begins with the chapter law number and ends with "providing an effective date," and encompasses the short title. *Cf. State v. Kaufman*, 430 So. 2d 904, 907 (Fla. 1983). "[F]ormerly the title of an act was not considered a part of it and, anciently, acts had no title prefixed at all. . . . [" *State ex rel. Flink v.*] *Canova*, 94 So. 2d [181,] 183–84 [(Fla. 1957)]. . . .

Over the years, full titles have varied in length, some being relatively brief and others spanning pages. . . . Although article III, section 6 [of Florida's constitution] imposes the restriction that the subject be "briefly expressed in the title," we have remained deferential to the Legislature's choice to craft a title to an act with few words or many. Indeed, we noted as early as 1905 that although a lengthy full title may be "unduly drawn out . . . , cumbersome, and awkwardly worded," its length alone will not invalidate an act. . . . As noted above, in recent years full titles have consistently begun with the phrase "an act relating to" and ended with "providing an effective date."

Franklin v. State, 887 So. 2d 1063, 1074–75 (Fla. 2004).

Notes and Questions to Consider:

1. Do prior topics previously discussed in this text contribute to the fact that the Florida Legislature uses such lengthy, detailed titles when such verbosity is not constitutionally required? For instance, recall from our discussion of the legislative branch that the constitutionally required first reading of a bill is accomplished by publication in the chamber's journal of the bill's title. Also recall that, "[d]espite the Single Subject Rule discussed above, a statute will not be unconstitutional for embracing more than one subject if the title is sufficiently broad to connect it with the general subject matter of the enactment." Patrick John McGinley, Florida Municipal Law and Practice § 3:7 (2017-2018 ed.). Likewise, recall from our discussion of the canons of construction that "[o]ne indicator of a legislature's intent is the title of the law enacting the statute, ordinance, or resolution. The title of an act is not part of the basic act but . . . may be considered in determining the intent of the act. . . ." *Id.*

2. Lengthy titles may be the norm but a short title is not necessarily unconstitutional. Case law precedent holds that "the title need not contain a detailed explanation of every provision found in that title's law. So long as the matters addressed in the act are fairly related to the subject described in the title, the title is constitutionally sufficient." Patrick John McGinley, Florida Municipal Law and Practice § 3:7 (2017-2018 ed.).

9. Zoning Laws

Florida's supreme court holds that "[z]oning is a legislative function which reposes ultimately in the governing authority of a municipality." *Gulf & E. Dev. Corp. v. City of Fort Lauderdale*, 354 So. 2d 57, 59 (Fla. 1978). Therefore, in Florida, zoning laws are the province of counties, cities, towns, and villages but not the Florida Legislature. Any zoning law enacted by Florida's legislature would be invalid.

As to the validity of local zoning laws, both the U.S. Supreme Court and Florida's supreme court adopted a highly deferential standard of judicial review early in the history of local zoning. The U.S. Supreme Court held in *Village of Euclid, Ohio v. Ambler Realty Co.*, 272 U.S. 365, 388 (1926), that "[i]f the validity of the legislative classification for zoning purposes be fairly debatable, the legislative judgment must be allowed to control." Florida's supreme court adopted this same "fairly debatable" rule of law in *City of Miami Beach v. Ocean & Inland Co.*, 3 So. 2d 364 (1941). But see *Bd. of County Com'rs of Brevard County v. Snyder*, 627 So. 2d 469, 471 (Fla. 1993) (granting less deference to requests for rezoning).

Despite the deference to zoning laws granted by federal and Florida constitutional law, Florida's Growth Management Act requires local governments to enact a Comprehensive Plan. So local lawmaking is invalid if inconsistent with that Comprehensive Plan. Each county, city, town, or village must create and then gain the approval of the Florida Department of Community Affairs for a Comprehensive Plan that includes "principles, guidelines, and standards for the orderly and balanced future economic, social, physical, environmental, and fiscal development" of the local government's jurisdictional area. At the minimum, the local plan must include elements covering future land use; capital improvements generally; sanitary sewer, solid waste, drainage, potable water, and natural ground water aquifer protection specifically; conservation; recreation and open space; housing; traffic circulation; intergovernmental coordination; coastal management (for local government in the coastal zone); and mass transit (for local jurisdictions with 50,000 or more people). *See* Florida Statutes section 163.3177. In summary, a "comprehensive plan is intended to provide for the future use of land, which contemplates [achieving] a gradual and ordered growth." *Bd. of County Com'rs of Brevard County v. Snyder*, 627 So. 2d 469, 475 (Fla. 1993). The Comprehensive Plan results in a "zoning map."

Proposed ordinances changing the zoning map and affecting a parcel or parcels of land fewer than 10 acres in size require individualized notice before enactment. "A failure to strictly comply with the following notice requirements will invalidate the local zoning ordinance." Patrick John McGinley, Florida Municipal Law and Practice § 3:8 (2017-2018 ed.) The clerk of the governing body must notify by mail each real property owner whose land is affected and whose address is known by reference to the latest ad valorem tax records. That notice must be given at least 30 days prior to the public hearing. *See* Florida Statutes sections 125.66 and 166.041. This results in an increased requirement for notice before enactment of such a zoning map change as compared to the enactment of other laws or ordinances that do not require such individualized notice.

Not every law that affects land is a zoning ordinance. Consider the facts and holding of *City of Sarasota v. 35 S. Lemon, Inc.*, 722 So. 2d 268 (Fla. 2d DCA 1998).

City of Sarasota v. 35 S. Lemon, Inc.

Second District Court of Appeal of Florida, 1998
722 So. 2d 268

The City of Sarasota (the City) appeals the partial final summary judgment in favor of 35 S. Lemon, Inc. . . . The trial court determined that the City's Permitting Ordinance and Noise Ordinance were not enacted properly because the ordinances regulated land development and were subject to review by the City's local planning agency. We conclude that the Noise Ordinance regulates conduct and is not subject to review by the City's local planning agency; therefore, we reverse the partial final summary judgment.

In 1997, the City adopted the Noise Ordinance by amending chapter 20 of its City Code. This amendment affected the appellees because their restaurant and nightclub were zoned C–CBD.

The City also enacted the Permitting Ordinance on the same day as the Noise Ordinance. . . . These code changes adversely affected the music provided by the appellees at their restaurant and nightclub.

Both the Noise Ordinance and the Permitting Ordinance were adopted pursuant to the procedures set forth in [Florida's Municipal Home Rule Powers Act codified at] section 166.041(3)(a), Florida Statutes (1995). After the ordinances were adopted, the appellees were cited with several violations of the Noise Ordinance. The . . . trial court granted partial summary judgment finding that the Noise Ordinance was void because it was not reviewed by the City's local planning agency [which must review all zoning ordinances]. . . . The partial summary judgment further enjoined the City from enforcing the Noise Ordinance.

In the order, the trial court sets forth the definition of "land development regulation" as defined in section 163.3164(23), Florida Statutes (1995), and emphasized that portion of the statute which provides that a land development regulation includes "the making of any material change in the use of or appearance of any structure or land." The court then cited this court's opinion in *Lee County v. Lippi*, 693 So. 2d 686 (Fla. 2d DCA 1997), in support for finding that the Noise Ordinance was a land development regulation subject to review by the planning agency. We conclude that the trial court incorrectly applied *Lippi* to the facts in this case.

In *Lippi*, this court was asked to determine whether two ordinances were properly enacted under similar facts to this case. The first ordinance prohibited the use of water craft within a certain area of the shoreline. The second ordinance regulated the location for personal water craft rentals. This court determined that the first ordinance was "patently a regulatory ordinance, not subject to the review requirements" of the statute. *See id.* at 689. This court then determined that the second ordinance regulating the placement of rental businesses, which required some businesses to close and relocate, sufficiently impacted a previously permitted land use and should have been reviewed by the local planning agency. *See id.*

If the Noise Ordinance is a land development regulation within the meaning of section 163.3164(23), Florida Statutes (1995), then the ordinance was improperly enacted because the City failed to submit the proposed ordinance for review by the planning agency. If the ordinance is an attempt to regulate conduct, it is exempt from this review process. Here, the appellees' business is still able to operate according to its previous use. It simply has to comply with the noise level requirements. This case is more concerned with regulating conduct rather than with regulating land development. *See T.J.R. Holding Co., Inc. v. Alachua County*, 617 So. 2d 798 (Fla. 1st DCA 1993) (ordinance which prohibited nudity and sexual conduct, or simulated sexual conduct, within establishments serving alcoholic beverages, was not a land-use regulation).

We conclude that the Noise Ordinance is a regulatory ordinance which is not subject to the review requirements of chapter 163. Accordingly, we reverse the trial court's partial summary judgment and remand this case to the trial court to resolve other matters still pending in this case.

———————

Notes and Questions to Consider:

1. This case was not the end of the City of Sarasota's attempts to regulate amplified music. "Again, in 2000, the city imposed an absolute ban on amplified noise within certain zoning districts during specified hours of the day and night. Luckily for the city, the court struck down this ordinance, finding that the First Amendment prohibits cities from completely banning amplified music." Ashley Suarez, *The Great Mash-Up Debate: A Holistic Approach to Controlling Noise Pollution in Florida's Downtown Districts*, 14 Ave Maria L. Rev. 222, 230–31 (2016).

2. A Florida city commission enacts an ordinance prohibiting new building construction in the Central Business District greater than two stories high. Was it required to provide individualized notice by mail to all landowners 30 days prior to enacting this ordinance?

3. A Florida city commission enacts an ordinance prohibiting nudity within establishments in the Central Business District that sell or serve alcohol. Was it required to provide individualized notice by mail to all landowners 30 days prior?

10. Inconsistency between State and Local Law

Recall the potential for overlap in the eligible subject matter for lawmaking by the Florida Legislature and local legislatures. Florida's legislature, its counties, its cities, its towns, and its villages can enact ordinances on many of the exact same topics as one another. This is true even if one is within the territorial jurisdiction of another. With more than one legislating body enacting laws on many of the same topics at the same time and over the same territory, inconsistencies may arise.

Perhaps in order to address this problem of inconsistency, Florida's Municipal Home Rule Powers Act gives counties and municipalities broad power to govern "to the extent *not inconsistent* with general or special law." So a Florida county, city, town, or village would need a source of legislative power other than the Municipal Home Rule Powers Act in order to enact a law that is inconsistent. An inconsistent law would fall unless something other than the Municipal Home Rule Powers Act enables such a law. But when is a local law inconsistent?

Generally speaking, inconsistency occurs in one of two ways: via preemption or via conflict of law. Florida's supreme court explains these two ways as follows:

> First, a county [or other municipal corporation] cannot legislate in a field if the subject area has been preempted to the State. *See City of Hollywood v.*

Mulligan, 934 So. 2d 1238, 1243 (Fla. 2006). "Preemption essentially takes a topic or a field in which local government might otherwise establish appropriate local laws and reserves that topic for regulation exclusively by the legislature." *Id.* (quoting *Phantom of Clearwater[, Inc. v. Pinellas County]*, 894 So. 2d [1011] , 1018 [(Fla. 2d DCA 2005)]). Second, in a field where both the State and local government can legislate concurrently, a county [or other municipal corporation] cannot enact an ordinance that directly conflicts with a state statute.

Orange County v. Singh, 289 So. 2d 668 (Fla. 2019). Let us first discuss inconsistency via a conflict of law, and then inconsistency via other types of preemption.

a. Inconsistency Via Conflict of Law

This type of inconsistency exists when the law impermissibly conflicts with a higher sovereign's law. Florida's supreme court explains that:

There is conflict between a local ordinance and a state statute when the local ordinance cannot coexist with the state statute. *See City of Hollywood*, 934 So. 2d at 1246; *see also State ex rel. Dade County v. Brautigam*, 224 So. 2d 688, 692 (Fla. 1969) (explaining that "inconsistent" as used in article VIII, section 6(f) of the Florida Constitution "means contradictory in the sense of legislative provisions which cannot coexist"). Stated otherwise, "[t]he test for conflict is whether 'in order to comply with one provision, a violation of the other is required.'" *Browning v. Sarasota Alliance for Fair Elections, Inc.*, 968 So. 2d 637, 649 (Fla. 2d DCA 2007). . . .

Orange County v. Singh, 289 So. 2d 668 (Fla. 2019). Although this quotation from Florida's supreme court addresses specifically a conflict of laws between the state and a county, the same rule of law applies to a conflict between a county and another municipal corporation such as a city, town, or village. As FLORIDA MUNICIPAL LAW AND PRACTICE explains:

County and municipal ordinances are inferior to laws of the state and must not conflict with any controlling provision of a state statute. A local government ordinance must not specifically conflict with a state statute. Similarly, a municipal ordinance may not conflict with a county ordinance if the county has reserved such power to itself. As discussed earlier, the Florida Constitution permits Florida's counties to be chartered or non-chartered. A county's enactment of a charter creates situations where charter county laws prevail over conflicting municipal laws. They prevail whenever the charter county law is a regulatory ordinance. They also prevail on other topics whenever the "supremacy clause" in the charter of the charter county states so.

Conflicts of law can arise under Florida's governmental structure of overlapping sovereigns of state, county, and municipal government. Yet, two or more laws addressing the same subject or behavior need not be found to be conflicting. Divergent local and state legislation may coexist without conflict. The mere fact that local and state laws address the same or similar subject matter does not mandate a finding of conflict.

The Supreme Court of Florida holds that the test to determine whether there is such a conflict is whether one must violate one provision in order to comply with the other. . . .

. . . A municipality cannot forbid what the Florida Legislature has expressly licensed, authorized, or required. A municipality cannot authorize what the Florida Legislature has expressly forbidden. A municipality may provide a penalty less severe than that imposed by a state statute for the same offense or violation.

Patrick John McGinley, FLORIDA MUNICIPAL LAW AND PRACTICE § 3:11 (2017-2018 ed.).

b. Inconsistency Via Preemption

This type of inconsistency exists when a lawmaking body with the power to preempt others from legislating on a particular subject, topic, or field of law exercises that power expressly or impliedly by enacting a law that preempts the field. FLORIDA MUNICIPAL LAW AND PRACTICE reminds us that a Florida city, town, or village "may not make any law on a matter preempted to the state or county government by the Florida Constitution, by general law, or pursuant to a county charter" and also reminds us that "a county may not make any law on a matter preempted to the state." Patrick John McGinley, FLORIDA MUNICIPAL LAW AND PRACTICE § 3:10 (2017-2018 ed.). The reason for this is that "[p]reemption is a matter of consistency. If the state preempts by creating a legislative scheme, then the various local governments must not add their own legislation in that area because to do so would render local laws inconsistent with the State Constitution or a state statute."

(1). Preemption of Local Law by State Law

The mere fact that a state law and a local law address the same topic does not mean that the state law preempts. Some Florida statutes contemplate the enactment of local ordinances to supplement or fulfill the intent of the statute. Other Florida statutes address the particular subject, topic, or field of law but do not fully preempt the field. One must analyze the legislation to determine whether it preempts.

In any instance of potential preemption, one must look for express preemption or implied preemption. Commentators suggest that "cases in which the courts have found express state preemption are rare." *See* Judge James R. Wolf and Sarah Harley Bolinder, *The Effectiveness of Home Rule: A Preemption and Conflict Analysis*, FLORIDA BAR JOURNAL, June 2009 at 92. "Implied preemption" occurs if a legislative scheme is so pervasive that it occupies the entire field, creating a danger of a conflict between local and state laws, as illustrated by the 1991 decision of the Supreme Court of Florida in *Florida Power Corp. v. Seminole County*, 635 So. 2d 96 (Fla. 1st DCA 1994), cause dismissed, 641 So. 2d 1345 (Fla. 1994).

Express preemption arises out of statements appearing in the plain text of the law that preempts. The specificity of the language needed for express preemption can be described as follows. "Express pre-emption requires a specific statement; the preemption cannot be made by implication nor by inference." *Board of Trustees of City of Dunedin Mun. Firefighters Retirement System v. Dulje*, 453 So. 2d 177, 178 (Fla. 2d DCA 1984). Therefore, express preemption exists when one or more statements in a law do more than imply an intent to preempt the field. "An 'express' reference is one which is distinctly stated and not left to inference." *Edwards v. State*, 422 So. 2d 84, 85 (Fla. 2d DCA 1982). Although the preemption must be "specific," "not made by implication," and "distinctly stated" in order to be an express preemption, nevertheless, "[t]he preemption need not be explicit so long as it is clear that the legislature has clearly preempted local regulation of the subject." *Tribune Co. v. Cannella*, 458 So. 2d 1075 (Fla. 1984). What is required is that the express preemption "be accomplished by clear language stating that intent." *Phantom of Clearwater, Inc. v. Pinellas County*, 894 So. 2d 1011, 1018 (Fla. 2d DCA 2005).

Florida Municipal Law and Practice tells us that:

> One might think, and indeed one Florida court held, that "[i]n cases where the Legislature expressly or specifically preempts an area, there is no problem with ascertaining what the Legislature intended." Yet, things are not always that simple. As commentators have noted:

> Even in cases of express preemption, it is unlikely that a specific portion of a state statute expressly declaring preemption will directly address the exact action contemplated by the local government. It is more likely that the state statute will demonstrate an intent to occupy a field of regulation. The court must then examine whether the local government action is within the scope of the preemption.

Patrick John McGinley, Florida Municipal Law and Practice § 3:10 (2017-2018 ed.).

(2). Preemption of Local Law by Another Local Law

The mere fact that a county law and the law of a municipality located within that county (city, town, or village) address the same topic does not mean that the county law preempts. Such a case of potential preemption cannot be decided merely on the basis that one type of local government "stands higher than a municipality upon the ladder of governmental hierarchy. . . ." *City of Temple Terrace v. Hillsborough Ass'n for Retarded Citizens, Inc.*, 322 So. 2d 571, 577 (Fla. 2d DCA 1975), aff'd, 332 So. 2d 610 (Fla. 1976). If preemption exists, then sometimes the county preempts the city, town, or village; but sometimes the city, town, or village preempts the county. Florida Municipal Law and Practice explains:

> Recall that under the Florida Constitution, Florida's counties may be chartered or non-chartered. A county's enactment of a charter may be a means by which the county broadens its preemption power over municipalities.

This is true because, although state law may continue to prevail over conflicting county laws regardless of whether the county has a charter, charter county laws can prevail over conflicting municipal laws. They prevail whenever the charter county law is a regulatory ordinance. They also prevail on other topics whenever the "supremacy clause" in the charter of the charter county states so. For non-charter counties, county laws do not prevail over conflicting municipal laws.

Patrick John McGinley, Florida Municipal Law and Practice § 3:10 (2017-2018 ed). Florida Jurisprudence 2d expresses the same idea as follows:

The charter of a county must provide which will prevail in the event of conflict between county and municipal ordinances. With respect to non-charter counties, a county ordinance that conflicts with a municipal ordinance is not effective within the municipality to the extent of the conflict. A county ordinance need not yield in incorporated areas of the county when it is not identical in scope to a city ordinance. . . .

Where a county ordinance is adopted under a constitutional amendment and home rule charter of government, it supersedes municipal charters and ordinances when in conflict with them except where the charter specifically provides otherwise.

12A Fla. Jur 2d Counties, Etc. § 229.

11. General Laws, Special Laws, and General Laws of Local Application

Florida's legislature may make general laws or special laws. A special law applies to particular persons or things; a general law relates to subjects, persons, or things as a class. *Lawnwood Med. Ctr., Inc. v. Seeger*, 990 So. 2d 503, 509 (Fla. 2008). Another name for a special law is a "general law of local application." Florida's supreme court tells us that "[a] general law of local application is a law that uses a classification scheme based on population or some other criterion so that its application is restricted to particular localities." *City of Miami Beach v. Frankel*, 363 So. 2d 555, 558 (Fla. 1978). So a "general law of local application," and a "special law," are one and the same.

Special laws have valid purposes. For example, once the electors of a county hold a referendum that approves their county charter, Florida's legislature may pass a special law enacting that county's charter. That charter then becomes the charter for that particular county, but not for any other county. In this way, special laws empower local governments to have unique charters. This is just one example of the Florida Legislature's permissible use of a special law.

Special laws have restrictions as to their procedure for enactment and as to their permissible topics. Florida's constitution contains an individualized notice requirement, so that those affected by the special law either are given notice in advance of its enactment or are empowered to hold a referendum before the special law becomes effective. *See* Art. III, sec. 10, Fla. Const. Florida's constitution contains an itemized list of topics for which special laws are impermissible. *See* Art. III, sec. 11, Fla. Const. The relevant language reads:

ARTICLE III, SECTION 10. *Special laws.*—No special law shall be passed unless notice of intention to seek enactment thereof has been published in the manner provided by general law. Such notice shall not be necessary when the law, except the provision for referendum, is conditioned to become effective only upon approval by vote of the electors of the area affected.

ARTICLE III, SECTION 11. *Prohibited special laws.*—

(a) There shall be no special law or general law of local application pertaining to:

(1) election, jurisdiction or duties of officers, except officers of municipalities, chartered counties, special districts or local governmental agencies;

(2) assessment or collection of taxes for state or county purposes, including extension of time therefor, relief of tax officers from due performance of their duties, and relief of their sureties from liability;

(3) rules of evidence in any court;

(4) punishment for crime;

(5) petit juries, including compensation of jurors, except establishment of jury commissions;

(6) change of civil or criminal venue;

(7) conditions precedent to bringing any civil or criminal proceedings, or limitations of time therefor;

(8) refund of money legally paid or remission of fines, penalties or forfeitures;

(9) creation, enforcement, extension or impairment of liens based on private contracts, or fixing of interest rates on private contracts;

(10) disposal of public property, including any interest therein, for private purposes;

(11) vacation of roads;

(12) private incorporation or grant of privilege to a private corporation;

(13) effectuation of invalid deeds, wills or other instruments, or change in the law of descent;

(14) change of name of any person;

(15) divorce;

(16) legitimation or adoption of persons;

(17) relief of minors from legal disabilities;

(18) transfer of any property interest of persons under legal disabilities or of estates of decedents;

(19) hunting or fresh water fishing;

(20) regulation of occupations which are regulated by a state agency; or

(21) any subject when prohibited by general law passed by a three-fifths vote of the membership of each house. Such law may be amended or repealed by like vote.

(b) In the enactment of general laws on other subjects, political subdivisions or other governmental entities may be classified only on a basis reasonably related to the subject of the law.

The difference between a general law and a special law is illustrated by Florida's supreme court's decision in *License Acquisitions, LLC v. Debary Real Estate Holdings, LLC*, 155 So. 3d 1137 (Fla. 2014).

License Acquisitions, LLC v. Debary Real Estate Holdings, LLC

Supreme Court of Florida, 2014
155 So. 3d 1137

LABARGA, C.J.

This case is before the Court on appeal from a decision of the First District Court of Appeal . . . which held section 550.054(14)(a), Florida Statutes (2010), to be an invalid special law. This Court has jurisdiction of the appeal under article V, section 3(b)(1) of the Florida Constitution. For the following reasons, we reverse the First District and hold that section 550.054(14)(a) is a valid general law.

Facts

. . . [T]he First District's per curiam decision declar[ed] section 550.054(14)(a) to be invalid as a special law enacted without either providing advance notice of intent to enact the law or conditioning the law's effectiveness upon a referendum of the electors of the areas affected in violation of article III, section 10, of the Florida Constitution. . . .

[S]ection 550.054(14) provides as follows:

(14)(a) Any holder of a permit to conduct jai alai may apply to the division [of pari-mutuel wagering] to convert such permit to a permit to conduct greyhound racing in lieu of jai alai if:

1. Such permit is located in a county in which the division has issued only two pari-mutuel permits pursuant to this section;

2. Such permit was not previously converted from any other class of permit; and

3. The holder of the permit has not conducted jai alai games during a period of 10 years immediately preceding his or her application for conversion under this subsection.

(b) The [Division of Business and Professional Regulation, or DBPR], upon application from the holder of a jai alai permit meeting all conditions of this section, shall convert the permit and shall issue to the permitholder a permit to conduct greyhound racing. . . .

§ 550.054(14), Florida Statutes (2010).

West Volusia Racing, Inc. (West Volusia Racing), and License Acquisitions, LLC (License Acquisitions), applied for the conversion of their jai alai permits under section 550.054(14)(a) on the day section 550.054 became effective. Approximately three weeks later, the DBPR granted the applications. Shortly thereafter, Debary Real Estate Holdings, LLC (Debary), instituted a declaratory judgment action alleging in pertinent part that section 550.054(14) is an unconstitutional special law—a law designed to operate upon particular persons or things, or one that purports to operate upon classified persons or things when classification is not permissible or the classification adopted is illegal—enacted without notice or conditioning the law's effectiveness upon a referendum. The appellants argued that the statute is a general law—a law that operates uniformly within a permissible classification and is not subject to the notice or referendum requirements of article III, section 10, of the Florida Constitution. Specifically, Debary alleged that section 550.054(14)(a) 1. was only applicable to two jai alai permits and that the classification adopted was not rationally related to the purpose of the statute because the statute would never be capable of application to additional parties. Therefore, according to Debary, the classification adopted was illegal. . . .

. . . At the time of the statute's enactment, there were twenty-one total section 550.054 permits existing in nine counties in Florida, eleven of which were jai alai permits. West Volusia Racing and License Acquisitions held jai alai permits that were eligible for conversion at the time of the statute's enactment because the permits were dormant for ten years and were located in counties where the DBPR had issued exactly two [pari-mutuel] permits. . . . Thus, the appellees contended that the statute was invalid as a special law enacted under the guise of a general law. . . .

Analysis

Special Law v. General Law

"A law that operates universally throughout the state, uniformly upon subjects as they may exist throughout the state, or uniformly within a permissible classification is a general law." *[Department of Business Regulation v.] Classic Mile, Inc.*, 541 So. 2d [1155,] 1157 [(Fla. 1989)]. A special law is one designed to operate upon particular persons or things, or one that purports to operate upon classified persons or things when classification is not permissible or the classification adopted is illegal; a local law is one relating to, or designed to operate only in, a specifically indicated part of the State, or one that purports to operate within a classified territory when classification is not permissible or the classification is illegal. *Id.* Article III, section 10, of the Florida Constitution prohibits the Legislature from passing a special law without either providing advance notice of intent to enact the law or conditioning the law's effectiveness upon a referendum of the electors of the areas affected. A special law, however, is not converted into a general law by the Legislature's treating it and passing it as a general law. *Id.* . . .

A statutory classification scheme must bear a reasonable relationship to the purpose of the statute in order for the statute to constitute a valid general law. *Id.* . . . Statutes that employ arbitrary classification schemes are not valid as general laws. *Id.* A statute is invalid if "'the descriptive technique is employed merely for identification rather than classification.'" *Id.* . . . Ultimately, the criterion that determines if a reasonable relationship exists between the classification adopted and the purpose of the statute is whether the classification is potentially open to additional parties. *Id.* . . . ; *see also Ocala Breeders' Sales Co., Inc. v. Fla. Gaming Ctrs., Inc.*, 731 So. 2d 21, 25 (Fla. 1st DCA 1999) ("If it is possible in the future for others to meet the criteria set forth in the statute, then it is a general law and not a special law."). A classification scheme is not considered closed "merely because it is unlikely that it will include anyone else." *Fla. Dep't of Bus. & Prof'l Regulation v. Gulfstream Park Racing Ass'n, Inc.*, 967 So. 2d 802, 808–09 (Fla. 2007). However, a classification scheme is not considered open "merely because there is a theoretical possibility that some day it might include someone else. That approach would undermine the constitutional requirements for the adoption of special laws. . . . *[T]he proper standard is whether there is a reasonable possibility that the class will include others.*" *Id.* at 809.

The parties do not dispute that the Legislature did not provide notice of its intent to enact the statute or condition its effectiveness on a referendum of the electors of the areas affected. Thus, the issue on appeal to this Court is whether section 550.054(14)(a) is unconstitutional as a special law passed under the guise of a general law. The question of whether a law is a special or general law is a legal question subject to de novo review. *Gulfstream Park Racing*, 967 So. 2d at 806. . . . "Although our review is de novo, statutes come clothed with a presumption of constitutionality and must be construed whenever possible to effect a constitutional outcome." *Lewis v. Leon Cnty.*, 73 So. 3d 151, 153 (Fla. 2011). "To overcome the presumption, the invalidity must appear beyond reasonable doubt, for it must be assumed the [L]egislature intended to enact a valid law." *Id.* . . .

The . . . statute when enacted and at the time of the trial court proceedings only applied to License Acquisitions and West Volusia Racing. The [parties disagree as to] whether there is a reasonable possibility that the class is open to additional parties. . . .

[In determining whether the statute creates a reasonable possibility that the class is open to additional parties in the future, t]he Court is obligated to accord legislative acts a presumption of constitutionality and to construe challenged legislation to effect a constitutional outcome whenever reasonably possible. . . . "[E]ven where the statute is reasonably susceptible of two interpretations, one of which would render it invalid and the other valid, we must adopt the constitutional construction." . . . *Miami Dolphins, Ltd. v. Metro. Dade Cnty.*, 394 So. 2d 981, 988 (Fla. 1981) ("Given that an interpretation upholding the constitutionality of the act is available to this Court, it must adopt that construction.") . . . .

The appellants [allege the statute offers the following constitutional construction. The appellants] claim that adoption of their suggested interpretations would result in a class open for conversion to all of the remaining permits except one — thus a total of ten of the eleven existing permits at the time of the statute's enactment — without a change in the law. Indeed, review of the record demonstrates that Hillsborough County had three total section 550.054 permits, one of which was a dormant jai alai permit; Gadsden County had a dormant jai alai permit, but it previously converted and could never be eligible; Miami-Dade County and Broward County both had two active jai alai permits, and five total section 550.054 permits; St. Lucie County had one active jai alai permit and no other section 550.054 permits; Hamilton County had one active jai alai permit and no other section 550.054 permits; Marion County had one active jai alai permit and no other section 550.054 permits; and two other counties, possibly Bay County and Dixie County, did not presently have any 550.054 permits and could legally acquire a permit without violating the mileage restrictions in section 550.054(2) noted above. Thus, only one current jai alai permit holder would be ineligible, and two counties without a present jai alai permit holder could conceivably join the class. Accordingly, the class is open to additional parties pursuant to this construction of the statute, which renders the statute a valid general law. *See Classic Mile*, 541 So. 2d at 1157 ("A statutory classification scheme must bear a reasonable relationship to the purpose of the statute in order for the statute to constitute a valid general law.") . . . .

This case, when considered in light of our precedent, supports our conclusion that this statute is a valid general law pursuant to this construction of the statute. In *Sanford-Orlando Kennel Club*, this Court considered whether a statute that permitted the conversion of any harness racing track to dog racing was an unconstitutional special law. 434 So. 2d at 880–81. Pursuant to the statute, a harness racing track could be converted to a dog racing track if that track earned a certain amount of average daily income over a period of years and generated a certain amount of tax revenue for the state. *Id.* at 880. Although the statute's classification scheme only applied to the two then-existing permits, the Court held that the classification scheme was a general law. The Court noted that "[a] general law operates uniformly, not because it operates upon every person in the state, but because every person brought under the law is affected by it in a uniform fashion.

Uniformity of treatment within the class is not dependent upon the number of persons in the class." *Id.* at 881. Further, the Court reasoned that the controlling point in evaluating the statute's constitutionality was that "even though this class did in fact apply to only one track, it is open and has the potential of applying to other tracks." *Id.* at 882.

In *Biscayne Kennel Club, Inc. v. Fla. State Racing Comm'n*, 165 So. 2d 762 (Fla. 1964), this Court considered the constitutionality of a statute that provided "for the transfer, under certain conditions, of existing racing permits to allow establishment of harness racing operations in counties which have by previous referendum for two years approved the operation of race track pari-mutuel pools, excluding those having more than one horse track permit or one with an average daily pari-mutuel pool less than a specified minimum." *Id.* at 763–64. The Court upheld the classification because a number of Florida counties could, by future referendum, acquire racing establishments and have "not more than one horse track with a daily pool above the minimum set." *Id.* at 764.

Other cases from this Court holding a statute unconstitutional largely involved classification schemes that were clearly applicable to only one individual, entity, or geographic area. *See, e.g., Gulfstream Park*, 967 So. 2d at 809 (addressing a statute that prohibited thoroughbred permit holders from engaging in intertrack wagering in "any area of the state where there are three or more horserace permitholders within 25 miles of each other," and holding that it was unconstitutional because there was no reasonable possibility that these conditions would ever exist in another part of the state); *City of Miami v. McGrath*, 824 So. 2d 143, 146, 151 (Fla. 2002) (addressing a statute which authorized only municipalities with populations of more than 300,000 on a date certain to impose a parking tax, and holding that the statute was a special law because its express terms limited its application and excluded any other municipalities from joining the class in the future); *Classic Mile*, 541 So. 2d at 1158–59 (declaring statute unconstitutional because conditions only applied to Marion County, could never apply to others, and the appellants made no attempt to demonstrate a reasonable relationship between the classification and the subject of the statute); *W. Flagler Kennel Club*, 153 So. 2d at 8 (holding the statute applicable only to Broward County and noting that the appellants failed to attempt to demonstrate a reasonable relationship between the classification and the subject of the statute). It is also noted that in *Gulfstream Park*, this Court held that "a statute that appears to apply to one . . . area at the time of enactment may still be considered a general law if it could be applied to other . . . areas in the future." 967 So. 2d at 808. As discussed above, although section 550.054(14) (a) applied to two permits at the time of enactment, it could be applied to other permits in the future.

. . . Accordingly, we agree with the appellants' interpretation of the statute because it is a fair construction of the statute that is consistent with legislative intent and results in a determination that the statute is a valid general law.

Conclusion

Based on the foregoing, we reverse the First District's decision holding section 550.054(14)(a) unconstitutional and . . . we hold that section 550.054(14)(a) is a valid general law. . . .

It is so ordered.

———————

Notes and Questions to Consider:

1. The court heard two plausible interpretations of the relevant statute. It chose one interpretation over the other so that the statute could be upheld as constitutional. Was this the proper result?

2. On November 6, 2018, Floridians enacted the following amendment to Florida's constitution:

> *Prohibition on racing of and wagering on greyhounds or other dogs.*—The humane treatment of animals is a fundamental value of the people of the State of Florida. After December 31, 2020, a person authorized to conduct gaming or pari-mutuel operations may not race greyhounds or any member of the *Canis Familiaris* subspecies in connection with any wager for money or any other thing of value in this state, and persons in this state may not wager money or any other thing of value on the outcome of a live dog race occurring in this state. The failure to conduct greyhound racing or wagering on greyhound racing after December 31, 2018, does not constitute grounds to revoke or deny renewal of other related gaming licenses held by a person who is a licensed greyhound permitholder on January 1, 2018, and does not affect the eligibility of such permitholder, or such permitholder's facility, to conduct other pari-mutuel activities authorized by general law. By general law, the legislature shall specify civil or criminal penalties for violations of this section and for activities that aid or abet violations of this section.

Art. X, § 32, Fla. Const.

E. Quasi-Legislative Power

Article IV of Fla's Constitution requires that "the laws be faithfully executed" by the executive branch. Can it essentially make law by enacting administrative rules?

Florida's Administrative Procedures Act (APA), which is codified at Florida Statutes chapter 120, empowers or requires every "agency"—a term that is broadly defined by the APA—to engage in "rulemaking." "Rule-making is a quasi-legislative function, as opposed to an adjudicative proceeding." *Booker Creek Preservation, Inc. v. Southwest Florida Water Management District*, 534 So. 2d 419, 422 (Fla. 5th DCA 1988). The APA defines a "rule" as follows:

"Rule" means each agency statement of general applicability that implements, interprets, or prescribes law or policy or describes the procedure or practice requirements of an agency and includes any form which imposes any requirement or solicits any information not specifically required by statute or by an existing rule. The term also includes the amendment or repeal of a rule. . . .

§ 120.52(15), Fla. Stat. (2003). Stated somewhat differently, "rules" are "statement[s] of general applicability that implement[ ], interpret[ ], or prescribe[ ] law or policy or describe[ ] the procedure or practice requirements of an agency." § 120.52(16), Fla. Stat. (2010). Accordingly, "[w]hen an agency promulgates a rule having the force of law, it acts in place of the legislature." *Whiley v. Scott*, 79 So. 3d 702, 710 (Fla. 2011) Florida's supreme court acknowledges that agency rulemaking pursuant to this statutory authority constitutes the performance of a quasi-legislative function. *Id.* (citing *General Telephone Co. of Fla. v. Fla. Public Service Comm'n*, 446 So. 2d 1063, 1066 (Fla. 1984)).

Florida's supreme court observes that "[r]ulemaking is a derivative of lawmaking. An agency is empowered to adopt rules if two requirements are satisfied. First, there must be a statutory grant of rulemaking authority, and second, there must be a specific law to be implemented." *Id.* at 710. Under the APA, an agency lacks the power to create standard practices and procedures without first having a statute enabling it to do so, then writing down the practice, publishing it, getting public input, and allowing the public to challenge the practice or procedure—all before adopting the practice. By so doing, Floridians have a weapon against "red tape."

For example, if a Floridian is stymied by an agency practice that has not been promulgated as a rule, the affected Floridian can file a "rule challenge," which is a quasi-judicial administrative law action arising out of the APA. The rule challenge is not filed in a court or law but instead is filed with the Florida Division of Administrative Hearings. The burden is upon the affected Floridian to prove that the agency has adopted a standard practice that was not promulgated as a rule as required under the APA. The relief available to a successful challenger can include compelling the agency to engage in rulemaking or in declaring the agency's practice inapplicable to the challenger.

***

Notes and Questions to Consider:

1. The courts give greater deference to quasi-legislative actions than to quasi-judicial actions. "The scope of review of the quasi-legislative function of rulemaking is more limited than that with respect to quasi-judicial action. . . ." *Brewster Phosphates v. State, Dept. of Envtl. Regulation*, 444 So. 2d 483, 486 (Fla. 1st DCA 1984). Why, in your opinion, would such deference be warranted?

2. Why might a successful challenger in a rule challenge under Florida's Administrative Procedures Act want to compel the agency to engage in rulemaking?

Chapter 11

Executive Power

A. Florida's Executive Branch

Perhaps Florida's executive branch is best described as the branch that executes, or carries out, the requirements of the law. Its role under Florida's constitution is described in this excerpt from Daniel Webster & Donald L. Bell, *First Principles for Constitution Revision*, 22 Nova L. Rev. 391 (1997):

The Executive Branch

The executive branch is responsible for executing the laws the legislative branch creates. While there is, as Locke suggested, an area of executive "prerogative" that arises from the Legislature's inability to foresee all circumstances in which immediate action might be required, the executive risks being discredited whenever it acts without explicit legislative authorization. Consequently, it is constrained to act only in those ways unlikely to create public controversy.

In establishing the executive branch of government, the Florida Constitution goes further than most other constitutions to protect the public from tyranny by assigning certain duties and responsibilities to particular officers and agencies of the government. Unlike the constitutions of some other states, the Florida Constitution does not vest all executive power in the state's Governor. It establishes the Governor as the state's chief executive officer, but then proceeds to divide the executive power among a wide range of other executive officers and agencies.

Florida's Constitution . . . has an elected Cabinet. . . . Not unexpectedly, it has been a source of vexation to many governors, including the current one, that the Office of Governor must share its power with members of the cabinet who may be political opponents. However, establishing some competition at the highest levels of executive decision making sometimes causes an extraordinary level of inquiry and public debate to surround those decisions.

In those areas of policy that require them to work with the cabinet, Florida's governors are undoubtedly more restrained and less capricious in making decisions. This provides some worthwhile protection for the people. . . .

The division of executive and legislative branch power does not stop with the cabinet. The Florida Constitution creates a multitude of constitutional agencies, offices, and commissions. These offices and agencies vary in the extent to which they are subject to the Governor's power and some agencies even have a measure of independence from legislative oversight. These additional distributions of power were intended to protect the people from tyranny. However, where any of these offices is not subject to an adequate system of checks and balances, they can become tyrannies within their area of authority. . . .

Notes and Questions to Consider:

1. Where is the line between executing the law and creating the law?

2. In the discussion of Florida's executive branch in the excerpt above, the authors refer to Florida's elected cabinet. In the next subsection of this chapter, we consider this fact more closely.

B. Elected Cabinet

Unlike the federal Constitution, where the president's cabinet are appointed by the president and confirmed by the U.S. Senate, Florida's cabinet is elected by the people. Article IV of Florida's constitution provides:

SECTION 4. *Cabinet.*—

(a) There shall be a cabinet composed of an attorney general, a chief financial officer, and a commissioner of agriculture. In addition to the powers and duties specified herein, they shall exercise such powers and perform such duties as may be prescribed by law. In the event of a tie vote of the governor and cabinet, the side on which the governor voted shall be deemed to prevail.

(b) The attorney general shall be the chief state legal officer. There is created in the office of the attorney general the position of statewide prosecutor. The statewide prosecutor shall have concurrent jurisdiction with the state attorneys to prosecute violations of criminal laws occurring or having occurred, in two or more judicial circuits as part of a related transaction, or when any such offense is affecting or has affected two or more judicial circuits as provided by general law. The statewide prosecutor shall be appointed by the attorney general from not less than three persons nominated by the judicial nominating commission for the supreme court, or as otherwise provided by general law.

(c) The chief financial officer shall serve as the chief fiscal officer of the state, and shall settle and approve accounts against the state, and shall keep all state funds and securities.

(d) The commissioner of agriculture shall have supervision of matters pertaining to agriculture except as otherwise provided by law.

(e) The governor as chair, the chief financial officer, and the attorney general shall constitute the state board of administration, which shall succeed to all the power, control, and authority of the state board of administration established pursuant to Article IX, Section 16 of the Constitution of 1885, and which shall continue as a body at least for the life of Article XII, Section 9(c).

(f) The governor as chair, the chief financial officer, the attorney general, and the commissioner of agriculture shall constitute the trustees of the internal improvement trust fund and the land acquisition trust fund as provided by law.

(g) The governor as chair, the chief financial officer, the attorney general, and the commissioner of agriculture shall constitute the agency head of the Department of Law Enforcement.

Notes and Questions to Consider:

1. Can an elected cabinet create controversy within the executive branch? Consider this commentary from the *West Virginia Law Review*:

> In forty-three states, including West Virginia [and Florida], the executive department operates under the supervision of an elected Governor and elected executive department officers. The holders of these constitutional executive department offices may be members of differing political parties.... [B]ecause each is an independently elected executive officer, each may possess significantly different perspectives as to desirable policies under prevailing law.

Patrick C. McGinley, *Separation of Powers, State Constitutions & the Attorney General: Who Represents the State?*, 99 W. Va. L. Rev. 721, 722 (1997).

2. Although Florida's governor's cabinet is composed of separately elected officials, Florida's lieutenant governor is elected on the same ticket as the governor. The people elect their governor and lieutenant governor, and elect the other members of the cabinet, "each for a term of four years beginning on the first Tuesday after the first Monday in January of the succeeding year. In primary elections, candidates for the office of governor may choose to run without a lieutenant governor candidate. In the general election, all candidates for the offices of governor and lieutenant governor shall form joint candidacies in a manner prescribed by law so that each voter shall cast a single vote for a candidate for governor and a candidate for lieutenant governor running together." Art. IV, sec. 5, Fla. Const.

3. Florida's constitution imposes qualifications upon those who would run for governor or lieutenant governor: "When elected, the governor, lieutenant governor and each cabinet member must be an elector not less than thirty years of age who has resided in the state for the preceding seven years." Art. IV, sec. 5, Fla. Const.

4. Also, term limits are imposed as follows: "No person who has, or but for resignation would have, served as governor or acting governor for more than six years

in two consecutive terms shall be elected governor for the succeeding term." Art. IV, sec. 5, Fla. Const.

C. Enumerated Powers of the Governor

Article IV of Florida's constitution provides:

SECTION 1. Governor.—

(a) The supreme executive power shall be vested in a governor, who shall be commander-in-chief of all military forces of the state not in active service of the United States. The governor shall take care that the laws be faithfully executed, commission all officers of the state and counties, and transact all necessary business with the officers of government. The governor may require information in writing from all executive or administrative state, county or municipal officers upon any subject relating to the duties of their respective offices. The governor shall be the chief administrative officer of the state responsible for the planning and budgeting for the state.

(b) The governor may initiate judicial proceedings in the name of the state against any executive or administrative state, county or municipal officer to enforce compliance with any duty or restrain any unauthorized act.

(c) The governor may request in writing the opinion of the justices of the supreme court as to the interpretation of any portion of this constitution upon any question affecting the governor's executive powers and duties. The justices shall, subject to their rules of procedure, permit interested persons to be heard on the questions presented and shall render their written opinion not earlier than ten days from the filing and docketing of the request, unless in their judgment the delay would cause public injury.

(d) The governor shall have power to call out the militia to preserve the public peace, execute the laws of the state, suppress insurrection, or repel invasion.

(e) The governor shall by message at least once in each regular session inform the legislature concerning the condition of the state, propose such reorganization of the executive department as will promote efficiency and economy, and recommend measures in the public interest.

(f) When not otherwise provided for in this constitution, the governor shall fill by appointment any vacancy in state or county office for the remainder of the term of an appointive office, and for the remainder of the term of an elective office if less than twenty-eight months, otherwise until the first Tuesday after the first Monday following the next general election.

SECTION 2. *Lieutenant governor.*—

There shall be a lieutenant governor, who shall perform such duties pertaining to the office of governor as shall be assigned by the governor, except when otherwise provided by law, and such other duties as may be prescribed by law.

SECTION 3. *Succession to office of governor; acting governor.* —

(a) Upon vacancy in the office of governor, the lieutenant governor shall become governor. Further succession to the office of governor shall be prescribed by law. A successor shall serve for the remainder of the term.

(b) Upon impeachment of the governor and until completion of trial thereof, or during the governor's physical or mental incapacity, the lieutenant governor shall act as governor. Further succession as acting governor shall be prescribed by law. Incapacity to serve as governor may be determined by the supreme court upon due notice after docketing of a written suggestion thereof by three cabinet members, and in such case restoration of capacity shall be similarly determined after docketing of written suggestion thereof by the governor, the legislature or three cabinet members. Incapacity to serve as governor may also be established by certificate filed with the custodian of state records by the governor declaring incapacity for physical reasons to serve as governor, and in such case restoration of capacity shall be similarly established.

. . .

SECTION 8. *Clemency.* —

(a) Except in cases of treason and in cases where impeachment results in conviction, the governor may, by executive order filed with the custodian of state records, suspend collection of fines and forfeitures, grant reprieves not exceeding sixty days and, with the approval of two members of the cabinet, grant full or conditional pardons, restore civil rights, commute punishment, and remit fines and forfeitures for offenses.

(b) In cases of treason the governor may grant reprieves until adjournment of the regular session of the legislature convening next after the conviction, at which session the legislature may grant a pardon or further reprieve; otherwise the sentence shall be executed.

(c) There may be created by law a parole and probation commission with power to supervise persons on probation and to grant paroles or conditional releases to persons under sentences for crime. The qualifications, method of selection and terms, not to exceed six years, of members of the commission shall be prescribed by law.

———————

Notes and Questions to Consider:

1. Note that, as an exception to the "case and controversy" requirements of Florida law, Florida's constitution empowers Florida's governor to seek an advisory opinion from Florida's supreme court "as to the interpretation of any portion of this constitution upon any question affecting the governor's executive powers and duties." *See* art. IV, sec. 1(c), Fla. Const. The same exception is extended to Florida's attorney general for the purpose of requesting a ruling from Florida's supreme court as to the validity of any initiative petition seeking to amend Florida's constitution

under the procedures of Section 3 of Article XI of Florida's constitution. *See* art. IV, section 10, Fla. Const. Was it wise to except these officers from the case and controversy requirement for these purposes?

2. Note that "the governor shall fill by appointment any vacancy in state or county office for the remainder of the term of an appointive office, and for the remainder of the term of an elective office if less than twenty-eight months. . . ." Art. IV, sec. 1(f), Fla. Const. For this reason, when a Florida court judge dies, resigns, or otherwise leaves before finishing enough of the term of office, the governor appoints a replacement to finish the term from the list of names provided by the Judicial Nominating Commission. Florida Jurisprudence 2d describes the process as follows:

> The Governor is required to fill each vacancy in a judicial office by appointment for a term specified by statute. The Governor is to select from among no less than three nor more than six persons nominated by the appropriate judicial nominating commission. . . .

> The Florida Constitution requires that a judge's former seat be filled via gubernatorial appointment rather than the election process where filling the seat with an elected judge would mean that the office would remain vacant for an extended time.

> . . . The Governor is required to make an appointment to fill the vacancy within 60 days after the nominations have been certified to him or her. The legal duty imposed on the Governor by these provisions is enforceable by mandamus. The Governor is without authority under the constitution to reject the certified list of the Judicial Nominating Commission and request that a new list be certified.

13 Fla. Jur 2d Courts and Judges § 295 (2018).

3. Note that Florida's lieutenant governor's powers are not enumerated but instead "shall be assigned by the governor, except when otherwise provided by law, and such other duties as may be prescribed by law." Art. IV, sec. 2, Fla. Const. Like the vice president under the federal constitution, the lieutenant governor becomes governor upon the death or disability of the governor. *See* art. IV, sec. 3(a) — (b), Fla. Const.

D. Faithful Execution of the Laws

Article IV, Section 1(a), of Florida's constitution, states in pertinent part that Florida's "governor shall take care that the laws be faithfully executed. . . ." For further power to faithfully execute the laws, Article IV, Section 7, of Florida's constitution provides that Florida's "governor may suspend from office any state officer not subject to impeachment . . . for malfeasance, misfeasance, neglect of duty, drunkenness, incompetence, permanent inability to perform official duties, or commission of a felony."

Without running afoul of Florida's constitution, can the laws of the state of Florida grant Florida's governor the power to assure the faithful execution of the laws by taking an action less than removing a state officer from office? Consider the case of *Ayala v. Scott*, 224 So. 3d 755, 761 (Fla. 2017).

Ayala v. Scott

Supreme Court of Florida, 2017
224 So. 3d 755

Aramis Donell Ayala, State Attorney for Florida's Ninth Judicial Circuit, petitions this Court for a writ of quo warranto, challenging Governor Rick Scott's authority under section 27.14(1), Florida Statutes (2016), to reassign the prosecution of death-penalty eligible cases in the Ninth Circuit to Brad King, State Attorney for Florida's Fifth Judicial Circuit. We have jurisdiction. See article V, § 3(b)(8), Fla. Const. For the reasons below, we deny Ayala's petition.

Background

At a March 15, 2017, press conference, Ayala announced that she "will not be seeking [the] death penalty in the cases handled in [her] office." Several times during the same press conference, Ayala reiterated her intent to implement a blanket "policy" of not seeking the death penalty in any eligible case because, in her view, pursuing death sentences "is not in the best interest of th[e] community or in the best interest of justice," even where an individual case "absolutely deserve[s] [the] death penalty."

In response to Ayala's announcement, Governor Rick Scott issued a series of executive orders reassigning the prosecution of death-penalty eligible cases pending in the Ninth Circuit to King. In support of these orders, the Governor cited his duty as Florida's chief executive officer under article IV, section 1(a), of the Florida Constitution to "take care that the laws be faithfully executed" and his authority under section 27.14(1), Florida Statutes, to assign state attorneys to other circuits "if, for any . . . good and sufficient reason, the Governor determines that the ends of justice would be best served." The reassignment orders do not direct King to pursue the death penalty in any particular case, and in a statement filed in this Court, King has sworn that the Governor made no attempt to influence his decision as to whether the circumstances of any of the reassigned cases warrant pursuing the death penalty.

After unsuccessfully seeking a stay of the reassignment orders in the Ninth Circuit, Ayala filed this petition for a writ of quo warranto challenging the Governor's authority to reassign the cases at issue to King. The record reflects that Ayala and her office have abided by the lower courts' denial of her motion and fully cooperated with King.

Analysis

Ayala argues that the Governor exceeded his authority under section 27.14 by reassigning death-penalty eligible cases in the Ninth Circuit to King over her objection because article V, section 17, of the Florida Constitution makes Ayala "the prosecuting officer of all trial courts in [the Ninth] [C]ircuit." While quo warranto is the proper vehicle to challenge the Governor's authority to reassign these cases to King, see *Fla. House of Representatives v. Crist*, 999 So. 2d 601, 607 (Fla. 2008), Ayala is not entitled to relief because the Governor did not exceed his authority on the facts of this case.

As Florida's chief executive officer, the Governor is vested with the "supreme executive power" and is charged with the duty to "take care that the laws be faithfully executed." Art. IV, § 1(a), Fla. Const. Florida law facilitates the Governor's discharge of this duty, among other ways, through state attorney assignments. Specifically, section 27.14(1), the constitutionality of which Ayala concedes, provides:

> If any state attorney is disqualified to represent the state in any investigation, case, or matter pending in the courts of his or her circuit or *if, for any other good and sufficient reason, the Governor determines that the ends of justice would be best served, the Governor may, by executive order filed with the Department of State,* either order an exchange of circuits or of courts between such state attorney and any other state attorney or *order an assignment of any state attorney to discharge the duties of the state attorney with respect to one or more specified investigations, cases, or matters, specified in general in the executive order of the Governor.* Any exchange or assignment of any state attorney to a particular circuit shall expire 12 months after the date of issuance, unless an extension is approved by order of the Supreme Court upon application of the Governor showing good and sufficient cause to extend such exchange or assignment.

§ 27.14(1), Fla. Stat. (2016) (emphasis added).

This Court has previously recognized that the Governor has broad authority to assign state attorneys to other circuits pursuant to section 27.14:

> It is the duty of the Governor under Fla. Const. F.S.A., art. IV, § 1(a) in the exercise of his executive power to "take care that the laws be faithfully executed." The exercise of this power and the performance of this duty are clearly essential to the orderly conduct of government and the execution of the laws of this State. An executive order assigning a state attorney is exclusively within the orbit of authority of the Chief Executive when exercised within the bounds of the statute. See *Kirk v. Baker*, 224 So. 2d 311 (Fla. 1969). The Governor is given broad authority to fulfill his duty in taking "care that the laws be faithfully executed," and he should be required to do no more than make a general recitation as to his reasons for assigning a state attorney to another circuit.

Finch v. Fitzpatrick, 254 So. 2d 203, 204–05 (Fla. 1971); see also *Austin v. State ex rel. Christian*, 310 So. 2d 289, 293 (Fla. 1975) ("The statutes authorizing assignments of state attorneys should be broadly and liberally construed so as to complement and implement the duty of the Governor under the Constitution of the State of

Florida to 'take care that the laws be faithfully executed.'" (quoting art. IV, § 1(a), Fla. Const.)).

Accordingly, this Court reviews challenges to the Governor's exercise of his "broad discretion in determining 'good and sufficient reason' for assigning a state attorney to another circuit," *Finch*, 254 So. 2d at 205, similar to the way in which it reviews exercises of discretion by the lower courts. Compare *Johns v. State*, 197 So. 791, 796 (1940) ("If the Governor should abuse [the assignment] power, by arbitrarily and without any reason whatsoever [for] making such an assignment, it might be that his action could be inquired into by writ of quo warranto. . . ."); with *McFadden v. State*, 177 So. 3d 562, 567 (Fla. 2015) ("Discretion is abused only when the trial court's decision is 'arbitrary, fanciful, or unreasonable.'" (quoting *Gonzalez v. State*, 990 So. 2d 1017, 1033 (Fla. 2008))).

Applying this well-established standard of review to the facts of this case, the executive orders reassigning the death-penalty eligible cases in the Ninth Circuit to King fall well "within the bounds" of the Governor's "broad authority." *Finch*, 254 So. 2d at 204–05. Far from being unreasoned or arbitrary, as required by section 27.14(1), the reassignments are predicated upon "good and sufficient reason," namely Ayala's blanket refusal to pursue the death penalty in any case despite Florida law establishing the death penalty as an appropriate sentence under certain circumstances. See generally § 921.141, Fla. Stat. (2017).

Notwithstanding the Governor's compliance with all of the requirements of section 27.14(1), however, Ayala and her amici urge this Court to invalidate the reassignment orders by viewing this case as a power struggle over prosecutorial discretion. We decline the invitation because by effectively banning the death penalty in the Ninth Circuit—as opposed to making case-specific determinations as to whether the facts of each death-penalty eligible case justify seeking the death penalty—Ayala has exercised no discretion at all. As New York's high court cogently explained, "adopting a 'blanket policy'" against the imposition of the death penalty is "in effect refusing to exercise discretion" and tantamount to a "functional[ ] veto" of state law authorizing prosecutors to pursue the death penalty in appropriate cases. *Johnson v. Pataki*, 91 N.Y.2d 214, 668 N.Y.S.2d 978, 691 N.E.2d 1002, 1007 (1997).

Although *Johnson* applied New York law, the standards to which this Court holds its own judicial officers establish that Ayala's actions have the same impact under Florida law. For example, our trial judges may not "*refuse* to exercise discretion" or "rely on an inflexible rule for a decision that the law places in the judge's discretion." *Barrow v. State*, 27 So. 3d 211, 218 (Fla. 4th DCA 2010), approved, 91 So. 3d 826 (Fla. 2012). Instead, exercising discretion demands an individualized determination "exercised according to the exigency of the case, upon a consideration of the attending circumstances." *Barber v. State*, 5 Fla. 199, 206 (Fla. 1853) (Thompson, J., concurring).

Thus, under Florida law, Ayala's blanket refusal to seek the death penalty in any eligible case, including a case that "absolutely deserve[s] [the] death penalty" does not reflect an exercise of prosecutorial discretion; it embodies, at best, a misunderstanding of Florida law. Cf. *Doe v. State*, 499 So. 2d 13, 14 (Fla. 3d DCA 1986) (holding "the trial court failed to exercise its independent sentencing discretion" in light of its erroneous view of the law); see also *Taylor v. State*, 38 So. 380, 383 (1905) (recognizing that "a failure of the state's interests" occurs where "the regular state attorney is unwilling or refuses to act").

Moreover, while Ayala's blanket prohibition against the death penalty provided the Governor with "good and sufficient reason" to reassign the cases at issue to King, also important to our holding is that the Governor did not attempt to decide which cases are deserving of the death penalty. The Governor's orders do not direct King to seek the death penalty in any of the reassigned cases, and King has sworn that the Governor has not attempted to interfere with his determination as to whether to pursue the death penalty in any case. Rather, consistent with the Governor's constitutional duty, effectuated pursuant to his statutory assignment authority, the executive orders ensure the faithful execution of Florida law by guaranteeing that the death penalty — while never mandatory — remains an option in the death-penalty eligible cases in the Ninth Circuit, but leaving it up to King, as the assigned state attorney, to determine whether to seek the death penalty on a case-by-case basis.

On these facts, the Governor has not abused his broad discretion in reassigning the cases at issue to King.

Conclusion

The executive orders reassigning death-penalty eligible cases in the Ninth Circuit to King do not exceed the Governor's authority on the facts of this case. Therefore, we deny Ayala's petition.

It is so ordered.

Notes and Questions to Consider:

1. Did the court in *Ayala v. Scott* overlook a separation of powers issue? A footnote, omitted from the opinion as transcribed above, suggests the issue was considered but rejected as follows. The court noted that, in *Fulk v. State*, 417 So. 2d 1121 (Fla. 5th DCA 1982), Florida's Fifth District Court of Appeal holds that "[a]lthough state attorneys, like all attorneys, are officers of the court, the execution of criminal statutes by enforcement, including prosecution, is an executive function of government. The state attorney, when acting as a prosecuting officer under Article V, section 17, of the Florida Constitution and under chapter 27 of the Florida Statutes, is performing an executive function and not a judicial function." *Id.* at 1126 (Cowart, J., concurring specially) (footnote omitted). Therefore, according to the footnote in *Ayala v. Scott*, the holding of *Fulk v. State* explains why the facts of *Ayala v. Scott* did not raise an issue regarding the separation of powers. Instead, Florida's supreme

court viewed this case as raising the issue of the scope of Florida's executive power. A dissenting opinion disagreed. Do you agree?

2. In light of *Ayala v. Scott*, what is a Florida elected official, who holds the power of discretion as part of their elected powers, supposed to do when faced with a law that the elected official finds morally repugnant?

3. *Ayala v. Scott* involved an elected prosecutor's discomfort with the death penalty. Florida law grants a prosecutor the discretion to seek the death penalty for crimes of first-degree murder, felony murder, capital drug trafficking, and capital sexual battery. The laws of many nations forbid the use of a death penalty, and the beliefs of many faiths are troubled by the use of the death penalty. For example, prior to 2018, paragraph 2267 of *The Catechism of the Catholic Church* stated that "[t]he traditional teaching of the Church does not exclude, presupposing full ascertainment of the identity and responsibility of the offender, recourse to the death penalty, when this is the only practicable way to defend the lives of human beings effectively against the aggressor." *Id.* at para. 2267. Commentators interpreted this paragraph to mean that "[w]hile the Catholic Church does not condemn the death penalty as intrinsically evil . . . because of the Church's high value of human life, the circumstances under which the death penalty is morally acceptable are rare." Bill Piatt, Catholic Legal Perspectives 185 (2d ed. 2015). In 1995, Saint Pope John Paul II cast doubt upon the future viability of the death penalty, writing in *Evangelium Vitae* that governments "ought not go to the extreme of executing the offender except in cases of absolute necessity: in other words, when it would not be possible otherwise to defend society. Today however, as a result of steady improvements in the organization of the penal system, such cases are very rare, if not practically non-existent." In 2011, Pope Emeritus Benedict XVI wrote in his Apostolic Exhortation *Africae Munus* that "I draw the attention of society's leaders to the need to make every effort to eliminate the death penalty. . . ." In 2018, Pope Francis approved the following new draft of paragraph 2267 of the Catechism of the Catholic Church:

> *The Death Penalty*
>
> 2267. Recourse to the death penalty on the part of legitimate authority, following a fair trial, was long considered an appropriate response to the gravity of certain crimes and an acceptable, albeit extreme, means of safeguarding the common good.
>
> Today, however, there is an increasing awareness that the dignity of the person is not lost even after the commission of very serious crimes. In addition, a new understanding has emerged of the significance of penal sanctions imposed by the state. Lastly, more effective systems of detention have been developed, which ensure the due protection of citizens but, at the same time, do not definitively deprive the guilty of the possibility of redemption.
>
> Consequently, the Church teaches, in the light of the Gospel, that "the death penalty is inadmissible because it is an attack on the inviolability and

dignity of the person", and she works with determination for its abolition worldwide.[1]

What are your personal beliefs about the death penalty today? Are your views of the death penalty different today because "more effective systems of detention have been developed, which ensure the due protection of citizens"? *See id.* What do you make of the results of surveys, such as the one in Northwestern University School of Law's Spring 2009 issue of the *Journal of Criminal Law and Criminology?* It "report[s] results from a survey of the world's leading criminologists that asked their expert opinions on whether the empirical research supports the contention that the death penalty is a superior deterrent. The findings demonstrate an overwhelming consensus among these criminologists that the empirical research conducted on the deterrence question strongly supports the conclusion that the death penalty does not add deterrent effects to those already achieved by long imprisonment." Michael L. Radelet & Traci L. Lacock, *Do Executions Lower Homicide Rates?: The Views of Leading Criminologists*, 99 J. Crim. L. & Criminology 489, 489–90 (2009).

E. Quasi-Executive Power

"While the general executive power of the state is vested in the executive branch, and chiefly in the Governor, the Legislature [or the state constitution itself] may delegate ministerial or quasi-executive powers. . . ." Jack K. Levin, 8 Mɪᴄʜ. Pʟ. & Pʀ. §60:20 (2d ed., Mar. 2019 update).

One example of quasi-executive power delegated by Florida's constitution is the discretionary power of prosecutors, as held by *Valdes v. State*, 728 So. 2d 736 (Fla. 1999):

Valdes v. State
Supreme Court of Florida, 1999
728 So. 2d 736

Frank Valdes appeals the trial court's summary denial of his motion for postconviction relief, filed pursuant to Florida Rule of Criminal Procedure 3.850. . . .

Valdes was found guilty and sentenced to death for the 1987 murder of a corrections officer. . . . The murder occurred during an aborted attempt by Valdes and his accomplice to assist a friend in escaping police custody. The Court unanimously affirmed the conviction and sentence on appeal. . . .

[The motion for post-conviction relief] stated one claim, as follows:

---

1. https://press.vatican.va/content/salastampa/en/bollettino/pubblico/2018/08/02/180802a .html

> The Defendant's rights . . . have been denied to him by and through the
> Florida Supreme Court's effectuation of an unauthorized amendment to
> the Judiciary article of Florida's Constitution—delegating away its pros-
> ecutorial arm (i.e., State Attorneys) to the Executive branch—resulting in
> the Defendant's wrongful prosecution, convictions, and sentences, which
> rights arise directly and/or are guaranteed against invasion by . . . the Flor-
> ida Constitution. . . .

[T]he merits of this claim . . . [are] fatally flawed in an important respect.
Article V, section 17, *specifically provides* that state attorneys are the prosecuting officers of all trials in each circuit. This Court has long held that as the prosecuting
officer, the state attorney has "complete discretion" in the decision to charge and
prosecute, *Cleveland v. State*, 417 So. 2d 653, 654 (Fla. 1982), and the judiciary cannot interfere with this "discretionary executive function." *State v. Bloom*, 497 So. 2d
2, 3 (Fla. 1986).

As this Court explained in *The Office of the State Attorney v. Parrotino*, 628 So.
2d 1097, 1099 (Fla. 1993), state attorneys fulfill a unique role, which is both quasi-
judicial and quasi-executive. This unique role is due to the tradition of their exclusive discretion in prosecution, combined with their status as officers of the court.
The office of state attorney thus "shares some attributes of the executive" by virtue of
its power as the prosecuting authority to determine whom and how to prosecute, as
well as some attributes of the judicial branch, such as judicial immunity. *Id.* at 1099
n. 2. Nothing about the *placement* of the constitutional provision in article V providing for the creation of the state attorneys undermines these long-held principles. . . .

Based on the foregoing, the trial court's summary denial of Valdes' petition is
affirmed. . . .

Notes and Questions to Consider:

1. *Valdes v. State* holds that "[n]othing about the *placement* of the constitutional
provision in Article V providing for the creation of the state attorneys undermines
these long-held principles." So the placement argument was a losing argument, but
was it a frivolous argument? Consider the fact that Florida's constitution addresses
executive powers in Article IV, but creates state attorneys in Article V with its creation of Florida's judicial branch.

2. "Regardless of the method of review, the court exercises a more limited review
of quasi-executive or quasi-legislative action than of quasi-judicial action." *Broward
County v. Admin. Comm'n*, 321 So. 2d 605, 610 (Fla. 1st DCA 1975). In your opinion,
why would it be appropriate to show such deference to quasi-executive action?

Chapter 12

Judicial Powers

A. Florida's Judicial Branch

The role of Florida's judicial branch is described in this excerpt from Daniel Webster & Donald L. Bell, *First Principles for Constitution Revision*, 22 Nova L. Rev. 391 (1997):

Even when ruled by a king, "[b]etwixt subject and subject . . . there must be measures, laws, and judges. . . ." The third branch of government, the judiciary, which has been called the least dangerous branch, was developed in society to substitute for two powers that people had in nature. The first is the power to do whatever one sees fit to assure self preservation. The second is the power to punish those who attempt to infringe the right of self preservation. . . .

Article V of the Florida Constitution establishes a system of courts and judges consistent with the fundamental purpose of the judiciary by establishing that all judicial officers of the state shall be "conservators of the peace." As Tocqueville explained:

> The great end of justice is to substitute the notion of right for that of violence. . . . The moral force which courts of justice possess renders the use of physical force very rare and is frequently substituted for it; but if force proves to be indispensable, its power is doubled by its association with the idea of law.

Thus, the principal function of the judiciary is public and private dispute resolution. The courts have the power under article V to review the constitutionality of legislative acts. But, like the other branches of government, the courts are confined to the exercise of those powers assigned to them under the constitution. The courts must take care that, in rendering their opinions, they do not go beyond the Legislature's intent, thereby creating new laws of their own. Similarly, it is beyond the power of the courts to execute the laws.

Notes and Questions to Consider:

1. In the discussion of Florida's judicial branch in the excerpt above, the authors note that "Article V of the Florida Constitution establishes a system of courts and judges." Why would Florida need to create, maintain, and fund a system of courts and judges when the U.S. Constitution already creates a federal one?

2. The discussion above ends with the authors' opinion that: "Our judiciary would be more restrained if we had a more restrained constitution. Thus, [we] should consider making changes [to Florida's constitution] that move [it] in a direction more conducive to judicial restraint." Do you agree?

B. Florida's State Court System

Just as Article III of the U.S. Constitution creates a federal court system, Article V of Florida's constitution creates Florida's system of state courts. In relevant part, Article V provides:

SECTION 1. Courts.—The judicial power shall be vested in a supreme court, district courts of appeal, circuit courts and county courts. No other courts may be established by the state, any political subdivision or any municipality. The legislature shall, by general law, divide the state into appellate court districts and judicial circuits following county lines. Commissions established by law, or administrative officers or bodies may be granted quasi-judicial power in matters connected with the functions of their offices. The legislature may establish by general law a civil traffic hearing officer system for the purpose of hearing civil traffic infractions. The legislature may, by general law, authorize a military court-martial to be conducted by military judges of the Florida National Guard, with direct appeal of a decision to the District Court of Appeal, First District.

SECTION 2. Administration; practice and procedure.— . . . The supreme court shall adopt rules for the practice and procedure in all courts including the time for seeking appellate review, the administrative supervision of all courts, the transfer to the court having jurisdiction of any proceeding when the jurisdiction of another court has been improvidently invoked, and a requirement that no cause shall be dismissed because an improper remedy has been sought. . . .

SECTION 3. Supreme court.—

(a) ORGANIZATION.—The supreme court shall consist of seven justices. Of the seven justices, each appellate district shall have at least one justice elected or appointed from the district to the supreme court who is a resident of the district at the time of the original appointment or election. Five justices shall constitute a quorum. The concurrence of four justices shall be necessary to a decision. When recusals for cause would prohibit the court from convening because of the requirements of this section, judges assigned to temporary duty may be substituted for justices.

(b) JURISDICTION.—The supreme court:

(1) Shall hear appeals from final judgments of trial courts imposing the death penalty and from decisions of district courts of appeal declaring invalid a state statute or a provision of the state constitution.

(2) When provided by general law, shall hear appeals from final judgments entered in proceedings for the validation of bonds or certificates of indebtedness and shall

review action of statewide agencies relating to rates or service of utilities providing electric, gas, or telephone service.

(3) May review any decision of a district court of appeal that expressly declares valid a state statute, or that expressly construes a provision of the state or federal constitution, or that expressly affects a class of constitutional or state officers, or that expressly and directly conflicts with a decision of another district court of appeal or of the supreme court on the same question of law.

(4) May review any decision of a district court of appeal that passes upon a question certified by it to be of great public importance, or that is certified by it to be in direct conflict with a decision of another district court of appeal.

(5) May review any order or judgment of a trial court certified by the district court of appeal in which an appeal is pending to be of great public importance, or to have a great effect on the proper administration of justice throughout the state, and certified to require immediate resolution by the supreme court.

(6) May review a question of law certified by the Supreme Court of the United States or a United States Court of Appeals which is determinative of the cause and for which there is no controlling precedent of the supreme court of Florida.

(7) May issue writs of prohibition to courts and all writs necessary to the complete exercise of its jurisdiction.

(8) May issue writs of mandamus and quo warranto to state officers and state agencies.

(9) May, or any justice may, issue writs of habeas corpus returnable before the supreme court or any justice, a district court of appeal or any judge thereof, or any circuit judge.

(10) Shall, when requested by the attorney general pursuant to the provisions of Section 10 of Article IV, render an advisory opinion of the justices, addressing issues as provided by general law. . . .

SECTION 4. District courts of appeal.—

(a) ORGANIZATION.—There shall be a district court of appeal serving each appellate district. Each district court of appeal shall consist of at least three judges. Three judges shall consider each case and the concurrence of two shall be necessary to a decision.

(b) JURISDICTION.—

(1) District courts of appeal shall have jurisdiction to hear appeals, that may be taken as a matter of right, from final judgments or orders of trial courts, including those entered on review of administrative action, not directly appealable to the supreme court or a circuit court. They may review interlocutory orders in such cases to the extent provided by rules adopted by the supreme court.

(2) District courts of appeal shall have the power of direct review of administrative action, as prescribed by general law.

(3) A district court of appeal or any judge thereof may issue writs of habeas corpus returnable before the court or any judge thereof or before any circuit judge within the territorial jurisdiction of the court. A district court of appeal may issue writs of mandamus, certiorari, prohibition, quo warranto, and other writs necessary to the complete exercise of its jurisdiction. To the extent necessary to dispose of all issues in a cause properly before it, a district court of appeal may exercise any of the appellate jurisdiction of the circuit courts. . . .

SECTION 5. Circuit courts.—

(a) ORGANIZATION.—There shall be a circuit court serving each judicial circuit.

(b) JURISDICTION.—The circuit courts shall have original jurisdiction not vested in the county courts, and jurisdiction of appeals when provided by general law. They shall have the power to issue writs of mandamus, quo warranto, certiorari, prohibition and habeas corpus, and all writs necessary or proper to the complete exercise of their jurisdiction. Jurisdiction of the circuit court shall be uniform throughout the state. They shall have the power of direct review of administrative action prescribed by general law.

SECTION 6. County courts.—

(a) ORGANIZATION.—There shall be a county court in each county. There shall be one or more judges for each county court as prescribed by general law.

(b) JURISDICTION.—The county courts shall exercise the jurisdiction prescribed by general law. Such jurisdiction shall be uniform throughout the state. . . .

. . .

SECTION 8. Eligibility.—No person shall be eligible for office of justice or judge of any court unless the person is an elector of the state and resides in the territorial jurisdiction of the court. No justice or judge shall serve after attaining the age of seventy years except upon temporary assignment or to complete a term, one-half of which has been served. No person is eligible for the office of justice of the supreme court or judge of a district court of appeal unless the person is, and has been for the preceding ten years, a member of the bar of Florida. No person is eligible for the office of circuit judge unless the person is, and has been for the preceding five years, a member of the bar of Florida. . . .

. . .

SECTION 10. Retention; election and terms.—

(a) Any justice or judge may qualify for retention by a vote of the electors in the general election next preceding the expiration of the justice's or judge's term in the manner prescribed by law. If a justice or judge is ineligible or fails to qualify for retention, a vacancy shall exist in that office upon the expiration of the term being served by the justice or judge. When a justice or judge so qualifies, the ballot shall read substantially as follows: "Shall Justice (or Judge) (name of justice or judge) of the (name of the court) be retained in office?" If a majority of the qualified electors voting within the territorial jurisdiction of the court vote to retain, the justice or judge shall be retained for a term of six years. . . .

SECTION 11. Vacancies.—

(a) Whenever a vacancy occurs in a judicial office to which election for retention applies, the governor shall fill the vacancy. . . .

SECTION 12. Discipline; removal and retirement.— . . .

(1) There shall be a judicial qualifications commission vested with jurisdiction to investigate and recommend to the Supreme Court of Florida the removal from office of any justice or judge whose conduct, during term of office . . . demonstrates a present unfitness to hold office, and to investigate and recommend the discipline of a justice or judge whose conduct, during term of office . . . warrants such discipline. For purposes of this section, discipline is defined as any or all of the following: reprimand, fine, suspension with or without pay, or lawyer discipline. . . .

SECTION 13. Prohibited activities.—All justices and judges shall devote full time to their judicial duties. They shall not engage in the practice of law or hold office in any political party. . . .

SECTION 14. Funding.—

(a) All justices and judges shall be compensated only by state salaries fixed by general law. . . .

(b) All funding for the offices of the clerks of the circuit and county courts performing court-related functions, [with certain enumerated exceptions], shall be provided by adequate and appropriate filing fees for judicial proceedings and service charges and costs for performing court-related functions as required by general law. Selected salaries, costs, and expenses of the state courts system may be funded from appropriate filing fees for judicial proceedings and service charges and costs for performing court-related functions, as provided by general law. . . .

(c) No county or municipality, except as provided in this subsection, shall be required to provide any funding for the state courts system, state attorneys' offices, public defenders' offices, court-appointed counsel or the offices of the clerks of the circuit and county courts performing court-related functions. Counties shall be required to fund the cost of communications services, existing radio systems, existing multi-agency criminal justice information systems, and the cost of construction or lease, maintenance, utilities, and security of facilities for the trial courts, public defenders' offices, state attorneys' offices, and the offices of the clerks of the circuit and county courts performing court-related functions. Counties shall also pay reasonable and necessary salaries, costs, and expenses of the state courts system to meet local requirements as determined by general law.

———

Notes and Questions to Consider:

1. Currently, Florida's 67 counties are divided into twenty judicial circuits, each of which consists of at least a single county and some of which as many as six counties. No county falls within more than one judicial circuit. The judicial circuits are all within one of five territorial District Courts of Appeal. The geographic jurisdiction of Florida's five District Courts of Appeal are:

First DCA: 1st, 2nd, 3rd, 8th and 14th Circuit Courts (as well as statewide jurisdiction over orders of the Florida Division of Administrative Hearings Offices of the Judges of Compensation Claims, which is the administrative agency that adjudicates claims of injured workers seeking benefits from employers under Florida's Workers' Compensation Law)

Second DCA: 6th, 10th, 12th, 13th and 20th Circuit Courts

Third DCA: 11th and 16th Circuit Courts

Fourth DCA: 15th, 17th and 19th Circuit Courts

Fifth DCA: 5th, 7th, 9th and 18th Circuit Courts.

The First DCA is in Tallahassee. The Second DCA is the only Florida district court of appeal that operates from two fixed locations: Lakeland and Tampa. The Third DCA is in Miami. The Fourth DCA is in West Palm Beach. The Fifth DCA is in Daytona Beach. Florida's supreme court is located at 500 S. Duval St., Tallahassee, FL 32399.

2. Note how Florida's court system is funded. Does this seem adequate? What can Florida's court system do if funding proves inadequate in any given year?

3. Note further that each court in Florida's court system is given authority to issue certain "writs." Those are discussed in greater detail later in this chapter.

C. Jurisdiction of Florida's Courts

The Florida Statutes provide the following jurisdiction of Florida's county courts as of May 24, 2019:

Florida Statutes section 34.01. *Jurisdiction of county court.* —

(1) County courts shall have original jurisdiction:

(a) In all misdemeanor cases not cognizable by the circuit courts.;

(b) Of all violations of municipal and county ordinances.;

(c) Of all actions at law, except those within the exclusive jurisdiction of the circuit courts, in which the matter in controversy does not exceed, exclusive of interest, costs, and attorney fees:

1. If filed on or before December 31, 2019, the sum of $15,000.

2. If filed on or after January 1, 2020, the sum of $30,000.

3. If filed on or after January 1, 2023, the sum of $50,000.

(d) Of disputes occurring in the homeowners' associations as described in s. 720.311(2)(a), which shall be concurrent with jurisdiction of the circuit courts. . . .

The Florida Statutes provide the following appellate jurisdiction of Florida's circuit courts as of May 24, 2019:

Florida Statutes section 26.012. *Jurisdiction of circuit court.* —

(1) Circuit courts shall have jurisdiction of appeals from county courts except:

(a) Appeals of county court orders or judgments where the amount in controversy is greater than $15,000. This paragraph is repealed on January 1, 2023.

(b) Appeals of county court orders or judgments declaring invalid a state statute or a provision of the State Constitution.

(c) Orders or judgments of a county court which are certified by the county court to the district court of appeal to be of great public importance and which are accepted by the district court of appeal for review.

Circuit courts shall have jurisdiction of appeals from final administrative orders of local government code enforcement boards. . . .

———————

Notes to Consider:

1. The statutes quoted above implement Article V, Section 5 of Florida's constitution (providing that Florida's "circuit courts shall have original jurisdiction not vested in the county courts, and jurisdiction of appeals when provided by general law") and Article V, Section 6 (providing that Florida's "county courts shall exercise the jurisdiction prescribed by general law.").

2. The statutes quoted above reflect amendments made in June 2019 expanding the amount-in-controversy jurisdiction of Florida's county courts and the appellate jurisdiction of Florida's circuit courts. House Bill 337, which is the bill that was signed into law, provides that "[t]he amendments to the jurisdiction of a court made by this act shall apply with respect to the date of filing the cause of action, regardless of when the cause of action accrued." *See* section 32 of 2019 Fla. Sess. Law Serv. Ch. 2019-58 (C.S.C.S.H.B. 337).

D. Extraordinary Writs

Article V of the Constitution of the State of Florida empowers all Florida state courts except county courts to issue certain "writs." What is a writ, and how is it used? The February 2006 issue of the FLORIDA BAR JOURNAL provides this introduction to writ practice in Florida:

Under Florida law, unless an order completely disposes of judicial labor on a claim or falls within the narrow, enumerated categories of appealable nonfinal orders, a litigant must wait until a case is over before obtaining the right to appeal. In some circumstances, however, certain orders subject a litigant to irreparable harm and require immediate review. Perhaps a trial court has ordered immediate disclosure of materials protected by attorney-client or trade secret privileges, or denied a motion to dismiss a premature claim for punitive damages or a motion to disqualify. In such instances, and others, a litigant may be able to obtain immediate review and issuance of a common law writ, which is ingrained in our common law tradition and has evolved with our judicial framework. Understanding the general principles governing common law writs provides a litigant with unique tools that are both practical and extraordinary.

Original Proceedings Described in Rule 9.100

Florida Rule of Appellate Procedure 9.100 describes the courts' original jurisdiction to issue common law writs. The rule identifies writs of mandamus, prohibition, quo warranto, certiorari, habeas corpus, and all writs necessary to the complete exercise of the courts' jurisdiction. Each of these writs warrants individual discussion, but certain general principles are universally applicable. An original writ proceeding is initiated by filing a petition directly within the appellate forum, with the appropriate filing fee, rather than by filing a notice of appeal in the lower tribunal. Fla. R. App. P. 9.100(b). In many cases, this shortens the time frame for preparing necessary materials for seeking review because certain extraordinary writ petitions must be filed within 30 days following rendition of the challenged order. Because the clerk does not transmit a record in writ proceedings, parties wishing to include record materials must file an appendix with the petition. Fla. R. App. P. 9.100(i) & 9.220.

Unlike an appellate proceeding, the party seeking a writ is identified as the petitioner and all other parties as respondents. Fla. R. App. P. 9.100(b). Neither the trial court nor other decision-making body should be named as a respondent. Fla. R. App. P. 9.100(c)(4). Furthermore, a respondent should not respond to an original writ petition unless the court issues an order to show cause or otherwise requires a response. Fla. R. App. P. 9.100(e)(3) & (h). Once a response is served, the petitioner has 20 days to serve a reply and supplemental appendix, if any. Fla. R. App. P. 9.100(k). An original petition dispenses with many of the stylistic requirements for an appellate brief, such as tables of contents and authorities; however, a petitioner and respondent must adhere to the font, page size, and page limit requirements and provide certificates of service and typeface compliance. Fla. R. App. P. 9.100(1).4

Jack R. Reiter, *Common Law Writs: From the Practical to the Extraordinary*, FLA. B.J., February 2006, at 32.

This introduction outlines the pleading requirements for each of the various writs. But the substantive elements of each writ are different, and its use is also different. Therefore, we examine each in turn with excerpts from FLORIDA ELEMENTS OF AN ACTION (with internal footnotes and citations omitted).

1. Writ of Mandamus

Elements of the Prima Facie Case for a Writ of Mandamus
from FLORIDA ELEMENTS OF AN ACTION

by Patrick John McGinley
21 Fla. Prac. § 1701:1
© 2017 by Thomson Reuters

A petition for writ of mandamus is an action seeking to remedy a government's failure to do something it is supposed to do. Mandamus is a proceeding to enforce a clear legal right to the performance of a clear legal duty.

A petition for mandamus seeks the entry of a writ of mandamus. If the court finds the petition is sufficient on its face, the court must issue an order for the respondent to show cause why the requested writ should not be issued, and this order bears the confusing name of an "alternative writ of mandamus."

If granted, a writ of mandamus is an enforceable command from a court directed to the government or a representative of the government (such as an inferior court, public officer, or governmental entity) requiring it to perform an act that it has a legal duty to perform because of its official position. Therefore, a mandamus action is a means by which to seek a court order commanding a government official to do something he is legally obliged to do.

The six required elements for a writ of mandamus are:

(1) the petitioner has a clear and certain legal right

(2) to the performance of a particular duty

(3) by a government or a representative of the government

(4) whose performance of that duty is ministerial and not discretionary,

(5) who has failed to perform despite an adequate request, and

(6) who has left the petitioner with no other legal method for obtaining relief.

The following paragraphs provide guidance as to how to plead and prove each of these six required elements.

Clear Legal Right:

Mandamus is proper to enforce a right which is clearly and certainly established in the law. This means that an action for mandamus may not be used to litigate the existence of a right. Nor may mandamus be used to litigate the entitlement to a right. Florida law is well settled that mandamus may only be used to enforce a right already clearly and certainly established in the law. For example, mandamus can be used to compel the state to issue the petitioner a license or permit to which the petitioner is entitled. But mandamus cannot be used to compel the state to issue the license in a particular form or to issue one type of license over another.

Duty to Act:

A petition for writ of mandamus must allege a respondent's breach of an indisputable legal duty to act. The required duty has been described as one that is "clear and indisputable." It must be a duty owed to the public, and not a duty that arises from private rights. Mandamus cannot be used to enforce private rights or duties.

Arm of Government:

Mandamus may only be issued against a government or against a person that may act in an official government capacity. "Mandamus does not lie to enforce private rights by compelling one private party to discharge a duty owed to another. The legal obligations of one citizen to another can be enforced in the courts but not by the use of an extraordinary remedy such as mandamus."

Examples of entities properly subject to a writ of mandamus include Florida's governor, a Florida state agency, a Florida regulatory bureau such as the Florida Public Service Commission, the Florida Department of Corrections, a Florida jail or civil commitment center, a Florida police force or law enforcement agency, a Florida county, a Florida judge or court, the county Supervisor of Voter Registration, a Canvassing Board of Elections or its members, and similar public entities and officers.

It is noteworthy that the 1959 decision of Florida's Third District Court of Appeal in *State ex rel. Fussell v. McLendon* granted mandamus against the president of a nongovernmental corporation. This decision does not explicitly address the issue that the president of a private corporation is not a government or a person who can act in an official government capacity. The Supreme Court of Florida was not asked to review this decision. A close reading of the text of this decision suggests that the respondent failed to object on the grounds that he was neither a government nor an arm of the government.

It is also noteworthy that individuals or entities who are alleged to be properly subjected to a writ of mandamus, and who respond by alleging the completion of the requested ministerial act instead of responding by questioning whether they are properly subjected to a writ of mandamus, have by so doing acknowledged that they are the proper subjects to such a writ. Stated somewhat differently, any question as to whether the court has jurisdiction over certain respondents named in the mandamus proceeding is dissipated when, instead of attempting to show cause why the writ should not issue, the respondents certify to the court that they have taken the ministerial action that the petition for writ of mandamus seeks.

Ministerial Act:

The writ of mandamus may be used to compel the performance of a ministerial duty imposed by law. Discretionary authority cannot be the subject of the writ. A duty or act is defined as "ministerial" when there is no room for the exercise of discretion, and the performance being required is directed by law.

When a court order requires a respondent not to take an act, then the request for the respondent to take an action "which contradicted the administrative order could not be considered a ministerial duty . . . so as to be subject to requirement of performance through a mandamus action."

Typically, when an agency of government is delegated rule-making authority by the Florida Legislature, the choice of the contents of the rule is a discretionary decision and not a ministerial one.

Action Requested Yet Not Done:

A petition for writ of mandamus is legally insufficient if it fails to allege that petitioner previously demanded performance from the respondent. The prerequisite demand for performance must be an adequate demand, which under certain factual circumstances will mean that the petitioner must first turn to the available administrative remedies. Options available to the petitioner seeking mandamus include alleging that he had exhausted his administrative remedies, or attaching any documents showing that he had pursued any administrative remedies, or alleging that no administrative remedies existed. Mandamus "may be used to compel the performance of a ministerial duty imposed by law where it has not been performed as the law requires," and therefore, the respondent's failure to complete a ministerial act, or the respondent's failure to do the act properly, may justify the issuance of a writ of mandamus.

No Other Remedy:

"In order for a petition for a writ of mandamus to be granted, it must be shown that the petitioner . . . has no other legal method for redressing the wrong or of obtaining the relief to which he is entitled." Therefore, a writ of mandamus "will not ordinarily issue when other legal remedies are available." This is true even when the other legal remedies may be more burdensome. "As an exception to this rule, however, the supreme court has held that the appellate courts may exercise discretion to issue writs of mandamus to address pure issues of law relating to the constitutionality of statutes."

Id. at § 1701:1.

2. Writ of Prohibition

Elements of the Prima Facie Case for a Writ of Prohibition from FLORIDA ELEMENTS OF AN ACTION

by Patrick John McGinley
21 Fla. Prac. § 1702:1
© 2017 by Thomson Reuters

A writ of prohibition is an original action filed with an appellate court seeking a discretionary remedy to prevent a lower court or tribunal from improperly exercising its judicial power. "Prohibition" is that process by which a superior court exercises its discretion to prevent an inferior court (or tribunal possessing judicial or quasi-judicial powers) from exceeding its jurisdiction in matters over which it has cognizance or usurping matters not within its jurisdiction to hear or determine.

A petition for prohibition seeks the entry of a writ of prohibition. If the court finds the petition is sufficient on its face, the court may in its discretion issue an order for the respondent to show cause why the requested writ should not be issued, and this order bears the archaic name of an "order nisi."

If granted, a writ of prohibition is an enforceable command from a court directed to the lower court or tribunal preventing it from performing certain acts. Therefore, a prohibition action is a means by which to seek a greater court's order preventing a lesser tribunal from doing something it should be forbidden to do.

The five required elements for a writ of prohibition are:

(1) an inferior court or quasi-judicial tribunal

(2) will make but has not yet made

(3) an unauthorized use of its judicial or quasi-judicial power

(4) that will cause the petitioner a harm for which there is no other appropriate and adequate remedy, and therefore,

(5) the reviewing court should exercise its discretion to stop this harm from happening.

The following paragraphs provide guidance as to how to plead and prove each of these five required elements.

Inferior Court or Tribunal:

The petition for writ of prohibition may only be issued by a superior court having appellate and supervisory jurisdiction over the entity whose action petitioner seeks to prohibit. So the first inquiry is whether the court where the petition for writ of prohibition has been filed qualifies as "superior." Additionally, the entity to be prohibited must be shown to be a lower court or a lower tribunal possessing judicial or quasi-judicial power. So the second inquiry is whether the entity sought to be prohibited is an "inferior court or quasi-judicial tribunal."

The reviewing court is the appropriate "superior," first of all, if it is the next highest court that holds appellate and supervisory jurisdiction over the allegedly inferior court or quasi-judicial tribunal. This means that to prohibit a county court, the petition for writ of prohibition should be filed in the circuit court that shares geographic jurisdiction with that county court. Prohibition of a circuit court is properly sought in the district court of appeal from which appellate jurisdiction over that circuit lies. Each of Florida's five District Courts of Appeal are empowered by the Florida Constitution to issue writs of prohibition. Prohibition of a district court of appeal is properly sought in the Supreme Court of Florida.

The reviewing court is the appropriate "superior," second of all, if it holds subject matter jurisdiction over the issues in the writ of prohibition. This may require "skipping over" the first highest superior court and instead filing the petition for writ of prohibition with that court's superior if restrictions upon subject matter jurisdiction warrant such a filing. For example, a petition for writ of prohibition cannot empower a court to review any subject matter over which it otherwise lacks subject matter jurisdiction. Thus, a district court of appeal cannot review judicial assignments by original writ because the Florida Supreme Court has exclusive jurisdiction to review judicial assignments, thereby compelling a petitioner to file his writ of prohibition against a circuit court chief judge not with the district court of appeal but instead with the Florida Supreme Court. "The 1980 amendment to Article V, Section 3(b)(7) of the Florida Constitution appears to permit the Florida Supreme Court to issue writs of prohibition to any court. However, the Court traditionally has accepted jurisdiction to issue these writs to circuit courts only when it ultimately would have appellate or discretionary jurisdiction over the matter."

The second inquiry of whether the entity sought to be prohibited is an "inferior court or quasi-judicial tribunal" grows complex if the entity is not a court. Because a court is always deemed to be acting in either a judicial or quasi-judicial capacity, any future action of a court is an act that may potentially be restrained by a successful petition for writ of prohibition. In a case seeking prohibition of a tribunal or agency, that entity may or may not be acting in a judicial or quasi-judicial capacity. The petitioner must plead and prove that it is doing so because only that type of future action may potentially be restrained by a successful petition for writ of prohibition. Stated somewhat differently, the potentially restrained act must be judicial or quasi-judicial in nature.

For example, an agency or commission that investigates and makes recommendations to another entity is not acting in a judicial or quasi-judicial nature.

Unauthorized Use of Judicial Power:

This element is one of jurisdiction. Indeed, the English law origins of the writ of prohibition are said to arise to safeguard the jurisdiction of the king's court against encroachments of other courts. Yet, prohibition is not available to prevent an erroneous exercise of jurisdiction, but instead is only available to prevent an unauthorized one.

A clear distinction is drawn between assumption of jurisdiction to which the court has no legal claim and erroneous exercise of jurisdiction with which it is invested. Prohibition does not lie for errors that may be redressed by appeal. It does not lie to prevent a subordinate court from deciding erroneously, or from enforcing an erroneous judgment, in a case in which it has a right to adjudicate. In the application of the principle, it matters not whether the court below has decided correctly or erroneously; its jurisdiction of the matter in controversy being conceded, prohibition will not lie to prevent an erroneous exercise of that jurisdiction. Therefore, prohibition may not be used to divest a lower tribunal of jurisdiction to hear and determine the question of its own jurisdiction; nor may it be used to test the correctness of a lower tribunal's ruling on jurisdiction where the existence of jurisdiction depends on controverted facts that the inferior tribunal has jurisdiction to determine.

Prohibition may only be granted when it is shown that a lower court or tribunal is without jurisdiction or attempting to act in excess of its jurisdiction. For example, a petition for a writ of prohibition is an appropriate action for challenging a trial court judge's denial of a motion to recuse or disqualify himself from a case over which he presides. It is also an appropriate action for challenging the head of a state agency's denial of a motion to disqualify himself from an administrative proceeding where he acts in a quasi-judicial capacity.

Perhaps a good example of when prohibition lies arises in the context of Florida's Workers' Compensation Law. It provides no-fault benefits if the injured employee is covered by that law, and creates administrative law tribunals for adjudicating the amount of those benefits. A circuit court could be subject to a writ of prohibition if it attempts to adjudicate the amount of those benefits. But a circuit court cannot be subject to a writ of prohibition when it attempts to adjudicate a personal injury action and the defense asserts that the plaintiff's exclusive remedy is under the workers' compensation law. This is because the circuit court has jurisdiction to decide that question even if it is wrong. The decision will often turn upon the facts, and the court from which the writ of prohibition is sought is in no position to ascertain the facts. Thus, prohibition may not be employed to raise the defense of workers' compensation immunity, but prohibition would lie if a claimant sought to recover workers' compensation by filing suit in circuit court because the court would have no jurisdiction to entertain a workers' compensation benefits action. Perhaps this example helps illustrate the line between what use of judicial power may be subject to a writ of prohibition and what may not.

Action About to Occur:

Prohibition is a preventative, rather than a corrective remedy. It acts only to prevent the commission of an act, and is not an appropriate remedy to revoke an order already issued.

Thus, a petition for a writ of prohibition is appropriate to forestall an impending injury when damage is likely to follow. Prohibition is preventive and not corrective in that it commands the one to whom it is directed not to do the thing which the supervisory court is informed the lower tribunal is about to do.

A writ of prohibition serves only to prevent the commission of an act. Because prohibition's purpose is to prevent the doing of something, not to compel the undoing of something already done, it cannot be used to revoke an order that has already been entered.

Harm for Which There Is No Other Adequate Remedy:

The Florida Supreme Court had held that the writ of prohibition "is very narrow in scope and operation and must be employed with caution and utilized only in emergency cases to prevent an impending injury where there is no other appropriate and adequate legal remedy." Stated somewhat differently, a writ of prohibition is appropriate "to forestall an impending injury where no other appropriate and adequate legal remedy exists and only when damage is likely to follow." For example, "[p]rohibition is also inappropriate if the parties have the right to remedy the wrong by direct appeal." Likewise, if a statute provides a remedy, then resorting to a writ of prohibition would be inappropriate.

Reviewing Court Is Convinced to Exercise Its Discretion:

In Florida, the courts have consistently determined, in accord with the historical understanding and background of the writ of prohibition, that it is meant to be very narrow in scope, to be employed with great caution and utilized only in emergencies. Thus, it might be said that a fifth required element of a successful writ of prohibition is proof of facts that persuade the reviewing court to exercise this discretionary power. The Supreme Court of Florida holds that "[p]rohibition is not a writ of right, but, rather, is a discretionary writ." This means that "the reviewing court is not required to grant a petition for writ of prohibition merely because it would be an appropriate remedy."

Appeal or Review of Grant or Denial of Writ of Prohibition:

An order on a petition for writ of prohibition is reviewable by certiorari.

Id. at § 1702:1 (footnotes omitted).

3. Writ of Quo Warranto

Elements of the Prima Facie Case for a Writ of Quo Warranto from FLORIDA ELEMENTS OF AN ACTION

by Patrick John McGinley
21 Fla. Prac. § 1703:1
© 2017 by Thomson Reuters

A petition for writ of quo warranto is an action to challenge "the exercise of some right or privilege, the peculiar powers of which are derived from the state." Statutes exist empowering the Florida Attorney General to bring petitions for writ of quo warranto, but the right to bring such a petition is not the Attorney General's alone. Quo warranto proceedings seek the enforcement of a public right, so "the people" are the real party to the action and the person bringing suit "need not show that he has any real or personal interest in it." Also, the person bringing the petition for quo warranto need not show he suffers any harm. Thus, actions in the nature of quo warranto to question the authority for the exercise of rights, privileges, and powers derived from the state can be brought by any person. A statutory exception exists for a quo warranto action challenging an election or a right to hold office arising from that election, for the person making such a quo warranto challenge must be either the Florida Attorney General or, if that attorney refuses to bring the suit, then it must be a person claiming the right to hold that office. . . .

. . . The four elements of an action for quo warranto are:

(1) A Florida official, government agency, or other alleged recipient of a power or right that is derived from the State of Florida

(2) has or will exercise that power

(3) but such use is or will be legally improper

(4) and therefore, the court should exercise its discretion to grant this discretionary writ.

The following paragraphs provide guidance as to how to plead and prove each of these four required elements.

Government or Right of Government:

The writ of quo warranto historically has been used to determine whether a state officer or agency has improperly exercised a power or right derived from the State. Examples of uses of quo warranto include challenging a public defender's authority to file a class action on behalf of juveniles in federal court, questioning the legality of a Florida city's actions regarding annexation ordinances, challenging the power and authority of a particular state attorney, ousting land from a municipality which should not properly have become a part of that municipality, or challenging the Florida governor's right to actions such as signing a compact with a Native American tribe, declaring a special session of the Florida Legislature, or declaring its topic.

Yet the use of quo warranto is only limited to state officers and agencies when the petition for writ of quo warranto is filed with the Supreme Court of Florida. Before Florida's five district courts of appeal and its 20 circuit courts, quo warranto is available to challenge "the exercise of some right or privilege, the peculiar powers of which are derived from the state." So the respondent need not have state power, but only needs to be using such power. For example, a citizen landowner who fenced off for himself a state-owned island in Kissimmee can be subjected to a writ of quo warranto because that citizen claims for himself the right to exclude others from the state's public lands, a right which accrues (if at all) from the state. . . .

Petitions for a writ of quo warranto historically have been filed after a public official has acted. . . . [I]t can be used to challenge a person's right to continue to hold a public office. It may also be used to challenge one's continued ability to hold a franchise of government.

Court Should Exercise Discretion to Grant Writ:

Because the Constitution provides that an appropriate court "may" issue a writ of quo warranto, the Supreme Court of Florida holds that this language renders the court's exercise of quo warranto jurisdiction discretionary. Stated somewhat differently, a petitioner's proof of entitlement to such a writ need not result in the court's issuance of that writ. Thus, a well-pled petition for writ of quo warranto should contain adequate proof to convince the court to exercise its discretion to issue this discretionary writ.

While holding that quo warranto relief is discretionary, the Supreme Court also offers some guidance as to when to exercise that discretion. A court may choose to consider extraordinary writ petitions "where the functions of government would be adversely affected absent an immediate determination by this Court." On the other hand, a court would most likely "decline jurisdiction and transfer or dismiss writ petitions which . . . raise substantial issues of fact or present individualized issues that do not require immediate resolution by this Court, or are not the type of case in which an opinion from this Court would provide important guiding principles for the other courts of this State."

Id. at § 1703:1 (footnotes omitted).

The use of, and a limitation upon, Florida's writ of quo warranto is illustrated by the following case of *League of Women Voters of Fla. v. Scott*, 232 So. 3d 264 (Fla. 2017). A special interest group petitioned for a writ of quo warranto against then-Governor Rick Scott to prohibit him from filling three upcoming judicial vacancies on Florida's supreme court. The factual basis was because Governor Scott's term concludes at the end of the day on the first Monday in January, which is the same day that the Justices' terms end. Governor Scott intended to make the appointments on his last day. The special interest group sought to stop him.

League of Women Voters of Florida v. Scott

Supreme Court of Florida, 2017
232 So. 3d 264

This case is before the Court on the petition of the League of Women Voters of Florida (the League) for a writ of quo warranto. Because the issue presented is not ripe for consideration, we dismiss the petition.

The League asks this Court to issue a writ of quo warranto against Governor Rick Scott prohibiting him from "filling any judicial vacancies on Florida's appellate courts that occur due to terms expiring in January 2019." The League's basis for filing the petition is Governor Scott's December 2016 announcement of intent to appoint the replacements for three justices of this Court. However, use of the writ to address prospective conduct is not appropriate.

Quo warranto is used "to determine whether a state officer or agency has improperly exercised a power or right derived from the State," *Fla. House of Representatives v. Crist*, 999 So. 2d 601, 607 (Fla. 2008), and the history of the extraordinary writ reflects that petitions for relief in quo warranto are properly filed only after a public official has acted. In *Swoope v. City of New Smyrna*, 98 Fla. 1082, 125 So. 371 (1929), we explained that a challenge to an individual's exercise of official authority

> will not be determined by bill in chancery, such a case being regarded as appropriately falling within the jurisdiction of the common law courts by proceedings in quo warranto. And since this remedy is applicable the moment an office or franchise is usurped, an injunction will not lie to prevent the usurpation, even though the respondent has not yet entered upon the office or assumed to exercise its functions. In such case the party aggrieved should wait until an actual usurpation has occurred, and then seek his remedy in quo warranto.

Id. at 372. A party must wait until a government official has acted before seeking relief pursuant to quo warranto because a threatened exercise of power which is allegedly outside of that public official's authority may not ultimately occur. To address whether quo warranto relief is warranted under such premature circumstances would amount to an impermissible advisory opinion based upon hypothetical facts.

We previously considered whether issuance of the writ was appropriate in situations where the state officer or agency had already acted. For example, in *Whiley v. Scott*, 79 So. 3d 702, 705 (Fla. 2011), we reviewed a completed action, in that the challenged executive order had already been issued. The same is true of *State ex rel. Butterworth v. Kenny*, 714 So. 2d 404, 406 (Fla. 1998), receded from on other grounds by *Darling v. State*, 45 So. 3d 444 (Fla. 2010), where we considered the authority of the Office of the Capital Collateral Regional Counsel for the Northern and Southern Regions to represent death row inmates in civil rights actions. Most recently, in *Ayala v. Scott*, 224 So .3d 755, 756–57 (Fla. 2017), we held that quo warranto was an appropriate vehicle for the state attorney for the Ninth Judicial Circuit to challenge a series of executive orders that reassigned the prosecution of a number of pending death-penalty eligible cases to the state attorney of another judicial circuit.

Although Governor Scott announced his intent to appoint the replacements for three justices of this Court, clearly no appointments have been made. To use quo warranto to review an action which is merely contemplated but not consummated, as in the present case, would require this Court to depart from the historical application of the writ. This we decline to do. Until some action is taken by the Governor, the matter the League seeks to have resolved is not ripe, and this Court lacks jurisdiction to determine whether quo warranto relief is warrantcd.

Based upon the foregoing, the petition is hereby dismissed.

LABARGA, C.J., and CANADY, POLSTON, and LAWSON, JJ., concur.

QUINCE, J., concurring in result only.

While I agree with the majority's conclusion that the "issue presented is not ripe for consideration," majority op. at 264, I also agree with Justice Lewis that this Court could properly review a petition for quo warranto prior to the actual appointment of a new justice. I write separately to clarify what I believe to be an improper focus in both opinions and to highlight the concessions made by Governor Scott's counsel during oral argument regarding the Governor's authority to make these appointments.

The majority currently states:

> Although Governor Scott announced his intent to appoint the replacements for three justices to this Court, *clearly no appointments have been made.* To use quo warranto to review an action *which is merely contemplated but not consummated,* as in the present case, would require this Court to depart from the historical application of the writ. This we decline to do. *Until some action is taken by the Governor,* the matter the League seeks to have resolved is not ripe, and this Court lacks jurisdiction to determine whether quo warranto relief is warranted.

Majority op. at 266 (emphasis added). First, the majority implies that the action would not be ripe until the Governor makes an appointment ("clearly, no appointments have been made . . . merely contemplated but not consummated"). However, the majority then appears to suggest that only "some action" would be necessary for this Court to consider the Governor's authority to make said action. Majority op. at 266. This inconsistent language creates unnecessary confusion about when a future petition for quo warranto would be ripe for this Court's consideration. This confusion is compounded by Justice Lewis' dissent, which also focuses on the presumption that the issue may only become ripe once the Governor has made an appointment. See Dissenting op. at 269 ("The majority's statement today that the appointment must be consummated before quo warranto applies. . . .").

Furthermore, the majority ignores that we have previously granted a petition for a writ of quo warranto challenging the Governor's authority to endeavor to fill a judicial vacancy. *Lerman v. Scott*, No. SC16-783, 2016 WL 3127708 (Fla. Jun. 3, 2016). In *Lerman*, the petitioners sought the writ of quo warranto "to show by what authority [Governor Scott] has endeavored to fill a vacancy, created by the Resign to Run statute, in the office of county court judge, in Group 11 of the Fifteenth Judicial Circuit, through an appointment." Petition at 1, 2016 WL 2760518, *Lerman v. Scott*, No. SC16–783. We granted the writ in *Lerman* because Governor Scott acted by requesting the Judicial Nominating Commission to provide a list of names for his consideration to make an appointment. *Lerman*, 2016 WL 3127708, at *1 ("The Governor shall not utilize the Fifteenth Judicial Circuit Judicial Nominating Commission to perform any functions related to nominating candidates for this judicial office."). Thus, unlike the dissent's characterization of *Lerman*, we were not merely responding to an announced intention, dissenting op. at 268–69, but did find an action short of an actual appointment by which the petitioner could question the Governor's authority. Under this Court's precedent, we have the authority to act prior to the Governor's making an appointment that is contrary to law.

On the merits of the instant petition, at oral argument in this Court, Governor Scott's counsel conceded that "the Governor's term concludes at the end of the day on [the first] Monday" in January, "the same day that the Justices' terms end." The Governor's counsel further conceded that if the justices do not leave before the end of their terms and "if the new governor's term has begun, then the new governor would have the authority to make the appointment." This position is the same as that taken by the majority of Florida voters in 2014 in response to a proposed constitutional amendment which would have required the Governor "to prospectively fill vacancies in a judicial office."

The Governor's concession reflects Florida law. Under the Florida Constitution, when a vacancy occurs in a judicial office to which election for retention applies, "the governor shall fill the vacancy by appointing for a term ending on the first Tuesday after the first Monday in January of the year following the next general election." Art. V, § 11(a), Fla. Const. However, a vacancy exists only "upon the expiration of the term being served by the justice." Art. V, § 10(a), Fla. Const. We have explained that this provision "expressly provides that a vacancy in a merit retention judicial office does not occur *until the end* of the judge or justice's term." *Advisory Op. to Governor re Judicial Vacancy Due to Mandatory Retirement*, 940 So. 2d 1090, 1091 (Fla. 2006) (emphasis added).

Moreover, under article IV, section 5(a), of the Florida Constitution, a governor's term does not begin until "the first Tuesday after the first Monday in January" of the year following the general election. As noted in an appendix to the instant petition filed in this Court, Governors Bush, Crist, and Scott all took the oath of office well before the first Tuesday after the first Monday in January so as to assume gubernatorial duties immediately on the first day of their respective terms. See App. to Pet'rs' Reply at 2–4.

Although not before us, the Governor also conceded that a declaratory action would be appropriate to challenge his endeavor to replace the retiring justices. I agree. Moreover, while I agree with the majority that it is not appropriate for us to rule on the petition at this time, I do not agree that it would only become appropriate to do so after Governor Scott has consummated an appointment. Furthermore, the concession made by the Governor during oral argument effectively answers the question raised in the petition.

PARIENTE, J., concurs.

LEWIS, J., dissenting.

It is most unfortunate that the majority finds it necessary to summarily dismiss this common law action to protect our State from blatantly unconstitutional actions for reasons other than a proper analysis of the law and do so directly contrary to the application of quo warranto in this judicial appointment context in 2016 in *Lerman v. Scott*, No. SC16-783, 2016 WL 3127708 *1 (Fla. June 3, 2016), in which the entire Court either concurred or concurred in result. It is even more regrettable and distressing that future Floridians have lost the ability to protect themselves and society from clearly unconstitutional action. The Florida Constitution requires devoted protection and the Florida citizens deserve better. Contrary to Florida law and the general common law, the majority has now announced that the challenged conduct must have already produced a constitutional crisis and calamitous result before illegal acts of government officials are subject to quo warranto review or relief. Florida law has generally recognized that quo warranto is available to prevent significant impacts on the operation of government, *Whiley v. Scott*, 79 So. 3d 702, 708 (Fla. 2011), but the majority now negates that common sense, reasonable, and logical analysis to require that illegal and unconstitutional conduct which produces disarray must have already occurred to allow judicial action. While writs of quo warranto may be applied to acts of state officials that have already been committed, the writ is not foreclosed as an avenue of relief for threatened and imminent future actions of state officials, based on the clear Florida law.

As recently as the summer of 2016, this Court granted a petition for writ of quo warranto in response to an announced intention by a Governor to appoint (not having already appointed) a judicial officer to fill a position vacated by a judge seeking higher office. *Lerman*, 2016 WL 3127708, at *1. County Court Judge Johnson resigned pursuant to the Resign to Run statute and Lerman submitted the necessary paperwork to become a candidate for the judicial position previously held by Judge Johnson. Governor Scott, as he has done here, announced that he was going to make an appointment to the position held by Judge Johnson. Lerman filed a petition for writ of quo warranto in this Court to prevent Governor Scott from appointing or attempting to appoint a person to the position previously held by Judge Johnson contrary to law. This Court granted the petition for quo warranto and ordered the position filled by election. *Id.* This Court further ordered that any functions related to the future appointment of candidates for this position terminate. *Id.* The majority's statement today that the appointment must be "consummated" before quo warranto applies is simply incorrect, contrary to common sense, and, in my view, dangerous. Majority op. at 266.

Under the majority view, elected politicians can announce their intentions and plan to engage in all types of illegal and harmful conduct but no relief is available until the illegal and harmful act has already inflicted its damage. Magnificent trees cut, pristine waters fouled, and unthinkable harm inflicted upon our citizens, which may not be prevented when the actor plans and even announces his intentions. Today, we have a new test. The writ is only available when the illegal act is taken and harm is actually inflicted — at times even irreparable harm.

The majority simply ignores that the Supreme Court of Vermont has recently granted a petition for writ of quo warranto under virtually identical circumstances as we face here. *Turner v. Shumlin*, 163 A.3d 1173 (Vt. 2017). In Vermont, the former Governor announced his intention to appoint the replacement for a current Supreme Court Justice who decided not to seek retention for another term. *Id.* at 1176. The Justice's term would not expire until after the current Governor's term had expired. *Id.* The same argument was made in Vermont as is advanced by the majority here that the court could not act until an illegal appointment was actually made. *Id.* at 1177. In rejecting the principle announced by the majority here, the Supreme Court of Vermont recognized that the circumstances were not conjectural, hypothetical, or abstract. *Id.* The announced intentions were concrete and unequivocal. *Id.* Understanding that there is a fundamental interest in ensuring that the constitutional process is sound, the court held that the Governor could not constitutionally appoint the Justice in question's replacement. *Id.* at 1188. We must all heed the closing words from the Vermont Supreme Court:

> We reach our decision having in mind the overarching principles of our democracy: the integrity of our governing institutions and the people's confidence in them.

Id.

Today, the majority opinion has chosen to cherrypick only certain rules with regard to writs of quo warranto, while ignoring the clear precedent from Florida and other jurisdictions that have emphasized the notion that the writ can be appropriate in cases of threatened or attempted action by a state official. *State ex rel. Bruce v. Kiesling*, 632 So. 2d 601, 603 (Fla. 1994) ("[W]e note that the common law remedy of quo warranto is employed either to determine the right of an individual to hold public office or to challenge a public officer's attempt to exercise some right or privilege derived from the State."); *State ex rel. Ervin v. Jacksonville Expressway Auth.*, 139 So. 2d 135, 137 (Fla. 1962) ("It is a proper function of the Attorney General, in the interest of the public, to test the exercise, or threatened exercise, of power by such a corporate state agency through the process of a quo warranto proceeding."); *Adm'r, Retreat Hosp. v. Johnson*, 660 So. 2d 333, 339 (Fla. 4th DCA 1995) ("The remedy of quo warranto is designed to challenge a public officer's attempt to exercise some right or privilege derived from the state.").

Notes and Questions to Consider:

1. The majority rules that a writ of quo warranto is not available until after the respondent acts. The respondent's stated intention to act is insufficient. What are the advantages and disadvantages to this rule?

2. The facts of this case involved an incumbent chief executive, his desire to fill a supreme court seat, and an attempt to keep the seat open until the incumbent was replaced by his successor. Are not those the same facts that fairly recently occurred on the national stage? In March 2016, outgoing U.S. President Barak Obama nominated federal appellate Judge Merrick Garland to fill a vacant seat on the U.S. Supreme Court, but the U.S. Senate, led by majority leader Mitch McConnell, successfully prevented Judge Garland's appointment and kept the seat open for the incoming president to fill. Would the result had been the same if this played out in Florida instead of the national stage?

3. Three of the justices deciding this case are the justices that the governor intends to replace. Although technically this may not have caused a conflict of interest, did it not place the governor and his counsel in an awkward position? Does it impact your answer to know that Governor Scott campaigned on a platform of promising to appoint more conservative judges and the three outgoing justices are often considered to be more liberal judges? If you were the governor's attorney, would you have discussed the possibility of filing a motion to recuse or disqualify the personally affected justices?

4. Under Florida's constitution, when does a vacancy occur in a judicial office to which election for retention applies? For the answer, see the fifth or sixth paragraph of Justice Quince's concurring opinion above.

5. Under Florida's constitution, when does a newly elected Florida governor's term begin? For the answer, see the next-to-last paragraph of Justice Quince's concurring opinion.

6. Justice Quince's concurring opinion cites to *Advisory Opinion to Governor re Judicial Vacancy Due to Mandatory Retirement*, 940 So. 2d 1090, 1091 (Fla. 2006). Under what circumstances can Florida's supreme court issue an advisory opinion?

7. Justice Quince writes: "the Governor also conceded that a declaratory action would be appropriate to challenge his endeavor to replace the retiring justices. I agree." Why do you think the League of Women Voters filed a petition for writ of quo warranto, the proper place for which was Florida's supreme court, instead of filing a complaint for declaratory judgment, the proper place for which was Florida's Circuit Court for the Second Judicial Circuit in and for Leon County, Florida?

8. Judge Quince's concurrence, and the second paragraph of Justice Lewis' dissent, reference "the Resign to Run statute." This refers to Florida Statutes section 99.012, an enabling statute for the sentence in the Florida Constitution's Article II, Section 5 that reads:

> No person shall hold at the same time more than one office under the government of the state and the counties and municipalities therein, except that a notary public or military officer may hold another office, and any officer may be a member of a constitution revision commission, taxation and budget reform commission, constitutional convention, or statutory body having only advisory powers.

Id. at clause 2. Section 99.012, as amended in 2018, provides in relevant part:

> "Officer" means a person, whether elected or appointed, who has the authority to exercise the sovereign power of the state pertaining to an office recognized under the State Constitution or laws of the state. . . . No officer may qualify as a candidate for another state, district, county, or municipal public office if the terms or any part thereof run concurrently with each other without resigning from the office he or she presently holds. . . . The resignation is irrevocable. . . . The written resignation must be submitted at least 10 days prior to the first day of qualifying for the office he or she intends to seek. . . . The resignation must be effective no later than the earlier of the following dates: 1. The date the officer would take office, if elected; or 2. The date the officer's successor is required to take office.

Id. at subsection (1). The 2018 amendment extended these requirements to certain officers becoming candidates for one of various federal offices.

4. Constitutional Writ (the "All Writs" Power)

Elements of the Prima Facie Case for a Constitutional Writ (An "All Writs" Claim)
from FLORIDA ELEMENTS OF AN ACTION

by Patrick John McGinley
21 Fla. Prac. § 1704:1
© 2017 by Thomson Reuters

Events transpiring now or in the future may sometimes affect a court's jurisdiction. Florida law provides a limited means to proactively thwart such events. A petition for constitutional writ is an original action filed to preserve a court's jurisdiction that has already been invoked or to protect a court's jurisdiction that likely will be invoked in the future. It is often called an "all writs" action due to the language appearing in the enabling article of the Florida Constitution (granting courts the power to issue "all writs necessary" to preserve their jurisdiction). This doctrine of "all writs" is not an independent basis for a court's jurisdiction, but rather, its use is restricted to preserving jurisdiction that exists now or is likely to exist in the future. Therefore, "[i]n practice, stay of lower court proceedings is the most common occasion for invoking the all writs power."

The elements of an action for a constitutional writ under the "all writs necessary" clauses of Article V of the Florida Constitution are:

(1) The court has jurisdiction now, or is likely to have such jurisdiction in the future;

(2) Events are transpiring that are a threat to that jurisdiction; and

(3) The court should exercise its discretionary authority to protect its jurisdiction.

Present or Future Jurisdiction:

The Supreme Court of Florida holds that the "all writs necessary" provisions of Article V of the Florida Constitution empower courts in their discretion to "issue all writs necessary to aid the Court in exercising its 'ultimate jurisdiction.'" For this reason, "[t]he use of the all writs section is not limited to pending cases; it may be used as well to protect the future exercise of [a court's] jurisdiction." As one commentator describes it:

Although a constitutional writ may be properly characterized as an ancillary remedy, the scope of its application is not limited to cases that have already been filed in the appellate court. A constitutional writ may be issued in connection with a case that will become the subject of the jurisdiction of the appellate court in the future. . . . Stated otherwise, the all writs provisions may be used as an aid to the ultimate jurisdiction of an appellate court, just as it may be used as an adjunct to an existing exercise of the court's jurisdiction. The use of a writ to protect a future claim is limited, however, to those situations in which an action threatens the potential jurisdiction of the court.

Thus, for "all writs" purposes, a court has present or future jurisdiction if a proceeding is pending or likely will be pending before the appellate court on another jurisdictional basis.

Events Threaten Jurisdiction:

Jurisdiction may be said to be threatened if the failure of the court to contemporaneously grant relief, enter a stay or impose an injunction to preserve the status quo will likely affect the court's "ultimate jurisdiction."

The events threatening jurisdiction must be things done or allowed to be done by a court or an agency acting in a quasi-judicial capacity.

Perhaps the most obvious threat arises when an appellate court has decided a case, issued its mandate, and remanded the case to the lower tribunal for further proceedings in accordance with the appellate decision and mandate, yet the lower tribunal fails to comply. The filing of a petition for constitutional writ is an appropriate action to seek to remedy such a threat to the appellate court's jurisdiction.

Yet the required threat to the court's current or future jurisdiction is not limited to the facts of a prior appeal and a current appellate mandate. Any other situation of a court or quasi-judicial tribunal taking actions that threaten a court's present or future jurisdiction might also be the subject of a petition for constitutional writ. Case law precedent provides examples of such situations.

For example, the Supreme Court of Florida is vested with jurisdiction in the second year following each decennial census to either review a legislative plan of apportionment or actually devise a plan of apportionment depending upon whether the legislature succeeds in passing an appropriate apportionment bill within the time limits. The Governor's actions to shorten those time limits therefore will likely affect the Supreme Court's "ultimate jurisdiction" to review or devise a plan of apportionment, thereby creating jurisdiction under the "all writs" clause of Article V of the Florida Constitution for the Court to enter a constitutional writ to the governor.

As another example, the Supreme Court of Florida holds to itself the power to regulate the practice of law in Florida. A statute empowered the Florida Public Employees Relations Commission with certain powers to regulate who practices law and how lawyers behave before PERC. In reviewing a petition for constitutional writ seeking to stop PERC's action in reviewing an application from a lawyer's group, the Supreme Court denied the constitutional writ as premature but acknowledged its possible future ability to grant one if PERC were to enact rules affecting the Supreme Court's ultimate jurisdiction to regulate the practice of law in Florida.

Court Should Exercise Its Discretion to Enter the Writ So as to Preserve Its Jurisdiction:

A petition for constitutional writ seeks the court to exercise its discretionary jurisdiction. Thus, it might be said that the last required element of a successful petition for constitutional writ is to allege and prove facts that persuade the court to exercise this discretionary power.

Id. at § 1704:1 (footnotes omitted).

5. Writ of Certiorari

Elements of the Prima Facie Case for a Writ of Certiorari from FLORIDA ELEMENTS OF AN ACTION

by Patrick John McGinley
21 Fla. Prac. § 1705:1
© 2017 by Thomson Reuters

Certiorari is a "special mechanism" by which a superior court under quite limited circumstances can review either a quasi-judicial act, or review the progress of a pending judicial case, so that the higher court can be made fully aware of the "events below and evaluate the proceedings for regularity." In Florida state courts, a petition for writ of certiorari has three potential uses: to appeal from certain orders that are not eligible for an appeal under the Florida Rules of Appellate Procedure; to appeal from the outcome of a prior petition for writ of certiorari; or to seek review of certain quasi-judicial actions of local government entities or state agencies over whom the Florida Administrative Procedure Act does not apply when appellate jurisdiction for such entities is not otherwise conferred by law. All three uses bear the name Certiorari, are often called "cert," and can properly be referred to by the name Common Law Certiorari. Yet the three uses are different enough in kind and in legal standards to warrant proposing three different names: Certiorari from Interlocutory Orders (a type of First-Tier Certiorari), Certiorari from Quasi-Judicial Acts (another type of First-Tier Certiorari), and Second-Tier Certiorari (a type of Certiorari review of a prior Certiorari proceeding). Before we discuss each separately, we first identify the source of authority for certiorari review, and then discuss some criteria common to each of the three types of certiorari.

Source of Authority

The Supreme Court of the State of Florida does not have authority under the Constitution of the State of Florida to grant or deny petitions for writs of certiorari. Florida's Circuit Courts are granted such authority under Article V, Section 5, and Florida's District Courts of Appeal are granted such authority under Article V, Section 4 of the state Constitution. The omission of the Supreme Court of Florida from having the authority to grant certiorari review is the result of a 1980 amendment to the Florida Constitution that achieved its intent to remove the Florida Supreme Court's certiorari jurisdiction.

Jurisdiction

Regarding the authority of a District Court of Appeal to grant a petition for writ of certiorari, the Constitution of the State of Florida provides, in relevant part:

Art. V, § 4. District Courts of Appeal . . .

(b) (3) . . . may issue writs of mandamus, certiorari, prohibition, quo warranto and other writs necessary to the complete exercise of its jurisdiction.

Regarding the authority of a Circuit Court to grant a petition for writ of certiorari, the Constitution of the State of Florida provides, in relevant part:

Art. V, § 5. Circuit Courts . . .

(b) . . . have . . . power to issue writs of mandamus, quo warranto, certiorari, prohibition . . . and other writs necessary to the complete exercise of its jurisdiction.

Venue

Although both a circuit court and a district court of appeal may have constitutional jurisdiction, the proper venue for filing the petition for writ of certiorari is the circuit court if the case or controversy at issue did not occur in circuit court. For example, the circuit court with geographic jurisdiction over the intended recipient of the writ of certiorari is the proper venue if the case or controversy at issue occurred in County Court, before a local government entity, or before a state agency. The circuit court routinely assigns such petitions to its appellate division. Of course, if the case or controversy from which certiorari is sought occurred in the state circuit court, then the District Court of Appeal with geographic jurisdiction over that circuit is the proper venue for filing the petition for writ of certiorari. Perhaps this language from a 1966 decision of Florida's Second District Court of Appeal best describes venue for extraordinary writs such as certiorari:

The jurisdiction to issue such writs initially follows the route of direct appellate jurisdiction. . . . The jurisdiction of this court to issue such writs might at first blush be construed to be without limitation or restriction, but we do not so conclude. . . . The provisions of the constitution granting this court jurisdiction to issue such writs must be construed to mean that such jurisdiction is limited to those causes in which a direct appeal to this court would be allowed as a matter of right at a later stage of the proceedings below. Any other interpretation would permit a picking and choosing of courts by litigants and the usurpation by one court of the jurisdiction of another, thereby disrupting the carefully laid pattern of appellate jurisdiction set forth in the constitution. We, therefore, hold that jurisdiction of this court to issue writs of mandamus, certiorari, prohibition and quo warranto, insofar as they apply to a court exercising the judicial power of the state, is limited to those causes then pending in which this court has direct appellate jurisdiction.

Certiorari from Interlocutory Orders

In this type of first-tier certiorari review, a petition for writ of certiorari may be used to review certain types of judicial orders that are not otherwise subject to review at this time via an immediate appeal. Such a judicial order may be called "interlocutory" because it is not a final decree, does not prevent the underlying litigation from continuing, allows the trial court to maintain control of and jurisdiction over the underlying suit, and is entered prior to a final judgment. The Florida Rules of Appellate Procedure lists those final and non-final orders from which an appeal may be taken immediately, and most if not all interlocutory orders are absent from that list. For such an order, certiorari may be an option, and if so, an independent review of that order may occur in the appellate court while the underlying lawsuit remains pending in the trial court.

"Very few categories of non-final orders qualify for the use of this extraordinary writ" of Certiorari from an Interlocutory Order. "Whether the appellate court will entertain the petition [for Certiorari from an Interlocutory Order] depends not only on the seriousness of the error in the lower tribunal, but also on the need for immediate relief." For this reason, the petitioner bears the burden to prove the following three elements:

(1) a departure from the essential requirements of the law,

(2) resulting in material injury for the remainder of the case

(3) that cannot be corrected on post-judgment appeal.

This is the customary order for listing the three elements, but they are listed in reverse order because "[t]he last two elements are jurisdictional and must be analyzed before the court may even consider the first element."

The last two elements require that "the appellate court must focus on the threshold jurisdictional question: whether there is a material injury that cannot be corrected on appeal, otherwise termed as irreparable harm." It is a waste of appellate judicial resources for the appellate court to take certiorari jurisdiction when an adequate remedy exists upon plenary appeal. Thus, these two elements require a showing that there is no adequate remedy on appeal. For example, "[a]n order of abatement is properly reviewable by writ of certiorari, because there is no adequate remedy for the delay caused by abatement after final judgment."

But "[i]f the harm caused by an erroneous order can be corrected by an award of damages or if it can be redressed on appeal from the final order in some other way, the reviewing court will likely decline to review the order by certiorari. The fact that the aggrieved party will be forced to spend time and money on a trial that is claimed to be unnecessary is not regarded as an irreparable injury." Thus, "[t]he expenditure of time and money to litigate a case that would be dismissed if the petition were granted is not an irreparable injury."

Pre-trial discovery orders are frequent fodder for attempts at this type of first-tier certiorari review. "For a denial of discovery to constitute material, irreparable harm, thus conferring certiorari jurisdiction, the denial must 'effectively eviscerate[ ] a party's claim, defense, or counterclaim.'" Such an evisceration would mean that there would be no adequate appellate remedy because "there is no practical way to determine after judgment how the requested discovery would have affected the outcome of the proceedings." On the other hand, an order erroneously granting impermissible discovery constitutes irreparable harm only when it is "one that would let the 'cat out of the bag' and provide the opponent material that could be used by an unscrupulous litigant to injure another person." For this reason, "[o]rders improperly requiring the disclosure of trade secrets or other proprietary information often create irreparable harm and are thus appropriate for certiorari review." But also for this reason, not every erroneous discovery order creates certiorari jurisdiction because some orders are subject to adequate redress on appeal from the final judgment. In 1995, the Supreme Court of Florida disapproved contrary decisions from the appellate courts to the extent they could be interpreted as "automatically equating irrelevant discovery requests with irreparable harm."

Irreparable harm was found in such diverse situations as:

- orders denying sovereign immunity
- granting or denying a discharge of a lis pendens upon real property
- granting discovery of attorney-client privileged information
- granting or denying disqualification of counsel,
- granting discovery of documents protected from discovery by the work-product privilege
- requiring an automobile insurer to produce portions of its adjusters' claims files to a medical care provider,
- revealing medical information of non-party patients,
- disregarding federal medical record privacy laws,
- compelling a paternity test,
- compelling, in a family law case, the ex-husband to submit to a psychosocial and substance abuse evaluation and compelling his production of such confidential records,
- excluding videographers or attorneys from attending compulsory medical examinations,
- granting a stay or abatement of the litigation,
- disclosing a corporation's trade secrets,
- revealing clergy communications

- failing to release a mentally ill defendant who could not be restored to competency to stand trial,

- failing to follow "law of the case,"

- requiring a party to produce for discovery records for which a statute creates a legal privilege against disclosure.

- requiring a party's business clients to produce documents when the clients had no connection to the claims in the lawsuit and the production may interfere with the party's relationship with his clients.

Irreparable harm was not found in situations such as:

- a trial court's failure to approve a party's contingency attorney fee contract

- a trial court granting discovery of the insurer's irrelevant and privileged claim log after all privileged information was redacted from the log,

- a discovery ruling that is erroneous but that can be remedied on appeal,

- an order granting discovery that is "overbroad, irrelevant, or burdensome."

- discovery of a party's financial information when there is a financial issue in the case and that financial discovery is relevant and reasonably calculated to lead to admissible evidence,

Once certiorari jurisdiction exists because the petitioner showed the presence of an irreparable harm, then—and only then—the court must determine whether the petitioner meets his burden under the first element of showing that the order "departed from the essential requirements of law—something that is more than just a legal error." "[A] petitioner can demonstrate a departure from the essential requirements of the law by showing 'that the trial court made an error so serious that it amounts to a miscarriage of justice.'" This means that the reviewing court "should not be as concerned with the mere existence of legal error as much as with the seriousness of the error." Adequate notice of the proceedings, and an appropriate opportunity to be heard, are certainly among the essential requirements of law. Thus, "Certiorari is often the proper remedy to challenge a pretrial order that has the effect of denying a party a procedural right" that may result in denying the petitioner her constitutional right to due process of law in the proceedings below. For example, the Florida Supreme Court finds that Florida Statutes section 768.72 (1995) "creates a substantive legal right not to be subjected to a punitive damages claim and ensuing financial worth discovery until the trial court makes a determination that there is a reasonable evidentiary basis for recovery of punitive damages." Therefore, the Florida Supreme Court "concluded that certiorari jurisdiction is appropriate to review whether a trial judge has conformed with the procedural requirements of section 768.72 but not so broad as to encompass review of the sufficiency of the evidence when the trial judge has followed the procedural requirements of section 768.72."

The essential requirements of law expand further than such procedural due process concerns, but quite limitedly. For example, when "the trial court reached the right result, albeit for the wrong reasons, the [court] did not depart from the essential requirements of law." For there to be a departure from the essential requirements of substantive law, the law must be settled and clear in that area. "[T]he clearly established law which if violated by an inferior court authorizes a [reviewing] court of appeal to grant certiorari review, can derive from a variety of legal sources including case law dealing with the same issue, an interpretation or application of a statute, a procedural rule, or a constitutional provision." For example, the failure to conduct an in-camera inspection of the discovery materials a party asserts are protected by the work-product privilege constitutes a departure from the essential requirements of law subject to certiorari relief. Likewise, it is a departure from the essential requirements of the law applicable to dependency proceedings when the trial court entered an order that relieved the father from complying with the tasks enumerated in an earlier case plan approved by the court, when a recent recurrence of violence in the presence of the child contradicted the claim that the father no longer needed the services in the case plan, nothing in the record supported the elimination of any of the services or the amendment of the case plan, and the elimination of the tasks and services comprising the plan exposed the child to more of the same harm that prompted the filing of the dependency petition. Other examples of departures from the essential requirements of law include granting an order of abatement that effectively amounts to a dismissal of the plaintiff's complaint, ordering a non-resident defendant to appear in the state for an independent medical examination to determine his capacity to testify and ordering juror interviews without determining whether any information elicited through those interviews will entitle the moving party to a new trial.

Yet the petitioner's success in obtaining jurisdiction and proving a departure from the essential requirements of law might not result in his success in obtaining certiorari. The reviewing "court may refuse to grant a petition for common-law certiorari even though there may have been a departure from the essential requirements of law." "It is this discretion which is the essential distinction between review by appeal and review by common-law certiorari." The writ is discretionary.

Certiorari from Quasi-Judicial Acts

In this type of first-tier certiorari review, a petition for writ of certiorari may be used to seek review of certain quasi-judicial actions of local government entities or agencies over whom the Florida Administrative Procedure

Act does not apply when appellate jurisdiction over such entities is not otherwise conferred by law. "Although termed 'certiorari' review, review at this level is not discretionary but rather is a matter of right and is akin in many respects to a plenary appeal." So a significant difference between this type of first-tier certiorari review and Certiorari from Interlocutory Orders is that this type of first-tier review gives the petitioner an absolute right to be heard on the merits of his certiorari claim.

But this type of certiorari is limited to quasi-judicial acts. Local government entities or agencies perform functions that may be legislative, quasi-legislative, quasi-executive, or quasi-judicial. "It is the character of the hearing that determines whether or not board action is legislative or quasi-judicial. . . . Generally speaking, legislative action results in the formulation of a general rule of policy, whereas judicial action results in the application of a general rule of policy." Stated somewhat differently, a "judicial or quasi judicial act determines the rules of law applicable, and the rights affected by them, in relation to past transactions. On the other hand, a quasi-legislative or administrative order prescribes what the rule of requirement of administratively determined duty shall be with respect to transactions to be executed in the future, in order that same shall be considered lawful. But even so, quasi legislative and quasi executive orders, after they have already been entered, may have a quasi judicial attribute if capable of being arrived at and provided by law to be declared by the administrative agency only after express statutory notice, hearing, and consideration of evidence to be adduced as a basis for the making thereof." This means that an action is quasi-judicial when a local government entity or an agency "exercised a statutory power given it to make a decision having a judicial character or attribute and consequent upon some notice or hearing provided to be had before it as a condition for the rendition of the particular decision made. Unless, therefore, a particular decision complained of can be said to have a judicial quality or attribute sufficient to stamp it as a quasi-judicial, as distinguished from a quasi-legislative or quasi-executive commission function, certiorari, which is a remedy limited solely to judicial or quasi-judicial determinations, will not lie." In Florida, "[i]t is not within the power of the Legislature to change the nature of a judicial function by merely creating another agency to participate in its performance." So, like local government entities, Florida state agencies commit quasi-judicial acts when their behavior meets these definitions of quasi-judicial.

With regard to such quasi-judicial acts, certiorari provides two levels of review. "Once the local agency has ruled . . . the parties may seek review in the court system, twice. First, a party may seek certiorari review in circuit court, i.e., 'first-tier' certiorari review. Although termed 'certiorari' review, review at this level is not discretionary but rather is a matter of right and is akin in many respects to a plenary appeal. . . . Next, a party may seek certiorari review of the circuit court decision in the district court, i.e., 'second-tier' certiorari review. Review at this level is circumscribed and is similar in scope to true common law certiorari review."

In the initial (or first-tier) certiorari review from such a quasi-judicial local act, the circuit court applies the following legal standard when determining whether to quash the local act:

(1) whether procedural due process is accorded,

(2) whether the essential requirements of the law have been observed, and

(3) whether the administrative findings and judgment are supported by competent, substantial evidence.

Note that, unlike any other type of certiorari review, this first-tier certiorari review of a quasi-judicial local act examines whether competent, substantial evidence supports the quasi-judicial findings and judgment. Also note that, unlike all other attempts at certiorari review, the petitioner is entitled to such review "as of right," meaning this instance of certiorari review is not a discretionary act for the reviewing court but instead more closely resembles a plenary appeal where the reviewing court is obliged to grant relief upon a proper showing of entitlement to relief.

Regarding the first and second elements of first-tier certiorari from a quasi-judicial act, they are interpreted consistently with the similarly phrased requirements for first-tier certiorari from an interlocutory order discussed above. Regarding the third element, "[c]ompetent substantial evidence is tantamount to legally sufficient evidence." When answering the inquiry as to whether there is competent substantial evidence, "[t]he circuit court's task is to review the record for evidence that supports the agency's decision, not that which rebuts it."

Second-Tier Certiorari

After either type of first-tier certiorari, be it a certiorari from an interlocutory order or a certiorari from a quasi-judicial local act, any further appellate review is also via a petition for writ of certiorari. This is because Article V of the Florida Constitution grants Florida's District Courts of Appeal "jurisdiction to hear appeals, that may be taken as a matter of right, from final judgments or orders" yet an opinion issued as to whether to grant or deny a writ of certiorari does not meet the technical definition of either a "judgment" or an "order." So the appellate court's review of the grant or denial of certiorari is itself via certiorari, and thus, it is often called Second-Tier Certiorari.

"Second-tier certiorari review is not a matter of right and . . . second-tier review is so extraordinarily limited." The decision as to whether to grant any type of relief upon second-tier certiorari is purely at the discretion of the district court of appeal reviewing the case, and "[t]he district courts should use this discretion cautiously so as to avert the possibility of common-law certiorari being used as a vehicle to obtain a second appeal."

On second-tier certiorari review, "appellate courts must exercise caution not to expand certiorari jurisdiction to review the correctness of the circuit court's decision." This is because "the departure from the essential requirements of law necessary for the issuance of a writ of certiorari is something more than a simple legal error." Second-tier certiorari is appropriate "only when there has been a violation of a clearly established principle of law resulting in a miscarriage of justice."

Id. at § 1705:1 (footnotes omitted). The limited review provided by a second-tier certiorari is represented well by the facts and holding of *Futch v. Florida Dept. of Highway Safety & Motor Vehicles*, 189 So. 3d 131 (Fla. 2016).

Futch v. Florida Dept. Of Highway Safety & Motor Vehicles
Supreme Court of the State of Florida, 2016
189 So. 3d 131

Nils Futch seeks review of the decision of the Fifth District Court of Appeal in *Futch v. Department of Highway Safety & Motor Vehicles*, 142 So. 3d 910 (Fla. 5th DCA 2014), on the ground that it expressly and directly conflicts with two decisions of the Second District Court of Appeal in *Department of Highway Safety & Motor Vehicles v. Robinson*, 93 So. 3d 1090 (Fla. 2d DCA 2012), and *McLaughlin v. Department of Highway Safety & Motor Vehicles*, 128 So. 3d 815 (Fla. 2d DCA 2012), and a decision of the First District Court of Appeal in *Department of Highway Safety & Motor Vehicles v. Edenfield*, 58 So. 3d 904 (Fla. 1st DCA 2011), on a question of law. We have jurisdiction. See art. V, § 3(b)(3), Fla. Const. Because the Fifth District inappropriately granted certiorari review, we quash the district court's decision and remand for reinstatement of the circuit court's decision.

During a traffic stop, Futch allegedly refused to submit to a blood-alcohol test. The Department of Highway Safety and Motor Vehicles ("DHSMV") suspended Futch's driver license for one year, effective March 15, 2013. Futch sought review of the driver license suspension. See §§ 322.2615, 322.64, Fla. Stat. (2012). During the administrative review, the hearing officer refused to permit Futch's counsel to ask more than two questions of Futch's expert witness. The hearing officer subsequently upheld the suspension. On certiorari review of the administrative decision, the circuit court found that the hearing officer's actions denied Futch due process, and invalidated the suspension. *Futch v. Dep't of Highway Safety & Motor Vehs.*, 21 Fla. L. Weekly Supp. 16, 18 (Fla. 7th Cir.Ct. Sept. 3, 2013). On second-tier certiorari review of the circuit court's decision, the Fifth District agreed with the circuit court that the hearing officer violated Futch's due process by refusing to allow his expert to testify. See *Futch*, 142 So. 3d at 915. However, the Fifth District held that the circuit court was required to remand the case back to DHSMV for another administrative hearing, and "that the circuit court misapplied the law when it directed DHSMV to set aside the suspension and reinstate Futch's driver's license." *Id.* at 916.

"Appellate courts must exercise caution not to expand certiorari jurisdiction to review the correctness of the circuit court's decision." *Nader v. Dep't of Highway Safety & Motor Vehs.*, 87 So. 3d 712, 723 (Fla. 2012); see also *Haines City Cmty. Dev. v. Heggs*, 658 So. 2d 523, 526 (Fla. 1995). "The departure from the essential requirements of law necessary for the issuance of a writ of certiorari is something more than a simple legal error." *Allstate Ins. Co. v. Kaklamanos*, 843 So. 2d 885, 889 (Fla. 2003). Certiorari is appropriate "only when there has been a violation of a clearly established principle of law resulting in a miscarriage of justice." *Id.*

Here, the Fifth District inappropriately exercised its certiorari jurisdiction to review the circuit court order. We reassert that "second-tier certiorari should not be used simply to grant a second appeal; rather, it should be reserved for those situations when there has been a violation of a clearly established principle of law resulting in a miscarriage of justice." *Nader*, 87 So. 3d at 717; see also *Kaklamanos*, 843 So. 2d at 889. There was no miscarriage of justice here. Accordingly, because the Fifth District was without jurisdiction, we quash the decision below and remand for reinstatement of the circuit court's decision.

It is so ordered.

LABARGA, C.J., and PARIENTE, LEWIS, and QUINCE, JJ., concur.

CANADY, J., dissents with an opinion, in which POLSTON, J., concurs.

CANADY, J., dissenting.

Although I acknowledge that the Fifth District did not state that the granting of second-tier certiorari relief requires a showing that the circuit court violated a clearly established principle of law resulting in a miscarriage of justice, I nevertheless would approve the result reached by the district court.

On second-tier certiorari review, the district court must consider "whether the circuit court afforded procedural due process and whether the circuit court applied the correct law. . . . [T]hese two components are merely expressions of ways in which the circuit court decision may have departed from the essential requirements of the law." *Haines City Cmty. Dev. v. Heggs*, 658 So. 2d 523, 530 (Fla. 1995). A district court may only exercise its discretion to grant second-tier certiorari relief when the circuit court "has violated a clearly established principle of law resulting in a miscarriage of justice." *Custer Med. Ctr. v. United Auto. Ins. Co.*, 62 So. 3d 1086, 1092 (Fla. 2010).

When a circuit court reviewing an administrative order determines that certiorari relief is warranted, the court has only one option — namely, to "quash the order reviewed." *Broward Cty. v. G.B.V. Int'l, Ltd.*, 787 So. 2d 838, 844 (Fla. 2001). And when an order is quashed on certiorari review, "it leaves the subject matter, that is, the controversy pending before the tribunal, commission, or administrative authority, as if no order or judgment had been entered. " *G.B.V.*, 787 So. 2d at 844. The law is clearly established that "the reviewing court has no power when exercising its jurisdiction in certiorari to enter a judgment on the merits of the controversy under consideration, nor to direct the tribunal, commission, or administrative authority to enter any particular order or judgment." Id. Consistent with these principles of law, the Fifth District "ha[s] consistently held that when a circuit court quashes a hearing officer's order on due process grounds, the matter is to be remanded to the hearing officer for further proceedings." *Futch*, 142 So. 3d at 915.

In this case, the Fifth District correctly recognized that this clearly established principle of law required the circuit court to remand the case for another administrative hearing. See, e.g., *G.B.V.*, 787 So. 2d at 844. Accordingly, because the circuit court invalidated the suspension of Futch's driver license—without the authority to do so—instead of quashing the order and remanding the case, the circuit court disregarded this Court's precedent and the Fifth District's precedent requiring that the matter be remanded for further proceedings. In doing so, the circuit court violated a clearly established principle of law.

Although the Fifth District did not expressly hold that the circuit court's violation of this clearly established principle of law resulted in a miscarriage of justice, I would conclude that the circuit court's error resulted in a miscarriage of justice that is "sufficiently egregious or fundamental to merit the extra review and safeguard provided by certiorari." *Heggs*, 658 So. 2d at 531. Specifically, the circuit court's error denied DHSMV the opportunity for the suspension of Futch's driver license to be properly considered by the hearing officer on the merits. The circuit court's error also resulted in a miscarriage of justice because it has precedential value in the Seventh Judicial Circuit, could affect many other administrative proceedings in that circuit, and substantially deprives DHSMV of its opportunity to sustain driver license suspensions in that circuit. Moreover, in holding that "no miscarriage of justice" occurred under the facts of this case, the majority has arguably created a scenario immune from second-tier certiorari review in which any circuit court in the State of Florida can invalidate any administrative driver license suspension on the sole basis that an evidentiary error violates due process. Majority op. at 132.

The circuit court not only transgressed the limitations on the authority of a court granting first-tier certiorari relief but also violated a cardinal rule of the appellate process. When an error made in a ruling on an evidentiary question is identified in a review proceeding, the result is not an automatic victory for the party aggrieved by the error. It is an "elementary" principle of the appellate process that "where findings are infirm because of an erroneous view of the law, a remand is the proper course unless the record permits only one resolution of the factual issue." *Pullman-Standard v. Swint*, 456 U.S. 273, 292 (1982). Indeed, no principle of the appellate process is more firmly-fixed and well-understood. The majority's conclusory decision contravening this principle holds the potential for much mischief.

In sum, the Fifth District was justified in granting certiorari relief because the circuit court violated a clearly established principle of law resulting in a miscarriage of justice. I dissent.

POLSTON, J., concurs.

6. Writ of Habeas Corpus

Florida's constitution provides that "[t]he writ of habeas corpus shall be grantable of right, freely and without cost. It shall be returnable without delay, and shall never be suspended unless, in case of rebellion or invasion, suspension is essential to the public safety." Art. I, § 13, Fla. Const.

Florida's supreme court, in an opinion quoting heavily from Florida's First District Court of Appeal, provides a detailed recitation of the history and use of the "Great Writ," the writ of habeas corpus, in *Henry v. Santana*, 62 So. 2d 1122 (Fla. 2011).

Henry v. Santana
Supreme Court of Florida, 2011
62 So. 3d 1122

This case is before the Court for review of the decision of the First District Court of Appeal in *Santana v. Henry*, 12 So. 3d 843 (Fla. 1st DCA 2009). The district court certified that its decision is in direct conflict with the decision of the Third District Court of Appeal in *Pope v. State*, 898 So. 2d 253 (Fla. 3d DCA 2005). We have jurisdiction. *See* art. V, § 3(b)(4), Fla. Const.

The issue presented is whether a court may sua sponte dismiss a petition for a writ of habeas corpus, in which a prisoner is seeking immediate release, based upon the petitioner's failure to allege exhaustion of administrative remedies. As further explained below, we hold that such a petition may not be dismissed on such grounds where the issue of the petitioner's failure to exhaust administrative remedies has not been raised by the parties.

Facts and Procedural Background

On June 24, 2008, Santana, an inmate, filed a pro se petition for writ of habeas corpus in the circuit court in Jackson County, alleging that he was entitled to immediate release. He filed the petition against Mark Henry, warden of the facility in Jackson County where he was housed. Santana's claim concerned the sentences that were imposed on October 4, 2007, following his violation of probation (VOP). The relevant facts are set forth in the district court opinion below:

> Runner O. Santana appeals the dismissal of his petition for writ of habeas corpus alleging "that he is entitled to immediate release when properly credited with time served" and requesting "issuance of an Order com[m]anding the Florida Department of Corrections . . . to immediately

release" him. Without prior notice to the parties or input from them, the trial court summarily dismissed the petition. It reasoned, in part, that Mr. Santana failed to exhaust administrative remedies, although the Department of Corrections (DOC) never raised this below. . . .

The petition below alleges that, after his probation (in three separate cases) was revoked, Mr. Santana was sentenced anew on October 4, 2007, receiving three concurrent prison sentences. In case No. 95–CF–4926, the petition alleges, he was sentenced to six years in prison with credit for 2,023 days, to be followed by two years' probation; in case No. 96–CF–9601 to 60.75 months with credit for 831 days; and in case No. 96–CF–10668 to six years with credit for 1,682 days. In addition, against each sentence, the petition alleges, he was awarded "credit for time served at the State Hospital," and a separate credit for 142 days for time spent in jail before the revocation hearing. . . .

Attached to the petition are the sentencing documents, as well as a transcript of the sentencing hearing.

Santana v. Henry, 12 So. 3d 843, 844–45 (Fla. 1st DCA 2009) (footnotes omitted).

The district court framed the issue before it narrowly, as follows:

At issue is whether the habeas court properly dismissed the petition on its own motion without hearing from the authorities alleged to hold the petitioner unlawfully. We are not concerned here with mere conditions of confinement, or gain-time calculations not affecting DOC's current right to hold the petitioner, or anything less than a state prisoner's alleged right to immediate release from custody.

Id. at 845–46 (citations omitted). The district court then addressed the traditional role of the writ of habeas corpus versus the role of the doctrine of exhaustion of administrative remedies and held that the trial court erred in dismissing Santana's habeas petition on the basis of a technicality not raised by the parties—i.e., Santana's failure to allege that he had exhausted his administrative remedies:

In any event, we hold the trial court erred by dismissing Mr. Santana's petition for writ of habeas corpus on the basis of a technicality—an assumed pleading defect—that was not raised by the parties. It is not clear DOC would have defended in this fashion, left to its own devices. "A trial judge may not sua sponte dismiss an action based on affirmative defenses not raised by proper pleadings." *Liton Lighting v. Platinum Television Group, Inc.*, 2 So. 3d 366, 367 (Fla. 4th DCA 2008).

Santana, 12 So. 3d at 847–48 (citations omitted). The district court ruled as follows:

Mindful that the "writ of habeas corpus is the fundamental instrument for safeguarding individual freedom against arbitrary and lawless state action," *Harris v. Nelson*, 394 U.S. 286, 290–91 (1969), we reverse and remand with directions that the trial court issue an order to show cause to the Department of Corrections before proceeding further.

Santana, 12 So. 3d at 844–45 (citations omitted). The district court certified conflict with *Pope v. State*, 898 So. 2d 253 (Fla. 3d DCA 2005). DOC sought review in this Court, which was granted.

Analysis

The writ of habeas corpus, or the Great Writ, is a high prerogative writ and, when properly issued, supersedes all other writs. *State ex rel. Perky v. Browne*, 142 So. 247, 248 (1932). The writ, which literally means "that you have the body," is a writ of inquiry and has traditionally been used to compel the custodian of the prisoner to bring the body of the prisoner into court so that the legality of the detention might be tested. This Court in *State ex rel. Deeb v. Fabisinski*, 152 So. 207 (1933), addressed the deep roots of the writ in Anglo-American jurisprudence:

> The great writ, known commonly by the name of "habeas corpus," was a high prerogative writ known to the common law, the object of which was the liberation of those who were imprisoned without sufficient cause. *See Ex parte Watkins*, 3 Pet. (U.S.) 193, 7 L.Ed. 650 [(1830)].

> It is a writ of inquiry upon matters of which the state itself is concerned in aid of right and liberty. . . .

> The name of the writ is "habeas corpus ad subjiciendum et recipiendum." It is not an action or suit, but is a summary remedy open to the person detained. It is civil rather than criminal in nature and is a legal and not equitable remedy. *See Ex parte Watkins, supra; Ex parte Bollman*, 4 Cranch (U.S.) 75, 2 L.Ed. 554 [(1807)].

> . . . [W]hile the writ had been in use in England from remote antiquity, it was often assailed by kings who sought tyrannical power and the benefits of the writ were in a great degree eluded by time-serving judges who assumed a discretionary power in awarding or refusing it and were disposed to support royal and ministerial usurpations. Owing to such abuses, the writ became powerless to release persons imprisoned without any cause assigned. In the fight by the people against the abuses of the writ, petitions of rights were submitted to the king, and during the reign of Charles I, A.D. 1641, provisions were enacted intended to make the writ effectual. These activities were, however, in vain. At last, in 1679, the Statute 31 Chas. II, chap. 2, was enacted. That act is known as the [H]abeas [C]orpus [A]ct. That act has been substantially incorporated into the jurisprudence of every state in the Union and the right to it secured by their Constitutions. The Constitution of the United States provides that the privilege of the writ of habeas corpus shall not be suspended except in certain circumstances. Article 1, §9, par. 2, U.S. Const.

> . . .

> The great writ of habeas corpus is the one mentioned in Magna Charta in the year 1215; the writ which alone was the subject of the acts of 16 Chas.

I and 31 Chas. II. It was the writ referred to in the Declaration of Independence and secured to the people of this country by the Constitution of the United States and the Constitutions of the different states.

Fabisinski, 152 So. at 209–10. This Court subsequently in *Allison v. Baker*, 11 So. 2d 578 (1943), reiterated the basic purpose of the writ:

The writ of habeas corpus is a high prerogative writ of ancient origin designed to obtain immediate relief from unlawful imprisonment without sufficient legal reasons. Essentially, it is a writ of inquiry and is issued to test the reasons or grounds of restraint and detention. The writ is venerated by all free and liberty loving people and recognized as a fundamental guaranty and protection of their right of liberty.

Id. at 579.

Given the basic purpose and fundamental importance of the writ, this Court has long recognized the necessity of informality and tolerance with regard to the pleading requirements for the writ:

The writ of habeas corpus is a writ of right. It is sometimes issued upon very informal application. *Ex parte Pells*, 9 So. 833 [(1891)]. Neither the right to the writ nor the right to be discharged from custody in a proper case is made to depend upon meticulous observance of the rules of pleading. The purpose of bringing the petitioner before the court is to inquire into the legality of his detention, and if during the proceedings it appears formally or informally to the court's satisfaction that the person is unlawfully deprived of his liberty and is illegally detained in custody against his will he will be discharged.

Ex parte Amos, 112 So. 289, 291–92 (1927). This Court has emphasized this need for informality repeatedly:

[H]istorically, habeas corpus is a high prerogative writ. It is as old as the common law itself and is an integral part of our own democratic process. The procedure for the granting of this particular writ is not to be circumscribed by hard and fast rules or technicalities which often accompany our consideration of other processes. If it appears to a court of competent jurisdiction that a man is being illegally restrained of his liberty, it is the responsibility of the court to brush aside formal technicalities and issue such appropriate orders as will do justice. In habeas corpus the niceties of the procedure are not anywhere near as important as the determination of the ultimate question as to the legality of the restraint.

Anglin v. Mayo, 88 So. 2d 918, 919–20 (Fla. 1956). This Court has gone so far as to rule that "[n]o formal application for habeas corpus is required." *Martin v. State*, 166 So. 467, 467 (1936).

The gravamen of the issue before the Court is whether the writ of habeas corpus should be encumbered by a pleading requirement regarding the exhaustion of administrative remedies in those cases where an inmate is seeking immediate release. DOC contends that unless the inmate first exhausts administrative remedies, he or she will be unable to file an informed petition because the petition will be based on mere speculation concerning the inmate's term of imprisonment and release date. DOC also contends that if the inmate fails to exhaust administrative remedies, the courts too will be operating in the dark in the same respect. DOC contends that the district court's ruling below will encourage inmates to file free habeas petitions instead of utilizing the Department's internal grievance procedure. In brief, it appears that DOC, for its own purposes, would prefer to respond to such inmate inquiries via its own internal grievance procedure rather than respond to orders to show cause issued by the courts. In light of the above authorities, however, it appears that DOC's proposed pleading requirement is antithetical to the basic purpose and fundamental importance of the writ.

In the decision under review, the district court addressed at length the traditional role of the writ of habeas corpus in relation to the doctrine of exhaustion of remedies:

> "The writ of habeas corpus is a high prerogative writ of ancient origin designed to obtain immediate relief from unlawful imprisonment without sufficient legal reasons. Essentially, it is a writ of inquiry and is issued to test the reasons or grounds of restraint and detention. The writ is venerated by all free and liberty loving people and recognized as a fundamental guaranty and protection of their right of liberty." *Allison v. Baker*, 11 So. 2d 578, 579 (1943). "The great writ has its origins in antiquity and its parameters have been shaped by suffering and deprivation. It is more than a privilege with which free men are endowed by constitutional mandate; it is a writ of ancient right." *Jamason v. State*, 447 So. 2d 892, 894 (Fla. 4th DCA 1983). "[H]istorically, habeas corpus is a high prerogative writ. It is as old as the common law itself and is an integral part of our own democratic process." *Anglin v. Mayo*, 88 So. 2d 918, 919 (Fla. 1956).
>
> By comparison, judicial abstention in favor of exhaustion of administrative remedies is a relatively recent invention. The doctrine of exhaustion of remedies counsels against judicial intervention in the decision-making function of the executive branch in certain circumstances. Whether to require exhaustion of administrative remedies is a question of judicial "policy rather than power." *Gulf Pines Mem'l Park, Inc. v. Oaklawn Mem'l Park, Inc.*, 361 So. 2d 695, 699 (Fla. 1978). *See also State, Dep't of Revenue v. Brock*, 576 So. 2d 848, 850 (Fla. 1st DCA 1991) ("[T]he doctrine requiring the exhaustion of administrative remedies is not jurisdictional. The exhaustion requirement is a court-created prudential doctrine; it is a matter of policy, not of power." (citations omitted)).
>
> Notions of administrative autonomy have been thought to require that agencies be given the opportunity to discover and correct their own errors, even after a case has reached the courts for judicial review of agency action.

In some contexts, judicial restraint may be necessary "to support the integrity of the administrative process and to allow the executive branch to carry out its responsibilities as a co-equal branch of government." [*Key Haven Associated Enters., Inc. v. Bd. of Trs. of the Internal Improvement Trust Fund*, 427 So. 2d 153, 157 (Fla. 1982)]. When an agency has discretion to exercise, it should of course be allowed to make discretionary decisions. If a party succeeds in vindicating its rights in the administrative process, thus obviating the need for judicial intervention, judicial resources are conserved; and immediate judicial access can weaken the effectiveness of an agency by encouraging people to ignore its procedures.

But the rationales for requiring exhaustion of administrative remedies diminish and disappear where an executive branch agency has little or no discretion to exercise and little or no expertise to bring to bear. The Department of Corrections does have discretion in deciding, for example, the conditions of confinement, and does have its own procedures on this subject deserving of judicial deference. On the other hand, the DOC has no discretion about which prisoners to release upon expiration of their sentences. Sentencing is a power, obligation, and prerogative of the courts, not the DOC.

> . . .

> . . . While the general rule is that exhaustion of administrative remedies is an affirmative defense, *see* Sylvia H. Walbolt, Matthew J. Conigliaro & J. Andrew Meyer, *Florida Civil Practice before Trial*, § 25.34 at 25–30 (7th ed. 2004) ("Affirmative defenses to extraordinary writs include impossibility or lack of power to perform, laches, unclean hands, absence of parties whose substantial rights would be affected, illegality of purpose, detriment to the public interest, mootness, and failure to exhaust administrative remedies. *See* FLORIDA APPELLATE PRACTICE § 20.38 (Fla. Bar CLE 5th ed. 2003)"), moreover, in the prisoner habeas context, it has been held that certain petitions must allege exhaustion of administrative remedies in order to be facially sufficient. But none of the cases to which our attention has been drawn has laid down such a pleading requirement for petitions for writ of habeas corpus alleging entitlement to immediate release. The petitioners in [the other cases] sought relief from conditions of confinement or restoration of forfeited gain time, not immediate release from the DOC's custody.

Santana, 12 So. 3d at 846–47 (citations omitted).

The district court held that the trial court erred in dismissing Santana's habeas petition based on a technicality not raised by the parties, and the court then noted the following:

> The general rule that pleadings ought not be dismissed on grounds no party urges has special force when the pleading is a petition for writ of habeas

corpus. "The scope and flexibility of the writ—its capacity to reach all manner of illegal detention—its ability to cut through barriers of form and procedural mazes—have always been emphasized and jealously guarded by courts and lawmakers. The very nature of the writ demands that it be administered with the initiative and flexibility essential to insure that miscarriages of justice within its reach are surfaced and corrected." *Harris v. Nelson*, 394 U.S. 286, 291 (1969). When a petition for writ of habeas corpus alleging that the petitioner is entitled to immediate release sets out plausible reasons and a specific factual basis in some detail, the custodian should be required to respond to the petition.

Santana, 12 So. 3d at 848 (citations omitted).

The district court added as a postscript the following passage explaining its ruling further:

If in this case the petition had not been summarily denied and the trial court had instead ordered the DOC to show cause why Mr. Santana's petition should not be granted, the DOC might have resisted by moving to dismiss on exhaustion of administrative remedies grounds or for failure to allege exhaustion but it might also have decided that the petition was meritorious and released the petitioner. "The procedure for the granting of this particular writ [i.e., habeas corpus] is not to be circumscribed by hard and fast rules or technicalities which often accompany our consideration of other processes. If it appears to a court of competent jurisdiction that a man is being illegally restrained of his liberty, it is the responsibility of the court to brush aside formal technicalities and issue such appropriate orders as will do justice. In habeas corpus the niceties of the procedure are not anywhere near as important as the determination of the ultimate question as to the legality of the restraint." *Anglin*, 88 So. 2d at 919–20.

Santana, 12 So. 3d at 848 (brackets in original).

In light of the constitutional and statutory authorities and precedent from this Court noted above, we conclude that the district court below ruled correctly, and we hold that a petition for a writ of habeas corpus, in which a prisoner is seeking immediate release, may not be dismissed based upon the petitioner's failure to allege exhaustion of administrative remedies where such failure has not been raised by the parties.

Conclusion

Based on the above, we approve the First District Court of Appeal's decision below and disapprove the Third District Court of Appeal's decision in *Pope v. State*, 898 So. 2d 253 (Fla. 3d DCA 2005), to the extent it is inconsistent with this opinion.

It is so ordered.

Notes and Questions to Consider:

1. Although Florida's constitution grants more than one court the authority to consider a petition for writ of habeas corpus, this does not mean that a prisoner may file for habeas corpus in each of these courts addressing the one same incarceration. In *Florida Parole & Prob. Comm'n v. Baker*, 346 So. 2d 640 (Fla. 2d DCA 1977), a prisoner filed but did not win a petition for writ of habeas corpus before Florida's Second District Court of Appeal. So the prisoner filed another petition for writ of habeas corpus, this time with the circuit court. He won. The state appealed to Florida's Second District Court of Appeal, and they reversed, holding:

> The circuit, district and supreme courts have concurrent jurisdiction in habeas corpus. It is well established that a petitioner may not have three direct, repetitious applications for habeas corpus available to him upon the same subject matter. The two petitions both involve the same subject matter and, in fact, the petition filed in the circuit court was filed prior to this court's denial of appellee's petition for rehearing.

> For the reasons stated above we hold that the defense of res judicata is established on this record.

> The order appealed granting the writ of habeas corpus and ordering appellee released is hereby reversed and the cause remanded.

Id. at 641.

2. Florida Rule of Criminal Procedure 3.850(m) assists prisoners in determining the proper court for filing a petition for writ of habeas corpus. That rule provides:

> *Habeas Corpus.* An application for writ of habeas corpus on behalf of a prisoner who is authorized to apply for relief by motion pursuant to this rule shall not be entertained if it appears that the applicant has failed to apply for relief, by motion, to the court that sentenced the applicant or that the court has denied the applicant relief, unless it also appears that the remedy by motion is inadequate or ineffective to test the legality of the applicant's detention.

E. Quasi-Judicial Power

Does Florida's constitution restrict judicial power solely to Florida's judiciary? To answer this question, first consider Article V of Florida's constitution, where it states:

> SECTION 1. *Courts.* — [J]udicial power shall be vested in a Sup. Ct., [DCA's], circuit courts and county courts. No other courts may be established by the state, any political subdivision or any municipality. . . . *Commissions established by law, or administrative officers or bodies may be granted quasi-judicial power in matters connected with the functions of their offices.*

As the italicized language reveals, judicial power can be extended to other branches of government to use in matters connected with the functions of their offices. When judicial power is authorized, but is used by an entity other than Florida's judiciary, we call that use "quasi-judicial."

Therefore, by use of quasi-judicial powers, an administrative officer or body can hear a Floridian's complaint, consider the sworn testimony of the complainant and other witnesses, allow for cross-examination, accept documents into evidence, and issue an individualized ruling based upon the testimony and evidence, all without violating Florida's separation of powers.

———————

Note and Question to Consider:

1. Of all the quasi-powers, quasi-judicial power is according the least deference by Florida's Courts. "Regardless of the method of review, the court exercises a more limited review of quasi-executive or quasi-legislative action than of quasi-judicial action." *Broward County v. Admin. Comm'n*, 321 So. 2d 605, 610 (Fla. 1st DCA 1975). In your opinion, why would this be appropriate?

Chapter 13

Separation of Powers, Sovereign Immunity, and Delegation

A. Separation of Powers

In Florida's constitution as in the U.S. Constitution, government consists of three branches: an executive, a legislative, and a judicial. Article II of Florida's constitution provides:

> *SECTION 3. Branches of government.*— The powers of the state government shall be divided into legislative, executive and judicial branches. No person belonging to one branch shall exercise any powers appertaining to either of the other branches unless expressly provided herein.

This language is an explicit requirement for a separation of powers, unlike the U.S. Constitution, where such a separation is implicit.

Why separate powers in this way? One purpose for Florida's separation of powers is summarized and criticized in this excerpt from Daniel Webster & Donald L. Bell, *First Principles for Constitution Revision*, 22 Nova L. Rev. 391 (1997):

> In framing a government which is to be administered by men over men, the great difficulty lies in this: You must first enable the government to control the governed; and in the next place oblige it to control itself." The Federalist No. 51 at 322 (James Madison) (Clinton Rossiter ed., 1961). Tyranny arises most easily when all power is concentrated in the hands of a single person or in the hands of just a few. A constitution that divides power in numerous ways and in numerous directions will best serve the constitutional function of protecting against tyranny. . . .

> . . . About his vision for the federal system, Madison commented:

> In the compound republic of America, the power surrendered by the people is first divided between two distinct governments, and then the portion allotted to each subdivided among distinct and separate departments. Hence a double security arises to the rights of the people. The different governments will control each other, at the same time that each will be controlled by itself. . . .

> The Florida Constitution, unlike its federal counterpart, contains an explicit separation of powers requirement. The purpose of this provision

was to limit the extent to which any branch of government may perform functions assigned by the constitution to another branch. . . .

Under Florida's doctrine against encroachment, no branch of government may encroach on the powers delegated to another branch by the constitution. For example, the Legislature cannot reserve to itself the right to execute the laws it creates because the power to execute the laws is reserved to the executive branch. . . .

A concordant policy, the doctrine of non-delegation, was intended to prevent the Legislature from delegating its lawmaking power to either of the other two branches of government. [T]he doctrine forbids the Legislature from delegating its core functions without any guidance or limits as to how those functions are to be exercised.

Notes and Questions to Consider:

1. Florida's supreme court holds: "We must zealously guard America's traditional separation of powers in the legislative, executive and judicial bodies of government; for that time tested formula will fail if each does not 'check and balance' the other." *Municipal Court, City of Fort Lauderdale v. Patrick*, 254 So. 2d 193, 194 (Fla. 1971). In the context of the separation of powers among the legislative, executive, and judicial branches, what is meant by "checks and balances"?

2. Florida's supreme court, in *Bush v. Schiavo*, 885 So. 2d 321 (Fla. 2004), observed that Florida case law precedent:

> "has traditionally applied a strict separation of powers doctrine," *State v. Cotton*, 769 So. 2d 345, 353 (Fla. 2000), and has explained that this doctrine "encompasses two fundamental prohibitions. The first is that no branch may encroach upon the powers of another. The second is that no branch may delegate to another branch its constitutionally assigned power." *Chiles v. Children A, B, C, D, E, & F*, 589 So. 2d 260, 264 (Fla. 1991).

Id. at 329 (citation omitted). Florida case law is replete with examples of laws or actions of government that Florida's courts held constitutionally infirm because one branch encroached upon the power of another. *See* John F. Cooper, Tishia A. Dunham & Carlos L. Woody, Florida Constitutional Law: Cases and Materials (Carolina Academic Press 5th ed. 2013) (citing *Florida House of Representatives v. Crist*, 999 So. 2d 601 (Fla. 2008) as an example of encroachment by Florida's executive upon the legislative; *Office of the State Attorney for the Eleventh Judicial Circuit v. Polites*, 904 So. 2d 527 (Fla. 3d DCA 2005) as an example of encroachment by Florida's judicial upon the executive; *Jones v. Chiles*, 638 So. 2d 48 (Fla. 1994) as an example of encroachment by Florida's legislative upon the executive; *McNeil v. Canty*, 12 So. 3d 215 (Fla. 2009) as an example of encroachment by Florida's executive upon the judicial; and *Bush v. Schiavo*, 885 So. 2d 321 (Fla. 2004) as an example of encroachment by Florida's legislative upon the judicial).

3. As noted in this text in its separate chapters addressing executive power, judicial power, and judicial power, and legislative power, Florida's constitution, in a proper circumstance, allows for the use of quasi-executive, quasi-judicial, or quasi-legislative power. Despite these allowances, violations of the separation of powers can occur. The following case law provides some examples.

1. Dissention among the Branches

Florida House of Representatives v. Crist, 999 So. 2d 601 (Fla. 2008) is a story of dissention between and among Florida's branches of government. The story begins with a federal law empowering Native American tribes to negotiate a compact with a state. Florida's legislature's only response to the tribe was inaction. Florida's governor acted when Florida's legislature would not act, and when he did, Florida's legislature complained to Florida's judicial branch that the governor's actions were improper. As we follow this story, the opinion illustrates several concepts important to Florida's separation of powers.

Florida House of Representatives v. Crist
Supreme Court of Florida, 2008
999 So. 2d 601

CANTERO, J.

After almost sixteen years of sporadic negotiations with four governors, in November 2007 the Seminole Indian Tribe of Florida signed a gambling "compact" (a contract between two sovereigns) with Florida Governor Charles Crist. The compact significantly expands casino gambling, also known as "gaming," on tribal lands. For example, it permits card games such as blackjack and baccarat that are otherwise prohibited by law. In return, the compact promises substantial remuneration to the State.

The Florida Legislature did not authorize the Governor to negotiate the compact before it was signed and has not ratified it since. To the contrary, shortly after the compact was signed, the Florida House of Representatives and its Speaker, Marco Rubio, filed in this Court a petition for a writ of quo warranto disputing the Governor's authority to bind the State to the compact. We have exercised our discretion to consider such petitions, *see* art. V, § 3(b)(8), Fla. Const., and now grant it on narrow grounds. We hold that the Governor does not have the constitutional authority to bind the State to a gaming compact that clearly departs from the State's public policy by legalizing types of gaming that are illegal everywhere else in the state.

In the remainder of this opinion, we describe the history of Indian gaming compacts in general and the negotiations leading up to the compact at issue. We then explain our jurisdiction to consider the petition. Finally, we discuss the applicable constitutional provisions, statutes, and cases governing our decision.

I. The Factual and Legal Background

We analyze the compact in the context of the federal regulations authorizing it as well as the background of the negotiations in this case. We first review the statutory foundation for the compact: the Indian Gaming Regulatory Act, 25 U.S.C. §§ 2701–2721 (2000) (IGRA). Next, we detail the history of the Tribe's attempts to negotiate a compact with the State. Finally, we explain the compact's relevant terms.

A. IGRA

Indian tribes are independent sovereigns. The Indian Commerce Clause of the United States Constitution grants only Congress the power to override their sovereignty on Indian lands. U.S. Const., art. I, § 8, cl. 3 ("The Congress shall have Power . . . [t]o regulate Commerce with . . . the Indian Tribes."); *see also California v. Cabazon Band of Mission Indians*, 480 U.S. 202, 207, 107 S.Ct. 1083, 94 L.Ed.2d 244 (1987) (noting that tribal sovereignty is subordinate only to the federal government). Before IGRA, states had no role in regulating Indian gaming. *See Cabazon*, 480 U.S. at 202, 107 S.Ct. 1083.

Congress enacted IGRA in 1988. Among other things, the statute provides "a statutory basis for the operation of gaming by Indian tribes as a means of promoting tribal economic development, self-sufficiency, and strong tribal governments." 25 U.S.C. § 2702(1). IGRA divides gaming into three classes: Class I includes "social games solely for prizes of minimal value." *Id.* § 2703(6). Class II includes "the game of chance commonly known as bingo" and "non-banked" card games — that is, games in which participants play against only each other; the host facility (the "house") has no stake in the outcome. *Id.* § 2703(7). Class III — the only type relevant here — comprises all other types of gaming, including slot machines, pari-mutuel wagering (such as horse and greyhound racing), lotteries, and "banked" card games — such as baccarat, blackjack (twenty-one), and *chemin de fer* — in which participants play against the house. *Id.* § 2703(6)-(8).

IGRA permits Class III gaming on tribal lands, but only in limited circumstances. It is lawful *only* if it is (1) authorized by tribal ordinance, (2) "located in a State that permits such gaming for any purpose by any person, organization, or entity," and (3) "conducted in accordance with a Tribal–State compact entered into by the Indian tribe and the State . . . *that is in effect.*" *Id.* § 2710(d)(1) (emphasis added).

IGRA provides for tribes to negotiate compacts with their host states. Upon a tribe's request, a state "*shall* negotiate with the Indian tribe in good faith to enter into such a compact." *Id.* § 2710(d)(3)(A) (emphasis added). If the parties successfully negotiate a compact and the Secretary of the Department of the Interior (Department) approves it, the compact takes effect "when notice of approval by the Secretary" is published in the Federal Register. *Id.* § 2710(d)(3)(B), (8).

If negotiations fail, IGRA allows a tribe to sue the state in federal court. If the state continues to refuse consent, the Secretary may "prescribe . . . procedures" permitting Class III gaming. *See id.* § 2710(d)(7)(B)(vii). The United States Supreme Court has held, however—in a case involving the Seminole Tribe's attempts to offer Class III gaming in Florida—that IGRA did not abrogate the states' Eleventh Amendment immunity. *See Seminole Tribe of Fla. v. Florida*, 517 U.S. 44, 47, 116 S.Ct. 1114, 134 L.Ed.2d 252 (1996). Therefore, states need not consent to such lawsuits. The Department later created an alternative procedure under which, when a tribe cannot negotiate a compact and a state asserts immunity, the Secretary may prescribe Class III gaming. *See* Class III Gaming Procedures, 64 Fed.Reg. 17535–02 (Apr. 12, 1999) (codified at 25 C.F.R. pt. 291 (2007)). At least one federal court, however, has held that the Secretary lacked authority to promulgate such regulations. *See Texas v. United States*, 497 F.3d 491, 493 (5th Cir. 2007), *petition for cert. filed sub nom. Kickapoo Traditional Tribe of Texas v. Texas*, 76 U.S.L.W. 3471 (U.S. Feb. 25, 2008) (No. 07–1109). Therefore, their validity remains questionable.

B. The Negotiations between the Tribe and the State

With this statutory framework in mind, we briefly describe the protracted history of the Seminole Tribe's efforts to negotiate a compact for conducting Class III gaming in Florida. These negotiations spanned sixteen years and four different governors.

The Seminole Indian Tribe is a federally recognized Indian tribe whose reservations and trust lands are located in the State. The Tribe currently operates Class II gaming facilities, offering low stakes poker games and electronically aided bingo games. The Tribe first sought a compact allowing it to offer Class III gaming in 1991. That January, the Tribe and Governor Lawton Chiles began negotiations, but they ultimately proved fruitless. That same year, the Tribe filed suit in federal court alleging that the State had failed to negotiate in good faith. As noted earlier, the Supreme Court ultimately ruled that the State could assert immunity, and it did. *See Seminole Tribe*, 517 U.S. at 47, *aff'g Seminole Tribe of Fla. v. Fla.*, 11 F.3d 1016 (11th Cir. 1994).

Over the next several years, the Tribe repeatedly petitioned the Department to establish Class III gaming procedures. In 1999, the Department did so. It found the Tribe eligible for the procedures and called an informal conference, which was held in Tallahassee that December. At the State's suggestion, however, the Tribe agreed to suspend the conference, though only temporarily. In January 2001, the Secretary issued a twenty-page decision allowing the Tribe to offer a wide range of Class III games. When the State requested clarification, however, the Secretary withdrew the decision. The delay continued. Finally, five years later—in May 2006—the Department reconvened the conference in Hollywood, Florida, and in September of that year warned that if the Tribe and the State did not execute a compact within 60 days, the Department would issue Class III gaming procedures. Despite the parties' failure to negotiate a compact, however, the Department never issued procedures.

Apparently exasperated with the slow progress of the procedures, in March 2007 the Tribe sued the Department in federal court. *See Seminole Tribe of Fla. v. United States*, No. 07–60317–CIV, 2007 WL 5077484 (S.D. Fla. filed Mar. 6, 2007). The Department then urged Governor Crist to negotiate a compact, warning that if a compact was not signed by November 15, 2007, the Department would finally issue procedures. Under the proposed procedures, the State would not receive any revenue and would have no control over the Tribe's gaming operations. The Tribe would be authorized to operate slot machines and "card games," defined as "a game or series of games of poker (other than Class II games) which are played in a *non-banking* manner." (Emphasis added.) Notably, the alternative procedures would *not* have permitted the Tribe to operate banked card games such as blackjack.

On November 14—the day before the deadline—the Governor agreed to a compact with the Tribe (Compact). Five days later, the House and its Speaker, Marco Rubio, filed this petition disputing the Governor's authority to bind the State to the Compact without legislative authorization or ratification. We allowed the Tribe to join the action as a respondent.

On January 7, 2008, upon publication of the Secretary's approval, the Compact went into effect. *See* Notice of Deemed Approved Tribal–State Class III Gaming Compact, 73 Fed.Reg. 1229 (Jan. 7, 2008). The parties agree, however, that the Secretary's approval does not render the petition moot.

C. The Compact

The Compact recites that the Governor "has the authority to act for the State with respect to the negotiation and execution of this Compact." It covers a period of twenty-five years and allows the Tribe to offer specified Class III gaming at seven casinos in the State. It establishes the terms, rights, and responsibilities of the parties regarding such gaming. We discuss only its more relevant provisions.

The Compact authorizes the Tribe to conduct "covered gaming," which includes several types of Class III gaming: slot machines; any banking or banked card game, including baccarat, blackjack (twenty-one), and *chemin de fer*; high stakes poker games; games and devices authorized for the state lottery; and any new game authorized by Florida law. The Compact expressly does *not* authorize roulette- or craps-style games. The gaming is limited to seven casinos on tribal lands in six areas of the state: Okeechobee, Coconut Creek, Hollywood (two), Clewiston, Immokalee, and Tampa. Compact pt. IV.B., at 7–8.

The Compact grants the Tribe the exclusive right to conduct certain types of gaming. That is, the Tribe may conduct some Class III gaming, such as banked card games, that is prohibited under state law. Based on that "partial but substantial exclusivity," the Tribe must pay the State a share of the gaming revenue. That share is based in part on amounts that increase at specified thresholds: when the Compact becomes effective, the State receives $50 million. Over the first twenty-four months of operation, it will receive another $175 million. Thereafter, for the third twelve months of operation the State will receive $150 million, and for each twelve-month cycle after that, a minimum of $100 million. If the State breaches the exclusivity provision, however—by legalizing any Class III gaming currently prohibited under state law—the Tribe may cease its payments. The Compact (attached as an appendix to this opinion) is thirty-seven pages long and contains several other provisions we need not detail here.

II. Jurisdiction

Before discussing the issue presented, we first address our jurisdiction. The House and Speaker Rubio have filed in this Court a petition for writ of quo warranto. The Governor contends that this Court lacks jurisdiction because the House does not seek either to remove him from office or to enjoin the future exercise of his authority. We conclude, however, that these are not the only grounds for issuing such a writ.

The Florida Constitution authorizes this Court to issue writs of quo warranto to "state officers and state agencies." Art. V, § 3(b)(8), Fla. Const. The term "quo warranto" means "by what authority." This writ historically has been used to determine whether a state officer or agency has improperly exercised a power or right derived from the State. *See Martinez v. Martinez*, 545 So. 2d 1338, 1339 (Fla. 1989); *see also* art. V, § 3(b)(8), Fla. Const. Here, the Governor is a state officer. The House challenges the Governor's authority to unilaterally execute the Compact on the State's behalf.

The Governor argues that because he already has signed the Compact, quo warranto relief is inappropriate. But the writ is not so limited. In fact, petitions for the writ historically have been filed *after* a public official has acted. *See, e.g., Chiles v. Phelps*, 714 So. 2d 453, 455 (Fla. 1998) (holding that the Legislature and its officers exceeded their authority in overriding the Governor's veto); *State ex rel. Butterworth v. Kenny*, 714 So. 2d 404, 406 (Fla. 1998) (issuing the writ after the Capital Collateral Regional Counsel had filed a federal civil rights suit, concluding that it had no authority to file it). The Governor's execution of the Compact does not defeat our jurisdiction.

The concurring-in-result-only opinion expresses concern that by considering a more narrow issue than the Governor's authority to execute IGRA compacts in general — that is, whether the Governor has the authority to bind the State to a compact that violates Florida law — we are expanding our quo warranto jurisdiction to include issues normally reserved for declaratory judgment actions. In prior quo warranto cases, however, we have considered separation-of-powers arguments normally reviewed in the context of declaratory judgments, such as whether the Governor's action has usurped the Legislature's power, "where the functions of government would be adversely affected absent an immediate determination by this Court." *Phelps*, 714 So. 2d at 457; *see also Martinez*, 545 So. 2d at 1339 (holding quo warranto appropriate to test the governor's power to call special sessions); *Orange County v. City of Orlando*, 327 So. 2d 7 (Fla. 1976) (holding that the legality of city's actions regarding annexation ordinances can be inquired into through quo warranto).

In this case, the Secretary has approved the Compact and, absent an immediate judicial resolution, it will be given effect. In fact, according to news reports, the Tribe already has begun offering blackjack and other games at the Seminole Hard Rock Hotel and Casino. *See* Amy Driscoll, "Casino Gambling: Amid glitz, blackjack's in the cards," THE MIAMI HERALD, June 23, 2008, at B1. Thus, if indeed the Governor has exceeded his constitutional authority, a compact that violates Florida law will, nevertheless, become effective in seven casinos located on tribal lands located in the state. As in *Phelps*, therefore, the importance and immediacy of the issue justifies our deciding this matter now rather than transferring it for resolution in a declaratory judgment action.

III. Discussion of Law

We now discuss the law that applies to this inter-branch dispute. In deciding whether the Governor or the Legislature has the authority to execute a compact, we first define a "compact" and its historical use in Florida. We then discuss how other jurisdictions have resolved this issue. Next, we review the relevant provisions of our own constitution. Finally, we explain our conclusion that the Governor lacked authority under our state's constitution to execute the Compact because it changes the state's public policy as expressed in the criminal law and therefore infringes on the Legislature's powers.

A. Compacts and Their Use in Florida

A compact is essentially a contract between two sovereigns. *Texas v. New Mexico*, 482 U.S. 124, 128 (1987); *see Black's Law Dictionary* 298 (8th ed. 1999) (defining a compact as "[a]n agreement or covenant between two or more parties, esp[ecially] between governments or states"). The United States Supreme Court has described compacts as "a supple device for dealing with interests confined within a region." *State ex rel. Dyer v. Sims*, 341 U.S. 22, 27 (1951). The United States Constitution provides that "[n]o State shall, without the Consent of Congress . . . enter into any Agreement or Compact with another State, or with a foreign Power." U.S. Const. art. I, § 10. IGRA establishes the consent of Congress to execute gaming compacts, but requires federal approval before they become effective. *See* 25 U.S.C. § 2710(d)(8).

Like many states, Florida has executed compacts on a range of subjects, including environmental control, water rights, energy, and education—more than thirty in all. The vast majority were executed with other states. In most cases, the Legislature enacted a law. *See, e.g.*, § 372.831, Fla. Stat. (2007) ("The Wildlife Violator Compact is created and entered into with all other jurisdictions legally joining therein in the form substantially as follows[.]"); § 257.28 (Interstate Library Compact); § 252.921 (Emergency Management Assistance Compact); § 322.44 (Driver License Compact). In others, the Legislature authorized the Governor to execute a compact in the form provided in a statute. *See, e.g.*, § 370.19, Fla. Stat. (2007) ("The Governor of this state is hereby authorized and directed to execute a compact on behalf of the State of Florida with any one or more of [the following states] . . . legally joining therein in the form substantially as follows [.]"); § 370.20 (containing the same authorization and establishing the terms for the Gulf States Marine Fisheries Compact); § 403.60 (using the same authorization language for the Interstate Environmental Control Compact, establishing its terms, and "signi[fying] in advance" the

Legislature's "approval and ratification of such compact"). In a few—including a compact among the State, the Tribe, and the South Florida Water Management District regulating water use on Tribal lands—the Legislature by statute approved and ratified the compact. § 285.165, Fla. Stat. (2007). Thus, by tradition at least, it is the Legislature that has consistently either exercised itself or expressly authorized the exercise of the power to bind the State to compacts. We have found no instance in which the governor has signed a compact without legislative involvement.

Although tradition bears some relevance, it does not resolve the question of which branch actually has the constitutional authority to execute compacts in general and gaming compacts in particular. As explained above, the Compact here governs Class III gaming on certain tribal lands in Florida. The issue is whether, regardless of whether the Governor bucked tradition, he had constitutional authority to execute the Compact without the Legislature's prior authorization or, at least, subsequent ratification.

B. How Other Courts Have Answered the Question

Although Florida has not addressed a governor's authority to bind a state to an IGRA compact, other states have. . . .

In all these cases, to determine which branch had the authority to bind the state to the compact, courts analyzed the nature and effect of the IGRA compact at issue and compared it to the powers the state constitution delegated to the respective branches. The courts found the compacts within the legislative power because they created or assigned new duties to agencies, conflicted with state law, changed state law, or restricted the legislature's power. Finally, recognizing that state legislative power is limited only by the state and federal constitutions, several courts have ascribed to the legislature, rather than the executive, any residual power on which the state constitutions were silent. *See Clark*, 904 P.2d at 25; *Pataki*, 766 N.Y.S.2d at 668 n. 11, 798 N.E.2d at 1061 n. 11. We now review our own state constitution in the context of IGRA's provisions and the Compact signed in this case.

C. Florida Constitutional Provisions

The House contends that several of the Compact's provisions encroach on the Legislature's law- and policy-making powers. To answer the question, we first review the separation-of-powers provisions of the Florida Constitution and our interpretations of it. We then discuss one specific provision on which the Governor relies: the "necessary business" clause.

1. The Florida Constitution's Delegation and Separation of Powers

The Florida Constitution generally specifies the relative powers of the three branches of government. Article II, section 3 provides innocuously that "[t]he powers of the state government shall be divided into legislative, executive and judicial branches. No person belonging to one branch shall exercise any powers appertaining to either of the other branches unless expressly provided herein." In construing our constitution, we have "traditionally applied a strict separation of powers doctrine." *Bush v. Schiavo*, 885 So. 2d 321, 329 (Fla. 2004) (quoting *State v. Cotton*, 769 So. 2d 345, 353 (Fla. 2000)).

These provisions are not specific, however. In fact, as we first noted 100 years ago, the state constitution does not exhaustively list each branch's powers. *State v. Atlantic Coast Line R.R. Co.*, 47 So. 969, 974 (1908). Both the Governor and the House concede that the state constitution does not expressly grant *either* branch the authority to execute compacts.

We must therefore expand our analysis beyond the plain language of the constitution. We have held that the powers of the respective branches "are those so defined . . . or such as are inherent or so recognized by immemorial governmental usage, and which involve the exercise of primary and independent will, discretion, and judgment, subject not to the control of another department, but only to the limitations imposed by the state and federal Constitutions." *Id.* at 974. A branch has "the inherent right to accomplish all objects naturally within the orbit of that department, not expressly limited by the fact of the existence of a similar power elsewhere or the express limitations in the constitution." *Sun Ins. Office, Ltd. v. Clay*, 133 So. 2d 735, 742 (Fla. 1961) (quoting *In re Integration of Neb. State Bar Ass'n*, 275 N.W. 265, 266 (1937)). As we noted over seventy-five years ago, what determines whether a particular function is legislative, executive, or judicial "so that it may be exercised by appropriate officers of the proper department" is not "the name given to the function or to the officer who performs it" but the "essential nature and effect of the governmental function to be performed." *Florida Motor Lines v. Railroad Comm'rs*, 129 So. 876, 881 (1930).

The House argues that, precisely because the state constitution does not expressly grant the governor authority to execute compacts, such authority belongs to the Legislature. In other words, the "residual" power — that is, powers not specifically assigned to the governor — belongs to the Legislature. Albeit many years ago and under different circumstances, we have implied as much. *See State ex rel. Green v. Pearson*, 14 So. 2d 565, 567 (1943) ("The legislative branch looks to the Constitution not for sources of power but for limitations upon power. But if such limitations are not found to exist, its discretion reasonably exercised may not be disturbed by the judicial branch of the government."); *State ex rel. Cunningham v. Davis*, 166 So. 289, 297 (1936) ("The test of legislative power is constitutional restriction; what the people have not said in their organic law their representatives shall not do, they may do."). And, as we noted above, other state courts have ascribed to their legislatures any residual power on which the state constitutions were silent. *See Clark*, 904 P.2d at 25; *Pataki*, 766 N.Y.S.2d at 668, n. 11, 798 N.E.2d at 1061 n. 11.

We need not decide, however, whether the authority to bind the state to compacts always resides in the legislature. Although the line of demarcation is not always clear, we have noted that "the legislature's exclusive power encompasses questions of fundamental policy and the articulation of reasonably definite standards to be used in implementing those policies." *B.H. v. State*, 645 So. 2d 987, 993 (Fla. 1994); *see also Askew v. Cross Key Waterways*, 372 So. 2d 913, 925 (Fla. 1978) (stating that under the nondelegation doctrine, "fundamental and primary policy decisions shall be made by members of the legislature"). Therefore, even if the Governor has authority to execute compacts, its terms cannot contradict the state's public policy, as expressed in its laws.

2. IGRA and the "Necessary Business" Clause

The Governor argues that his authority to execute the Compact derives from article IV, section 1 of the Florida Constitution. That provision states in part that "[t]he governor shall take care that the laws be faithfully executed . . . and transact all necessary business with the officers of government." Art. IV, § 1(a), Fla. Const. The Governor submits that the phrase "transact all necessary business with the officers of government" includes negotiating with the Tribe and that he cannot ignore the federal directive to "negotiate"; therefore, negotiating the Compact was "necessary business" under IGRA.

IGRA provides that a tribe seeking to offer Class III gaming must "request [that] the State . . . enter into negotiations" for a compact and that the "State shall negotiate with the Indian tribe in good faith." 25 U.S.C. § 2710(d)(3)(A). The Governor is therefore correct that IGRA requires states to negotiate. As other courts have recognized, however, nowhere does IGRA equate "the state" with "the governor." *See Seminole Tribe*, 517 U.S. at 75 n. 17 (contrasting IGRA's "repeated[ ] refer[ences] exclusively to 'the State'" with other federal statutes directed at a state's governor and concluding that "the duty imposed by the Act . . . is not of the sort likely to be performed by an individual state executive officer or even a group of officers"); *Seminole Tribe*, 11 F.3d at 1029 ("IGRA uniformly addresses itself to 'the State'; not once does it impose duties or responsibilities on a particular officer of the state (e.g., the governor, the legislature, etc.).)." In addition, when a state fails to negotiate, a tribe must sue the *state*, not the governor. *Seminole Tribe*, 517 U.S. at 74–75 (holding that Congress intended § 2710(d)(3) to be enforced against the state, not the governor); *Seminole Tribe*, 11 F.3d at 1029 ("[T]hese suits are not against officials in an attempt to force them to follow federal law.").

More importantly, a State's "duty to negotiate" under IGRA cannot be enforced. A state may avoid its duty, as Florida has effectively done, by asserting its immunity. *Seminole Tribe*, 517 U.S. at 47, 116 S.Ct. 1114. Therefore, although IGRA requires a state to negotiate, it does not impose any duty on a state's governor. Moreover, IGRA does not prescribe the terms of a compact, *see* 25 U.S.C. § 2710(d), and it does not confer on the governor the authority to bind the state to a compact or act in contravention to state law. In other words, IGRA does not grant a governor, or any state actor, any powers beyond those provided by the state's constitution and laws. *See Clark*, 904 P.2d at 26 ("We do not agree that Congress, in enacting the IGRA, sought to invest state governors with powers in excess of those that the governors possess under state law.").

We express no opinion on whether the "necessary business" clause may ever grant the governor authority to bind the State to an IGRA compact. We do conclude, however, that the clause does not authorize the governor to execute compacts contrary to the expressed public policy of the state or to create exceptions to the law. Nor does it change our conclusion that "the legislature's exclusive power encompasses questions of fundamental policy and the articulation of reasonably definite standards to be used in implementing those policies." *B.H.*, 645 So. 2d at 993.

We now discuss why, in authorizing conduct prohibited by state law, the Governor exceeded his authority.

D. The Compact Violates the Separation of Powers

The House claims that the Compact violates the separation of powers on a number of grounds. We find one of them dispositive. The Compact permits the Tribe to conduct certain Class III gaming that is prohibited under Florida law. Therefore, the Compact violates the state's public policy about the types of gambling that should be allowed. We hold that, whatever the Governor's authority to execute compacts, it does not extend so far. The Governor does not have authority to agree to legalize in some parts of the state, or for some persons, conduct that is otherwise illegal throughout the state.

We first discuss whether state laws in general, and gaming laws in particular, apply to Indian tribes. We next discuss Florida law on gaming. We then address the House's argument that IGRA prohibits compacts from expanding the gaming allowed under state law. Finally, we explain why the Governor lacked authority to bind the State to a compact, such as this one, that contradicts state law.

1. State Gaming Laws Apply to the Tribe

Generally, state laws do not apply to tribal Indians on Indian reservations unless Congress so provides. *McClanahan v. State Tax Comm'n of Ariz.*, 411 U.S. 164, 170, 93 S.Ct. 1257, 36 L.Ed.2d 129 (1973). Therefore, the extent to which a state may enforce its criminal laws on tribal land depends on federal authorization. *See Seminole Tribe of Fla. v. Butterworth*, 658 F.2d 310, 312 (5th Cir. 1981). Congress has, however, conferred on the states the authority to assume jurisdiction over crimes committed on tribal land, *see* Act of Aug. 15, 1953, Pub.L. No. 280 § 6, 67 Stat. 588, 590 (1953), and Florida has assumed such jurisdiction. *See* ch. 61–252, §§ 1–2, at 452–53, Laws of Fla. (codified at § 285.16, Fla. Stat. (2007)); *see also* § 285.16(2), Fla. Stat. (2007) ("The civil and criminal laws of Florida shall obtain on all Indian reservations in this state and shall be enforced in the same manner as elsewhere throughout the state."); Op. Att'y Gen. Fla. 94–45 (1994) (discussing the state's jurisdiction over Indian reservations). The state's law is therefore enforceable on tribal lands to the extent it does not conflict with federal law. *See* Op. Att'y Gen. Fla. 94–45 (1994); *see also Hall v. State*, 762 So. 2d 936, 936–38 (Fla. 2d DCA 2000) (holding that the circuit court had jurisdiction over a vehicular homicide on an Indian reservation); *State v. Billie*, 497 So. 2d 889, 892–95 (Fla. 2d DCA 1986) (holding that a Seminole

Indian was properly charged under state criminal law with killing a Florida panther on tribal land). In regard to gambling in particular, federal law provides that, except as provided in a tribal-state compact, state gambling laws apply on tribal lands. *See* 18 U.S.C. § 1166(a) (2000).

Based on these state and federal provisions, what is legal in Florida is legal on tribal lands, and what is illegal in Florida is illegal there. Absent a compact, any gambling prohibited in the state is prohibited on tribal land.

2. Florida's Gaming Laws

It is undisputed that Florida permits limited forms of Class III gaming. The state's constitution authorizes the state lottery, which offers various Class III games, and now permits slot machines in Miami-Dade and Broward Counties. *See* art. X, §§ 7, 15, Fla. Const. For a long time, the State also has regulated pari-mutuel wagering — for example, on dog and horse racing. *See* ch. 550, Fla. Stat. (2007) (governing pari-mutuel wagering).

It is also undisputed, however, that the State prohibits all other types of Class III gaming, including lotteries not sponsored by the State and slot machines outside Miami-Dade and Broward Counties. Florida law distinguishes between nonbanked (Class II) card games and banked (Class III) card games. A "banking game" is one "in which the house is a participant in the game, taking on players, paying winners, and collecting from losers or in which the cardroom establishes a bank against which participants play." § 849.086(2)(b); *see* § 849.086(1), Fla. Stat. (deeming banked games to be "casino gaming"). Florida law authorizes cardrooms at pari-mutuel facilities for games of "poker or dominoes," but only if they are played "in a nonbanking manner." § 849.086(2), Fla. Stat.; *see* § 849.086(1)-(3). Florida law prohibits banked card games, however. *See* § 849.086(12)(a), (15)(a). Blackjack, baccarat, and *chemin de fer* are banked card games. They are therefore illegal in Florida.

3. Does IGRA Permit Compacts to Expand Gaming?

Contrary to Florida law, the Compact allows banked card games such as blackjack, baccarat, and *chemin de fer*. The House argues that the Compact therefore violates IGRA itself, which permits Class III gaming *only* if the state "permits such gaming for any purpose by any person, organization, or entity." 25 U.S.C. § 2710(d)(1). The Governor, on the other hand, contends that, once state law permits *any* Class III gaming, a compact may allow *all* Class III gaming.

The meaning of the phrase "permits such gaming" has been heavily litigated. The question is whether, when state law permits some Class III games to be played, a tribe must be permitted to conduct only those particular games or all Class III games. *See* Kathryn R. L. Rand, *Caught in the Middle: How State Politics, State Law, and State Courts Constrain Tribal Influence over Indian Gaming*, 90 MARQ. L. REV. 971, 983 (2007) (citing cases). The Secretary's interpretation of this provision supports the House's argument. *See* Class III Gaming Procedures, 63 Fed.Reg. 3289,

3293 (Jan. 22, 1998) (Proposed Rules) ("IGRA thus makes it unlawful for Tribes to operate particular Class III games that State law completely and affirmatively prohibits."). So do a majority of federal courts. *See, e.g., Rumsey Indian Rancheria of Wintun Indians v. Wilson*, 64 F.3d 1250, 1258 (9th Cir. 1994) ("[A] state need only allow Indian tribes to operate games that others can operate, but need not give tribes what others cannot have."); *see also Cheyenne River Sioux Tribe v. South Dakota*, 3 F.3d 273, 279 (8th Cir. 1993) (stating that IGRA "does not require the state to negotiate with respect to forms of gaming it does not presently permit"); *but see Lac du Flambeau Band of Lake Superior Chippewa Indians v. Wisconsin*, 770 F.Supp. 480, 486 (W.D.Wis. 1991) ("Congress did not intend the term 'permits such gaming' to limit the tribes to the specific types of gaming activity actually in operation in a state."). Our Attorney General has agreed with the majority interpretation. *See* Op. Att'y Gen. Fla. 2007–36 at 3 (2007) ("[I]n light of the greater weight of federal case law and the Department of the Interior's interpretation of IGRA, Class III gaming activities subject to mandatory negotiations between a state and an Indian tribe do not include those specifically prohibited by state law.").

Whether the Compact violates IGRA, however, is a question we need not and do not resolve. Given our narrow scope of review on a writ of quo warranto, the issue here is only whether the Florida Constitution grants the Governor the authority to unilaterally bind the State to a compact that violates public policy. We conclude that *even if* the Governor is correct that IGRA permits the expansion of gaming on tribal lands beyond what state law permits, such an agreement represents a significant change in Florida's public policy. It is therefore precisely the type of action particularly within the Legislature's power. We now discuss that issue.

4. The Compact Violates Florida's Public Policy on Gaming

Article II, section 3 of the Florida Constitution prohibits the executive branch from usurping the powers of another branch. Enacting laws—and especially criminal laws—is quintessentially a legislative function. *See State v. Barquet*, 262 So. 2d 431, 433 (Fla. 1972) ("The lawmaking function is the chief legislative power."). By authorizing the Tribe to conduct "banked card games" that are illegal throughout Florida—and thus illegal for the Tribe—the Compact violates Florida law. *See Chiles v. Children A, B, C, D, E, & F*, 589 So. 2d 260, 264 (Fla. 1991) ("This Court has repeatedly held that, under the doctrine of separation of powers, the legislature may not delegate the power to enact laws or to declare what the law shall be to any other branch."). The Governor's action therefore encroaches on the legislative function and was beyond his authority. Nor does it matter that the Compact is a contract between the State and the Tribe. Neither the Governor nor anyone else in the executive branch has the authority to execute a contract that violates state criminal law. *Cf. Local No. 234, United Assoc. of Journeymen & Apprentices of Plumbing & Pipefitting Industry v. Henley & Beckwith, Inc.*, 66 So. 2d 818, 821 (Fla. 1953) ("[A]n agreement that is violative of a provision of a constitution or a valid statute, or an agreement which cannot be performed without violating such a constitutional or statutory provision, is illegal and void."); *City of Miami v. Benson*, 63 So. 2d 916, 923 (Fla. 1953) ("The contract in question, that is, the acceptance by the City of the proposal made by its agent, employee or advisor, to purchase the bonds, is contrary to public policy and is, therefore, void.").

IV. Conclusion

We conclude that the Governor's execution of a compact authorizing types of gaming that are prohibited under Florida law violates the separation of powers. The Governor has no authority to change or amend state law. Such power falls exclusively to the Legislature. Therefore, we hold that the Governor lacked authority to bind the State to a compact that violates Florida law as this compact does. We need not resolve the broader issue of whether the Governor ever has the authority to execute compacts without either the Legislature's prior authorization or, at least, its subsequent ratification. Because we believe the parties will fully comply with the dictates of this opinion, we grant the petition but withhold issuance of the writ.

It is so ordered.

Notes and Questions to Consider:

1. Which branch of Florida's government does *Florida House of Representatives v. Crist* hold to be the branch that determines the public policy of the state of Florida? What impact could this have on Florida's other two branches?

2. Recall that an extraordinary writ like a writ of quo warranto is a discretionary remedy, and so, a party that proves its entitlement to such a writ may still be denied issuance of that writ by the court. Indeed, here in *Florida House of Representatives v. Crist*, Florida's supreme court found that the House of Representatives was entitled to such a writ yet the court withheld its issuance. In what way was this in deference to the separation of powers?

3. *Florida House of Representatives v. Crist* attempts to tackle some of the nuances of the sovereignty of Native Americans. Some commentators once said, "The nuances of tribal sovereign immunity ... are recommended only for the brave." David Getches, Charles Wilkinson, Robert Williams & Matthew Fletcher, CASES AND MATERIALS ON FEDERAL INDIAN LAW 315 (2d ed. 1986). One of the points raised was to classify the agreement between the governor and the tribe as a "compact." What is a compact?

4. The federal Constitution states: "The Congress shall have Power ... To regulate Commerce ... with the Indian Tribes...." Art. 1, §8, clause 3, U.S. Const. "This phrase ... has been interpreted to mean that the states lack jurisdiction over Native American reservation activity until granted that authority by the federal government." Patrick John McGinley, FLORIDA MUNICIPAL LAW AND PRACTICE §6:3 (2017-2018 ed.). Section 7 of former "Public Law 280 [formerly codified at 18 USC §1162 and 28 USC §1360] granted Florida and other states the right to assume criminal and civil jurisdiction by legislative enactment...." *Id.* Under that

authority, Florida's legislature enacted Florida Statutes section § 285.16 in 1961 and that law endures. It provides:

> *Civil and criminal jurisdiction; Indian reservation. —*
>
> *(1) The State of Florida hereby assumes jurisdiction over criminal offenses committed by or against Indians or other persons within Indian reservations and over civil causes of actions between Indians or other persons or to which Indians or other persons are parties rising within Indian reservations.*
>
> *(2) The civil and criminal laws of Florida shall obtain on all Indian reservations in this state and shall be enforced in the same manner as elsewhere throughout the state.*

§ 285.16, Fla. Stat. Was it wise and fair for Florida to erode Native American sovereignty in this way?

5. Florida Statutes section 285.16 attempts to draw a line between civil and criminal laws. Is the line always so bright? Consider *Bryan v. Itasca County*, 426 U.S. 373 (1976) (assuming to divide all laws into either criminal or civil) and *California v. Cabazon Band of Mission Indians*, 426 U.S. 373 (1987) (acknowledging the division attempted in *Bryan v. Itasca County* did not always work, and proposing instead a division between civil/regulatory versus criminal/prohibitory).

6. *Florida House of Representatives v. Crist* holds that, unless there is a tribal-state compact allowing gambling, any gambling prohibited in Florida is prohibited on tribal land. Likewise, *Crist* holds that the tribal-state gaming compact violated state law by authorizing the tribe to conduct "banked card games" that were illegal throughout Florida, and therefore, illegal for the tribe. In light of Florida Statutes section 285.16, could the court have ruled any other way?

7. *Florida House of Representatives v. Crist* holds that Florida's supreme court has quo warranto jurisdiction alleging a violation of the separation of powers, and has that jurisdiction even after the act has occurred. This holding defeated the governor's defense that the House could have acted sooner and failed to act in time. Is it necessary for one to wait and suffer the harm inflicted by a violation of the separation of powers before one may seek quo warranto relief? Consider this holding from footnote 1 of *League of Women Voters of Florida v. Scott*, 232 So. 3d 264 (Fla. 2017):

> We recognize that [*Florida House of Representatives v.*] *Crist* contained language suggesting the writ could be used to prohibit future conduct. *See, e.g.,* 999 So. 2d at 607 ("The Governor contends that this Court lacks jurisdiction because the House does not seek either to remove him from office or to enjoin the future exercise of his authority. We conclude, however, that these are not the only grounds for issuing such a writ."). However, the history of quo warranto as well as our precedent belie any suggestion to this effect. In *Crist*, we explained that "petitions for the writ historically have been filed *after* a public official has acted," and the disputed act had already

occurred. *Id.* In that case, the Florida House of Representatives challenged the execution by Governor Charles Crist of a compact with the Seminole Indian Tribe of Florida. . . .

Id. at 265 n.1.

8. Article IV, Section 1 of Florida's constitution states that "[t]he supreme executive power shall be vested in a governor, who shall . . . transact all necessary business with the officers of government." *Florida House of Representatives v. Crist* holds that this "necessary business" clause of Florida's constitution does not authorize Florida's governor to execute compacts contrary to the expressed public policy of the state or to create exceptions to state law. Does this make the authority of Florida's governor different that the authority of a U.S. President? Consider, for example, the proposed "Development, Relief, and Education for Alien Minors" Act, or "DREAM" Act, that failed to pass in the U.S. Congress from 2009 through 2012. It would have prevented deportation of certain "Dreamers" and made them eligible for work permits. After Congress did not pass that law, the U.S. president issued an executive branch memorandum on June 15, 2012. It deferred action on deportation of "Dreamers" and made them eligible for work permits. In a way, the presidential action implemented a public policy that the national legislature decided not to implement. Does Florida's governor have a similar power to implement a public policy that Florida's legislature decides not to implement, or would that be a violation of Florida's separation of powers? *See Florida House of Representatives v. Crist*, 999 So. 2d at 614–17 (holding that Florida's governor lacked authority to bind Florida to a compact that departed from our state's public policy by legalizing types of gaming that were illegal everywhere else in the state).

2. Cooperation among the Branches

Just as the tale of dissention among the branches in *Florida House of Representatives v. Crist* illustrated many lessons about Florida's separation of powers, so too can a tale of cooperation among the branches. This tale begins in 1976, when Florida's legislature enacted the first codified rules of evidence for Florida's courts. Perhaps Florida's supreme court could have rejected Florida's legislature's enactment of an evidence code for Florida's courts. Instead, Florida's supreme court held that "[r]ules of evidence may in some instances be substantive law and, therefore, the sole responsibility of the legislature. In other instances, evidentiary rules may be procedural and the responsibility of this Court." *In re Fla. Evidence Code*, 372 So. 2d 1369, 1369 (Fla. 1979). The court therefore chose to adopt the rules.

Over the next 37 years, Florida's judiciary continued to accept Florida's legislature's occasional amendments to Florida's evidence code. That spirit of cooperation ended in the 2000s when an amendment to the evidence code by the Legislature was held to violate the constitutional right to confront one's accusers in a criminal case. Then, as explained in Florida Workers' Compensation:

> In 2013, the Florida Legislature modified the Florida Evidence Code at Florida Statutes section 90.702 "to adopt the standards for expert testimony in the courts of this state as provided in *Daubert v. Merrell Dow Pharmaceuticals, Inc.*, 509 U.S. 579 (1993), *General Electric Co. v. Joiner*, 522 U.S. 136 (1997), and *Kumho Tire Co., Ltd. v. Carmichael*, 526 U.S. 137 (1999), and to no longer apply the standard in *Frye v. United States*, 293 F. 1013 (D.C.Cir. 1923)." *Frye* and *Daubert* are competing methods for a trial judge to determine the reliability of expert testimony before allowing it to be admitted into evidence. By amending section 90.702, the Legislature signaled its intent "to tighten the rules for admissibility of expert testimony."

Patrick John McGinley, Florida Workers' Compensation § 42:12 (2019 ed.).

With that background in mind, we pick up this story with the decision in *DeLisle v. Crane Co.*, 258 So. 3d 1219 (Fla. 2018). But *DeLisle* does not end our tale. A few months later, with three Florida Supreme Court justices having retired and three new appointees having taken their place, Florida's supreme court spoke again in *In re Amendments to Florida Evidence Code*, SC19-107, 2019 WL 2219714 (Fla. May 23, 2019). Below, we start with *DeLisle*, and finish with *In re Amendments*.

DeLisle v. Crane Co.

Supreme Court of Florida, 2018
258 So. 3d 1219

... After developing mesothelioma, [a disease that can be caused by exposure to asbestos,] DeLisle filed a personal injury action against ... Crane, Lorillard Tobacco Co., and Hollingsworth & Vose Co. ("H & V").

At trial, DeLisle presented evidence that he was exposed to asbestos fibers from sheet gaskets.... Crane, a valve and pump manufacturer, used "Cranite" sheet gaskets containing chrysotile asbestos fibers. DeLisle also testified that he smoked Original Kent cigarettes with asbestos-containing "Micronite" filters from 1952 to 1956. These cigarettes were produced by Lorillard's predecessor, and the filters were supplied by a former subsidiary of H & V. The filters contained crocidolite asbestos....

The parties hotly disputed causation, and even DeLisle's own experts did not agree on which products produced sufficient exposure to asbestos to constitute a substantial contributing factor to DeLisle's disease....

Appellees challenged each expert's opinions under section 90.702, Florida Statutes, which adopted the *Daubert* test for expert testimony.... Following *Daubert* hearings, the trial court admitted each expert's testimony....

Following three days of deliberation, the jury awarded DeLisle $8 million in damages....

Crane appealed ...

The Fourth District reviewed the admission of the testimony of the experts under *Daubert v. Merrell Dow Pharmaceuticals, Inc.*, 509 U.S. 579 (1993), and found that the trial court "failed to properly exercise its gatekeeping function. . . ." The Fourth District reversed for a new trial. . . . DeLisle sought review by this Court, which was granted.

The Florida Legislature and the Florida Supreme Court have worked in tandem for nearly forty years to enact and maintain codified rules of evidence. This arrangement between the branches to avoid constitutional questions of separation of powers continued uninterrupted from the Evidence Code's inception until 2000. In the instant case, we are asked to determine whether chapter 2013-107, section 1, Laws of Florida, which revised section 90.702, Florida Statutes (2015), and which we previously declined to adopt, to the extent it was procedural, infringes on this Court's rulemaking authority. We find that it does. Therefore, we reverse the Fourth District and remand for reinstatement of the final judgment.

The Florida Legislature enacted the first codified rules of evidence in 1976. . . . In 1979, we adopted the Florida Evidence Code, to the extent that the code was procedural. . . . We recognized that "[r]ules of evidence may in some instances be substantive law and, therefore, the sole responsibility of the legislature. In other instances, evidentiary rules may be procedural and the responsibility of this Court." . . . We therefore chose to adopt the rules, "[t]o avoid multiple appeals and confusion in the operation of the courts caused by assertions that portions of the evidence code are procedural and, therefore, unconstitutional because they had not been adopted by this Court under its rule-making authority." *Id.* Since then, we have traditionally continued to adopt the code, to the extent it is procedural, to avoid the issue of whether the Evidence Code is substantive in nature and therefore within the province of the Legislature or procedural in nature and therefore within the province of this Court. . . .

Until 2000, the working arrangement between the Legislature and the Florida Supreme Court remained intact. However, in *In re Amendments to the Florida Evidence Code*, 782 So. 2d 339 (Fla. 2000), this Court for the first time declined to adopt, to the extent they were procedural, amendments to section 90.803, Florida Statutes (1997). *Id.* (declining to adopt chapter 98-2, section 1, Laws of Florida, amending section 90.803(22), Florida Statutes, which allows the admission of former testimony although the declarant is available as a witness, in part because of concerns about its constitutionality). We then considered the constitutionality of the provision in *State v. Abreu*, 837 So. 2d 400 (Fla. 2003), determining that the revised statute was unconstitutional because it infringed on a defendant's right to confront witnesses. *Id.* at 406.

Since then, we have only rarely declined to adopt a statutory revision to the Evidence Code. . . .

Generally, the Legislature has the power to enact substantive law while this Court has the power to enact procedural law. *See Allen v. Butterworth*, 756 So. 2d 52, 59

(Fla. 2000). Substantive law has been described as that which defines, creates, or regulates rights—"those existing for their own sake and constituting the normal legal order of society, i.e., the rights of life, liberty, property, and reputation." *In re Fla. Rules of Criminal Procedure*, 272 So. 2d 65, 65 (Fla. 1972) (Adkins, J., concurring). Procedural law, on the other hand, is the form, manner, or means by which substantive law is implemented. *Id.* at 66 (Adkins, J., concurring). Stated differently, procedural law "includes all rules governing the parties, their counsel and the Court throughout the progress of the case from the time of its initiation until final judgment and its execution." *Allen v. Butterworth*, 756 So. 2d 52, 60 (Fla. 2000) . . . . "It is the method of conducting litigation involving rights and corresponding defenses." *Haven Federal Savings & Loan Ass'n v. Kirian*, 579 So. 2d 730, 732 (Fla. 1991) (citing *Skinner v. City of Eustis*, 147 Fla. 22, 2 So. 2d 116 (1941)).

The distinction between substantive and procedural law, however, is not always clear. For example, a law is considered to be substantive when it both creates and conditions a right. *See . . . Jackson v. Fla. Dep't of Corr.*, 790 So. 2d 381, 383–84 (Fla. 2000) (holding that the Legislature could properly limit the right of indigents to proceed without payment of costs); *Caple v. Tuttle's Design-Build, Inc.*, 753 So. 2d 49, 54 (Fla. 2000) (holding that a statute creating the right to petition for mortgage payment receipts during foreclosure proceedings and establishing the grounds for granting such a petition was constitutional); *School Bd. of Broward Cty. v. Price*, 362 So. 2d 1337 (Fla. 1978) (holding that section 230.23(9)(d)(2), Florida Statutes (1977), set the bounds of a substantive right conditioned on a waiver and was therefore not an unconstitutional infringement of the Court's power to set procedural rules). However, when procedural aspects overwhelm substantive ones, the law may no longer be considered substantive. . . .

Here, the Legislature sought to adopt *Daubert* and cease the application of *Frye* to expert testimony. In *Frye v. United States*, 293 F. 1013 (D.C. Cir. 1923), a short opinion, the Court of Appeals for the District of Columbia pronounced that . . . "the thing from which the deduction is made must be sufficiently established to have gained general acceptance in the particular field in which it belongs." *Id.* This rule— that expert testimony should be deduced from generally accepted scientific principles—has been the standard in Florida cases and, today, we reaffirm that it is still the standard. *See, e.g., . . . Bundy v. State*, 471 So. 2d 9, 13 (Fla. 1985) (describing the *Frye* test as one in which "the results of mechanical or scientific testing are not admissible unless the testing has developed or improved to the point where experts in the field widely share the view that the results are scientifically reliable as accurate").

[W]e formally adopted *Frye* . . . [in] *Stokes v. State*, 548 So. 2d 188, 195 (Fla. 1989) . . . . [where] we noted:

> [A] courtroom is not a laboratory, and as such it is not the place to conduct scientific experiments. If the scientific community considers a procedure or process unreliable for its own purposes, then the procedure must be considered less reliable for courtroom use.

Stokes, 548 So. 2d at 193–94. We note that we adopted the *Frye* test irrespective of the Evidence Code, which was in place at the time.

In *Hadden v. State*, 690 So. 2d 573 (Fla. 1997), we rejected the argument that the Legislature's enactment and this Court's subsequent adoption of the Evidence Code replaced the *Frye* standard with the balancing test that existed in the code. . . .

After decades of the federal courts' applying *Frye*, Congress revised the Federal Rules of Evidence. The revision was addressed by the United States Supreme Court in 1993. In *Daubert v. Merrell Dow Pharmaceuticals*, 509 U.S. 579 (1993), the United States Supreme Court determined the appropriate standard for admitting expert scientific testimony in a federal trial. *Id.* at 582. The Supreme Court ultimately agreed . . . that *Frye* had been superseded by the adoption of the revised Federal Rules of Evidence. *Id.* at 587.

The Court explained its decision, stating, "[I]n order to qualify as 'scientific knowledge,' an inference or assertion must be derived by the scientific method." *Daubert*, 509 U.S. at 590. The inquiry derived from *Daubert* is a flexible one, as emphasized by the Supreme Court. *Id.* at 594. "The focus, of course, must be solely on principles and methodology, not on the conclusions that they generate." *Id.* at 595. . . .

. . . In short, in *Daubert*, the United States Supreme Court found that otherwise probative and scientifically valid evidence was being excluded under the *Frye* standard and the change in rule 702 was necessary to permit additional relevant evidence to be considered even if it was based on scientific methods or principles that were not yet generally accepted.

Nevertheless, in *Brim v. State*, 695 So. 2d 268 (Fla. 1997), we unanimously emphasized that we continue to apply *Frye*. . . . We opined:

> Despite the federal adoption of a more lenient standard in *Daubert v. Merrell Dow Pharmaceuticals, Inc.*, 509 U.S. 579 (1993), we have maintained the higher standard of reliability as dictated by *Frye*. . . .

Brim, 695 So. 2d at 271–72 (footnote omitted).

Following our repeated affirmations of the *Frye* rule, in 2013 the Legislature amended section 90.702 to incorporate *Daubert* in[to] the Florida Rules of Evidence. The amendment revised the statute to read as follows:

> 90.702 *Testimony by experts.* — If scientific, technical, or other specialized knowledge will assist the trier of fact in understanding the evidence or in determining a fact in issue, a witness qualified as an expert by knowledge, skill, experience, training, or education may testify about it in the form of an opinion or otherwise, if:
>
> (1) The testimony is based upon sufficient facts or data;
>
> (2) The testimony is the product of reliable principles and methods; and

(3) The witness has applied the principles and methods reliably to the facts of the case.

§ 90.702, Fla. Stat. (as amended by ch. 2013-107, § 1, Laws of Fla.).

Article II, section 3 of the Florida Constitution prohibits one branch of government from exercising any of the powers of the other branches. Further, article V, section 2(a) provides this Court the exclusive authority to "adopt rules for the practice and procedure in all courts." Art. V, § 2(a), Fla. Const. The Legislature may only repeal the rules of this Court by "general law enacted by two-thirds vote of the membership of each house of the legislature." *Id.* . . . The vote here did not meet the requirement. The House passed the bill with a majority, 70 to 41 (or 58.3% of the membership). The Senate passed the bill with more than the necessary two-thirds vote, 30 to 9 (or 75% of the membership). *Id.*

We have previously found that the Legislature exceeded its authority in adopting statutes we found to infringe on the authority of this Court to determine matters of practice or procedure. . . .

In *Jackson v. Florida Department of Corrections*, 790 So. 2d 381 (Fla. 2000), we explained that a statute can have both substantive provisions and procedural requirements and "[i]f the procedural requirements conflict with or interfere with the procedural mechanisms of the court system, they are unconstitutional under both a separation of powers analysis, and because [they intrude upon] the exclusive province of the Supreme Court pursuant to the rulemaking authority vested in it by the Florida Constitution." *Id.* at 384 (citing art. II, § 3, art. V, § 2, Fla. Const.; *State v. Garcia*, 229 So. 2d 236, 238 (Fla. 1969)) . . . .

In *State v. Raymond*, 906 So. 2d 1045 (Fla. 2005), we determined that section 907.041(4)(b), Florida Statutes (2000), providing that a person charged with a dangerous crime was prohibited from receiving a nonmonetary pretrial release, was purely procedural and, therefore, an unconstitutional violation of the separation of powers clause. "It is a well-established principle that a statute which purports to create or modify a procedural rule of court is constitutionally infirm." *Id.* at 1048. . . . Further, "where there is no substantive right conveyed by the statute, the procedural aspects are not incidental; accordingly, such a statute is unconstitutional." *Id.* at 1049. . . .

Section 90.702, Florida Statutes, as amended in 2013, is not substantive. It does not create, define, or regulate a right. Indeed, while we have stated that the Florida Evidence Code contains both substantive and procedural rights, this statute is one that solely regulates the action of litigants in court proceedings. *See, e.g., Glendening v. State*, 536 So. 2d 212, 215 (Fla. 1988) (determining that section 90.803(23), Florida Statutes (1985), concerning out-of-court statements, was procedural for the purposes of ex post facto analysis).

Our consideration of the constitutionality of the amendment does not end with our determination that the provision was procedural. For this Court to determine that the amendment is unconstitutional, it must also conflict with a rule of this Court. *See Haven Fed. Sav. & Loan Ass'n v. Kirian*, 579 So. 2d 730, 732–33 (Fla. 1991) ("Where this Court promulgates rules relating to the practice and procedure of all courts and a statute provides a contrary practice or procedure, the statute is unconstitutional to the extent of the conflict.") . . . A procedural rule of this Court may be pronounced in caselaw. . . . While the Legislature purports to have pronounced public policy in overturning *Marsh*, we hold that the rule announced in *Stokes* and reaffirmed in *Marsh* was a procedural rule of this Court that the Legislature could not repeal by simple majority.

The expert testimony in this case was properly admitted [under *Frye*] and should not have been excluded by the Fourth District. . . .

For the foregoing reasons, we quash the Fourth District's decision. Furthermore, because the causation of mesothelioma is neither new nor novel, the trial court's acceptance of the expert testimony was proper. We therefore remand to the Fourth District with instructions to remand to the trial court to reinstate the final judgment. . . .

It is so ordered.

———————

As promised in the introductory paragraphs preceding *DeLisle*, our tale does not end with *DeLisle*. We pick up our tale just a few months later when Florida's supreme court decided *In re Amendments to Florida Evidence Code*, SC19-107, 2019 WL 2219714 (Fla. May 23, 2019):

In re: Amendments to Florida Evidence Code

Supreme Court of Florida, 2019
SC19-107, 2019 WL 2219714

The Court, according to its exclusive rulemaking authority pursuant to article V, section 2(a) of the Florida Constitution, adopts chapter 2013-107, sections 1 and 2, Laws of Florida (*Daubert* amendments), which amended sections 90.702 (Testimony by experts) and 90.704 (Basis of opinion testimony by experts), Florida Statutes, of the Florida Evidence Code to replace the *Frye* standard for admitting certain expert testimony with the *Daubert* standard, the standard for expert testimony found in Federal Rule of Evidence 702.

In *In re Amendments to Florida Evidence Code*, 210 So. 3d 1231, 1239 (Fla. 2017), at the recommendation of The Florida Bar's Code and Rules of Evidence Committee (Committee), which occurred by a close vote of 16–14, the majority of this Court previously declined to adopt the *Daubert* amendments, to the extent that they are procedural, solely "due to the constitutional concerns raised" by the Committee members and commenters who opposed the amendments. Without now readdressing the correctness of this Court's ruling in *DeLisle v. Crane Co.*, 258 So. 3d 1219, 1221, 1229 (Fla. 2018), we note that the decision determined that section 90.702 of the Florida Evidence Code, as amended by section 1 of chapter 2013-107, is procedural in nature. *DeLisle* did not address the amendment to section 90.704 made by section 2 of chapter 2013-107. Therefore, the Court has not determined the extent to which that amendment may be procedural.

As noted by *In re Amendments to Florida Evidence Code*, 210 So. 3d at 1236–37, the *Daubert* amendments were considered by The Florida Bar's Code and Rules of Evidence Committee. The Committee provided majority and minority reports against and in favor of the Court's adoption of the *Daubert* amendments. The Board of Governors of The Florida Bar approved the Committee's recommendation, and extensive comments were received in response to the published recommendation. The Court held oral argument in the case. Because of the extensive briefing and arguments on this issue previously made to the Court, and mindful of the resources of parties, members of The Florida Bar, and the judiciary, we revisit the outcome of the recommendation on the *Daubert* amendments without requiring the process to be repeated.

We now recede from the Court's prior decision not to adopt the Legislature's *Daubert* amendments to the Evidence Code and to retain the *Frye* standard. As Justice Polston has explained, the "grave constitutional concerns" raised by those who oppose the amendments to the Code appear unfounded:

> [T]he United States Supreme Court decided *Daubert v. Merrell Dow Pharmaceuticals, Inc.*, 509 U.S. 579 (1993), in 1993, and the standard has been routinely applied in federal courts ever since. The clear majority of state jurisdictions also adhere to the *Daubert* standard. *See* 1 *McCormick on Evidence* § 13 (7th ed. June 2016 Supp.). In fact, there are 36 states that have rejected *Frye* in favor of *Daubert* to some extent. *See* Charles Alan Wright & Victor Gold, 29 *Federal Practice and Procedure* § 6267, at 308–09 n.15 (2016). Has the entire federal court system for the last 23 years as well as 36 states denied parties' rights to a jury trial and access to courts? Do only Florida and a few other states have a constitutionally sound standard for the admissibility of expert testimony? Of course not.
>
> As a note to the federal rule of evidence explains, "[a] review of the caselaw after *Daubert* shows that the rejection of expert testimony is the exception rather than the rule." Fed. R. Evid. 702 advisory committee's note to 2000 amendment. "*Daubert* did not work a 'sea-change over federal evidence law,' and 'the trial court's role as gatekeeper is not intended to serve as a replacement for the adversary system.'" *Id.* . . .
>
> Furthermore, I know of no reported decisions that have held that the *Daubert* standard violates the constitutional guarantees of a jury trial and access to courts. To the contrary, there is case law holding that the *Daubert* standard does not violate the constitution. *See, e.g., Junk v. Terminix Int'l Co.*, 628 F.3d 439, 450 (8th Cir. 2010) (rejecting legal merit of the constitutional claim "that the district court violated [appellant's] Seventh

Amendment right to a jury trial by improperly weighing evidence in the course of its *Daubert* rulings" and explaining that "Junk does not cite any case for the notion that a proper *Daubert* ruling violates a party's right to a jury trial"); *E.I. du Pont de Nemours & Co. v. Robinson*, 923 S.W.2d 549, 558 (Tex. 1995) (rejecting claim "that allowing the trial judge to assess the reliability of expert testimony violates [the parties'] federal and state constitutional rights to a jury trial by infringing upon the jury's inherent authority to assess the credibility of witnesses and the weight to be given their testimony"); *see also Gen. Elec. Co. v. Joiner*, 522 U.S. 136, 142–43, 118 S.Ct. 512, 139 L.Ed.2d 508 (1997) (rejecting "argument that because the granting of summary judgment in this case was 'outcome determinative,' it should have been subjected to a more searching standard of review" and explaining that, while "disputed issues of fact are resolved against the moving party[,] . . . the question of admissibility of expert testimony is not such an issue of fact").

Accordingly, the . . . "grave constitutional concerns" regarding the *Daubert* standard are unfounded.

In re Amends. to Fla. Evidence Code, 210 So. 3d 1231, 1242–43 (Polston, J., concurring in part and dissenting in part). While we find Justice Polston's observations instructive in deciding to now adopt the Legislature's *Daubert* amendments, we do not decide, in this rules case, the constitutional or other substantive concerns that have been raised about the amendments. Those issues must be left for a proper case or controversy.

Additionally, as outlined in the Committee minority report, the *Daubert* amendments remedy deficiencies of the *Frye* standard. Whereas the *Frye* standard only applied to expert testimony based on new or novel scientific techniques and general acceptance, *Daubert* provides that "the trial judge must ensure that any and all scientific testimony or evidence admitted is not only relevant, but reliable." *Daubert*, 509 U.S. at 589 (holding that the Federal Rules of Evidence superseded *Frye*). Moreover, also as argued in the minority report, the *Daubert* amendments will create consistency between the state and federal courts with respect to the admissibility of expert testimony and will promote fairness and predictability in the legal system, as well as help lessen forum shopping.

Accordingly, in accordance with this Court's exclusive rule-making authority and longstanding practice of adopting provisions of the Florida Evidence Code as they are enacted or amended by the Legislature, we adopt the amendments to sections 90.702 and 90.704 of the Florida Evidence Code made by chapter 2013-107, sections 1 and 2. Effective immediately upon the release of this opinion, we adopt the amendments to section 90.702 as procedural rules of evidence and adopt the amendment to section 90.704 to the extent it is procedural.

It is so ordered.

———————

Notes and Questions to Consider:

1. In *DeLisle*, Florida's supreme court declines to replace the *Frye* rule with *Daubert*. A few months later and with three retiring Supreme Court justices having been replaced with new justices, Florida's supreme court replaces *Frye* with *Daubert* in its *In re Amendments* decision. To what extent was the different outcome attributable to changed circumstances, and to what extent was it attributable to changed personnel?

2. Noting that Florida's constitution makes judicial rulemaking the sole province of Florida's supreme court, is it wrong if the difference is due to changed personnel?

B. Sovereign Immunity

One result of the separation of powers is the concept of sovereign immunity. Judicial relief can be denied in a suit against a governmental entity if the entity possesses sovereign immunity as to the claims in that suit. Florida's supreme court explains:

> Florida law has enunciated three policy considerations that underpin the doctrine of sovereign immunity. First is the preservation of the constitutional principle of separation of powers. *See Commercial Carrier Corp. v. Indian River County*, 371 So. 2d 1010, 1022 (Fla. 1979) (stating that "certain functions of coordinate branches of government may not be subjected to scrutiny by judge or jury as to the wisdom of their performance"). Second is the protection of the public treasury. *See Spangler v. Fla. State Tpk. Auth.*, 106 So. 2d 421, 424 (Fla. 1958) (explaining that "immunity of the sovereign is a part of the public policy of the state[, which] is enforced as a protection of the public against profligate encroachments on the public treasury"). Third is the maintenance of the orderly administration of government. *See State Rd. Dep't v. Tharp*, 1 So. 2d 868, 869 (Fla. 1941) ("If the State could be sued at the instance of every citizen, the public service would be disrupted and the administration of government would be bottlenecked.").

Am. Home Assur. Co. v. Nat'l R.R. Passenger Corp., 908 So. 2d 459, 471 (Fla. 2005).

1. Sovereign Immunity Defined

"Sovereign immunity, or crown immunity, is a legal doctrine by which the sovereign or state cannot commit a legal wrong and is immune from civil suit or criminal prosecution." Patrick John McGinley, FLORIDA MUNICIPAL LAW AND PRACTICE § 7:2 (2017-2018 ed.).

The Federalist Papers explain the basis of, and the argument in support for, sovereign immunity as follows:

It is inherent in the nature of sovereignty not to be amenable to the suit of an individual without its consent. This is the general sense, and the general practice of mankind; and the exemption, as one of the attributes of sovereignty, is now enjoyed by the government of every State in the Union. Unless, therefore, there is a surrender of this immunity in the plan of the convention, it will remain with the States, and the danger intimated must be merely ideal. The circumstances which are necessary to produce an alienation of State sovereignty . . . flows from the obligations of good faith. The contracts between a nation and individuals are only binding on the conscience of the sovereign, and have no pretensions to a compulsive force. They confer no right of action, independent of the sovereign will. To what purpose would it be to authorize suits against States for the debts they owe? How could recoveries be enforced? It is evident, it could not be done without waging war against the contracting State; and to ascribe to the federal courts, by mere implication, and in destruction of a pre-existing right of the State governments, a power which would involve such a consequence, would be altogether forced and unwarrantable.

Id. (citing The Federalist No. 81, p. 487 (C. Rossiter ed. 1961) (A. Hamilton) (cited with approval in *Seminole Tribe of Florida v. Florida*, 517 U.S. 44 (1996)).

FLORIDA MUNICIPAL LAW AND PRACTICE describes two historical rules of sovereign immunity, and the current state of sovereign immunity, as follows:

The doctrine of sovereign immunity comprises two distinct rules, which are not always separately recognized: font of law and font of justice. The one rule holds that the King or the Crown, as the font of law, is not bound by the law's provisions. The other provides that the King or the Crown, as the font of justice, is not subject to suit in its own courts. The font of law rule puts the sovereign beyond the reach of its laws. The font of justice rule puts the sovereign beyond the jurisdiction of its courts.

The font of law implements the ancient maxim that "the King can do no wrong." Professor Jaffe has argued this expression "originally meant precisely the contrary to what it later came to mean," that is, "'it meant that the king must not, was not allowed, not entitled, to do wrong.'" In any event, and as either Presidents Nixon or Clinton might readily attest, it is clear that the idea of the sovereign and its minions being in this sense "above the law" has not survived in American law.

The font of justice implements the idea that the sovereign's courts are not to be used against the sovereign. It took its common-law form in the high Middle Ages. "At least as early as the 13th century, during the reign of Henry III (1216–1272), it was recognized that the king could not be sued in his own courts." . . . "By the time of Bracton (1268) it was settled doctrine that the King could not be sued *eo nomine* in his own courts."

The significance of the font of justice doctrine in the nascent American law is less clear, however, than its early development and steady endurance in England might suggest. Some colonial governments might have enjoyed some such immunity. However, historians dispute the scope (and even the existence) of this governmental immunity in pre-Revolutionary America.

Whatever the scope of sovereign immunity might have been in the Colonies, however, or during the period of the Confederation, the proposal to establish a National Government under the Constitution drafted in 1787 presented a prospect unknown to the common law prior to the American experience: the States would become parts of a system in which sovereignty over even domestic matters would be divided or parceled out between the States and the Nation, the latter to be invested with its own judicial power and the right to prevail against the States whenever their respective substantive laws might be in conflict. With this prospect in mind, the drafters of the 1787 federal Constitution had several options. The federal Constitution could have addressed state sovereign immunity by eliminating whatever sovereign immunity the States previously had, as to any matter subject to federal law or jurisdiction. It could have addressed state sovereign immunity by recognizing an analogue to the old immunity in the new context of federal jurisdiction, but subject to abrogation as to any matter within that jurisdiction. It could have enshrined a doctrine of inviolable state sovereign immunity in the text, thereby giving it constitutional protection in the new federal jurisdiction.

Yet, the 1787 draft, in fact, said nothing on the subject, and it was this very silence that occasioned some, though apparently not widespread, dispute among the framers and others over whether ratification of the Constitution would preclude a state sued in federal court from asserting sovereign immunity as it could have done on any matter of nonfederal law litigated in its own courts. As it has come down to us, the discussion gave no attention to congressional power under the proposed Article I but focused entirely on the limits of the judicial power provided in Article III. Likewise, although the jurisdictional bases together constituting the judicial power of the national courts under § 2 of Article III included questions arising under federal law and cases between states and individuals who are not citizens, it was only upon the latter citizen-state diversity provisions that preratification questions about state immunity from suit or liability centered.

This brings us to the notion of state sovereign immunity in its modern and present form. Presently, there is little to no notion of immunizing the font of law insofar as it is abhorrent to modern American notions of justice that any one or thing be held wholly beyond the fair reach of the rule of law. Yet, immunizing the font of law persists insofar as the sovereign when writing the law might write itself to be exempt from the full restrictions or penalties imposed by that law. When a bill as so written is passed into law by the people's legislators, the people's sovereign becomes exempt from that new law because the people have held their sovereign to be exempt from that law. Such font of law exemptions may be upheld, or may fall, depending upon whether a higher power or higher constitution might govern. Font of justice immunizations are even more common and perhaps more accepted by modernity. In the modern system of geographically overlapping state courts and federal courts, which in and of themselves may be overlapped by specialty courts or regulatory agencies of various subject matter jurisdictions, it, perhaps, seems less offensive to the modern ear to hear that a particular claim might be barred from adjudication in a particular court. For this reason or others, it seems more and more common for the people to accept a new law exempting their sovereign from the jurisdiction of a particular court or courts. Such a sovereign may find itself immunized completely, unless the sovereign itself agrees to hold the jurisdiction of another court to be even higher than the sovereign's domestic courts. American domestic sovereigns appear more diligent in immunizing themselves from foreign jurisdictions than some other modern nation-states. Treaties such as those creating the Court of Justice of the European Communities or creating the European Economic Union may be examples of foreign nation-states' greater willingness to yield sovereign immunity than is currently popular domestically.

It has been said in some jurisdictions that the doctrine of governmental immunity from suit is currently in disfavor, that courts are disposed to hear an action against the state unless good reason stands in the way, and that the current trend of legislative policy and judicial thought is toward the abandonment of the doctrine of governmental immunity. Florida has not followed this view, and still generally follows the rule, under the law of sovereign immunity, that a suit may not be maintained against the state of Florida without its consent.

Id.

Notes and Questions to Consider:

1. Why in the modern era would a concept such as sovereign immunity still exist? Imagine that sovereign immunity did not exist, and a jury is so offended by the action or inaction of the state of Florida that it awards damages against the state in the amount of twenty billion dollars. Where would the state of Florida obtain that money? What Florida bills and obligations would be unpaid in order to satisfy that judgment? What government services would Florida stop providing in order to satisfy that judgment? Does this scenario illustrate how it might be in the best interest of Floridians for the state of Florida to have sovereign immunity?

2. Certainly it is practical for the state of Florida to have sovereign immunity, but in your opinion, is it equitable? Imagine a plaintiff who is injured catastrophically by the negligence of the state of Florida and for whom all experts agree has suffered economic damages in the form of wage loss and future medical care in the amount of $12,000,000. Imagine that Florida's sovereign immunity caps that damage award at $300,000. Does sovereign immunity create a fair result for such a plaintiff?

3. In the scenario from the last question, has sovereign immunity achieved its goal of protecting the public treasury in such an instance? After the plaintiff's $300,000 award is exhausted, will the plaintiff turn to public assistance to finance the balance of the plaintiff's future financial needs? Will this adversely affect the public treasury?

2. Sovereign Immunity as an Inherent Power

Florida's constitution addresses sovereign immunity in its Article X, where it states:

> SECTION 13. *Suits against the state.*— Provision may be made by general law for bringing suit against the state as to all liabilities now existing or hereafter originating.

This section of "the Florida Constitution provides that the Legislature can abrogate the state's sovereign immunity." *Am. Home Assur. Co. v. Nat'l R.R. Passenger Corp.*, 908 So. 2d 459, 471 (Fla. 2005). Note that neither this section, nor any other section of Florida's constitution, purports to create Florida's sovereign immunity. Instead, the authors of this section write from the perspective of Florida's sovereign immunity pre-existing Florida's constitution. This section constitutes a potential waiver of that pre-existing sovereign immunity insofar as it authorizes Florida's legislature to waive or not waive the state's sovereign immunity upon terms set by the Legislature. Only Florida's legislature has authority to enact a general law that waives the state's sovereign immunity. *Id.* (citing *Manatee County v. Town of Longboat Key*, 365 So. 2d 143, 147 (Fla. 1978). "Further, any waiver of sovereign immunity must be clear and unequivocal." *Id.* (citing, inter alia, *Rabideau v. State*, 409 So. 2d 1045, 1046 (Fla. 1982). "[W]aivers of sovereign immunity . . . must [be] strictly construe[d] . . . [and] the waiver . . . will not be found as a product of inference or implication." *Id.* at 471–72. Stated somewhat differently, "sovereign immunity is the rule, rather than the exception" in Florida. *Pan-Am Tobacco Corp. v. Department of Corrections*, 471 So. 2d 4, 5 (Fla. 1984).

Florida's supreme court noted the following principles of sovereign immunity under Florida law:

> sovereign immunity applies to actions where the state is a party, unless the Legislature waives this immunity by general law; in the torts context, the Legislature has authorized a limited waiver of state sovereign immunity through [Florida Statutes] section 768.28; and in *Pan-Am Tobacco Corp. v.*

> *Department of Corrections*, 471 So. 2d 4, 5 (Fla. 1984), this Court held that these statutory limitations do not apply in actions brought against the state for breach of contract.

Am. Home Assur. Co. v. Nat'l R.R. Passenger Corp., 908 So. 2d 459, 467 (Fla. 2005).

From these principles, we can identify who is immune and from what they are immune. By "who," we mean the state, its counties, and its municipal corporations (meaning its cities, towns, and villages). By "what," we mean either a claim arising under state or federal law. Claims arising under state law would be claims created by a Florida Statute or the common law of the state of Florida. Claims arising under federal law would be claims created by the United States Code, the Code of Federal Regulations, or federal common law to the limited extent it still exists after *Erie v. Thompkins*, 304 U.S. 64 (1938) (holding that "federal common law exists only in such narrow areas as those concerned with the rights and obligations of the United States, interstate and international disputes implicating the conflicting rights of States or our relations with foreign nations, and admiralty cases.").

Seen from this perspective, Florida's sovereign immunity raises three separate issues: (1) Is the state of Florida or its counties or its municipal corporations immune from state law claims? (2) Is the state of Florida immune from a federal law claim? (3) Are Florida's counties, municipal corporations or entities they create immune from a federal law claim? We address each issue in turn.

a. Sovereign Immunity of the State, Counties, or Municipal Corporations from State Law Claims

To answer this question, we must first answer it under the common law, and then acknowledge how the Florida Statutes alter the common law.

First, without regard to the statutory alterations of the common law, the general rule of common law sovereign immunity is that the immunity of the state is total, but the immunity of counties and municipal corporations is not. Under the common law before it is altered by statute, the state of Florida is immune, and counties are immune unless Florida's legislature by general law provides otherwise, but municipal corporations (cities, towns, and villages) are not immune. For example, common law sovereign immunity did not protect a municipal corporation conducting "proprietary functions," meaning functions that a private entity can perform, and that are not uniquely for the benefit of the general public, such as operating an automobile or machinery, hiring and supervising employees, commercial activities, or administering local and internal affairs within its territory.

This is the common law of statutory immunity, but it is altered by the Florida Statutes. Recall that Article X, Section 13 of Florida's constitution provides that "[p]rovision may be made by general law for bringing suit against the state as to all liabilities now existing or hereafter originating." Florida's legislature has made various provisions in the Florida Statutes that alter the common law of statutory immunity.

Perhaps the most noteworthy example is the statute applicable to tort claims arising out of state law. That statute is amended quite regularly, and as of 2018 reads in relevant part as follows:

> The state and its agencies and subdivisions shall be liable for tort claims ... but liability shall not include punitive damages or [prejudgment] interest. . . . Neither the state nor its agencies or subdivisions shall be liable to pay a claim or a judgment by any one person which exceeds the sum of $200,000 or ... when totaled with all other claims or judgments ... exceeds the sum of $300,000. . . . [T]hat portion of the judgment that exceeds these amounts ... may be paid in part or in whole only by further act of the Legislature. . . .
>
> No attorney may charge, demand, receive, or collect, for services rendered, fees in excess of 25 percent of any judgment or settlement. . . .
>
> No officer, employee, or agent of the state or of any of its subdivisions shall be held personally liable in tort or named as a party ... unless such officer, employee, or agent acted in bad faith or with malicious purpose or in a manner exhibiting wanton and willful disregard of human rights, safety, or property. . . . The exclusive remedy for injury or damage suffered as a result of an act, event, or omission of an officer, employee, or agent of the state or any of its subdivisions or constitutional officers shall be by action against the governmental entity ... unless such act or omission was committed in bad faith or with malicious purpose or in a manner exhibiting wanton and willful disregard of human rights, safety, or property. The state or its subdivisions shall not be liable in tort for the acts or omissions of an officer, employee, or agent committed while acting outside the course and scope of her or his employment or committed in bad faith or with malicious purpose or in a manner exhibiting wanton and willful disregard of human rights, safety, or property.

§ 768.28, Fla. Stat. (2018).

In explaining how the common law of sovereign immunity operates considering Florida Statutes section 768.28, former Florida Supreme Court Justice Raoul Cantero wrote the following:

> I write to further explain the historical differences in our state constitution and our common law between the sovereign immunity of the state and that of municipalities. As I explain below, these common law differences dictate that the sovereign immunity of municipalities must be construed strictly, whereas the immunity of the state must be construed more broadly. . . .
>
> [Florida's Municipal Home Rule Powers Act provides] broad powers conferred on municipalities to "exercise *any* power for municipal purposes, except when expressly prohibited by law." § 166.021(1), Fla. Stat. (1993) (emphasis added). [Therefore], unlike the effect of section 768.28 on the

immunity of the state, the statute actually granted partial immunity to municipalities that did not previously exist. Because the immunity the statute grants municipalities is in derogation of the common law, it must be strictly construed.

The state and municipalities differ in the degree of their historical sovereign immunity. Under the common law, the state's immunity was total. See *Cauley v. City of Jacksonville*, 403 So. 2d 379, 381 (Fla. 1981); *Spangler v. Fla. State Tpk. Auth.*, 106 So. 2d 421, 422 (Fla. 1958) (holding that the state and its agencies are immune from suit); *Smith v. City of Arcadia*, 2 So. 2d 725, 728 (Fla. 1941) ("The State cannot be sued. . . .") . . . ; *State Road Dep't of Fla. v. Tharp*, 1 So. 2d 868, 869 (Fla. 1941) ("[The] State cannot be sued without its consent. As to tort actions, the rule is universal and unqualified unless relaxed by the State. . . ."). [Florida's] 1868 Constitution granted [Florida's] Legislature the power to waive it. See *id.* (citing art. IV, § 19, Fla. Const. (1868) (now art. X, § 13, Fla. Const.)). However, the Legislature declined to act until 1973, when it adopted section 768.28. See Ch. 73–313, Laws of Fla.

In contrast to the state, municipalities never enjoyed total immunity from suit. See *Cauley*, 403 So. 2d at 381–83 (recognizing that state sovereign immunity "remained in full force until section 768.28's enactment" while municipal sovereign immunity became subject to many exceptions before the waiver statute); *Woodford v. City of St. Petersburg*, 84 So. 2d 25, 26 (Fla. 1955) (holding that a municipality exercising a proprietary function is liable in the same manner as private corporations); *City of Tampa v. Easton*, 198 So. 753, 754 (Fla. 1940) ("Unlike a county, a municipality is not a subdivision of the State with subordinate attributes of sovereignty in the performance of governmental functions. . . ."); *City of Tallahassee v. Fortune*, 3 Fla. 19 (1850) (distinguishing precedent from the United States and England and holding that an action for trespass may lie against a municipal corporation); see also *Cauley*, 403 So. 2d at 382–84 (outlining the development of municipal sovereign immunity law in Florida from *Fortune* through the enactment of section 768.28).

Before section 768.28, questions of whether municipal sovereign immunity applied were analyzed as follows:

1) as to those municipal activities which fall in the category of proprietary functions a municipality has the same tort liability as a private corporation;

2) as to those activities which fall in the category of governmental functions ". . . a municipality is liable in tort, under the doctrine of respondent [sic] superior, [. . .] only when such tort is committed against one with whom the agent or employee is in privity, or with whom he is dealing or is otherwise in contact in a direct transaction or confrontation."

3) as to those activities which fall in the category of judicial, quasi-judicial, legislative, and quasi-legislative functions, a municipality remains immune.

Cauley, 403 So. 2d at 383 (quoting *Gordon v. City of West Palm Beach*, 321 So. 2d 78, 80 (Fla. 4th DCA 1975)) (citations omitted); see also *Commercial Carrier Corp. v. Indian River County*, 371 So. 2d 1010, 1015 (Fla. 1979) (reviewing the history of municipal sovereign immunity and recognizing that before section 768.28 a municipality would be held liable for torts committed in the performance of proprietary acts).

Essentially, the state and its agencies, on the one hand, and municipalities, on the other, arrived at section 768.28 from opposite directions: the state from a status of near-total immunity; and municipalities from a status of near-nonexistent immunity. In fact, when the statute was first enacted, its effect on municipalities was unclear. In 1976, the Attorney General issued an opinion that "municipalities possessed no aspect of the state's sovereign immunity from tort liability upon which the waiver contained in section 768.28, and the limitations specified therein, could operate." Op. Att'y Gen. Fla. 76–41 (1976). In other words, the Attorney General opined that section 768.28, including its limitation on the amount of damages, did not apply to municipalities because they did not enjoy any immunity from tort suits that could be waived. The Legislature quickly amended section 768.28 by adding the following language in subsection 5: "The limitations of liability set forth in this subsection shall apply to the state and its agencies and subdivisions whether or not the state or its agencies or subdivisions possessed sovereign immunity prior to July 1, 1974." Ch. 77–86, § 1, Laws of Fla.

Section 768.28, therefore, affected the State and counties differently than it did municipalities. As to the State, the statute waived its sovereign immunity up to specified limits. As to municipalities, the statute granted them immunity from judgments above those limits.

Section 768.28 nullified the common law affecting both the state and municipalities, and therefore must be strictly construed. See *Carlile v. Game & Fresh Water Fish Comm'n*, 354 So. 2d 362, 364 (Fla. 1977). But it nullified the common law in different ways. As to the state and its agencies, the statute waives traditional immunity. As to municipalities, however, it grants partial immunity. Therefore, in construing the statute strictly, it must be construed in favor of granting immunity to the state, but against granting it to a municipality.

Am. Home Assur. Co. v. Nat'l R.R. Passenger Corp., 908 So. 2d 459, 477–78 (Fla. 2005) (Justice Cantero concurring).

This explains how sovereign immunity works for the state, its counties, and its municipal corporations (cities, towns, and villages) regarding state law tort claims.

What about state law breach of contract claims? That question is answered by *Pan-Am Tobacco Corp. v. Dep't of Corr.*, 471 So. 2d 4 (Fla. 1984):

Pan-Am Tobacco Corp. v. Department of Corrections
Supreme Court of Florida, 1984
471 So. 2d 4

... Pan-Am Tobacco Corp. entered into a written contract with the Department of Corrections. Pan-Am was to provide vending machines in six correctional facilities. The contract provided that Department of Corrections could cancel the contract for unsatisfactory performance by Pan-Am if it gave Pan-Am sixty days' written notice and thirty days within which to correct any deficiencies. Additionally, the contract provided for liquidated damages. Department of Corrections canceled the contract on thirty days' written notice, specifying no deficiencies in Pan-Am's performance and giving no time within which to correct any deficiencies. Pan-Am brought suit ... and the First District Court of Appeal ... certified as a matter of great public importance the following question:

> When a state agency improperly rescinds an express executory contract with
> a private vendor who suffers a loss of profit as a consequence, may the state
> invoke sovereign immunity as a bar to an action on the breach of contract?

... We answer the question in the negative. ...

In Florida, sovereign immunity is the rule, rather than the exception, as evidenced by article X, section 13 of the Florida Constitution: "Provision may be made by general law for bringing suit against the state as to all liabilities now existing or hereafter originating."

In section 768.28, Florida Statutes (1981), the legislature has explicitly waived sovereign immunity in tort. There is no analogous waiver in contract. Nonetheless, the legislature has, by general law, explicitly empowered various state agencies to enter into contracts. *See e.g.*, §§ 23.017, 153.62(11), 163.370, 230.22(4), 337.19(1), Fla. Stat. (1981). Additionally, it has authorized certain goals and activities which can only be achieved if state agencies have the power to contract for necessary goods and services. *See e.g.*, §§ 20.315, 945.215, Fla. Stat. (1981).

It is basic hornbook law that a contract which is not mutually enforceable is an illusory contract. *Howard Cole & Co. v. Williams*, 27 So. 2d 352 (1946). Where one party retains to itself the option of fulfilling or declining to fulfill its obligations under the contract, there is no valid contract and neither side may be bound. ...

Where the legislature has, by general law, authorized entities of the state to enter into contract or to undertake those activities which, as a matter of practicality, require entering into contract, the legislature has clearly intended that such contracts be valid and binding on both parties. As a matter of law, the state must be obligated to the private citizen or the legislative authorization for such action is void and meaningless. We therefore hold that where the state has entered into a contract fairly authorized by the powers granted by general law, the defense of sovereign immunity will not protect the state from action arising from the state's breach of that contract.

We recognize that in so holding we recede from a line of cases holding that the state may not be sued in contract without express consent to the suit. *See, e.g., Gay v. Southern Builders, Inc.*, 66 So. 2d 499 (Fla. 1953), *Bloxham v. Florida Central and Peninsular Railroad*, 17 So. 902 (Fla. 1895). Nonetheless, we note that this is not the first time this Court has looked to the legislative intent in general law to find a sovereign amenable to suit. *Manatee County v. Town of Longboat Key*, 365 So. 2d 143 (Fla. 1978) (where the legislature clearly intended the county to participate in resolution of taxation dispute and the county ignored its statutory duty, courts had jurisdiction to fashion a remedy in equity).

We would also emphasize that our holding here is applicable only to suits on express, written contracts into which the state agency has statutory authority to enter. Accordingly, the decision of the district court is quashed and this cause is remanded for further proceedings.

It is so ordered.

Notes and Questions to Consider:

1. How can the outcome of *Pan-Am v. Department of Corrections* be reconciled with these prior rulings from Florida's supreme court:

a. Any waiver of sovereign immunity "must be 'clear and unequivocal.'" *Arnold v. Shumpert*, 217 So. 2d 116, 120 (Fla. 1968)?

b. "The only way that the State can give its consent to be made a party defendant to a suit is by legislative act." *Suits v. Hillsborough County*, 2 So. 2d 353, 357 (Fla. 1941)?

2. *Pan-Am v. Department of Corrections* holds that, "where the state has entered into a contract fairly authorized by the powers granted by general law, the defense of sovereign immunity will not protect the state from action arising from the state's breach of contract." What Florida Statute says so? Prior to the decision in *Pan-Am v. Department of Corrections*, what Florida case law precedent said so?

3. The holding of *Pan-Am v. Department of Corrections* explicitly overrules all contrary prior decisions, including one decided back in 1895. When the Department of Corrections breached the contract in the 1980s, did they not have a right to rely on case law precedent dating back more than 85 years?

4. After Florida's supreme court decided *Pan-Am v. Department of Corrections*, none of the parties sought review from the United States Supreme Court. Under the "adequate and independent" doctrine as interpreted by *Michigan v. Long* and discussed in Chapter 1 of this text, would the U.S. Supreme Court have jurisdiction to review *Pan-Am v. Department of Corrections*?

b. Sovereign Immunity of the State from Federal Claims

The supremacy of federal law means that the sovereign immunity of the state of Florida from federal law claims depends on federal law. The Eleventh Amendment to the U.S. Constitution provides, in relevant part, that the "[j]udicial power of the United States shall not be construed to extend to any suit . . . against one of the United States by Citizens of another State, or by Citizens or Subjects of any Foreign State."

"Despite the limited categories of suits barred by the [Eleventh] Amendment's literal language, the [U.S.] Supreme Court has long interpreted the Amendment as expressive of the broader proposition that a state has immunity from suits brought by her own citizens as well as by those of another states." *Duncan v. University of Texas Health Science Center at Houston*, 469 Fed. Appx. 364, 366 (5th Cir. 2012). Therefore, as FLORIDA MUNICIPAL LAW AND PRACTICE explains, "[b]ecause Florida has sovereign immunity, the U.S. Congress cannot use its powers under Article I of the federal Constitution to subject Florida or any other state to suit in federal court without the state's consent." Patrick John McGinley, FLORIDA MUNICIPAL LAW AND PRACTICE § 7:3 (2018-2019 ed.). However, that treatise adds:

> Exceptions arise when the text of the federal Constitution allows the U.S. Congress to abrogate state sovereign immunity, and Congress passes a law that properly utilizes that power. For example, the bankruptcy clause of Article I of the U.S. Constitution was properly implemented by Congress to abrogate state sovereign immunity. As another example, the 14th Amendment to the federal Constitution gives Congress the power to abrogate state immunity from suit to the extent necessary to protect the civil rights granted by the Constitution. Therefore, conduct by persons acting under color of state law which violates 14th Amendment civil rights protected by 42 U.S.C. § 1983 cannot be immunized by state law.

Id. Note that 42 U.S.C. section 1983, which is part of the federal Civil Rights Act, provides in relevant part:

> Every person who, under color of any statute, ordinance, regulation, custom, or usage, of any State or Territory or the District of Columbia, subjects, or causes to be subjected, any citizen of the United States or other person within the jurisdiction thereof to the deprivation of any rights, privileges, or immunities secured by the Constitution and laws, shall be liable to the party injured in an action at law, suit in equity, or other proper proceeding for redress.

Therefore, although it is true that a state like Florida cannot be sued in federal court on a federal claim without Florida's permission, that permission can be implied. By Florida signing the federal Constitution, Florida implied its permission to be sued in federal court on a federal claim when the text of the federal Constitution empowers such a claim and an act of the U.S. Congress properly implements that power. *See* Patrick John McGinley, Florida Municipal Law and Practice §7:3 (2018-2019 ed.). This is why the debtor's filing of a federal bankruptcy petition is sufficient to cause an automatic stay of a pending state lawsuit, and is why a state becomes liable for violating the civil rights of its citizens under the federal Civil Rights Act.

As for state officers and those individuals acting under color of state law, sovereign immunity does not prevent the issuance of injunctive relief against them and their behavior in violating a federal law or a federal constitutional right, as per the U.S. Supreme Court's 1908's decision in *Ex parte Young*, 209 U.S. 123 (1908). "The basic doctrine of *Ex parte Young* can be simply stated. A federal court is not barred by the Eleventh Amendment from enjoining state officers from acting unconstitutionally, either because their action is alleged to violate the Constitution directly or because it is contrary to a federal statute or regulation that is the supreme law of the land." Alan Wright, Arthur R. Miller, et al., 17A Fed. Prac. & Proc. Juris. §4232 (3d ed.) (April 2019 update). But just like states, state officers acting within their official capacity are immune from suits for damages in federal court without their consent. *See id.* at §4232 n.2.

c. Sovereign Immunity of Counties and Municipal Corporations from Federal Claims

Do Florida's counties, cities, towns, and villages enjoy sovereign immunity from federal law claims? "The Eleventh Amendment does not protect counties, cities, or other local governmental units so long as they are not the alter ego of the state . . . and the *Young* rule is not needed to sue those governmental units or their officers." Alan Wright, Arthur R. Miller, et al., 17A Fed. Prac. & Proc. Juris. §4232 (3d ed.) (April 2019 update). To see this rule in action, consider *Town of Lake Clarke Shores v. Page*, 569 So. 2d 1256 (Fla. 1990).

Town of Lake Clarke Shores v. Page
Supreme Court of Florida, 1990
569 So. 2d 1256

. . . We review the opinion of the Fourth District Court of Appeal in *Page v. Valentine*, 552 So .2d 212 (Fla. 4th DCA 1989), in which we accepted jurisdiction based on conflict with *Howlett ex rel. Howlett v. Rose*, 537 So. 2d 706 (Fla. 2d DCA), *review denied*, 545 So. 2d 1367 (Fla. 1989), *rev'd*, 496 U.S. 356 (1990). We have jurisdiction. Art. V, §3(b)(3), Fla. Const.

The respondent, Alan Page, sued the petitioner, Town of Lake Clarke Shores (Town), under 42 U.S.C. §1983. . . . In his complaint Page alleged that he was formerly a police officer with the Lake Clarke Shores Police Department. He claimed that his employment was terminated because Town officials were "discontented" by a letter published in *The Palm Beach Post* in which Page expressed his opinion about the effects of stress on police officers. The trial court dismissed the action against the Town holding that the court had no subject matter jurisdiction over § 1983 actions due to Florida's sovereign immunity doctrine. The Fourth District Court of Appeal reversed, relying on *City of Riviera Beach v. Langevin*, 522 So. 2d 857 (Fla. 4th DCA 1987), *review dismissed*, 536 So. 2d 243 (Fla. 1988), and *Southern Alliance Corp. v. City of Winter Haven*, 505 So. 2d 489 (Fla. 2d DCA 1987).

We agree with the court below that state trial courts do have subject matter jurisdiction over § 1983 actions against municipalities. The United States Supreme Court recently decided *Howlett ex rel. Howlett v. Rose*, 496 U.S. 356 (1990), reversing the very decision upon which the Town relies. In that case, the Supreme Court reaffirmed its ruling in *Will v. Michigan Department of State Police*, 491 U.S. 58 (1989), that "an entity with Eleventh Amendment immunity is not a 'person' within the meaning of § 1983." *Howlett*, 110 S.Ct. at 2437. Therefore, "the State and arms of the State, which have traditionally enjoyed Eleventh Amendment immunity, are not subject to suit under § 1983 in either federal court or state court." *Id.* However, the Court further stated that

> since the Court has held that municipal corporations and similar governmental entities are "persons," see *Monell v. New York City Dept. of Social Services*, 436 U.S. 658, 663 (1978); cf. *Will*, 491 U.S. at 58 n. 9; *Mt. Healthy City Board of Education v. Doyle*, 429 U.S. 274, 280–281 (1977), a state court entertaining a § 1983 action must adhere to that interpretation. "Municipal defenses—including an assertion of sovereign immunity—to a federal right of action are, of course, controlled by federal law." *Owen v. City of Independence*, 445 U.S. [622] at 647 n. 30 [(1980)]. "By including municipalities within the class of 'persons' subject to liability for violation of the Federal Constitution and laws, Congress—the supreme sovereign on matters of federal law—abolished whatever vestige of the State's sovereign immunity the municipality possessed." *Id.*, at 647–648 (footnote omitted).

Id. . . . The Supreme Court pointed out that the Second District Court of Appeal had erroneously extended this Court's decision in *Hill v. Department of Corrections*, 513 So. 2d 129 (Fla. 1987), *cert. denied*, 484 U.S. 106 (1988), *holding limited*, *Howlett ex rel. Howlett v. Rose*, 496 U.S. 356 (1990), which involved a state agency, to a suit against a municipality.

Therefore, we approve the opinion below and remand for further proceedings.

It is so ordered.

Note and Question to Consider:

1. This case explains that the federal Civil Rights Act makes "persons" liable for violations under federal law. That Act, instead of defining "persons" to include only natural persons, also includes a "municipality" within its definition of the word "persons." This led Florida's supreme court in *Town of Lake Clarke Shores v. Page* to hold: "By including municipalities within the class of 'persons' subject to liability

for violation of the Federal Constitution and laws, Congress—the supreme sovereign on matters of federal law—abolished whatever vestige of the State's sovereign immunity the municipality possessed." Why was a federal statutory definition enough to abrogate a state's inherent power of sovereign immunity?

C. Delegation

Florida's executive, legislative, and judicial branches of government may delegate their power, but they may not abdicate their power. Any delegation of authority "requires an intelligible principle to be laid down for the guidance of an administrative official in the performance of his duties." *Phillips Petroleum Co. v. Anderson*, 74 So. 2d 544, 547 (Fla. 1954).

1. Delegation of Legislative Powers

In *Whiley v. Scott*, 79 So. 3d 702 (Fla. 2011), a citizen was successful in challenging Florida's governor's authority to reign in agency rulemaking by proving his involvement in that rulemaking ran afoul of the proper delegation of legislative powers.

Whiley v. Scott
Supreme Court of Florida, 2011
79 So. 3d 702

This case is before the Court on the petition of Rosalie Whiley for a writ of quo warranto seeking an order directing Respondent, the Honorable Rick Scott, Governor of the State of Florida, to demonstrate that he has not exceeded his authority. . . . In exercising our discretion to resolve this matter, we grant relief and specifically hold that the Governor impermissibly suspended agency rulemaking to the extent that Executive Orders 11–01 and 11–72 include a requirement that the Office of Fiscal Accountability and Regulatory Reform (OFARR) must first permit an agency to engage in the rulemaking which has been delegated by the Florida Legislature. . . .

[I.] Background

On January 4, 2011, Governor Scott issued "Executive Order Number 11–01 (Suspending Rulemaking and Establishing the Office of Fiscal Accountability and Regulatory Reform)," which created that office (OFARR) within the Executive Office of the Governor. OFARR is tasked with the goal of ensuring that agency-created rules do not hinder government performance and that they are fiscally responsible. . . . The Secretary of State was ordered not to publish any rulemaking notices in the Florida Administrative Weekly absent authorization from OFARR. . . .

II. Discussion

Our precise task in this case is to decide whether the Governor has overstepped his constitutional authority by issuing executive orders which contain certain limitations and suspensions upon agencies relating to their delegated legislative rulemaking authority. . . .

[Florida's] Legislature has delegated specific responsibilities to agency heads, such as the authority to determine whether to go forward with proposing, amending, repealing, or adopting rules. See § 120.54(3)(a)(1), Fla. Stat. (2010) . . . . This authority of the agency head cannot be delegated or transferred. See § 120.54(1)(k), Fla. Stat. (2010). Thus, rulemaking is a legislative function. See *Sims v. State*, 754 So. 2d 657, 668 (Fla. 2000) ("[T]he Legislature may 'enact a law, complete in itself, designed to accomplish a general public purpose, and may expressly authorize designated officials within definite valid limitations to provide rules and regulations for the complete operation and enforcement of the law within its expressed general purpose.'") . . . The Legislature delegates rulemaking authority to state agencies because they usually have expertise in a particular area for which they are charged with oversight. . . . Accordingly, the Legislature may specifically delegate, to some extent, its rulemaking authority to the executive branch "to permit administration of legislative policy by an agency with the expertise and flexibility needed to deal with complex and fluid conditions." *Microtel, Inc. v. Fla. Pub. Serv. Comm'n.*, 464 So. 2d 1189, 1191 (Fla. 1985); see also § 120.536(1), Fla. Stat. (2010).

To determine whether the executive orders encroach upon the legislative delegations of rulemaking authority, the Court must first consider the established procedure for rulemaking. When adopting rules, the agencies must specifically conform to the rulemaking procedure enacted by the Legislature as the Florida Administrative Procedure Act in chapter 120, Florida Statutes. . . .

The foregoing leads the Court to conclude that the Governor's executive orders at issue here, to the extent each suspends and terminates rulemaking by precluding notice publication and other compliance with Chapter 120 absent prior approval from OFARR—contrary to the Administrative Procedure Act—infringe upon the very process of rulemaking and encroach upon the Legislature's delegation of its rulemaking power as set forth in the Florida Statutes. . . .

III. Conclusion

We distinguish between the Governor's constitutional authority with respect to the provisions of the executive orders pertaining to review and oversight of rulemaking within the executive agencies under his control, and the Legislature's lawmaking authority under article III, section 1 of the Florida Constitution. The Legislature retains the sole right to delegate rulemaking authority to agencies, and all provisions in both Executive Order 11–01 or 11–72 that operate to suspend rulemaking contrary to the APA constitute an encroachment upon a legislative function. We grant Whiley's petition but withhold issuance of the writ of quo warranto. We trust that any provision in Executive Order 11–72 suspending agency compliance with the APA, i.e., rulemaking, will not be enforced against an agency at this time, and until such time as the Florida Legislature may amend the APA or otherwise delegate such rulemaking authority to the Executive Office of the Governor.

It is so ordered.

2. Delegation of Judicial Powers

In *Pearce v. State*, 968 So. 2d 92 (Fla. 2d DCA 2007), Florida's Second District Court of Appeal agreed that a Florida Statute resulted in an improper delegation of judicial powers.

Pearce v. State

Second District Court of Appeal of Florida, 2007
968 So. 2d 92

Kelvin Pearce challenges a restitution order imposed after he pleaded guilty to petit theft, a first-degree misdemeanor. §812.014(2)(e), Fla. Stat. (2000). He argues—and the State concedes—that the trial court erred when it authorized Mr. Pearce's probation officer to establish a payment schedule for the restitution amount. We agree and reverse the restitution order in part with directions.

The Restitution Order & Subsequent Orders

At Mr. Pearce's April 26, 2006, sentencing and restitution hearing, the trial court withheld adjudication on the petit theft offense. The trial court imposed a sentence of twelve months' probation, and it ordered Mr. Pearce to pay $10,515 in restitution to the victim. Notably, the trial court delegated the matter of establishing a payment schedule to Mr. Pearce's probation officer. Mr. Pearce timely filed his notice of appeal.

On November 20, 2006, Mr. Pearce filed a motion to correct sentencing error under Florida Rule of Criminal Procedure 3.800(b)(2). Mr. Pearce did not contest the amount of the restitution award, but he argued that the trial court erred when it authorized his probation officer to determine a schedule for the restitution payments. The trial court agreed, and on January 25, 2007, it filed an order granting Mr. Pearce's motion and awarding him a new restitution hearing. On February 7, 2007, the circuit court set a restitution payment schedule at $250 per month. Finally, on April 12, 2007, the circuit court entered an order modifying the terms of Mr. Pearce's probation so that any restitution amount outstanding at the end of his one-year probationary term would be converted to a lien.

Analysis

As the State concedes, the trial court erred in its original restitution order when it delegated to Mr. Pearce's probation officer the authority for determining the restitution payment schedule. Florida courts have long held that the determination of a restitution payment schedule is a judicial responsibility that cannot be delegated. *Lewellen v. State*, 685 So. 2d 1367, 1368 (Fla. 2d DCA 1996); *Douglas v. State*, 664 So. 2d 1099, 1099 (Fla. 2d DCA 1995); *Guinn v. State*, 652 So. 2d 902, 902 (Fla. 2d DCA 1995); *Briggs v. State*, 647 So. 2d 182, 182 (Fla. 1st DCA 1994); *see also Thomas v.*

State, 635 So. 2d 1009, 1010 (Fla. 1st DCA 1994) (finding error where the trial court revoked probation based on the defendant's failure "to follow a payment schedule established, not by the trial court, but by the probation officer"). In addition, while the trial court clearly intended to correct its error when it granted Mr. Pearce's rule 3.800(b)(2) motion, we note that sixty-six days had elapsed from November 20, 2006 (the day Mr. Pearce filed his motion) to January 25, 2007 (the day the order granting the motion was filed). Consequently, Mr. Pearce's motion was deemed denied by rule when the trial court failed to dispose of it within sixty days — i.e., by January 19, 2007. *See* Fla. R.Crim. P. 3.800(b)(1)(B). For these reasons, we affirm the restitution order to the extent that it established the restitution amount, but we reverse the restitution order to the extent that it delegated to the probation officer the determination of the payment schedule.

Because the circuit court did not file an order ruling on the motion within the sixty-day time period, its jurisdiction to correct the error terminated on January 19, 2007. Thus the January 25 order granting Mr. Pearce's motion, the February 7 order setting the restitution payment schedule at $250 per month, and the April 12 order converting all outstanding restitution amounts to a lien are nullities. *Whitmore v. State*, 910 So. 2d 308, 308 (Fla. 2d DCA 2005); *Sessions v. State*, 907 So. 2d 572, 573 (Fla. 1st DCA 2005). Accordingly, we vacate these orders.

Conclusion

To summarize, we affirm Mr. Pearce's judgment and sentence, and we affirm the portion of the restitution order that establishes the restitution amount. We reverse the restitution order to the extent that it delegates authority to Mr. Pearce's probation officer to determine the restitution payment schedule. We vacate the three orders entered after January 19, 2007, and we remand with directions to conduct a new restitution hearing to determine the appropriate method for Mr. Pearce to satisfy the remainder of his restitution obligation.

Affirmed in part, reversed in part, and remanded with directions.

Chapter 14

Government Transparency and Accountability

A. Florida's Sunshine Laws

A series of amendments to Florida's constitution require transparency and accountability—or "sunshine" if you will—in the operations of Florida's state and local governments. These amendments, combined with some Florida Statutes applying the concepts found in these constitutional amendments, commonly are called Florida's Sunshine Law. Florida's supreme court notes that Florida's "Sunshine Law was enacted in the public interest to protect the public from 'closed door' politics and, as such, the law must be broadly construed to effect its remedial and protective purpose." *Wood v. Marston*, 442 So. 2d 934, 938 (Fla. 1983).

Public records, open meetings, transparency, and public accountability were not always the norm in the state of Florida. Perhaps this is best illustrated by the group of Florida state senators in the 1950s known as the Pork Chop Gang. They were a group of North Florida Democrats who dominated the Florida State Senate due to a late-nineteenth century apportionment rule that gave disproportionate voting power to rural districts. They were known to meet on the Isola River at lobbyist Rayburn Horn's fish camp to play poker and drink whiskey. During legislative sessions, the Pork Chop Gang lived and plotted together at Tallahassee's Cherokee Hotel, Floridan Hotel, and The Duval Hotel. Although Florida law did not make this behavior illegal at that time, this behavior came under increasing criticism from then-Governor LeRoy Collins and newspapermen like then-Editor of THE TAMPA TRIBUNE James Clendinen. *See* Patrick John McGinley, FLORIDA MUNICIPAL LAW AND PRACTICE § 10:2 (2017-18 ed.).

Part of the criticism was that decisions about legislative actions and laws were being made at these informal gatherings. When the Pork Chop Gang lived and plotted together as to how to cast their block of legislative votes, the public could not attend. No notes were kept. No dissenting voices were heard. The public could not participate in any meaningful way. The Pork Chop Gang's legislative power block was inaccessible and largely unaccountable.

In 1967, the Florida Legislature took a step forward toward government transparency and accountability by revising and somewhat strengthening Florida's Sunshine Laws, which at the time were statutes only and were not self-executing constitutional amendments. For this reason and others, the 1967 legislation had its limits. It did not apply to Florida's legislative or judicial branches of state government. It applied only to Florida's executive branch and to local governments, including counties, municipalities, and districts. In 1978, the Constitution Revision Commission proposed elevating these laws to constitutional status and applying them to records and meetings of the Legislature. That proposal was not adopted. *Id.* at § 10:2.

Then in November 1990, an amendment to Florida's constitution added Article III, § 4 bringing accountability, open government, and sunshine to the Florida Legislature. It provides, in relevant part, that:

> (e) The rules of procedure of each house shall provide that all legislative committee and subcommittee meetings of each house, and joint conference committee meetings, shall be open and noticed to the public. The rules of procedure of each house shall further provide that all prearranged gatherings, between more than two members of the legislature, or between the governor, the president of the senate, or the speaker of the house of representatives, the purpose of which is to agree upon formal legislative action that will be taken at a subsequent time, or at which formal legislative action is taken, regarding pending legislation or amendments, shall be reasonably open to the public. All open meetings shall be subject to order and decorum. This section shall be implemented and defined by the rules of each house, and such rules shall control admission to the floor of each legislative chamber and may, where reasonably necessary for security purposes or to protect a witness appearing before a committee, provide for the closure of committee meetings. Each house shall be the sole judge for the interpretation, implementation, and enforcement of this section.

The plain language of this subsection (e) requires that all legislative committee and subcommittee meetings be open to the public. Outside of these legislative meetings, all prearranged gatherings with more than two legislators must be open to the public also. Likewise, meetings between the governor, the president of the Senate, or the speaker of the House of Representatives for the purpose of agreeing upon formal legislative action fall under the definition of "public meetings." The definition of "formal legislative action" was not provided in the Constitution but was left to legislative rule. The amendment leaves each house of the Legislature as the "sole judge for the interpretation, implementation, and enforcement" of this section. As such, the Legislature is insulated from any judicial enforcement of this section. *Id.* at § 10:2.

In November 1992, an amendment to Florida's constitution took a giant leap forward toward greater accountability, open government, and sunshine. Florida's constitution was amended to add Article I, section 24 that brought requirements of transparency and public access to all branches of Florida government. In relevant part, those 1992 amendments to Article I, section 24 provide:

> (a) Every person has the right to inspect or copy any public record made or received in connection with the official business of any public body,

officer, or employee of the state, or persons acting on their behalf, except with respect to records exempted pursuant to this section or specifically made confidential by this Constitution. This section specifically includes the legislative, executive, and judicial branches of government and each agency or department created thereunder; counties, municipalities, and districts; and each constitutional officer, board, and commission, or entity created pursuant to law or this Constitution.

(b) All meetings of any collegial public body of the executive branch of state government or of any collegial public body of a county, municipality, school district, or special district, at which official acts are to be taken or at which public business of such body is to be transacted or discussed, shall be open and noticed to the public and meetings of the legislature shall be open and noticed as provided in Article III, Section 4(e), except with respect to meetings exempted pursuant to this section or specifically closed by this Constitution.

(c) This section shall be self-executing. The legislature, however, may provide by general law passed by a two-thirds vote of each house for the exemption of records from the requirements of subsection (a) and the exemption of meetings from the requirements of subsection (b), provided that such law shall state with specificity the public necessity justifying the exemption and shall be no broader than necessary to accomplish the stated purpose of the law. The legislature shall enact laws governing the enforcement of this section, including the maintenance, control, destruction, disposal, and disposition of records made public by this section, except that each house of the legislature may adopt rules governing the enforcement of this section in relation to records of the legislative branch. Laws enacted pursuant to this subsection shall contain only exemptions from the requirements of subsections (a) or (b) and provisions governing the enforcement of this section, and shall relate to one subject.

(d) All laws that are in effect on July 1, 1993, that limit public access to records or meetings shall remain in force, and such laws apply to records of the legislative and judicial branches, until they are repealed. Rules of court that are in effect on the date of adoption of this section that limit access to records shall remain in effect until they are repealed.

Note how these amendments impose transparency, open meetings, and public records requirements upon virtually all branches of Florida's state government, all Florida local governments, and all Florida officers, agencies, boards, and employees. FLORIDA MUNICIPAL LAW AND PRACTICE describes the effect of these amendments as follows:

Subsection (a) ensures the right of public access to any public record not exempted in the manner set out in the amendment, made or received in connection with the official business of any public body, officer, or employee of the state, or persons acting on their behalf.

Subsection (b) requires that all meetings of any collegial public body of the executive branch or collegial bodies of local governments, at which official acts are to be taken or at which the business of the entity is to be transacted or discussed, must be open and noticed to the public. On the contrary, legislative meetings are open and noticed as provided in Article III, section 4(e), which operates quite differently. As to the executive branch and local government collegial bodies, any gathering of two or more members to discuss a matter that may foreseeably come before that body is considered a public meeting and must be noticed and open. On the other hand, Article III, section 4(e) requires that only legislative committees, subcommittees, and conference committees must be open and noticed.

Subsection (c) grants the Legislature the power to enact general laws governing the enforcement of this section and to enact exemptions to the requirements for public access. Any law creating an exemption: (1) must state with specificity the public necessity justifying the exemption; (2) may be no broader than necessary to accomplish the stated purpose of the exemption; and (3) may contain no other subject except exemptions and provisions governing the enforcement of this section and must relate to a single subject.

See Patrick John McGinley, FLORIDA MUNICIPAL LAW AND PRACTICE § 10:2 (2017-18 ed.). "These constitutional amendments give great strength to Florida's Sunshine Law." *Id.*

Supplementing these amendments to Florida's constitution, Florida Statutes section 268.011 add additional requirements of transparency, accountability, and openness. In relevant part, Florida Statutes section 268.011 provides:

(1) All meetings of any board or commission of any state agency or authority or of any agency or authority of any county, municipal corporation, or political subdivision, except as otherwise provided in the Constitution, at which official acts are to be taken are declared to be public meetings open to the public at all times, and no resolution, rule, or formal action shall be considered binding except as taken or made at such meeting. The board or commission must provide reasonable notice of all such meetings.

(2) The minutes of a meeting of any such board or commission of any such state agency or authority shall be promptly recorded, and such records shall be open to public inspection. The circuit courts of this state shall have jurisdiction to issue injunctions to enforce the purposes of this section upon application by any citizen of this state.

(3)

(a) Any public officer who violates any provision of this section is guilty of a noncriminal infraction, punishable by fine not exceeding $500.

(b) Any person who is a member of a board or commission or of any state agency or authority of any county, municipal corporation, or political subdivision who knowingly violates the provisions of this section by attending a meeting not held in accordance with the provisions hereof is guilty of a misdemeanor of the second degree, punishable as provided in s. 775.082 or s. 775.083.

(c) Conduct which occurs outside the state which would constitute a knowing violation of this section is a misdemeanor of the second degree, punishable as provided in s. 775.082 or s. 775.083.

(4) Whenever an action has been filed against any board or commission of any state agency or authority or any agency or authority of any county, municipal corporation, or political subdivision to enforce the provisions of this section or to invalidate the actions of any such board, commission, agency, or authority, which action was taken in violation of this section, and the court determines that the defendant or defendants to such action acted in violation of this section, the court shall assess a reasonable attorney's fee against such agency, and may assess a reasonable attorney's fee against the individual filing such an action if the court finds it was filed in bad faith or was frivolous. Any fees so assessed may be assessed against the individual member or members of such board or commission; provided, that in any case where the board or commission seeks the advice of its attorney and such advice is followed, no such fees shall be assessed against the individual member or members of the board or commission. However, this subsection shall not apply to a state attorney or his or her duly authorized assistants or any officer charged with enforcing the provisions of this section.

(5) Whenever any board or commission of any state agency or authority or any agency or authority of any county, municipal corporation, or political subdivision appeals any court order which has found said board, commission, agency, or authority to have violated this section, and such order is affirmed, the court shall assess a reasonable attorney's fee for the appeal against such board, commission, agency, or authority. Any fees so assessed may be assessed against the individual member or members of such board or commission; provided, that in any case where the board or commission seeks the advice of its attorney and such advice is followed, no such fees shall be assessed against the individual member or members of the board or commission.

(6) All persons subject to subsection (1) are prohibited from holding meetings at any facility or location which discriminates on the basis of sex, age, race, creed, color, origin, or economic status or which operates in such a manner as to unreasonably restrict public access to such a facility.

(7) Whenever any member of any board or commission of any state agency or authority or any agency or authority of any county, municipal corporation, or political subdivision is charged with a violation of this section and is

subsequently acquitted, the board or commission is authorized to reimburse said member for any portion of his or her reasonable attorney's fees.

(8) Notwithstanding the provisions of subsection (1), any board or commission of any state agency or authority or any agency or authority of any county, municipal corporation, or political subdivision, and the chief administrative or executive officer of the governmental entity, may meet in private with the entity's attorney to discuss pending litigation to which the entity is presently a party before a court or administrative agency, provided that the following conditions are met:

(a) The entity's attorney shall advise the entity at a public meeting that he or she desires advice concerning the litigation.

(b) The subject matter of the meeting shall be confined to settlement negotiations or strategy sessions related to litigation expenditures.

(c) The entire session shall be recorded by a certified court reporter. The reporter shall record the times of commencement and termination of the session, all discussion and proceedings, the names of all persons present at any time, and the names of all persons speaking. No portion of the session shall be off the record. The court reporter's notes shall be fully transcribed and filed with the entity's clerk within a reasonable time after the meeting.

(d) The entity shall give reasonable public notice of the time and date of the attorney-client session and the names of persons who will be attending the session. The session shall commence at an open meeting at which the persons chairing the meeting shall announce the commencement and estimated length of the attorney-client session and the names of the persons attending. At the conclusion of the attorney-client session, the meeting shall be reopened, and the person chairing the meeting shall announce the termination of the session.

(e) The transcript shall be made part of the public record upon conclusion of the litigation.

As a reading of this statute and the prior constitutional amendments show, "there are three basic requirements of Florida's Sunshine Law: (1) meetings of public boards or commissions must be open to the public; (2) reasonable notice of such meetings must be given; and (3) minutes of the meetings must be taken and promptly recorded." Patrick John McGinley, FLORIDA MUNICIPAL LAW AND PRACTICE § 10:2 (2017-18 ed.).

B. Applicability of Florida's Sunshine Law and Definition of "Public Record"

To whom does Florida's Sunshine Laws apply, and what exactly is a "public record" under that law? To answer these questions, keep in mind that Florida's Sunshine Law, "having been enacted for the public benefit, should be interpreted most favorably to the public." *Canney v. Board of Public Instruction of Alachua Cty.*, 278 So. 2d 260 (Fla. 1973). Florida's Sunshine Law "must be broadly construed to [advance] its remedial and protective purpose." *Wood v. Marston*, 442 So. 2d 934 (Fla. 1983). Importantly, Florida's Sunshine Law "should be construed so as to frustrate all evasive devices." *Palm Beach v. Gradison*, 296 So. 2d 473 (Fla. 1974).

Perhaps the answers to these questions are best illustrated by Florida's First District Court of Appeal's 2009 decision in *National Collegiate Athletic Association v. Associated Press*, 18 So. 3d 1201 (Fla. 1st DCA 2009), review denied, 37 So. 3d 848 (2010).

National Collegiate Athletic Association v. Associated Press

First District Court of Appeal of Florida, 2009
18 So. 3d 1201

The National Collegiate Athletic Association (NCAA) appeals a final judgment requiring it to disclose certain documents under Florida's Sunshine Law to The Associated Press and other news organizations. We find no error in the decision by the trial court. Accordingly, we affirm.

Records created and maintained by the NCAA are not generally subject to public disclosure. However, the documents at issue in this case were examined by lawyers for a public agency, Florida State University, and used in the course of the agency's business. Because the documents were received in connection with the transaction of official business by an agency, they are public records. The NCAA has failed to show that an exception applies under state or federal law, and thus the records must be disclosed.

I.

The events leading to the present controversy began when the University became aware of allegations that a learning specialist and an academic tutor had provided improper assistance to a number of students, some of whom were participating in athletic programs. The University engaged the services of a private firm to conduct an internal investigation on its behalf. After the completion of a comprehensive self-investigation of academic misconduct, the University reported its findings to the NCAA.

Several months later, the NCAA issued a notice of allegations to the University. The effect of the notice was to formally initiate a disciplinary proceeding regarding the misconduct the University had previously reported to the NCAA. The University submitted a response to the allegations, and the case was called up for a hearing before the NCAA's Committee on Infractions. The transcript of the hearing before the committee has not been made public.

Thereafter, the NCAA's Committee on Infractions issued an infractions report. It imposed penalties against the University for the academic misconduct, including an order that certain athletic victories be vacated. The report was provided to the

University in paper form, and, after the names of the students had been redacted, the report was made public.

The University then retained the Gray-Robinson law firm to file an appeal to the NCAA from the penalties imposed by the committee. Because the work of the committee was done in private, the lawyers had to make an arrangement with the NCAA to obtain access to the records relevant to the enforcement proceeding. The arrangement was as follows. The NCAA put images of the transcript of the October 28, 2008, hearing and other records on a secure Internet website. Lawyers for GrayRobinson signed a confidentiality agreement with the NCAA promising not to disclose any information they obtained from the website. The NCAA then gave the lawyers a password they could use to obtain the information from the website.

This is the system the NCAA uses with all of its member institutions [. . .] as part of an effort to go "paperless." [Julie Roe, the Director of Enforcement for the NCAA,] referred to the secure website as the "custodial website." Authorized representatives of member institutions could go to the website to obtain access to information they needed to resolve their disputes with the NCAA, and, at the same time, the NCAA could avoid public disclosure of confidential sources of information used in its investigations.

After they had signed the confidentiality agreement, the lawyers at GrayRobinson examined the transcript of the hearing before the Committee on Infractions. The lawyers then used the information in the transcript to prepare the University's appeal to the NCAA. They filed the initial brief on behalf of the University, and the Committee on Infractions filed a written response. The response was submitted to the NCAA as a part of the appeal. It was considered to be the property of the NCAA and it was not disclosed to the public.

The Associated Press sought disclosure of documents in the NCAA disciplinary proceeding and appeal and, when the request was denied, they filed suit under Florida's Sunshine Law against the NCAA, Florida State University, its President, and the GrayRobinson law firm.

The public records case was tried before the court. Two documents were at issue in the litigation: the transcript of the hearing before the NCAA Committee on Infractions and the Committee's response to the University's appeal. The plaintiffs argued that both documents were "public records" under Florida's Sunshine Law. The NCAA argued that the documents were not public records.

The trial court concluded that the transcript and response were public records because they were received by an agency of the state government. The court ordered the immediate disclosure of the transcript and response, but the NCAA appealed to this court, and the judgment by the trial court was stayed pending the disposition of the appeal.

II.

The issues presented in this appeal are governed by the organic law of the state. The Florida Constitution creates a broad right to inspect the records of any state or local governmental body. Article I, section 24(a) of the Florida Constitution grants "[e]very person . . . the right to inspect or copy any public record made or received in connection with the official business of any public body, officer or employee of the state, or persons acting on their behalf." The right to inspect a public record in Florida is not one that is merely established by legislation, it is a right demanded by the people.

Article I, section 24(c) of the Florida Constitution provides that the right to inspect public records shall be "self-executing." Legislation is not required to implement the right, but section 24(c) expressly grants authority to the Florida Legislature to "enact laws governing the enforcement of this section." The rights created by the constitution may be enforced under the procedures in the public records law, Chapter 119, Florida Statutes. The opening sentence of the law declares that "[i]t is the policy in this state that all state, county and municipal records are open for personal inspection and copying by any person" and that "[p]roviding access to public records is a duty of each agency."

Florida courts construe the public records law liberally in favor of the state's policy of open government. If there is any doubt about the application of the law in a particular case, the doubt is resolved in favor of disclosing the documents.

a.

With these principles in mind, we address whether the transcript and response are public records. We begin by observing that the public records law is not limited to paper documents but that it applies, as well, to documents that exist only in digital form. Florida's Sunshine Law makes it clear that the public records law applies to documents maintained on a computer in the same way that it would apply to those kept in a file cabinet. This section notes the increased dependency on computerized records and it directs that "each agency must provide reasonable access to records electronically maintained." It goes on to conclude that the automation of public records "must not erode the right of access to those records."

To determine whether a particular document qualifies as a public record the court must look first to the definition given in the law itself. Section 119.011(12) defines the term "public record" as:

> all documents, papers, letters, maps, books, tapes, photographs, films, sound records, data processing software, or other material, regardless of the physical form, characteristic or means of transmission, made or received pursuant to law or ordinance in connection with the transaction of official business.

By this definition, a document may qualify as a public record under the statute if it was prepared by a private party, so long as it was "received" by a government agent and used in the transaction of public business.

The Florida Supreme Court provided additional guidance to the lower courts in *Shevin v. Byron, Harless, Schaffer, Reid & Associates, Inc.*, 379 So. 2d 633 (Fla. 1980).

In that case, the court defined the term "record" as used in section 119.011(12) as "any material prepared in connection with official agency business which is intended to perpetuate, communicate, or formalize knowledge of some type." *Shevin*, 379 So. 2d at 640. This definition was intended "to give content to the public records law" by attributing a meaning to the term "record" that is "consistent with common understanding of the term." *Shevin* at 640.

Based on these authorities, we conclude that the transcript and response are public records. Although these documents were prepared and maintained by a private organization, they were "received" by agents of a public agency and used in connection with public business. The purpose of the transcript was to perpetuate the information presented to the infractions committee, in the event the parties wished to appeal the sanction imposed by the committee. The response was designed to communicate information to the body that would hear the appeal within the NCAA.

The term "received" in section 119.011(12) refers not only to a situation in which a public agent takes physical delivery of a document, but also to one in which a public agent examines a document residing on a remote computer. If that were not the case, a party could easily circumvent the public records laws. The appeal by the University is a matter of public concern. It is not transformed into a private matter merely because the documents the University lawyers used to prepare the appeal reside on a computer owned by a private organization. The definition of a public record does not turn on the sender's method of transmission.

Our conclusion that the transcript and response became public records when they were examined by state lawyers and used for a public purpose is supported by the decision of the Second District Court of Appeal in *Times Publishing Co. v. City of St. Petersburg*, 558 So. 2d 487 (Fla. 2d DCA 1990). That case involved negotiations between the Chicago White Sox and the City of St. Petersburg for the use of the Suncoast Dome. The documents pertaining to the negotiations were prepared and maintained exclusively by the White Sox, but they were examined by agents for the City under a confidentiality agreement. The court held that the documents were subject to disclosure under the public records law because they were examined by agents for the City and used in the course of its business.

These principles apply with equal force here. It is true, as the NCAA points out, that the documents at issue in *Times Publishing* were modified at the request of the City, but that is a distinction without a difference. A document that is used in the course of public business is a public record under the definition in section 119.011(12) if it was made by a public official or if was received by the official. If it was received, that is enough. It is not necessary to also show that it was made, partly made, or modified in some way by the official.

We would be more inclined to accept the NCAA's argument that viewing is not the equivalent of receiving if the documents at issue had not been directly related to the work these lawyers were doing for the state. If the GrayRobinson lawyers had used their password to look at the disciplinary records of a student athlete from a private school in New York, the NCAA would have a good argument that the record did not become public merely because it was "viewed" by someone who happened to work for the State of Florida. The point overlooked in the NCAA's argument, however, is that the records in this case were examined and used for an official state purpose.

The GrayRobinson lawyers signed a confidentiality agreement with the NCAA, but that has no impact on our decision that the transcript and response are public records. A public record cannot be transformed into a private record merely because an agent of the government has promised that it will be kept private. Nor is it material that the NCAA had an expectation that the documents would remain private. As we explained in *Sepro Corp. v. Florida Department of Environmental Protection*, 839 So. 2d 781, 784 (Fla. 1st DCA 2003), "[A] private party cannot render public records exempt from disclosure merely by designating information it furnishes a governmental agency confidential." The right to examine these records is a right belonging to the public; it cannot be bargained away by a representative of the government.

In limited but well-defined circumstances, a record created and maintained by a private organization can be subject to disclosure as a public record on an agency theory. For example, if a private entity is acting on behalf of the state or local government and creates a document that reflects the business of the governmental entity, the document can become a public record. In *News and Sun-Sentinel Co. v. Schwab, Twitty & Hanser Architectural Group, Inc.*, 596 So. 2d 1029 (Fla. 1992), the supreme court set out a nine-factor test to determine whether records held by a private party must be disclosed under the public record act on the theory that the private party is acting on behalf of the government.

The critical question in this line of cases is whether the private party is a "private agency, person, partnership, corporation or business entity acting on behalf of [a] public agency " that has therefore become an "agency," as defined in section 119.011(2) Florida Statutes. The common feature of all of the cases in this line of authority is that they all involve efforts to determine whether a private entity has assumed the role of the government. Typically, the private entity has a contract with the government and performs a public function in the course of its duties under the contract. The private entity is acting not as a business adversary to the government but as a surrogate for the government.

The issue in the present case is much less complicated. The transcript and response are public records because they were received by agents of the state and used in the course of the state's business. We need not apply the nine-factor test in *Schwab* to come to this conclusion. Nor is it necessary to decide whether the NCAA became a public "agency" in its own right under section 119.011(2) by stepping into the shoes of the University and assuming a public duty of the University. The documents at issue in this case became public records by a much more direct route: they were received by agents of the University and used in connection with the University's business. The legal status of these records is no different than it would be if they had been prepared by the University's lawyers and if the only existing copies were in the NCAA's possession.

The enforcement of the public records law is also relatively straightforward in a situation like this. Section 119.07(1)(a), Florida Statutes states that "every person who has custody of a public record shall permit the record to be inspected and copied by any person desiring to do so. . . ." The plain meaning of this statute is that the public records law can be enforced against any person who has custody of public records, whether that person is employed by the public agency creating or receiving the records or not. It makes no difference that the records in question are in the hands of a private party. If they are public records, they are subject to compelled disclosure under the law.

b.

We come now to the final argument on appeal, that the public records law is unconstitutional as applied under the facts of this case. The NCAA contends that the law as applied here violates its rights under the dormant Commerce Clause and under the First Amendment right to freedom of association. These arguments lack merit.

The Commerce Clause states: "The Congress shall have Power . . . To regulate Commerce . . . among the several States. . . ." U.S. Const., Art. I, §8, cl. 3. The United States Supreme Court has recognized that this affirmative grant of authority to Congress also encompasses an implicit or "dormant" limitation on the authority of the States to enact legislation affecting interstate commerce. See *Hughes v. Oklahoma*, 441 U.S. 322, 326 (1979). The United States Supreme Court has adopted a two-tiered test to determine whether a state law violates the dormant Commerce Clause. If a statute "directly regulates or discriminates against interstate commerce, or [if] its effect is to favor in-state economic interests over out-of-state interests," the court may declare it unconstitutional as applied, without further inquiry. *Brown-Forman Distillers, Inc. v. New York State Liquor Authority*, 476 U.S. 573, 578–79 (1986). However, if the statute regulates evenhandedly and if it has only an indirect effect on interstate commerce, the court must determine whether the state's interest is legitimate and, if so, whether the burden on interstate commerce exceeds the local benefits.

The public records law does not attempt to regulate or discriminate against interstate commerce. It does not deal with the subject of commerce at all. Nor does the application of the law in this case favor in-state economic interests over out-of-state interests. The law would apply in the same way we have applied it here if a private Florida corporation doing business entirely within the borders of the state had provided information to a public official and if the information had then been used in connection with public business.

We are not persuaded that the Public Records law has an indirect effect on interstate commerce, but even if some effect had been established, we could not say that the law violates the dormant Commerce Clause. The Public Records law implements a right guaranteed to members of the public under the Florida Constitution and it therefore promotes a state interest of the highest order. The negligible impact the law might have on interstate commerce clearly does not outweigh the goal of ensuring open government.

The NCAA relies on *NCAA v. Miller*, 10 F.3d 633 (9th Cir. 1993), and *NCAA v. Roberts*, 1994 WL 750585 (N.D.Fla. 1994), in support of its dormant Commerce Clause argument, but these cases are distinguishable. Both involve state statutes purporting to regulate disciplinary proceedings by college athletic associations. In contrast, the public records law is a law of general application; it does not single out athletic associations.

The NCAA's claim that the application of the Florida public records law would impair its ability to function also assumes that the law imposes a burden that would not be imposed in other states. That is not the case. Many other states also define a public record broadly to include records that are connected with the business of the government yet are not in the hands of a public agent. Some statutes are like the one in Florida, in that they refer to documents that were made or "received" by a public agent in connection with public business. Others are even broader, in that they refer to documents that were "used" by a public agent in the course of public business. We do not suggest that the analysis would be precisely the same in every state, but merely that Florida law is not so distinctive that it would force the NCAA to change the way it does business. This case arose in Florida, but it is likely that the NCAA would be dealing with the same issue had it arisen most anywhere in the United States.

The argument that the application of the Florida public records law violates the NCAA's right to freedom of association under the First Amendment is also unavailing. We acknowledge that the NCAA is a private voluntary organization and that it enjoys the freedom of association guaranteed by the First Amendment, but the NCAA has not shown that the application of the Florida public records law impairs that right. The application of the Florida public records law could not, by any stretch of the imagination, require the NCAA to admit or reject certain institutions. Nor does it require the NCAA to reject the values it wishes to express. The law may prevent the NCAA from conducting secret proceedings against a public school in this state, but that does not impair the NCAA's freedom of expression or its freedom of association.

III.

In summary, we hold that the application of the Florida public records law does not violate any constitutional right under the facts of this case, that the transcript of the hearing before the Committee on Infractions and the Committee's response are public records, and that these documents are not exempt from disclosure under state or federal law. For these reasons, we affirm the judgment of the trial court and order the disclosure of the transcript, and the response in its original form.

Affirmed.

Notes and Questions to Consider:

1. The holding in *NCAA v. Associated Press* does not mean that the records of all private corporations and nongovernmental entities are made public by Florida's Sunshine Law. Sunshine applies to Florida's state and local governments and agencies, but generally does not apply to private entities. The exception is when the private entity steps into the shoes of the government and assumes the duty to provide a governmental service. This can occur, for example, when the private entity has a contract with the government and performs a public function in the course of its duties under the contract. The nine-factor *Schwab* test, named after the Florida Supreme Court decision in *News and Sun-Sentinel Co. v. Schwab, Twitty & Hanser Architectural Group, Inc.*, 596 So. 2d 1029 (Fla. 1992), determines whether the private entity's actions are sufficient to make its records public under Florida's Sunshine Law. The critical question answered by the nine-factor *Schwab* test is whether the private party is a "private agency, person, partnership, corporation or business entity acting on behalf of a public agency " that has therefore become an "agency," as defined in section 119.011(2) Florida Statutes. The nine-factor *Schwab* test is satisfied only in these limited but well-defined circumstances. How is it beneficial that Florida's Sunshine Law is not generally applicable to private entities?

2. What if the *Schwab* test did not exist and the records in possession of private entities were never subject to public inspection under Florida's Sunshine Law? How would that contradict the purposes of Florida's Sunshine Law? How would that thwart the goal that Florida's Sunshine Law "should be construed so as to frustrate all evasive devices?"

3. Note that *NCAA v. Associated Press* did not need to enumerate and apply the nine-factor *Schwab* test. The court found it unnecessary to decide whether the NCAA was acting on behalf of a public agency as required by *Schwab*. Instead, the court found that the state (specifically, the Florida State University) acted on its own. Specifically, the lawyers of GrayRobinson, acting for their state client, the University, examined the NCAA's records in order to defend the state. That means the records were received by agents of the state and used in the course of the state's business. This is enough to qualify those particular records of the NCAA as public records under Florida's Sunshine Law. Does that mean that every one of the NCAA's records must now be open to inspection by the public?

4. Were you surprised by the holding that the Florida State University was a "public agency" subject to the requirements of Florida's Sunshine Law? Case law precedent interprets "public agency" quite expansively, as seen from this condensed version of the list of public entities appearing in Patrick John McGinley, FLORIDA ELEMENTS OF AN ACTION § 2101:1 (2016-17 edition): "every board of commission of the state, or of any county or political subdivision; boards created by interlocal agreement; the State Fair Authority; school advisory councils; committees to help screen public job applicants; a mayor's group of concerned citizens advising on legislation; a liaison between a mayor's office and a Chamber of Commerce; the

postelection transition team of a newly elected official; private organizations that were created by a public entity to serve it; entities assisting the Florida Department of Corrections with its corrections work programs. . . ." How does an expansive definition of "public agency" help advance the purposes of Florida's Sunshine Law?

5. Did you notice that the public agency need not have actual possession of the document for it to become subject to public disclosure under Florida's Sunshine Law? Instead, *NCAA v. Associated Press* held it was enough that the public agency (or, more precisely, the lawyers representing the public agency) used and examined the document in the course of the state's business. Does this make it difficult for public agencies to keep track of what documents are public documents?

6. Were you surprised that the public agency need not create the document that is subject to public disclosure under Florida's Sunshine Law. Most public websites and letters sent by public agencies warn the public that any correspondence or email sent to the public agency becomes a public record under Florida's Sunshine Law.

C. Exceptions to, and Exclusions from, Florida's Sunshine Law

Fans of Florida's Sunshine Law allege that "Florida's Sunshine Law has long been lauded as one of the best in the nation." *See, e.g.,* John Cooper, *Sending the Wrong Message: Technology, Sunshine Law, and the Public Record in Florida,* 39 Stetson L. Rev. 411 (Winter 2010). If this is true, then perhaps it is because "Florida's Sunshine Law has fewer exemptions than most other states' open meetings statutes." Sandra F. Chase and Christina Locke, *The Government-in-the-Sunshine Law Then and Now: Model for Implementing New Technologies Consistent with Florida's Position as a Leader in Open Government,* 35 Fla. St. U. L. Rev. 245 (Winter 2008).

The applicability of Florida's Sunshine Law and the restrictions it imposes are interpreted broadly, whereas the few exceptions to Florida's Sunshine Law are interpreted narrowly. One might say that "coverage is expressed generally; exemptions are identified explicitly." *Wood v. Marston,* 442 So. 2d 934, 938 (Fla. 1983). Perhaps these words from Florida's supreme court say it best: "The principle to be followed is very simple: When in doubt, the members of any board, agency, authority or commission should follow the open-meeting policy of the State." *Town of Palm Beach v. Gradison,* 296 So. 2d 473, 477 (Fla. 1974).

Florida's constitution empowers the Florida Legislature to enact exceptions to public access, but any such exception is facially unconstitutional unless it (1) specifies the public necessity for the exception, (2) is not broader than necessary to accomplish the stated necessity, and (3) does not contain any other subject matter other than the exceptions and their enforcement.

Unless the Florida Legislature enacts such an exception, then in general, only two limited exceptions exist: the "use-of-staff" exception, and the "fact-finding" exception. Both exemptions are narrow in scope and ultimately turn on whether there was actual or apparent decision-making authority, as explained in this excerpt from FLORIDA MUNICIPAL LAW AND PRACTICE:

> The "use-of-staff" exception can be said to be the broader of the two exceptions because it is available to any governmental group or entity. Its purpose is to allow government officials to have clerical assistants who ultimately bear no responsibility or authority of their own, but who help the government official carry out his or her responsibility and authority. As a general rule, government officials may call upon staff members for factual information and advice without being subject to the Sunshine Law's requirements. Also, a Sunshine violation does not occur when a governmental executive uses staff for a fact-finding and advisory function in fulfilling his or her duties. This exception to the Sunshine Law only applies to staff meetings that are informal, where the discussions were "merely informational," where none of the staff members attending the meetings had any decision-making authority during the meetings, and where no formal action was taken or possibly could have been taken at the meetings. However, if one or more of the staff committee members are delegated any decision-making authority, then the committee as a whole loses its exemption from the Sunshine Law because it stands in the shoes of such public officials from whom the authority was delegated. Stated somewhat differently, if a staff committee has been delegated any decision-making authority in addition to mere fact-finding or information-gathering, then the Sunshine Law applies to the committee. Thus, it is the nature of the act performed by the staff committee, and not the makeup of the committee or the proximity of the act to the final decision, that determines whether a committee composed of staff is subject to the Sunshine Law. For this reason, the use-of-staff exception may never apply when the government official and the staff he consulted made joint decisions. Likewise, the use-of-staff exception may never apply when the government official has delegated part of his or her decision-making authority to a staff member.
>
> The very limited "fact-finding" exception applies only to advisory committees. Such a committee (by whatever name they may be called by the board or entity that created it) is exempt from Florida's Sunshine Law only if the committee has been delegated mere "information-gathering or fact-finding authority" by its board and does not have any "decision-making authority" whatsoever. Where the committee has been delegated decision-making authority, the committee's meetings must be open to public scrutiny, regardless of the review procedures eventually used by the traditional governmental body. The question of decision-making authority is broadly answered to find such authority for Sunshine Law purposes even when the authority is limited to giving nonbinding advice to the entity who has sole decision-making power. Only when a group, on behalf of a public entity,

functions solely as a fact finder or information gatherer with no decision-making authority or decision-recommending role can that group be considered exempt from Florida's Sunshine Law.

For this reason, the "fact-finding exception" is further restricted to be available only to the appointing entity's qualifying fact-finding committee and never to the appointing entity itself. This is true even when the appointing board steps down from its decision-making role to embark on a purely fact-finding mission because despite this stated restriction, the board nevertheless remains the ultimate decision-making governmental authority. Note that the requirement that certain board meetings must be open to the public does not imply that the board could meet privately to discuss other matters.

Patrick John McGinley, FLORIDA MUNICIPAL LAW AND PRACTICE § 10:3 (2017-18 ed.) (internal footnotes and quotation marks omitted).

Concerns for equity or great need will not justify a judicially created exception to Florida's Sunshine Law, as is illustrated by *Neu v. Miami Herald Publishing Co.*, 462 So. 2d 821 (Fla. 1985). In *Neu*, Florida's then-existing version of the Sunshine Law conflicted with the Florida Evidence Code, Florida's attorney-client privilege, and the *Rules Regulating The Florida Bar*. The facts of *Neu* involved a governmental entity that was a party to a lawsuit. Sometimes, state and local governments get sued. What if a government entity subject to the open government requirements of Florida's Sunshine Laws wants to meet with its defense attorneys in private to discuss the litigation and its potential settlement? What if the defending governmental unit wants to hear its defense attorney's opinion as to the likelihood of winning the case and the attorney's opinion as to the proper settlement amount? Should such a meeting be open to the public so that the newspaper can report about such opinions—and the plaintiff can learn about them, too? *Neu v. Miami Herald* discusses the application of Florida's Sunshine Laws to such a situation at a time before the Florida Legislature amended the Sunshine Law to provide for private meetings.

Neu v. Miami Herald Publishing Company

Supreme Court of Florida, 1985
462 So. 2d 821

The state attorney and THE MIAMI HERALD sought a declaratory judgment that a proposed meeting between the city council and its attorney to discuss pending litigation was subject to the open meeting provisions of the Sunshine Law, section 286.011, Florida Statutes (1981). Relying on *Bassett v. Braddock*, 262 So. 2d 425 (Fla. 1972), the trial court concluded that the proposed meeting was neither official nor formal action under section 286.011 and, thus, there was no requirement that the meeting be open to the public. On appeal, the district court reversed [and] distinguished *Bassett* on the basis that it dealt with a different question arising under a constitutional exception to the Sunshine Law. The district court also rejected the argument that the attorney-client privilege provisions of the Florida Evidence Code granted an exception for closed meetings because, in the court's view, section 286.011(1) limited exceptions to the Sunshine Law to those created by the constitution. Because of the continuing significance of the issue, the court certified the following question of great public importance:

> Whether the Sunshine Law applies to meetings between a City Council and the City Attorney held for the purpose of discussing the settlement of pending litigation to which the city is a party.

We answer the question affirmatively and approve the decision of the district court.

Before turning to the dispositive questions, we dispose of two peripheral questions which have been raised. First, the city council devised a procedure whereby representatives of the press and the state attorney, among others, were to be admitted to the meeting and a record maintained which would later be released to the public. The representatives attending the meeting would be pledged to respect the confidentiality of the cases discussed in the meeting until the cases had been resolved. Whatever merits there may be in this procedural attempt to compromise the competing values between open meetings and private discussion with an attorney, the procedure has no legal impact. Under the Sunshine Law, a meeting is either fully open or fully closed; there are no intermediate categories.

Second, the district court opinion suggests that in enacting the Sunshine Law the legislature, by the use of the words "except as otherwise provided in the constitution," established a requirement that future legislatures could not establish statutory exceptions to the open meeting requirements of the Sunshine Law. This is, of course, incorrect. A legislature may not bind the hands of future legislatures by prohibiting amendments to statutory law.

Turning now to the dispositive questions, the trial court concluded, and petitioners urge, that our decision in *Bassett* creates an exception to the Sunshine Law permitting governmental bodies to meet privately with their attorneys to discuss pending litigation. In *Bassett*, we held that an attorney representing a governmental body could meet privately with employee representatives to negotiate a collective bargaining agreement, and that the governmental body could meet privately with its attorney representative to instruct and consult on the negotiations. We agree that much of our rationale in *Bassett* would appear to support the proposition that private consultations are permitted with attorneys representing governmental bodies in pending litigation. Indeed, we went so far as to comment that "where the negotiator is an *attorney* that certainly he is entitled to consult with the Board on matters regarding preliminary advices." *Bassett*, 262 So. 2d at 428 (emphasis in original). Despite the broadness of such language, our decision was restricted to and rested on what we saw to be a constitutional exception to the Sunshine Law, to wit: the Article I, section 6 right of public employees to bargain collectively.

Petitioners urge that opening up the consultation of the governmental body with its attorney to its adversary in pending litigation gives the adversary an unfair advantage which can be used to secure unmerited or excessive judgments or settlements against the public. There is a good deal of wisdom in petitioners' argument but, as will be made clear below, we have no constitutional or statutory authority to create an exception to the Sunshine Law for governmental bodies to meet privately with their attorneys to discuss pending litigation.

Petitioners next urge that [the] attorney/client privilege [allows] governmental bodies [to] meet privately with their attorneys. Although we agree that the legislature has the authority to exempt such meetings from the Sunshine Law, we do not agree that it has done so. [The attorney-client privilege as codified in Florida Statutes] Section 90.502(1)(c) provides that "[a] communication between lawyer and client is 'confidential' if it is not intended to be disclosed to third persons. . . ." The Law Revision Council Note to section (1), Florida Statutes Annotated 90.502 (1979), comments that "[w]hen the communication is made in public . . . the intent to keep the communication confidential is lacking and the privilege cannot be claimed." The Sunshine Law explicitly provides for public meetings; communications at such public meetings are not confidential and no attorney/client privilege can arise therefrom. In construing legislation, courts should not assume that the legislature acted pointlessly. *Sharer v. Hotel Corp. of America*, 144 So. 2d 813, 817 (Fla. 1962).

Petitioners next urge, alternatively, that reading section 286.011 to deny them a right to private meetings with their attorney places section 286.011 in conflict with Florida Bar Code of Professional Responsibility [the predecessor to the *Rules Regulating The Florida Bar*], and infringes on the constitutional authority of this Court under Article V, section 15, Florida Constitution to regulate the practice of law. Petitioners cite *Times Pub. Co. v. Williams*, 222 So. 2d 470 (Fla. 2d DCA 1969), in support. We disagree and disapprove that portion of *Times Publishing Co.* which holds that the legislature is without authority to regulate the relationship of public bodies with their attorneys. We note first that Disciplinary Rule 4-101 and Ethical Consideration 4-2 both provide that an attorney may divulge communications with his client when required by law. Further, as we noted above, there are no confidential communications to protect when the communications occur in a public meeting. Finally, the attorney/client privilege belongs to the client, not the attorney. The legislature has plenary constitutional authority to regulate the activities of political subdivisions and can require, as it has done in section 286.011, that meetings be open to the public. The attorney's right to invoke the attorney/client privilege is derivative of the client's right to that privilege. Under the circumstances, it would truly be a case of the tail wagging the dog to hold that an attorney, or this Court, could require closed meetings of public bodies, contrary to statutory law, based on the Code of Professional Responsibility.

Petitioners also urge that they have a due process right under the Fourteenth Amendment to the United States Constitution to privately consult with their attorney. We will not make any sweeping pronouncements on the distinction between due process rights of governmental entities and private persons. It is enough to say that the legislature has the power to require open meetings and that petitioners' argument has been rejected by the United States Supreme Court. *Williams v. Mayor and City Council of Baltimore*, 289 U.S. 36 (1933).

One can argue and reargue whether the broad reading of the Sunshine Law is politically wise. We have no interest in nor responsibility for debating political questions. As we said in *Wait v. Florida Power & Light Co.*, 372 So. 2d 420, 424 (Fla. 1979):

> This argument should be addressed to the legislature. Courts deal with the construction and constitutionality of legislative determinations, not their wisdom. In this case, we are confined to a determination of the legislature's intent.

The certified question is answered in the affirmative and the decision of the district court approved.

It is so ordered.

———————

Notes and Questions to Consider:

1. Sometimes the requirements of Florida's Sunshine Law may conflict with other laws, such as is seen in *Neu v. Miami Herald*, where the open meetings requirements of the Sunshine Law conflicted with the Florida Evidence Code, the attorney-client privilege, and the *Rules Regulating The Florida Bar*. Generally speaking, when such a conflict exists, does Florida's Sunshine Law prevail?

2. The holding of *Neu v. Miami Herald* constitutes an unequitable result from the perspective of the governmental entity that is the defendant in the lawsuit. The advice from its attorney about that suit will be made public. Newspapers and others may spread that information far and wide. The opposing counsels in the suit, and their clients, may learn what advice the defendant's lawyers gave the governmental defendant. On the other hand, the governmental defendant does not learn what advice the opposing counsels are giving to the opposing party. Are such inequities sufficient to permit a judicially created exception to Florida Sunshine Law?

3. *Neu v. Miami Herald* interpreted the 1985 version of Florida's Sunshine Law, which had not yet been amended to provide a procedure for government officials to meet privately with defense attorneys. In the first of the two "peripheral questions" addressed near the beginning of *Neu*, the court considers and rejects the city council's makeshift solution for complying with Florida's Sunshine Law yet preserving the attorney-client privilege. Why did the court find this makeshift solution impermissible?

4. *Neu* ends with the admonition that the question of whether Florida's Sunshine Law was politically wise is one for the legislature not the courts. Did the legislature act? As discussed in Part A of this chapter, the current version of Florida's Sunshine Law contains an exception intended to preserve the attorney-client privilege in situations similar to *Neu v. Miami Herald*. Florida Statutes section 286.011(8) provides

in relevant part that the governmental entity may meet in private with the entity's attorney to discuss pending litigation provided that the following conditions are met:

(a) The entity's attorney requests it.

(b) The discussion is confined to settlement or litigation expenditures.

(c) The discussion is recorded by a certified court reporter who records the start and stop time, all discussions, and the names of all persons present and all persons speaking. No portion of the session shall be off the record. The court reporter's notes shall be fully transcribed and filed with the entity's clerk within a reasonable time after the meeting.

(d) The entity gives reasonable public notice of the time and date of the attorney-client session and the names of persons who will be attending. The session shall commence at an open meeting at which the persons chairing the meeting shall announce the commencement and estimated length of the attorney-client session and the names of the persons attending. At the conclusion of the attorney-client session, the meeting shall be reopened, and the person chairing the meeting shall announce the termination of the session.

(e) The transcript shall be made part of the public record upon conclusion of the litigation.

D. Audio or Video Recording of Government Gatherings or Meetings

Clearly, a record of government gatherings or meeting is contemplated by the Florida Sunshine Law's requirement that the government make "minutes" of the meeting, promptly record them into the public record, and make that public record open to public inspection. But "minutes" are not a verbatim transcript, and "minutes" do not record every single word or action.

What if the news, or even just a citizen, wants to make a complete audio or video recording of a gathering or meeting of government officials? Some people do not wish to be recorded. Some people act awkwardly once they know they are being recorded. The effect of Florida's Sunshine Law upon the ability to record what is said and observed at government gatherings and meetings is illustrated by the following case of *Pinellas County Sch. Bd. v. Suncam, Inc.*, 829 So. 2d 989 (Fla. 2d DCA 2002).

Pinellas County School Board v. Suncam, Inc.

Florida's Second District Court of Appeal, 2002
829 So. 2d 989

The Pinellas County School Board appeals from a final judgment which determined that the board had committed a violation of the Florida Sunshine Law, section 286.011, Florida Statutes (2001). We affirm.

The facts are not in dispute. The Pinellas County School Board scheduled a public meeting of the Special Services Selection Committee for the purpose of evaluating applications of general contractors for the remodeling, renovation, and new construction of Gibbs High School in Pinellas County. It is agreed that the board complied with all other requirements of the Florida Sunshine Law, section 286.011, Florida Statutes (2001), with the exception of denying the request of Suncam, Inc. to videotape the proceedings.

The asserted justification for denial by the board was that participants in the meeting would not act normally while being videotaped and that this would impair the work of the committee. It is agreed that the videotaping itself would be unobtrusive. It is also agreed that although the board vacillated on whether to allow videotaping, in the final analysis, videotaping was permitted solely at the discretion of the board through its superintendent. The ultimate issue for our determination is whether the board retains unfettered authority to deny videotaping of its otherwise public meeting. We answer the question in the negative, but limit our response to the sufficiency of the board's stated reason for not allowing videotaping in this instance.

The Sunshine Law was enacted to protect the public from "closed door" politics. See *Wood v. Marston*, 442 So. 2d 934, 938 (Fla. 1983). As a result, the law "must be broadly construed to effect its remedial and protective purpose." *Id.* "The breadth of such right is virtually unfettered. . . ." *Lorei v. Smith*, 464 So. 2d 1330, 1332 (Fla. 2d DCA 1985). In *Hough v. Stembridge*, 278 So. 2d 288, 289 (Fla. 3d DCA 1973), the Third District held that violation of the Sunshine Law can occur where a state agency meets and violates the "statute's spirit, intent, and purpose." Thus, although the statute does not explicitly provide for the video recording of public meetings, the refusal to allow such recording certainly violates the "statute's spirit, intent, and purpose."

This specific issue was addressed by the attorney general several years ago. Op. Att'y. Gen. Fla. 91–28 (1991). See *Beverly v. Div. of Beverage of Dep't of Bus. Regulation*, 282 So. 2d 657 (Fla. 1st DCA 1973) (holding opinions of Florida's Attorney General are entitled to great weight in construing the law of the state, but are not binding on the district court of appeal). The attorney general stated: "A municipality may not prohibit a citizen from video taping the meetings of the city council through the use of nondisruptive video recording devices." The attorney general concluded its opinion with the following statement:

> In previously considering a similar issue, this office stated that a rule which prohibits the use of all tape recorders, including silent taping devices that are neither distracting nor disruptive, was in conflict with the public policy of the state as interpreted under Florida Statutes section 286.011. While a public board may adopt reasonable rules and policies to ensure the orderly conduct of its public meeting and to require orderly behavior on the part of those attending, rules prohibiting the use of silent or nondisruptive tape recording devices would appear to be unreasonable and arbitrary and, therefore, invalid.

Moreover, the Legislature in Florida Statutes section 934.02(1) appears to implicitly recognize the public's right to silently record public meetings. Chapter 934, the Security of Communications Law, regulates the interception of oral communication. Section 934.02(2), however, defines "oral communication" as specifically excluding "public oral communication uttered at a public meeting."

Op. Att'y. Gen. Fla. 91–28 (footnotes omitted).

We determine that the board was in violation of the Florida Sunshine Law in the instant case and, therefore, affirm the final judgment.

Affirmed and remanded for proceedings pursuant to this opinion.

———————

Notes and Questions to Consider:

1. Nowadays, it seems like everyone has a phone in their pocket or bag, and those phones can be used to make audio or video recordings. Does Florida's Sunshine Law entitle Floridians to use their phones to make an audio or video recording of Florida government gatherings or meetings? Can people record the government gathering surreptitiously? In addressing these questions, FLORIDA MUNICIPAL LAW AND PRACTICE summarizes Florida case law precedent as follows:

> Regarding the public's available means for making a record of or recording a municipal meeting, the municipality or its board may adopt reasonable rules and policies which ensure the orderly conduct of a public meeting and require orderly behavior on the part of those persons attending that meeting.
>
> Despite this power, it may not ban the use of nondisruptive recording devices. Therefore, the public may record the meeting using any nondisruptive means, including secret or covert methods of an audio or video recording.

Patrick John McGinley, FLORIDA MUNICIPAL LAW AND PRACTICE § 10:7 (2017-18 ed.) (footnotes omitted).

2. How does permitting the audio and video recording of government gatherings or meetings further the Florida Sunshine Law's goals of transparency and accountability?

3. By permitting surreptitious audio or video recordings, does the Florida Sunshine Law discourage—or to borrow a phrase from federal First Amendment jurisprudence, have a "chilling effect" upon—public debate or free speech at government meetings?

4. What if some people who attend public meetings wish to make a statement to the government "off the record." How can this be achieved in compliance with Florida's Sunshine Law?

E. Public Notice of Government Gatherings or Meetings

One requirement of Florida's Sunshine Law is for the government to provide "due public notice" of all government gatherings or meetings. What exactly does that require? Consider the following Opinion of the Florida attorney general.

Florida Attorney General Advisory Opinion

NUMBER: AGO 73-170

Date: May 17, 1973

Re: Sunshine Law—Meaning of Term "Due Public Notice"

To: Jack Faircloth, Clerk, Circuit Court, Bonifay

Prepared by: Henry George White, Assistant Attorney General

Question:

What is the meaning of the term "due public notice" in s. 125.001, Florida Statutes, as that term relates to the provisions of the Florida Sunshine Law?

Summary:

The meaning of the term "due public notice" is variable, depending on the facts of each situation. The purpose of notice is to apprise individuals or the public generally of the pendency of matters which may affect their personal or property rights and afford them the opportunity to appear and present their views. The nature of the proceeding at which these rights are to be affected, the nature of the rights themselves, the applicable statutory provisions, and other surrounding circumstances will influence the notice requirements of each case. But in every case the notice must reasonably convey all the information required in that situation and it must afford a reasonable time for interested persons to make an appearance if they wish.

[Discussion:]

The Government in the Sunshine Law is a policy declaration by the legislature that all meetings of public bodies at which official acts are to be taken shall be open to the public. Implicit in this policy is the requirement that the public have notice of such meetings. While the Sunshine Law does not expressly mention notice, the cases construing it do speak of the public's right "to be present and to be heard," *Board of Public Instruction of Broward County v. Doran*, 224 So. 2d 693 (Fla. 1969), and the right of "public scrutiny and participation," *City of Miami Beach v. Berns*, 245 So. 2d 38 (Fla. 1971). It is axiomatic that the right "to be present and to heard" has little meaning or value unless the public is informed that particular matters are pending and can choose whether or not to attend and participate in a meeting. An understanding of the purpose of notice assists in the formulation of a functional definition of that term.

There is no precise definition of or formula for due notice which is applicable to every situation. Due notice is a relative term, the meaning and sufficiency of which can be ascertained only in reference to the particular facts and circumstances upon which it bears. Notice which is adequate under normal conditions may be impractical or impossible in emergency situations. So the purpose behind the requirement of notice, the events about which notice is given, and the nature of the rights affected will determine what is required in each case.

I have previously stated in AGO 071-32 that any meeting which is subject to the provisions of the Sunshine Law must be preceded by:

> "a reasonable and ample period of notice to the public and representatives of the press so that they may attend the meeting if they wish. Both the period of notice of the meeting and the method of promulgating the notice to the public must be performed in strict accordance with legislative requirements when these requirements exist; where there is no legislative prescription, then the serving of notice and the promulgation of the notice must be given in a reasonable manner calculated to timely inform the public."

Accord: Attorney General Opinions 071-346 and 072-400.

As noted above, Florida's Sunshine Law requires "due public notice" of regular or special meetings of the board of county commissioners, but the type or period of notice required in this situation is not covered by the statute. As the statute does not identify the prerequisites for adequate notice, the criteria outlined above will come into play. Thus, even though Florida Statutes section 125.66(2) requires at least fifteen days' notice of an intention to enact a county ordinance, and prescribes the manner in which the notice of intention must be given, such notice will not satisfy the requirements of Florida's Sunshine Law unless there is proper notice of the time and place of the meeting at which such action is to be taken by the board of county commissioners. Similarly, Florida Statutes section 125.66(3) allows a waiver of the notice requirements by a four-fifths vote of the county commissioners declaring that an emergency exists and that the immediate enactment of an ordinance is necessary. Nevertheless, this section, read with Florida's Sunshine Laws, contemplates that due notice of the time and place of the regular or special meeting at which the emergency enactment is acted upon will have been given.

In sum: In every situation in which some type of notice is required, the content of the notice and the method of promulgating it will be influenced by applicable statutory requirements and by what the particular circumstances may fairly and reasonable dictate or require. If the purpose for notice is kept in mind, together with the character of the event about which notice is to be given and the nature of the rights to be affected, the essential requirements for notice in that situation will suggest themselves. Good faith adherence to those guidelines will assure that the notice requirements of each situation will be satisfied.

———————

Notes and Questions to Consider:

1. The opinion above is not a court opinion. It is an opinion of the attorney general of the state of Florida. Article IV of Florida's constitution authorizes Florida's attorney general to issue formal legal opinions at the request of such public officials on questions relating to the application of state law. The opinion was issued to the inquiring Florida Clerk of the Circuit Court, who may be an elected public official under Article VIII, Section 1(d) of Florida's constitution. Then, in accordance with Florida's Sunshine Law, the opinion became public. What precedential value do these attorney general opinions hold? *Browning v. Fla. Prosecuting Attorneys Ass'n, Inc.*, 56 So. 3d 873 (Fla. 1st DCA 2011) states that "Attorney General opinions are not binding on Florida courts and can be rejected. However, this court has previously held Attorney General opinions are entitled to great weight in construing the law of this State. Furthermore, the fact that two different Attorney Generals have reached the same conclusion with respect to the exact issue now before us lends considerable persuasive influence to their opinions and weighs heavily in favor of our conclusion herein." *Id.* at 878 n.2 (internal citations and quotes omitted).

2. The concept of procedural due process of law, as embodied in the Fifth and Fourteenth Amendments to the U.S. Constitution, imposes upon state governments, at a minimum, the requirements of providing adequate notice and an opportunity to be heard. In light of these minimum federal requirements, are the notice requirements of Florida's Sunshine Law superfluous, or does Florida's Sunshine Law increase these federal minimums?

3. This attorney general opinion number AGO 73-170 concludes by stating: "If the purpose for notice is kept in mind, together with the character of the event about which notice is to be given and the nature of the rights to be affected, the essential requirements for notice in that situation will suggest themselves." To what extent is this an actionable, bright-line rule? FLORIDA MUNICIPAL LAW AND PRACTICE attempts to answer that question as follows:

> Florida's Sunshine Law does not state with specificity what is required in order for the public to have received a timely and proper notice of a hearing. Florida courts have so far declined to create a bright-line rule or an explicit time period for providing notice, but instead hold only that "reasonable notice" of a public meeting is mandatory. Like any legal standard based upon the notion of reasonableness, the actions necessary depend upon the circumstances. For example, the court found that a six-days' notice of a city commission meeting did not violate Florida's Sunshine Law. Likewise, the court found that a three-days' notice constituted reasonable notice of a meeting of the city of Perry's City Council, where it considered renovating and upgrading certain aspects of its utility system. A three-days' notice was again found reasonable when notice of a city's special meeting held on Monday, September 15, was posted at city hall and faxed to the media on

Friday, September 12. However, a 90-minutes' notice of a city commission's special meeting was once found inadequate.

Clearly, the meaning of "reasonable notice" will vary depending on the fact situation, but the purpose of requiring "reasonable notice" is to apprise the public of the pendency of matters that might affect their rights, afford them the opportunity to appear and present their views, and afford them a reasonable time to attend the meeting if they wish. Perhaps, with this purpose in mind, a reasonable notice may be devised based upon the circumstances presented.

Patrick John McGinley, Florida Municipal Law and Practice § 10:4 (2017-18 ed.).

4. Do the notice requirements imposed by Florida's Sunshine Laws entitle the government to receive notice from the Floridian of the fact that the Floridian will make an audio or video recording of a government gathering or meeting?

It was once said, and is oft repeated, that "life is what happens to us while we are busy making other plans." Allen Saunders, Reader's Digest Magazine, Jan. 1957. Can an unforeseen event, or even a perceived emergency, justify the government's omission of the usual advance notice of a public meeting? Consider the decision of Florida's First District Court of Appeal in *Rhea v. City of Gainesville*, 574 So. 2d 221 (Fla. 1st DCA 1991).

Rhea v. City of Gainesville
First District Court of Appeal of Florida, 1991
574 So. 2d 221

Appellant, Darnell Rhea, appeals the trial court's dismissal with prejudice of his amended complaint. We reverse.

The record indicates that, on February 20, 1990, the mayor of Gainesville called a special meeting of the Gainesville City Commission. The meeting was held that afternoon at 3:00 p.m. The minutes of the 3:00 p.m. meeting indicate that all members of the local news media were contacted regarding the special meeting no later than 1:35 p.m. that day. The purpose of the meeting was to respond to the upcoming appointment by the Alachua County legislative delegation of a committee to study the operation of Gainesville Regional Utilities. At the meeting, discussion was had and a motion was passed authorizing the mayor to write to the delegation conveying the Commission's position on the issue and offering the Commission's support.

On March 9, 1990, appellant (a resident of Alachua County) filed a complaint against the City purporting to allege that the February 20, 1990, meeting had been held without proper notice to the public, and was therefore in violation of the "Sunshine Law" (section 286.011, Florida Statutes). The City filed a motion to dismiss for failure to state a cause of action, and the motion was granted with leave to amend.

On May 4, 1990, appellant filed an amended complaint requesting the court find that the meeting violated the notice requirement, that it void all formal action taken at the meeting, and that it award appellant costs pursuant to section 286.011(4). The City again moved to dismiss for failure to allege facts establishing a violation of section 286.011 and, on June 12, 1990, the court dismissed the amended complaint with prejudice, finding "the acts complained of by the plaintiff are not formal actions contemplated within the provisions of Florida Statute 286.011."

Although the statute does not contain a specific notice requirement, it has been held that "reasonable notice" of a public meeting is mandatory in order for the meeting to be public in essence. In *Yarbrough v. Young*, 462 So. 2d 515 (Fla. 1st DCA 1985), this court found that three days' notice of a meeting constituted reasonable notice. In a 1973 attorney general's opinion, it was stated that the meaning of the term "due public notice" would vary depending on the fact situation, but that its purpose was to apprise the public of the pendency of matters that might affect their rights, afford them the opportunity to appear and present their views, and afford them a reasonable time to make an appearance if they wished. Op. Atty. Gen., 73-170, May 17, 1973.

The Florida Supreme Court held that the Sunshine Law covers "any gathering of the members where the members deal with some matter on which foreseeable action will be taken by the board." *Board of Public Instruction of Broward County v. Doran*, 224 So. 2d 693, 698 (Fla. 1969). Further, the Second District has held that "[e]very step in the decision-making process, including the decision itself, is a necessary preliminary to formal action. It follows that each such step constitutes an 'official act,' an indispensable requisite to 'formal action,' within the meaning of the act." *Times Pub. Co. v. Williams*, 222 So. 2d 470, 473 (Fla. 2d DCA 1969).

Under the above authorities, we find appellant's amended complaint to have stated a sufficient cause of action under section 286.011, by making a prima facie showing that the Commission held a public meeting at which official acts or formal action took place, without providing reasonable notice to the public. We therefore reverse the dismissal of the amended complaint, and remand for further proceedings.

F. Restrictions upon the Location of Government Gatherings or Meetings

Florida's supreme court holds: "A secret meeting occurs when public officials meet at a time and place to avoid being seen or heard by the public." *City of Miami Beach v. Berns*, 245 So. 2d 38, 41 (Fla. 1971). Perhaps for this reason, Florida's supreme court interprets Florida's Sunshine Law to impose restrictions upon the location of public meetings held by state or municipal governmental entities.

In the private sector, employers and other entities sometimes hold off-site workshops, company outings that involve both work and entertainment, and the like.

In the public sector, does Florida's Sunshine Law allow such activities? This is the question raised in the case of *Rhea v. School Board of Alachua County*, 636 So. 2d 1383 (Fla. 1st DCA 1994), which proposes a "balancing of interests" test.

Rhea v. School Board of Alachua County

First District Court of Appeal of Florida, 1994
636 So. 2d 1383

Darnell Rhea (Rhea) appeals a summary judgment entered in favor of the Alachua County School Board (Board). The trial court found that the Board's workshop held in Orlando, Florida, on December 3, 1991, did not violate section 286.011, Florida Statutes (1991), commonly known as the "Government in the Sunshine Law." We reverse.

The Board announced, during its regular November meeting, that it intended to conduct a workshop for Board members in Orlando on December 3, 1991, to take advantage of the fact that all the members already would be in Orlando to attend the semi-annual convention of the Florida School Boards Association. The Board also advertised the meeting by placing a detailed notice in the *Gainesville Sun* newspaper on November 26, 1991, stating that the meeting was "a public workshop to which all persons are invited." The Board met on the evening of December 3, 1991, as planned, at the Twin Towers Hotel in Orlando.

Rhea filed a complaint on May 29, 1992, seeking injunctive and declaratory relief against the Board, alleging that the Board violated section 286.011 in holding a Board meeting in a place located outside the geographical boundaries of the Board's district, that is, Alachua County, and more than 100 miles from Gainesville, the Board's headquarters.

Both parties moved for summary judgment. Rhea's affidavit stated that he would have attended the meeting but for the fact it was held outside Alachua County, over 100 miles from him. The Board attached a copy of the minutes of the workshop and two affidavits in support of its motion. One affidavit was from a Board member, who stated that the Orlando workshop was open to the public at all times, that is, the meeting was held in a public meeting room, the room had sufficient space for those in attendance, and the meeting was properly noticed. The second affidavit was from the Board's attorney, who stated that the workshop occurred in a hotel public meeting room, the door to which was left open throughout the session. Moreover, the hotel's staff was advised to direct anyone who inquired about the meeting to the appropriate location.

The Board properly concedes that the school board workshop held in Orlando was a "public meeting" for purposes of the Sunshine Law. The Board, however, denies that any violation of that law took place. Section 286.011(1) provides in relevant part:

> All meetings of any board ... at which official acts are to be taken are declared public meetings *open to the public* at all times, and no resolution,

> rule, or formal action shall be considered binding except as taken or made
> at such meeting.

(Emphasis added.) The mere fact that a meeting is held in a public room does not make it public within the meaning of the Sunshine Law. For a meeting to be "public," it is essential that the public be given advance notice and a reasonable opportunity to attend.

Adequacy of notice is not an issue in this case. Rhea challenges instead the scope of the word "public," as contemplated by the Sunshine Law. Rhea contends "public" refers to the constituency of the public entity that is convening. The "public" for the Alachua County School Board, therefore, would be members of Alachua County, as opposed to members of Orange County or the Florida public at large. Rhea argues that by meeting outside Alachua County, at a hotel more than 100 miles from its headquarters, the Board denied reasonable access to its public.

Section 286.011 does not define the word "public." Applying the plain and ordinary meaning of the word to the instant case, the relevant "public," the community that would be affected by the Board's official actions, is Alachua County. The Alachua County school board represents the entire county, and the relevant community is Alachua County. Thus, whether the Orlando Board workshop was sufficiently "open to the public" depends on whether Alachua County residents had a "reasonable opportunity" to attend the meeting.

Rhea urges this court to fashion an absolute rule which would prohibit any Board workshop from being held under any circumstances at a site more than 100 miles from the usual meeting place. We can envision circumstances which would warrant the conduct of a workshop beyond the county boundaries and perhaps even more than 100 miles from the usual meeting place. Thus, we decline to adopt a bright line test which would resolve every dispute on this issue. Rather, we hold that a balancing of interests test is the most appropriate method by which to determine which interest predominates in a given case. The interests of the public in having a reasonable opportunity to attend a Board workshop must be balanced against the Board's need to conduct a workshop at a site beyond the county boundaries. A significant and obvious factor to be considered in the weighing process is the extent of the distance from the usual meeting place to the out-of-county workshop, an issue which both parties to this cause addressed extensively. We conclude that the greater the distance, the heavier the burden is upon the Board to demonstrate a need for the alternate site. It follows that the shorter the distance, the lighter the burden is upon the Board to justify the out-of-county site.

Another factor to be considered is any good faith action by the Board to minimize the expense and inconvenience of the public in attending an out-of-county workshop. For example, an offer by the Board to provide transportation for the public at the Board's expense, would serve to mitigate the disadvantage to the public, thus enhancing the weight of the Board's position in the matter.

We would ordinarily expect a Board workshop to be held within the county boundaries for reasons of sound logic and common sense. However, when a perceived need to do otherwise arises, the Board must apply the balancing of interests test.

The foregoing factors are not intended to be all-inclusive. Any consideration of the balancing process must focus upon the issue of whether the Board's need for a workshop at a particular geographical site is outweighed by the resulting barriers which tend to prevent public attendance. Thus, any factor or circumstance which impacts thereon must be considered on a case-by-case basis.

When applying this balancing test to the circumstances of the instant case, we conclude that the Board's workshop held at a hotel in Orlando, Florida, on December 3, 1991, did not afford the citizens of Alachua County a reasonable opportunity to attend. There was nothing peculiar about the Orlando site, that is, there was nothing physically located there, nor any activity taking place, which necessitated the Board's observation or discussion at that particular location. The only reason for holding the workshop in Orlando was because the Board members were already assembled at the same hotel for a semi-annual meeting of the Florida School Boards Association. The only advantage to the Board was the elimination of travel time and expense ordinarily incurred by Board members and staff in making the usual trip from home or office to the regular meeting site in Gainesville on an alternate date. We consider this to be an insignificant advantage. When compared to the disadvantages visited upon the public in terms of additional time and expense of travel, we conclude that the balancing process weighs heavily in favor of a finding that the public was denied a reasonable opportunity to attend the workshop. While the failure of the Board to mitigate any of the barriers would ordinarily be significant, the need for the workshop in Orlando was such that we do not believe that even significant mitigation could have overcome the minimal need for the workshop at that site.

We accordingly REVERSE and REMAND for consistent proceedings.

———————————

Notes and Questions to Consider:

1. In *Rhea v. School Board of Alachua County*, the School Board's Orlando meeting was open to the public. So why did the court hold that it violated Florida's Sunshine public meeting requirement?

2. When we examined the Florida Sunshine Law's notice requirements in the subsection of this text above, we questioned whether those requirements created an actionable, bright-line rule. Can the same criticism be raised as to these requirements about the location of meetings?

3. Does the location of the meeting violate Florida's Sunshine Law if the room is too small for the number of people who choose to attend? Citing to an unpublished

opinion from Florida's Fifth District Court of Appeal, Florida Municipal Law and Practice opines that:

> The public entity violates the Sunshine Law if it does not provide ample space for the meeting. This does not mean that the room hosting the meeting must be large enough for an unexpected crowd, but that reasonable access be granted to all regardless of the size of the crowd. For example, in the case of a Water Management District meeting which drew an overflow crowd, the district did not violate the Sunshine Law even though not all members of the public were able to enter the meeting room. The district board was holding its meeting at the board's usual meeting place and therefore had not moved the meeting to inconvenience the crowd. Once noting the size of the turnout, the district chose its largest available room. Also, the district board set up a computer with external speakers so that those who were not able to enter the meeting room could view and hear the proceedings. These types of accommodations yield compliance with the Sunshine Law even when the size of the room exceeds the size of the crowd attending.

Patrick John McGinley, Florida Municipal Law and Practice § 10:5 (2017-18 ed.).

4. Does the location of the meeting violate Florida's Sunshine Law if it is hard to hear the speakers? Consider this advice from the Florida Attorney General's Office as published in the 2012 version of their Government in the Sunshine Manual:

> A violation of the Sunshine Law may occur if, during a recess of a public meeting, board members discuss issues before the board in a manner not generally audible to the public attending the meeting. Although such a meeting is not clandestine, it nonetheless violates the letter and spirit of the law. *Rackleff v. Bishop*, No. 89-235 (Fla. 2d Cir. Ct. March 5, 1990). And see Opinion of the Florida Attorney General number AGO 71-159, stating that discussions of public business which are audible only to "a select few" who are at the table with the board members may violate the "openness" requirement of the law.

Office of Fla. Atty. Gen., Government in the Sunshine Manual Vol. 34 (2012 Electronic Edition).

5. Florida's supreme court describes the Florida Sunshine Law's right of the public to attend government meetings as an "inalienable" right. *Board of Public Instruction of Broward County v. Doran*, 224 So. 2d 693 (Fla. 1969). Does the balance-of-interests test in *Rhea v. School Board of Alachua County* adequately protect a right so cherished as to be declared inalienable?

6. Florida experiences hurricanes and foul weather on a recurring basis. Under Florida's Sunshine Law as interpreted by *Rhea v. School Board of Alachua County*, to what extent would the weather be a permissible factor in setting the location of a government meeting? How would it affect the balance of interests?

G. Sunshine Law Restrictions upon the Location of Government Gatherings or Meetings

Did you notice a strange thing in common between the last two cases we read? Compare the name of the appellant in the case appearing immediately above with the name of the appellant in the case immediately preceding it. See how the later case is called *Rhea v. School Board of Alachua County*, 636 So. 2d 1383 (Fla. 1st DCA 1994)? And the former case is called in *Rhea v. City of Gainesville*, 574 So. 2d 221 (Fla. 1st DCA 1991)? See how both cases begin with *Rhea*? That is because, in both cases, the appellant is one and the same: Mr. Darnell Rhea.

It appears that Mr. Darnell Rhea is no stranger to the courtrooms of Florida. Assuming WestLaw is correct, then other reported decisions appear also to involve Mr. Darnell Rhea, perhaps including *Rhea v. Dist. Bd. of Trustees of Santa Fe Coll.*, 109 So. 3d 851 (Fla. 1st DCA 2013); *Rhea v. Bradford County Prop. Appraiser*, 106 So. 3d 933 (Fla. 1st DCA 2013); *Grover v. Bradford County Sheriff's Office*, 90 So. 3d 277 (Fla. 1st DCA 2012) (listing "Darnell Rhea" as a co-appellant); *Hess v. Sch. Bd. of Alachua County*, 704 So. 2d 523 (Fla. 1st DCA 1997) (listing "Darnell Rhea" as a co-appellant); and *Sch. Bd. of Alachua County v. Rhea*, 661 So. 2d 331, 332 (Fla. 1st DCA 1995) (a subsequent appeal from an order addressing attorney fees entered after remand from 636 So. 2d 1383). More than one of Mr. Rhea's cases involved Florida's Sunshine Law, and more than one of Mr. Rhea's cases involved Mr. Rhea having lawyers who represented him.

How can one Floridian afford to bring so much litigation under Florida's Sunshine Law? Perhaps Mr. Rhea found pro bono lawyers who, like Mr. Rhea, appear to be dedicated to the public interest and are staunch defenders of Florida's constitution.

But it is at least theoretically possible that Mr. Rhea's lawyers were not intending to work for free, and possible that an economic incentive might be present for Mr. Rhea's lawyers. Consider the following remedies, sanctions, and damage awards that may be available upon a successful litigation under Florida's Sunshine Law:

- Entry of a declaratory judgment holding the action taken in violation of Florida's Sunshine Law to be null, void, and unenforceable

- A noncriminal infraction, punishable by a fine not exceeding $500 (awardable against any public officer)

- A second-degree misdemeanor for knowingly attending a meeting held in violation of the Sunshine Law (awardable against any person who is a member of a board or commission or of any state agency or authority of any county, municipal corporation, or political subdivision)

- A second-degree misdemeanor for conduct occurring outside the state that would constitute a knowing violation of Florida's Sunshine Law

- Reasonable attorney fees against the guilty agency

- Reasonable attorney fees against the guilty individuals (i.e., against the individual member or members of such board or commission; provided, that in any case where the board or commission seeks the advice of its attorney and such advice is followed, no such fees shall be assessed against the individual member or members of the board or commission. However, this subsection shall not apply to a state attorney or his or her duly authorized assistants or any officer charged with enforcing the provisions of this section)
- Taxable costs of the litigation (awardable against the nonprevailing party or parties)

Note that these remedies enumerated above can involve attorney fee awards. The entitlement to attorney fees under Florida's Sunshine Law is usually a "one-way street," so-to-speak, in that the court must award fees against the government if the Floridian prevails, but the court must not award fees against the Floridian unless the court finds that action was filed in bad faith or was frivolous.

Notes and Questions to Consider:

1. Do the potential attorney fee awards available under Florida's Sunshine Law improperly incentivize the filing and pursuit of litigation? Or do they merely reimburse victims of violations of Florida's constitution?

2. If you were a Florida attorney, and your potential new client were the victim of a violation of Florida's Sunshine Law, could you represent her on a contingency fee basis? If so, then, would you?

H. Inadvertent Meetings and Unforeseen Gatherings

Even an inadvertent meeting or unforeseen gathering of public officials is subject to the requirements of Florida's Sunshine Law if government business reasonably could be discussed or is discussed. The meeting or gathering might have been intended for another purpose, but nevertheless, can be subject to Florida's Sunshine Law. For example, consider the mediation that occurred under a federal court rule requiring confidentiality at issue in the case of *Brown v. Denton*, 152 So. 3d 8 (Fla. 1st DCA 2014).

Brown v. Denton
First District Court of Appeal of Florida, 2014.
152 So. 3d 8

In this consolidated appeal, the appellants, Mayor Alvin Brown (the Mayor), the City of Jacksonville (the City), and the Jacksonville Police and Fire Pension Fund Board of Trustees (the Board), appeal an order granting summary final judgment in favor of the appellee, Frank Denton (Denton). Finding no grounds for reversible error, we affirm.

In February 2013, Randall Wyse, who was employed as the fire district chief and who also served as the Chief Negotiator for the Firefighters' Union—the Jacksonville Association of Fire Fighters Local 122, IAFF (JAFF)—along with several other plaintiffs, filed suit against the City and the Board in the United States District Court for the Middle District of Florida. In March 2013, the City, the Board, and the plaintiffs voluntarily sought mediation in the federal case. For the next few months, several closed-door mediation sessions were held at a stipulated mediator's office in Gainesville, Florida. Although not parties to the federal litigation, the JAFF and the Fraternal Order of Police Lodge 5–30 (FOP and, collectively with JAFF, the Unions) attended the mediation sessions. No party informed the federal court that the negotiations would entail collective bargaining or that the provisions of the Florida Statutes and Constitution may require such collective bargaining to be conducted in public. There was no public notice of the mediation sessions nor was any transcript made of the proceedings.

The end result of the private mediation sessions was a Mediation Settlement Agreement (MSA), which, on its face, changed the specific, defined pension benefits of City employees in the Unions. The signatories to the MSA included: the Mayor's Chief of Staff, General Counsel for the City, Wyse (who signed "individually" and also as the President/Chief Negotiator of JAFF), the Executive Director of the Pension Fund, legal counsel for the Pension Fund, legal counsel for the Unions, and the President/Chief Negotiator of FOP as well as the remaining federal plaintiffs. The parties were to use their best efforts to obtain approval from their respected officials necessary for implementation of the MSA. It was also undisputed that the parties intended to seek further mediation if the MSA were not adopted.

In May 2013, the Mayor held a press conference announcing an agreement on retirement reform with the Unions. An ordinance was subsequently introduced to the City Council seeking approval of the MSA. In July 2013, the City Council voted down the proposed ordinance and, therefore, decided not to adopt the MSA.

In August 2013, Denton, an editor of THE FLORIDA TIMES–UNION newspaper in Jacksonville, filed a verified amended complaint for declaratory and injunctive relief in circuit court against the Mayor, in his official capacity, the City, and the Board. The complaint alleged that the closed-door mediation sessions constituted collective bargaining negotiations that, under section 447.605(2), Florida Statutes (2013), were conducted in violation of Florida's Sunshine Law as codified in section 286.011, Florida Statutes (2013). The complaint sought a declaration that the MSA was void ab initio and that a Sunshine Law violation occurred and would continue to occur were the mediation sessions allowed to continue. Finally, the complaint sought an injunction prohibiting the defendants from adopting, performing, or implementing the MSA and from engaging in future mediation.

Following motions for summary judgment on the issues, on December 31, 2013, the circuit court entered an order granting summary final judgment in favor of Denton. The circuit court found that it had jurisdiction to determine whether collective bargaining had been held in compliance with the Sunshine Law and to enjoin further violations. The circuit court found that in negotiating the MSA, the City and the Board made changes to the terms of the employee pension benefits, which were a mandatory subject of collective bargaining, and, absent a clear waiver, were required to be conducted in the sunshine. The circuit court found that the Board acted as the Unions' representative and bargaining agent in the negotiations or the Unions themselves participated to some degree in negotiating the MSA. As such, the circuit court held that the federal mediation sessions violated the Sunshine Law, voided the MSA *ab initio*, and enjoined "the parties from conducting further proceedings entailing collective bargaining of the police officer and firefighter pension funds in private outside of the sunshine." The circuit court further held,

> The Local Rules for the Middle District of Florida require that mediations be privileged. Given the parameters of the Sunshine Law and its place within the Florida Constitution, however, it is appropriate that the parties be ordered to inform a federal court that they are obligated to comply with Florida's Sunshine Law requirements and further ordered to take all reasonable steps to seek a waiver of the local federal rules in order to comply with this Court's judgment, the Constitution of the State of Florida, and applicable Florida laws mandating Government in the Sunshine. If, after fully complying with this Court's judgment, the parties nevertheless are ordered by the federal court to conduct mediations in private, the Supremacy Clause of the United States Constitution requires that the parties comply with the federal court's order.

The appellants then individually initiated appeals, between them challenging the circuit court's jurisdiction, its determination that collective bargaining occurred, its determination that the entities present at the mediation sessions had the ability to collectively bargain pension benefits, and its determination that the Board acted as the Unions' bargaining agent. They also argued that the circuit court's order violated the rule of confidentiality of mediation sessions, principles of comity, and the Supremacy Clause. We are not persuaded that any of these issues require reversing Judge Wallace's well-reasoned and sound order.

The Sunshine Law provides a right of access to government. See Art. 1, § 24, Fla. Const.; § 286.011, Fla. Stat. (2013). It was enacted in the public interest to protect the public from "closed door" politics. See *Pinellas Cnty. Sch. Bd. v. Suncam, Inc.*, 829 So. 2d 989, 990 (Fla. 2d DCA 2002) (citing *Wood v. Marston*, 442 So. 2d 934, 938 (Fla. 1983)). The Sunshine Law is to be liberally construed to give effect to its public purpose, and exemptions should be narrowly construed. See *Bd. of Pub. Instruction of Broward Cnty. v. Doran*, 224 So. 2d 693, 699 (Fla. 1969). In addition, it should be construed so as to frustrate all evasive devices. See *City of Miami Beach v. Berns*, 245 So. 2d 38, 41 (Fla. 1971).

Chapter 447, Part II, Florida Statutes (PERA), governs collective bargaining of public employees. Section 447.605(2), Florida Statutes (2013), provides:

> The collective bargaining negotiations between a chief executive officer, or his or her representative, and a bargaining agent shall be in compliance with the provisions of Florida Statutes section 286.011.

Thus, once the collective bargaining process begins, whenever one side or any of its representatives at any time meets with the other side or any of its representatives to discuss anything relevant to the terms and conditions of the employer-employee relationship, such a meeting is subject to the Sunshine Law. *City of Fort Myers v. News-Press Publ'g Co., Inc.*, 514 So. 2d 408, 412 (Fla. 2d DCA 1987).

The matters here were presented to the circuit court in the context of violations of the Sunshine Law. Considering and determining Sunshine Law violations are within the circuit court's purview. See § 286.011(2), Fla. Stat. (2013) (vesting jurisdiction to enforce the public meeting requirements in the circuit courts). While the circuit court made some determinations regarding collective bargaining, those determinations were not dispositive of any issues particularly relating to the collective bargaining process itself so as to fall under PERC's exclusive jurisdiction. Rather, they constituted necessary threshold determinations in the context of whether the mediation sessions triggered application of the Sunshine Law. Cf. *Miami Ass'n of Firefighters Local 587 v. City of Miami*, 87 So. 3d 93 (Fla. 3d DCA 2012) (finding that the union was required to exhaust its administrative remedies with PERC before seeking relief in circuit court where the claims against the City raised violations of both chapter 447, Florida Statutes, and the Sunshine Law).

The circuit court found that the Board acted as the Unions' bargaining agent in the mediation sessions, which, in the context of the Sunshine Law, was a proper finding. The circuit court focused on the fact that section 447.605(2) requires collective bargaining to be conducted in the sunshine when negotiations involve a "bargaining agent." Considering the definition of bargaining agent in section 447.203(12), Florida Statutes (2013), the circuit court found that it included more than just PERC-certified bargaining agents as it also included the certified entities' "representative." Thus, the fact that the Board had not been formally designated as the Unions' bargaining agent did not necessarily mean that it did not function as a representative of the Unions so as to qualify as a "bargaining agent" for purposes of Sunshine Law application.

With regard to whether collective bargaining occurred during the mediation sessions, the circuit court found that the parties negotiated pension benefits, an undisputed mandatory subject of collective bargaining. The circuit court appropriately considered the parties that went in to the closed-door mediation sessions and the end product, which by its terms made changes to employee pension benefits. As further evidence of the changes made by the MSA, the circuit court recognized that the Mayor held a press conference announcing an agreement on retirement reform with the Unions. The fact that the MSA was tentative and conditioned upon further approval does not cure any prior Sunshine Law violation as the purpose of the Sunshine Law is to "prevent at nonpublic meetings the crystallization of secret decisions to a point just short of ceremonial acceptance." *Zorc v. City of Vero Beach*, 722 So. 2d 891, 896 (Fla. 4th DCA 1998) (citing *Town of Palm Beach v. Gradison*, 296 So. 2d 473, 477 (Fla. 1974)). The circuit court's findings with regard to the parties as well as the nature of the mediation sessions were supported by the record such that they should not be disturbed on appeal.

With regard to the remedy ordered, the circuit court took appropriate care in recognizing the federal court's supremacy and the limited scope of the Sunshine Law issue before it. The circuit court narrowly crafted its remedy to respect the interplay between Sunshine Law principals and federal mediation.

We affirm the order on appeal under the broad public policy of Florida's Sunshine Law. We cannot condone hiding behind federal mediation, whether intentionally or unintentionally, in an effort to thwart the requirements of the Sunshine Law. Caution should be taken to comply with the Sunshine Law, and compliance should be the default rather than the exception. See *Gradison*, 296 So. 2d at 477 ("The principle to be followed is very simple: When in doubt, the members of any board, agency, authority or commission should follow the open-meeting policy of the State."). By holding closed-door negotiations that resulted in changes to public employee's pension benefits, the appellants ignored an important party who also had the right to be in the room—the public.

AFFIRMED.

Notes and Questions to Consider:

1. Although the mediation at issue in *Brown v. Denton* was convened by the lawsuit's parties voluntarily, nevertheless, it was convened due to a pending lawsuit in the United States District Court for the Middle District of Florida, was held as part of that lawsuit, and was governed by the Middle District's rules requiring privilege and confidentiality. How, then, did such a "meeting" violate Florida's Sunshine Laws?

2. Could a "meeting" happen inadvertently yet still be subject to the open government and transparency requirements of Florida's Sunshine Laws? Consider the following advice given to local government officials by the Florida Association of Counties:

> The Sunshine Law applies to any function where two members of the same board are present. It applies to all assemblies or meetings, whether structured or casual. . . .

> The Sunshine Law may also apply where there is communication between two or more members of the same board, but no actual meeting. . . .

> The Attorney General's Office has found that private discussions via e-mail between board members about board business are prohibited under

the Sunshine Law. Similarly, the use of a website blog or message board . . . triggers the requirements of the Florida Sunshine Law. . . .

. . . The Florida Attorney General has determined that, while there is nothing prohibiting a board or commission from posting comments on the local government's Facebook page, members must not engage in any discussion of matters that could foreseeably come before the board or commission for official action. Thus, engaging in an exchange of ideas or discussions on a Facebook page or Twitter site could become a violation of the Florida Sunshine Laws.

Herbert W.A. Thiele, *Sunshine, Public Meetings, and Open Records Law* in Florida Association of Counties, Florida County Government Guide (2010).

Chapter 15

Elections, Taxation, Finance, and Education

A. Elections

Article VI of Florida's constitution discusses suffrage and elections. As to the regulation of Florida's elections, Article VI provides:

> SECTION 1. *Regulation of elections.* — All elections by the people shall be by direct and secret vote. General elections shall be determined by a plurality of votes cast. Registration and elections shall, and political party functions may, be regulated by law; however, the requirements for a candidate with no party affiliation or for a candidate of a minor party for placement of the candidate's name on the ballot shall be no greater than the requirements for a candidate of the party having the largest number of registered voters.

Is the election process of any state more infamous than Florida's? In *Bush v. Gore*, 531 U.S. 98 (2000), "[s]even Justices of the [Supreme] Court [of the United States] agree[d] that there are constitutional problems with" Florida's election system. *Id.* at 111. The U.S. Supreme Court held that in Florida, a simple recount "cannot be conducted in compliance with the requirements of equal protection and due process without substantial additional work." *Id.* at 110. The "additional work" omitted by Florida seemed to be quite basic regulatory tasks: "the adoption (after opportunity for argument) of adequate statewide standards for determining what is a legal vote, and practicable procedures to implement them, but also orderly judicial review of any disputed matters that might arise." *Id.* at 110.

Nearly two decades later, has Florida solved its infirmities in the regulation of its elections? Consider the case of *Orange County v. Singh*, 268 So. 3d 668 (Fla. 2019).

Orange County v. Singh

Supreme Court of Florida, 2019
268 So. 3d 668

Respondents' Joint Motion to Recall Mandate is hereby granted. The opinion of this Court dated January 4, 2019, is hereby withdrawn, and this opinion is substituted in its place. *See* § 43.44, Fla. Stat. (2018) ("An appellate court may, as the circumstances and justice of the case may require, reconsider, revise, reform, or modify its own opinions and orders for the purpose of making the same accord with law and justice."); Fla. R. Jud. Admin. 2.205(b)(5). In light of the substituted opinion, we hereby deny Respondents' Joint Motion for Clarification.

We have for review the Fifth District Court of Appeal's decision in *Orange County v. Singh*, 230 So. 3d 639 (Fla. 5th DCA 2017), which affirmed a trial court judgment invalidating an Orange County ordinance. Because home-rule counties may not enact ordinances on subjects preempted to the State and inconsistent with general law, we approve the decision of the Fifth District.

I. Background

. . . On August 19, 2014, the Orange County Board of Commissioners enacted an ordinance proposing an amendment to the Orange County Charter to provide for term limits and nonpartisan elections for six county constitutional officers—clerk of the circuit court, comptroller, property appraiser, sheriff, supervisor of elections, and tax collector. The ordinance provided for the following ballot question to be presented for further approval:

CHARTER AMENDMENT PROVIDING FOR TERM LIMITS AND NON-PARTISAN ELECTIONS FOR COUNTY CONSTITUTIONAL OFFICERS

For the purpose of establishing term limits and nonpartisan elections for the Orange County Clerk of the Circuit Court, Comptroller, Property Appraiser, Sheriff, Supervisor of Elections and Tax Collector, this amendment provides for county constitutional officers to be elected on a nonpartisan basis and subject to term limits of four consecutive full 4-year terms.

_____ Yes

_____ No

The ballot question appeared on the November 4, 2014[,] ballot and was approved by the majority of Orange County voters. As a result, the relevant portions of section 703 of the Orange County Charter were amended (as underlined) to read:

B. Except as may be specifically set forth in the Charter, the county officers referenced under Article VIII, Section 1(d) of the Florida Constitution and Chapter 72–461, Laws of Florida, shall not be governed by the Charter but instead governed by the Constitution and laws of the State of Florida. The establishment of nonpartisan elections and term limits for county constitutional officers shall in no way affect or impugn their status as independent constitutional officers, and shall in no way imply any authority by the board whatsoever over such independent constitutional officers.

C. Elections for all county constitutional offices shall be non-partisan. No county constitutional office candidate shall be required to pay any party assessment or be required to state the party of which the candidate is a member. All county constitutional office candidates' names shall be placed on the ballot without reference to political party affiliation.

In the event that more than two (2) candidates have qualified for any single county constitutional office, an election shall be held at the time of the first primary election and, providing no candidate receives a majority of the votes cast, the two (2) candidates receiving the most votes shall be placed on the ballot for the general election.

D. Any county constitutional officer who has held the same county constitutional office for the preceding four (4) full consecutive terms is prohibited from appearing on the ballot for reelection to that office; provided, however, that the terms of office beginning before January 1, 2015, shall not be counted.

Prior to the November 4, 2014, election, three Orange County constitutional officers—the sheriff, property appraiser, and tax collector (collectively "Appellees")—filed a suit for declaratory and injunctive relief against Orange County, challenging the underlying county ordinance as well as the ballot title and summary. After the election, in ruling on competing summary judgment motions, the trial court upheld the portion of the charter amendment providing for term limits, but struck down that portion providing for nonpartisan elections. The trial court concluded that Orange County was prohibited from regulating nonpartisan elections for county constitutional officers because that subject matter was preempted to the Legislature.

. . . On appeal, the Fifth District affirmed the trial court's judgment. . . . The Fifth District held that section 97.0115, Florida Statutes, expressly preempts the Orange County ordinance requiring nonpartisan elections for county constitutional officers. [*Singh*, 230 So. 3d] at 641–42. The Fifth District reasoned that the Legislature regulates elections generally through the Florida Election Code and "enacted section 97.0115, which expressly provides that all matters set forth in the Florida Election Code were preempted" to the Legislature. *Id.* at 642. The Fifth District further reasoned that chapter 105, Florida Statutes, "set forth provisions and procedures specific to nonpartisan elections," and "chapter 105 did not authorize counties to hold nonpartisan elections for the county constitutional officers that are the subject of the charter amendment at issue." *Id.*

II. The Florida Election Code

Article VI, section 1 of the Florida Constitution provides that "[r]egistration and elections shall, and political party functions may, be regulated by law[.]" *See Grapeland Heights Civic Ass'n v. City of Miami*, 267 So. 2d 321, 324 (Fla. 1972) ("[I]t necessarily follows that 'law' *in our constitution* means an enactment by the State Legislature . . . —not by a City Commission or any other political body."). The Legislature regulates elections through the Florida Election Code, which encompasses chapters 97-106, Florida Statutes (2018). Importantly, the Florida Election Code contains express language of preemption as section 97.0115 states that "[a]ll matters set forth in chapters 97-105 are preempted to the state, except as otherwise specifically authorized by state or federal law." The Florida Election Code further explains that the Secretary of State, as "the chief election officer of the state," is to "[o]btain and maintain uniformity in the interpretation and implementation of the election laws." § 97.012(1), Fla. Stat. (2018).

The Florida Election Code generally contemplates partisan elections. In other words, candidates nominated by political parties in the primary election are to appear on the general election ballot for most offices. *See* § 101.151(2)(c), Fla. Stat. (2018) ("Each nominee of a political party chosen in a primary shall appear on the general election ballot in the same numbered group or district as on the primary election ballot."). In fact, section 97.021(29) (emphasis added), defines a "[p]rimary election" as "an election held preceding the general election for the purpose of nominating a party nominee to be voted for in the general election to fill a national, state, *county*, or district office."

Specifically, section 100.051 provides that "[t]he supervisor of elections of each county shall print on ballots to be used in the county at the next general election the names of candidates who have been nominated by a political party and the candidates who have otherwise obtained a position on the general election ballot in compliance with the requirements of this code." In addition to the candidates nominated by political parties, no-party affiliation candidates, minor political party candidates, and spaces for write-in candidates may be listed on the general election ballot and may compete for the same offices as the major political party candidates in compliance with the Florida Election Code. § 99.0955, Fla. Stat. (2018); § 99.096, Fla. Stat. (2018); § 99.061(4)(b), Fla. Stat. (2018).

Regarding qualifying for nomination or election to county offices in particular, section 99.061(2) (emphasis added) provides that "each person seeking to qualify for nomination or election to a county office . . . shall file his or her qualification papers with, and pay the qualifying fee, which shall consist of the filing fee and election assessment, *and party assessment*, if any has been levied, to, the supervisor of elections of the county, or shall qualify by the petition process pursuant to s. 99.095." The same subsection also states that "the supervisor of elections shall remit to the secretary of the state executive committee of *the political party to which the candidate belongs* the amount of the filing fee, two-thirds of which shall be used to promote *the candidacy of candidates for county offices* and the candidacy of members of the Legislature." *Id.* (emphasis added).

Regarding timing, section 100.031, Florida Statutes (2018), provides that "[a] general election shall be held in each county on the first Tuesday after the first Monday in November of each even-numbered year." Section 100.061, Florida Statutes (2018), states that "a primary election for nomination of candidates of political parties shall be held on the Tuesday 10 weeks prior to the general election." Further, section 100.041(1), Florida Statutes (2018) (emphasis added), lists the following offices, including several county constitutional offices, that are to be chosen at the general election after a primary election:

> State senators shall be elected for terms of 4 years, those from odd-numbered
> districts in each year the number of which is a multiple of 4 and those from

even-numbered districts in each even-numbered year the number of which is not a multiple of 4. Members of the House of Representatives shall be elected for terms of 2 years in each even-numbered year. *In each county, a clerk of the circuit court, sheriff, superintendent of schools, property appraiser, and tax collector shall be chosen by the qualified electors at the general election in each year the number of which is a multiple of 4.* The Governor and the administrative officers of the executive branch of the state shall be elected for terms of 4 years in each even-numbered year the number of which is not a multiple of 4. The terms of state offices other than the terms of members of the Legislature shall begin on the first Tuesday after the first Monday in January after said election. The term of office of each member of the Legislature shall begin upon election.

See also § 98.015(1), Fla. Stat. (2018) ("A supervisor of elections shall be elected in each county at the general election in each year the number of which is a multiple of four for a 4-year term commencing on the first Tuesday after the first Monday in January succeeding his or her election.").

However, while the Florida Election Code contemplates elections for most offices to include candidates nominated by political parties, it also specifies that elections for certain offices must be nonpartisan. Pursuant to section 97.021(22), Florida Statutes (2018), "'Nonpartisan office' means an office for which a candidate is prohibited from campaigning or qualifying for election or retention in office based on party affiliation." Then, chapter 105, entitled "Nonpartisan Elections," provides that judicial officers and school board members are nonpartisan offices. Candidates for judicial offices (or those seeking retention) are "prohibited from campaigning or qualifying for such [offices] based on party affiliation." § 105.011(2), Fla. Stat. (2018). Furthermore, section 105.09(1), Florida Statutes (2018), states that "[n]o political party or partisan political organization shall endorse, support, or assist any candidate in a campaign for election to judicial office." Section 105.035(1), Florida Statutes (2018), also explains that "[a] person seeking to qualify for election to the office of circuit judge or county court judge or the office of school board member may qualify for election to such office by means of the petitioning process prescribed in this section." And section 105.041(3)-(4), Florida Statutes (2018), states that "[n]o reference to political party affiliation shall appear on any ballot with respect to any nonpartisan office or candidate," while "[s]pace shall be made available on the general election ballot" for write-in candidates for circuit and county court judge as well as school board members.

Regarding timing of the nonpartisan elections, section 105.051(1)(b), Florida Statutes (2018), provides that elections for judicial officers and school board members are to be conducted during the primary election with the possibility of a runoff during the general election:

> If two or more candidates, neither of whom is a write-in candidate, qualify for such an office, the names of those candidates shall be placed on the ballot at the primary election. If any candidate for such office receives a

majority of the votes cast for such office in the primary election, the name of the candidate who receives such majority shall not appear on any other ballot unless a write-in candidate has qualified for such office. An unopposed candidate shall be deemed to have voted for himself or herself at the general election. If no candidate for such office receives a majority of the votes cast for such office in the primary election, the names of the two candidates receiving the highest number of votes for such office shall be placed on the general election ballot. If more than two candidates receive an equal and highest number of votes, the name of each candidate receiving an equal and highest number of votes shall be placed on the general election ballot. In any contest in which there is a tie for second place and the candidate placing first did not receive a majority of the votes cast for such office, the name of the candidate placing first and the name of each candidate tying for second shall be placed on the general election ballot.

Additionally, the nonpartisan chapter of the Florida Election Code, chapter 105, specifies that the retention elections of appellate judges are to take place during the general election. § 105.051(2), Fla. Stat. (2018).

Notably, chapter 105 does not include any county constitutional officers as nonpartisan. The specific references to the county constitutional officers in the Florida Election Code are in its more general provisions in which candidates nominated by political parties may appear on the general ballot. Moreover, although the Florida Election Code expressly allows for municipal elections to vary from its requirements pursuant to an ordinance or charter so long as the variance does not conflict with "any provision in the Florida Election Code that expressly applies to municipalities," § 100.3605(1), Florida Statutes (2018), there is no similar allowance for county elections.

III. The Orange County Ordinance Is Expressly Preempted and in Conflict

Orange County contends that the ordinance at issue in this case is not expressly preempted by or in conflict with the Florida Election Code. We disagree.

In *Phantom of Brevard, Inc. v. Brevard County*, 3 So. 3d 309, 314 (Fla. 2008), this Court explained the following standards regarding whether a county ordinance is preempted by or in conflict with a statute:

Pursuant to our Constitution, chartered counties have broad powers of self-government. *See* art. VIII, § 1(g), Fla. Const. Indeed, under article VIII, section 1(g) of the Florida Constitution, chartered counties have the broad authority to "enact county ordinances not inconsistent with general law." *See also* David G. Tucker, *A Primer on Counties and Municipalities, Part I*, FLA. B.J., Mar. 2007, at 49. However, there are two ways that a county ordinance can be inconsistent with state law and therefore unconstitutional. First, a county cannot legislate in a field if the subject area has been preempted to the State. *See City of Hollywood v. Mulligan*, 934 So. 2d 1238, 1243 (Fla. 2006). "Preemption essentially takes a topic or a field in which local government might otherwise establish appropriate local laws and reserves that topic for regulation exclusively by the legislature." *Id.* (quoting *Phantom of Clearwater[, Inc. v. Pinellas County]*, 894 So. 2d [1011], 1018 [(Fla. 2d DCA 2005)]). Second, in a field where both the State and local government can legislate concurrently, a county cannot enact an ordinance that directly conflicts with a state statute. *See Tallahassee Mem'l Reg'l Med. Ctr., Inc. v. Tallahassee Med. Ctr., Inc.*, 681 So. 2d 826, 831 (Fla. 1st DCA 1996). Local "ordinances are inferior to laws of the state and must not conflict with any controlling provision of a statute." *Thomas v. State*, 614 So. 2d 468, 470 (Fla. 1993); *Hillsborough County v. Fla. Rest. Ass'n*, 603 So. 2d 587, 591 (Fla. 2d DCA 1992) ("If [a county] has enacted such an inconsistent ordinance, the ordinance must be declared null and void."); *see also Rinzler v. Carson*, 262 So. 2d 661, 668 (Fla. 1972) ("A municipality cannot forbid what the legislature has expressly licensed, authorized or required, nor may it authorize what the legislature has expressly forbidden.").

There is conflict between a local ordinance and a state statute when the local ordinance cannot coexist with the state statute. *See City of Hollywood*, 934 So. 2d at 1246; *see also State ex rel. Dade County v. Brautigam*, 224 So. 2d 688, 692 (Fla. 1969) (explaining that "inconsistent" as used in article VIII, section 6(f) of the Florida Constitution "means contradictory in the sense of legislative provisions which cannot coexist"). Stated otherwise, "[t]he test for conflict is whether 'in order to comply with one provision, a violation of the other is required.'" *Browning v. Sarasota Alliance for Fair Elections, Inc.*, 968 So. 2d 637, 649 (Fla. 2d DCA 2007) (quoting *Phantom of Clearwater*, 894 So. 2d at 1020), *review granted*, No. SC07-2074 (Fla. Nov. 29, 2007).

In this case, the Florida Election Code expressly preempts the Orange County ordinance requiring nonpartisan elections for its county constitutional officers. Section 97.0115 provides that "[a]ll matters set forth in chapters 97-105 are preempted to the state, except as otherwise specifically authorized by state or federal law." As explained above, the Florida Election Code contemplates partisan elections for most offices, and it does not specifically authorize otherwise for county constitutional officers. Furthermore, article VIII, section 1(d) of the Florida Constitution does not expressly label the election of county constitutional officers as "partisan" or "nonpartisan." Therefore, this constitutional provision is not an exception to the preemption language contained in section 97.0115.

The Florida Election Code contains detailed provisions specific to county constitutional officers and county elections, provisions that are within the portions of the code providing for partisan elections. Section 100.041 states that "[i]n each county, a clerk of the circuit court, sheriff, superintendent of schools, property appraiser, and tax collector shall be chosen by the qualified electors at the general election in each year the number of which is a multiple of 4." *See also* § 100.031, Fla. Stat. ("A general election shall be held in each county . . . to choose a successor to each elective . . . county . . . officer. . . ."); § 98.015 (1), Fla. Stat. ("A supervisor of elections shall be elected in each county at the general election . . ."). Further, section 100.051 expressly provides that candidates listed on the general election ballot are "candidates who have been nominated by a political party *and* the candidates who have otherwise obtained a position on the general election ballot in compliance with the requirements of this code." (Emphasis added.)

In contrast, the Orange County ordinance provides as follows:

> Elections for all county constitutional offices shall be non-partisan. No county constitutional office candidate shall be required to pay any party assessment or be required to state the party of which the candidate is a member. All county constitutional offices candidates' names shall be placed on the ballot without reference to party affiliation.

Singh, 230 So. 3d at 640–41 (quoting amended charter).

The portion of the ordinance that requires elections for county constitutional officers to be held during the primary election conflicts with section 100.041, which requires county constitutional officers to appear on the general election ballot. It also conflicts with section 98.015, Florida Statutes, which separately addresses the election of the supervisor of elections. *See* § 98.015, Fla. Stat. ("A supervisor of elections shall be elected in each county at the general election . . .").

Even if the portion of the Orange County ordinance that requires such an election to be held during the primary election is severed, a glaring and unconstitutional conflict remains. The Orange County ordinance prohibits a candidate for county constitutional office from being referenced on the ballot by party or seeking nomination by a party during the primary election. However, the Florida Election Code expressly provides for nomination of candidates for county office by their respective political parties during the primary election. *See* § 99.061(2), Fla. Stat. (candidates for county offices may qualify for nomination or election by filing the qualifying papers and paying "the filing fee and election assessment, and party assessment"); § 97.021(29), Fla. Stat. (defining "[p]rimary election" as "an election held preceding the general election for the purpose of nominating a party nominee to be voted for in the general election to fill a national, state, county, or district office"); § 100.051, Fla. Stat. (explaining that candidates listed on the general election ballot include those "candidates who have been nominated by a political party"); *see also* § 100.031, Fla. Stat. ("A general election shall be held in each county . . . to choose a successor to each elective . . . county . . . officer. . . ."); § 100.041(1), Fla. Stat. ("In each county, a clerk of the circuit court, sheriff, superintendent of schools, property appraiser, and tax collector shall be chosen by the qualified electors at the general election in each year the number of which is a multiple of 4."); § 98.015(1), Fla. Stat. ("A supervisor of elections shall be elected in each county at the general election. . . ."). Therefore, by banning a candidate for county constitutional office from running by party or seeking nomination by party, the ordinance directly conflicts with the Florida Election Code. And this Court has explained that a local government "cannot forbid what the legislature has expressly licensed, authorized or required." *Rinzler*, 262 So. 2d at 668.

Accordingly, because the Orange County ordinance prohibits candidates from running based on their party affiliation or seeking the nomination of their party during the primary election, which is expressly provided for in the Florida Election Code, the ordinance directly conflicts with the Florida Election Code. It also conflicts with the Florida Election Code's requirement that the candidates for county constitutional officers appear on the general election ballot.

IV. Conclusion

As explained above, the Florida Election Code expressly preempts the Orange County ordinance, an ordinance that is in direct conflict with the Florida Election Code regarding whether candidates nominated by major political parties in the primary election may appear on the general election ballot for county constitutional officers. Therefore, we approve the decision of the Fifth District, which held that the Florida Election Code preempts the Orange County ordinance requiring nonpartisan elections for county constitutional officers.

It is so ordered.

CANADY, C.J., and POLSTON, LAWSON, LAGOA, LUCK, and MUÑIZ, JJ., concur.

LABARGA, J., dissents with an opinion.

LABARGA, J., dissenting.

In [a previous order entered in this same case,] this Court held that the Florida Election Code does not expressly preempt the home rule authority of Orange County to determine that its constitutional officers be elected in a general election without partisan affiliation. I concurred in that decision, and I continue to agree with the analysis and conclusion reached by the earlier majority. Accordingly, I dissent from the current majority's holding that the nonpartisan-election portion of the Orange County ordinance is preempted by the Florida Election Code and to the decision of the majority to recall the mandate issued in this case.

1. Electors and Disqualification

As the term "elector" is used in Florida's constitution, it means someone who is eligible to vote in an election. *See Harris v. Baden*, 17 So. 2d 608 (Fla. 1944). A "disqualification" is something that makes someone ineligible to be an elector. See *id.*

Article VI of Florida's constitution says the following about electors and their potential disqualification.

> SECTION 2. *Electors.*—Every citizen of the United States who is at least eighteen years of age and who is a permanent resident of the state, if registered as provided by law, shall be an elector of the county where registered.

SECTION 3. *Oath.*—Each eligible citizen upon registering shall subscribe the following: "I do solemnly swear (or affirm) that I will protect and defend the Constitution of the United States and the Constitution of the State of Florida, and that I am qualified to register as an elector under the Constitution and laws of the State of Florida."

SECTION 4. *Disqualifications.*—

(a) No person convicted of a felony, or adjudicated in this or any other state to be mentally incompetent, shall be qualified to vote or hold office until restoration of civil rights or removal of disability. Except as provided in subsection (b) of this section, any disqualification from voting arising from a felony conviction shall terminate and voting rights shall be restored upon completion of all terms of sentence including parole or probation.

(b) No person convicted of murder or a felony sexual offense shall be qualified to vote until restoration of civil rights.

(c) No person may appear on the ballot for re-election to any of the following offices:

    (1) Florida representative,

    (2) Florida senator,

    (3) Florida Lieutenant governor,

    (4) any office of the Florida cabinet,

    (5) U.S. Representative from Florida [but see note 1 below], or

    (6) U.S. Senator from Florida [but see note 1 below]

if, by the end of the current term of office, the person will have served (or, but for resignation, would have served) in that office for eight consecutive years.

Notes and Questions to Consider:

1. Note that the language in Florida's constitution in Article VI, Section 4, about term limits violates the U.S. Constitution as applied to candidates for the U.S. Congress. In *U.S. Term Limits, Inc. v. Thornton*, 514 U.S. 779 (1995), the U.S. Supreme Court considered a similar term limit appearing in the Arkansas Constitution. The court affirmed the Arkansas Supreme Court's ruling that the term limits imposed upon candidates for the United States Congress was a violation of the U.S. Constitution. Specifically, the court held that states cannot impose qualifications upon candidates for the U.S. Senate or U.S. House of Representatives in addition to those imposed by the U.S. Constitution. The Tenth Amendment to the U.S. Constitution did not reserve such power to the states. Could Florida impose such term limits in a way that would not violate the U.S. Constitution?

2. Note that the language in Article VI, Section 4, stating "any disqualification from voting arising from a felony conviction shall terminate and voting rights shall be restored upon completion of all terms of sentence including parole or probation," and the language surrounding it, were the result of Amendment 4 that passed in 2018.

2. Primary, General, and Special Elections

Regarding primary, general, and special elections, Florida's constitution's Article VI provides:

SECTION 5. *Primary, general, and special elections.* —

(a) A general election shall be held in each county on the first Tuesday after the first Monday in November of each even-numbered year to choose a successor to each elective state and county officer whose term will expire before the next general election and, except as provided herein, to fill each vacancy in elective office for the unexpired portion of the term. A general election may be suspended or delayed due to a state of emergency or impending emergency pursuant to general law. Special elections and referenda shall be held as provided by law.

(b) If all candidates for an office have the same party affiliation and the winner will have no opposition in the general election, all qualified electors, regardless of party affiliation, may vote in the primary elections for that office.

SECTION 6. *Municipal and district elections.* —Registration and elections in municipalities shall, and in other governmental entities created by statute may, be provided by law.

SECTION 7. *Campaign spending limits and funding of campaigns for elective state-wide office.* — It is the policy of this state to provide for state-wide elections in which all qualified candidates may compete effectively. A method of public financing for campaigns for state-wide office shall be established by law. Spending limits shall be established for such campaigns for candidates who use public funds in their campaigns. The legislature shall provide funding for this provision. General law implementing this paragraph shall be at least as protective of effective competition by a candidate who uses public funds as the general law in effect on January 1, 1998.

B. Taxation

Florida's constitution considers the rights of taxpayers to be fundamental enough to warrant mentioning in the Declaration of Rights—the same preferred placement given to religious freedom, the freedom of speech and press, the right to assemble, the right to work, and the right to due process. Specifically, Article I of Florida's constitution reads:

SECTION 25. Taxpayer's Bill of Rights. — By general law the legislature shall prescribe and adopt a Taxpayers' Bill of Rights that, in clear and concise language, sets forth taxpayers' rights and responsibilities and government's responsibilities to deal fairly with taxpayers under the laws of this state. This section shall be effective July 1, 1993.

Can Florida be called a "tax haven?" Famously, Florida is one of just a few U.S. states that do not impose a state income tax. Florida's constitution contains language restricting taxes and making new tax laws harder to enact. Consider this subsection of Article VII of Florida's constitution:

SECTION 19. Supermajority vote required to impose, authorize, or raise state taxes or fees. —

(a) SUPERMAJORITY VOTE REQUIRED TO IMPOSE OR AUTHORIZE NEW STATE TAX OR FEE. No new state tax or fee may be imposed or authorized by the legislature except through legislation approved by two-thirds of the membership of each house of the legislature and presented to the Governor for approval pursuant to Article III, Section 8.

(b) SUPERMAJORITY VOTE REQUIRED TO RAISE STATE TAXES OR FEES. No state tax or fee may be raised by the legislature except through legislation approved by two-thirds of the membership of each house of the legislature and presented to the Governor for approval pursuant to Article III, Section 8.

(c) APPLICABILITY. This section does not authorize the imposition of any state tax or fee otherwise prohibited by this Constitution, and does not apply to any tax or fee imposed by, or authorized to be imposed by, a county, municipality, school board, or special district.

(d) DEFINITIONS. As used in this section, the following terms shall have the following meanings:

(1) "Fee" means any charge or payment required by law, including any fee for service, fee or cost for licenses, and charge for service.

(2) "Raise" means:

a. To increase or authorize an increase in the rate of a state tax or fee imposed on a percentage or per mill basis;

b. To increase or authorize an increase in the amount of a state tax or fee imposed on a flat or fixed amount basis; or

c. To decrease or eliminate a state tax or fee exemption or credit.

(e) SINGLE-SUBJECT. A state tax or fee imposed, authorized, or raised under this section must be contained in a separate bill that contains no other subject.

Florida's aversion to taxation does not end there. Article VII of Florida's constitution contains the following restrictions:

SECTION 5. Estate, inheritance and income taxes. —

(a) NATURAL PERSONS. No tax upon estates or inheritances or upon the income of natural persons who are residents or citizens of the state shall be levied by the state, or under its authority, in excess of the aggregate of amounts which may be allowed to be credited upon or deducted from any similar tax levied by the United States or any state.

(b) OTHERS. No tax upon the income of residents and citizens other than natural persons shall be levied by the state, or under its authority, in excess of 5% of net income, as defined by law, or at such greater rate as is authorized by a three-fifths (3/5) vote of the membership of each house of the legislature or as will provide for the state the maximum amount which may be allowed to be credited against income taxes levied by the United States and other states. There shall be exempt from taxation not less than five thousand dollars ($5,000) of the excess of net income subject to tax over the maximum amount allowed to be credited against income taxes levied by the United States and other states. . . .

In addition to these restrictions upon taxation, much of Florida's constitution is dedicated to restricting or forbidding the power to tax. Article VII, Sections 1 through 9, of Florida's constitution addresses various forms of taxation. Consider these restrictions upon taxation that read, in relevant part, as follows:

SECTION 1. Taxation; appropriations; state expenses; state revenue limitation. —

(a) No tax shall be levied except in pursuance of law. No state ad valorem taxes shall be levied upon real estate or tangible personal property. All other forms of taxation shall be preempted to the state except as provided by general law.

(b) Motor vehicles, boats, airplanes, trailers, trailer coaches and mobile homes, as defined by law, shall be subject to a license tax for their operation in the amounts and for the purposes prescribed by law, but shall not be subject to ad valorem taxes.

(c) No money shall be drawn from the treasury except in pursuance of appropriation made by law.

. . . (e) Except as provided herein, state revenues collected for any fiscal year shall be limited to state revenues allowed under this subsection for the prior fiscal year plus an adjustment for growth. As used in this subsection, "growth" means an amount equal to the average annual rate of growth in Florida personal income over the most recent twenty quarters times the state revenues allowed under this subsection for the prior fiscal year. . . . State revenues allowed under this subsection for any fiscal year may be increased by a two-thirds vote of the membership of each house of the legislature in a separate bill that contains no other subject and that sets forth the dollar amount by which the state revenues allowed will be increased. . . .

SECTION 2. Taxes; rate. — All ad valorem taxation shall be at a uniform rate within each taxing unit, except the taxes on intangible personal property may be at different rates but shall never exceed two mills on the dollar of assessed value; provided, as to any obligations secured by mortgage, deed of trust, or other lien on real estate wherever located, an intangible tax of not more than two mills on the dollar may be levied by law to be in lieu of all other intangible assessments on such obligations.

SECTION 3. Taxes; exemptions. —

(a) All property owned by a municipality and used exclusively by it for municipal or public purposes shall be exempt from taxation. A municipality, owning property outside the municipality, may be required by general law to make payment to the taxing unit in which the property is located. Such portions of property as are used predominantly for educational, literary, scientific, religious or charitable purposes may be exempted by general law from taxation.

(b) There shall be exempt from taxation, cumulatively, to every head of a family residing in this state, household goods and personal effects to the value fixed by general law, not less than one thousand dollars, and to every widow or widower or person who is blind or totally and permanently disabled, property to the value fixed by general law not less than five hundred dollars.

(c) Any county or municipality may, for the purpose of its respective tax levy and subject to the provisions of this subsection and general law, grant community and economic development ad valorem tax exemptions to new businesses and expansions of existing businesses. . . .

(d) Any county or municipality may, for the purpose of its respective tax levy and subject to the provisions of this subsection and general law, grant historic preservation ad valorem tax exemptions to owners of historic properties. . . .

(e) By general law and subject to conditions specified therein:

(1) Twenty-five thousand dollars of the assessed value of property subject to tangible personal property tax shall be exempt from ad valorem taxation.

(2) The assessed value of solar devices or renewable energy source devices subject to tangible personal property tax may be exempt from ad valorem taxation, subject to limitations provided by general law.

(f) There shall be granted an ad valorem tax exemption for real property dedicated in perpetuity for conservation purposes, including real property encumbered by perpetual conservation easements or by other perpetual conservation protections, as defined by general law.

(g) By general law and subject to the conditions specified therein, each person who receives a homestead exemption as provided in section 6 of this article; who was a member of the United States military or military reserves, the United States Coast Guard or its reserves, or the Florida National Guard; and who was deployed during the preceding calendar year on active duty outside the continental United States, Alaska, or Hawaii in support of military operations designated by the legislature shall receive an additional exemption equal to a percentage of the taxable value of his or her homestead property. The applicable percentage shall be calculated as the number of days during the preceding calendar year the person was deployed on active duty outside the continental United States, Alaska, or Hawaii in support of military operations designated by the legislature divided by the number of days in that year. . . .

Notes and Questions to Consider:

1. Florida's legislature enacted the constitutionally required Taxpayer's Bill of Rights in 1992. It enumerates 21 distinct rights, including:

The right to available information and prompt, accurate responses to questions and requests for tax assistance;

The right to request assistance from a taxpayers' rights advocate who may issue a stay order if a taxpayer has suffered or is about to suffer irreparable loss as a result of an action by the Florida Department of Revenue;

The right to be represented or advised by counsel or other qualified representatives;

The right to seek review, through formal or informal proceedings, of any adverse decisions;

The right to have the taxpayer's tax information kept confidential unless otherwise specified by law;

The right to an action at law within the limitations of Florida Statutes section 768.28, relating to sovereign immunity, to recover damages against the state or the Department of Revenue for injury caused by the wrongful or negligent act or omission of a department officer or employee; (see s. 768.28); and

The right of the taxpayer or the department, as the prevailing party in a judicial or administrative action brought or maintained without the support of justiciable issues of fact or law, to recover all costs of the administrative or judicial action, including reasonable attorney's fees.

See Florida Statutes section 213.015.

2. As seen in the excerpts from Article VII of Florida's constitution that are quoted above, the state lacks the power of ad valorem taxation, and ad valorem taxation is the only valid method of taxation possessed by local governments such as counties, cities, towns, villages, and districts. What is meant by "ad valorem?"

Florida's supreme court, in *Smith v. Am. Airlines, Inc.*, 606 So. 2d 618, 621 n.2 (Fla. 1992), holds that "the term itself means '[a] tax imposed on the value of property.'" The Court notes that "[t]he more common ad valorem tax is that imposed by states, counties, and cities [is up]on real estate." *Id.* However, as noted by the Court, "the definition does not end there, but goes on to add that '[a]d valorem taxes, can, however, be imposed upon personal property.'" *Id.*

3. As to the ad valorem taxation of personal property, note that Florida's constitution at Article VII provides two important exemptions. "Twenty-five thousand dollars of the assessed value of property subject to tangible personal property tax shall be exempt from ad valorem taxation." *Id.* at sec. 3. "Motor vehicles, boats, airplanes, trailers, trailer coaches and mobile homes, as defined by law, shall be subject to a license tax for their operation in the amounts and for the purposes prescribed by law, but shall not be subject to ad valorem taxes." *Id.* at sec. 1.

4. Note that the means by which ad valorem taxation is computed is in "millage rates" which is often abbreviated as "mills." Millage "rates shall be stated in terms of dollars and cents per thousand dollars of assessed property value." § 200.001, Fla. Stat. That means that one mill represents the amount of tax per every $1,000 of a property's assessed value. To convert millage rates to dollar rate amounts, divide each mill rate by 1,000. Then, multiply the result by the property's taxable value to compute the property tax.

5. Estate taxes are imposed by Florida's legislature upon a limited number of estates. It is avoided by the size of the estate, not by the drafting of the estate plan, because "[t]he estate tax is a tax on the privilege of transferring property at death and is charged on the entire estate of the deceased regardless of the manner of its distribution." 53 Fla. Jur 2d Taxation § 1865 (June 2019 update). One commentator summarizes the operation of Estate Tax Law of Florida, Florida Statutes chapter 198, as follows:

> The Florida estate tax is directly linked to the federal estate tax. Therefore, if no federal estate tax is due, then no Florida estate tax would be due.... [A] resident decedent is subject to Florida estate tax equal to the credit for state death taxes provided in Internal Revenue Code § 2011, less any death taxes paid to another state.... [A] nonresident decedent is subject to the Florida estate tax on the pro rata share of the credit for state death taxes provided in IRC § 2011, based upon the ratio of the taxable Florida property over the federal gross estate.
>
> Personal representatives may be called on to: 1) file Florida estate tax returns; 2) request refunds of Florida estate tax; 3) claim credits for prior transfers of tax in related estates; 4) comply with tax recapture provisions; 5) seek deferral of estate tax payment in certain circumstances; 6) receive release from estate tax liens on property; and 7) claim benefits of Florida generation-skipping transfer tax provisions. The personal representative of a decedent's estate is required to file an estate tax return with the Florida

Department of Revenue (DOR) . . . contingent upon the value of the federal gross estate. If the value of the decedent's federal gross estate . . . is less than the decedent's remaining applicable exclusion amount, then the personal representative may . . . file an Affidavit of No Florida Estate Tax Due. . . . This affidavit should be filed in the county in which the decedent owned real estate.

After the personal representative files the Florida estate tax return with the DOR, the DOR will require a copy of the Internal Revenue Service federal estate tax closing letter to determine the amount of the Florida estate tax due. The federal estate tax closing letter provides the credit for state death taxes and the amount of the credit for prior transfers.

Benjamin A. Jablow, *The Ins and Outs of the Florida Estate Tax*, Fla. B.J., January 2005, at 41.

6. Gross receipts taxes may be enacted by Florida's legislature despite Florida's constitution's restriction against personal income taxes. For example, "Florida imposes a gross receipts tax on utility and communications services." 53 Fla. Jur 2d Taxation § 1926 (June 2019 update). As another example, under Florida's "Insurance Code, insurers must pay to the Department of Revenue a tax on insurance premiums, premiums for title insurance, or assessments, including membership fees and policy fees and gross deposits received from subscribers to reciprocal or interinsurance agreements, and on annuity premiums or considerations received during the preceding calendar year." 53 Fla. Jur 2d Taxation § 1980 (June 2019 update). A gross receipts tax differs from a sales tax, which is imposed upon buyers, because a gross receipts tax is imposed upon sellers instead. Florida's supreme court, in interpreting Florida's constitution, holds that:

No provision of the Constitution forbids the imposition of license or privilege taxes on the right to do business in the state and also on the gross receipts of such business. Both of these exactions are in the nature of license or privilege or occupational taxes. . . . By imposing a license tax as a condition precedent to the right to do intrastate business in the state, and also a tax upon the gross receipts of such business, the Legislature has not violated the Constitution or exceeded its powers; and it is not material whether the two taxes are imposed by one or by different statutes, enacted concurrently or at different times. The policy disclosed in the exactions made is not subject to judicial review.

Pullman Co. v. Knott, 69 So. 703, 704 (Fla. 1915). As to a state's authority to do so, considering the federal Constitution's Commerce Clause:

Like other specific taxes, gross receipts taxes involving interstate commerce are . . . valid as long as:

(1) there is a substantial nexus between the taxed activity and the taxing state;

(2) the tax is fairly apportioned to the taxing state in order to avoid multiple taxation of the receipts;

(3) the tax does not discriminate against interstate commerce; and

(4) the tax is fairly related to the services provided by the State imposing the tax.

50 Fla. Jur 2d Taxation § 248.

7. Excise taxes are within the taxing power of Florida's legislature. "An 'excise tax' is any tax that does not fall within the classification of a poll tax or a property tax and that embraces every form of burden not laid directly upon persons or property." 53 Fla. Jur 2d Taxation § 2017 (June 2019 update). Unlike sales taxes that apply to all items not exempted, excise taxes apply only to enumerated items. Whereas sales taxes are computed always as a percentage of the purchase price, excise taxes are computed either on a per-unit basis or as a percentage of the purchase price. For example, "a tax on the purchase of electricity, gas, water, and telephone service is an excise tax." *Id.* As another example, Florida's "doc stamp tax," codified at Florida Statutes chapter 201, taxes documents that transfer an interest in Florida real property such as deeds, and documents containing written obligations to pay money such as promissory notes and mortgages. Such documents are unenforceable unless the doc stamp tax is paid. The tax is paid to the Clerk of Court when the document is recorded, or if unrecorded, is paid to the Florida Department of Revenue. Florida's counties may impose a surtax of their own on doc stamp taxes imposed upon deeds, except for single-family residences. See §§ 125.0167, 201.02, and 201.031, Fla. Stat. "The requirements as to uniformity and valuation do not ordinarily apply to excises. . . . [T]he only organic limitations upon the state are that due process, equal protection, and contract rights must be observed and that interstate commerce may not be burdened nor federal functions interfered with." 53 Fla. Jur 2d Taxation § 2019 (June 2019 update).

8. Sales and use taxes are imposed by Florida's legislature, plus a local option. Local option sales taxes are a surtax that increase Florida's sales tax on a regional basis, thereby making the sales tax rate vary throughout the state. In addition to the local option sales tax, other local option taxes permitted by Florida's legislature include discretionary sales surtaxes, fuel taxes, transient rental taxes, tourist development or impact taxes, convention development taxes, food and beverage taxes, and municipal resort taxes.

9. Does the state of Florida, its agencies, its counties, and its municipal corporations pay taxes to the state of Florida? Florida's supreme court holds that:

> [G]overnmentally owned property is generally excluded from taxation, through either immunity or exemption. An exemption presupposes an ability to tax, whereas an immunity implies the absence of that ability. See *Greater Orlando Aviation Auth. v. Crotty*, 775 So. 2d 978, 980 (Fla. 5th DCA 2000). The state and counties are immune from taxation. See *Canaveral Port Auth. v. Dep't of Revenue*, 690 So. 2d 1226, 1228 (Fla. 1996);

Park-N-Shop, Inc. v. Sparkman, 99 So. 2d 571, 573 (Fla. 1957). Unlike counties, municipalities are not subdivisions of the state and are therefore subject to taxation absent an exemption. See *Greater Orlando Aviation Auth.*, 775 So.2d at 980.

> Article VII, section 3(a) of the Florida Constitution confers on property owned by municipalities an exemption from ad valorem taxation under certain circumstances. To qualify for the exemption in article VII, section 3(a), the property must be both owned by a municipality and used exclusively by the municipality for municipal or public purposes.

Florida Dept. of Revenue v. City of Gainesville, 918 So. 2d 250, 255 (Fla. 2005).

1. Power to Tax

"To impose, levy, and collect a tax is an exercise of the sovereign power" of a state. *Prevost v. Greneaux*, 60 U.S. 1, 3 (1856). States claim an inherent power to tax. As long ago as 1873, the Supreme Court of the United States held: "This power belongs in this country to the legislative sovereignty, State or National. In the case . . . [of state taxation, the] power must be derived from the legislature of the State. . . . [T]he State [can] delegated the power . . . by special statute or . . . vest the power in some other tribunal." *Heine v. Bd. of Levee Com'rs*, 86 U.S. 655, 661 (1873).

The Supreme Court of the United States recognized a state's broad power to tax, subject to certain restrictions, when it held:

> The power of taxation, however vast in its character and searching in its extent, is necessarily limited to subjects within the jurisdiction of the State. These subjects are persons, property, and business. Whatever form taxation may assume, whether as duties, imposts, excises, or licenses, it must relate to one of these subjects. It is not possible to conceive of any other, though as applied to them, the taxation may be exercised in a great variety of ways. It may touch property in every shape, in its natural condition, in its manufactured form, and in its various transmutations. And the amount of the taxation may be determined by the value of the property, or its use, or its capacity, or its productiveness. It may touch business in the almost infinite forms in which it is conducted, in professions, in commerce, in manufactures, and in transportation. Unless restrained by provisions of the Federal Constitution, the power of the State as to the mode, form, and extent of taxation is unlimited, where the subjects to which it applies are within her jurisdiction.

In re State Tax on Foreign-Held Bonds, 82 U.S. 300, 319 (1872).

Federal law imposes additional restrictions upon a state legislature's inherent power to tax. A state tax must be for a public purpose. *Citizens' Sav. & Loan Ass'n v. City of Topeka*, 87 U.S. 655 (1874). The Import-Export Clause of the U.S. Constitution prevents states from levying "any Imposts or Duties on Imports or Exports" and says that "[n]o Tax or Duty shall be laid on Articles exported from any State." Art. I, § 10, clause 2, U.S. Const.

Federal law also restricts a state's power to impose taxes extraterritorially. The so-called Dormant Commerce Clause, or Negative Commerce Clause, found by U.S. Supreme Court precedent to arise from Article I, Section 8, clause 3 of the U.S. Constitution, would mean that no state can impose any tax on interstate commerce unless that tax has a substantial nexus with the taxing state, is nondiscriminatory between in-state and out-of-state activity, is fairly apportioned to tax only the state's fair share of interstate activity, and is fairly related to services provided by the state, with the taxpayer enjoying state-provided services while in the state. *See generally Complete Auto Transit, Inc. v. Brady*, 430 U.S. 274 (1977). However, an out-of-state seller's physical presence in the taxing state is not necessary for the state to require the seller to collect and remit its sales tax. *S. Dakota v. Wayfair, Inc.*, 138 S. Ct. 2080 (2018) (overruling *Quill Corp. v. North Dakota By and Through Heitkamp*, 504 U.S. 298 (1992)).

Florida's constitution requires the state to raise "sufficient revenue to defray the expenses of the state for each fiscal period." Art. VII, § 1, Fla. Const. Of course, this does not empower the state to confiscate wealth, assets, or property without due process of law. *Green v. Frazier*, 253 U.S. 233, 234 (1920) ("The only ground of attack involving the validity of the [state's tax] which requires our consideration concerns the alleged deprivation of rights secured to the plaintiffs by the Fourteenth Amendment to the federal Constitution. It is contended that taxation under the laws in question has the effect of depriving plaintiffs of property without due process of law."). Indeed, Florida's constitution is clear: "No tax shall be levied except in pursuance of law." Art. VII, § 1, Fla. Const.

Florida's supreme court holds that Florida's legislature has an inherent power to tax as follows:

As the Florida Constitution and the case law of this State evidence, the State, through the legislative branch of the government, possesses an inherent power to tax, and a municipality may exercise a taxing power only to the extent to which such power has been specifically granted to it by general law. See Fla. Constitution, Article VII, s 1(a); *Housing Authority of Plant City v. Kirk*, 231 So. 2d 522, (Fla. 1970); and *City of Miami Beach v. Lansburgh*, 218 So. 2d 519 (Fla. 3d DCA 1969). The right to determine the subjects of taxation and exemptions therefrom is within the [Florida] Legislature's prerogative in the exercise of its sovereign power. But this right is subject to the controlling constitutional limitations. *Cassady v. Consolidated Naval Stores, Inc.*, 119 So. 2d 35 (Fla. 1960). This Court has held in *City of Tampa et al. v. Birdsong*, [261 So. 2d 1 (Fla. 1972), that] municipalities may not impose a particular tax unless specifically authorized by general law to do so.

Belcher Oil Co. v. Dade County, 271 So. 2d 118, 122 (Fla. 1972). Stated somewhat differently, Florida's supreme court holds that "taxation by a city[, town, or village] must be expressly authorized either by the Florida Constitution or grant of the Florida Legislature." *State v. City of Port Orange*, 650 So. 2d 1, 3 (Fla. 1994). Florida's supreme court holds also that "the Florida Constitution authorizes municipalities to impose only ad valorem taxation 'except as provided by general law,' see art. VII, § 1(a), Fla. Const . . ." *City of Gainesville v. State*, 863 So. 2d 138, 143 n.3 (Fla. 2003).

When a local government is delegated the power to tax, what restrictions exist upon the use of that tax revenue? This issue was considered by Florida's attorney general in the following attorney general opinion number AGO 93-12.

Florida Attorney General Advisory Opinion
NUMBER: AGO 93-12
Date: February 9, 1993

Subject: Distribution of local option gas tax

To: Honorable J.E. Cooksey, Chairman, Jefferson County Board of County Commissioners . . .

[Question:]

Must a county share local option gas tax levied pursuant to s. 336.025, F.S. (1992 Supp.), with an eligible municipality within the county, when the county is using such tax proceeds to fund infrastructure rather than transportation? . . .

In sum:

A county eligible to levy a local option gas tax pursuant to s. 336.025, F.S. (1992 Supp.), must distribute the proceeds to eligible municipalities as directed therein, regardless of whether the funds are used for infrastructure.

[Analysis:]

Section 336.025, F.S. (1992 Supp.), allows counties to impose a local option gas tax upon every gallon of motor fuel and special fuel sold in a county and taxed under the provisions of Part I or Part II, Ch. 206, F.S. (1992 Supp.). Only those municipalities and counties eligible for participation in the distribution of moneys under Parts II and VI of Ch. 218, F.S., are eligible to receive moneys under this section. [Section 336.025(6), F.S. (1992 Supp.). Part II, Ch. 218, F.S., the Florida Revenue Sharing Act of 1972, allows those units of local government meeting the requirements in s. 218.23, F.S., to share in tax proceeds deposited in the revenue sharing trust funds created pursuant to the act. Part VI, Ch. 218, F.S., allows eligible county or municipal governments to receive a portion of the local government half-cent sales tax provided therein.]

A county may levy the tax by ordinance adopted by a majority vote of the governing body or approval by referendum. Under this procedure,

"[t]he county may, prior to June 1, establish by interlocal agreement with one or more of the municipalities located therein, representing a majority of the population of the incorporated area within the county, a distribution formula for dividing the entire proceeds of the local option gas tax among the county government and all eligible municipalities within the county." (e.s.)

In the absence of an interlocal agreement, the county may, prior to June 10, adopt a resolution of intent to levy the tax. If no interlocal agreement or resolution is adopted, municipalities representing more than 50 percent of the county population may, prior to June 20, adopt uniform resolutions approving the local option tax, establishing the duration of the levy and the rate authorized, and setting the date for a countywide referendum on whether to impose the tax. In the event the tax is levied by county resolution or by uniform resolutions of the municipalities, the proceeds of the tax must be distributed "among the county government and eligible municipalities based on the transportation expenditures of each for the immediately preceding 5 fiscal years." Any newly incorporated municipality which is eligible for participation in the distribution of moneys under Parts II and VI, Ch. 218, F.S., located in a county levying the local option gas tax is also entitled to receive a share of the tax revenues.

The Legislature has made it clear, by the plain language of the statute, that proceeds from the local option gas tax are to be distributed among the county government and the eligible municipalities within the county. Where the Legislature has prescribed the manner in which a thing is to be done, it is, in effect, a prohibition against its being done in any other way.

Generally, local option gas tax proceeds received pursuant to s. 336.025, F.S. (1992 Supp.), may be used by the county and municipal governments only for transportation expenditures. However, s. 336.025(8), F.S. (1992 Supp.), provides that counties with a population of 50,000 or less on April 1, 1992, may use the tax proceeds to fund infrastructure projects, if consistent with the county's comprehensive plan and only after the local government, prior to the fiscal year in which the funds will be used, has held a duly noticed public hearing and adopted a resolution certifying that the local government has met all of the transportation needs identified in its comprehensive plan.

Thus, under the specified conditions, a county with a population of 50,000 or less may use the proceeds from the local option gas tax to fund infrastructure projects. There is nothing in the statute, however, indicating that a county using its gas tax proceeds for infrastructure purposes is entitled to all of the proceeds from the gas tax in the county, to the exclusion of the municipalities eligible to receive distributions pursuant to s. 336.025, F.S. (1992 Supp.). Absent such authority, it does not appear that Jefferson County may alter the distribution of proceeds from the local option gas tax to deprive eligible municipalities of their share of the tax proceeds.

Accordingly, a county eligible to levy a local option gas tax pursuant to s. 336.025, F.S. (1992 Supp.), must distribute the proceeds to eligible municipalities within the county as directed therein, regardless of whether the funds are used for transportation or infrastructure. . . .

———————

Notes and Questions to Consider:

1. Florida's attorney general's opinion quoted above interprets the statute where Florida's legislature gave Florida's local governments the option to levy a surtax (the "half-penny sales tax"). What gave Florida's legislature the right to require the revenue gained from that surtax to be distributed in the way described in the opinion?

2. Is it wise for a state legislature to impose tax and expenditure limitations upon local governments? Consider this commentator's analysis:

> Empirical research on tax and expenditure limitations (TELs) has found several broad effects[:]
>
> *Reduced Role of the Property Tax*
>
> TELs have contributed to the reduction in property taxes as a percentage of personal income and in the role of property taxes in funding local government. . . .
>
> *Increased Role for Nontax Revenue Sources*
>
> TELs appear to have contributed to an increase in the role of assessments, fees (including development impact fees) and user and service charges in funding local governments. . . .
>
> *Shift in Power to the States*
>
> TELs imposed on local governments may have contributed to a shift in power to the states. The fiscal limits on local governments are typically more stringent than those imposed upon the states, and they have made local governments more dependent on state aid. . . .
>
> *Reduction in Local Revenue Growth*
>
> Even with the growth in intergovernmental aid, new taxes, and nontax local revenues, TELs appear to have reduced local revenue growth. . . . [F]or the most part, revenues in states with TELs have grown more slowly than in states without them. . . .

Richard Briffault, *State and Local Finance*, in G. Alan Tarr & Robert F. Williams, STATE CONSTITUTIONS FOR THE TWENTY-FIRST CENTURY, vol. 3, pp. 225–28 (State University of New York Press, 2006).

3. Article VII of Florida's constitution contains the following restrictions and requirements regarding laws requiring counties or municipalities to spend funds or limit their ability to raise or receive state tax revenue:

> *SECTION 18. Laws requiring counties or municipalities to spend funds or limiting their ability to raise revenue or receive state tax revenue. —*

(a) No county or municipality shall be bound by any general law requiring such county or municipality to spend funds or to take an action requiring the expenditure of funds unless the legislature has determined that such law fulfills an important state interest and unless: funds have been appropriated that have been estimated at the time of enactment to be sufficient to fund such expenditure; the legislature authorizes or has authorized a county or municipality to enact a funding source not available for such county or municipality on February 1, 1989, that can be used to generate the amount of funds estimated to be sufficient to fund such expenditure by a simple majority vote of the governing body of such county or municipality; the law requiring such expenditure is approved by two-thirds of the membership in each house of the legislature; the expenditure is required to comply with a law that applies to all persons similarly situated, including the state and local governments; or the law is either required to comply with a federal requirement or required for eligibility for a federal entitlement, which federal requirement specifically contemplates actions by counties or municipalities for compliance.

(b) Except upon approval of each house of the legislature by two-thirds of the membership, the legislature may not enact, amend, or repeal any general law if the anticipated effect of doing so would be to reduce the authority that municipalities or counties have to raise revenues in the aggregate, as such authority exists on February 1, 1989.

(c) Except upon approval of each house of the legislature by two-thirds of the membership, the legislature may not enact, amend, or repeal any general law if the anticipated effect of doing so would be to reduce the percentage of a state tax shared with counties and municipalities as an aggregate on February 1, 1989. The provisions of this subsection shall not apply to enhancements enacted after February 1, 1989, to state tax sources, or during a fiscal emergency declared in a written joint proclamation issued by the president of the senate and the speaker of the house of representatives, or where the legislature provides additional state-shared revenues which are anticipated to be sufficient to replace the anticipated aggregate loss of state-shared revenues resulting from the reduction of the percentage of the state tax shared with counties and municipalities, which source of replacement revenues shall be subject to the same requirements for repeal or modification as provided herein for a state-shared tax source existing on February 1, 1989.

(d) Laws adopted to require funding of pension benefits existing on the effective date of this section, criminal laws, election laws, the general appropriations act, special appropriations acts, laws reauthorizing but not expanding then-existing statutory authority, laws having insignificant fiscal impact, and laws creating, modifying, or repealing noncriminal infractions, are exempt from the requirements of this section.

(e) The legislature may enact laws to assist in the implementation and enforcement of this section.

4. A state's inherent, sovereign power to tax is vested with the state's legislature. Under Florida's constitution, the Florida Legislature's right to impose taxes and to use tax revenues is subject to constraint, including the following constraints benefitting local governments that appear in Article VII:

SECTION 7. Allocation of pari-mutuel taxes. — Taxes upon the operation of pari-mutuel pools may be preempted to the state or allocated in whole or in part to the counties. When allocated to the counties, the distribution shall be in equal amounts to the several counties.

SECTION 8. Aid to local governments. — State funds may be appropriated to the several counties, school districts, municipalities or special districts upon such conditions as may be provided by general law. These conditions may include the use of relative ad valorem assessment levels determined by a state agency designated by general law.

SECTION 9. Local taxes. —

(a) Counties, school districts, and municipalities shall, and special districts may, be authorized by law to levy ad valorem taxes and may be authorized by general law to levy other taxes, for their respective purposes, except ad valorem taxes on intangible personal property and taxes prohibited by this constitution.

(b) Ad valorem taxes, exclusive of taxes levied for the payment of bonds and taxes levied for periods not longer than two years when authorized by vote of the electors who are the owners of freeholds therein not wholly exempt from taxation, shall not be levied in excess of the following millages upon the assessed value of real estate and tangible personal property: for all county purposes, ten mills; for all municipal purposes, ten mills; for all school purposes, ten mills; for water management purposes for the northwest portion of the state lying west of the line between ranges two and three east, 0.05 mill; for water management purposes for the remaining portions of the state, 1.0 mill; and for all other special districts a millage authorized by law approved by vote of the electors who are owners of freeholds therein not wholly exempt from taxation. A county furnishing municipal services may, to the extent authorized by law, levy additional taxes within the limits fixed for municipal purposes.

5. Are the restrictions upon state taxation that are imposed by the U.S. Constitution and by federal law onerous? Consider the opinion of these two commentators:

The authority of the sovereign states to establish and operate systems of taxation for the purpose of collecting revenue to fund state and local governmental functions is affected by [these] provisions of the federal constitution[:]

(1). The Commerce Clause. See, e.g., *Bacchus Imports, Ltd. v. Dias*, [468 U.S. 263] (1984).

(2). The Export Import Clause. See, e.g., *Michelin Tire Corp. v. Wages*, [423 U.S. 889] (1976).

(3). The Supremacy Clause. See, e.g., *Maryland v. Louisiana*, [452 U.S. 456] (1981).

(4). The Due Process Clause of the Fourteenth Amendment. See, e.g., *Standard Pressed Steel Co. v. Washington Dept. of Revenue*, [419 U.S. 560] (1975).

(5) The Equal Protection Clause of the Fourteenth Amendment. See, e.g., *Exxon Corp. v. Eagerton*, [464 U.S. 801] (1983).

(6). The Privileges and Immunities Clause of Article IV, Section 2 of the United States Constitution. See, e.g., *Austin v. New Hampshire*, [419 U.S. 822] (1975)

While this list appears onerous at first glance, the federal courts have historically exhibited great deference toward the states in local revenue matters. This deference has apparently been motivated by federalism concerns.

Thomas C. Marks, Jr. and John F. Cooper, STATE CONSTITUTIONAL LAW IN A NUT-SHELL 244–45 (2003).

2. Nontax Revenue Sources

Florida's supreme court defines a "tax" as "an enforced burden imposed by sovereign right for the support of the government, the administration of law, and the exercise of various functions the sovereign is called on to perform." *State v. City of Port Orange*, 650 So. 2d 1, 3 (Fla. 1994).

Not every financial obligation imposed by a sovereign meets this definition of a "tax." Governmental entities that lack the power to tax may impose financial obligations that do not meet the definition of "tax," if that entity is granted such a power by a Florida Statute, or if that entity possesses Home Rule Powers. To be valid, these non-tax financial obligations must meet certain requirements, as illustrated by the case of *Morris v. City of Cape Coral*, 163 So. 3d 1174 (Fla. 2015) involving a Florida city's imposition of a special assessment upon city landowners for the cost of running the local fire department.

Morris v. City of Cape Coral
Supreme Court of Florida, 2015
163 So. 3d 1174

This case arises from a final judgment validating the City of Cape Coral's special assessment to provide fire protection services. We have jurisdiction. See art.

V, § 3(b)(2), Fla. Const. The City of Cape Coral ("City" or "Cape Coral") passed an ordinance levying a special assessment against all real property in the city, both developed and undeveloped. The assessment has two tiers—one for all property and a second that applies only to developed property. Scott Morris and other property owners (collectively referred to as either "Morris" or "Property Owners") appeal the validation, arguing that the two-tier methodology is arbitrary, [and] that the assessment violates existing law. . . . Because we find that Cape Coral properly exercised its authority to issue a special assessment to fund fire protection services and that the assessment does not violate existing law, we affirm the order of validation.

<h2 style="text-align:center">Facts</h2>

In April 2013, Cape Coral authorized its city manager to hire Burton & Associates ("Burton") to prepare a study relating to a non-ad valorem assessment to fund the City's fire protection services. Burton presented its findings in a report dated June 10, 2013, which the City accepted. The report recommended a two-tier assessment, reasoning that all parcels in the city benefited from fire protection services and that developed property received an added benefit of protection from losses. Burton calculated the costs to maintain the facilities, equipment, and personnel necessary to provide fire protection services on a 24-hour-per-day, 365-days-per-year basis to all parcels in the city (exclusive of Emergency Medical Services costs). These costs represented seventy percent of the total fire protection services cost and were to be evenly distributed among all parcels. The costs for fuel, equipment maintenance, actual response to a fire, and other related operations were associated with protection from loss of structures.

At a June 10, 2013, public meeting, the City read and approved an Assessment Ordinance, which was again read and approved at the July 15, 2013, meeting. The City also passed a Note Ordinance at the same meeting. Thereafter, the Initial Assessment Resolution was adopted on July 29, 2013, and the Final Assessment Resolution was adopted on August 26, 2013. On August 28, 2013, the City filed its complaint to validate the debt under Chapter 75, Florida Statutes. The trial court issued an Order to Show Cause on September 11, 2013, which provided the time and date of the hearing. The Order to Show Cause was published in the local newspaper twenty days prior to the hearing and again the following week.

The trial court held the Show Cause hearing on October 7, 2013. Eight property owners appeared in opposition to the special assessment. The hearing was initially scheduled to last an hour, with each party given three minutes to present its argument. The trial court realized this was insufficient time and extended the hearing for two additional days. . . .

On December 11, 2013, the trial court entered its final judgment of validation. The judgment found, in pertinent part:

> (1) that the City of Cape Coral has the legal authority to issue the bond and assess properties within its jurisdiction as requested, (2) that the intended purpose of the bond is legal, to wit, it shall provide a continuation or

provision of fire safety related service for all affected parcels, and (3) that the issuance of the bond and its related process comply with all essential elements and requirements of law, including reasonable apportionment.

[Four] property owners[] filed a Notice of Appeal with this Court on February 18, 2014.

Standard of Review

This Court's scope of review is limited to: (1) whether the municipality has the authority to issue the assessment; (2) whether the purpose of the assessment is legal; and (3) whether the assessment complies with the requirements of the law. See *City of Winter Springs v. State*, 776 So. 2d 255, 257 (Fla. 2001) (citations omitted).

"[A] valid special assessment must meet two requirements: (1) the property assessed must derive a special benefit from the service provided; and (2) the assessment must be fairly and reasonably apportioned according to the benefits received." *Sarasota Cnty. v. Sarasota Church of Christ*, 667 So. 2d 180, 183 (Fla. 1995) (citing *City of Boca Raton v. State*, 595 So. 2d 25, 30 (Fla. 1992)). "These two prongs both constitute questions of fact for a legislative body rather than the judiciary." *Id.* at 183. The standard to be applied to both prongs is that the legislative findings should be upheld unless the determination is arbitrary. *Id.* at 184. "Even an unpopular decision, when made correctly, must be upheld." *Winter Springs*, 776 So. 2d at 261.

Analysis

. . . The authority to issue special assessments under a municipality's home rule powers was addressed by this Court in *Boca Raton*. In *Boca Raton*, after providing a history of home rule authority, we determined that

> a municipality may now exercise any governmental, corporate, or proprietary power for a municipal purpose except when expressly prohibited by law, and a municipality may legislate on any subject matter on which the legislature may act [with exceptions]. . . . Therefore, it would appear that the City of Boca Raton can levy its special assessment unless it is expressly prohibited. . . .

Boca Raton, 595 So. 2d at 28. . . . Accordingly, . . . there is no question that the City had the legal authority to levy the special assessment.

Further, we have previously upheld the validity of special assessments to fund fire protection services. See, e.g., *Lake Cnty. v. Water Oak Mgmt. Corp.*, 695 So. 2d 667 (Fla. 1997); *S. Trail Fire Control Dist., Sarasota Cnty. v. State*, 273 So. 2d 380 (Fla. 1973); *Fire Dist. No. 1 of Polk Cnty. v. Jenkins*, 221 So. 2d 740 (Fla. 1969).

The Property Owners allege that the benefit from the fire protection services is a general one, and not a specific benefit. To support their argument, the Property Owners rely on our decision in *St. Lucie County — Fort Pierce Fire Prevention & Control District v. Higgs*, 141 So. 2d 744 (Fla. 1962), for their contention that assessments levied on property for maintenance and operation of fire prevention services constitutes a tax. See *Higgs*, 141 So. 2d at 746. In *Higgs*, this Court agreed with the circuit court's finding that a particular assessment to fund fire services was invalid because "no parcel of land was specially or peculiarly benefited in proportion to its value. . . ." *Id.*

However, in 1997, we held that solid waste disposal and fire protection services funded by a special assessment did provide a special benefit. *Water Oak Mgmt.*, 695 So. 2d at 668. Therein, the Fifth District Court of Appeal found Lake County's assessment invalid under this Court's decision in *Higgs* because everyone in the county had access to fire protection services and so was not a special benefit. We found that the Fifth District had misconstrued our decision in *Higgs*, stating:

> In evaluating whether a special benefit is conferred to property by the services for which the assessment is imposed, the test is not whether the services confer a "unique" benefit or are different in type or degree from the benefit provided to the community as a whole; rather, the test is whether there is a "logical relationship" between the services provided and the benefit to real property.

Water Oak Mgmt., 695 So. 2d at 669 (citing *Whisnant v. Stringfellow*, 50 So. 2d 885 (Fla. 1951) (footnote omitted); *Crowder v. Phillips*, 1 So. 2d 629 (1941)). Noting our decision in *Fire District No. 1*, we found that "fire protection services do, at a minimum, specially benefit real property by providing for lower insurance premiums and enhancing the value of the property. Thus, there is a 'logical relationship' between the services provided and the benefit to real property." *Water Oak Mgmt.*, 695 So. 2d at 669. We then clarified that our decision in *Higgs* turned not on the benefit prong, but on the apportionment prong. *Id*. at 670.

In this case, Cape Coral has established that the assessed property receives a special benefit. In the Assessment Ordinance, the City made the following statement:

Legislative Determinations of Special Benefit:

> It is hereby ascertained and declared that the Fire Protection services, facilities, and programs provide a special benefit to property because Fire Protection services possess a logical relationship to the use and enjoyment of property by: (1) protecting the value and integrity of the improvements, structures, and unimproved land through the provision of available Fire Protection services; (2) protecting the life and safety of intended occupants in the use and enjoyment of property; (3) lowering the cost of fire insurance by the presence of a professional and comprehensive Fire Protection program within the City and limiting the potential financial liability for uninsured or underinsured properties; and (4) containing and extinguishing the spread of fire incidents occurring on property, including but not limited to unimproved property, with the potential to spread and endanger the structures and occupants of property.

Likewise, the experts retained by Cape Coral determined that all parcels in the City received a special benefit from the City's fire protection services and facilities. In its report, Burton reasoned that the response-readiness of the fire department benefitted all parcels by raising property value and marketability, limiting liability by containing fire and preventing its spread to other parcels, ensuring immediate response, and heightening the use and enjoyment of all properties. These findings are similar to the reasons we accepted in *Water Oak Mgmt.* See *Water Oak Mgmt.*, 695 So. 2d at 669 ("[F]ire protection services do, at a minimum, specially benefit real property by providing for lower insurance premiums and enhancing the value of the property."). Thus, the facts of the present case lie squarely within the facts of *Water Oak Mgmt.* Only the methodology differs.

The Property Owners question the validity of Tier 1 and Tier 2 of the assessment. In short, the Property Owners argue that the assessment is not properly apportioned. We have instructed:

> To be legal, special assessments must be directly proportionate to the benefits to the property upon which they are levied and this may not be inferred from a situation where all property in a district is assessed for the benefit of the whole on the theory that individual parcels are peculiarly benefited in the ratio that the assessed value of each bears to the total value of all property in the district.

Higgs, 141 So. 2d at 746. In other words, the assessment cannot be in excess of the proportional benefits. *S. Trail Fire Control Dist.*, 273 So. 2d at 384. And, the proportional benefits cannot be calculated by the ratio of the value of the assessed property against the value of all property. See *Water Oak Mgmt.*, 695 So. 2d at 670 (explaining that the decision in *Higgs* turned on whether the land was benefitted in proportion to its value, stating: "the assessment in that case was actually a tax because it had been wrongfully apportioned based on the assessed value of the properties rather than on the special benefits provided to the properties."). However, this Court has also held that "[t]he mere fact that some property is assessed on an area basis, and other property is assessed at a flat rate basis, does not in itself establish the invalidity of the special assessment." *S. Trail Fire Control Dist.*, 273 So. 2d at 384.

To this end, the Property Owners allege that Tier 1 of the assessment is invalid because it equally assesses all property and therefore is not proportional. The Property Owners further argue that Tier 2 of the assessment, being based on the value of any structures and improvements on a parcel, amounts to nothing more than a tax. In other words, the Property Owners allege that the City's chosen methodology is arbitrary and does not properly apportion the costs. We find that the City's methodology is not arbitrary. See *Sarasota Church of Christ*, 667 So. 2d at 184 ("[L]egislative determination as to the existence of special benefits and as to the apportionment of the costs of those benefits should be upheld unless the determination is arbitrary.").

In the present case, the City contracted for a study to determine the best method to apportion the costs of fire services. By adopting the approach recommended in the study, the City has attempted to apportion the costs based on both the general availability of fire protection services to everyone (Tier 1) and the additional benefit of improved property owners of protecting structures from damage (Tier 2).

We have not previously addressed a bifurcated approach to fire service assessments. However, this sort of approach closely resembles the approach we approved in *Sarasota Church of Christ*.

In *Sarasota Church of Christ*, we considered the validity of special assessments against developed property for stormwater management services. There, undeveloped property was not assessed at all, residential property was assessed at a flat rate per number of individual dwelling units on the property, and non-residential property was assessed based on a formula. Specifically, "[t]his method for apportionment focuse[d] on the projected stormwater discharge from developed parcels based on the amount of 'horizontal impervious area' assumed for each parcel and divide[d] the contributions based on varying property usage." This Court held that "this method of apportioning the costs of the stormwater services is not arbitrary and bears a reasonable relationship to the benefits received by the individual developed properties. . . ." *Sarasota Church of Christ*, 667 So. 2d at 186.

The Tier 2 formula for improved properties is akin to the formula in *Sarasota Church of Christ* for determining the assessment against commercial property. Like that of *Sarasota County*, the City's methodology reasonably relates to the additional benefits received by improved properties. The formula contemplates that each improved parcel benefits differently because the cost to replace the respective structure differs. The use of the property appraiser's structure value is reasonable because the property appraiser is statutorily required to use a replacement cost to determine this value. See § 193.011(5), Fla. Stat. (2014). We find that this is a reasonable approach to apportionment and not arbitrary.

As we have stated, "[t]he manner of the assessment is immaterial and may vary within the district, as long as the amount of the assessment for each tract is not in excess of the proportional benefits as compared to other assessments on other tracts." *Boca Raton*, 595 So. 2d at 31 (quoting *S. Trail Fire Control Dist.*, 273 So. 2d at 384). In fact, we have acknowledged:

> No system of appraising benefits or assessing costs has yet been devised that is not open to some criticism. None have attained the ideal position of exact equality, but, if assessing boards would bear in mind that benefits actually accruing to the property improved in addition to those received by the community at large must control both as to the benefits prorated and the limit of assessments for cost of improvement, the system employed would be as near the ideal as it is humanly possible to make it.

Id. (quoting *City of Ft. Myers v. State*, 117 So. 97, 104 (Fla. 1928)). The methodology at issue here was found by the trial court to be "valid, non-arbitrary and considered established insofar as the [opposing parties] failed to present any competent, persuasive evidence to dispute or call into reasonable question [the court's] findings and determinations." A review of the record supports the trial court's determination. . . .

Likewise, the Property Owners have failed to establish that they were denied procedural due process. The Property Owners have not alleged that the City failed to provide notice or denied the Property Owners a meaningful opportunity to be heard. In addition to the validation hearing, the City publicly discussed the special assessment at four public meetings, for which notice was provided. At the validation hearing, the trial court extended the time for the Property Owners to voice their concerns. Based on the foregoing, the Property Owners have not established that they were denied procedural due process. . . .

Conclusion

For the foregoing reasons, we affirm the final judgment of validation. . . .

Notes and Questions to Consider:

1. What is a special assessment, and why would a municipal corporation impose one? Commentators explain that:

> Special assessments and ad valorem property taxes are similar—for example, payment is mandatory and they are both levied on real property—but they are not the same. The central distinction is that "special assessments must confer a specific benefit upon the land burdened by the assessment," while property taxes do not. . . .
>
> . . . A special assessment is validly imposed . . . if it meets a two-prong test established by caselaw. Under the "special benefit" prong, all of the assessed parcels must receive a special benefit from the improvements or services to be financed by the special assessment revenues. Under the "fair apportionment" prong, the cost of the improvements or services "'must be fairly and reasonably apportioned'" among the parcels receiving the special benefit. . . . The question is whether the amount assessed for each property is reasonably proportional to the benefit the property receives.
>
> . . . A city's legislative determinations of fair apportionment are presumptively valid, and courts must review them under a highly deferential standard. A court cannot disturb a city's legislative determination unless it is arbitrary.

Susan Churuti, Chris Roe, Ellie Neiberger, Tyler Egbert & Zach Lombardo, *The Line between Special Assessments and Ad Valorem Taxes:* Morris v. City of Cape Coral, 45 STETSON L. REV. 471, 472–74 (2016).

2. What satisfies the first prong of the two-prong test for the validity of a special assessment, the "special benefit" prong? It is satisfied when "that portion of the community which is required to bear it [must] receive[] some special or peculiar benefit in the enhancement of value of the property against which it is imposed as a result of the improvement made with the proceeds of the special assessment. It is limited to the property benefited, is not governed by uniformity, and may be determined legislatively or judicially." *Klemm v. Davenport*, 129 So. 904, 907 (Fla. 1930). Stated somewhat differently, "the property of the taxpayer [must be] deemed by

the legislative authority to be benefited over and beyond the general benefit to the community, and it is imposed and collected as an equivalent for that benefit and to pay for the improvement in whole or in part. . . . The purpose for which such assessment is imposed must, of course, be public in its nature as distinguished from one designed solely for private benefit." *Atl. Coast Line R. Co. v. City of Lakeland*, 115 So. 669, 683–84 (Fla. 1927).

3. What satisfies the second prong of the two-prong test for validity of a special assessment, the "fair apportionment" prong? *See St. Lucie County-Fort Pierce Fire Prevention & Control Dist. v. Higgs*, 141 So. 2d 744, 746 (Fla. 1962) ("To be legal, special assessments must be directly proportionate to the benefits to the property upon which they are levied and this may not be inferred from a situation where all property in a district is assessed for the benefit of the whole on the theory that individual parcels are peculiarly benefited in the ratio that the assessed value of each bears to the total value of all property in the district.")

4. In *Morris v. City of Cape Coral*, the city lacked the power to tax its residents for fire services. Yet the city created a financial liability for all property owners (Tier 1) and additional liability for owners of developed property (Tier 2) to pay for fire services and labeled it all as a "special assessment." Florida's supreme court held that neither Tier 1 nor Tier 2 met the definition of a "tax," and that both tiers met the legal requirements for a "special assessment." Is this just a matter of semantics? Florida's supreme court holds that the "power of a municipality to tax should not be broadened by semantics . . ." *State v. City of Port Orange*, 650 So. 2d 1, 3 (Fla. 1994). Therefore, a financial liability that meets the definition of a "tax" cannot be levied just by labeling it as a special assessment. "[I]n Florida's Constitution, the voters have placed a limit on ad valorem millage available to municipalities, art. VII, § 9, Fla. Const.; made homesteads exempt from taxation up to minimum limits, art. VII, § 9, Fla. Const.; and exempted from levy those homesteads specifically delineated in article X, section 4 of the Florida Constitution. These constitutional provisions cannot be circumvented by creativity." *Id.* at 4.

5. Why can a Florida governmental entity forbidden to impose a tax still be able to impose a special assessment? In the 1950s, Florida's supreme court held that "obligations secured solely by special assessments do not come within the prohibition of Article IX, Section 6 of [Florida's] Constitution, since, historically, a pledge of special assessments has never been considered to be a 'pledge of the taxing power.'" *City of Orlando v. State*, 67 So. 2d 673, 674 (Fla. 1953). Fifty years later, Florida's supreme court held again that "[s]pecial assessments are not taxes because they confer a special benefit on the land burdened by the assessment." *City of Gainesville v. State*, 863 So. 2d 138, 143 n.3 (Fla. 2003).

6. Sovereign immunity protects Florida from liability to counties, municipal corporations, and districts who might enact a special assessment. Therefore, neither the state of Florida, nor its state agencies, may be liable for a special assessment unless a law passed by Florida's legislature permits it. *City of Gainesville v. State*, 863 So. 2d 138, 143 n.3 (Fla. 2003).

7. In lieu of a special assessment, another funding method used by Florida's governmental entities who lack the power to tax is a user fee. Examples include utility fees for sewer or electric, park pavilion rental fees, permits, licenses, and the like. "User fees are charges based upon the proprietary right of the governing body permitting the use of the instrumentality involved. Such fees share common traits that distinguish them from taxes: they are charged in exchange for a particular governmental service which benefits the party paying the fee in a manner not shared by other members of society, . . . and they are paid by choice, in that the party paying the fee has the option of not utilizing the governmental service and thereby avoiding the charge." *City of Gainesville v. State*, 863 So. 2d 138, 143 n.3 (Fla. 2003). Therefore, a financial obligation meets the definition of a "user fee" if it is an avoidable charge, paid voluntarily, in return for use of a thing or service provided by the governmental entity. To be valid, user fees must meet the following requirements. The fee must bear a rational relationship to the per capita cost of the thing or service. The fee must be used by the governing body toward its expense in owning, maintaining, or providing the thing or service. Home Rule Powers, whether granted by the state constitution or the state legislature, are sufficient authority for imposing user fees. If the governmental entity has Home Rule Powers, then an enabling statute from Florida's legislature is not a necessary prerequisite to charging user fees. *See id.*

3. Just Valuation

Article VII, Section 4 of Florida's constitution requires that ad valorem taxation be calculated by multiplying the millage rate by the "just valuation" of the property. Florida's supreme court holds that "[t]he 'just valuation' at which property must be assessed under the Constitution . . . is synonymous with fair market value, i.e., the amount a purchaser willing but not obliged to buy would pay to a seller who is willing but not obliged to sell." *S. Bell Tel. & Tel. Co. v. Dade County*, 275 So. 2d 4, 8 (Fla. 1973).

The text of Florida's constitution mandates that certain types of land are taxed below their "just valuation" as follows:

> *SECTION 4. Taxation; assessments.* — By general law regulations shall be prescribed which shall secure a just valuation of all property for ad valorem taxation, provided:
>
> (a) Agricultural land, land producing high water recharge to Florida's aquifers, or land used exclusively for noncommercial recreational purposes may be classified by general law and assessed solely on the basis of character or use.
>
> (b) . . . [L]and used for conservation purposes shall be classified by general law and assessed solely on the basis of character or use.
>
> (c) Pursuant to general law tangible personal property held for sale as stock in trade and livestock may be valued for taxation at a specified percentage

of its value, may be classified for tax purposes, or may be exempted from taxation.

. . . (i) The legislature, by general law and subject to conditions specified therein, may prohibit the consideration of the following in the determination of the assessed value of real property:

(1) Any change or improvement to real property used for residential purposes made to improve the property's resistance to wind damage.

(2) The installation of a solar or renewable energy source device.

(j)

(1) The assessment of the following working waterfront properties shall be based upon the current use of the property:

a. Land used predominantly for commercial fishing purposes.

b. Land that is accessible to the public and used for vessel launches into waters that are navigable.

c. Marinas and drystacks that are open to the public.

d. Water-dependent marine manufacturing facilities, commercial fishing facilities, and marine vessel construction and repair facilities and their support activities. . . .

Other than these exceptions to the "just valuation" enumerated in the text of Florida's constitution, what are the guiding principles for Florida's calculation of the "just valuation" of property for ad valorem taxation? Consider the case of *Straughn v. GAC Properties, Inc.*, 360 So. 2d 385, 386–87 (Fla. 1978) involving a property owner whose undeveloped parcel of land lies partially in one Florida county and partially in another.

Straughn v. GAC Properties, Inc.

Supreme Court of Florida, 1978
360 So. 2d 385

The narrow question presented in this case is whether . . . to compel equalization of ad valorem tax valuations where real property situated in one county is assessed on the basis of a higher value than that assigned to allegedly identical property located in another county.

GAC Properties owns a large tract of undeveloped land on both sides of the Osceola-Polk County line. The Polk County tax appraiser valued that portion of the property in his jurisdiction for 1975 at $300 per lot, while the Osceola County appraiser valued the lands in his domain at $560 per lot. GAC Properties sued[, alleging] . . . that the discrepancy violates the "just valuation" requirement of Article VII, Section 4, Florida Constitution. . . .

. . . [We held in previous decisions that] inter-county assessment uniformity is not required by the Constitution, and that variations even between adjacent counties are not a basis for lowering tax assessments which are neither greater than 100% of fair market value nor unequally or improperly determined in relation to other properties within the same county. These principles flow from the constitutional directive that Florida's counties each have their own tax appraiser. . . . [Florida's L]egislature has in recent years endeavored to equalize real property tax assessments among the counties by developing statewide valuation standards, . . . [but] the ability of the legislature to harmonize tax assessments throughout the state[:]

> must remain conditioned by the Constitution's directive that a class of county officers are assigned the primary responsibility to perform assessment functions. At best the legislative goal can be achieved only incrementally through cooperative efforts of the assessors and the Department, and by the development of procedures which will accommodate the responsibilities of both.

[*Spooner v. Askew*, 345 So. 2d 1055, 1059–60 (Fla. 1976).]

We decline to hold, merely on the basis of an allegation that different values have been assigned to adjacent properties of like character in different counties, that a taxpayer can claim a violation of the "just valuation" requirement [of Florida's constitution] . . . .

Notes and Questions to Consider:

1. *Straughn v. GAC Properties* involved just a single parcel of land which happened to lie in two separate counties. One county said it was worth $300, and the other, $500. How did it arise that this one parcel would be assigned two different values using the same applicable law?

2. The opinion references the constitutional requirement that each county have its own property appraiser. Indeed, Florida's constitution provides: "There shall be elected by the electors of each county, for terms of four years, . . . a tax collector, [and] a property appraiser. . . ." Art. VIII, § 1, Fla. Const. How did the property appraiser's status as a constitutional officer impact the outcome of *Straughn v. GAC Properties*?

3. hy did the court not find a violation of the "just valuation" requirement when two different values were assigned to the one parcel, and the one owner paid different taxes to the two counties? Consider the fact that at least one noted treatise opines: "The mandate of just valuation for property taxation has as one of its goals the uniformity of treatment of taxpayers." 51A Fla. Jur 2d Taxation § 943 (June 2019 update).

4. The opinion also references a "recent" attempt by Florida's legislature to equalize real property tax assessments. After *Straughn v. GAC Properties*, how could such a goal ever be achieved?

4. Assessment

What are the procedural requirements for assessing ad valorem taxes in Florida, and to what level of judicial review can these assessments be subjected? These questions are answered well in a decision by a bankruptcy court applying Florida law correctly in an order adjudicating the claim of the Pasco County Tax Collector in the case of *In re Litestream Techs.*, LLC, 337 B.R. 705 (Bankr. M.D. Fla. 2006).

In re: Litestream Technologies, LLC

United States Bankruptcy Court for the
Middle District of Florida, 2006
337 B.R. 705

This is a contested matter, under Bankruptcy Code Section 505(a), to determine the amount of the Pasco County Tax Collector's claim for 2004 tangible personal property taxes—filed in the amount of $61,472.96. The claim is based on an assessed valuation by the County's Property Appraiser.

The Liquidating Trustee for the estate, who is holding sufficient cash to pay the claim, and the purchaser of the debtor's Pasco County operations challenged the claim, arguing that the underlying assessment exceeds "just valuation." For the reasons set forth in more detail below, the Court concludes that the assessment was made in accordance with state law and will not be overturned or modified.

Background

. . . The debtor built and operated fiber optic telecommunications systems (for telephone, cable television, and internet connection) in developing residential communities in Pasco and St. Johns Counties. Its assets consisted of franchise rights in each county, agreements with developers, system equipment and infrastructure, and about 1,100 consumers' subscription contracts [hereinafter called "the Pasco Assets"] . . . .

In April 2004, before the sale of the Pasco Assets, the debtor filed a Tangible Personal Property Tax Return with the Pasco County Tax Appraiser. . . . On the form, the debtor self-reported its "estimate of fair market value" as "$3,343,786," based on its total installed costs. . . .

The Property Appraiser then utilized the "cost approach" to value the assets that the debtor had reported in its 2003 and 2004 tax returns. The Property Appraiser examined these assets by categories and then adjusted the debtor's reported values. . . . These adjustments resulted in an aggregate assessed value of $3,109,878.

The Purchaser and the Liquidating Trustee contend that the assessed value is excessive: they argue that it was error for the Property Appraiser to ignore the price, $3,130,000, which was paid for all of the Pasco Assets. . . .

Discussion

. . . The Property Appraiser is required to appraise all taxable property as of January 1 of the current tax year. Florida Statutes, Section 192.042. The assessment is to be made at "just value." Fla. Const. Art. VII, § 4.

In turn, Florida law requires property appraisers to consider eight statutory factors to arrive at "just value." Section 193.011, Florida Statutes (2004). The property appraiser must consider all of these factors, but has discretion in weighing them and calculating the assessed value. *In re Liuzzo*, 204 B.R. at 238 (citing *Valencia Center, Inc. v. Bystrom*, 543 So. 2d 214, 216 (Fla. 1989)).

Florida law also recognizes a "presumption of correctness" of an assessment, so long as the eight statutory factors have been considered. *Mazourek v. Wal-Mart Stores, Inc.*, 831 So. 2d 85, 89 (Fla. 2002). The burden is on the party challenging the assessment to overcome this presumption, by demonstrating that the property appraiser has failed to properly consider the Section 193.011 factors[:]

> The method of valuation and the weight to be given each factor is left to the appraiser's discretion, and the decision will not be disturbed on review as long as each factor has been lawfully considered and the assessed value is within the range of reasonable appraisals. Because there are so many well-recognized approaches for arriving at an appraisal, the Appraiser's decision may be overturned only if there is *no reasonable hypothesis to support it.*

Mazourek v. Wal-Mart Stores, Inc., 831 So.2d at 91 (emphasis added).

The Property Appraiser did not abuse his discretion by utilizing the "cost approach" to value the debtor's tangible property. . . .

Conclusion

The cost approach, as employed by the Property Appraiser in this case, is an appropriate method of valuing the debtor's cable system. The Property Appraiser did not abuse his discretion in calculating the assessed value by starting with the debtor's self-reported value and adjusting it for depreciation and replacement cost. Therefore, the 2004 tangible tax assessment will not be overturned or modified.

Notes and Questions to Consider:

1. Ultimately, in determining the "just value" of the property, the property appraiser's goal is to determine what a willing buyer, who has a desire to buy but is under no obligation to do so, would pay a willing seller, with a desire to sell but under no obligation to do so, in an arm's-length transaction. Sales of comparable properties, within a short distance of the subject property, are one such indication of that value but those sale prices must be adjusted to account for the unique attributes of the properties. Florida's supreme court notes: "When no actual sale has occurred, [Florida law] requires the assessor to place himself in the position of the parties to a hypothetical sale of the property, to consider all of the factors they would regard as

important in fixing the price of the property and to arrive at an opinion of value." *S. Bell Tel. & Tel. Co. v. Dade County*, 275 So. 2d 4, 8 (Fla. 1973).

2. The opinion makes reference to "eight statutory factors." These are codified in Florida Statutes chapter 193, which, from September 2008 to the present, reads:

> 193.011. *Factors to consider in deriving just valuation.* — In arriving at just valuation as required under s. 4, Art. VII of the State Constitution, the property appraiser shall take into consideration the following factors:
>
> (1) The present cash value of the property, which is the amount a willing purchaser would pay a willing seller, exclusive of reasonable fees and costs of purchase, in cash or the immediate equivalent thereof in a transaction at arm's length;
>
> (2) The highest and best use to which the property can be expected to be put in the immediate future and the present use of the property, taking into consideration the legally permissible use of the property, including any applicable judicial limitation, local or state land use regulation, or historic preservation ordinance, and any zoning changes, concurrency requirements, and permits necessary to achieve the highest and best use, and considering any moratorium imposed by executive order, law, ordinance, regulation, resolution, or proclamation adopted by any governmental body or agency or the Governor when the moratorium or judicial limitation prohibits or restricts the development or improvement of property as otherwise authorized by applicable law. The applicable governmental body or agency or the Governor shall notify the property appraiser in writing of any executive order, ordinance, regulation, resolution, or proclamation it adopts imposing any such limitation, regulation, or moratorium;
>
> (3) The location of said property;
>
> (4) The quantity or size of said property;
>
> (5) The cost of said property and the present replacement value of any improvements thereon;
>
> (6) The condition of said property;
>
> (7) The income from said property; and
>
> (8) The net proceeds of the sale of the property, as received by the seller, after deduction of all of the usual and reasonable fees and costs of the sale, including the costs and expenses of financing, and allowance for unconventional or atypical terms of financing arrangements. When the net proceeds of the sale of any property are utilized, directly or indirectly, in the determination of just valuation of realty of the sold parcel or any other parcel under the provisions of this section, the property appraiser, for the purposes of such determination, shall exclude any portion of such net proceeds attributable to payments for household furnishings or other items of personal property.

§ 193.011, Fla. Stat.

5. "Save Our Homes" Amendment Supplements the Common Homestead Tax Exemption

As you may recall from a prior chapter in this text discussing Florida's common homestead tax exemption, it is not self-executing. Instead, Florida homesteaders must apply for the homestead tax exemption in a timely and proper manner. *See Zingale v. Powell*, 885 So. 2d 277, 285 (Fla. 2004).

Another benefit accruing to homesteaders who successfully apply for Florida's homestead tax exemption is the benefit of an amendment to Florida's constitution known as Save Our Homes. Florida's supreme court notes that "article VII, section 4(c) of the Florida Constitution, known as the 'Save Our Homes' amendment, . . . limits the annual change in property tax assessments on homestead exempt property to three percent of the previous assessment or the change in the Consumer Price Index, whichever is less." *Zingale v. Powell*, 885 So. 2d 277, 279 (Fla. 2004). Stated somewhat differently, Save Our Homes limits the annual increase of the homesteader's property tax to a certain percentage of last year's property tax bill. A subsequent amendment to Florida's constitution makes this tax savings "portable" so that moving from one tax-qualified homestead to another tax-qualified homestead results in bringing the benefits of that prior tax cap to the new homestead. If the former residence is retained not sold, it may qualify for a nonhomestead cap on annual increases. For the homesteader who is a longtime resident, these tax savings can be substantial.

What is required to maintain these ongoing tax benefits? Consider the case of *Orange County Prop. Appraiser v. Sommers*, 84 So. 3d 1277 (Fla. 5th DCA 2012).

Orange County Property Appraiser v. Sommers
Fifth District Court of Appeal of Florida, 2012
84 So. 3d 1277

This case of first impression compels us to consider what the innocent looking phrase, "placed on the tax roll," means with respect to the ten per cent cap on increases in the assessment of continuously owned nonhomestead residential real property that previously enjoyed the status of homestead property. The phrase is found in section 193.1554(3), Florida Statutes (2010). The trial court concluded that the phrase meant that the homestead value of continuously owned residential property remained in place even after the property no longer bore a homestead classification, and that the assessment on the property could not be increased by more than the ten per cent limit found in section 193.1554(3). The appellants, Orange County Property Appraiser and Orange County Tax Collector, appeal the final judgment finding that the 2009 assessed value of the residential property owned by the appellees, Bernard D. Sommers and Arlene P. Sommers, was incorrect. We conclude that the trial court misinterpreted the statute and reverse.

The facts are neither complicated, nor contested. Mr. and Mrs. Sommers owned a home in Maitland, Florida, from 1960 to 2010. They continuously resided in that house from the date of purchase until they moved to a different residence in November 2008. Although they were not living in the home, they still owned it until January 2010, at which time they sold it. It is uncontested that the house was not homestead from the day Mr. and Mrs. Sommers moved out in 2008, to the day it was sold in 2010.

In 2008, the property enjoyed the homestead exemption because it was the Sommers' residence on January 1st of that year. The Property Appraiser assessed the home in 2008 in compliance with the "Save Our Homes" assessment cap contained in Article VII, Subsection 4(d) of the Florida Constitution, and implemented in section 193.155(1), Florida Statutes (2010). The assessment cap on the Sommers' property, assessed as homestead, was three per cent. After applying the homestead exemption with the Save Our Homes cap, the Property Appraiser assessed the taxable value of the Sommers' home for that year at $134,060.

In 2009, because Mr. and Mrs. Sommers no longer lived in the home, the property became a "nonhomestead residential" property for ad valorem tax purposes. The Property Appraiser assessed the Sommers' home as of January 1, 2009, using the just value or fair market value standard, at $279,955. Compared to the taxable value of the homestead in 2008 of $134,060, the assessment in 2009, was an increase in the taxable value of the home of $145,895, or 108.1%.

Mr. and Mrs. Sommers disputed the 2009 assessment and filed a petition with the Orange County Value Adjustment Board ("VAB"), seeking relief. They paid their taxes in full, but under protest. At the VAB hearing before a special magistrate, the Sommers argued that because the Property Appraiser had increased the assessment of their now nonhomestead residential property by an amount in excess of ten per cent of the previous-year assessment, the Appraiser had violated the ten per cent cap imposed on assessment increases for that classification of property under newly adopted Subsection 4(g) of Article VII of the Florida Constitution and section 193.1554, Florida Statutes. The Property Appraiser countered that he properly assessed the Sommers' nonhomestead residential property at its just value for 2009 and that only in 2010 would the Sommers' property be subject to the ten per cent cap on assessment increases pursuant to section 193.1554.

. . . The section of the Florida Constitution governing the valuation of real property for ad valorem tax purposes and a number of statutes concerning the same matter must be spread upon the table in order to understand the arguments of the parties. We begin with the constitution.

The Florida Constitution mandates the just valuation of all property for ad valorem tax purposes. Art. VII, § 4, Fla. Const.; *Bystrom v. Whitman*, 488 So. 2d 520, 521 (Fla. 1986). General law provides, concomitantly, that all real property shall be assessed according to its just value on January 1 of each year. See § 192.042(1), Fla. Stat. Homestead property is treated somewhat differently in that it is benefitted by a number of tax breaks after it is justly valued. See, e.g., § 196.031, Fla. Stat. (2010).

In the event of a termination of homestead status, however, real property must be assessed as provided by general law. Art. VII, §4(d)(6).

Article VII, Section 4(g), of the Florida Constitution considers the subject of nonhomestead residential property. It provides:

(g) For all levies other than school district levies, assessments of residential real property, as defined by general law, which contains nine units or fewer and *which is not subject to the assessment limitations set forth in subsections (a) through (d) [including the homestead exemption]* shall change only as provided in this subsection.

(1) Assessments subject to this subsection shall be changed annually on the date of assessment provided by law; *but those changes in assessments shall not exceed ten percent (10%) of the assessment for the prior year.*

We have added emphasis to certain provisions of this passage because it is informative with regard to the codification by the legislature of its requirements. Section 4(g) essentially defines nonhomestead residential property as being residential real property of fewer than nine units which is not accorded homestead treatment for real property tax purposes. That is to say, in order to be classified as nonhomestead residential property and to receive the benefit of the ten per cent tax increase limitation, a parcel of real estate cannot at the same time be subject to the homestead exemption.

Section 193.1554, Florida Statutes, which implements these constitutional requirements, provides in pertinent part:

(1) As used in this section, the term "nonhomestead residential property" means residential real property that contains nine or fewer dwelling units, including vacant property zoned and platted for residential use, *and that does not receive the exemption under [Florida Statutes section] 196.031* (the homestead exemption).

(2) For all levies other than school district levies, nonhomestead residential property shall be assessed at just value as of January 1, 2008. Property placed on the tax roll after January 1, 2008, shall be assessed at just value as of January 1 of the year in which the property is placed on the tax roll.

(3) Beginning in 2009, or *the year following the year the property is placed on the tax roll*, whichever is later, the property shall be reassessed annually on January 1. *Any change resulting from such reassessment may not exceed 10 percent of the assessed value of the property for the prior year.*

(4) If the assessed value of the property as calculated under subsection (3) exceeds the just value, the assessed value of the property shall be lowered to the just value of the property.

(Emphasis added).

In accordance with the constitution, the statute also underscores that nonhomestead residential real property is a parcel that has nine or fewer units and which does not already enjoy a homestead exemption. Thus, if a property is homestead property, it cannot by definition also enjoy the ten per cent limitation for nonhomestead property. The conflict in the present case, however, stems from the words "placed on the tax roll" found in subsection (3). It says that nonhomestead residential property is subject to the ten per cent increase limitation beginning in the "year following the year the property is placed on the tax roll."

More specifically, the issue before us is whether the ten per cent cap applies to residential property that changes its classification from homestead to nonhomestead, but does not change ownership. Orange County argues that Mr. and Mrs. Sommers cannot enjoy the Save Our Homes cap on their property once it was no longer their homestead. Thus, according to Orange County, once the house became a nonhomestead property, the assessor was required to assess the house at its just or fair market value. Only in subsequent years would it be the beneficiary of the ten per cent cap. Otherwise, the property which is currently not entitled to the Save Our Homes discount, would inherently benefit from that discount if the 2008 homestead value of the house was utilized as the base value, so long as it continued to be owned by Mr. and Mrs. Sommers.

The Sommerses argue to the contrary that section 193.1554(3), Florida Statutes, which governs nonhomestead residential property, does not allow an assessment that exceeds ten per cent of the assessed value for the property for the prior year. They insist that their house has been on the tax roll since 1960, albeit as a homestead property, and that the simple change in the classification of the property does not put it on the tax roll anew. That is, the Sommers say their property was "placed on the tax roll" in 1960, not in 2008.

While we certainly understand the position adopted by Mr. and Mrs. Sommers, we conclude that the legislature did not intend a single piece of residential property to be entitled to both the homestead exemption and tax cap and the ten per cent nonhomestead tax cap at the same time. Article VII, Section 4(g) and section 193.1554(2) simply do not contemplate a single parcel receiving the benefit of both exemptions at the same time. The appellants are, therefore, correct that once the property changes classification from homestead to nonhomestead, it must then be revalued at its fair market value for ad valorem tax purposes before it can receive the benefit of the ten percent limitation in future tax years.

The architecture of the ad valorem tax structure within Florida confirms this conclusion. When real property first becomes classified as homestead, it is "assessed at just value as of January 1st of the year following the establishment of the homestead. . . ." See Art. VII, §4(d)(4), Fla. Const. Analogously, when lands classified as agricultural are diverted to nonagricultural use, or are no longer used for agriculture, or are rezoned to a nonagricultural use at the request of the owner, those lands must also be reclassified and reassessed at just value accordingly. See §193.461(4)(a), Fla. Stat. (2010). In similar fashion, nonhomestead residential property is also required to be assessed at just value on January 1st of the year following a change of ownership or control. See §193.1554(5), Fla. Stat. (2010). The pattern is clear. . . .

Accordingly, the judgment is reversed and remanded for action consistent with this opinion.

REVERSED and REMANDED.

––––––––––

Notes and Questions to Consider:

1. In *Orange County Property Appraiser v. Sommers*, the court notes that the taxpayers asserted that their tax was improperly assessed at too high an amount. Then the taxpayers paid the tax anyway "under protest," and thereafter, initiated formal proceedings challenging the amount of the tax. Why did the taxpayers pay the tax despite believing it to be illegal? Consider this section of Article VII of Florida's constitution:

> *SECTION 13. Relief from illegal taxes.*—Until payment of all taxes which have been legally assessed upon the property of the same owner, no court shall grant relief from the payment of any tax that may be illegal or illegally assessed.

2. The taxpayers' claim was based upon the Save Our Homes Amendment, found in Article VII, Section 4, of Florida's constitution. It caps annual increases of common homestead property tax as follows: "changes in assessments shall not exceed the lower of the following: (a). Three percent (3%) of the assessment for the prior year. (b). The percent change in the Consumer Price Index . . . as initially reported by the United States Department of Labor, Bureau of Labor Statistics." What do you believe motivated Florida's electors to enact this amendment to Florida's constitution?

3. Regarding common homestead tax property that becomes nonhomestead and the effect upon the common homestead tax exemption, Florida's constitution states: "In the event of a termination of homestead status, the property shall be assessed as provided by general law." Art. VII, sec. 4, Fla. Const. Why not leave the common homestead tax exemption in place despite the termination of the homestead status?

4. Regarding the effect of home improvements upon the common homestead tax exemption, Florida's constitution states: "Changes, additions, reductions, or improvements to homestead property shall be assessed as provided for by general law; provided, however, after the adjustment for any change, addition, reduction, or improvement, the property shall be assessed as provided in this subsection." Art. VII, sec. 4, Fla. Const. It also provides:

> A county may, in the manner prescribed by general law, provide for a reduction in the assessed value of homestead property to the extent of any increase in the assessed value of that property which results from the construction or reconstruction of the property for the purpose of providing living quarters for one or more natural or adoptive grandparents or parents of the owner of the property or of the owner's spouse if at least one of the grandparents or parents for whom the living quarters are provided is

62 years of age or older. Such a reduction may not exceed the lesser of the following:

(1) The increase in assessed value resulting from construction or reconstruction of the property.

(2) Twenty percent of the total assessed value of the property as improved.

Art. VII, sec. 4, Fla. Const.

5. Florida's constitution contains other homestead and nonhomestead tax benefits reducing ad valorem taxation in Article VII, Section 4, subsections (d) through (h); and Article VII, Section 6, subsections (a) through (h). Many address specific groups of people. For example, consider the following subsections of Article VII, Section 6:

SECTION 6. Homestead exemptions. —

. . . (c) By general law and subject to conditions specified therein, the Legislature may provide to renters, who are permanent residents, ad valorem tax relief on all ad valorem tax levies. Such ad valorem tax relief shall be in the form and amount established by general law.

(d) The legislature may, by general law, allow counties or municipalities, for the purpose of their respective tax levies and subject to the provisions of general law, to grant either or both of the following additional homestead tax exemptions:

(1) An exemption not exceeding fifty thousand dollars to a person who has the legal or equitable title to real estate and maintains thereon the permanent residence of the owner, who has attained age sixty-five, and whose household income, as defined by general law, does not exceed twenty thousand dollars; or

(2) An exemption equal to the assessed value of the property to a person who has the legal or equitable title to real estate with a just value less than two hundred and fifty thousand dollars, as determined in the first tax year that the owner applies and is eligible for the exemption, and who has maintained thereon the permanent residence of the owner for not less than twenty-five years, who has attained age sixty-five, and whose household income does not exceed the income limitation prescribed in paragraph (1).

The general law must allow counties and municipalities to grant these additional exemptions, within the limits prescribed in this subsection, by ordinance adopted in the manner prescribed by general law, and must provide for the periodic adjustment of the income limitation prescribed in this subsection for changes in the cost of living.

(e) Each veteran who is age 65 or older who is partially or totally permanently disabled shall receive a discount from the amount of the ad valorem tax otherwise owed on homestead property the veteran owns and resides in if the disability was combat related and the veteran was honorably discharged upon separation from military service. The discount shall be in a percentage equal to the percentage of the veteran's permanent, service-connected disability as determined by the United States Department of Veterans Affairs. To qualify for the discount granted by this subsection, an applicant must submit to the county property appraiser, by March 1, an official letter from the United States Department of Veterans Affairs stating the percentage of the veteran's service-connected disability and such evidence that reasonably identifies the disability as combat related and a copy of the veteran's honorable discharge. If the property appraiser denies the request for a discount, the appraiser must notify the applicant in writing of the reasons for the denial, and the veteran may reapply. The Legislature may, by general law, waive the annual application requirement in subsequent years. This subsection is self-executing and does not require implementing legislation.

(f) By general law and subject to conditions and limitations specified therein, the Legislature may provide ad valorem tax relief equal to the total amount or a portion of the ad valorem tax otherwise owed on homestead property to:

(1) The surviving spouse of a veteran who died from service-connected causes while on active duty as a member of the United States Armed Forces.

(2) The surviving spouse of a first responder who died in the line of duty.

(3) A first responder who is totally and permanently disabled as a result of an injury or injuries sustained in the line of duty. Causal connection between a disability and service in the line of duty shall not be presumed but must be determined as provided by general law. For purposes of this paragraph, the term "disability" does not include a chronic condition or chronic disease, unless the injury sustained in the line of duty was the sole cause of the chronic condition or chronic disease.

As used in this subsection and as further defined by general law, the term "first responder" means a law enforcement officer, a correctional officer, a firefighter, an emergency medical technician, or a paramedic, and the term "in the line of duty" means arising out of and in the actual performance of duty required by employment as a first responder.

C. Finance

Florida's constitution, at Article VII, Sections 10 through 19, imposes restrictions on Florida's ability to incur debt, pledge credit, or finance projects. State constitutions typically include such restrictions, even though the U.S. Constitution does not. As one commentator noted:

This state constitutional focus on governmental finance differs sharply from the federal Constitution's relative indifference to public finance. The Constitution simply authorizes Congress "to lay and collect taxes, duties, imposts, and excises to pay the debts and provide for the common defense and the general welfare of the United States" and "to borrow money on the credit of the United States." Beyond those brief statements, the Constitution imposes two minor procedural constraints on federal spending and taxation: All bills for raising revenue must originate in the House of Representatives, and no money may be drawn from the Treasury "but in consequences of appropriations made by law; and a regular statement and account of the receipts and expenditures of all public money shall be published from time to time." There are also a handful of substantive constitutional constraints on federal taxation: "All duties, imposts, and excises shall be uniform throughout the United States." Taxes and duties on exports are barred; so, too, direct or capitation taxes are barred unless apportioned among the states according to population. The apportionment requirement, however, was modified by the 16th Amendment to authorize federal taxation on incomes without regard to apportionment. There are no constitutional limits on borrowing at all.

Where the federal Constitution primarily empowers Congress to raise and spend money, the state constitutions operate to limit state and local government financial support for private sector activities, and to protect state and local taxpayers from the burdens of state and local debt and taxation. In effect, they constitutionalize both the separation of the public from the private sector and the norm of financially limited government.

Richard Briffault, *State and Local Finance*, in G. Alan Tarr & Robert F. Williams, STATE CONSTITUTIONS FOR THE TWENTY-FIRST CENTURY, vol. 3, pp. 211–12 (State University of New York Press, 2006).

It is with this background that we examine Florida's constitution's Article VII, its restrictions upon pledging credit, and its requirements for state and local bonds.

1. Permissible Purposes for Pledging Credit

Florida's constitution restricts Florida's state and local governments from pledging credit in Article VII, which, in relevant part, provides:

> SECTION 10. Pledging credit. — Neither the state nor any county, school district, municipality, special district, or agency of any of them, shall become a joint owner with, or stockholder of, or give, lend or use its taxing power or credit to aid any corporation, association, partnership or person; but this shall not prohibit laws authorizing:

(a) the investment of public trust funds;

(b) the investment of other public funds in obligations of, or insured by, the United States or any of its instrumentalities;

(c) the issuance and sale by any county, municipality, special district or other local governmental body of (1) revenue bonds to finance or refinance the cost of capital projects for airports or port facilities, or (2) revenue bonds to finance or refinance the cost of capital projects for industrial or manufacturing plants to the extent that the interest thereon is exempt from income taxes under the then existing laws of the United States, when, in either case, the revenue bonds are payable solely from revenue derived from the sale, operation or leasing of the projects. If any project so financed, or any part thereof, is occupied or operated by any private corporation, association, partnership or person pursuant to contract or lease with the issuing body, the property interest created by such contract or lease shall be subject to taxation to the same extent as other privately owned property.

(d) a municipality, county, special district, or agency of any of them, being a joint owner of, giving, or lending or using its taxing power or credit for the joint ownership, construction and operation of electrical energy generating or transmission facilities with any corporation, association, partnership or person.

What restrictions upon government financing result from these clauses in Florida's constitution? The answer to that question is well-illustrated by the following case of *N. Palm Beach County Water Control Dist. v. State*, 604 So. 2d 440, 447 (Fla. 1992) where the dissent took issue with Florida's supreme court's approval of the public financing of a private country club's multi-million dollar "Caribbean island" landscaping and the public financing of the guard gates erected to prevent the public from enjoying the country club's landscaping.

Northern Palm Beach County Water Control District v. State of Florida

Supreme Court of Florida, 1992
604 So. 2d 440

This is an appeal from a final judgment which declined to validate water control and improvement bonds proposed to be issued by the Northern Palm Beach Water Control District (District). We have jurisdiction pursuant to article V, section 3(b)(2) of the Florida Constitution, and chapter 75, Florida Statutes (1989).

The District is a drainage district organized and existing under [the] Laws of Florida. . . . The District sought validation of water control and improvement bonds to finance on-site road improvements in . . . the JDM Country Club[. It] is being developed by Hansen-Florida II, Inc., and will include single family residences, multifamily housing, park areas, and three golf courses.

The . . . improvements, which are the subject of this appeal, include interior or on-site road improvements such as paving, striping, signs, landscaping, irrigation, bridges, an overpass, culverts, street lighting, security gatehouses, and a secondary drainage system consisting of storm drain pipes, inlets, manholes and surface drainage. . . .

In December 1989, the Board of Supervisors of the District adopted a general bond resolution which authorized the issuance of Water Control and Improvement Bonds . . . in a principal amount not to exceed $16,312,500. The bond resolution provided that the bonds "shall not be general obligations or indebtedness" of the District, but instead are "special obligations payable solely" from, and secured by, a first lien and pledge of the proceeds of the drainage tax levied on the lands in [the JDM Country Club]. In March 1990, the Board of Supervisors adopted a resolution levying a $42,625,000 drainage tax on the lands in [the JDM Country Club]. . . . The amount levied consisted of an initial assessment of $18,125,000, plus the $24,500,000 interest estimated to accrue on the bonds.

After the bond validation hearing, the circuit court entered a final judgment which declined to validate the bonds because "[t]he intended use of the proceeds of this bond issue serves no valid public purpose." . . .

The scope of judicial inquiry in bond validation proceedings is limited to the following issues: 1) determining if the public body has the authority to issue the bonds; 2) determining if the purpose of the obligation is legal; and 3) ensuring that the bond issuance complies with the requirements of law. *Taylor v. Lee County*, 498 So.2d 424 (Fla. 1986). Only two questions are presented for our consideration here: 1) whether the revenue bond proceeds will be used for a valid public purpose, and 2) whether the District has complied with the requirements of its enabling legislation in issuing the bonds.

As to the first issue, the State contends that these bonds violate article VII, section 10 of the Florida Constitution, which prohibits the District from using its taxing power or pledging public credit to aid private enterprise, and that no valid public purpose can be served by financing the construction of roadways within a private development where public access will be limited by security gatehouses. The District asserts that in enacting chapters 59–994 and 89–462 the legislature found a public purpose in designating roads for the exclusive use and benefit of a unit of development and its residents.

Article VII, section 10 of the Florida Constitution prohibits the state and its subdivisions, including special districts such as this water control district, from using its taxing power or pledging public credit to aid any private person or entity. However, if the project falls within one of the four subsections of article VII, section 10, then no constitutional prohibition is involved. *See Linscott v. Orange County Indus. Dev. Auth.*, 443 So. 2d 97 (Fla. 1983). The on-site road improvements planned for [the JDM Country Club] do not fall within these four subsections. Thus, in order to determine if the bonds run afoul of the constitution, we must first determine whether the District's taxing power or pledge of credit is involved. If either is involved, then the improvements must serve a paramount public purpose. *See Orange County Indus. Dev. Auth. v. State*, 427 So. 2d 174 (Fla. 1983). However, if we conclude that neither is involved, then the paramount public purpose test is not applicable and "it is enough to show only that a public purpose is served." *Linscott*, 443 So.2d at 101. . . .

As to the public purposes actually served by these bonds, we note that the roadway improvements at issue will provide access to the water management facilities and aid in the development of the reclaimed lands. However, the fact that public access to the roads will be limited raises a question of whether the stated public purposes are only incidental to a primary private purpose, the development of [the JDM Country Club] by Hansen-Florida II, Inc. "A broad, general public purpose . . . will not constitutionally sustain a project that in terms of direct, actual use, is purely a private enterprise." *Orange County*, 427 So. 2d at 179. In *Orange County*, the Court found that the expansion of a television station's broadcast facilities did not serve a paramount public purpose even though the public would receive a number of benefits from the proposed expansion. However, the Court also noted that the presence of public ownership would be a significant factor in a finding of public purpose. *Id.*

In this case, the District will retain ownership of the roadways in question. This public ownership coupled with the legislative declaration of public purpose contained in the District's enabling legislation leads us to the conclusion that the on-site road improvements serve a public purpose. Thus, the proposed water control and improvement bonds are not prohibited by article VII, section 10 of the Florida Constitution. . . .

Accordingly, we reverse the final judgment and remand with directions that the bond issue be approved.

It is so ordered.

OVERTON, BARKETT, GRIMES and HARDING, JJ., concur.

SHAW, C.J., dissents with an opinion, in which KOGAN, J., concurs.

McDONALD, J., dissents.

SHAW, C.J., dissenting.

The majority opinion trips lightly over the matter of how public financing of the construction and beautification of a private country club roadway serves a valid public purpose within the purview of article VII, section 10, Florida Constitution. I would affirm the trial court's judgment invalidating the bonds.

I. Facts

A. Private Country Club

The Northern Palm Beach Water Control District ("District"), a public drainage district of the State of Florida, proposes to issue $16,312,500 in government revenue bonds to pay for the construction and maintenance of approximately 24,000 feet of roadway within Unit of Development No. 31, otherwise known as the JDM Country Club ("Club"), a planned 1,313-acre private golf and tennis club. The District's Board of Supervisors ("Board") adopted a formal Water Management Plan ("Plan") for the Club, which provides in part:

> The Unit 31 site, known as JDM Country Club, is being developed as a Planned Community District under the procedures and requirements of the City of Palm Beach Gardens Code of Ordinances. The development will include [2,384 single family dwelling units], park areas and three golf courses.

The homes within the Club will occupy prime residential sites abutting, or lying in close proximity to, the fairways and greens of the three golf courses and, according to Paul Urschalitz, the District's security expert, will vary in price from a quarter-million to over a million dollars apiece:

> Q. Would you anticipate looking at the type homes—did you have a chance to get an idea of what type of homes they're going to put in there?
>
> A. Yes.
>
> Q. What type of price range homes did you look at?
>
> A. I think they're listed in this document, two hundred and fifty thousand to over a million. . . .

In addition to the roadway itself, the District will pay for extensive roadway improvements within the Club. Tracy Bennett, the District's engineer, testified:

> The onsite roadway improvements include paving of the roadways, the striping, the signage, landscaping with the roadways, irrigation to maintain the landscaping and sodding, bridges, an overpass, culverts, street lighting, security gatehouses, and secondary drainage system consisting of storm drainage pipes, inlets, manholes and surface drainage.

B. "Caribbean Island" Motif

The District's Plan calls for extensive roadside landscaping paid for by the District to enhance the private Club's "Caribbean Island" theme[:]

> Extensive landscaping within the onsite roadway rights-of-way system is planned. . . . The overall theme of the development is to provide a Caribbean Island effect. Strong emphasis in the roadway planting will be on various palm species 20 to 30 feet high with a full-canopied backdrop, accented with dwarf palms and a wide variety of blooming groundcover plants. The remaining open areas will be sodded. The most intensive landscaping treatment is the median, followed by right-of-way adjacent to a development parcel, then right-of-way adjacent to lake open areas. . . .

According to the Plan, the initial cost to the District of this garden-like landscaping is vast. The Plan states . . . [that] the District, a public entity, will pay nearly six million dollars in initial roadside landscaping costs—more than the cost of the entire roadway itself—to promote the private Club's "Caribbean Island" motif.

This amounts to almost *one and one-half million dollars of landscaping per mile of proposed roadway* for the private Club.

C. Security Gatehouses

In addition to the "Caribbean Island" landscaping and other improvements noted above, the District will also pay for the construction and maintenance of three gatehouses to be staffed by security personnel to block all public access to the private Club. The District's official Plan provides:

> In addition, the Board of Supervisors has the power to provide, control ingress and egress, and maintain roads for the exclusive use and benefit of a Unit of Development and its landowners, residents and invitees.

> The onsite roadway system [is] planned for the exclusive use and benefit of [the Club] and its landowners, residents, and invitees. . . .

Peter Pimental, executive director of the District, testified as follows:

> A. Want me to explain? What we proposed to do is construct these gatehouses as Mr. Bennett testified and with those gatehouses would be the security people who would control the ingress and egress to the project and those people or persons who have reason to be inside would be allowed inside the project. Those that have no purpose or no reason to be there, will not be permitted to just wander through the project.

> Q. How would you define "reason to be there?"

> A. There would be service directed, service oriented persons, residents, invitees, guests, police, fire, emergency service, all of those would have access to the project.

> Q. So if I was out on a Sunday afternoon driving around, just wanted to ride through the District, I would be restricted under your rules?

> A. Yes.

> Q. So it is not open to the public at all?

> A. Perhaps not. . . .

Thus, all on-site improvements within the Club—including the landscaping and roadway itself—that are paid for by the public District will be closed to the general public.

D. Financing

To pay for the District's proposed on-site improvements within the Club, the Board adopted a general bond resolution that authorizes issuance of Water Control and Improvement Bonds in a principal amount not to exceed $16,312,500. The resolution provides that the bonds shall not be general obligations or indebtedness of the District, but shall instead be special obligations payable solely from, and secured by, a first lien and pledge of the proceeds of a drainage tax levied on the lands of the Club. The Board subsequently adopted a resolution levying a $42,625,000 drainage tax on the lands of the Club in proportion to the benefits to be derived from the construction of the improvements. The tax, which consists of an initial assessment of $18,125,000 plus $24,500,000 interest expected to accrue on the bonds, will be paid solely by the landowners within the Club. The landowners will thus ultimately foot the bill for the District's proposed roadway improvements within the Club.

The bonds will be issued in the denomination of $5,000, or multiples thereof, will mature within 30 years, and significantly, will pay interest periodically (twice a year) from the District to bondholders at a rate to be determined later. In paying this interest, the Board covenants that it will comply with specific requirements of the federal tax code concerning the tax status of certain government bonds. These provisions, which are designed to stimulate funding for public projects, specify that interest payments by state and local governments to their investors may be tax-exempt for the investors. The Board's bond resolution states:

> Section 4.08. *Compliance with Tax Requirements.* The Issuer hereby covenants and agrees, for the benefit of the Owners from time to time of the Bonds, to comply with the requirements applicable to it contained in Section 103 and Part IV of Subchapter B of Chapter 1 of the Code and to the extent necessary to preserve the exclusion of interest on the Bonds from gross income for federal income tax purposes.

Because the District's interest payments to bondholders will be tax-exempt for the holders, the bonds will be readily marketable even though the District may offer the bonds at an interest rate substantially below that of privately-issued, taxable securities. This reduced interest rate will minimize the District's financial obligations to bondholders and the resulting tax obligations of the Club's landowners.

II. The Applicable Law

In *Taylor v. Lee County*, 498 So. 2d 424, 425 (Fla. 1986), Justice McDonald explained the nature of this Court's inquiry in bond validation proceedings:

> The scope of judicial inquiry in bond validation proceedings is limited. Specifically, courts should: 1) determine if a public body has the authority to issue the subject bonds; 2) determine if the purpose of the obligation is legal; and 3) ensure that the authorization of the obligations complies with the requirements of law.

In the present case, we are concerned primarily with whether the purpose of the District's bonds is legal.

Article VII, section 10, Florida Constitution, bars governments within Florida from using their taxing power or credit to aid private corporations or persons:

> *SECTION 10. Pledging credit.* — Neither the state nor any county, school district, municipality, special district, or agency of any of them, shall become a joint owner with, or stockholder of, or give, lend or use its taxing power or credit to aid any corporation, association, partnership or person. . . .

The purpose of section 10 is to prevent state government from using its vast resources to monopolize, or otherwise "destroy," a segment of private enterprise, and also "to protect public funds and resources from being exploited in assisting or promoting private ventures when the public would be at most only incidentally benefited." *Bannon v. Port of Palm Beach Dist.*, 246 So. 2d 737, 741 (Fla. 1971). To pass constitutional muster, a government bond issue must serve a truly public purpose, i.e., it must bestow a benefit on society exceeding that which is normally attendant to any successful business venture. . . .

III. Conclusion

Simply designating a project "public" by legislative fiat does not necessarily make it so, especially where uncontroverted facts attest otherwise. A quote from Lewis Carroll makes the point:

> "I don't know what you mean by 'glory,'" Alice said.

> Humpty Dumpty smiled contemptuously. "Of course you don't—till I tell you. I meant 'there's a nice knock-down argument for you!'"

> "But 'glory' doesn't mean 'a nice knock-down argument,'" Alice objected.

> "When I use a word," Humpty Dumpty said, in rather a scornful tone, "it means just what I choose it to mean—neither more nor less."

> "The question is," said Alice, "whether you can make words mean so many different things."

> "The question is," said Humpty Dumpty, "which is to be master—that's all."

Lewis Carroll, *Through the Looking Glass* 113 (Dial Books for Young Readers, NAL Penguin, Inc. 1988) (1872). Under our constitutional system of government in Florida, courts, not legislators or water control districts, are the ultimate "masters" of the constitutional meaning of such terms as "public purpose" in judicial proceedings.

While a restricted roadway may serve a valid public purpose under certain circumstances, I conclude that no reasonable and sufficient public purpose is served by issuance of government bonds to finance the construction and landscaping of roadways within the private JDM Country Club. The extraordinarily expensive roadside landscaping to enhance the "Caribbean Island" motif of the private residences and golf courses within the Club would serve virtually no reasonable public purpose even if the Club were to be open to the general public. The fact that security gatehouses will be erected for the sole purpose of barring the public from the premises renders any alleged benefit to the public from the landscaping or roadway moot.

It is perfectly clear to me that the District's bond project serves a simple, very private, purpose. It allows the owners of the proposed 2,384 residences within the Club to capitalize on a massive tax-break, intended for public projects, in financing the construction of a luxurious environment for their own private use. The undertaking smacks of state-sponsored, economic apartheid. I can conceive of few more private projects.

Rather than relying on . . . this Court's own examination of a cold record, I would place great weight on the reasoned judgment of the respected trial judge, for he alone had the opportunity to personally observe—on both direct and cross-examination—the demeanor of many of the Club's main functionaries, and he is far more familiar with the local circumstances surrounding this issue. Sufficient competent evidence supports his ruling.

I would affirm the trial court's judgment invalidating the bonds.

————————

Notes and Questions to Consider:

1. Many of the facts of *N. Palm Beach County Water Control Dist. v. State* are missing from the majority's decision and appear only in the dissent. Why would the majority have omitted these facts?

2. The majority opinion cites to prior precedent in *Linscott v. Orange County Indus. Dev. Auth.*, 443 So. 2d 97 (Fla. 1983) to identify the legal standard for applying Article VII, Section 10's prohibition upon the state and its subdivisions, including special districts such as this water control district, from using its taxing power or pledging public credit to aid any private person or entity. Under *Linscott*, first we determine if the project falls within one of these four enumerated of Article VII, Section 10, for which no constitutional prohibition applies: (a) the investment of public trust funds; (b) the investment of other public funds in obligations of, or insured by, the United States or any of its instrumentalities; (c) revenue bonds to finance or refinance the cost of capital projects for airports or port facilities, or for industrial or manufacturing plants to the extent that the interest thereon is exempt from income taxes under the then existing laws of the United States; or (d) the joint ownership, construction, and operation of electrical energy generating or transmission facilities. Second, we determine if the taxing power or pledge of credit is involved. If so, then the thing the bonds finance must serve a paramount public purpose. If not, then "it is enough to show only that a public purpose is served." *Linscott*, 443 So.2d at 101.

2. Types and Purposes of State and Municipal Bonds

States, counties, municipal corporations, and state-created districts borrow money by issuing a debt instrument called a municipal bond. *See, e.g.*, chapter 215, Fla. Stat. Municipal bonds are popular among certain investors who are eligible for their exemption from certain federal income tax liabilities. Municipal bonds were often popular before the Great Recession, and still somewhat popular thereafter, because "the municipal bond market has traditionally been viewed as a relatively safe market where credit risk was not a primary concern. . . ." Ming-Jie Wang, *Credit Default Swaps on Municipal Bonds: A Double-Edged Sword?*, 35 Yale J. on Reg. 301, 302 (2018). One commentator provides this primer on municipal bonds and how they work:

> Three types of municipal bonds exist: general obligation bonds, revenue bonds, and short-term debt securities. General obligation bonds are backed

by the issuer's "full faith and credit," meaning the issuer can tax residents to provide revenue for repayment of the bonds. Revenue bonds are used to fund specific projects. Unlike general obligation bonds, the specific project's revenue repays the revenue bonds' obligations. Conduit bonds are a special form of revenue bonds, and municipalities issue them on behalf of a third party. As its name indicates, short-term debt securities mature quickly, within thirteen months. These securities provide funds for the gap in "time when expenses occur and when [other] revenues become available." General obligation bonds and revenue bonds, however, remain the most common.

Charlotte W. Rhodes, *Living in a Material World: Defining "Materiality" in the Municipal Bond Market and Rule 15c2-12*, 72 WASH. & LEE L. REV. 1989, 1994–97 (2015).

As the commentator notes, federal regulation of municipal bonds is limited insofar as federal law regulates municipal bonds only indirectly. For example, federal law "prohibits the SEC or the MSRB from requiring municipal issuers to file disclosures before municipal offerings." *Id.* (citing 15 U.S.C. § 78o-4(d)(1)-(2) (2012)).

So it may be surprising that state regulation of municipal bonds has relatively recent origins, according to these commentators:

> From 1837 through 1840, the American economy experienced a deep depression. In 1840, many of the state public improvement projects ceased construction due to economic setbacks. As a result, the states felt the dual wrath of declining revenues occasioned by the depression and unrelenting debt service requirements. Consequently, many states found themselves with non-income producing, partially funded projects, with the obligation to fully repay the outstanding indebtedness. From 1841 to 1842, nine separate states, including Florida, Illinois, Indiana, Michigan and Pennsylvania, were unable to resist the economic pressures and defaulted on their bonds. For example, the state of Mississippi alone defaulted on $7,000,000 worth of state bonds in 1841. The state continued to repudiate the bonds, and in 1875 the Mississippi Constitution was amended to include a specific provision prohibiting the state from repaying any of these bonds. *See* Mississippi Constitution of 1875, Article XII, Section 5.

> These developments fueled a popular movement for revenue reform at the state level. As a result of the relative success of this movement, most state constitutions currently contain some restrictions on the issuance of state debt. . . .

Thomas C. Marks, Jr. and John F. Cooper, STATE CONSTITUTIONAL LAW IN A NUTSHELL 245–46 (2003).

Florida's constitution, at Article VII, contains the following restrictions upon government bonds:

SECTION 11. State bonds; revenue bonds. —

(a) State bonds pledging the full faith and credit of the state may be issued only to finance or refinance the cost of state fixed capital outlay projects authorized by law, and purposes incidental thereto, upon approval by a vote of the electors; provided state bonds issued pursuant to this subsection may be refunded without a vote of the electors at a lower net average interest cost rate. The total outstanding principal of state bonds issued pursuant to this subsection shall never exceed fifty percent of the total tax revenues of the state for the two preceding fiscal years, excluding any tax revenues held in trust under the provisions of this constitution.

(b) Moneys sufficient to pay debt service on state bonds as the same becomes due shall be appropriated by law.

(c) Any state bonds pledging the full faith and credit of the state issued under this section or any other section of this constitution may be combined for the purposes of sale.

(d) Revenue bonds may be issued by the state or its agencies without a vote of the electors to finance or refinance the cost of state fixed capital outlay projects authorized by law, and purposes incidental thereto, and shall be payable solely from funds derived directly from sources other than state tax revenues.

(e) Bonds pledging all or part of a dedicated state tax revenue may be issued by the state in the manner provided by general law to finance or refinance the acquisition and improvement of land, water areas, and related property interests and resources for the purposes of conservation, outdoor recreation, water resource development, restoration of natural systems, and historic preservation.

(f) Each project, building, or facility to be financed or refinanced with revenue bonds issued under this section shall first be approved by the Legislature by an act relating to appropriations or by general law.

SECTION 12. Local bonds. —Counties, school districts, municipalities, special districts and local governmental bodies with taxing powers may issue bonds, certificates of indebtedness or any form of tax anticipation certificates, payable from ad valorem taxation and maturing more than twelve months after issuance only:

(a) to finance or refinance capital projects authorized by law and only when approved by vote of the electors who are owners of freeholds therein not wholly exempt from taxation; or

(b) to refund outstanding bonds and interest and redemption premium thereon at a lower net average interest cost rate.

SECTION 14. Bonds for pollution control and abatement and other water facilities. —

(a) When authorized by law, state bonds pledging the full faith and credit of the state may be issued without an election to finance the construction of air and water pollution control and abatement and solid waste disposal facilities and other water facilities authorized by general law (herein referred to as "facilities") to be operated by any municipality, county, district or authority, or any agency thereof (herein referred to as "local governmental agencies"), or by any agency of the State of Florida. Such bonds shall be secured by a pledge of and shall be payable primarily from all or any part of revenues to be derived from operation of such facilities, special assessments, rentals to be received under lease-purchase agreements herein provided for, any other revenues that may be legally available for such purpose, including revenues from other facilities, or any combination thereof (herein collectively referred to as "pledged revenues"), and shall be additionally secured by the full faith and credit of the State of Florida.

(b) No such bonds shall be issued unless a state fiscal agency, created by law, has made a determination that in no state fiscal year will the debt service requirements of the bonds proposed to be issued and all other bonds secured by the pledged revenues exceed seventy-five per cent of the pledged revenues.

(c) The state may lease any of such facilities to any local governmental agency, under lease-purchase agreements for such periods and under such other terms and conditions as may be mutually agreed upon. The local governmental agencies may pledge the revenues derived from such leased facilities or any other available funds for the payment of rentals thereunder; and, in addition, the full faith and credit and taxing power of such local governmental agencies may be pledged for the payment of such rentals without any election of freeholder electors or qualified electors.

(d) The state may also issue such bonds for the purpose of loaning money to local governmental agencies, for the construction of such facilities to be owned or operated by any of such local governmental agencies. Such loans shall bear interest at not more than one-half of one per cent per annum greater than the last preceding issue of state bonds pursuant to this section, shall be secured by the pledged revenues, and may be additionally secured by the full faith and credit of the local governmental agencies.

(e) The total outstanding principal of state bonds issued pursuant to this section 14 shall never exceed fifty per cent of the total tax revenues of the state for the two preceding fiscal years.

SECTION 15. Revenue bonds for scholarship loans. —

(a) When authorized by law, revenue bonds may be issued to establish a fund to make loans to students determined eligible as prescribed by law and who have been admitted to attend any public or private institutions of higher learning, junior colleges, health related training institutions, or vocational training centers, which are recognized or accredited under terms and conditions prescribed by law. Revenue bonds issued pursuant to this section shall be secured by a pledge of and shall be payable primarily from payments of interest, principal, and handling charges to such fund from the recipients of the loans and, if authorized by law, may be additionally secured by student fees and by any other moneys in such fund. There shall be established from the proceeds of each issue of revenue bonds a reserve account in an amount equal to and sufficient to pay the greatest amount of principal, interest, and handling charges to become due on such issue in any ensuing state fiscal year.

(b) Interest moneys in the fund established pursuant to this section, not required in any fiscal year for payment of debt service on then outstanding revenue bonds or for maintenance of the reserve account, may be used for educational loans to students determined to be eligible therefor in the manner provided by law, or for such other related purposes as may be provided by law.

SECTION 16. Bonds for housing and related facilities. —

(a) When authorized by law, revenue bonds may be issued without an election to finance or refinance housing and related facilities in Florida, herein referred to as "facilities."

(b) The bonds shall be secured by a pledge of and shall be payable primarily from all or any part of revenues to be derived from the financing, operation or sale of such facilities, mortgage or loan payments, and any other revenues or assets that may be legally available for such purposes derived from sources other than ad valorem taxation, including revenues from other facilities, or any combination thereof, herein collectively referred to as "pledged revenues," provided that in no event shall the full faith and credit of the state be pledged to secure such revenue bonds.

(c) No bonds shall be issued unless a state fiscal agency, created by law, has made a determination that in no state fiscal year will the debt service requirements of the bonds proposed to be issued and all other bonds secured by the same pledged revenues exceed the pledged revenues available for payment of such debt service requirements, as defined by law.

SECTION 17. Bonds for acquiring transportation right-of-way or for constructing bridges. —

(a) When authorized by law, state bonds pledging the full faith and credit of the state may be issued, without a vote of the electors, to finance or refinance the cost of acquiring real property or the rights to real property for state roads as defined by law, or to finance or refinance the cost of state bridge construction, and purposes incidental to such property acquisition or state bridge construction.

(b) Bonds issued under this section shall be secured by a pledge of and shall be payable primarily from motor fuel or special fuel taxes, except those defined in Section 9(c) of Article XII, as provided by law, and shall additionally be secured by the full faith and credit of the state.

(c) No bonds shall be issued under this section unless a state fiscal agency, created by law, has made a determination that in no state fiscal year will the debt service requirements of the bonds proposed to be issued and all other bonds secured by the same pledged revenues exceed ninety percent of the pledged revenues available for payment of such debt service requirements, as defined by law. For the purposes of this subsection, the term "pledged revenues" means all revenues pledged to the payment of debt service, excluding any pledge of the full faith and credit of the state.

Notes and Questions to Consider:

1. Note that Florida's constitution refers to several types of bonds without defining them. Florida's legislature provides the following definitions in Florida Statutes chapter 215:

> (1). "General obligation bonds," which are obligations secured by the full faith and credit of a governmental unit or payable from the proceeds of ad valorem taxes of a governmental unit.

> (2). "Revenue bonds," which are obligations of a governmental unit issued to pay the cost of a self-liquidating project or improvements thereof, or combination of one or more projects or improvements thereof, and payable from the earnings of such project and any other special funds authorized to be pledged as additional security therefor, except for bonds issued to finance projects under part II [the Florida Industrial Development Financing Act], part III [Industrial Development Authorities], or part V [Housing Finance Authorities] of chapter 159 or health facilities under part III of chapter 154.

> (3). "Bond anticipation notes," which are notes issued by a governmental unit in anticipation of the issuance of general obligation or revenue bonds.

> (4). "Limited revenue bonds," which are obligations issued by a governmental unit to pay the cost of a project or improvement thereof, or combination of one or more projects or improvements thereof, and payable from funds of a governmental unit, exclusive of ad valorem taxes, special assessments, or earnings from such projects or improvements.

> (5). "Special assessment bonds," which are bonds that provide for capital improvements and are paid in whole or in part by levying and collecting special assessments on the abutting, adjoining, contiguous, or other specially benefited property.

§ 215.84, Fla. Stat. (2019).

2. General obligation bonds are backed by the "full faith and credit" of the issuing entity. Revenue bonds are not. Which type of bond would be preferable to the risk-averse investor? Which might be preferable to the investor seeking a higher yield?

3. For what purposes can the state issue a general obligation bond? Consider, for example, Article VII, Section 11 of Florida's constitution (stating that "[s]tate bonds pledging the full faith and credit of the state may be issued only to finance or refinance the cost of state fixed capital outlay projects authorized by law, and purposes incidental thereto . . .").

4. When does Florida's legislature need the approval of Florida's electors in order to issue a general obligation bond? Consider Florida's constitution at Article VII in Section 11 where it provides that "[s]tate bonds pledging the full faith and credit of the state may be issued only . . . upon approval by a vote of the electors; provided

state bonds issued pursuant to this subsection may be refunded without a vote of the electors at a lower net average interest cost rate."

5. For what purposes can counties, school districts, municipalities, special districts, and local governmental bodies with taxing powers issue long-term bonds (meaning bonds maturing more than 12 months after issuance) payable from ad valorem taxation? Consider Article VII, Section 12 (restricting such bonds to these purposes: (a) to finance or refinance capital projects authorized by law and only when approved by vote of the electors who are owners of freeholds therein not wholly exempt from taxation; or (b) to refund outstanding bonds and interest and redemption premium thereon at a lower net average interest cost rate).

D. Education

The text of the U.S. Constitution does not address the topic of education. The fact that states provide state-sponsored education implicates other federal rights, perhaps most notably the right not to suffer discrimination at school found in cases such as *Brown v. Board of Education*, where the U.S. Supreme Court held:

> Today, education is perhaps the most important function of state and local governments. Compulsory school attendance laws and the great expenditures for education both demonstrate our recognition of the importance of education to our democratic society. It is required in the performance of our most basic public responsibilities, even service in the armed forces. It is the very foundation of good citizenship. Today it is a principal instrument in awakening the child to cultural values, in preparing him for later professional training, and in helping him to adjust normally to his environment. In these days, it is doubtful that any child may reasonably be expected to succeed in life if he is denied the opportunity of an education. Such an opportunity, where the state has undertaken to provide it, is a right which must be made available to all on equal terms.

Brown v. Bd. of Ed. of Topeka, Shawnee County, Kan., 347 U.S. 483, 493 (1954), supplemented sub nom. *Brown v. Bd. of Educ. of Topeka, Kan.*, 349 U.S. 294 (1955). Despite the importance of an education as noted in *Brown v. Board of Education*, the Court did not hold that an education is a fundamental right. Indeed, in *San Antonio Indep. Sch. Dist. v. Rodriguez*, 411 U.S. 1 (1973), the Court declined to recognize the right to an education as a fundamental right. The Court held:

> Education, of course, is not among the rights afforded explicit protection under our Federal Constitution. Nor do we find any basis for saying it is implicitly so protected. As we have said, the undisputed importance of education will not alone cause this Court to depart from the usual standard for reviewing a State's social and economic legislation.

Id. at 35.

The text of state constitutions address the topic of education. "Today, each state's constitution has provisions concerning public education. . . . In terms of free education, the majority of states have a clause in their constitution establishing a free system of public schools; however, the interpretation of 'free' beyond tuition varies across states. Some states have extended the meaning of 'free public education' to include school supplies and materials, while others have determined that such items are not included." Kate Barnes, *"Free" Education: The Inclusion of Educational Materials and Supplies as Part of the Right to Free Education*, 40 J.L. & EDUC. 373 (2011).

Florida's constitution addresses the topic of education in its Article IV. It begins with this phrase: "The education of children is a fundamental value of the people of the State of Florida. It is, therefore, a paramount duty of the state to make adequate provision for the education of all children residing within its borders." Art. IX, § 1, Fla. Const. Does this mean that, if Florida's schools are failing to adequately educate Florida's children, then Florida's legislature is empowered to create a system to remedy that failure? Consider *Bush v. Holmes*, 919 So. 2d 392 (Fla. 2006).

Bush v. Holmes

Supreme Court of Florida, 2006
919 So. 2d 392

Because a state statute was declared unconstitutional by the First District Court of Appeal, this Court is required by the Florida Constitution to hear this appeal. See art. V, § 3(b)(1), Fla. Const. The issue we decide is whether the State of Florida is prohibited by the Florida Constitution from expending public funds to allow students to obtain a private school education in kindergarten through grade twelve, as an alternative to a public school education. The law in question, now codified at section 1002.38, Florida Statutes (2005), authorizes a system of school vouchers and is known as the Opportunity Scholarship Program (OSP).

Under the OSP, a student from a public school that fails to meet certain minimum state standards has two options. The first is to move to another public school with a satisfactory record under the state standards. The second option is to receive funds from the public treasury, which would otherwise have gone to the student's school district, to pay the student's tuition at a private school. The narrow question we address is whether the second option violates a part of the Florida Constitution requiring the state to both provide for "the education of all children residing within its borders" and provide "by law for a uniform, efficient, safe, secure, and high quality system of free public schools that allows students to obtain a high quality education." Art. IX, § 1(a), Fla. Const. . . .

Our inquiry begins with the plain language of the second and third sentences of article IX, section 1(a) of the Constitution. The relevant words are these: "It is . . . a paramount duty of the state to make adequate provision for the education of all children residing within its borders." Using the same term, "adequate provision," article IX, section 1(a) further states: "Adequate provision shall be made by law for a uniform, efficient, safe, secure, and high quality system of free public schools." . . .

Article IX, section 1(a) is a limitation on the Legislature's power because it provides both a mandate to provide for children's education and a restriction on the execution of that mandate. The second and third sentences must be read *in pari materia*, rather than as distinct and unrelated obligations. This principle of statutory construction is equally applicable to constitutional provisions. As we stated in construing a different constitutional amendment, the provision should "be construed as a whole in order to ascertain the general purpose and meaning of each part; each subsection, sentence, and clause must be read in light of the others to form a congruous whole." *Dep't of Envtl. Prot. v. Millender*, 666 So. 2d 882, 886 (Fla. 1996); see also *Physicians Healthcare Plans, Inc. v. Pfeifler*, 846 So. 2d 1129, 1134 (Fla. 2003).

The second sentence of article IX, section 1(a) provides that it is the "paramount duty of the state to make adequate provision for the education of all children residing within its borders." The third sentence of article IX, section 1(a) provides a restriction on the exercise of this mandate by specifying that the adequate provision required in the second sentence "shall be made by law for a uniform, efficient, safe, secure and high quality system of *free public schools.*" (Emphasis supplied.) The OSP violates this provision by devoting the state's resources to the education of children within our state through means other than a system of free public schools. . . .

The dissent considers our use of rules of construction such as "in pari materia" . . . unnecessary to discern the meaning of a provision that the dissent considers clear and unambiguous. "Ambiguity suggests that reasonable persons can find different meanings in the same language." *Forsythe v. Longboat Key Beach Erosion Control Dist.*, 604 So. 2d 452, 455 (Fla. 1992). It is precisely because the amendment is not clear and unambiguous regarding public funding of private schools that we look to accepted standards of construction applicable to constitutional provisions. See *Joshua v. City of Gainesville*, 768 So. 2d 432, 435 (Fla. 2000) (stating that "if the language of the statute is unclear, then rules of statutory construction control"); *Zingale*, 885 So. 2d at 282, 285 (applying rules of statutory construction, including "in pari materia," to constitutional provisions); *Caribbean Conservation Corp. v. Florida Fish & Wildlife Conservation Comm'n*, 838 So. 2d 492, 501 (Fla. 2003) (same). "*In pari materia*" [is an] objective principle to apply in our analysis.

Although parents certainly have the right to choose how to educate their children, article IX, section (1)(a) does not, as the Attorney General asserts, establish a "floor" of what the state can do to provide for the education of Florida's children. The provision mandates that the state's obligation is to provide for the education of Florida's children, specifies that the manner of fulfilling this obligation is by providing a uniform, high quality system of free public education, and does not authorize additional equivalent alternatives. . . .

Reinforcing our determination that the state's use of public funds to support an alternative system of education is in violation of article IX, section 1(a) is the limitation of the use of monies from the State School Fund set forth in article IX, section 6. That provision states that income and interest from the State School Fund may be appropriated "only to the support and maintenance of free public schools." Art. IX, §6, Fla. Const. It is well established that "[e]very provision of [the constitution] was inserted with a definite purpose and all sections and provisions of it must be construed together, that is, *in pari materia*, in order to determine its meaning, effect, restraints, and prohibitions." *Thomas v. State ex rel. Cobb*, 58 So. 2d 173, 174 (Fla. 1952); see also *Caribbean Conservation Corp.*, 838 So. 2d at 501 ("[I]n construing multiple constitutional provisions addressing a similar subject, the provisions 'must be read *in pari materia* to ensure a consistent and logical meaning that gives effect to each provision.'") (quoting *Advisory Opinion to the Governor–1996 Amendment 5 (Everglades)*, 706 So. 2d 278, 281 (Fla. 1997)). Reading sections 1(a) and 6 of article IX *in pari materia* evinces the clear intent that public funds be used to support the public school system, not to support a duplicative, competitive private system.

Further, in reading article IX as a whole, we note the clear difference between the language of section 1(a) and that of section 1(b), which was adopted in 2002 and provides in full:

> Every four-year-old child in Florida *shall be provided by the State a high quality pre-kindergarten learning opportunity in the form of an early childhood development and education program which shall be voluntary, high quality, free, and delivered according to professionally accepted standards.* An early childhood development and education program means an organized program designed to address and enhance each child's ability to make age appropriate progress in an appropriate range of settings in the development of language and cognitive capabilities and emotional, social, regulatory and moral capacities through education in basic skills and such other skills as the Legislature may determine to be appropriate.

(Emphasis supplied.) Although this provision requires that the pre-kindergarten learning opportunity must be free and delivered according to professionally accepted standards, noticeably absent is a requirement that the state provide this opportunity by a particular means. Thus, in contrast to the Legislature's obligation under section 1(a) to make adequate provision for kindergarten through grade twelve education through a system of free public schools, the Legislature is free under section 1(b) to provide for pre-kindergarten education in any manner it desires, consistent with other applicable constitutional provisions. . . .

Because we conclude that section 1002.38 violates article IX, section 1(a) of the Florida Constitution, we disapprove the First District's decision in *Holmes I*. . . . In order not to disrupt the education of students who are receiving vouchers for the current school year, our decision shall have prospective application to commence at the conclusion of the current school year.

It is so ordered.

WELLS, ANSTEAD, LEWIS, and QUINCE, concur.

BELL, J., dissents with an opinion, in which CANTERO, J., concurs.

BELL, J., dissenting.

"[N]othing in article IX, section 1 clearly prohibits the Legislature from allowing the well-delineated use of public funds for private school education, particularly in circumstances where the Legislature finds such use is necessary." *Bush v. Holmes*, 767 So. 2d 668, 675 (Fla. 1st DCA 2000) (footnote omitted). This conclusion, written by Judge Charles Kahn for a unanimous panel of the First District Court of Appeal, is the only answer this Court is empowered to give to the constitutional question the majority has decided to answer. Therefore, I dissent.

In its construction of this constitutional provision, the majority asserts that it "follow[s] principles parallel to those guiding statutory construction," yet its reasoning fails to adhere to the most fundamental of these principles. It fails to evince any presumption that the OSP is constitutional or any effort to resolve every doubt in favor of its constitutionality. Therefore, I begin this dissent by stating the fundamental principles that should direct any determination of whether the OSP violates article IX, section 1. Next, I address the text of article IX, section 1. I will show that this text is plain and unambiguous. Because article IX is unambiguous, it needs no interpretation, and it is inappropriate to use maxims of statutory construction to justify an exclusivity not in the text. Finally, I find no record support for the majority's presumption that the OSP prevents the State from fulfilling its mandate to make adequate provision for a uniform system of free public schools.

I. Fundamental Principles of State Constitutional Jurisprudence

. . . This judicial deference to duly enacted legislation is derived from three "first principles" of state constitutional jurisprudence. First, the people are the ultimate sovereign. . . . Second, unlike the federal constitution, our state constitution is a limitation upon the power of government rather than a grant of that power. *Chiles v. Phelps*, 714 So. 2d 453, 458 (Fla. 1998) . . . . This means that the Legislature has general legislative or policy-making power over such issues as the education of Florida's children except as those powers are specifically limited by the constitution. Id. (recognizing that "[t]he legislature's power is inherent, though it may be limited by the constitution"); see also *State ex rel. Green v. Pearson*, 153 Fla. 314, 14 So. 2d 565, 567 (1943) ("It is a familiarly accepted doctrine of constitutional law that the power of the Legislature is inherent. . . . The legislative branch looks to the Constitution not for sources of power but for limitations upon power."). Third, because general legislative or policy-making power is vested in the legislature, the power of judicial review over legislative enactments is strictly limited. Specifically, when a legislative enactment is challenged under the state constitution, courts are without authority to invalidate the enactment unless it is clearly contrary to an express or necessarily implied prohibition within the constitution. *Chapman v. Reddick*, 41 Fla. 120, 25 So. 673, 677 (1899) ("[U]nless legislation duly passed be clearly contrary to some express or implied prohibition contained [in the constitution], the courts have no authority to pronounce it invalid.").

Because of these three "first principles," statutes like the OSP come to courts with a strong presumption of constitutionality. *State v. Jefferson*, 758 So. 2d 661, 664 (Fla. 2000) ("[w]henever possible, statutes should be construed in such a manner so as to avoid an unconstitutional result"); see also *State ex rel. Shevin v. Metz Const. Co., Inc.*, 285 So. 2d 598, 600 (Fla. 1973) ("It is elementary that a statute is clothed with a presumption of constitutional validity"). . . . [A]rticle IX, section 1, when read in light of these fundamental principles, the OSP does not violate any express or necessarily implied provision of article IX, section 1(a) of the Florida Constitution. . . .

[T]he majority's reading of article IX, section 1 *in pari materia* with article IX, section 6 certainly supports the importance of the public school system in this State. However, it does not imply an absolute prohibition against the use of public funds to provide parents with children in a public school that is not properly educating their child with the option of placing that child in a private school. In fact, in the more than 150 years that section 6 has been a part of Florida's Constitution, it has never been interpreted as preventing the State from using public funds to provide education through private schools. Historical records indicate that Florida provided public funds to private schools until, at least, 1917. See, e.g., Thomas Everette Cochran, History of Public-School Education in Florida 25 (1921) (indicating the State provided $3,964 to private academies in 1860); Nita Katharine Pyburn, Documentary History of Education in Florida: 1822–1860, 27 (1951) (recognizing that it was relatively common for the State to fund private academies, the "accepted form of secondary education" through general revenues); Richard J. Gabel, *Public Funds for Church and Private Schools* 638, 639 n. 3 (May 1937) (Ph.D. dissertation, Catholic University of America) (relying on historical documents to find that Florida use[d] public funds to provide private education until at least 1917). In addition, a commentary on the proposed 1958 constitutional revision described the education article as "authoriz[ing] a system of uniform free public schools, and also permit[ting] the legislature to provide assistance for 'other non-sectarian schools.'" Manning J. Dauer, *The Proposed New Florida Constitution: An Analysis* 16 (1958). When the Florida House of Representatives considered language for the 1968 constitution, it rejected a proposal to add a section to article IX that would have limited the Legislature's use of education funds by preventing any state money from going to sectarian schools. See 3 Minutes: Committee of the Whole House, Constitutional Revision 34 (1967) (proposed art. IX, § 7, Fla. Const).

Consequently, I can find no justification for the majority's assertion that reading article IX, section 1 *in pari materia* with article IX, section 6 justifies its conclusion that article IX, section 1 must be interpreted to restrict the Legislature from applying public funds to private schools. . . .

Therefore, I agree with Judge Kahn and his two colleagues in the First District Court of Appeal's first opinion regarding this dispute over the OSP. "Nothing in article IX, section 1 clearly prohibits the Legislature from allowing the well-delineated use of public funds for private school education, particularly in circumstances where the Legislature finds such use is necessary." *Bush*, 767 So. 2d at 675. The Opportunity Scholarship Program does not violate article IX, section 1 of Florida's Constitution.

CANTERO, J., concurs.

Notes and Questions to Consider:

1. Both the opinion of the court, and the dissent of Justice Bell, apply the *in pari materia* canon of construction to the state constitutional language at issue. Why, then, did the court and the dissenting justice reach different conclusions as to whether the statute was constitutional?

2. Assuming the use of the same canon of construction permissibly could lead to opposite results, of what good use is that canon in aiding in the proper interpretation of a state constitution? Or in providing judicial restraint of those judges who interpret that constitution? Commentators lament: "The canons of construction have been criticized for their subjectivity." John F. Cooper, Tichia A. Dunham & Carlos L. Woody, FLORIDA CONSTITUTIONAL LAW: CASES AND MATERIALS (Carolina Academic Press, 5th ed., 2013) at 29 & n.55 (citing Karl N. Llwewllyn, *Remarks on the Theory of Appellate Decision and the Rules and Canons About How Statutes Are to Be Construed*, 3 VAND. L. REV. 395 (1950)).

3. The majority holds that "[i]n order not to disrupt the education of students who are receiving vouchers for the current school year, our decision shall have prospective application to commence at the conclusion of the current school year." Did this really prevent the disruption of the education of students receiving vouchers? What about those students who were forced, after the end of the current school year, to complete the rest of their school years at a failing school?

4. To what extent was the outcome of *Bush v. Holmes* the result of Florida's Blaine Amendment, and to what extent was the outcome the result of other requirements in Florida's constitution? Stated somewhat differently, to amend Florida's constitution to overrule *Bush v. Holmes*, what parts of Florida's constitution need amending?

Chapter 16

Criminal Justice and Procedure

A. Trial by Jury

The Constitution of the State of Florida discusses a Floridian's right to jury in the following paragraphs (emphasis added):

Section 11. Prohibited special laws. —

(a) There shall be no special law or general law of local application pertaining to: . . . (5) **petit juries, including compensation of jurors**, except establishment of jury commissions; . . .

Section 15. Prosecution for crime; offenses committed by children. —

(a) No person shall be tried for capital crime without presentment or indictment by a **grand jury**, or for other felony without such presentment or indictment or an information under oath filed by the prosecuting officer of the court, except persons on active duty in the militia when tried by courts martial.

(b) When authorized by law, a child as therein defined may be charged with a violation of law as an act of delinquency instead of crime and tried without a jury or other requirements applicable to criminal cases. Any child so charged shall, upon demand made as provided by law before a trial in a juvenile proceeding, be tried in an appropriate court as an adult. A child found delinquent shall be disciplined as provided by law.

Section 16. Rights of accused and of victims. —

(a) In all criminal prosecutions the accused shall, upon demand, be informed of the nature and cause of the accusation, and shall be furnished a copy of the charges, and shall have the right to have compulsory process for witnesses, to confront at trial adverse witnesses, to be heard in person, by counsel or both, and to have a speedy and public **trial by impartial jury** in the county where the crime was committed. If the county is not known, the indictment or information may charge venue in two or more counties conjunctively and proof that the crime was committed in that area shall be sufficient; but before pleading the accused may elect in which of those counties the trial will take place. Venue for prosecution of crimes committed beyond the boundaries of the state shall be fixed by law.

(b) Victims of crime or their lawful representatives, including the next of kin of homicide victims, are entitled to the right to be informed, to be present, and to be heard when relevant, at all crucial stages of criminal proceedings, to the extent that these rights do not interfere with the constitutional rights of the accused. . . .

Section 22. Trial by jury.— The right of trial by jury shall be secure to all and remain inviolate. The qualifications and the number of jurors, not fewer than six, shall be fixed by law.

The concept of a jury is not new. Indeed, at least one legal commentator can trace its history to "15 centuries before Christ." Such is the language used in the following educational and entertaining article from the April 1961 edition of the Texas Law Review.

The Jury

By Jack Pope
39 Tex. L. Rev. 426

. . . Independently, coincidentally, and rather frequently the notion of popular and representative assistance in the administration of justice has appeared in the affairs of many nations. Something inherent in man and his sense of justice has inclined him toward the idea that qualified citizens should have an active part in matters which we now can more distinctly classify as investigating committees, administrative bodies, or even the measuring of justice in gross. Indistinct yearning for popular participation in the affairs of justice have brooded over the spirits of many people, but only once did the idea survive the onslaughts of the centuries and develop historical continuity. The struggle for survival by the institution we call the jury is truly the epic of our law.

From Antiquity to Magna Carta

Fifteen centuries before Christ, Moses selected one man from each of the tribes of Israel which were encamped in the wilderness of Paran and sent them to spy out the land of Canaan. He charged them to inspect the land and its people, whether they be strong or weak, few or many; whether the land be good or bad, fat or lean, wooded or not; in what cities the people dwell, and whether they live in tents or in strongholds. Forty days later, the twelve returned with a divided opinion. Ten favored retreat; Caleb and Joshua voted for conquest. The twelve spies could hardly be called a jury, but certainly they possessed rudimentary characteristics of a jury. For example, they were selected by the public authority from the neighborhood, they were charged with respect to the limits of their duty, there were twelve of them, they were permitted to weigh the facts by free debate and deliberation, and they made a return of their divided decision to the public power.

Eleven hundred years later, Socrates was condemned to death by a Greek jury, called a dicast. Five hundred and one jurors served in that famous trial, and Plato in his *Apology* tells us that a change of thirty votes would have resulted in his acquittal.

With such a large number of jurors one might suppose that anyone who happened to be in the public square would be eligible to serve, but this is not so. Qualifications among the Athenians were significant, for only citizens and property holders could serve. Each year six thousand citizens were selected by lot, and these were divided into groups of five hundred. Certain cases required a dicast of only two hundred Athenians, but more important cases required as many as two thousand. When a case came on for trial, the dicast that would hear the trial was selected by lot in order to avoid possible bribery. The decisions of the dicast were final. The trial of cases by great popular assemblies was a characteristic of the age of Pericles, and in 451 B.C. he enacted laws under which jurors received pay for their service. The jurors were put upon oath to give a verdict according to their honest opinions. The peculiar size of the Athenian juries defeated the development of the idea of deliberation, and Greek law failed to discern the difference between judicial and legislative matters as well as matters of law and those of fact, but their modes of proof were rather enlightened.

Rome contributed much to law generally and to the system of proofs but added very little to the idea of trial by jury. Trials were before magistrates who originally were possessed of *imperium*, a power similar to that of a military commander-in-chief. But early in the days of the republic, as a check upon this power, the citizens of Rome could appeal to the *populus Romanus*. Two centuries before Christ, citizens outside of Rome were accorded citizenship with the right of appeal. Even soldiers were later granted the right to appeal to the popular assembly. This right of appeal was a source of freedom to the people, but, in the days of the Empire, these popular trials succumbed to the great powers of imperial officials. Rome achieved a clearer distinction between justice and politics and also public and private wrongs. It also discovered the administrative value of an inquest as a means to investigate and seek out criminals.

Along the eastern Mediterranean the Sanhedrin exercised authority over both spiritual and temporal matters, functioning as the highest judicial body of the Jews. Its origin may be traced to the time of Jehoshaphat. There were seventy-one members consisting of the chief priests, the scribes or lawyers, and the elders. The elders were the heads of families and were the representatives of the laity. The Sanhedrin heard, deliberated and passed judgment on matters of law and of fact until it was swept away in 70 A.D. by the destruction of Jerusalem by Titus.

Thirteen centuries after Christ, Alfonso the Learned published *Las Siete Partidas*. We again find the jury foreshadowed, but it made little progress and contributed no new ideas. A body of twelve men summoned by the king or his representative would select sea captains below the rank of Admiral, and also alfa queques, who were the appointed officials to negotiate for the ransom of captives.

The jury, Forsyth tells us, arose "silently and gradually out of the usages of a state of society which has forever passed away." He says that trial by jury "does not owe its existence to any positive law: it is not the creature of an Act of Parliament establishing the form and defining the functions of the new tribunal." . . .

Characteristics of the Jury Emerge

. . . Of what purpose is a jury if judges may usurp their functions? Judges were now experts in the law, and they were also the ones who managed, supervised, charged, and corrected the juries. Judges possessed the power to grant new trials, to fine, and to imprison. It was not until the seventeenth century that the jury, within its sphere of duties, won its independence from overbearing judges. The problem came into focus during the famous trial of William Penn for conducting a Quaker meeting. Penn and another were charged with unlawful assembly. The judge, bent on compelling a conviction, kept an English jury confined for three days without food or water. Chief Justice Vaughan, in the famous Bushell's Case of 1670 freed the jurors and explained that there was no use for a jury if it may be controlled by the notions of the judge. By this landmark decision, jurors were emancipated from judges on fact decisions. One of the great but little discussed checks and balances of our governmental system is this separation of functions of judge and jury over law and fact.

The great characteristics of the jury were isolated and understood by the time of Blackstone. Mingled with praise and criticism, the *Commentaries* give us a complete picture of the eighteenth century jury. The trial was presided over by a judge who was under oath and subject to uniform law. Jurors were selected from the county in which the cause arose and where the jurors lived, the summoning officer was under oath, and the parties were afforded ample notice so they might investigate the qualifications of the jurors. The whole array could be challenged in case of partiality by the selecting officers or the intermeddling of either party. Jurors were selected from the array at random from slips of paper on which the names of jurors were written, and jurors could be challenged for causes which are remarkably familiar. Proofs to the jury were by witnesses' testimony tendered upon oath in open court, and witnesses were sworn not only to tell the truth, but all of it. Objections to the evidence were publicly ruled upon by the judge, and errors in ruling were preserved by bills of exception. The judge charged the jury who then withdrew for private deliberation and confinement until they returned a unanimous verdict. Special issues were frequently used. Blackstone expressed displeasure with several practices of his time which were barbaric. The judge could still deprive jurors of food, water, heat, light and rest in order to coerce a unanimous verdict. If the judge needed to depart before a verdict was received, he would place the jurors in a cart and drive them around the circuit with him. Thus Blackstone described that institution which "ever will be looked upon as the glory of the English law."

The Jury Comes to America

. . . All of the states were using juries of varying forms prior to the Declaration of Independence. Several states, following the Declaration, assured their own freedoms by including Bills of Rights in their constitutions. The Articles of Confederation asserted no authority over individuals, but the congress in its approval of the Northwest Ordinance, agreed with the territory to protect certain fundamental rights including the right to trial by jury. Drafted by September 1787, ratified by March 1789, the Constitution was soon amended by the Bill of Rights as promised.

The body of the Constitution did not overlook that institution which had protected Americans from the Stuart judges. It specifically provided for a jury in trials of crimes. There was no constitutional provision for a civil jury. Hamilton forcefully argued that juries in civil actions were not abolished simply because there was no specific provision for them, but the issue was resolved in the Seventh Amendment with a provision for civil juries.

The right to a jury is enthroned in three of the Amendments to the Constitution. In the case of capital or otherwise infamous crimes, the Fifth Amendment provides that no person need answer a charge unless on a presentment or indictment of a Grand Jury. It was a long road from the Prankish inquest to the Bill of Rights. By the Sixth Amendment, citizens are afforded a trial which is public, speedy and before an impartial jury where the crime was committed. The trial is by proofs of witnesses and the accused may have compulsory process and an attorney. In a single sentence is pressed the fruit of a struggle for human rights which spans the centuries. The Seventh Amendment assures citizens of trials in civil suits at common law which involve as much as twenty dollars and denies a judge the power to decide matters of pure fact.

The centuries have poured content and meaning into the simple word, "jury," that was incorporated into the Constitution. Concepts that once were confused, by the time of the constitutional fathers, were isolated, separated and defined. No single feature makes a jury; it takes all of them. Assembled under the term, "jury," are these received ideas: (1) Citizens may participate in the administration of justice. (2) The administration of justice is a specialized branch of government. (3) There is a difference between an accusing and a trial jury. (4) Jurors are selected by the public authority, (5) and perform their services under the sanction of an oath. (6) They must possess certain qualifications and be from the vicinity of the dispute, (7) and their qualifications may be challenged by the litigants. (8) Some persons are entitled to an exemption [from jury service]. (9) Historically, twelve persons composed a jury. (10) Jurors are not witnesses or investigators, but (11) evidence must be presented before them in open court. (12) The judge may instruct and charge the jury (13) before they withdraw to deliberate (14) in private. (15) The jury's function is to decide the facts — not the law, and (16) in that sphere, it is independent of the judge. (17) The jury may return a special verdict, but (18) verdicts must be unanimous, and (19) returned in open court. (20) Judges may exercise corrective control over juries in cases of misconduct or corruption.

Conclusion

One may wonder how the jury survived at all. . . .

Tested against almost all known obstacles and filtered by the centuries, the jury is now workable and acceptable to judges, to the public, the jury itself, and a feasible body of law. It is one of the most durable and stubborn of all human institutions. The clans and tribes where it originated have dissolved into unrecorded history and are long forgotten. Kingdoms and world empires arose and vanished, but the jury held on. It outlasted oppression, intrigue and absolutism at many hands. It survived civil wars, revolutions and conquests. One by one, many practices appeared to challenge the jury's right of survival—compurgation, ordeal, trial by battle, inquisition, torture, witchcraft, sorcery, the Star Chamber. They are gone, but the jury tenaciously held on. Dialects were absorbed into languages and tongues which once lived and are now dead. The jury endured. . . .

. . . The jury did not cross the channel to the continent, but it was transplanted to America. It has withstood every ordeal of the ages; it has been tested in the battles of freedom, and free peoples of the world are today its strongest compurgators.

This story of people's interest and participation in the administration of justice through a system of trial by jury is truly the epic of our law.

Notes and Questions to Consider:

1. Author Jack Pope, when discussing the characteristics of a jury, discussed the famous trial of William Penn (of the family from whom the U.S. state of Pennsylvania takes its name). To what extent is the method of compelling a conviction used by the trial judge in William Penn's case still available to trial judges today?

2. Just before the conclusion of the excerpt, author Jack Pope enumerates 20 ideas that constitute the notion of a fair jury system. Are all of those 20 ideas embodied in the Constitution of the State of Florida? Are all of them in use in Florida today?

3. As we can see from Jack Pope's article, a jury often consisted of 12 jurors. Yet Florida provides for fewer. The Supreme Court of the United States addressed this situation in *Williams v. Florida*, 399 U.S. 78 (1970):

Williams v. Florida

Supreme Court of the United States, 1970
399 U.S. 78, 90 S.Ct. 1893, 26 L.Ed.2d 446

Mr. Justice White delivered the opinion of the Court.

Prior to his trial for robbery in the State of Florida, petitioner . . . filed a pretrial motion to impanel a 12-man jury instead of the six-man jury provided by Florida law in all but capital cases. That motion too was denied. Petitioner was convicted as charged and was sentenced to life imprisonment. . . . [P]etitioner claims that his Fifth and Sixth Amendment rights had been violated. We granted certiorari. . . .

In *Duncan v. Louisiana*, 391 U.S. 145 (1968), we held that the Fourteenth Amendment guarantees a right to trial by jury in all criminal cases that—were they to be tried in a federal court—would come within the Sixth Amendment's guarantee. Petitioner's trial for robbery on July 3, 1968, clearly falls within the scope of that holding. See *Baldwin v. New York*, 399 U.S. 66 (1970); *DeStefano v. Woods*, 392 U.S. 631 (1968). The question in this case then is whether the constitutional guarantee of a trial by 'jury' necessarily requires trial by exactly 12 persons, rather than some lesser number—in this case six. We hold that the 12-man panel is not a necessary ingredient of 'trial by jury,' and that respondent's refusal to impanel more than the six members provided for by Florida law did not violate petitioner's Sixth Amendment rights as applied to the States through the Fourteenth.

We had occasion in *Duncan v. Louisiana*, supra, to review briefly the oft-told history of the development of trial by jury in criminal cases. That history revealed a long tradition attaching great importance to the concept of relying on a body of one's peers to determine guilt or innocence as a safeguard against arbitrary law enforcement. That same history, however, affords little insight into the considerations that gradually led the size of that body to be generally fixed at 12. Some have suggested that the number 12 was fixed upon simply because that was the number of the presentment jury from the hundred, from which the petit jury developed. Other, less circular but more fanciful reasons for the number 12 have been given, 'but they were all brought forward after the number was fixed,' and rest on little more than mystical or superstitious insights into the significance of '12.' Lord Coke's explanation that the 'number of twelve is much respected in holy writ, as 12 apostles, 12 stones, 12 tribes, etc.,' is typical. In short, while sometime in the 14th century the size of the jury at common law came to be fixed generally at 12, that particular feature of the jury system appears to have been a historical accident, unrelated to the great purposes which gave rise to the jury in the first place. The question before us is whether this accidental feature of the jury has been immutably codified into our Constitution.

This Court's earlier decisions have assumed an affirmative answer to this question. The leading case so construing the Sixth Amendment is *Thompson v. Utah*, 170 U.S. 343 (1898). There the defendant had been tried and convicted by a 12-man jury for a crime committed in the Territory of Utah. A new trial was granted, but by that time Utah had been admitted as a State. The defendant's new trial proceeded under Utah's Constitution, providing for a jury of only eight members. This Court reversed the resulting conviction, holding that Utah's constitutional provision was an ex post facto law as applied to the defendant. In reaching its conclusion, the Court announced that the Sixth Amendment was applicable to the defendant's trial when Utah was a Territory, and that the jury referred to in the Amendment was a jury 'constituted, as it was at common law, of twelve persons, neither more nor less.' *Id.* at 349. Arguably unnecessary for the result, this announcement was supported simply by referring to the Magna Carta, and by quoting passages from treatises which noted—what has already been seen—that at common law the jury did indeed consist of 12. Noticeably absent was any discussion of the essential step in the argument: namely, that every feature of the jury as it existed at common law—whether incidental or essential to that institution—was necessarily included in the Constitution wherever that document referred to a 'jury.' Subsequent decisions have reaffirmed the announcement in *Thompson* often in dictum and usually by relying—where there was any discussion of the issue at all—solely on the fact that the common-law jury consisted of 12. . . .

While 'the intent of the Framers' is often an elusive quarry, the relevant constitutional history casts considerable doubt on the easy assumption in our past decisions that if a given feature existed in a jury at common law in 1789, then it was necessarily preserved in the Constitution. Provisions for jury trial were first placed in the Constitution in Article III's provision that '(t)he Trial of all Crimes . . . shall be by Jury; and such Trial shall be held in the State where the said Crimes shall have been committed.' The 'very scanty history (of this provision) in the records of the Constitutional Convention' sheds little light either way on the intended correlation between Article III's 'jury' and the features of the jury at common law. Indeed, pending and after the adoption of the Constitution, fears were expressed that Article III's provision failed to preserve the common-law right to be tried by a 'jury of the vicinage.' That concern, as well as the concern to preserve the right to jury in civil as well as criminal cases, furnished part of the impetus for introducing amendments to the Constitution that ultimately resulted in the jury trial provisions of the Sixth and Seventh Amendments. As introduced by James Madison in the House, the Amendment relating to jury trial in criminal cases would have provided that:

> The trial of all crimes . . . shall be by an impartial jury of freeholders of the vicinage, with the requisite of unanimity for conviction, of the right of challenge, and other accustomed requisites. . . .

The Amendment passed the House in substantially this form, but after more than a week of debate in the Senate it returned to the House considerably altered. While records of the actual debates that occurred in the Senate are not available, a letter from Madison to Edmund Pendleton on September 14, 1789, indicates that one of the Senate's major objections was to the 'vicinage' requirement in the House version. A conference committee was appointed. As reported in a second letter by Madison on September 23, 1789, the Senate remained opposed to the vicinage requirement, partly because in its view the then-pending judiciary bill—which was debated at the same time as the Amendments—adequately preserved the common-law vicinage feature, making it unnecessary to freeze that requirement into the Constitution. 'The Senate,' wrote Madison:

> are . . . inflexible in opposing a definition of the locality of Juries. The vicinage they contend is either too vague or too strict a term; too vague if depending on limits to be fixed by the pleasure of the law, too strict if limited to the county. It was proposed to insert after the word Juries, 'with the accustomed requisites,' leaving the definition to be construed according to the judgment of professional men. Even this could not be obtained. . . . The Senate suppose, also, that the provision for vicinage in the Judiciary bill will sufficiently quiet the fears which called for an amendment on this point.

The version that finally emerged from the Committee was the version that ultimately became the Sixth Amendment, ensuring an accused:

> the right to a speedy and public trial, by an impartial jury of the State and district wherein the crime shall have been committed, which district shall have been previously ascertained by law . . .

Gone were the provisions spelling out such common-law features of the jury as 'unanimity,' or 'the accustomed requisites.' And the 'vicinage' requirement itself had been replaced by wording that reflected a compromise between broad and narrow definitions of that term, and that left Congress the power to determine the actual size of the 'vicinage' by its creation of judicial districts.

Three significant features may be observed in this sketch of the background of the Constitution's jury trial provisions. First, even though the vicinage requirement was as much a feature of the common-law jury as was the 12-man requirement, the mere reference to 'trial by jury' in Article III was not interpreted to include that feature. Indeed, as the subsequent debates over the Amendments indicate, disagreement arose over whether the feature should be included at all in its common-law sense, resulting in the compromise described above. Second, provisions that would have explicitly tied the 'jury' concept to the 'accustomed requisites' of the time were eliminated. Such action is concededly open to the explanation that the 'accustomed requisites' were thought to be already included in the concept of a 'jury.' But that explanation is no more plausible than the contrary one: that the deletion had some substantive effect. Indeed, given the clear expectation that a substantive change would be [affected] by the inclusion or deletion of an explicit 'vicinage' requirement, the latter explanation is, if anything, the more plausible. Finally, contemporary legislative and constitutional provisions indicate that where Congress wanted to leave no doubt that it was incorporating existing common-law features of the jury system, it knew how to use express language to that effect. Thus, the Judiciary bill, signed by the President on the same day that the House and Senate finally agreed on the form of the Amendments to be submitted to the States, provided in certain cases for the narrower 'vicinage' requirements that the House had wanted to include in the Amendments. And the Seventh Amendment, providing for jury trial in civil cases, explicitly added that 'no fact tried by a jury, shall be otherwise re-examined in any Court of the United States, than according to the rules of the common law.'

We do not pretend to be able to divine precisely what the word 'jury' imported to the Framers, the First Congress, or the States in 1789. It may well be that the usual expectation was that the jury would consist of 12, and that hence, the most likely conclusion to be drawn is simply that little thought was actually given to the specific question we face today. But there is absolutely no indication in 'the intent of the Framers' of an explicit decision to equate the constitutional and common-law characteristics of the jury. Nothing in this history suggests, then, that we do violence to the letter of the Constitution by turning to other than purely historical considerations to determine which features of the jury system, as it existed at common law, were preserved in the Constitution. The relevant inquiry, as we see it, must be the function that the particular feature performs and its relation to the purposes of the jury trial. Measured by this standard, the 12-man requirement cannot be regarded as an indispensable component of the Sixth Amendment.

The purpose of the jury trial, as we noted in *Duncan*, is to prevent oppression by the Government. 'Providing an accused with the right to be tried by a jury of his

554   16 · CRIMINAL JUSTICE AND PROCEDURE

peers gave him an inestimable safeguard against the corrupt or overzealous prosecutor and against the compliant, biased, or eccentric judge.' *Duncan*, 391 U.S. at 156.
Given this purpose, the essential feature of a jury obviously lies in the interposition
between the accused and his accuser of the commonsense judgment of a group of
laymen, and in the community participation and shared responsibility that results
from that group's determination of guilt or innocence. The performance of this role
is not a function of the particular number of the body that makes up the jury. To
be sure, the number should probably be large enough to promote group deliberation, free from outside attempts at intimidation, and to provide a fair possibility for
obtaining a representative cross-section of the community. But we find little reason
to think that these goals are in any meaningful sense less likely to be achieved when
the jury numbers six, than when it numbers 12—particularly if the requirement of
unanimity is retained. And, certainly the reliability of the jury as a factfinder hardly
seems likely to be a function of its size.

It might be suggested that the 12-man jury gives a defendant a greater advantage
since he has more 'chances' of finding a juror who will insist on acquittal and thus
prevent conviction. But the advantage might just as easily belong to the State, which
also needs only one juror out of twelve insisting on guilt to prevent acquittal. What
few experiments have occurred—usually in the civil area—indicate that there is
no discernible difference between the results reached by the two different-sized
juries. In short, neither currently available evidence nor theory suggests that the 12-
man jury is necessarily more advantageous to the defendant than a jury composed
of fewer members.

Similarly, while in theory the number of viewpoints represented on a randomly
selected jury ought to increase as the size of the jury increases, in practice the difference between the 12-man and the six-man jury in terms of the cross-section of the
community represented seems likely to be negligible. Even the 12-man jury cannot
insure representation of every distinct voice in the community, particularly given
the use of the peremptory challenge. As long as arbitrary exclusions of a particular
class from the jury rolls are forbidden, see, e.g., *Carter v. Jury Commission*, 396 U.S.
320, 329–30 (1970), the concern that the cross-section will be significantly diminished if the jury is decreased in size from 12 to six seems an unrealistic one.

We conclude, in short, as we began: the fact that the jury at common law was
composed of precisely 12 is a historical accident, unnecessary to effect the purposes
of the jury system and wholly without significance 'except to mystics.' *Duncan*, 391
U.S. at 182 (Harlan, J., dissenting). To read the Sixth Amendment as forever codify-
ing a feature so incidental to the real purpose of the Amendment is to ascribe a blind
formalism to the Framers which would require considerably more evidence than we
have been able to discover in the history and language of the Constitution or in the
reasoning of our past decisions. We do not mean to intimate that legislatures can
never have good reasons for concluding that the 12-man jury is preferable to the
smaller jury, or that such conclusions—reflected in the provisions of most States and
in our federal system—are in any sense unwise. Legislatures may well have their own

views about the relative value of the larger and smaller juries, and may conclude that, wholly apart from the jury's primary function, it is desirable to spread the collective responsibility for the determination of guilt among the larger group. In capital cases, for example, it appears that no State provides for less than 12 jurors—a fact that suggests implicit recognition of the value of the larger body as a means of legitimating society's decision to impose the death penalty. Our holding does no more than leave these considerations to Congress and the States, unrestrained by an interpretation of the Sixth Amendment that would forever dictate the precise number that can constitute a jury. Consistent with this holding, we conclude that petitioner's Sixth Amendment rights, as applied to the States through the Fourteenth Amendment, were not violated by Florida's decision to provide a six-man rather than a 12-man jury. The judgment of the Florida District Court of Appeal is

Affirmed.

B. Searches, Seizures, and Probable Cause

The Constitution of the State of Florida discusses a Floridian's right to be free from certain searches and seizures by or for the state when it provides the following in Article I:

> **SECTION 12. Searches and seizures.**— The right of the people to be secure in their persons, houses, papers and effects against unreasonable searches and seizures, and against the unreasonable interception of private communications by any means, shall not be violated. No warrant shall be issued except upon probable cause, supported by affidavit, particularly describing the place or places to be searched, the person or persons, thing or things to be seized, the communication to be intercepted, and the nature of evidence to be obtained. This right shall be construed in conformity with the 4th Amendment to the United States Constitution, as interpreted by the United States Supreme Court. Articles or information obtained in violation of this right shall not be admissible in evidence if such articles or information would be inadmissible under decisions of the United States Supreme Court construing the 4th Amendment to the United States Constitution.

Williams v. State of Florida

Fifth District Court of Appeal of Florida, 2004
869 So. 2d 750

Joerg F. Jaeger of Jaeger & Blankner, Orlando, for Appellant.

Charles J. Crist, Jr., Attorney General, Tallahassee, and Rebecca Rock McGuigan, Assistant Attorney General, Daytona Beach, for Appellee.

SAWAYA, C.J.

Zarek L. Williams appeals the judgment and sentences entered in accordance with a jury verdict finding him guilty of trafficking in 400 grams or more of cocaine, possession of a firearm in the commission of a felony, carrying a concealed firearm, and possession of drug paraphernalia. Williams argues that because the charges stem from an unreasonably prolonged traffic stop, the trial court erred in denying his motions to suppress. Specifically, Williams raises two issues that have merit: 1) the initial stop exceeded the time necessary to write the citation; and 2) Williams was illegally detained after he was issued the citation. We agree and reverse.

While on routine patrol, the arresting officer stopped Williams at 7:38 p.m. for a window tint violation and an obscured tag. A minute-and-a-half later, the officer requested back-up. Four minutes after the stop, the officer requested a drug dog, which arrived at 8:13 p.m. Ten minutes after the stop, the officer ran Williams' date of birth through the teletype and immediately received a response that no warrants were outstanding for Williams. Thirty-five minutes after the stop, the officer issued Williams a citation for the window tint violation. The record reveals that the citation the officer issued to Williams had been partially filled out before the stop even took place. [The officer testified at the suppression hearing that he is a "slow writer" and in order to expedite the process of issuing citations, he fills in portions of a number of citations ahead of time. Specifically, he fills in the year, the county, the city and signs the citations. The "county traffic court" information was pre-stamped on the citation. The only information that the officer had to fill out at the time of the stop was the information obtained from Williams' driver's license and the VIN from the car. The officer testified that filling out this information on the citation took thirty-five minutes, during which he called for a drug-sniffing dog to be brought to the scene.] After Williams was handed the citation and his driver's license, he was asked to step to the median so the drug dog could sweep the car. The dog alerted and Williams was arrested.

Williams claims that he was detained far longer than necessary for the officer to issue the citation and, therefore, the search of his vehicle via the drug dog was improper. Williams notes that there is no evidence that the officer had any basis for suspecting criminal activity when he stopped Williams or when issuing the citation to him. Therefore, Williams claims the trial court erred in denying his motion to suppress. We agree. An individual who is stopped for the commission of a traffic infraction may be subjected to a canine search of the exterior of the vehicle so long as it is done within the time required to issue a citation. *Eldridge v. State*, 817 So. 2d 884 (Fla. 5th DCA 2002); *Maxwell v. State*, 785 So. 2d 1277 (Fla. 5th DCA 2001) (citing *Cresswell v. State*, 564 So. 2d 480 (Fla. 1990)); *Welch v. State*, 741 So. 2d 1268 (Fla. 5th DCA 1999). In *Eldridge*, we further explained that the time to issue a citation "should last no longer than is necessary to write the citation and, when necessary, to make the license, tag, insurance and registration checks as long as that information can be obtained within a reasonable period of time." 817 So. 2d at 887 (citations omitted).

In the instant case, it took thirty-five minutes for the officer to obtain the necessary information and write the citation. We conclude, based on the facts and circumstances of this case, that this time far exceeded that which was necessary to issue the citation to Williams. Because Williams was illegally detained at the time the canine search began, the search was improper, and the drugs, paraphernalia and firearm were illegally seized and therefore inadmissible in evidence. *Eldridge*; *Maxwell*. Hence, the trial court erred in denying the motion to suppress.

Moreover, we cannot ignore the fact that the officer actually had completed the citation and handed it to Williams before the drug dog performed the search of the vehicle. Even if it was reasonable to take thirty-five minutes to obtain the necessary information and issue the citation, the stop had ended before Williams was directed to step to the median, citation in hand, so the dog could proceed with the search. Because the stop had ended before the drug search by the dog began and because the officer had no basis for suspecting criminal activity, the continued detention of Williams was illegal. Accordingly, we reverse the order denying the motion to suppress and remand with directions to discharge Williams.

REVERSED AND REMANDED.

ORFINGER and MONACO, JJ., concur.

———————

Notes and Questions to Consider:

1. Perhaps a routine traffic stop is more like a brief stop under *Terry v. Ohio*, 392 U.S. 1 (1968), than an arrest. Why was it relevant that the initial stop exceeded the time necessary to write the automobile citation? How did this implicate a constitutional right of the driver?

2. Was this 2004 decision of a Florida state court a harbinger of a future ruling of the Supreme Court of the United States? Eleven years later, the U.S. Supreme Court decided *Rodriguez v. United States*, 135 S. Ct. 1609, 191 L. Ed. 2d 492 (2015). There, a policeman finished issuing the citation to the driver but then delayed the occupants of the vehicle for another seven to eight minutes to do a walk around with a canine. The Federal Court of Appeals held this to be a *de minimis* infringement on liberty that did not violate any constitutional rights. The U.S. Supreme Court reversed, holding that "a police stop exceeding the time needed to handle the matter for which the stop was made violates the Constitution's shield against unreasonable seizures. A seizure justified only by a police-observed traffic violation, therefore, 'become[s] unlawful if it is prolonged beyond the time reasonably required to complete th[e] mission' of issuing a ticket for the violation." 135 S. Ct. at 1612 (citing *Illinois v. Caballes*, 543 U.S. 405 (2005)).

3. What if the officer's work issuing the citation is completed, or reasonably should be completed, but then the officer develops a reasonable suspicion about this driver about another matter?

———————

Tobin v. State of Florida

First District Court of Appeal of Florida, 2014
146 So. 3d 159

MARSTILLER, J.

We have for review the trial court's denial of Appellant's dispositive motion to suppress evidence he was driving with a suspended or revoked license, which led the court to find Appellant in violation of community control. Because the deputy sheriff who stopped Appellant's vehicle lacked the reasonable, articulable suspicion of criminal activity necessary to justify what the court determined—and the State conceded—was an investigatory stop, we conclude the court erred in denying the motion to suppress.

Appellant was on two years' community control, followed by two years' probation, for committing battery on a law enforcement officer and resisting an officer with violence. On the night in question, the Okaloosa County Sheriff's Office received two anonymous calls complaining of a disturbance at a particular residence or business located at the end of a privately-maintained road. The Sheriff's Office had received complaints in the past about disturbances at the property; some complaints were founded, some were not. The first anonymous call that night indicated firearms may be involved. When deputies investigated, they found no disturbance. Sometime later, a second call came in reporting a disturbance at the property, this time alleging someone on the property was overheard shouting "Shoot me now!" Two deputies responded, each in his own cruiser. The first deputy to arrive saw a vehicle leaving the property as he approached, and radioed to the second deputy, who was nearer to the intersection of the private road and the public street, to stop the vehicle. The second deputy, seeing the vehicle coming directly toward him, activated the blue lights on his cruiser, causing the then-unknown driver to stop his vehicle "beak to beak" with the cruiser. When Appellant began to get out of the vehicle, the deputy directed him to stay put. The deputy testified at the suppression hearing he did so because of concerns, based on the anonymous call, that a firearm may be present. Upon approaching the vehicle, however, the deputy recognized Appellant, knew he was on community control, and knew his driver's license was suspended. At that point, he arrested Appellant for driving with a suspended license. The deputy also smelled alcohol on Appellant's breath and found a cup containing an alcoholic beverage in the passenger or back seat of Appellant's vehicle.

The State later filed an affidavit of violation of community control based on the new law violation and failure to abstain from using alcohol. Upon denying Appellant's motion to suppress, the trial court found only the new law violation proven, revoked Appellant's community control on that basis, and entered judgment sentencing him to 36 months in prison.

It is well settled that, to effect a constitutionally-permissible investigatory stop, a law enforcement officer must have a well-founded, articulable suspicion that the person stopped has committed, is committing, or is about to commit a crime. § 901.151, Fla. Stat. (2012), *Terry v. Ohio*, 392 U.S. 1 (1968); *Popple v. State*, 626 So. 2d 185, 186 (Fla. 1993); *Berry v. State*, 86 So. 3d 595, 598 (Fla. 1st DCA 2012). "Mere suspicion is not enough to support a [*Terry*] stop." *Popple*, 626 So. 2d at 186.

The parties assert that whether the deputy who stopped Appellant's vehicle had the requisite well-founded suspicion of criminal activity turns on how the anonymous calls are characterized. *See State v. Maynard*, 783 So. 2d 226, 228, (Fla. 2001). Appellant argues the calls were merely anonymous tips that, absent additional information obtained by the deputies, were not sufficiently reliable to justify the detention that occurred here. The State counters that the callers can be reasonably characterized as citizen informants whose calls are presumed reliable and generally are sufficient to support an investigatory detention without further corroboration.

"Reasonable suspicion ... is dependent upon both the content of information possessed by police and its degree of reliability. Both factors—quantity and quality—are considered in the 'totality of circumstances—the whole picture,' that must be taken into account when evaluating whether there is reasonable suspicion." *Alabama v. White*, 496 U.S. 325, 330 (1990) (quoting *United States v. Cortez*, 449 U.S. 411, 417). "'In analyzing whether third-party information can provide the requisite reasonable suspicion, courts have looked to the reliability of the informant as well as the reliability of the information provided.'" *Berry*, 86 So. 3d at 598 (quoting *D.P. v. State*, 65 So. 3d 123, 127 (Fla. 3d DCA 2011)). The less reliable the tip, the more independent corroboration will be required to establish reasonable suspicion. *White*, 496 U.S. at 330, 110 S.Ct. 2412. On the "spectrum of reliability," an anonymous tip has "relatively low" reliability. *Berry*, 86 So. 3d at 598; *see also State v. DeLuca*, 40 So. 3d 120, 124 (Fla. 1st DCA 2010). This is because "an anonymous tip alone seldom demonstrates the informant's basis of knowledge or veracity as ordinary citizens generally do not provide extensive recitations of the basis of their everyday observations and given that the veracity of persons supplying [such] tips" cannot be determined. *White*, 496 U.S. at 329. Thus, "[a]n anonymous tip requires that the information be 'sufficiently corroborated' by the officer to constitute reasonable suspicion[.]" *Berry*, 86 So. 3d at 598 (citing *State v. Evans*, 692 So. 2d 216, 218 (Fla. 4th DCA 1997)). A citizen informant, on the other hand, is presumed highly reliable because his or her "motivation in reporting illegality is the promotion of justice and public safety," and because the informant gives his or her name to police and "can be held accountable for the accuracy of the information given." *DeLuca*, 40 So. 3d at 124. Therefore, "[a] tip from a citizen informant is sufficient by itself to provide law enforcement with reasonable suspicion to conduct a *Terry* stop." *Berry*, 86 So. 3d at 599 (citing *State v. Maynard*, 783 So. 2d 226, 228 (Fla. 2001)).

Applying these principles to the facts in the instant case, we conclude the deputy who stopped Appellant's car did not have a well-founded suspicion of criminal activity needed to effect a lawful *Terry* stop. The disturbance calls that sent the deputies to the property on the night [in] question were anonymous tips bereft of any details indicating the information given was reliable. Indeed, the first call proved to be unfounded after deputies investigated. The second call, alleging someone was overheard yelling "Shoot me now," still did not provide any specific, articulable facts indicating that Appellant (or any other identifiable person, for that matter) was engaged in criminal activity. Thus, even if, as the State argues, we could characterize the callers as citizen informants, there still was insufficient information given to support a reasonable, articulable suspicion that a crime had been, or was being, committed. *See Florida v. J.L.*, 529 U.S. 266 (2000) (holding anonymous tip claiming person was carrying a gun insufficient, without more, to justify stop and frisk of the person); *Baptiste v. State*, 995 So. 2d 285 (Fla. 2008) (holding anonymous 911 call describing person and alleging person had waved firearm in public not sufficiently reliable to provide reasonable suspicion for investigative stop of person matching the description).

Because the anonymous calls provided neither the quantity nor the quality of information necessary to create reasonable suspicion, the deputies needed additional, independently-obtained information. They had none, for they had not yet begun to investigate the alleged disturbance when Appellant's car was stopped. Nor did they observe any behavior by Appellant to generate reasonable suspicion he was or had been engaged in criminal activity involving a firearm. Compare *Hudson v. State*, 41 So. 3d 948 (Fla. 2d DCA 2010) (finding reasonable suspicion where officers received anonymous call that a man was burglarizing cars in stadium parking lot, and observed person matching "vague description" carrying two duffel bags and hurriedly walking away from stadium) and *J.H. v. State*, 106 So. 3d 1001 (Fla. 3d DCA 2013) (finding no reasonable suspicion where officer responded to scene of fight reported by anonymous caller and observed no fight, but saw and stopped a youth matching description who was merely sweating and out of breath and appeared nervous).

If the second deputy's action could be characterized as attempting a consensual encounter with Appellant, see generally *Popple*, 626 So. 2d at 186, we could affirm the trial court's denial of Appellant's motion to suppress. But the deputy effected the stop of Appellant's car by activating the blue lights on his cruiser, positioning the cruiser on the road such that Appellant had to stop directly opposite, and ordering Appellant to remain in the car when he attempted to step out. "Although there is no litmus-paper test for distinguishing a consensual encounter from a seizure, a significant identifying characteristic of a consensual encounter is that the officer cannot hinder or restrict the person's freedom to leave or freedom to refuse to answer inquiries[.]" *Id.* at 187. On the other hand, "a person is seized if, under the circumstances, a reasonable person would conclude that he or she is not free to end the encounter and depart." *Id.* at 188. What occurred in this case was a seizure — an investigatory stop for which a reasonable, articulable suspicion of criminal activity *by Appellant* was required. Because the anonymous calls failed to provide deputies with the requisite level of suspicion, the stop of Appellant's car was unlawful, and the trial court should have granted the motion to suppress. Accordingly, we reverse the order of revocation of community control and the subsequent judgment and sentence, and direct the trial court to reinstate Appellant's community control.

REVERSED and REMANDED with directions. . . .

———————

Notes and Questions to Consider:

1. What is the court's rationale for concluding that "someone was overheard yelling 'Shoot me now'" does not yield a reasonable suspicion of criminal activity?

2. Would the court's logic hold true if that same yell had been heard inside a crowded theatre? What about if outside in an open, vacant field?

———————

State [of Florida] v. Teamer

Supreme Court of Florida, 2014
151 So. 3d 421

QUINCE, J.

This case is before the Court for review of the decision of the First District Court of Appeal in *Teamer v. State*, 108 So. 3d 664 (Fla. 1st DCA 2013). The district court certified that its decision is in direct conflict with the decision of the Fourth District Court of Appeal in *Aders v. State*, 67 So. 3d 368 (Fla. 4th DCA 2011). We have jurisdiction. *See* art. V, § 3(b)(4), Fla. Const. As we explain, we approve the First District's decision and disapprove that of the Fourth District.

Facts and Procedural History

On June 22, 2010, an Escambia County Deputy Sheriff observed Kerrick Teamer driving a *bright green* Chevrolet. *Teamer*, 108 So. 3d at 665. After noticing the car, the deputy continued on his patrol, driving into one of the neighborhoods in that area. Upon traveling back to where he had first seen Teamer, the deputy again observed Teamer driving the same car. The deputy then "ran" the number from Teamer's license plate through the Florida Department of Highway Safety and Motor Vehicles (DHSMV) database, as is customary for him while on patrol, and learned that the vehicle was registered as a *blue* Chevrolet. *Id.* The database did not return any information regarding the model of the vehicle. Based only on the color inconsistency, the deputy pulled the car over to conduct a traffic stop.

"Upon interviewing the occupants, the deputy learned that the vehicle had recently been painted, thus explaining the inconsistency." *Id.* However, during the stop, the deputy noticed a strong odor of marijuana emanating from the car and decided to conduct a search of the vehicle, Teamer, and the other passenger. *Id.* "Marijuana and crack cocaine were recovered from the vehicle, and about $1,100 in cash was recovered from [Teamer]. [He] was charged with trafficking in cocaine (between 28–200 grams), possession of marijuana (less than 20 grams), and possession of drug paraphernalia" (scales). *Id.*

On October 4, 2010, Teamer filed a motion to suppress the results of the stop as products of an unlawful, warrantless search. At the hearing on the motion to suppress, the deputy acknowledged that, in his training and experience, he had encountered individuals who would switch license plates and he could not verify a vehicle's identification number without pulling over the vehicle. *Id.* On cross-examination, the deputy acknowledged that the car was not reported stolen, he had not observed any other traffic violations or suspicious or furtive behavior, he was not "aware of any reports of stolen vehicles or swapped plates in the area," and "the only thing that was out of the ordinary was the inconsistency of the vehicle color from the registration." *Id.*

The trial court denied the motion to suppress, explaining that the rationale for the denial was that the deputy "had a legal right to conduct an investigatory stop when a registration search of the automobile license tag reflected a different color than the observed color of the vehicle." The trial court found that the deputy made the investigatory stop "because the registration was not consistent with the color of the vehicle" and that since "the vehicle was legally stopped for investigative purposes," the odor of marijuana that the officer smelled during the stop gave him probable cause to conduct a search. After a jury trial, Teamer was convicted on all three counts as charged in the information. The trial judge sentenced him to six years on count one and time served on the other two counts.

Teamer appealed, and the First District reversed the trial court's denial of Teamer's motion to suppress, certifying conflict with the Fourth District in *Aders. Id.* at 670. The First District acknowledged "that any discrepancy between a vehicle's plates and the registration may legitimately raise a concern that the vehicle is stolen or the plates were swapped from another vehicle," but found that such concern must be weighed "against a citizen's right under the Fourth Amendment to travel on the roads free from governmental intrusions." *Id.* at 667. The district court cited several cases demonstrating that color discrepancy is typically one of *several* factors constituting reasonable suspicion. *Id.* at 668. The First District then cited two non-binding cases for the principle that a color discrepancy alone does not provide reasonable suspicion for a stop. *Id.* at 668–69. Relying on those cases and other "somewhat analogous cases involving investigations of 'temporary tags,'" the district court ruled that a color discrepancy alone did not warrant an investigatory stop. *Id.* at 669–70. The court found that under the converse ruling, "every person who changes the color of [his or her] vehicle is continually subject to an investigatory stop so long as the color inconsistency persists." *Id.* at 670. The First District stated that it was "hesitant to license an investigatory stop" under such circumstances. *Id.*

Analysis

In reviewing a trial court's ruling on a motion to suppress, the trial court's determinations of historical facts are reversed only if not supported by competent, substantial evidence. *Connor v. State*, 803 So. 2d 598, 608 (Fla. 2001). However, the application of the law to those facts is subject to de novo review. *Id.* Further, this Court is required to construe Florida's constitutional right against unreasonable searches and seizures "in conformity with the [Fourth] Amendment to the United

States Constitution, as interpreted by the United States Supreme Court." Art. I, § 12, Fla. Const.; *Bernie v. State*, 524 So. 2d 988, 990–91 (Fla. 1988) ("[W]e are bound to follow the interpretations of the United States Supreme Court with relation to the [F]ourth [A]mendment. . . .").

The United States Supreme Court has "held that the police can stop and briefly detain a person for investigative purposes if the officer has a reasonable suspicion supported by articulable facts that criminal activity 'may be afoot,' even if the officer lacks probable cause." *United States v. Sokolow*, 490 U.S. 1, 7 (1989) (quoting *Terry v. Ohio*, 392 U.S. 1, 30 (1968)); *Popple v. State*, 626 So. 2d 185, 186 (Fla. 1993) ("[A] police officer may reasonably detain a citizen temporarily if the officer has a reasonable suspicion that a person has committed, is committing, or is about to commit a crime." (citing § 901.151, Fla. Stat. (1991))). However, a "police officer must be able to point to specific and articulable facts which, taken together with rational inferences from those facts, reasonably warrant" an investigatory stop. *Terry*, 392 U.S. at 21. The Supreme Court has described reasonable suspicion as "a particularized and objective basis for suspecting the particular person stopped of criminal activity." *United States v. Cortez*, 449 U.S. 411, 417 (1981). This standard requires "something more than an 'inchoate and unparticularized suspicion or hunch.'" *Sokolow*, 490 U.S. at 7 (quoting *Terry*, 392 U.S. at 27) (internal quotation marks omitted).

"Reasonableness, of course, depends 'on a balance between the public interest and the individual's right to personal security free from arbitrary interference by law officers.'" *Pennsylvania v. Mimms*, 434 U.S. 106, 109 (1977) (quoting *United States v. Brignoni-Ponce*, 422 U.S. 873, 878 (1975)); *State v. Diaz*, 850 So. 2d 435, 439 (Fla. 2003) ("The real test is one of reasonableness, which involves balancing the interests of the State with those of the motorist."). "When a search or seizure is conducted without a warrant, the government bears the burden of demonstrating that the search or seizure was reasonable." *Hilton v. State*, 961 So. 2d 284, 296 (Fla. 2007) (citing *United States v. Johnson*, 63 F.3d 242, 245 (3d Cir. 1995) ("As a general rule, the burden of proof is on the defendant who seeks to suppress evidence. However, once the defendant has established a basis for his motion, *i.e.*, the search or seizure was conducted without a warrant, the burden shifts to the government to show that the search or seizure was reasonable." (citation omitted))).

Reasonable suspicion must also be assessed based on "the totality of the circumstances—the whole picture," *Cortez*, 449 U.S. at 417; *United States v. Arvizu*, 534 U.S. 266, 277 (2002), and "from the standpoint of an objectively reasonable police officer," *Ornelas v. United States*, 517 U.S. 690, 696 (1996); *Arvizu*, 534 U.S. at 277. Thus, a police officer may draw inferences based on his own experience. *Ornelas*, 517 U.S. at 700; *Cortez*, 449 U.S. at 418 ("[A] trained officer draws inferences and makes deductions—inferences and deductions that might well elude an untrained person."). However, "the officer's subjective intentions are not involved in the determination of reasonableness." *Hilton*, 961 So. 2d at 294; *Whren v. United States*, 517 U.S. 806, 813 (1996) (recognizing the rejection of "any argument that the constitutional reasonableness of traffic stops depends on the actual motivations of the individual officers involved").

"[I]nnocent behavior will frequently provide the basis" for reasonable suspicion. *Sokolow*, 490 U.S. at 10; *see also Illinois v. Wardlow*, 528 U.S. 119, 125 (2000) (acknowledging this fact and recognizing that an officer can detain an individual to resolve an ambiguity regarding suspicious yet lawful or innocent conduct). "[T]he relevant inquiry is not whether particular conduct is innocent or guilty, but the degree of suspicion that attaches to particular types of noncriminal acts." *Sokolow*, 490 U.S. at 10 (internal quotation marks omitted). In the instant case, the State concedes that "the failure to update a vehicle registration to reflect a new color is not in specific violation of a Florida law." Thus, what degree of suspicion attaches to this noncriminal act?

To warrant an investigatory stop, the law requires not just a mere suspicion of criminal activity, but a reasonable, well-founded one. *Popple*, 626 So. 2d at 186 ("[A]n investigatory stop requires a well-founded, articulable suspicion of criminal activity."). In *Terry*, the stop was found appropriate because the officer "had observed [three men] go [t]hrough a series of acts, each of them perhaps innocent in itself, but which taken together warranted further investigation." *Terry*, 392 U.S. at 22. The U.S. Supreme Court described the scenario as follows:

> There is nothing unusual in two men standing together on a street corner, perhaps waiting for someone. Nor is there anything suspicious about people in such circumstances strolling up and down the street, singly or in pairs. Store windows, moreover, are made to be looked in. But the story is quite different where, as here, two men hover about a street corner for an extended period of time, at the end of which it becomes apparent that they are not waiting for anyone or anything; where these men pace alternately along an identical route, pausing to stare in the same store window roughly 24 times; where each completion of this route is followed immediately by a conference between the two men on the corner; where they are joined in one of these conferences by a third man who leaves swiftly; and where the two men finally follow the third and rejoin him a couple of blocks away.

Id. at 22–23. The Supreme Court found that "[i]t would have been poor police work indeed for an officer of 30 years' experience in the detection of thievery from stores in this same neighborhood to have failed to investigate this behavior further." *Id.* at 23. Thus each seemingly innocent activity in *Terry* had a cumulative effect of providing an officer with a reasonable suspicion.

Conversely, in *State v. Johnson*, 561 So. 2d 1139, 1142 (Fla. 1990), this Court rejected an officer's use of a self-created drug courier profile because "Florida law does not permit a profile based on factors that are little more than mundane or unremarkable descriptions of everyday law-abiding activities." We noted that a drug courier profile in a Supreme Court case was upheld "precisely because it described *unusual* conduct that set the defendant apart from other travelers and that strongly suggested concealed criminal conduct." *Id.* We invalidated the profile used in *Johnson* because "there was nothing at all unusual or out of the ordinary about the conduct that" fit within the profile. *Id.* at 1142–43. In so holding, we stated that individuals fitting within the officer's profile "simply cannot be described as an inherently 'suspicious' bunch." *Id.* at 1143. The innocent factors within the profile failed to create a reasonable suspicion.

Turning to the instant case, the sole basis here for the investigatory stop is an observation of one completely noncriminal factor, not several incidents of innocent activity combining under a totality of the circumstances to arouse a reasonable suspicion—as was the case in *Terry*. The discrepancy between the vehicle registration and the color the deputy observed does present an ambiguous situation, and the Supreme Court has recognized that an officer can detain an individual to resolve an ambiguity regarding suspicious yet lawful or innocent conduct. *Wardlow*, 528 U.S. at 125. However, the suspicion still must be a reasonable one. *Popple*, 626 So. 2d at 186 ("Mere suspicion is not enough to support a stop."). In this case, there simply are not enough facts to demonstrate reasonableness. Like the factors in *Johnson*, the color discrepancy here is not "inherently suspicious" or "unusual" enough or so "out of the ordinary" as to provide an officer with a reasonable suspicion of criminal activity, especially given the fact that it is not against the law in Florida to change the color of your vehicle without notifying the DHSMV.

The law allows officers to draw rational inferences, but to find reasonable suspicion based on this single noncriminal factor would be to license investigatory stops on nothing more than an officer's hunch. Doing so would be akin to finding reasonable suspicion for an officer to stop an individual for walking in a sparsely occupied area after midnight simply because that officer testified that, in his experience, people who walk in such areas after midnight tend to commit robberies. Without more, this one fact may provide a "mere suspicion," but it does not rise to the level of a reasonable suspicion. Neither does the sole innocent factor here—a color discrepancy—rise to such level. The deputy may have had a suspicion, but it was not a reasonable or well-founded one, especially given the fact that the driver of the vehicle was not engaged in any suspicious activity. Moreover, "the government provided no evidence to tip the scales from a mere hunch to something even approaching reasonable and articulable suspicion, despite attempting to justify a detention based on one observed incident of completely innocent behavior in a non-suspicious context." *United States v. Uribe*, 709 F.3d 646, 652 (7th Cir. 2013).

Reasonableness also "depends 'on a balance between the public interest and the individual's right to personal security free from arbitrary interference by law officers.'" *Mimms*, 434 U.S. at 109 (quoting *Brignoni-Ponce*, 422 U.S. at 878); *Diaz*, 850 So. 2d at 439 ("The real test is one of reasonableness, which involves balancing the interests of the State with those of the motorist."). In order to determine reasonableness, courts "must balance the nature and quality of the intrusion on the individual's Fourth Amendment interests against the importance of the governmental interests alleged to justify the intrusion." *United States v. Place*, 462 U.S. 696, 703 (1983); *Delaware v. Prouse*, 440 U.S. 648, 654 (1979) ("[T]he permissibility of a particular law enforcement practice is judged by balancing its intrusion on the individual's Fourth Amendment interests against its promotion of legitimate governmental interests."). Thus we must balance the nature and quality of the intrusion required to stop an individual and investigate a color discrepancy against the government's interest in finding stolen vehicles or enforcing vehicle registration laws.

In *Brignoni-Ponce*, the Supreme Court invalidated a roving patrol stop by Border Patrol agents near a closed checkpoint operation at the Mexican border. 422 U.S. at 886. In stopping the vehicle, the agents had relied on a single factor—"the apparent Mexican ancestry of the occupants." *Id.* at 885–86. As part of balancing the public interest with the motorist's rights, the Supreme Court outlined as the governmental interest preventing illegal aliens from entering this country. *Id.* at 878–80. However, despite the importance of that interest, the "modest" intrusion of a brief stop, and the absence of practical alternatives for policing the border, the Court found that the apparent Mexican heritage of the occupants did not provide reasonable suspicion for a stop. *Id.* at 881, 886. The Court stated, "The likelihood that any given person of Mexican ancestry is an alien is high enough to make Mexican appearance a relevant factor, but standing alone it does not justify stopping all Mexican-Americans to ask if they are aliens." *Id.* at 886–87; *cf. United States v. Martinez-Fuerte*, 428 U.S. 543, 557–59 (1976) (upholding stops for brief questioning at fixed checkpoints even with no reasonable suspicion of illegal aliens because although the need for such stops is as great as that in *Brignoni-Ponce*, a checkpoint stop is much less intrusive since "the generating of concern or even fright on the part of lawful travelers is appreciably less").

Similarly, in *Prouse*, the Supreme Court invalidated a random vehicle stop by roving patrol officers *solely* to confirm a driver's compliance with licensure and registration requirements. 440 U.S. at 659. The Court described the intrusion on the motorist's interests as follows:

> We cannot assume that the physical and psychological intrusion visited upon the occupants of a vehicle by a random stop to check documents is of any less moment than that occasioned by a stop by border agents on roving patrol. Both of these stops generally entail law enforcement officers signaling a moving automobile to pull over to the side of the roadway, by means of a possibly unsettling show of authority. Both interfere with freedom of movement, are inconvenient, and consume time. Both may create substantial anxiety. For Fourth Amendment purposes, we also see insufficient resemblance between sporadic and random stops of individual vehicles making their way through city traffic and those stops occasioned by roadblocks where all vehicles are brought to a halt or to a near halt, and all are subjected to a show of the police power of the community. At traffic checkpoints the motorist can see that other vehicles are being stopped, he can see visible signs of the officers' authority, and he is much less likely to be frightened or annoyed by the intrusion.

Id. at 657 (internal quotation marks omitted). The Court balanced that intrusion with the state's interests in apprehending stolen vehicles—which the Court characterized as indistinguishable from a "general interest in crime control"—and promoting roadway safety. *Id.* at 658–59. The Supreme Court held that given the alternative mechanisms available for enforcing traffic and vehicle safety regulations—the foremost of which being to act only upon observed violations—the incremental contribution to highway safety of the random stops in that case did not justify their intrusion on Fourth Amendment rights. *Id.* at 659.

The intrusion involved in the instant case is similar to that described in *Prouse*, especially considering that anyone who chooses to paint his or her vehicle a different color could be pulled over by law enforcement every time he or she drives it. *Prouse*, 440 U.S. at 662–63 ("Were the individual subject to unfettered governmental intrusion every time he entered an automobile, the security guaranteed by the Fourth Amendment would be seriously circumscribed."). Furthermore, the governmental interest here is not nearly as strong as that in *Brignoni-Ponce* of developing "effective measures to prevent the illegal entry of aliens at the Mexican border," 422 U.S. at 878–79, but is more like that in *Prouse*—"ensuring that . . . licensing, registration, and vehicle inspection requirements are being observed," 440 U.S. at 658. In fact, the Supreme Court described part of the interest at stake here—the apprehension of stolen vehicles—as indistinguishable "from the general interest in crime control." *Id.* at 659 n. 18.

Even more relevant is the Supreme Court's finding in *Brignoni-Ponce* that a single factor—the apparent Mexican ancestry of the vehicle's occupants—was not enough to furnish a reasonable suspicion that the occupants were illegal aliens. 422 U.S. at 885–86. Likewise, the likelihood that a color discrepancy such as that at issue here indicates a stolen vehicle *may* be high enough to make it a relevant factor, but standing alone, it does not justify initiating a stop to determine if the law has been violated. The deputy here needed more indicia of a violation to distinguish between an illegal transfer of license plates, for example, and a legal decision to paint one's vehicle. Conducting an investigatory stop based on a color discrepancy only when that discrepancy exists *in conjunction with* additional factors indicating potential criminal activity still protects the government's interests, while also preserving a motorist's right of freedom from arbitrary interference by law enforcement. We find that the governmental interest in this case is outweighed by Teamer's constitutional rights, and the investigatory stop was not warranted.

"Under the exclusionary rule announced by the United States Supreme Court, 'the Fourth Amendment bar[s] the use of evidence secured through an illegal search and seizure.'" *Hilton*, 961 So. 2d at 293 (alteration in original) (quoting *Mapp v. Ohio*, 367 U.S. 643, 648 (1961) (holding that the federal exclusionary rule applies to the states as well)). "Whether the exclusionary sanction is appropriately imposed in a particular case . . . is 'an issue separate from the question whether the Fourth Amendment rights of the party seeking to invoke the rule were violated by police conduct.'" *United States v. Leon*, 468 U.S. 897, 906 (1984) (quoting *Illinois v. Gates*, 462 U.S. 213, 223 (1983)).

The primary rationale behind the exclusionary rule is to deter law enforcement from violating constitutional rights. *Terry*, 392 U.S. at 12; *see also United States v.*

Calandra, 414 U.S. 338, 348 (1974) ("[T]he rule is a judicially created remedy designed to safeguard Fourth Amendment rights generally through its deterrent effect."). The instant case is not one in which the exclusionary rule "is powerless to deter invasions of constitutionally guaranteed rights [because] the police either have no interest in prosecuting or are willing to forgo successful prosecution in the interest of serving some other goal." *Terry*, 392 U.S. at 14. Applying the exclusionary rule here would have the required deterrent effect. *See, e.g., Prouse*, 440 U.S. at 651, 663 (affirming the trial court's judgment granting the defendant's motion to suppress).

Further, the State has not demonstrated that any exceptions apply. *Brown v. Illinois*, 422 U.S. 590, 604 (1975) (discussing whether to apply an exception to the exclusionary rule and stating that "the burden of showing admissibility rests, of course, on the prosecution"). The State argues a variation of the good faith exception to the exclusionary rule. This exception was first found to apply whenever a law enforcement officer conducts a search while relying, in good faith, upon a defective search warrant. *Leon*, 468 U.S. at 922; *Massachusetts v. Sheppard*, 468 U.S. 981, 987–89 (1984). Over time, however, the Supreme Court extended this exception to other factual scenarios, including searches where police acted in objectively reasonable reliance on binding judicial precedent. *Davis v. United States*, 131 S.Ct. 2419, 2428 (2011). However, the rule of *Davis* has no application to the present case because the *Aders* decision was issued on July 27, 2011 — more than one year *after* the stop of Teamer's vehicle. Thus *Aders* was not binding precedent on which the deputy could have relied.

Despite this fact, the State argues that the good faith exception should still apply because the deputy here "arrived at a conclusion shared by non-binding courts in other jurisdictions, and later shared by the Fourth District" in *Aders*. However, there are also nonbinding courts in other jurisdictions that have arrived at the exact opposite conclusion. *United States v. Uribe*, No. 2:10–cr–17–JMS–CMM, 2011 WL 4538407 (S.D.Ind. Sept. 28, 2011); *Commonwealth v. Mason*, 78 Va. Cir. 474 (Cir.Ct. 2009), *aff'd*, No. 1956–09–2, 2010 WL 768721 (Va.Ct.App. Mar. 9, 2010). We are satisfied that the exclusionary rule will have an appropriate deterrent effect in this case and that none of the exceptions to the rule apply.

Conclusion

Based on the foregoing, we disapprove the decision of the Fourth District in *Aders v. State*, 67 So. 3d 368 (Fla. 4th DCA 2011), and approve the First District's decision in *Teamer v. State*, 108 So. 3d 664 (Fla. 1st DCA 2013), reversing the trial court's judgment and sentence and ordering that Teamer be discharged.

It is so ordered.

LABARGA, C.J., and PARIENTE, LEWIS, and PERRY, JJ., concur.

CANADY, J., dissents with an opinion in which POLSTON, J., concurs.

CANADY, J., dissenting.

Because I conclude that the traffic stop of Kerrick Van Teamer's vehicle was based on a reasonable suspicion of criminal activity and that the trial court therefore correctly denied the motion to suppress, I dissent from the majority's approval of the First District Court of Appeal's decision reversing Teamer's judgment and sentence and ordering that he be discharged. I would quash the decision of the First District on review and approve the decision of the Fourth District in *Aders v. State*, 67 So. 3d 368 (Fla. 4th DCA 2011).

I.

"The Fourth Amendment permits brief investigative stops—such as the traffic stop in this case—when a law enforcement officer has 'a particularized and objective basis for suspecting the particular person stopped of criminal activity.'" *Navarette v. California*, 134 S.Ct. 1683, 1687 (2014) (quoting *United States v. Cortez*, 449 U.S. 411, 417–18 (1981)). This rule is rooted in *Terry v. Ohio*, 392 U.S. 1 (1968), where "the [Supreme] Court implicitly acknowledged the authority of the police to make a *forcible stop* of a person when the officer has reasonable, articulable suspicion that the person has been, is, or is about to be engaged in criminal activity." *United States v. Place*, 462 U.S. 696, 702 (1983).

The *Terry* rule recognizes that "[t]he Fourth Amendment requires 'some minimal level of objective justification' for making the stop." *United States v. Sokolow*, 490 U.S. 1, 7 (1989) (quoting *Immigration & Naturalization Serv. v. Delgado*, 466 U.S. 210, 217 (1984)). Reasonable suspicion thus requires "something more than an 'inchoate and unparticularized suspicion or "hunch."'" *Sokolow*, 490 U.S. at 7 (quoting *Terry*, 392 U.S. at 27). "A determination that reasonable suspicion exists, however, need not rule out the possibility of innocent conduct." *United States v. Arvizu*, 534 U.S. 266, 277 (2002). In permitting detentions based on reasonable suspicion, "*Terry* accepts the risk that officers may stop innocent people." *Illinois v. Wardlow*, 528 U.S. 119, 126 (2000). But when a stop lacks an objective basis, "the risk of arbitrary and abusive police practices exceeds tolerable limits." *Brown v. Texas*, 443 U.S. 47, 52 (1979). Courts making "reasonable-suspicion determinations . . . must look at the 'totality of the circumstances' of each case." *Arvizu*, 534 U.S. at 273.

The rule authorizing stops based on reasonable suspicion—which embodies an "exception to the probable-cause requirement"—rests on the Supreme Court's "balancing of the competing interests to determine the reasonableness of the type of seizure involved within the meaning of 'the Fourth Amendment's general proscription against unreasonable searches and seizures.'" *Place*, 462 U.S. at 703 (quoting *Terry*, 392 U.S. at 20). This balancing process involves weighing "the nature and quality of the intrusion on the individual's Fourth Amendment interests against the importance of the governmental interests alleged to justify the intrusion." *Id.* "A central concern in balancing these competing considerations in a variety of settings has been to assure that an individual's reasonable expectation of privacy is not subject to arbitrary invasions solely at the unfettered discretion of officers in the field." *Brown*, 443 U.S. at 51. The Supreme Court's categorical authorization of brief investigative detentions based on a reasonable suspicion of criminal activity flows from the conclusion that "[w]hen the nature and extent of the detention are minimally intrusive of the individual's Fourth Amendment interests, the opposing law enforcement interests can support a seizure based on less than probable cause." *Place*, 462 U.S. at 703.

II.

Here, the officer's suspicion was aroused by the discrepancy between the color of the vehicle driven by Teamer and the color that was indicated in the registration information for the vehicle associated with the license tag on Teamer's vehicle. Because of this discrepancy, a reasonable officer could suspect that the license tag may have been illegally transferred from the vehicle to which it was assigned. Although the color discrepancy was not necessarily indicative of illegality, it constituted "a particularized and objective basis for suspecting the particular person stopped of criminal activity." *Navarette*, 134 S.Ct. at 1687 (quoting *Cortez*, 449 U.S. at 417–18). The color discrepancy was "something more than an 'inchoate and unparticularized suspicion or "hunch."'" *Sokolow*, 490 U.S. at 7 (quoting *Terry*, 392 U.S. at 27, 88 S.Ct. 1868). I would therefore conclude that the officer had the "minimal level of objective justification" necessary to conduct a stop for the purpose of further investigating the discrepancy. *Sokolow*, 490 U.S. at 7 (quoting *Delgado*, 466 U.S. at 217).

"It is not uncommon for members of the same court to disagree as to whether the proper threshold for reasonable suspicion has been reached." William E. Ringel, *Searches & Seizures Arrests & Confessions* § 11:12 (Westlaw database updated March 2014). On the issue presented by this case, different courts have disagreed regarding whether the color discrepancy was sufficient to establish reasonable suspicion. Compare *Aders*, 67 So. 3d at 371 (holding that "[a] color discrepancy is enough to create a reasonable suspicion in the mind of a law enforcement officer of the violation of . . . criminal law"); *United States v. Uribe*, 709 F.3d 646 (7th Cir. 2013) (same); *Andrews v. State*, 289 Ga.App. 679, 658 S.E.2d 126 (2008) (same); *Smith v. State*, 713 N.E.2d 338 (Ind.Ct.App. 1999) (same); with *Van Teamer*, 108 So. 3d 664 (Fla. 1st DCA 2013) (holding that color discrepancy alone does not warrant an investigatory stop); *United States v. Uribe*, 2011 WL 4538407 (S.D.Ind. Sept. 28, 2011) (same); *Commonwealth v. Mason*, 2010 WL 768721 (Va.Ct.App. Mar. 9, 2010) (same). Different views on this question are no doubt influenced by divergent judgments regarding the likelihood that the color discrepancy had an innocent explanation — namely, the repainting of the vehicle after it was registered — and was not indicative of illegality. The courts in fact have no empirical basis for reaching a conclusion about that likelihood. But a stop predicated on such a color discrepancy unquestionably falls outside the category of "arbitrary invasions solely at the unfettered discretion of officers in the field." *Brown*, 443 U.S. at 51. A stop in such circumstances cannot fairly be called an "arbitrary and abusive" police practice. *Id.* at 52.

The crux of the majority's decision in this case is its conclusion that finding "reasonable suspicion based on this single noncriminal factor would be to license investigatory stops on nothing more than an officer's hunch." Majority op. at 428. This conclusion suggests a categorical rule that is not consistent with the framework established in the Supreme Court's Fourth Amendment jurisprudence. Although the totality of the circumstances must be taken into account in every case, that does not mean that an officer's reliance on a "single noncriminal factor"—such as the vehicle color discrepancy here—is the equivalent of a "hunch." The majority is wholly unjustified in categorizing an undeniably objective factor as a hunch. The majority's "effort to refine and elaborate the requirements of 'reasonable suspicion' in this case creates unnecessary difficulty in dealing with one of the relatively simple concepts embodied in the Fourth Amendment." *Sokolow*, 490 U.S. at 7–8.

The two cases on which the majority places primary reliance do not support the majority's line of analysis. In *United States v. Brignoni-Ponce*, 422 U.S. 873, 876 (1975), the Supreme Court considered "whether a roving patrol may stop a vehicle in an area near the border and question its occupants when the only ground for suspicion is that the occupants appear to be of Mexican ancestry." The Supreme Court concluded that "Mexican appearance" "standing alone . . . does not justify stopping all Mexican-Americans to ask if they are aliens." *Id.* at 887. The Supreme Court's rejection of stops based purely on ethnic classification does not support the conclusion that all stops where the officer relies on "a single noncriminal factor" are unconstitutional. Nor does *Delaware v. Prouse*, 440 U.S. 648, 655 (1979), where the Supreme Court rejected Delaware's argument "that patrol officers be subject to no constraints in deciding which automobiles shall be stopped for a license and registration check because the State's interest in discretionary spot checks as a means of ensuring the safety of its roadways outweighs the resulting intrusion on the privacy and security of the persons detained." *Prouse* thus does not address the issue of reasonable suspicion, and it sheds no light on whether reasonable suspicion existed in the case on review here.

III.

The officer's stop of Teamer did not transgress the requirements of the Fourth Amendment. The decision of the First District should be quashed, and Teamer's conviction and sentence should remain undisturbed.

POLSTON, J., concurs.

C. Searches, Seizures, and *Navarette v. California*

Recall that the protection against government search and seizure in the Constitution of the State of Florida states that this "right shall be construed in conformity with the 4th Amendment to the United States Constitution, as interpreted by the United States Supreme Court." Art. I, sec. 12, Fla. Const.

So this provision of the state constitution must be interpreted in light of *Navarette v. California*, 134 S. Ct. 1683, 188 L. Ed. 2d 680 (2014):

Navarette v. California

Supreme Court of the United States, 2014
134 S. Ct. 1683, 188 L. Ed. 2d 680

Justice Thomas delivered the opinion of the Court.

After a 911 caller reported that a vehicle had run her off the road, a police officer located the vehicle she identified during the call and executed a traffic stop. We hold that the stop complied with the Fourth Amendment because, under the totality of the circumstances, the officer had reasonable suspicion that the driver was intoxicated.

I

On August 23, 2008, a Mendocino County 911 dispatch team for the California Highway Patrol (CHP) received a call from another CHP dispatcher in neighboring Humboldt County. The Humboldt County dispatcher relayed a tip from a 911 caller, which the Mendocino County team recorded as follows: "'Showing southbound Highway 1 at mile marker 88, Silver Ford 150 pickup. Plate of 8–David–94925. Ran the reporting party off the roadway and was last seen approximately five [minutes] ago.'" App. 36a. The Mendocino County team then broadcast that information to CHP officers at 3:47 p.m.

A CHP officer heading northbound toward the reported vehicle responded to the broadcast. At 4:00 p.m., the officer passed the truck near mile marker 69. At about 4:05 p.m., after making a U-turn, he pulled the truck over. A second officer, who had separately responded to the broadcast, also arrived on the scene. As the two officers approached the truck, they smelled marijuana. A search of the truck bed revealed 30 pounds of marijuana. The officers arrested the driver, petitioner Lorenzo Prado Navarette, and the passenger, petitioner José Prado Navarette.

Petitioners moved to suppress the evidence, arguing that the traffic stop violated the Fourth Amendment because the officer lacked reasonable suspicion of criminal activity. Both the magistrate who presided over the suppression hearing and the Superior Court disagreed. Petitioners pleaded guilty to transporting marijuana and were sentenced to 90 days in jail plus three years of probation.

The California Court of Appeal affirmed, concluding that the officer had reasonable suspicion to conduct an investigative stop. The court reasoned that the content of the tip indicated that it came from an eyewitness victim of reckless driving, and that the officer's corroboration of the truck's description, location, and direction established that the tip was reliable enough to justify a traffic stop. Finally, the court concluded that the caller reported driving that was sufficiently dangerous to merit an investigative stop without waiting for the officer to observe additional reckless driving himself. The California Supreme Court denied review. We granted certiorari, and now affirm.

II

The Fourth Amendment permits brief investigative stops—such as the traffic stop in this case—when a law enforcement officer has "a particularized and objective basis for suspecting the particular person stopped of criminal activity." *United States v. Cortez*, 449 U.S. 411, 417–418 (1981); see also *Terry v. Ohio*, 392 U.S. 1, 21–22 (1968). The "reasonable suspicion" necessary to justify such a stop "is dependent upon both the content of information possessed by police and its degree of reliability." *Alabama v. White*, 496 U.S. 325, 330 (1990). The standard takes into account "the totality of the circumstances—the whole picture." *Cortez, supra*, at 417. Although a mere "hunch" does not create reasonable suspicion, *Terry, supra*, at 27, the level of suspicion the standard requires is "considerably less than proof of wrongdoing by a preponderance of the evidence," and "obviously less" than is necessary for probable cause, *United States v. Sokolow*, 490 U.S. 1, 7 (1989).

A

These principles apply with full force to investigative stops based on information from anonymous tips. We have firmly rejected the argument "that reasonable cause for a[n investigative stop] can only be based on the officer's personal observation, rather than on information supplied by another person." *Adams v. Williams*, 407 U.S. 143, 147 (1972). Of course, "an anonymous tip *alone* seldom demonstrates the informant's basis of knowledge or veracity." *White*, 496 U.S. at 329 (emphasis added). That is because "ordinary citizens generally do not provide extensive recitations of the basis of their everyday observations," and an anonymous tipster's veracity is "'by hypothesis largely unknown, and unknowable.'" *Ibid.* But under appropriate circumstances, an anonymous tip can demonstrate "sufficient indicia of reliability to provide reasonable suspicion to make [an] investigatory stop." *Id.* at 327.

Our decisions in *Alabama v. White*, 496 U.S. 325 (1990), and *Florida v. J.L.*, 529 U.S. 266 (2000), are useful guides. In *White*, an anonymous tipster told the police that a woman would drive from a particular apartment building to a particular motel in a brown Plymouth station wagon with a broken right tail light. The tipster further asserted that the woman would be transporting cocaine. 496 U.S. at 327. After confirming the innocent details, officers stopped the station wagon as it neared the motel and found cocaine in the vehicle. *Id.* at 331. We held that the officers' corroboration of certain details made the anonymous tip sufficiently reliable to create reasonable suspicion of criminal activity. By accurately predicting future behavior, the tipster demonstrated "a special familiarity with respondent's affairs," which in turn implied that the tipster had "access to reliable information about that individual's illegal activities." *Id.* at 332. We also recognized that an informant who is proved to tell the truth about some things is more likely to tell the truth about other things, "including the claim that the object of the tip is engaged in criminal activity." *Id.* at 331 (citing *Illinois v. Gates*, 462 U.S. 213, 244 (1983)).

In *J.L.*, by contrast, we determined that no reasonable suspicion arose from a bare-bones tip that a young black male in a plaid shirt standing at a bus stop was carrying a gun. 529 U.S. at 268. The tipster did not explain how he knew about the gun, nor did he suggest that he had any special familiarity with the young man's affairs. *Id.* at 271. As a result, police had no basis for believing "that the tipster ha[d] knowledge of concealed criminal activity." *Id.* at 272. Furthermore, the tip included no predictions of future behavior that could be corroborated to assess the tipster's credibility. *Id.* at 271. We accordingly concluded that the tip was insufficiently reliable to justify a stop and frisk.

B

The initial question in this case is whether the 911 call was sufficiently reliable to credit the allegation that petitioners' truck "ran the [caller] off the roadway." Even assuming for present purposes that the 911 call was anonymous, we conclude that the call bore adequate indicia of reliability for the officer to credit the caller's account. The officer was therefore justified in proceeding from the premise that the truck had, in fact, caused the caller's car to be dangerously diverted from the highway.

By reporting that she had been run off the road by a specific vehicle — a silver Ford F–150 pickup, license plate 8D94925 — the caller necessarily claimed eyewitness knowledge of the alleged dangerous driving. That basis of knowledge lends significant support to the tip's reliability. See *Gates, supra,* at 234 ("[An informant's] explicit and detailed description of alleged wrongdoing, along with a statement that the event was observed firsthand, entitles his tip to greater weight than might otherwise be the case"); *Spinelli v. United States,* 393 U.S. 410, 416 (1969) (a tip of illegal gambling is less reliable when "it is not alleged that the informant personally observed [the defendant] at work or that he had ever placed a bet with him"). This is in contrast to *J.L.,* where the tip provided no basis for concluding that the tipster had actually seen the gun. 529 U.S. at 271. Even in *White,* where we upheld the stop, there was scant evidence that the tipster had actually observed cocaine in the station wagon. We called *White* a "close case" because "[k]nowledge about a person's future movements indicates some familiarity with that person's affairs, but having such knowledge does not necessarily imply that the informant knows, in particular, whether that person is carrying hidden contraband." 529 U.S. at 271. A driver's claim that another vehicle ran her off the road, however, necessarily implies that the informant knows the other car was driven dangerously.

There is also reason to think that the 911 caller in this case was telling the truth. Police confirmed the truck's location near mile marker 69 (roughly 19 highway miles south of the location reported in the 911 call) at 4:00 p.m. (roughly 18 minutes after the 911 call). That timeline of events suggests that the caller reported the incident soon after she was run off the road. That sort of contemporaneous report has long been treated as especially reliable. In evidence law, we generally credit the proposition that statements about an event and made soon after perceiving that event are especially trustworthy because "substantial contemporaneity of event and statement negate the likelihood of deliberate or conscious misrepresentation." *Advisory Committee's Notes on Fed. Rule Evid. 803(1),* 28 U.S.C.App., p. 371 (describing the rationale for the hearsay exception for "present sense impression[s]"). A similar rationale applies to a "statement relating to a startling event" — such as getting run off the road — "made while the declarant was under the stress of excitement that it caused." Fed. Rule Evid. 803(2) (hearsay exception for "excited utterances"). Unsurprisingly, 911 calls that would otherwise be inadmissible hearsay have often been admitted on those grounds. See D. Binder, Hearsay Handbook §8.1, pp. 257–259 (4th ed. 2013–2014) (citing cases admitting 911 calls as present sense impressions); *id.* §9.1 at 274–275 (911 calls admitted as excited utterances). There was no indication that the tip in *J.L.* (or even in *White*) was contemporaneous with the observation of criminal activity or made under the stress of excitement caused by a startling event, but those considerations weigh in favor of the caller's veracity here.

Another indicator of veracity is the caller's use of the 911 emergency system. See Brief for Respondent 40–41, 44; Brief for United States as *Amicus Curiae* 16–18. A 911 call has some features that allow for identifying and tracing callers, and thus provide some safeguards against making false reports with immunity. See *J.L.*, *supra*, at 276, 120 S.Ct. 1375 (KENNEDY, J., concurring). As this case illustrates, 911 calls can be recorded, which provides victims with an opportunity to identify the false tipster's voice and subject him to prosecution, see, *e.g.*, Cal.Penal Code Ann. §653x (West 2010) (makes "telephon[ing] the 911 emergency line with the intent to annoy or harass" punishable by imprisonment and fine); see also §148.3 (2014 West Cum. Supp.) (prohibits falsely reporting "that an 'emergency' exists"); §148.5 (prohibits falsely reporting "that a felony or misdemeanor has been committed"). The 911 system also permits law enforcement to verify important information about the caller. In 1998, the Federal Communications Commission (FCC) began to require cellular carriers to relay the caller's phone number to 911 dispatchers. 47 CFR §20.18(d)(1) (2013) (FCC's "Phase I enhanced 911 services" requirements). Beginning in 2001, carriers have been required to identify the caller's geographic location with increasing specificity. §§20.18(e)-(h) ("Phase II enhanced 911 service" requirements). And although callers may ordinarily block call recipients from obtaining their identifying information, FCC regulations exempt 911 calls from that privilege. §§64.1601(b), (d)(4)(ii) ("911 emergency services" exemption from rule that, when a caller so requests, "a carrier may not reveal that caller's number or name"). None of this is to suggest that tips in 911 calls are *per se* reliable. Given the foregoing technological and regulatory developments, however, a reasonable officer could conclude that a false tipster would think twice before using such a system. The caller's use of the 911 system is therefore one of the relevant circumstances that, taken together, justified the officer's reliance on the information reported in the 911 call.

C

Even a reliable tip will justify an investigative stop only if it creates reasonable suspicion that "criminal activity may be afoot." *Terry*, 392 U.S. at 30. We must therefore determine whether the 911 caller's report of being run off the roadway created reasonable suspicion of an ongoing crime such as drunk driving as opposed to an isolated episode of past recklessness. See *Cortez*, 449 U.S. at 417 ("An investigatory stop must be justified by some objective manifestation that the person stopped is, or is about to be, engaged in criminal activity"). We conclude that the behavior alleged by the 911 caller, "viewed from the standpoint of an objectively reasonable police officer, amount[s] to reasonable suspicion" of drunk driving. *Ornelas v. United States*, 517 U.S. 690, 696 (1996). The stop was therefore proper.

Reasonable suspicion depends on "the factual and practical considerations of everyday life on which reasonable and prudent men, not legal technicians, act." *Id.*, at 695. Under that common sense approach, we can appropriately recognize certain driving behaviors as sound indicia of drunk driving. See, *e.g.*, *People v. Wells*, 38 Cal.4th 1078, 1081, 136 P.3d 810, 811 (2006) ("weaving all over the roadway"); *State v. Prendergast*, 103 Hawai'i 451, 452–453, 83 P.3d 714, 715–716 (2004) ("cross[ing] over the center line" on a highway and "almost caus[ing] several head-on collisions"); *State v. Golotta*, 178 N.J. 205, 209, 837 A.2d 359, 361 (2003) (driving "all over the road" and "weaving back and forth"); *State v. Walshire*, 634 N.W.2d 625, 626 (Iowa 2001) ("driving in the median"). Indeed, the accumulated experience of thousands of officers suggests that these sorts of erratic behaviors are strongly correlated with drunk driving. See Nat. Highway Traffic Safety Admin., THE VISUAL DETECTION OF DWI MOTORISTS 4–5 (Mar. 2010), online at http://nhtsa. gov/staticfiles/nti/pdf/808677.pdf (as visited Apr. 18, 2014, and available in Clerk of Court's case file). Of course, not all traffic infractions imply intoxication. Unconfirmed reports of driving without a seatbelt or slightly over the speed limit, for example, are so tenuously connected to drunk driving that a stop on those grounds alone would be constitutionally suspect. But a reliable tip alleging the dangerous behaviors discussed above generally would justify a traffic stop on suspicion of drunk driving.

The 911 caller in this case reported more than a minor traffic infraction and more than a conclusory allegation of drunk or reckless driving. Instead, she alleged a specific and dangerous result of the driver's conduct: running another car off the highway. That conduct bears too great a resemblance to paradigmatic manifestations of drunk driving to be dismissed as an isolated example of recklessness. Running another vehicle off the road suggests lane-positioning problems, decreased vigilance, impaired judgment, or some combination of those recognized drunk driving cues. See Visual Detection of DWI Motorists 4–5. And the experience of many officers suggests that a driver who almost strikes a vehicle or another object—the exact scenario that ordinarily causes "running [another vehicle] off the roadway"—is likely intoxicated. See *id.* at 5, 8. As a result, we cannot say that the officer acted unreasonably under these circumstances in stopping a driver whose alleged conduct was a significant indicator of drunk driving.

Petitioners' attempts to second-guess the officer's reasonable suspicion of drunk driving are unavailing. It is true that the reported behavior might also be explained by, for example, a driver responding to "an unruly child or other distraction." Brief for Petitioners 21. But we have consistently recognized that reasonable suspicion "need not rule out the possibility of innocent conduct." *United States v. Arvizu*, 534 U.S. 266, 277 (2002).

Nor did the absence of additional suspicious conduct, after the vehicle was first spotted by an officer, dispel the reasonable suspicion of drunk driving. Brief for

Petitioners 23–24. It is hardly surprising that the appearance of a marked police car would inspire more careful driving for a time. Cf. *Arvizu*, *supra*, at 275 ("[s]lowing down after spotting a law enforcement vehicle" does not dispel reasonable suspicion of criminal activity). Extended observation of an allegedly drunk driver might eventually dispel a reasonable suspicion of intoxication, but the 5-minute period in this case hardly sufficed in that regard. Of course, an officer who already has such a reasonable suspicion need not surveil a vehicle at length in order to personally observe suspicious driving. See *Adams v. Williams*, 407 U.S. at 147 (repudiating the argument that "reasonable cause for a[n investigative stop] can only be based on the officer's personal observation"). Once reasonable suspicion of drunk driving arises, "[t]he reasonableness of the officer's decision to stop a suspect does not turn on the availability of less intrusive investigatory techniques." *Sokolow*, 490 U.S. at 11. This would be a particularly inappropriate context to depart from that settled rule, because allowing a drunk driver a second chance for dangerous conduct could have disastrous consequences.

III

Like *White*, this is a "close case." 496 U.S. at 332. As in that case, the indicia of the 911 caller's reliability here are stronger than those in *J.L.*, where we held that a bare-bones tip was unreliable. 529 U.S. at 271. Although the indicia present here are different from those we found sufficient in *White*, there is more than one way to demonstrate "a particularized and objective basis for suspecting the particular person stopped of criminal activity." *Cortez*, 449 U.S. at 417–418. Under the totality of the circumstances, we find the indicia of reliability in this case sufficient to provide the officer with reasonable suspicion that the driver of the reported vehicle had run another vehicle off the road. That made it reasonable under the circumstances for the officer to execute a traffic stop. We accordingly affirm.

It is so ordered.

Justice SCALIA, with whom Justice GINSBURG, Justice SOTOMAYOR, and Justice KAGAN join, dissenting.

The California Court of Appeal in this case relied on jurisprudence from the California Supreme Court (adopted as well by other courts) to the effect that "an anonymous and uncorroborated tip regarding a possibly intoxicated highway driver" provides without more the reasonable suspicion necessary to justify a stop. *People v. Wells*, 38 Cal.4th l078, 1082, 136 P.3d 810, 812 (2006). See also, *e.g.*, *United States v. Wheat*, 278 F.3d 722, 729–730 (C.A.8 2001); *State v. Walshire*, 634 N.W.2d 625, 626–627, 630 (Iowa 2001). Today's opinion does not explicitly adopt such a departure from our normal Fourth Amendment requirement that anonymous tips must be corroborated; it purports to adhere to our prior cases, such as *Florida v. J.L.*, 529 U.S. 266 (2000), and *Alabama v. White*, 496 U.S. 325 (1990). Be not deceived.

Law enforcement agencies follow closely our judgments on matters such as this, and they will identify at once our new rule: So long as the caller identifies where the car is, anonymous claims of a single instance of possibly careless or reckless driving, called in to 911, will support a traffic stop. This is not my concept, and I am sure would not be the Framers', of a people secure from unreasonable searches and seizures. I would reverse the judgment of the Court of Appeal of California.

I

The California Highway Patrol in this case knew nothing about the tipster on whose word — and that alone — they seized Lorenzo and José Prado Navarette. They did not know her name. They did not know her phone number or address. They did not even know where she called from (she may have dialed in from a neighboring county, App. 33a–34a).

The tipster said the truck had "[run her] off the roadway," *id.*, at 36a, but the police had no reason to credit that charge and many reasons to doubt it, beginning with the peculiar fact that the accusation was anonymous. "[E]liminating accountability . . . is ordinarily the very purpose of anonymity." *McIntyre v. Ohio Elections Comm'n*, 514 U.S. 334, 385, 115 S.Ct. 1511, 131 L.Ed.2d 426 (1995) (SCALIA, J., dissenting). The unnamed tipster "can lie with impunity," *J.L., supra*, at 275, 120 S.Ct. 1375 (KENNEDY, J., concurring). Anonymity is especially suspicious with respect to the call that is the subject of the present case. When does a victim complain to the police about an arguably criminal act (running the victim off the road) without giving his identity, so that he can accuse and testify when the culprit is caught?

The question before us, the Court agrees, *ante*, at 1690–1691, is whether the "content of information possessed by police and its degree of reliability," *White*, 496 U.S. at 330, gave the officers reasonable suspicion that the driver of the truck (Lorenzo) was committing an ongoing crime. When the only source of the government's information is an informant's tip, we ask whether the tip bears sufficient "'indicia of reliability,'" *id.* at 328, to establish "a particularized and objective basis for suspecting the particular person stopped of criminal activity," *United States v. Cortez*, 449 U.S. 411, 417–418 (1981).

The most extreme case, before this one, in which an anonymous tip was found to meet this standard was *White, supra*. There the reliability of the tip was established by the fact that it predicted the target's behavior in the finest detail — a detail that could be known only by someone familiar with the target's business: She would, the tipster said, leave a particular apartment building, get into a brown Plymouth station wagon with a broken right tail light, and drive immediately to a particular motel. *Id.* at 327. Very few persons would have such intimate knowledge, and hence knowledge of the unobservable fact that the woman was carrying unlawful drugs was plausible. *Id.*, at 332. Here the Court makes a big deal of the fact that the tipster was dead right about the fact that a silver Ford F–150 truck (license plate 8D94925) was traveling south on Highway 1 somewhere near mile marker 88. But everyone in the world who saw the car would have that knowledge, and anyone who wanted the car stopped would have to provide that information. Unlike the situation in *White*, that generally available knowledge in no way makes it plausible that the tipster saw the car run someone off the road.

The Court says, *ante*, at 1689, that "[b]y reporting that she had been run off the road by a specific vehicle . . . the caller necessarily claimed eyewitness knowledge." So what? The issue is not how she claimed to know, but whether what she claimed to know was true. The claim to "eyewitness knowledge" of being run off the road supports *not at all* its veracity; nor does the amazing, mystifying prediction (so far short of what existed in *White*) that the petitioners' truck *would be heading south on Highway 1.*

The Court finds "reason to think" that the informant "was telling the truth" in the fact that police observation confirmed that the truck had been driving near the spot at which, and at the approximate time at which, the tipster alleged she had been run off the road. *Ante*, at 1689. According to the Court, the statement therefore qualifies as a "'present sense impression'" or "'excited utterance,'" kinds of hearsay that the law deems categorically admissible given their low likelihood of reflecting "'deliberate or conscious misrepresentation.'" *Ibid.* (quoting Advisory Committee's Notes on Fed. Rule Evid. 803(1), 28 U.S.C.App., p. 371). So, the Court says, we can fairly suppose that the accusation was true.

No, we cannot. To begin with, it is questionable whether either the "present sense impression" or the "excited utterance" exception to the hearsay rule applies here. The classic "present sense impression" is the recounting of an event that is occurring before the declarant's eyes, as the declarant is speaking ("I am watching the Hindenburg explode!"). See 2 K. Broun, McCormick on Evidence 362 (7th ed. 2013) (hereinafter McCormick). And the classic "excited utterance" is a statement elicited, almost involuntarily, by the shock of what the declarant is immediately witnessing ("My God, those people will be killed!"). See *id.* at 368–369. It is the immediacy that gives the statement some credibility; the declarant has not had time to dissemble or embellish. There is no such immediacy here. The declarant had time to observe the license number of the offending vehicle, 8D94925 (a difficult task if she was forced off the road and the vehicle was speeding away), to bring her car to a halt, to copy down the observed license number (presumably), and (if she was using her own cell phone) to dial a call to the police from the stopped car. Plenty of time to dissemble or embellish.

Moreover, even assuming that less than true immediacy will suffice for these hearsay exceptions to apply, the tipster's statement would run into additional barriers to admissibility and acceptance. According to the very Advisory Committee's Notes from which the Court quotes, cases addressing an unidentified declarant's present sense impression "indicate hesitancy in upholding the statement alone as sufficient" proof of the reported event. 28 U.S.C.App., at 371; see also 7 M. Graham, Handbook of Federal Evidence 19–20 (7th ed. 2012). For excited utterances as well, the "knotty theoretical" question of statement-alone admissibility persists— seemingly even when the declarant is known. 2 McCormick 368. "Some courts . . . have taken the position that an excited utterance is admissible only if other proof is presented which supports a finding of fact that the exciting event did occur. The issue has not yet been resolved under the Federal Rules." *Id.* at 367–368 (footnote omitted). It is even unsettled whether excited utterances of an unknown declarant are *ever* admissible. A leading treatise reports that "the courts have been reluctant to admit such statements, principally because of uncertainty that foundational requirements, including the impact of the event on the declarant, have been satisfied." *Id.* at 372. In sum, it is unlikely that the law of evidence would deem the mystery caller in this case "especially trustworthy," *ante*, at 1689.

Finally, and least tenably, the Court says that another "indicator of veracity" is the anonymous tipster's mere "use of the 911 emergency system," *ante*, at 1689. Because, you see, recent "technological and regulatory developments" suggest that the identities of unnamed 911 callers are increasingly less likely to remain unknown. *Ibid.* Indeed, the systems are able to identify "the caller's geographic location with increasing specificity." *Ibid.* Amici disagree with this, see Brief for National Association of Criminal Defense Lawyers et al. 8–12, and the present case surely suggests that *amici* are right—since we know neither the identity of the tipster nor even the county from which the call was made. But assuming the Court is right about the ease of identifying 911 callers, it proves absolutely nothing in the present case unless the anonymous caller was *aware* of that fact. "It is the tipster's *belief* in anonymity, not its *reality*, that will control his behavior." *Id.* at 10 (emphasis added). There is no reason to believe that your average anonymous 911 tipster is aware that 911 callers are readily identifiable.

II

All that has been said up to now assumes that the anonymous caller made, at least in effect, an accusation of drunken driving. But in fact she did not. She said that the petitioners' truck "'[r]an [me] off the roadway.'" App. 36a. That neither asserts that the driver was drunk nor even raises the *likelihood* that the driver was drunk. The most it conveys is that the truck did some apparently non-typical thing that forced the tipster off the roadway, whether partly or fully, temporarily or permanently. Who really knows what (if anything) happened? The truck might have swerved to avoid an animal, a pothole, or a jaywalking pedestrian.

But let us assume the worst of the many possibilities: that it was a careless, reckless, or even intentional maneuver that forced the tipster off the road. Lorenzo might have been distracted by his use of a hands-free cell phone, see Strayer, Drews & Crouch, *A Comparison of the Cell Phone Driver and the Drunk Driver*, 48 Human Factors 381, 388 (2006), or distracted by an intense sports argument with Jose, see D. Strayer et al., AAA Foundation for Traffic Safety, Measuring Cognitive Distraction in the Automobile 28 (June 2013), online at https://www .aaafoundation.org/ sites/default/files/MeasuringCognitiveDistractions.pdf as visited Apr. 17, 2014, and available in Clerk of Court's case file). Or, indeed, he might have intentionally forced the tipster off the road because of some personal animus, or hostility to her "Make Love, Not War" bumper sticker. I fail to see how reasonable suspicion of a *discrete instance* of irregular or hazardous driving generates a reasonable suspicion of *ongoing intoxicated driving*. What proportion of the hundreds of thousands—perhaps millions—of careless, reckless, or intentional traffic violations committed each day is attributable to drunken drivers? I say 0.1 percent. I have no basis for that except my own guesswork. But unless the Court has some basis in reality to believe that the proportion is many orders of magnitude above that — say 1 in 10 or at least 1 in 20 — it has no grounds for its unsupported assertion that the tipster's report in this case gave rise to a *reasonable suspicion* of drunken driving.

Bear in mind that that is the only basis for the stop that has been asserted in this litigation. The stop required suspicion of an ongoing crime, not merely suspicion of having run someone off the road earlier. And driving while being a careless or reckless person, unlike driving while being a drunk person, is not an ongoing crime. In other words, in order to stop the petitioners the officers here not only had to assume without basis the accuracy of the anonymous accusation but also had to posit an unlikely reason (drunkenness) for the accused behavior.

In sum, at the moment the police spotted the truck, it was more than merely "*possib[le]*" that the petitioners were not committing an ongoing traffic crime. *United States v. Arvizu*, 534 U.S. 266, 277 (2002) (emphasis added). It was overwhelmingly likely that they were not.

III

It gets worse. Not only, it turns out, did the police have no good reason *at first* to believe that Lorenzo was driving drunk, they had very good reason *at last* to know that he was not. The Court concludes that the tip, plus confirmation of the truck's location, produced reasonable suspicion that the truck not only had been *but still was* barreling dangerously and drunkenly down Highway 1. *Ante*, at 1690–1692. In fact, alas, it was not, and the officers knew it. They followed the truck for five minutes, presumably to see if it was being operated recklessly. And *that* was good police work. While the anonymous tip was not enough to support a stop for drunken driving under *Terry v. Ohio*, 392 U.S. 1 (1968), it was surely enough to counsel observation of the truck to see if it was driven by a drunken driver. But the pesky little detail left out of the Court's reasonable-suspicion equation is that, for the five minutes that the truck was being followed (five minutes is a *long* time), Lorenzo's driving was irreproachable. Had the officers witnessed the petitioners violate a single traffic law, they would have had cause to stop the truck, *Whren v. United States*, 517 U.S. 806, 810 (1996), and this case would not be before us. And not only was the driving *irreproachable*, but the State offers no evidence to suggest that the petitioners even did anything *suspicious*, such as suddenly slowing down, pulling off to the side of the road, or turning somewhere to see whether they were being followed. Cf. *Arvizu, supra*, at 270–271 (concluding that an officer's suspicion of criminality was enhanced when the driver, upon seeing that he was being followed, "slowed dramatically," "appeared stiff," and "seemed to be trying to pretend" that the patrol car was not there). Consequently, the tip's suggestion of ongoing drunken driving (if it could be deemed to suggest that) not only went uncorroborated; it was affirmatively undermined.

A hypothetical variation on the facts of this case illustrates the point. Suppose an anonymous tipster reports that, while following near mile marker 88 a silver Ford

F–150, license plate 8D949925, traveling southbound on Highway 1, she saw in the truck's open cab several five-foot-tall stacks of what was unmistakably baled cannabis. Two minutes later, a highway patrolman spots the truck exactly where the tip suggested it would be, begins following it, but sees nothing in the truck's cab. It is not enough to say that the officer's observation merely failed to corroborate the tipster's accusation. It is more precise to say that the officer's observation *discredited* the informant's accusation: The crime was supposedly occurring (and would continue to occur) in plain view, but the police saw nothing. Similarly, here, the crime supposedly suggested by the tip was ongoing intoxicated driving, the hallmarks of which are many, readily identifiable, and difficult to conceal. That the officers witnessed nary a minor traffic violation nor any other "sound indici[um] of drunk driving," *ante*, at 1690, strongly suggests that the suspected crime was *not* occurring after all. The tip's implication of continuing criminality, already weak, grew even weaker.

Resisting this line of reasoning, the Court curiously asserts that, since drunk drivers who see marked squad cars in their rearview mirrors may evade detection simply by driving "more careful[ly]," the "absence of additional suspicious conduct" is "hardly surprising" and thus largely irrelevant. *Ante*, at 1691–1692. Whether a drunk driver drives drunkenly, the Court seems to think, is up to him. That is not how I understand the influence of alcohol. I subscribe to the more traditional view that the dangers of intoxicated driving are the intoxicant's impairing effects on the body — effects that no mere act of the will can resist. See, *e.g.*, A. Dasgupta, THE SCIENCE OF DRINKING: HOW ALCOHOL AFFECTS YOUR BODY AND MIND 39 (explaining that the physiological effect of a blood alcohol content between 0.08 and 0.109, for example, is "sever[e] impair[ment]" of "[b]alance, speech, hearing, and reaction time," as well as one's general "ability to drive a motor vehicle"). Consistent with this view, I take it as a fundamental premise of our intoxicated-driving laws that a driver soused enough to swerve once can be expected to swerve again — and soon. If he does not, and if the only evidence of his first episode of irregular driving is a mere inference from an uncorroborated, vague, and nameless tip, then the Fourth Amendment requires that he be left alone.

. . .

The Court's opinion serves up a freedom-destroying cocktail consisting of two parts patent falsity: (1) that anonymous 911 reports of traffic violations are reliable so long as they correctly identify a car and its location, and (2) that a single instance of careless or reckless driving necessarily supports a reasonable suspicion of drunkenness. All the malevolent 911 caller need do is assert a traffic violation, and the targeted car will be stopped, forcibly if necessary, by the police. If the driver turns out not to be drunk (which will almost always be the case), the caller need fear no consequences, even if 911 knows his identity. After all, he never alleged drunkenness, but merely called in a traffic violation — and on that point his word is as good as his victim's.

Drunken driving is a serious matter, but so is the loss of our freedom to come and go as we please without police interference. To prevent and detect murder we do not allow searches without probable cause or targeted *Terry* stops without reasonable suspicion. We should not do so for drunken driving either. After today's opinion all of us on the road, and not just drug dealers, are at risk of having our freedom of movement curtailed on suspicion of drunkenness, based upon a phone tip, true or false, of a single instance of careless driving. I respectfully dissent.

———————

Notes and Questions to Consider:

1. When, if ever, must an anonymous tip be corroborated before law enforcement may act upon it?

2. The late Justice Scalia is renowned for his writing skills. To what extent does Justice Scalia's dissent reflect the power of the written word?

3. Imagine two policemen observe an orange car full of Floridians and desire to stop and search the car, but after the two policemen consult one another, they cannot conjure a legally sufficient reason to do so. The first policeman, believing the ends justify the means, leaves the presence of the second policeman and makes an anonymous 911 call like the one described in the case above. The second policeman, unaware of the actions of the first, is informed about the anonymous 911 call and based upon it stops and searches the orange car full of Floridians. Assuming the first policeman never takes responsibility for the 911 call, how can the rights of these Floridians be vindicated?

4. In the hypothetical above, what difference would it make if the anonymous 911 call described behavior that was not illegal but that the second policeman mistakenly believed to be illegal? Consider *Heien v. North Carolina*, 135 S.Ct. 530, 190 L.Ed.2d 475 (2014):

———————

Heien v. North Carolina
Supreme Court of the United States, 2014
135 S.Ct. 530, 190 L.Ed.2d 475

Chief Justice Roberts delivered the opinion of the Court.

The Fourth Amendment prohibits "unreasonable searches and seizures." Under this standard, a search or seizure may be permissible even though the justification for the action includes a reasonable factual mistake. An officer might, for example, stop a motorist for traveling alone in a high-occupancy vehicle lane, only to discover upon approaching the car that two children are slumped over asleep in the back seat. The driver has not violated the law, but neither has the officer violated the Fourth Amendment.

But what if the police officer's reasonable mistake is not one of fact but of law? In this case, an officer stopped a vehicle because one of its two brake lights was out, but a court later determined that a single working brake light was all the law required. The question presented is whether such a mistake of law can nonetheless give rise to the reasonable suspicion necessary to uphold the seizure under the Fourth Amendment. We hold that it can. Because the officer's mistake about the brake-light law was reasonable, the stop in this case was lawful under the Fourth Amendment.

I

On the morning of April 29, 2009, Sergeant Matt Darisse of the Surry County Sheriff's Department sat in his patrol car near Dobson, North Carolina, observing northbound traffic on Interstate 77. Shortly before 8 a.m., a Ford Escort passed by. Darisse thought the driver looked "very stiff and nervous," so he pulled onto the interstate and began following the Escort. A few miles down the road, the Escort braked as it approached a slower vehicle, but only the left brake light came on. Noting the faulty right brake light, Darisse activated his vehicle's lights and pulled the Escort over. App. 4–7, 15–16.

Two men were in the car: Maynor Javier Vasquez sat behind the wheel, and petitioner Nicholas Brady Heien lay across the rear seat. Sergeant Darisse explained to Vasquez that as long as his license and registration checked out, he would receive only a warning ticket for the broken brake light. A records check revealed no problems with the documents, and Darisse gave Vasquez the warning ticket. But Darisse had become suspicious during the course of the stop—Vasquez appeared nervous, Heien remained lying down the entire time, and the two gave inconsistent answers about their destination. Darisse asked Vasquez if he would be willing to answer some questions. Vasquez assented, and Darisse asked whether the men were transporting various types of contraband. Told no, Darisse asked whether he could search the Escort. Vasquez said he had no objection, but told Darisse he should ask Heien, because Heien owned the car. Heien gave his consent, and Darisse, aided by a fellow officer who had since arrived, began a thorough search of the vehicle. In the side compartment of a duffle bag, Darisse found a sandwich bag containing cocaine. The officers arrested both men. 366 N.C. 271, 272–273, 737 S.E.2d 351, 352–353 (2012); App. 5–6, 25, 37.

The State charged Heien with attempted trafficking in cocaine. Heien moved to suppress the evidence seized from the car, contending that the stop and search had violated the Fourth Amendment of the United States Constitution. After a hearing at which both officers testified and the State played a video recording of the stop, the trial court denied the suppression motion, concluding that the faulty brake light had given Sergeant Darisse reasonable suspicion to initiate the stop, and that Heien's subsequent consent to the search was valid. Heien pleaded guilty but reserved his right to appeal the suppression decision. App. 1, 7–10, 12, 29, 43–44.

The North Carolina Court of Appeals reversed. 214 N.C.App. 515, 714 S.E.2d 827 (2011). The initial stop was not valid, the court held, because driving with only one working brake light was not actually a violation of North Carolina law. The relevant provision of the vehicle code provides that a car must be "equipped with a stop lamp on the rear of the vehicle. The stop lamp shall display a red or amber light visible from a distance of not less than 100 feet to the rear in normal sunlight, and shall be actuated upon application of the service (foot) brake. The stop lamp may be incorporated into a unit with one or more other rear lamps." N.C. Gen.Stat. Ann. §20–129(g) (2007).

Focusing on the statute's references to "a stop lamp" and "[t]he stop lamp" in the singular, the court concluded that a vehicle is required to have only one working brake light—which Heien's vehicle indisputably did. The justification for the stop was therefore "objectively unreasonable," and the stop violated the Fourth Amendment. 214 N.C.App., at 518–522, 714 S.E.2d, at 829–831.

The State appealed, and the North Carolina Supreme Court reversed. 366 N.C. 271, 737 S.E.2d 351. Noting that the State had chosen not to seek review of the Court of Appeals' interpretation of the vehicle code, the North Carolina Supreme Court assumed for purposes of its decision that the faulty brake light was not a violation. *Id.*, at 275, 737 S.E.2d, at 354. But the court concluded that, for several reasons, Sergeant Darisse could have reasonably, even if mistakenly, read the vehicle code to require that both brake lights be in good working order. Most notably, a nearby code provision requires that "all originally equipped rear lamps" be functional. *Id.*, at 282–283, 737 S.E.2d, at 358–359 (quoting N.C. Gen.Stat. Ann. §20–129(d)). Because Sergeant Darisse's mistaken understanding of the vehicle code was reasonable, the stop was valid. "An officer may make a mistake, including a mistake of law, yet still act reasonably under the circumstances. . . . [W]hen an officer acts reasonably under the circumstances, he is not violating the Fourth Amendment." *Id.*, at 279, 737 S.E.2d, at 356.

The North Carolina Supreme Court remanded to the Court of Appeals to address Heien's other arguments for suppression (which are not at issue here). *Id.*, at 283, 737 S.E.2d, at 359. The Court of Appeals rejected those arguments and affirmed the trial court's denial of his motion to suppress. [*See*] 741 S.E.2d 1 (2013). The North Carolina Supreme Court affirmed in turn. 367 N.C. 163, 749 S.E.2d 278 (2013). We granted certiorari. 134 S.Ct. 1872, 188 L.Ed.2d 910 (2014).

II

The Fourth Amendment [to the United States Constitution] provides:

"The right of the people to be secure in their persons, houses, papers, and effects, against unreasonable searches and seizures, shall not be violated, and no Warrants shall issue, but upon probable cause, supported by Oath or affirmation, and particularly describing the place to be searched, and the persons or things to be seized."

A traffic stop for a suspected violation of law is a "seizure" of the occupants of the vehicle and therefore must be conducted in accordance with the Fourth Amendment. *Brendlin v. California*, 551 U.S. 249, 255–259, 127 S.Ct. 2400, 168 L.Ed.2d 132 (2007). All parties agree that to justify this type of seizure, officers need only "reasonable suspicion"—that is, "a particularized and objective basis for suspecting the particular person stopped" of breaking the law. *Prado Navarette v. California*, 134 S.Ct. 1683, 1687–88, 188 L.Ed.2d 680 (2014) (internal quotation marks omitted). The question here is whether reasonable suspicion can rest on a mistaken understanding of the scope of a legal prohibition. We hold that it can.

As the text indicates and we have repeatedly affirmed, "the ultimate touchstone of the Fourth Amendment is 'reasonableness.'" *Riley v. California*, 134 S.Ct. 2473, 2482, 189 L.Ed.2d 430 (2014) (some internal quotation marks omitted). To be reasonable is not to be perfect, and so the Fourth Amendment allows for some mistakes on the part of government officials, giving them "fair leeway for enforcing the law in the community's protection." *Brinegar v. United States*, 338 U.S. 160, 176, 69 S.Ct. 1302, 93 L.Ed. 1879 (1949). We have recognized that searches and seizures based on mistakes of fact can be reasonable. The warrantless search of a home, for instance, is reasonable if undertaken with the consent of a resident, and remains lawful when officers obtain the consent of someone who reasonably appears to be but is not in fact a resident. See *Illinois v. Rodriguez*, 497 U.S. 177, 183–186, 110 S.Ct. 2793, 111 L.Ed.2d 148 (1990). By the same token, if officers with probable cause to arrest a suspect mistakenly arrest an individual matching the suspect's description, neither the seizure nor an accompanying search of the arrestee would be unlawful. See *Hill v. California*, 401 U.S. 797, 802–805, 91 S.Ct. 1106, 28 L.Ed.2d 484 (1971). The limit is that "the mistakes must be those of reasonable men." *Brinegar, supra*, at 176, 69 S.Ct. 1302.

But reasonable men make mistakes of law, too, and such mistakes are no less compatible with the concept of reasonable suspicion. Reasonable suspicion arises from the combination of an officer's understanding of the facts and his understanding of the relevant law. The officer may be reasonably mistaken on either ground. Whether the facts turn out to be not what was thought, or the law turns out to be not what was thought, the result is the same: the facts are outside the scope of the law. There is no reason, under the text of the Fourth Amendment or our precedents, why this same result should be acceptable when reached by way of a reasonable mistake of fact, but not when reached by way of a similarly reasonable mistake of law.

The dissent counters that our cases discussing probable cause and reasonable suspicion, most notably *Ornelas v. United States*, 517 U.S. 690, 696–697, 116 S.Ct. 1657, 134 L.Ed.2d 911 (1996), have contained "scarcely a peep" about mistakes of law. *Post*, at 542–543 (opinion of Sotomayor, J.). It would have been surprising, of course, if they had, since none of those cases involved a mistake of law.

Although such recent cases did not address mistakes of law, older precedents did. In fact, cases dating back two centuries support treating legal and factual errors alike in this context. Customs statutes enacted by Congress not long after the founding authorized courts to issue certificates indemnifying customs officers against damages suits premised on unlawful seizures. See, *e.g.*, Act of Mar. 2, 1799, ch. 22, §89, 1 Stat. 695–696. Courts were to issue such certificates on a showing that the officer had "reasonable cause"—a synonym for "probable cause"—for the challenged seizure. *Ibid.*; see *Stacey v. Emery*, 97 U.S. 642, 646, 24 L.Ed. 1035 (1878);

United States v. Riddle, 5 Cranch 311, 3 L.Ed. 110 (1809). In *United States v. Riddle*, a customs officer seized goods on the ground that the English shipper had violated the customs laws by preparing an invoice that undervalued the merchandise, even though the American consignee declared the true value to the customs collector. Chief Justice Marshall held that there had been no violation of the customs law because, whatever the shipper's intention, the consignee had not actually attempted to defraud the Government. Nevertheless, because "the construction of the law was liable to some question," he affirmed the issuance of a certificate of probable cause: "A doubt as to the true construction of the *law* is as reasonable a cause for seizure as a doubt respecting the fact." *Id.*, at 313.

This holding—that reasonable mistakes of law, like those of fact, would justify certificates of probable cause—was reiterated in a number of 19th-century decisions. See, *e.g.*, *The Friendship*, 9 F.Cas. 825, 826 (No. 5,125) (C.C.D.Mass. 1812) (Story, J.); *United States v. The Reindeer*, 27 F.Cas. 758, 768 (No. 16,145) (C.C.D.R.I. 1848); *United States v. The Recorder*, 27 F.Cas. 723 (No. 16,130) (C.C.S.D.N.Y. 1849). By the Civil War, there had been "numerous cases in which [a] captured vessel was in no fault, and had not, under a true construction of the law, presented even ground of suspicion, and yet the captor was exonerated because he acted under an honest mistake of the law." *The La Manche*, 14 F.Cas. 965, 972 (No. 8,004) (D.Mass. 1863).

Riddle and its progeny are not directly on point. Chief Justice Marshall was not construing the Fourth Amendment, and a certificate of probable cause functioned much like a modern-day finding of qualified immunity, which depends on an inquiry distinct from whether an officer has committed a constitutional violation. See, *e.g.*, *Carroll v. Carman*, *ante*, at 7, 135 S.Ct. 348, 352 (2014) (*per curiam*). But Chief Justice Marshall was nevertheless explaining the concept of probable cause, which, he noted elsewhere, "in all cases of seizure, has a fixed and well known meaning. It imports a seizure made under circumstances which warrant suspicion." *Locke v. United States*, 7 Cranch 339, 348, 3 L.Ed. 364 (1813). We have said the phrase "probable cause" bore this "fixed and well known meaning" in the Fourth Amendment, see *Brinegar*, *supra*, at 175, and n. 14, 69 S.Ct. 1302, and *Riddle* illustrates that it encompassed suspicion based on reasonable mistakes of both fact and law. No decision of this Court in the two centuries since has undermined that understanding.

The contrary conclusion would be hard to reconcile with a much more recent precedent. In *Michigan v. DeFillippo*, 443 U.S. 31, 99 S.Ct. 2627, 61 L.Ed.2d 343 (1979), we addressed the validity of an arrest made under a criminal law later declared unconstitutional. A Detroit ordinance that authorized police officers to stop and question individuals suspected of criminal activity also made it an offense for such an individual "to refuse to identify himself and produce evidence of his identity." *Id.*, at 33, 99 S.Ct. 2627. Detroit police officers sent to investigate a report of public intoxication arrested Gary DeFillippo after he failed to identify himself. A search incident to arrest uncovered drugs, and DeFillippo was charged with possession of a controlled substance. The Michigan Court of Appeals ordered the suppression of the drugs, concluding that the identification ordinance was unconstitutionally vague and that DeFillippo's arrest was therefore invalid. *Id.*, at 34–35, 99 S.Ct. 2627.

Accepting the unconstitutionality of the ordinance as a given, we nonetheless reversed. At the time the officers arrested DeFillippo, we explained, "there was no controlling precedent that this ordinance was or was not constitutional, and hence the conduct observed violated a presumptively valid ordinance." *Id.*, at 37, 99 S.Ct. 2627. Acknowledging that the outcome might have been different had the ordinance been "grossly and flagrantly unconstitutional," we concluded that under the circumstances "there was abundant probable cause to satisfy the constitutional prerequisite for an arrest." *Id.*, at 37–38, 99 S.Ct. 2627.

The officers were wrong in concluding that DeFillippo was guilty of a criminal offense when he declined to identify himself. That a court only *later* declared the ordinance unconstitutional does not change the fact that DeFillippo's conduct was lawful when the officers observed it. See *Danforth v. Minnesota*, 552 U.S. 264, 271, 128 S.Ct. 1029, 169 L.Ed.2d 859 (2008). But the officers' assumption that the law was valid was reasonable, and their observations gave them "abundant probable cause" to arrest DeFillippo. 443 U.S., at 37, 99 S.Ct. 2627. Although DeFillippo could not be prosecuted under the identification ordinance, the search that turned up the drugs was constitutional.

Heien struggles to recast *DeFillippo* as a case solely about the exclusionary rule, not the Fourth Amendment itself. In his view, the officers' mistake of law resulted in a violation the Fourth Amendment, but suppression of the drugs was not the proper remedy. We did say in a footnote that suppression of the evidence found on DeFillippo would serve none of the purposes of the exclusionary rule. See *id.*, at 38, n. 3, 99 S.Ct. 2627. But that literally marginal discussion does not displace our express holding that the arrest was constitutionally valid because the officers had probable cause. See *id.*, at 40, 99 S.Ct. 2627. Nor, contrary to Heien's suggestion, did either *United States v. Leon*, 468 U.S. 897, 104 S.Ct. 3405, 82 L.Ed.2d 677 (1984), or *Illinois v. Gates*, 462 U.S. 213, 103 S.Ct. 2317, 76 L.Ed.2d 527 (1983), somehow erase that holding and transform *DeFillippo* into an exclusionary rule decision. See Brief for Petitioner 28–29. In *Leon*, we said *DeFillippo* paid "attention to the purposes underlying the exclusionary rule," but we also clarified that it did "not involv[e] the scope of the rule itself." 468 U.S., at 911–912, 104 S.Ct. 3405. As for *Gates*, only Justice White's separate opinion (joined by no other Justice) discussed *DeFillippo*, and it acknowledged that "*DeFillippo* did not modify the exclusionary rule itself" but instead "upheld the validity of an arrest." 462 U.S., at 256, n. 12, 103 S.Ct. 2317 (opinion concurring in judgment).

Heien is correct that in a number of decisions we have looked to the reasonableness of an officer's legal error in the course of considering the appropriate remedy for a constitutional violation, instead of whether there was a violation at all. See, *e.g.*, *Davis v. United States*, 131 S.Ct. 2419, 2429–30, 180 L.Ed.2d 285 (2011) (exclusionary rule); *Illinois v. Krull*, 480 U.S. 340, 359–360, 107 S.Ct. 1160, 94 L.Ed.2d 364 (1987) (exclusionary rule); *Wilson v. Layne*, 526 U.S. 603, 615, 119 S.Ct. 1692, 143 L.Ed.2d

818 (1999) (qualified immunity); *Anderson v. Creighton*, 483 U.S. 635, 641, 107 S.Ct. 3034, 97 L.Ed.2d 523 (1987) (qualified immunity). In those cases, however, we had already found or assumed a Fourth Amendment violation. An officer's mistaken view that the conduct at issue did *not* give rise to such a violation—no matter how reasonable—could not change that ultimate conclusion. See Brief for Respondent 29–31; Brief for United States as *Amicus Curiae* 30, n. 3. Any consideration of the reasonableness of an officer's mistake was therefore limited to the separate matter of remedy.

Here, by contrast, the mistake of law relates to the antecedent question of whether it was reasonable for an officer to suspect that the defendant's conduct was illegal. If so, there was no violation of the Fourth Amendment in the first place. None of the cases Heien or the dissent cites precludes a court from considering a reasonable mistake of law in addressing that question. Cf. *Herring v. United States*, 555 U.S. 135, 139, 129 S.Ct. 695, 172 L.Ed.2d 496 (2009) (assuming a Fourth Amendment violation while rejecting application of the exclusionary rule, but noting that "[w]hen a probable-cause determination was based on reasonable but mistaken assumptions, the person subjected to a search or seizure has not necessarily been the victim of a constitutional violation").

Heien also contends that the reasons the Fourth Amendment allows some errors of fact do not extend to errors of law. Officers in the field must make factual assessments on the fly, Heien notes, and so deserve a margin of error. In Heien's view, no such margin is appropriate for questions of law: The statute here either requires one working brake light or two, and the answer does not turn on anything "an officer might suddenly confront in the field." Brief for Petitioner 21. But Heien's point does not consider the reality that an officer may "suddenly confront" a situation in the field as to which the application of a statute is unclear—however clear it may later become. A law prohibiting "vehicles" in the park either covers Segways or not, see A. Scalia & B. Garner, Reading Law: The Interpretation of Legal Texts 36–38 (2012), but an officer will nevertheless have to make a quick decision on the law the first time one whizzes by.

Contrary to the suggestion of Heien and *amici*, our decision does not discourage officers from learning the law. The Fourth Amendment tolerates only *reasonable* mistakes, and those mistakes—whether of fact or of law—must be *objectively* reasonable. We do not examine the subjective understanding of the particular officer involved. Cf. *Whren v. United States*, 517 U.S. 806, 813, 116 S.Ct. 1769, 135 L.Ed.2d 89 (1996). And the inquiry is not as forgiving as the one employed in the distinct context of deciding whether an officer is entitled to qualified immunity for a constitutional or statutory violation. Thus, an officer can gain no Fourth Amendment advantage through a sloppy study of the laws he is duty-bound to enforce.

Finally, Heien and *amici* point to the well-known maxim, "Ignorance of the law is no excuse," and contend that it is fundamentally unfair to let police officers get away with mistakes of law when the citizenry is accorded no such leeway. Though this argument has a certain rhetorical appeal, it misconceives the implication of the maxim. The true symmetry is this: Just as an individual generally cannot escape criminal liability based on a mistaken understanding of the law, so too the government cannot impose criminal liability based on a mistaken understanding of the law. If the law required two working brake lights, Heien could not escape a ticket by claiming he reasonably thought he needed only one; if the law required only one, Sergeant Darisse could not issue a valid ticket by claiming he reasonably thought drivers needed two. But just because mistakes of law cannot justify either the imposition or the avoidance of criminal liability, it does not follow that they cannot justify an investigatory stop. And Heien is not appealing a brake-light ticket; he is appealing a cocaine-trafficking conviction as to which there is no asserted mistake of fact or law.

III

Here we have little difficulty concluding that the officer's error of law was reasonable. Although the North Carolina statute at issue refers to "*a* stop lamp," suggesting the need for only a single working brake light, it also provides that "[t]he stop lamp may be incorporated into a unit with one or more *other* rear lamps." N.C. Gen.Stat. Ann. § 20–129(g) (emphasis added). The use of "other" suggests to the everyday reader of English that a "stop lamp" is a type of "rear lamp." And another subsection of the same provision requires that vehicles "have all originally equipped rear lamps or the equivalent in good working order," § 20–129(d), arguably indicating that if a vehicle has multiple "stop lamp[s]," all must be functional.

The North Carolina Court of Appeals concluded that the "rear lamps" discussed in subsection (d) do not include brake lights, but, given the "other," it would at least have been reasonable to think they did. Both the majority and the dissent in the North Carolina Supreme Court so concluded, and we agree. See 366 N.C., at 282–283, 737 S.E.2d, at 358–359; *id.*, at 283, 737 S.E.2d, at 359 (Hudson, J., dissenting) (calling the Court of Appeals' decision "surprising"). This "stop lamp" provision, moreover, had never been previously construed by North Carolina's appellate courts. See *id.*, at 283, 737 S.E.2d, at 359 (majority opinion). It was thus objectively reasonable for an officer in Sergeant Darisse's position to think that Heien's faulty right brake light was a violation of North Carolina law. And because the mistake of law was reasonable, there was reasonable suspicion justifying the stop.

The judgment of the Supreme Court of North Carolina is

Affirmed.

Justice KAGAN, with whom Justice GINSBURG joins, concurring.

I concur in full in the Court's opinion, which explains why certain mistakes of law can support the reasonable suspicion needed to stop a vehicle under the Fourth Amendment. In doing so, the Court correctly emphasizes that the "Fourth Amendment tolerates only . . . *objectively* reasonable" mistakes of law. *Ante*, at 539. And the Court makes clear that the inquiry into whether an officer's mistake of law counts as objectively reasonable "is not as forgiving as the one employed in the distinct context of deciding whether an officer is entitled to qualified immunity." *Ibid.* I write separately to elaborate briefly on those important limitations.

First, an officer's "subjective understanding" is irrelevant: As the Court notes, "[w]e do not examine" it at all. *Ibid.* That means the government cannot defend an officer's mistaken legal interpretation on the ground that the officer was unaware of or untrained in the law. And it means that, contrary to the dissenting opinion in the court below, an officer's reliance on "an incorrect memo or training program from the police department" makes no difference to the analysis. 366 N.C. 271, 284, 737 S.E.2d 351, 360 (2012) (Hudson, J., dissenting). Those considerations pertain to the officer's subjective understanding of the law and thus cannot help to justify a seizure.

Second, the inquiry the Court permits today is more demanding than the one courts undertake before awarding qualified immunity. See Tr. of Oral Arg. 51 (Solicitor General stating that the two tests "require essentially the opposite" showings); Brief for Respondent 31–32 (making a similar point). Our modern qualified immunity doctrine protects "all but the plainly incompetent or those who knowingly violate the law." *Ashcroft v. al–Kidd*, 131 S.Ct. 2074, 2085, 179 L.Ed.2d 1149 (2011) (quoting *Malley v. Briggs*, 475 U.S. 335, 341, 106 S.Ct. 1092, 89 L.Ed.2d 271 (1986)). By contrast, Justice Story's opinion in *The Friendship*, 9 F.Cas. 825, 826 (No. 5,125)(C.C.D.Mass. 1812) (cited *ante*, at 537), suggests the appropriate standard for deciding when a legal error can support a seizure: when an officer takes a reasonable view of a "vexata questio" on which different judges "h[o]ld opposite opinions." See Brief for United States as *Amicus Curiae* 26 (invoking that language). Or to make the same point without the Latin, the test is satisfied when the law at issue is "so doubtful in construction" that a reasonable judge could agree with the officer's view. *The Friendship*, 9 F.Cas., at 826.

A court tasked with deciding whether an officer's mistake of law can support a seizure thus faces a straightforward question of statutory construction. If the statute is genuinely ambiguous, such that overturning the officer's judgment requires hard interpretive work, then the officer has made a reasonable mistake. But if not, not. As the Solicitor General made the point at oral argument, the statute must pose a "really difficult" or "very hard question of statutory interpretation." Tr. of Oral Arg. 50. And indeed, both North Carolina and the Solicitor General agreed that such cases will be "exceedingly rare." Brief for Respondent 17; Tr. of Oral Arg. 48.

The Court's analysis of Sergeant Darisse's interpretation of the North Carolina law at issue here appropriately reflects these principles. As the Court explains, see *ante*, at 540, the statute requires every car on the highway to have "a stop lamp," in the singular. N.C. Gen.Stat. Ann. § 20–129(g) (2007). But the statute goes on to state that a stop lamp (or, in more modern terminology, brake light) "may be incorporated into a unit with one or more *other* rear lamps," suggesting that a stop lamp itself qualifies as a rear lamp. *Ibid.* (emphasis added). And the statute further mandates that every car have "*all* originally equipped rear lamps . . . in good working order." § 20–129(d) (emphasis added). The North Carolina Court of Appeals dealt with the statute's conflicting signals in one way (deciding that a brake light is *not* a rear lamp, and so only one needs to work); but a court could easily take the officer's view (deciding that a brake light *is* a rear lamp, and if a car comes equipped with more than one, as modern cars do, all must be in working order). The critical point is that the statute poses a quite difficult question of interpretation, and Sergeant Darisse's judgment, although overturned, had much to recommend it. I therefore agree with the Court that the traffic stop he conducted did not violate the Fourth Amendment.

Justice SOTOMAYOR, dissenting.

The Court is, of course, correct that "the ultimate touchstone of the Fourth Amendment is 'reasonableness.'" *Riley v. California*, 134 S.Ct. 2473, 2482 (2014). But this broad statement simply sets the standard a court is to apply when it conducts its inquiry into whether the Fourth Amendment has been violated. It does not define the categories of inputs that courts are to consider when assessing the reasonableness of a search or seizure, each of which must be independently justified. What this case requires us to decide is whether a police officer's understanding of the law is an input into the reasonableness inquiry, or whether this inquiry instead takes the law as a given and assesses an officer's understanding of the facts against a fixed legal yardstick.

I would hold that determining whether a search or seizure is reasonable requires evaluating an officer's understanding of the facts against the actual state of the law. I would accordingly reverse the judgment of the North Carolina Supreme Court, and I respectfully dissent from the Court's contrary holding. . . .

. . . [W]hen we have talked about the leeway that officers have in making probable-cause determinations, we have focused on their assessments of facts. See, *e.g.*, *Terry v. Ohio*, 392 U.S. 1, 21–22 (1968) (framing the question as whether the "facts" give rise to reasonable suspicion). We have conceded that an arresting officer's state of mind does not factor into the probable-cause inquiry, "except for *the facts* that he knows." *Devenpeck v. Alford*, 543 U.S. 146, 153 (2004) (emphasis added). And we have said that, to satisfy the reasonableness requirement, "what is generally demanded of the many *factual determinations* that must regularly be made by agents of the government . . . is not that they always be correct, but that they always be reasonable." *Illinois v. Rodriguez*, 497 U.S. 177, 185 (1990) (emphasis added). There is scarcely a peep in these cases to suggest that an officer's understanding or conception of anything other than the facts is relevant.

This framing of the reasonableness inquiry has not only been focused on officers' understanding of the facts, it has been justified in large part based on the recognition that officers are generally in a superior position, relative to courts, to evaluate those facts and their significance as they unfold. In other words, the leeway we afford officers' factual assessments is rooted not only in our recognition that police officers operating in the field have to make quick decisions, see *id.*, at 186, 110 S.Ct. 2793, but also in our understanding that police officers have the expertise to "dra[w] inferences and mak[e] deductions . . . that might well elude an untrained person." *United States v. Cortez*, 449 U.S. 411, 418 (1981). When officers evaluate unfolding circumstances, they deploy that expertise to draw "conclusions about human behavior" much in the way that "jurors [do] *as factfinders.*" *Ibid.* (emphasis added).

The same cannot be said about legal exegesis. After all, the meaning of the law is not probabilistic in the same way that factual determinations are. Rather, "the notion that the law is definite and knowable" sits at the foundation of our legal system. *Cheek v. United States*, 498 U.S. 192, 199 (1991). And it is courts, not officers, that are in the best position to interpret the laws. . . .

. . . Traffic stops like those at issue here can be "annoying, frightening, and perhaps humiliating." *Terry*, 392 U.S. at 25; see *Delaware v. Prouse*, 440 U.S. 648, 657 (1979). We have nevertheless held that an officer's subjective motivations do not render a traffic stop unlawful. *Whren v. United States*, 517 U.S. 806 (1996). But we assumed in *Whren* that when an officer acts on pretext, at least that pretext would be the violation of an actual law. See *id.*, at 810 (discussing the three provisions of the District of Columbia traffic code that the parties accepted the officer had probable cause to believe had been violated). Giving officers license to effect seizures so long as they can attach to their reasonable view of the facts some reasonable legal interpretation (or misinterpretation) that suggests a law has been violated significantly expands this authority. Cf. *Barlow v. United States*, 7 Pet. 404, 411, 8 L.Ed. 728 (1833) (Story, J.) ("There is scarcely any law which does not admit of some ingenious doubt"). One wonders how a citizen seeking to be law-abiding and to structure his or her behavior to avoid these invasive, frightening, and humiliating encounters could do so.

In addition to these human consequences — including those for communities and for their relationships with the police — permitting mistakes of law to justify seizures has the perverse effect of preventing or delaying the clarification of the law. Under such an approach, courts need not interpret statutory language but can instead simply decide whether an officer's interpretation was reasonable. Indeed, had this very case arisen after the North Carolina Supreme Court announced its rule, the North Carolina Court of Appeals would not have had the occasion to interpret the statute at issue. Similarly, courts in the Eighth Circuit, which has been the only Circuit to include police mistakes of law in the reasonableness inquiry, have observed that they need not decide interpretive questions under their approach. See, *e.g.*, *United States v. Rodriguez-Lopez*, 444 F.3d 1020, 1022–1023 (C.A.8 2006). This result is bad for citizens, who need to know their rights and responsibilities, and it is bad for police, who would benefit from clearer direction. Cf. *Camreta v. Greene*, 131 S.Ct. 2020, 2031–32 (2011) (recognizing the importance of clarifying the law).

Of course, if the law enforcement system could not function without permitting mistakes of law to justify seizures, one could at least argue that permitting as much is a necessary evil. But I have not seen any persuasive argument that law enforcement will be unduly hampered by a rule that precludes consideration of mistakes of law in the reasonableness inquiry. After all, there is no indication that excluding an officer's mistake of law from the reasonableness inquiry has created a problem for law enforcement in the overwhelming number of Circuits which have adopted that approach. If an officer makes a stop in good faith but it turns out that, as in this case, the officer was wrong about what the law proscribed or required, I know of no penalty that the officer would suffer. See 366 N.C. 271, 286–288, 737 S.E.2d 351, 361–362 (2012) (Hudson, J., dissenting) (observing that "officers (rightfully) face no punishment for a stop based on a mistake of law"). Moreover, such an officer would likely have a defense to any civil suit on the basis of qualified immunity. See *Ashcroft v. al-Kidd*, 131 S.Ct. 2074, 2085 (2011) ("Qualified immunity gives government officials breathing room to make reasonable but mistaken judgments about open legal questions").

Nor will it often be the case that any evidence that may be seized during the stop will be suppressed, thanks to the exception to the exclusionary rule for good-faith police errors. See, *e.g.*, *Davis v. United States*, 131 S.Ct. 2419, 2427–28 (2011). It is true that, unlike most States, North Carolina does not provide a good-faith exception as a matter of state law, see *State v. Carter*, 322 N.C. 709, 721–724, 370 S.E.2d 553, 560–562 (1988), but North Carolina recognizes that it may solve any remedial problems it may perceive on its own, see *id.*, at 724, 370 S.E.2d, at 562; N.C. Gen.Stat. Ann. § 15A–974 (2013) (statutory good-faith exception). More fundamentally, that is a remedial concern, and the protections offered by the Fourth Amendment are not meant to yield to accommodate remedial concerns. Our jurisprudence draws a sharp "analytica[l] distinct[ion]" between the existence of a Fourth Amendment violation and the remedy for that violation. *Davis*, 131 S.Ct., at 2431.

In short, there is nothing in our case law requiring us to hold that a reasonable mistake of law can justify a seizure under the Fourth Amendment, and quite a bit suggesting just the opposite. I also see nothing to be gained from such a holding, and much to be lost.

III

In reaching the contrary conclusion, the Court makes both serious legal and practical errors. On the legal side, the Court barely addresses *Ornelas* and the other cases that frame the reasonableness inquiry around factual determinations. Instead, in support of its conclusion that reasonable suspicion "arises from the *combination* of an officer's understanding of the facts *and* his understanding of the relevant law," *ante*, at 536 (emphasis added), the Court first reaches to founding-era customs statutes and cases applying those statutes. It concedes, however, that these cases are "not directly on point" because they say nothing about the scope of the Fourth Amendment and are instead equivalents of our modern-day qualified immunity jurisprudence for civil damages. *Ante*, at 537.

The only link in the tenuous chain the Court constructs between those cases and this one that has anything to say about the Fourth Amendment is *Brinegar v. United States*, 338 U.S. 160 (1949). See *ante*, at 537–538. But all that our opinion in *Brinegar* actually says is that probable cause exists where "'the facts and circumstances within [the officers'] knowledge and of which they had reasonably trustworthy information [are] sufficient in themselves to warrant a man of reasonable caution in the belief that' an offense has been or is being committed." 338 U.S. at 175–176 (quoting *Carroll v. United States*, 267 U.S. 132, 162 (1925)). It thus states the uncontroversial proposition that the probable-cause inquiry looks to the reasonableness of an officer's understanding of the facts. Indeed, *Brinegar* is an odd case for the Court to rely on given that, like the cases I discussed above, it subsequently emphasizes that "the mistakes must be those of reasonable men, acting on *facts* leading sensibly to their conclusions of probability." 338 U.S. at 176 (emphasis added). Again, reasonable understandings of the facts, not reasonable understandings of what the law says. . . .

. . . To my mind, the more administrable approach—and the one more consistent with our precedents and principles—would be to hold that an officer's mistake of law, no matter how reasonable, cannot support the individualized suspicion necessary to justify a seizure under the Fourth Amendment. I respectfully dissent.

Notes and Questions to Consider:

1. How many times can the same officer make the same mistake of law and it still constitute a reasonable mistake sufficient to support the individualized suspicion necessary to justify a seizure?

2. When can a citizen make a reasonable mistake of law yet still avoid the adverse consequences that arise?

3. Can a series of innocent acts, none of which is sufficient by itself to support an individualized suspicion necessary to support a search, together add up to an individualized suspicion?

D. Pretrial Release and Detention

Article I, Section 14 of Florida's constitution provides:

> *Pretrial release and detention.*—Unless charged with a capital offense or an offense punishable by life imprisonment and the proof of guilt is evident or the presumption is great, every person charged with a crime or violation of municipal or county ordinance shall be entitled to pretrial release on reasonable conditions. If no conditions of release can reasonably protect the community from risk of physical harm to persons, assure the presence of the accused at trial, or assure the integrity of the judicial process, the accused may be detained.

E. Prosecution of Offenses Committed by Children

Article I, Section 15 of Florida's constitution provides:

> *Prosecution for crime; offenses committed by children.*—
>
> (a) No person shall be tried for capital crime without presentment or indictment by a grand jury, or for other felony without such presentment or

indictment or an information under oath filed by the prosecuting officer of the court, except persons on active duty in the militia when tried by courts martial.

(b) When authorized by law, a child as therein defined may be charged with a violation of law as an act of delinquency instead of crime and tried without a jury or other requirements applicable to criminal cases. Any child so charged shall, upon demand made as provided by law before a trial in a juvenile proceeding, be tried in an appropriate court as an adult. A child found delinquent shall be disciplined as provided by law.

F. Rights of Accused and of Victims

Article I, Section 16 of Florida's constitution provides:

Rights of accused and of victims. —

(a) In all criminal prosecutions the accused shall, upon demand, be informed of the nature and cause of the accusation, and shall be furnished a copy of the charges, and shall have the right to have compulsory process for witnesses, to confront at trial adverse witnesses, to be heard in person, by counsel or both, and to have a speedy and public trial by impartial jury in the county where the crime was committed. If the county is not known, the indictment or information may charge venue in two or more counties conjunctively and proof that the crime was committed in that area shall be sufficient; but before pleading the accused may elect in which of those counties the trial will take place. Venue for prosecution of crimes committed beyond the boundaries of the state shall be fixed by law.

(b) To preserve and protect the right of crime victims to achieve justice, ensure a meaningful role throughout the criminal and juvenile justice systems for crime victims, and ensure that crime victims' rights and interests are respected and protected by law in a manner no less vigorous than protections afforded to criminal defendants and juvenile delinquents, every victim is entitled to the following rights, beginning at the time of his or her victimization:

(1) The right to due process and to be treated with fairness and respect for the victim's dignity.

(2) The right to be free from intimidation, harassment, and abuse.

(3) The right, within the judicial process, to be reasonably protected from the accused and any person acting on behalf of the accused. However, nothing contained herein is intended to create a special relationship between the crime victim and any law enforcement agency or office absent a special relationship or duty as defined by Florida law.

(4) The right to have the safety and welfare of the victim and the victim's family considered when setting bail, including setting pretrial release conditions that protect the safety and welfare of the victim and the victim's family.

(5) The right to prevent the disclosure of information or records that could be used to locate or harass the victim or the victim's family, or which could disclose confidential or privileged information of the victim.

(6) A victim shall have the following specific rights upon request:

a. The right to reasonable, accurate, and timely notice of, and to be present at, all public proceedings involving the criminal conduct, including, but not limited to, trial, plea, sentencing, or adjudication, even if the victim will be a witness at the proceeding, notwithstanding any rule to the contrary. A victim shall also be provided reasonable, accurate, and timely notice of any release or escape of the defendant or delinquent, and any proceeding during which a right of the victim is implicated.

b. The right to be heard in any public proceeding involving pretrial or other release from any form of legal constraint, plea, sentencing, adjudication, or parole, and any proceeding during which a right of the victim is implicated.

c. The right to confer with the prosecuting attorney concerning any plea agreements, participation in pretrial diversion programs, release, restitution, sentencing, or any other disposition of the case.

d. The right to provide information regarding the impact of the offender's conduct on the victim and the victim's family to the individual responsible for conducting any presentence investigation or compiling any presentence investigation report, and to have any such information considered in any sentencing recommendations submitted to the court.

e. The right to receive a copy of any presentence report, and any other report or record relevant to the exercise of a victim's right, except for such portions made confidential or exempt by law.

f. The right to be informed of the conviction, sentence, adjudication, place and time of incarceration, or other disposition of the convicted offender, any scheduled release date of the offender, and the release of or the escape of the offender from custody.

g. The right to be informed of all postconviction processes and procedures, to participate in such processes and procedures, to provide information to the release authority to be considered before any release decision is made, and to be notified of any release decision regarding the offender. The parole or early release authority shall extend the right to be heard to any person harmed by the offender.

h. The right to be informed of clemency and expungement procedures, to provide information to the governor, the court, any clemency board, and other authority in these procedures, and to have that information considered before a clemency or expungement decision is made; and to be notified of such decision in advance of any release of the offender.

(7) The rights of the victim, as provided in subparagraph (6)a., subparagraph (6)b., or subparagraph (6)c., that apply to any first appearance proceeding are satisfied by a reasonable attempt by the appropriate agency to notify the victim and convey the victim's views to the court.

(8) The right to the prompt return of the victim's property when no longer needed as evidence in the case.

(9) The right to full and timely restitution in every case and from each convicted offender for all losses suffered, both directly and indirectly, by the victim as a result of the criminal conduct.

(10) The right to proceedings free from unreasonable delay, and to a prompt and final conclusion of the case and any related postjudgment proceedings.

a. The state attorney may file a good faith demand for a speedy trial and the trial court shall hold a calendar call, with notice, within fifteen days of the filing demand, to schedule a trial to commence on a date at least five days but no more than sixty days after the date of the calendar call unless the trial judge enters an order with specific findings of fact justifying a trial date more than sixty days after the calendar call.

b. All state-level appeals and collateral attacks on any judgment must be complete within two years from the date of appeal in non-capital cases and within five years from the date of appeal in capital cases, unless a court enters an order with specific findings as to why the court was unable to comply with this subparagraph and the circumstances causing the delay. Each year, the chief judge of any district court of appeal or the chief justice of the supreme court shall report on a case-by-case basis to the speaker of the house of representatives and the president of the senate all cases where the court entered an order regarding inability to comply with this subparagraph. The legislature may enact legislation to implement this subparagraph.

(11) The right to be informed of these rights, and to be informed that victims can seek the advice of an attorney with respect to their rights. This information shall be made available to the general public and provided to all crime victims in the form of a card or by other means intended to effectively advise the victim of their rights under this section.

(c) The victim, the retained attorney of the victim, a lawful representative of the victim, or the office of the state attorney upon request of the victim, may assert and seek enforcement of the rights enumerated in this section and any other right afforded to a victim by law in any trial or appellate court, or before any other authority with jurisdiction over the case, as a matter of right. The court or other authority with jurisdiction shall act promptly on such a request, affording a remedy by due course of law for the violation of any right. The reasons for any decision regarding the disposition of a victim's right shall be clearly stated on the record.

(d) The granting of the rights enumerated in this section to victims may not be construed to deny or impair any other rights possessed by victims. The provisions of this section apply throughout criminal and juvenile justice processes, are self-executing, and do not require implementing legislation. This section may not be construed to create any cause of action for damages against the state or a political subdivision of the state, or any officer, employee, or agent of the state or its political subdivisions.

(e) As used in this section, a "victim" is a person who suffers direct or threatened physical, psychological, or financial harm as a result of the commission or attempted commission of a crime or delinquent act or against whom the crime or delinquent act is committed. The term "victim" includes the victim's lawful representative, the parent or guardian of a minor, or the next of kin of a homicide victim, except upon a showing that the interest of such individual would be in actual or potential conflict with the interests of the victim. The term "victim" does not include the accused. The terms "crime" and "criminal" include delinquent acts and conduct.

G. Excessive Punishments

Article I, Section 17 of Florida's constitution provides:

Excessive punishments. — Excessive fines, cruel and unusual punishment, attainder, forfeiture of estate, indefinite imprisonment, and unreasonable detention of witnesses are forbidden. The death penalty is an authorized punishment for capital crimes designated by the legislature. The prohibition against cruel or unusual punishment, and the prohibition against cruel and unusual punishment, shall be construed in conformity with decisions of the United States Supreme Court which interpret the prohibition against cruel and unusual punishment provided in the Eighth Amendment to the United States Constitution. Any method of execution shall be allowed, unless prohibited by the United States Constitution. Methods of execution may be designated by the legislature, and a change in any method of execution may be applied retroactively. A sentence of death shall not be reduced on the basis that a method of execution is invalid. In any case in which an execution method is declared invalid, the death sentence shall remain in force until the sentence can be lawfully executed by any valid method. This section shall apply retroactively.

Chapter 17

Eminent Domain and Inverse Condemnation

The state of Florida has the power to take away its citizens' real or personal property, even including a citizen's home. Specifically, Article X, Section 6 of the Constitution of the State of Florida provides:

> **Eminent domain.** — No private property shall be taken except for a public purpose and with full compensation therefor paid to each owner. . . .

Note from the quotation above that under the Constitution of the State of Florida, eminent domain requires "full compensation" instead of "just compensation" as required under the Constitution of the United States.

Whether this is a distinction without a difference depends upon the jury who decides the eminent domain case. In Florida, eminent domain requires a bifurcated trial, where first the government bears the burden to prove its right to take the Floridian's property by showing its "reasonable necessity" to put eligible property to an acceptable "public purpose" as seen in the case law below.

A. Total Takings Test

With both the federal and state constitutions addressing eminent domain, the question arises whether there is room for any independent state law jurisprudence. So we present first a leading U.S. Supreme Court decision identifying the "total takings test" to pose the question as to whether room is left for state's rights. Then we present a Florida Supreme Court decision, followed by an opinion of Florida's District Court of Appeal interpreting the decisions of the federal and state Supreme Courts. Does an independent state jurisprudence exist in this area?

First, consider *Lucas v. South Carolina Coastal Council*, 505 U.S. 1003 (1992):

Lucas v. South Carolina Coastal Council
Supreme Court of the United States, 1992
505 U.S. 1003, 112 S.Ct. 2886, 120 L.Ed.2d 79

Justice SCALIA delivered the opinion of the Court.

In 1986, petitioner David H. Lucas paid $975,000 for two residential lots on the Isle of Palms in Charleston County, South Carolina, on which he intended to build single-family homes. In 1988, however, the South Carolina Legislature enacted the Beachfront Management Act, S.C.Code Ann. § 48–39–250 *et seq.* (Supp. 1990), which had the direct effect of barring petitioner from erecting any permanent habitable structures on his two parcels. See § 48–39–290(A). A state trial court found that this prohibition rendered Lucas's parcels "valueless." App. to Pet. for Cert. 37. This case requires us to decide whether the Act's dramatic effect on the economic value of Lucas's lots accomplished a taking of private property under the Fifth and Fourteenth Amendments requiring the payment of "just compensation." U.S. Const., Amdt. 5.

I

A

South Carolina's expressed interest in intensively managing development activities in the so-called "coastal zone" dates from 1977 when, in the aftermath of Congress's passage of the federal Coastal Zone Management Act of 1972, 86 Stat. 1280, as amended, 16 U.S.C. § 1451 *et seq.*, the legislature enacted a Coastal Zone Management Act of its own. See S.C. Code § 48–39–10 *et seq.* (1987). In its original form, the South Carolina Act required owners of coastal zone land that qualified as a "critical area" (defined in the legislation to include beaches and immediately adjacent sand dunes, § 48–39–10(J)) to obtain a permit from the newly created South Carolina Coastal Council (Council) (respondent here) prior to committing the land to a "use other than the use the critical area was devoted to on [September 28, 1977]." § 48–39–130(A).

In the late 1970s, Lucas and others began extensive residential development of the Isle of Palms, a barrier island situated eastward of the city of Charleston. Toward the close of the development cycle for one residential subdivision known as "Beachwood East," Lucas in 1986 purchased the two lots at issue in this litigation for his own account. No portion of the lots, which were located approximately 300 feet from the beach, qualified as a "critical area" under the 1977 Act; accordingly, at the time Lucas acquired these parcels, he was not legally obliged to obtain a permit from the Council in advance of any development activity. His intention with respect to the lots was to do what the owners of the immediately adjacent parcels had already done: erect single-family residences. He commissioned architectural drawings for this purpose.

The Beachfront Management Act brought Lucas's plans to an abrupt end. Under that 1988 legislation, the Council was directed to establish a "baseline" connecting the landward-most "point[s] of erosion . . . during the past forty years" in the region of the Isle of Palms that includes Lucas's lots. S.C. Code § 48–39–280(A)(2) (Supp. 1988). In action not challenged here, the Council fixed this baseline landward of Lucas's parcels. That was significant, for under the Act construction of occupiable improvements was flatly prohibited seaward of a line drawn 20 feet landward of, and parallel to, the baseline. § 48–39–290(A). The Act provided no exceptions.

B

Lucas promptly filed suit in the South Carolina Court of Common Pleas, contending that the Beachfront Management Act's construction bar effected a taking of his property without just compensation. Lucas did not take issue with the validity of the Act as a lawful exercise of South Carolina's police power, but contended that the Act's complete extinguishment of his property's value entitled him to compensation regardless of whether the legislature had acted in furtherance of legitimate police power objectives. Following a bench trial, the court agreed. Among its factual determinations was the finding that "at the time Lucas purchased the two lots, both were zoned for single-family residential construction and . . . there were no restrictions imposed upon such use of the property by either the State of South Carolina, the County of Charleston, or the Town of the Isle of Palms." App. to Pet. for Cert. 36. The trial court further found that the Beachfront Management Act decreed a permanent ban on construction insofar as Lucas's lots were concerned, and that this prohibition "deprive[d] Lucas of any reasonable economic use of the lots, . . . eliminated the unrestricted right of use, and render[ed] them valueless." *Id.*, at 37. The court thus concluded that Lucas's properties had been "taken" by operation of the Act, and it ordered respondent to pay "just compensation" in the amount of $1,232,387.50. *Id.*, at 40.

The Supreme Court of South Carolina reversed. It found dispositive what it described as Lucas's concession "that the Beachfront Management Act [was] properly and validly designed to preserve . . . South Carolina's beaches." 304 S.C. 376, 379, 404 S.E.2d 895, 896 (1991). Failing an attack on the validity of the statute as such, the court believed itself bound to accept the "uncontested . . . findings" of the South Carolina Legislature that new construction in the coastal zone—such as petitioner intended—threatened this public resource. *Id.*, at 383, 404 S.E.2d, at 898. The court ruled that when a regulation respecting the use of property is designed "to prevent serious public harm," *id.*, at 383, 404 S.E.2d, at 899 (citing, *inter alia*, *Mugler v. Kansas*, 123 U.S. 623 (1887)), no compensation is owing under the Takings Clause regardless of the regulation's effect on the property's value.

Two justices dissented. They acknowledged that our *Mugler* line of cases recognizes governmental power to prohibit "noxious" uses of property—*i.e.*, uses of property akin to "public nuisances"—without having to pay compensation. But they would not have characterized the Beachfront Management Act's "*primary* purpose [as] the prevention of a nuisance." 304 S.C., at 395, 404 S.E.2d, at 906 (Harwell, J., dissenting). To the dissenters, the chief purposes of the legislation, among them the promotion of tourism and the creation of a "habitat for indigenous flora and fauna," could not fairly be compared to nuisance abatement. *Id.*, at 396, 404 S.E.2d, at 906. As a consequence, they would have affirmed the trial court's conclusion that the Act's obliteration of the value of petitioner's lots accomplished a taking.

We granted certiorari.

II

As a threshold matter, we must briefly address the Council's suggestion that this case is inappropriate for plenary review. After briefing and argument before the South Carolina Supreme Court, but prior to issuance of that court's opinion, the Beachfront Management Act was amended to authorize the Council, in certain circumstances, to issue "special permits" for the construction or reconstruction of habitable structures seaward of the baseline. See S.C. Code §48–39–290(D)(1) (Supp. 1991). According to the Council, this amendment renders Lucas's claim of a permanent deprivation unripe, as Lucas may yet be able to secure permission to build on his property. "[The Court's] cases," we are reminded, "uniformly reflect an insistence on knowing the nature and extent of permitted development before adjudicating the constitutionality of the regulations that purport to limit it." *MacDonald, Sommer & Frates v. Yolo County*, 477 U.S. 340, 351 (1986). See also *Agins v. City of Tiburon*, 447 U.S. 255, 260 (1980). Because petitioner "has not yet obtained a final decision regarding how [he] will be allowed to develop [his] property," *Williamson County Regional Planning Comm'n v. Hamilton Bank of Johnson City*, 473 U.S. 172, 190 (1985), the Council argues that he is not yet entitled to definitive adjudication of his takings claim in this Court.

We think these considerations would preclude review had the South Carolina Supreme Court rested its judgment on ripeness grounds, as it was (essentially) invited to do by the Council. See Brief for Respondent 9, n. 3. The South Carolina Supreme Court shrugged off the possibility of further administrative and trial proceedings, however, preferring to dispose of Lucas's takings claim on the merits. Cf., *e.g.*, *San Diego Gas & Electric Co. v. San Diego*, 450 U.S. 621, 631–632 (1981). This unusual disposition does not preclude Lucas from applying for a permit under the 1990 amendment for *future* construction, and challenging, on takings grounds, any denial. But it does preclude, both practically and legally, any takings claim with respect to Lucas's *past* deprivation, *i.e.*, for his having been denied construction rights during the period before the 1990 amendment. See generally *First English Evangelical Lutheran Church of Glendale v. County of Los Angeles*, 482 U.S. 304 (1987) (holding that temporary deprivations of use are compensable under the Takings Clause). Without even so much as commenting upon the consequences of the South Carolina Supreme Court's judgment in this respect, the Council insists that permitting Lucas to press his claim of a past deprivation on this appeal would be improper, since "the issues of whether and to what extent [Lucas] has incurred a temporary taking ... have simply never been addressed." Brief for Respondent 11. Yet Lucas had no reason to proceed on a "temporary taking" theory at trial, or even to seek remand for that purpose prior to submission of the case to the South Carolina Supreme Court, since as the Act then read, the taking was unconditional and permanent. Moreover, given the breadth of the South Carolina Supreme Court's holding and judgment, Lucas would plainly be unable (absent our intervention now) to obtain further state-court adjudication with respect to the 1988–1990 period.

In these circumstances, we think it would not accord with sound process to insist that Lucas pursue the late-created "special permit" procedure before his takings claim can be considered ripe. Lucas has properly alleged Article III injury in fact in this case, with respect to both the pre-1990 and post-1990 constraints placed on the use of his parcels by the Beachfront Management Act. That there is a discretionary "special permit" procedure by which he may regain—for the future, at least—beneficial use of his land goes only to the prudential "ripeness" of Lucas's challenge, and for the reasons discussed we do not think it prudent to apply that prudential requirement here. See *Esposito v. South Carolina Coastal Council*, 939 F.2d 165, 168 (CA4 1991), cert. denied, 505 U.S. 1219 (1992). We leave for decision on remand, of course, the questions left unaddressed by the South Carolina Supreme Court as a consequence of its categorical disposition.

III

A

Prior to Justice Holmes's exposition in *Pennsylvania Coal Co. v. Mahon*, 260 U.S. 393 (1922), it was generally thought that the Takings Clause reached only a "direct appropriation" of property, *Legal Tender Cases*, 12 Wall. 457, 551, 20 L.Ed. 287 (1871), or the functional equivalent of a "practical ouster of [the owner's] possession," *Transportation Co. v. Chicago*, 99 U.S. 635, 642 (1879). See also *Gibson v. United States*, 166 U.S. 269, 275–276 (1897). Justice Holmes recognized in *Mahon*, however, that if the protection against physical appropriations of private property was to be meaningfully enforced, the government's power to redefine the range of interests included in the ownership of property was necessarily constrained by constitutional limits. 260 U.S. at 414–415. If, instead, the uses of private property were subject to unbridled, uncompensated qualification under the police power, "the natural tendency of human nature [would be] to extend the qualification more and more until at last private property disappear[ed]." *Id.*, at 415. These considerations gave birth in that case to the oft-cited maxim that, "while property may be regulated to a certain extent, if regulation goes too far it will be recognized as a taking." *Ibid.*

Nevertheless, our decision in *Mahon* offered little insight into when, and under what circumstances, a given regulation would be seen as going "too far" for purposes of the Fifth Amendment. In 70-odd years of succeeding "regulatory takings" jurisprudence, we have generally eschewed any "set formula" for determining how far is too far, preferring to "engag[e] in . . . essentially ad hoc, factual inquiries." *Penn Central Transportation Co. v. New York City*, 438 U.S. 104, 124 (1978) (quoting *Goldblatt v. Hempstead*, 369 U.S. 590, 594 (1962)). See Epstein, *Takings: Descent and Resurrection*, 1987 S.Ct. Rev. 1, 4. We have, however, described at least two discrete categories of regulatory action as compensable without case-specific inquiry into the public interest advanced in support of the restraint. The first encompasses regulations that compel the property owner to suffer a physical "invasion" of his property. In general (at least with regard to permanent invasions), no matter how minute the intrusion, and no matter how weighty the public purpose behind it, we have required compensation. For example, in *Loretto v. Teleprompter Manhattan CATV Corp.*, 458 U.S. 419 (1982), we determined that New York's law requiring landlords to allow television cable companies to emplace cable facilities in their apartment buildings constituted a taking, *id.* at 435–440, even though the facilities occupied at most only 1 ½ cubic feet of the landlords' property, see *id.* at 438, n. 16. See also *United States v. Causby*, 328 U.S. 256, 265 and n. 10 (1946) (physical invasions of airspace); cf. *Kaiser Aetna v. United States*, 444 U.S. 164 (1979) (imposition of navigational servitude upon private marina).

The second situation in which we have found categorical treatment appropriate is where regulation denies all economically beneficial or productive use of land. See *Agins*, 447 U.S., at 260; see also *Nollan v. California Coastal Comm'n*, 483 U.S. 825, 834 (1987); *Keystone Bituminous Coal Assn. v. DeBenedictis*, 480 U.S. 470, 495 (1987); *Hodel v. Virginia Surface Mining & Reclamation Assn., Inc.*, 452 U.S. 264, 295–296 (1981). As we have said on numerous occasions, the Fifth Amendment is violated when land-use regulation "does not substantially advance legitimate state interests *or denies an owner economically viable use of his land.*" *Agins, supra,* 447 U.S. at 260 (citations omitted) (emphasis added).

We have never set forth the justification for this rule. Perhaps it is simply, as Justice Brennan suggested, that total deprivation of beneficial use is, from the landowner's point of view, the equivalent of a physical appropriation. See *San Diego Gas & Electric Co. v. San Diego*, 450 U.S. at 652 (dissenting opinion). "[F]or what is the land but the profits thereof[?]" 1 E. Coke, Institutes, ch. 1, §1 (1st Am. ed. 1812). Surely, at least, in the extraordinary circumstance when *no* productive or economically beneficial use of land is permitted, it is less realistic to indulge our usual assumption that the legislature is simply "adjusting the benefits and burdens of economic life," *Penn Central Transportation Co.*, 438 U.S. at 124, in a manner that secures an "average reciprocity of advantage" to everyone concerned, *Pennsylvania Coal Co. v. Mahon*, 260 U.S. at 415. And the *functional* basis for permitting the government, by regulation, to affect property values without compensation—that "Government hardly could go on if to some extent values incident to property could not be diminished without paying for every such change in the general law," *id.* at 413—does not apply to the relatively rare situations where the government has deprived a landowner of all economically beneficial uses.

On the other side of the balance, affirmatively supporting a compensation requirement, is the fact that regulations that leave the owner of land without economically beneficial or productive options for its use—typically, as here, by requiring land to be left substantially in its natural state—carry with them a heightened risk that private property is being pressed into some form of public service under the guise of mitigating serious public harm. See, *e.g., Annicelli v. South Kingstown*, 463 A.2d 133, 140–141 (R.I. 1983) (prohibition on construction adjacent to beach justified on twin grounds of safety and "conservation of open space"); *Morris County Land Improvement Co. v. Parsippany-Troy Hills Township*, 40 N.J. 539, 552–553, 193 A.2d 232, 240 (1963) (prohibition on filling marshlands imposed in order to preserve region as water detention basin and create wildlife refuge). As Justice Brennan explained: "From the government's point of view, the benefits flowing to the public from preservation of open space through regulation may be equally great as from creating a wildlife refuge through formal condemnation or increasing electricity production through a dam project that floods private property." *San Diego Gas & Elec. Co., supra*, 450 U.S. at 652 (dissenting opinion). The many statutes on the books, both state and federal, that provide for the use of eminent domain to impose servitudes on private scenic lands preventing developmental uses, or to acquire such lands altogether, suggest the practical equivalence in this setting of negative regulation and appropriation. See, *e.g.*, 16 U.S.C. § 410ff–1(a) (authorizing acquisition of "lands, waters, or interests [within Channel Islands National Park] (including but not limited to scenic easements)"); § 460aa–2(a) (authorizing acquisition of "any lands, or lesser interests therein, including mineral interests and scenic easements" within Sawtooth National Recreation Area); §§ 3921–3923 (authorizing acquisition of wetlands); N.C. Gen.Stat. § 113A–38 (1990) (authorizing acquisition of, *inter alia*, "'scenic easements'" within the North Carolina natural and scenic rivers system); Tenn.Code Ann. §§ 11–15–101 to 11–15–108 (1987) (authorizing acquisition of "protective easements" and other rights in real property adjacent to State's historic, architectural, archaeological, or cultural resources).

We think, in short, that there are good reasons for our frequently expressed belief that when the owner of real property has been called upon to sacrifice *all* economically beneficial uses in the name of the common good, that is, to leave his property economically idle, he has suffered a taking.

B

The trial court found Lucas's two beachfront lots to have been rendered valueless by respondent's enforcement of the coastal-zone construction ban. Under Lucas's theory of the case, which rested upon our "no economically viable use" statements, that finding entitled him to compensation. Lucas believed it unnecessary to take issue with either the purposes behind the Beachfront Management Act, or the means chosen by the South Carolina Legislature to effectuate those purposes. The South Carolina Supreme Court, however, thought otherwise. In its view, the Beachfront Management Act was no ordinary enactment, but involved an exercise of South Carolina's "police powers" to mitigate the harm to the public interest that petitioner's use of his land might occasion. 304 S.C., at 384, 404 S.E.2d, at 899. By neglecting to dispute the findings enumerated in the Act or otherwise to challenge the legislature's purposes, petitioner "concede[d] that the beach/dune area of South Carolina's shores is an extremely valuable public resource; that the erection of new construction, *inter alia*, contributes to the erosion and destruction of this public resource; and that discouraging new construction in close proximity to the beach/dune area is necessary to prevent a great public harm." *Id.*, at 382–383, 404 S.E.2d, at 898. In the court's view, these concessions brought petitioner's challenge within a long line of this Court's cases sustaining against Due Process and Takings Clause challenges the State's use of its "police powers" to enjoin a property owner from activities akin to public nuisances. See *Mugler v. Kansas*, 123 U.S. 623 (1887) (law prohibiting manufacture of alcoholic beverages); *Hadacheck v. Sebastian*, 239 U.S. 394 (1915) (law barring operation of brick mill in residential area); *Miller v. Schoene*, 276 U.S. 272 (1928) (order to destroy diseased cedar trees to prevent infection of nearby orchards); *Goldblatt v. Hempstead*, 369 U.S. 590 (1962) (law effectively preventing continued operation of quarry in residential area).

It is correct that many of our prior opinions have suggested that "harmful or noxious uses" of property may be proscribed by government regulation without the requirement of compensation. For a number of reasons, however, we think the South Carolina Supreme Court was too quick to conclude that that principle decides the present case. The "harmful or noxious uses" principle was the Court's early attempt to describe in theoretical terms why government may, consistent with the Takings Clause, affect property values by regulation without incurring an obligation to compensate—a reality we nowadays acknowledge explicitly with respect to the full scope of the State's police power. See, *e.g., Penn Central Transportation Co.*, 438 U.S. at 125 (where State "reasonably conclude[s] that 'the health, safety, morals, or general welfare' would be promoted by prohibiting particular contemplated uses of land," compensation need not accompany prohibition); see also *Nollan v. California Coastal Comm'n*, 483 U.S. at 834–835 ("Our cases have not elaborated on the standards for determining what constitutes a 'legitimate state interest[,]' [but] [t]hey have made clear . . . that a broad range of governmental purposes and regulations satisfy these requirements"). We made this very point in *Penn Central Transportation Co.*, where, in the course of sustaining New York City's landmarks preservation program against a takings challenge, we rejected the petitioner's suggestion that *Mugler* and the cases following it were premised on, and thus limited by, some objective conception of "noxiousness":

"[T]he uses in issue in *Hadacheck, Miller*, and *Goldblatt* were perfectly lawful in themselves. They involved no 'blameworthiness, . . . moral wrongdoing or conscious act of dangerous risk-taking which induce[d society] to shift the cost to a pa[rt]icular individual.' Sax, *Takings and the Police Power*, 74 YALE L.J. 36, 50 (1964). These cases are better understood as resting not on any supposed 'noxious' quality of the prohibited uses but rather on the ground that the restrictions were reasonably related to the implementation of a policy—not unlike historic preservation—expected to produce a widespread public benefit and applicable to all similarly situated property." 438 U.S. at 133–134.

"Harmful or noxious use" analysis was, in other words, simply the progenitor of our more contemporary statements that "land-use regulation does not effect a taking if it 'substantially advance[s] legitimate state interests'. . . ." *Nollan, supra*, 483 U.S. at 834 (quoting *Agins v. Tiburon*, 447 U.S. at 260); see also *Penn Central Transportation Co., supra*, 438 U.S. at 127; *Euclid v. Ambler Realty Co.*, 272 U.S. 365, 387–388 (1926).

The transition from our early focus on control of "noxious" uses to our contemporary understanding of the broad realm within which government may regulate without compensation was an easy one, since the distinction between "harm-preventing" and "benefit-conferring" regulation is often in the eye of the beholder. It is quite possible, for example, to describe in *either* fashion the ecological, economic, and esthetic concerns that inspired the South Carolina Legislature in the present case. One could say that imposing a servitude on Lucas's land is necessary in order to prevent his use of it from "harming" South Carolina's ecological resources; or, instead, in order to achieve the "benefits" of an ecological preserve. Compare, *e.g., Claridge v. New Hampshire Wetlands Board*, 125 N.H. 745, 752, 485 A.2d 287, 292 (1984) (owner may, without compensation, be barred from filling wetlands because landfilling would deprive adjacent coastal habitats and marine fisheries of ecological support), with, *e.g., Bartlett v. Zoning Comm'n of Old Lyme*, 161 Conn. 24, 30, 282 A.2d 907, 910 (1971) (owner barred from filling tidal marshland must be compensated, despite municipality's "laudable" goal of "preserv[ing] marshlands from encroachment or destruction"). Whether one or the other of the competing characterizations will come to one's lips in a particular case depends primarily upon one's evaluation of the worth of competing uses of real estate. See Restatement (Second) of Torts §822, Comment *g*, p. 112 (1979) ("Practically all human activities unless carried on in a wilderness interfere to some extent with others or involve some risk of interference"). A given restraint will be seen as mitigating "harm" to the adjacent parcels or securing a "benefit" for them, depending upon the observer's evaluation of the relative importance of the use that the restraint favors. See Sax, *Takings and the Police Power*, 74 YALE L.J. 36, 49 (1964) ("[T]he problem [in this area] is not one of noxiousness or harm-creating activity at all; rather it is a problem of inconsistency between perfectly innocent and independently desirable uses"). Whether Lucas's construction of single-family residences on his parcels should be described as bringing "harm" to South Carolina's adjacent ecological resources thus depends principally upon whether the describer believes that the State's use interest in nurturing those resources is so important that *any* competing adjacent use must yield.

When it is understood that "prevention of harmful use" was merely our early formulation of the police power justification necessary to sustain (without compensation) *any* regulatory diminution in value; and that the distinction between regulation that "prevents harmful use" and that which "confers benefits" is difficult, if not impossible, to discern on an objective, value-free basis; it becomes self-evident that noxious-use logic cannot serve as a touchstone to distinguish regulatory "takings"—which require compensation—from regulatory deprivations that do not require compensation. *A fortiori* the legislature's recitation of a noxious-use justification cannot be the basis for departing from our categorical rule that total regulatory takings must be compensated. If it were, departure would virtually always be allowed. The South Carolina Supreme Court's approach would essentially nullify *Mahon*'s affirmation of limits to the noncompensable exercise of the police power. Our cases provide no support for this: None of them that employed the logic of "harmful use" prevention to sustain a regulation involved an allegation that the regulation wholly eliminated the value of the claimant's land. See *Keystone Bituminous Coal Assn.*, 480 U.S. at 513–514 (Rehnquist, C.J., dissenting).

Where the State seeks to sustain regulation that deprives land of all economically beneficial use, we think it may resist compensation only if the logically antecedent inquiry into the nature of the owner's estate shows that the proscribed use interests were not part of his title to begin with. This accords, we think, with our "takings" jurisprudence, which has traditionally been guided by the understandings of our citizens regarding the content of, and the State's power over, the "bundle of rights" that they acquire when they obtain title to property. It seems to us that the property owner necessarily expects the uses of his property to be restricted, from time to time, by various measures newly enacted by the State in legitimate exercise of its police powers; "[a]s long recognized, some values are enjoyed under an implied limitation and must yield to the police power." *Pennsylvania Coal Co. v. Mahon*, 260 U.S. at 413. And in the case of personal property, by reason of the State's traditionally high degree of control over commercial dealings, he ought to be aware of the possibility that new regulation might even render his property economically worthless (at least if the property's only economically productive use is sale or manufacture for sale). See *Andrus v. Allard*, 444 U.S. 51, 66–67 (1979) (prohibition on sale of eagle feathers). In the case of land, however, we think the notion pressed by the Council that title is somehow held subject to the "implied limitation" that the State may subsequently eliminate all economically valuable use is inconsistent with the historical compact recorded in the Takings Clause that has become part of our constitutional culture.

Where "permanent physical occupation" of land is concerned, we have refused to allow the government to decree it anew (without compensation), no matter how weighty the asserted "public interests" involved, *Loretto v. Teleprompter Manhattan CATV Corp.*, 458 U.S. at 426—though we assuredly *would* permit the government to assert a permanent easement that was a pre-existing limitation upon the land owner's title. Compare *Scranton v. Wheeler*, 179 U.S. 141, 163 (1900) (interests of "riparian owner in the submerged lands . . . bordering on a public navigable water" held subject to Government's navigational servitude) with *Kaiser Aetna v. United States*, 444 U.S. at 178–180 (imposition of navigational servitude on marina created and rendered navigable at private expense held to constitute a taking). We believe similar treatment must be accorded confiscatory regulations, *i.e.*, regulations that prohibit all economically beneficial use of land: Any limitation so severe cannot be newly legislated or decreed (without compensation), but must inhere in the title itself, in the restrictions that background principles of the State's law of property and nuisance already place upon land ownership. A law or decree with such an effect must, in other words, do no more than duplicate the result that could have been achieved in the courts—by adjacent landowners (or other uniquely affected persons) under the State's law of private nuisance, or by the State under its complementary power to abate nuisances that affect the public generally, or otherwise.

On this analysis, the owner of a lake-bed, for example, would not be entitled to compensation when he is denied the requisite permit to engage in a landfilling operation that would have the effect of flooding others' land. Nor the corporate owner of a nuclear generating plant, when it is directed to remove all improvements from its land upon discovery that the plant sits astride an earthquake fault. Such regulatory action may well have the effect of eliminating the land's only economically productive use, but it does not proscribe a productive use that was previously permissible under relevant property and nuisance principles. The use of these properties for what are now expressly prohibited purposes was *always* unlawful, and (subject to other constitutional limitations) it was open to the State at any point to make the implication of those background principles of nuisance and property law explicit. See Michelman, *Property, Utility, and Fairness, Comments on the Ethical Foundations of "Just Compensation" Law*, 80 Harv. L. Rev. 1165, 1239–1241 (1967). In light of our traditional resort to "existing rules or understandings that stem from an independent source such as state law" to define the range of interests that qualify for protection as "property" under the Fifth and Fourteenth Amendments, *Board of Regents of State Colleges v. Roth*, 408 U.S. 564, 577 (1972); see, *e.g., Ruckelshaus v. Monsanto Co.*, 467 U.S. 986, 1011–1012 (1984); *Hughes v. Washington*, 389 U.S. 290, 295 (1967) (Stewart, J., concurring), this recognition that the Takings Clause does not require compensation when an owner is barred from putting land to a use that is proscribed by those "existing rules or understandings" is surely unexceptional. When, however, a regulation that declares "off-limits" all economically productive or beneficial uses of land goes beyond what the relevant background principles would dictate, compensation must be paid to sustain it.

The "total taking" inquiry we require today will ordinarily entail (as the application of state nuisance law ordinarily entails) analysis of, among other things, the degree of harm to public lands and resources, or adjacent private property, posed by the claimant's proposed activities, see, *e.g.*, Restatement (Second) of Torts §§ 826, 827, the social value of the claimant's activities and their suitability to the locality in question, see, *e.g., id.*, §§ 828(a) and (b), 831, and the relative ease with which the alleged harm can be avoided through measures taken by the claimant and the government (or adjacent private landowners) alike, see, *e.g., id.*, §§ 827(e), 828(c), 830. The fact that a particular use has long been engaged in by similarly situated owners ordinarily imports a lack of any common-law prohibition (though changed circumstances or new knowledge may make what was previously permissible no longer so, see *id.*, § 827, Comment *g*. So also does the fact that other landowners, similarly situated, are permitted to continue the use denied to the claimant.

It seems unlikely that common-law principles would have prevented the erection of any habitable or productive improvements on petitioner's land; they rarely support prohibition of the "essential use" of land, *Curtin v. Benson*, 222 U.S. 78, 86 (1911). The question, however, is one of state law to be dealt with on remand. We emphasize that to win its case South Carolina must do more than proffer the legislature's declaration that the uses Lucas desires are inconsistent with the public interest, or the conclusory assertion that they violate a common-law maxim such as *sic utere tuo ut alienum non laedas*. As we have said, a "State, by *ipse dixit*, may not transform private property into public property without compensation. . . ." *Webb's Fabulous Pharmacies, Inc. v. Beckwith*, 449 U.S. 155, 164 (1980). Instead, as it would be required to do if it sought to restrain Lucas in a common-law action for public nuisance, South Carolina must identify background principles of nuisance and property law that prohibit the uses he now intends in the circumstances in which the property is presently found. Only on this showing can the State fairly claim that, in proscribing all such beneficial uses, the Beachfront Management Act is taking nothing.

The judgment is reversed, and the case is remanded for proceedings not inconsistent with this opinion. *So ordered.*

Notes and Questions to Consider:

1. Could the "background principles of the State's law of property and nuisance" vary from state to state? How does the state of Florida interpret these background principles under its state constitution in the area of eminent domain and reverse condemnation?

2. What are Florida's background principals of its state's law of property and nuisance? Perhaps the answer might be suggested by the case of *Conner v. Carlton*, 223 So. 2d 324 (Fla. 1969). Although it is not an eminent domain or reverse condemnation case, it holds that "in the exercise of its police power the state may summarily seize or destroy diseased cattle, contaminated food, obscene publications, illicit intoxicants, narcotics, prohibited weapons, gambling devices and paraphernalia, and other property that menaces the public health, safety or morals." If this is Florida's standard applicable to eminent domain and reverse condemnation, how could Florida jurisprudence differ from other states such as, for example, Colorado?

B. State's Police Power, Property Law, and Nuisance Law Put a Limit upon Inverse Condemnation

One might think of eminent domain and inverse condemnation (or "takings") as two sides of the same coin. In eminent domain, the government informs the citizen that the government is confiscating the citizen's land and begins the process of taking title to it and paying compensation for it. Whereas in a case of inverse condemnation, a citizen finds that a restriction placed upon his land that on its face does not appear to confiscate his land ends up confiscating enough of the landowner's rights that he can sue for compensation. But how much regulation is too much so as to constitute a "taking" or inverse condemnation? Consider the following case of *Village of Tequesta v. Jupiter Inlet Corp.*, 371 So. 2d 663 (Fla. 1979).

Village of Tequesta v. Jupiter Inlet Corp.
Supreme Court of Florida, 1979
371 So. 2d 663

ADKINS, Justice.

Pursuant to article V, section 3(b)(3), Florida Constitution, the Fourth District Court of Appeal in *Jupiter Inlet Corp. v. Village of Tequesta*, 349 So. 2d 216 (Fla. 4th

DCA 1977) certified to this Court as a matter of great public interest the following question:

> *Can a municipality be held responsible through inverse condemnation for a taking, from private ownership for public purposes, of underground shallow aquifer water, to the extent that the owner is deprived of the beneficial use of the aquifer?*

Jupiter Inlet Corporation, plaintiff in the trial court, will be referred to as Jupiter, and The Village of Tequesta, defendant in the trial court, will be referred to as Tequesta.

Jupiter owned property near Tequesta on which it planned to build a 120-unit condominium project, "Broadview." This property was located approximately 1,200 feet from Tequesta's well field number four. This well field contained seven wells, seventy-five to ninety feet deep, which pumped in excess of a million gallons of water a day from the shallow water aquifer to supply Tequesta residents with water. It was relatively inexpensive to withdraw water from the shallow-water aquifer.

As a result of the excessive amount of water withdrawn by Tequesta from the shallow-water aquifer, the fresh-water supply was endangered and salt water from the intercoastal waterway intruded into the shallow-water aquifer. There was testimony from a hydrologist that saltwater intrusion was caused by a reduction in the water levels in the interior to a point low enough that the fresh-water level could not withstand the pressure of the saltwater level in the intercoastal. The water which Tequesta withdrew came from the shallow-water aquifer beneath its property. Because Tequesta would not supply Jupiter water, it was necessary for Jupiter to secure a special exception from the county. Tequesta opposed the permit application and it was denied. Jupiter was not permitted to drill wells to withdraw water from the shallow-water aquifer because of the endangered condition of the aquifer due to the excessive withdrawals made by Tequesta.

The only means by which Jupiter could supply water to its property was to drill a well to the Floridan aquifer located 1,200 feet below the surface, at a substantially greater cost.

Jupiter instituted an action for inverse condemnation and injunction due to the excessive pumping by Tequesta. The theory of Jupiter's action was that due to depletion by Tequesta of the shallow-water aquifer beneath its property Jupiter was effectively deprived of the beneficial use of its property rights in the shallow-water aquifer.

Considering any factual conflicts in the light most favorable to Jupiter, the trial judge granted a summary judgment in favor of the Village of Tequesta. Viewing the facts in the same light as did the trial court, the district court of appeal said:

> The owner has been deprived by government action of the use and enjoyment of what was his, and so through a suit in inverse condemnation he can compel the government to pay for what it has taken.

349 So. 2d at 217. The district court of appeal then certified the above question to this Court for consideration.

The following hydrological statements are fully supported by F. Maloney, S. Plager, and F. Baldwin, WATER LAW AND ADMINISTRATION, page 141 (1968) (hereinafter referred to as Water Law) as well as the discussion in *City of St. Petersburg v. Southwest Florida Water Management District*, 355 So. 2d 796 (Fla. 2d DCA 1977).

Water-bearing zones under the earth's surface capable of receiving, storing, and transmitting water are called aquifers. Most aquifers in Florida are cavernous limestone or sand and shale beds. Aquifers are separated by relatively impervious layers of shales and clays which are called aquicludes.

There are two basic types of aquifers. One is the unconfined aquifer associated with the water table. It is free to rise and fall with the amount of rainfall and other surface-water influences such as rivers, lakes, irrigation, etc. Near the coast the water level in this aquifer fluctuates with the tidal action. It is referred to as the ground-water aquifer, water-table aquifer, and the shallow aquifer.

The other type of aquifer is an artesian aquifer. Water in this aquifer is confined within aquicludes. Water will either not pass through these aquicludes or will do so at a much slower rate than it can travel within the aquifer itself. Water enters artesian aquifers slowly through the surrounding aquiclude by virtue of fissures, sinkholes, or other openings in the aquiclude. Water in the artesian aquifer is under pressure. One artesian aquifer is known as the Floridan aquifer. It underlies most of the state and furnishes most of the well-water supplies of the state.

In an early decision, *Tampa Watchworks Co. v. Cline*, 37 Fla. 586, 20 So. 780 (1896), we made a classification of water passing over or through lands as follows:

> (1) In respect to surface streams which flow in a permanent, distinct, and well-defined channel from the lands of one owner to those of another; (2) in respect to surface waters, however originating, which, without any distinct or well-defined channel, by attraction, gravitation, or otherwise, are shed and pass from the lands of one proprietor to those of another; (3) subterranean streams which flow in a permanent, distinct, and well-defined channel from the lands of one to those of another proprietor; (4) subsurface waters which, without any permanent, distinct, or definite channel, percolate in veins or filter from the lands of one owner to those of another.

20 So. at 782.

Although we classified water as if its different physical states were separate and distinct, we recognize that these classes are interrelated parts of the hydrologic cycle. We are primarily concerned in this case with the rights of landowners in the shallow-water aquifer.

Ancient law gave no special consideration to ground water, treating all water like the air, the sea, and wild animals, as the property of no one or the property of everyone. Trelease, *Government Ownership and Trusteeship of Water*, 45 Calif. Law

Review 638, 640 (1957). Technological ignorance about the existence, origin, movement and course of percolating ground waters resulted in the so-called "English rule" which essentially allowed a land owner to take or interfere with percolating waters underlying his land, irrespective of any effects his use might have on ground water underlying his neighbors' lands. This doctrine, first enunciated in 1843 in an English case, *Acton v. Blundell*, 152 Eng.Rep. 1235 (1843) was based upon the maxim, "To whomsoever the soil belongs, he owns also to the sky and to the depths." See Water Law at 155. With the growth of hydrological capabilities in pumping technology, the English rule was repudiated in most American jurisdictions. See Annots. 29 A.L.R.2d 1354, 1361–65 (1953); 109 A.L.R. 395, 399–403 (1937); 55 A.L.R. 1385, 1398–1408 (1928), and cases cited therein. The so-called "American," or "reasonable use," rule rejected the "to the sky and to the depths" notion for another maxim, "use your own property so as not to injure that of another." See *Koch v. Wick*, 87 So. 2d 47 (Fla. 1956); *Cason v. Florida Power Co.*, 74 Fla. 1, 76 So. 535 (Fla. 1917); *Bassett v. Salisbury Manufacturing Co.*, 43 N.H. 569 (1862). The reasonable use rule adopted by most Eastern states, including Florida, was stated by one court as follows:

> (A) landowner, who, in the course of using his own land, obstructs, diverts, or removes percolating water to the injury of his neighbor . . . must be (making) a reasonable exercise of his proprietary right, i.e., such an exercise as may be reasonably necessary for some useful or beneficial purpose, generally relating to the land in which the waters are found.

Finley et ux. v. Teeter Stone, Inc., 251 Md. 428, 435, 248 A.2d 106, 111–12 (Md.App. 1968). See also Water Law at 158.

In applying the reasonable use rule this Court has not given definite answers as to the actual amount of water that may be taken by overlying land owners, nor have we considered the meaning of the term "ownership" as applied to percolating water.

In 93 C.J.S. Waters section 90, page 765 (1956), the rule is stated thus:

> There can be no ownership in seeping and percolating waters in the absolute sense, because of their wandering and migratory character, unless and until they are reduced to the actual possession and control of the person claiming them. Their ownership consists in the right of the owner of the land to capture, control, and possess them, to prevent their escape, if he can do so, from his land, and to prevent strangers from trespassing on his land in an effort to capture, control, or possess them. If percolating waters escape naturally to other lands, the title of the former owner is gone; while a landowner may prevent the escape of such waters from his land, if he can do so, yet he has no right to follow them into the lands of another and there capture, control, or reduce them to possession. (Footnotes omitted).

The common-law concept of absolute ownership of percolating water while it is in one's land gave him the right to abstract from his land all the water he could find there. On the other hand, it afforded him no protection against the acts of his neighbors who, by pumping on their own land, managed to draw out of his land all the water it contained. Thus the term "ownership" as applied to percolating water never meant that the overlying owner had a property or proprietary interest in the corpus of the water itself.

This necessarily follows from the physical characteristic of percolating water. It is migratory in nature and is a part of the land only so long as it is in it. There is a right of use as it passes, but there is no ownership in the absolute sense. It belongs to the overlying owner in a limited sense, that is, he has the unqualified right to capture and control it in a reasonable way with an immunity from liability to his neighbors for doing so. When it is reduced to his possession and control, it ceases to be percolating water and becomes his personal property. But if it flows or percolates from his land, he loses all right and interest in it the instant it passes beyond the boundaries of his property, and when it enters the land of his neighbor it belongs to him in the same limited way.

The right of the owner to ground water underlying his land is to the usufruct of the water and not to the water itself. The ownership of the land does not carry with it any ownership of vested rights to underlying ground water not actually diverted and applied to beneficial use.

In *Valls v. Arnold Industries, Inc. et al.*, 328 So. 2d 471, 473 (Fla. 2d DCA 1976) the court said:

> Water, oil, minerals and other substances of value which lie beneath the surface are valuable property rights which cannot be divested without due process of law and the payment of just compensation.

This case involved a post-trial apportionment award in condemnation as between fee-title owners and owners of reserved mineral rights. In order to effect a payment to the holders of the mineral rights, it was necessary for the court to find that these mineral rights were property rights and therefore subject to condemnation. The court relied upon *Copello v. Hart*, 293 So. 2d 734 (Fla. 1st DCA 1974) and *Dickinson et al. v. Davis et al.*, 224 So. 2d 262 (Fla. 1969). These cases held that minerals, gas, and oil are separate properties from the surface and may be conveyed and taxed separately. Neither case referred to property rights in water.

We overrule the dicta in *Valls*, supra, that water beneath the surface is a private property right which cannot be divested under any circumstances without due process of law and the payment of just compensation. The right to use water does not carry with it ownership of the water lying under the land. Of course, "property" in its strict legal sense "means that dominion or indefinite right of user and disposition which one may lawfully exercise over particular things or objects." *Tatum Brothers, etc. v. Watson*, 92 Fla. 278, 109 So. 623, 626 (1926). This "right of user" may be protected by injunction, *Koch v. Wick*, supra, or regulated by law, *Pounds v. Darling*, 75 Fla. 125, 77 So. 666 (1918); *Broward v. Mabry*, 58 Fla. 398, 50 So. 826 (1909), but the right of user is not considered "private property" requiring condemnation proceedings unless the property has been rendered useless for certain purposes. For example, in *Kendry et al. v. State Road Department*, 213 So. 2d 23 (Fla. 4th DCA

1968), the state agency caused such flooding on the owner's property that it was rendered useless for residential purposes. This was a "taking."

In the case Sub judice, Jupiter was only subjected to the consequential damages incurred when it was required to draw water from the Floridan aquifer instead of the shallow-water aquifer. It still had a "right of user."

There is a distinction when this right of user as to water has been invaded by circumstances showing an intentional invasion in an unreasonable manner or an unintentional invasion when the conduct was negligent, reckless, or ultrahazardous, resulting in a destruction of the right of user as to land.

For example, in *Labruzzo et ux. v. Atlantic Dredging & Const. Co. etc.*, 54 So. 2d 673 (Fla. 1951), plaintiff sued for damages for the interruption and diversion of the natural flow of the underground waters which fed plaintiff's spring. The defendant contended that there was no indication of the existence of a well-defined subterranean stream feeding plaintiff's spring. Therefore, the source of the spring should have been considered percolating waters, the flow of which had been interrupted by the defendant in the lawful and reasonable use of its property. Under the reasonable use rule, defendant contended that plaintiff had no cause of action. The trial judge agreed and, upon appeal, this Court reversed, saying:

> At the outset, it should be noted that we are not here dealing with a problem involving a proprietary competition over the water itself—that is to say, there is no conflict here between the respective rights of persons to make competing proprietary uses of subterranean waters to which they both have access. In such cases, the present trend among the courts of this country is away from the old common-law rule of unqualified and absolute right of a landowner to intercept and draw from his land the percolating waters therein; and the latter cases hold that the right of a landowner to subterranean waters percolating through his own land and his neighbor's lands is limited to a reasonable and beneficial use of such waters. . . .

> In the instant case, however, we are concerned with an interference with plaintiffs' use of the spring on their land, caused by conduct of the defendant not involving a competing use of water and in which the effect on the subterranean water is only incidental to the defendant's use of its land. Obviously, then, the rule of "reasonable use," as engrafted upon the old common-law rule of absolute and unqualified ownership of percolating waters, insofar as the proprietary beneficial use of the Water is concerned, has no application here where we are concerned with the proprietary use of Land, and in which the water is only incidentally affected. Under such circumstances, even at common law, a person was subject to liability for interference with another's use of water, either for (1) an intentional invasion when his conduct was unreasonable under the circumstances of the particular case, or (2) an unintentional invasion when his conduct was negligent, reckless or ultrahazardous. Restatement of Torts, Vol. IV, Section 849, and

Sections 822–840. In the absence, then, of surface indications, an interference with subterranean water is, or course, unintentional and Damnum absque injuria unless the conduct resulting therein is negligent, reckless or ultrahazardous. . . .

Since the allegations of plaintiffs' declaration must be taken as true on demurrer, it is clear that plaintiffs have stated a cause of action for an intentional invasion by defendant of their water rights, for which it must respond in damages if its conduct was unreasonable under the particular circumstances. . . . (Citations omitted).

54 So. 2d at 675–77.

Article X, section 6, of the Florida Constitution forbids the "taking" of private property except for a public purpose and with full compensation. Unlike the constitutions of several other states, the Florida Constitution does not expressly forbid "damage" to property with just compensation. *Arundel Corp. et al. v. Griffin et al.,* 89 Fla. 128, 103 So. 422 (1925).

When the governmental action is such that it does not encroach on private property but merely impairs its use by the owner, the action does not constitute a "taking" but is merely consequential damage and the owner is not entitled to compensation. *Selden et al. v. City of Jacksonville,* 28 Fla. 558, 10 So. 457 (1891).

In *Poe v. State Road Department,* 127 So. 2d 898, 901 (Fla. 1st DCA 1961) the court said:

It is universally recognized that injury by the condemnor to remaining land caused by obstructing, diverting or increasing the flow of surface waters, but which do not amount to a permanent deprivation by the owner of the use of such remaining lands, is a consequential damage resulting from the taking in an eminent domain proceeding, and must be recovered in that proceeding, if at all. (Footnote omitted).

If the damage suffered by the owner is the equivalent "of a taking" or an appropriation of his property for public use, then our constitution recognizes the owner's right to compel compensation. On the other hand, if the damage suffered is not a taking or an appropriation within the limits of our organic law, then the damages suffered are Damnum absque injuria and compensation therefor by the public agency cannot be compelled. *Weir v. Palm Beach County,* 85 So. 2d 865 (Fla. 1956).

The district court of appeal, in its opinion, relied upon *White v. Pinellas County,* 185 So. 2d 468 (Fla. 1966), as authority for the principle that a taking can occur when any property rights are involved. This case involved trees and shrubs located on the property which were used as a windbreak and a privacy screen. In *White* there was a physical invasion of the property when the state, through its agents, cut down large trees and shrubs. In the case Sub judice there was no physical invasion of Jupiter's property by the agents of Tequesta, so no compensation is due for consequential damage.

The cases relied upon by respondent involve situations where there was damage to the land itself, a result which does not exist in this case. *Cason v. Florida Power Co.*, supra, dealt with resulting damage to the fee because of the diversion of percolating water. *Koch v. Wick*, supra, dealt with damage to the fee by diversion of water therefrom to the point that the fee would become infertile and unsuitable for cultivation. In *State Road Department et al. v. Tharp*, 146 Fla. 745, 1 So. 2d 868 (1941), the construction of a highway embankment impeded the flow and raised the level of a millrace to such an extent as to destroy the use of plaintiff's grist mill. This was held to be a taking.

The "reasonable use" rule insofar as the proprietary beneficial use of water is concerned has no application where the court is concerned with the proprietary use of Land, and in which the water is only incidentally affected. See *Labruzzo v. Atlantic Dredging and Construction Co.*, supra.

Property owners have been successful in seeking relief under the theory of inverse condemnation against the appropriate authority as a result of the excessive noise from low-flying jet aircraft. See *Hillsborough County Aviation Authority v. Benitez*, 200 So. 2d 194 (Fla. 2d DCA 1967). The "taking" of an airspace above the land is not comparable to the "taking" of the water located in a ground aquifer beneath the land in the absence of a trespass on the land itself. The damage to the airspace was such as to deprive the property owners of all beneficial use of their property. The alleged damage to the shallow-water aquifer deprived Jupiter of no beneficial use of the land itself. Jupiter developed the property to its highest and best use and has suffered no more than consequential damage, which is not compensable through inverse condemnation.

The bare essential facts controlling this case are simple and direct. Tequesta utilized all of the available percolating water of the shallow-well aquifer in the area of Jupiter's land. Jupiter decided to become a competing user. This desire was thwarted because Tequesta had utilized all of the water which could be safely withdrawn from the shallow-well aquifer. This meant Jupiter had to go deeper to the Floridan aquifer to obtain its water and to spend more money than it would have if allowed to use the shallow-well aquifer. The costs were increased both in drilling and treatment of the water. It is a hydrologic impossibility to place a value upon the water which was withdrawn from underneath Jupiter's land.

It is incumbent upon Jupiter to show, not only a taking, but also that a private property right has been destroyed by governmental action. Jupiter did not have a constitutionally protected right in the water beneath its property. In the cases cited by Jupiter, the courts supported compensation for the taking of a use which was existent and of which a party was deprived. Jupiter seeks to be compensated for a use which it had never perfected to the point that it was in existence. Jupiter had a right to use the water, but the use itself is not existent until this right is exercised.

The property rights relative to waters that naturally percolate through the land of one owner to and through the land of another are correlative. Reasonableness could only be determined after the conflict arises between users. The "reasonableness" of a given use depends upon many variables such as: the reasonable demands of other users; the quantity of water available for use; the consideration of public policy. Even an allocation between conflicting users has no durability, for the decision by another land owner to exercise his previously neglected right to use water could easily render all other uses unreasonable. A person developing his own land could make a substantial investment with no way of determining whether reasonable use by others would limit or destroy his development right even though it was the first in time.

The judicial system was ill-equipped to deal with such conflict and became oriented to a case-by-case approach to solving disputes. This Court recognizes that all conflicts between competing users must be determined from the facts and circumstance of particular cases as they arise. *Cason v. Florida Power Co., supra.* This "right to use" is not "private property" as contemplated by article X, section 6, Florida Constitution requiring full compensation before taking for a public purpose.

The State of Florida operates under an administrative system of water management pursuant to the terms of the Florida Water Resources Act. Ch. 373, Fla. Stat. (1972). The law prior to the Florida Water Resources Act did not allow ownership in the corpus of the water, but only in the use of it. Even then, the use was bounded by the perimeters of reasonable and beneficial use. Legislation limiting the right to the use of the water is in itself no more objectionable than legislation forbidding the use of property for certain purposes by zoning regulations. *Village of Euclid v. Ambler Realty Co.*, 272 U.S. 365, 47 S.Ct. 114, 71 L.Ed. 303 (1926); 54 A.L.R. 1016 (1928).

The Florida Water Resources Act, in recognizing the need for conservation and control of the waters in the state (Section 373.016, Fla.Stat. (1973)) makes all waters in the state subject to regulation, unless otherwise specifically exempt. § 373.023(1) Fla. Stat. (1973). The Department of Environmental Regulation and the various water management districts are given the responsibility to accomplish the conservation, protection, management, and control of the waters of the state. § 373.016(3) Fla. Stat. (1973). In order to exercise such controls a permitting system is established which requires permits for consumptive use of water, exempting only "domestic consumption of water by individual users" from the requirements of a permit. § 373.219(1) Fla. Stat. (1973). Jupiter, in serving a 120-unit condominium, does not qualify as an individual user and thus must secure a permit in order to draw water from beneath its property. Without a permit Jupiter has no such property right to the use of water beneath its land for which, upon deprivation, it must be compensated through inverse condemnation.

The Water Resources Act of 1972 recognizes a right to use water under the common law as separate from the right to use water under a permit granted pursuant to the act. This is done by a provision concerning the termination of the common-law right and a transitional procedure. The holder of such a common-law water-use right was given two years to convert the common-law water right into a permit water right. § 373.226(3) Fla. Stat. (1973). In order to qualify for the initial permit under section 373.226(2) Florida Statutes (1973), the right must have been exercised prior to the implementation of the Florida Water Resources Act by a water management district with geographical jurisdiction in that area. Otherwise the right is abandoned and extinguished requiring a new application for a permit. Tequesta had acquired the permit and Jupiter was merely a proposed user. The Florida Water Resources Act makes no provision for the continuation of an unexercised common-law right to use water. Jupiter had perfected no legal interest to the use of the water beneath its land which would support an action in inverse condemnation.

Section 373.1961 Florida Statutes (1975) provides additional powers and duties for the governing boards of the water management district. Subsection (7) provides that the governing board:

> May acquire title to such interest as is necessary in real property, by purchase, gift, devise, lease, eminent domain, or otherwise, for *water production and transmission* consistent with this section. However, the district shall not use any of the eminent domain powers herein granted to acquire water and water rights already devoted to reasonable and beneficial use or any water production or transmission facilities owned by any county, municipality, or regional water supply authority. (Emphasis supplied).

Condemnation of "water rights" is not granted in the first sentence of this subsection. The authority granted is specifically limited to the acquisition of land for the purpose of constructing and operating well fields and other withdrawal facilities and for the right-of-way necessary for the transmission of water to consumers. The second sentence prohibits the use of eminent domain to acquire such "water rights" which were already being put to a reasonable and beneficial use. The statutory prohibition of the use of eminent domain in one situation cannot be used as authority for its use by implication in another, as the statute must be strictly construed. *Canal Authority v. Miller*, 243 So. 2d 193 (Fla. 1970). All that Section 373.1961(7) Florida Statutes (1975) accomplishes is to further protect presently existing legal uses of water. No implication can be drawn that this section intends to include any "water right" other than the permit that may be granted by a water management district. After all, if a use of water is both preexisting and also reasonable and beneficial, after two years, it must be either under permit or it is conclusively presumed to be abandoned. There was no necessity for the Water Resources Act to provide for the condemnation of an unexercised right to use water, as the owner became subject to the permit provisions of the law. There was no "taking" of this right.

In summary, we hold:

1. Prior to the adoption of the Water Resources Act, Florida followed the reasonable use rule; that is, a landowner, who, in the course of using his own land, removes percolating water to the injury of his neighbor, must be making a reasonable exercise of his proprietary rights, i.e., such an exercise as may be reasonably necessary for some useful or beneficial purpose, generally relating to the land in which the waters are found;

2. There was no ownership in the waters below the land, as the right of the owner to ground water underlying his land was to the use of the water and not to the water itself;

3. In applying the reasonable use rule, this Court has not given definite answers as to the actual amount of water that may be taken by overlying landowners;

4. The diversion of water from the shallow-water aquifer is not a "taking" or an appropriation of property for public use requiring condemnation proceeding unless there is a resulting damage to the land itself, for example, a diversion of water to the extent that the land becomes unsuitable for cultivation, raising the level of flowing waters to the extent that land is flooded, etc.;

5. The landowner does not have a constitutionally-protected property right in the water beneath the property, requiring compensation for the taking of the water when used for a public purpose;

6. Just as legislation may limit the use of property for certain purposes by zoning, so it is that the right to the use of the water may also be limited or regulated.

7. The Water Resources Act now controls the use of water and replaces the ad hoc judicial determination in water management districts where consumptive use permitting is in force.

8. Jupiter's remedy is only through proper application for a permit under the Florida Water Resources Act.

For the above reasons, we answer the certified question in the negative and hold that Tequesta cannot be held responsible for damages through inverse condemnation.

The decision of the district court of appeal is quashed and this cause is remanded with instructions to affirm the summary judgment entered by the trial judge in favor of Tequesta. . . .

***

Schick v. Florida Department of Agriculture

First District Court of Appeal of Florida, 1987
504 So. 2d 1318

JOANOS, Judge.

This is an appeal from a dismissal with prejudice of a claim for compensation for inverse condemnation. Three questions are presented for our review: (1) whether appellants may raise a claim for inverse condemnation for pollution of underground water in privately-owned wells, (2) whether appellants may maintain a tort claim against the state in regard to its conduct of the nematode eradication program, and (3) whether appellants may maintain a claim predicated on strict liability against the state. We affirm in part and reverse in part.

Appellants' initial 18-count complaint sought damages from the Florida Department of Agriculture (FDA) for ethylene dibromide (EDB) contamination. The complaint was dismissed pursuant to FDA's motion, with leave to file an amended complaint within twenty days. Appellants' second amended complaint was again met with a motion to dismiss based on allegations that appellants' claims were barred by the doctrine of sovereign immunity, and that the allegations of the complaint did not state a taking by FDA. The trial court dismissed the second amended complaint with prejudice, finding that its allegations were in substance identical to the allegations of each count of the first complaint. Thereafter, the trial court denied appellants' motion to alter or amend the order of dismissal.

The first question for our consideration is appellants' inverse condemnation claim for pollution of underground water in privately owned wells. The Florida Constitution bars the taking of private property except for public use, and then only after full compensation. Art. X, s. 6, Fla. Const.; *Village of Tequesta v. Jupiter Inlet Corporation*, 371 So. 2d 663, 669 (Fla.), *cert. denied*, 444 U.S. 965, 100 S.Ct. 453, 62 L.Ed.2d 377 (1979). Thus, a cause of action for inverse condemnation will lie against a government agency, which by its conduct or activities, has taken private property without a formal exercise of the power of eminent domain. *Pinellas County v. Brown*, 420 So. 2d 308, 309 (Fla. 2d DCA 1982), *petition for review denied*, 430 So. 2d 450 (Fla. 1983).

It is well settled that an action for inverse condemnation is available only in those instances where the "taking" has effectively deprived the owner of all reasonable and beneficial use and enjoyment of the property. *Graham v. Estuary Properties, Inc.*, 399 So. 2d 1374 (Fla.), *cert. denied*, 454 U.S. 1083, 102 S.Ct. 640, 70 L.Ed.2d 618 (1981); *City of Jacksonville v. Schumann*, 167 So. 2d 95 (Fla. 1st DCA 1964), *cert. denied*, 172 So. 2d 597 (Fla. 1965); *Florida Audubon Society v. Ratner*, 497 So. 2d 672 (Fla. 3d DCA 1986). Since there is no settled formula to determine when a valid exercise of the police power stops and an impermissible encroachment of private property rights begins, the determination must be made on a case by case basis.

In *Poe v. State Road Department*, 127 So. 2d 898, 900 (Fla. 1st DCA 1961), a taking was defined as:

> [1] entering upon private property for more than a momentary period and, [2] under the warrant or color of legal authority, [3] devoting it to a public use, or [4] otherwise appropriating or injuriously affecting it in such a way as substantially to oust the owner and deprive him of all beneficial enjoyment thereof.

Examples of conduct which constitute a taking of private property are: negligently permitting clay, sand, and silt to wash from a road embankment onto adjoining land in such quantities as to damage the land permanently and render it useless for any practical purposes; and construction of a highway embankment in a manner that impeded the flow and raised the level of a millrace to such an extent as to destroy the use of a grist mill. *Poe*, 127 So. 2d at 900.

The Fourth District held, in *Kendry v. State Road Department*, 213 So. 2d 23 (Fla. 4th DCA 1968), *cert. denied*, 222 So. 2d 752 (Fla. 1969), pursuant to *State Road Department v. Tharp*, 146 Fla. 745, 1 So. 2d 868 (1941), that to demonstrate a taking it was not necessary to show that all value in the property had been destroyed. In *Kendry* the governmental activity resulted in flooding of appellants' properties. The court found the second amended complaint clearly alleged the flooding rendered the properties useless for all residential purposes, and concluded therefore that the allegations were sufficient to demonstrate a taking. A similar result obtained in *Young v. Palm Beach County*, 443 So. 2d 450 (Fla. 4th DCA 1984). In *Young* the court held that the amended complaint which alleged a steady increase in airplane flights over a 14-year period, with the attendant noise which substantially interfered with the beneficial use and enjoyment of appellant's property, was adequate to state a cause of action for inverse condemnation. The court further found that appellant did not have to allege that the conditions complained of were reasonably expected to continue.

In this case, FDA relies on *Hillsborough County v. Gutierrez*, 433 So. 2d 1337 (Fla. 2d DCA 1983) to support its contention that appellants have not been deprived of all beneficial use of their property. In *Gutierrez*, the court found the flooding which damaged the Gutierrez residence did not constitute a "taking" because there had been no permanent invasion amounting to an appropriation. Instead, the evidence showed the parties were residing in their residence and the damage caused by the flooding had been remedied at their expense. On these facts, the court found the parties' use and enjoyment had been impaired, but they had not been substantially deprived of the beneficial use of their property.

We find the supreme court's opinion in *Village of Tequesta v. Jupiter Inlet Corporation* is instructive with respect to the circumstances of the instant case. In *Tequesta* the court said:

> The right of the owner to ground water underlying his land is to the usufruct of the water and not to the water itself. The ownership of the land does not carry with it any ownership of vested rights to underlying groundwater not actually diverted and applied to beneficial use.

Village of Tequesta, 371 So. 2d at 667. The court distinguished the "taking" of airspace above the land from the "taking" of water located in a ground aquifer, on the premise that the airspace damage worked to deprive the owners of all beneficial use of their property. In *Tequesta*, however, the alleged damage to the shallow water aquifer merely deprived a developer of access to an inexpensive water supply, thus the damage was not compensable through inverse condemnation. The court reasoned:

> It is incumbent upon Jupiter to show, not only a taking, but also that a private property right has been destroyed by governmental action. Jupiter did not have a constitutionally protected right in the water beneath its property. In the cases cited by Jupiter, the courts supported compensation for

> the taking of a use which was existent and of which a party was deprived. Jupiter seeks to be compensated for a use which it had never perfected to the point that it was in existence. Jupiter had a right to use the water, but the use itself is not existent until this right is exercised.

Id., 371 So. 2d at 670.

In the instant case, appellants allege in the second amended complaint that: (1) from 1961 until the summer of 1983, FDA applied EDB in amounts far in excess of the chemical manufacturer's recommended use and in excess of the amount allowed by the Environmental Protection Agency (EPA); (2) in the summer of 1983 the Florida Department of Environmental Regulation (DER) found appellants' water supply was contaminated; (3) the use of EDB was banned in Florida in 1983; (4) for more than ten years prior to 1983, EDB was known to be a highly toxic chemical, a potent mutagen, and a suspected carcinogen; (5) FDA's activities permanently deprived appellants of all reasonable beneficial use and enjoyment of their properties; and (6) the properties are residential, and without a clean water supply they are virtually worthless.

In this case, unlike the position of the developer in *Village of Tequesta*, appellants have been deprived of the *existing* use of the water in their wells and pipes. Appellants had exercised their constitutionally protected right of the existent use of the water in their wells up until 1983 when DER barred further use due to the EDB contamination. Accordingly, we find that appellants' second amended complaint alleges that substantial interference with the beneficial use and enjoyment of their property sufficient to state a cause of action for inverse condemnation.

The second question presented for our review is whether the doctrine of sovereign immunity precludes appellants' suit against FDA predicated on allegations of negligence in the conduct of the nematode eradication program. We note at the outset that enactment of section 768.28, Florida Statutes, "eliminated the immunity which prevented recovery for existing common law torts committed by the government." *Trianon Park Condominium Association, Inc. v. City of Hialeah*, 468 So. 2d 912, 914 (Fla. 1985). However, in *Commercial Carrier Corporation v. Indian River County*, 371 So. 2d 1010 (Fla. 1979), the court held that although section 768.28 evinces legislative intent to waive immunity on a broad basis, that waiver does not encompass "discretionary" governmental functions. The reason for this is the court's perception that "certain functions of coordinate branches of government may not be subjected to scrutiny by judge or jury as to the wisdom of their performance." *Id.*, 1022. To aid in identifying the functions which are not subject to a waiver of immunity, the supreme court adopted an analysis which distinguishes between "planning" and "operational" levels of decision-making by governmental agencies.

The planning level-operational level analysis adopted in *Commercial Carrier*, was utilized by the supreme court in *City of St. Petersburg v. Collom*, 419 So. 2d 1082 (Fla. 1982). In *Collom*, the court reasoned that—

> once a governmental entity creates a *known* dangerous condition which
> may not be readily apparent to one who could be injured by the condition
> and the governmental entity *has knowledge* of the presence of people likely
> to be injured, then the governmental entity must take steps to avert the
> danger or properly warn persons who may be injured by that danger. (cita-
> tion omitted). The failure of government to act in this type of circumstance
> is, in our view, a failure at the operational level.

City of St. Petersburg, 419 So. 2d at 1086. The court deemed it "unreasonable to
presume that a governmental entity, as a matter of policy in making a judgmen-
tal, planning-level decision, would knowingly create a trap or dangerous condition and intentionally fail to warn or protect the users of that improvement from
the risk." Therefore, it was considered "logical and reasonable to treat the failure
to warn or correct a known danger created by government as negligence at the
operational level." *Id. Accord Avallone v. Board of County Commissioners of Citrus
County*, 493 So. 2d 1002 (Fla. 1986); *Ralph v. City of Daytona Beach*, 471 So. 2d 1, 2
(Fla. 1983).

In *City of Daytona Beach v. Palmer*, 469 So. 2d 121 (Fla. 1985), the decisions of
firefighters regarding *how* to fight a fire were construed as "discretionary judgmen-
tal decisions which are inherent in this public safety function of fire protection." *Id.*,
123. However, the court went on to distinguish firefighting decisions —

> from *negligent conduct* resulting in personal injury while fire equipment is
> being driven to the scene of a fire or personal injury to a spectator from the
> negligent handling of equipment at the scene. Governmental entities are
> clearly liable for this type of conduct as a result of the enactment of section
> 768.28, Florida Statutes (1983).

Id. See also Hardie v. City of Gainesville, 482 So. 2d 394, 397 (Fla. 1st DCA 1985),
rev. denied, 488 So. 2d 67 (Fla. 1986), where this court held that maintenance and
operation of electrical service "involves operational activities for which there is no
sovereign immunity."

We have considered the analysis set forth in *Commercial Carrier* and *Trianon
Park* in the context of its pertinence to the nematode eradication program which is
the subject of the complaint in this case, and we recognize the inherent difficulty in
applying the suggested criteria. However, our examination of this record in light of
the criteria provided by the supreme court has led us to conclude that actual implementation of the program was a service designed, albeit indirectly, for the welfare
of the citizens of the state. Furthermore, excessive application of EDB is the type of
negligent conduct deemed operational in *City of Daytona Beach v. Palmer*. Thus, in
the final analysis, the FDA nematode eradication program weighs more heavily on
the side of an operational than a planning level governmental function.

The allegations of the complaint are consistent with a construction of the program as an operational level function. Accordingly, we find the complaint alleges
facts which indicate that sovereign immunity would not bar the suit.

As their final point, appellants urge us to find that the section 768.28 limited waiver of sovereign immunity does not encompass suits based on a theory of strict liability. The argument is an intriguing one, however, as FDA correctly argues, Florida's Tort Claims Act has adopted much of the language of the Federal Tort Claims Act, and in construing the extent of the waiver intended by the act, Florida courts have consulted federal decisions. *See Commercial Carrier Corporation v. Indian River County*, supra; *Hollis v. School Board of Leon County*, 384 So. 2d 661 (Fla. 1st DCA 1980).

The United States Supreme Court has held unequivocally that the Federal Tort Claims Act does not contemplate the imposition of strict liability of any kind upon the government. *Dalehite v. United States*, 346 U.S. 15, 73 S.Ct. 956, 97 L.Ed. 1427 (1953); *Laird v. Nelms*, 406 U.S. 797, 92 S.Ct. 1899, 32 L.Ed.2d 499, *reh. denied*, 409 U.S. 902, 93 S.Ct. 95, 34 L.Ed.2d 165 (1972). The Act expressly provides that sovereign immunity is waived only to the extent specified in the act, that is, liability will attach to the government in the same manner and to the same extent as to a private individual under like circumstances. Section 768.28, Fla. Stat. (1985); 28 Fla.Jur.2d, *Government Tort Liability*, sec. 11. Thus, the removal of sovereign immunity in tort actions does not impose strict liability in its place. 57 Am.Jur. 2d, *Municipal, School, and State Tort Liability*, sec. 54.

In summary, we find the allegations of the second amended complaint state a cause of action for inverse condemnation and establish operational level activities with respect to the nematode eradication program. Therefore, we reverse the final order with respect to these issues. We affirm the final order with respect to dismissal with prejudice of the claim founded on a theory of strict liability.

Accordingly, the order appealed is affirmed in part, reversed in part, and this cause is remanded with directions to allow appellants to proceed with their claim for compensation for inverse condemnation and with their tort claim against the state in regard to the conduct of the nematode eradication program. . . .

———————

Notes and Questions to Consider:

1. States may interpret their state constitutions to restrict the government from *damaging* a citizen's land or land rights. Does the state of Florida interpret its state constitution in this way?

2. Similarly, state constitutions may forbid the government from damaging land without paying the landowner just compensation. Does the Constitution of the State of Florida require payment in such a circumstance?

3. Under Florida Supreme Court precedent as interpreted by the Florida District Courts of Appeal, is the "right to use" land or its appurtenances the type of "private property" as contemplated by Article X, Section 6, of Florida's constitution as requiring full compensation before it is taken by the government for a public purpose?

4. The "Bert J. Harris, Jr. Private Property Rights Protection Act," or the "Harris Act" as it is sometimes called, is codified in chapter 70 of the Florida Statutes. It states:

> The Legislature recognizes that some laws, regulations, and ordinances of the state and political entities in the state, as applied, may inordinately burden, restrict, or limit private property rights without amounting to a taking under the State Constitution or the United States Constitution. The Legislature determines that there is an important state interest in protecting the interests of private property owners from such inordinate burdens. Therefore, it is the intent of the Legislature that, as a separate and distinct cause of action from the law of takings, the Legislature herein provides for relief, or payment of compensation, when a new law, rule, regulation, or ordinance of the state or a political entity in the state, as applied, unfairly affects real property.

§ 70.001(1), Fla. Stat. Why, in your opinion, would Florida's legislature deem such a law to be necessary?

Index

VICTIM RIGHTS, 596

VOTER INITIATIVES, 250–52

VOTING, 255–56, 292–94, 477–87

W

WATER, 277

WATER CONTROL DISTRICT, 531

WORK, right to, 124

WRITS
Generally, 353–91
all writ power, 370–72
certiorari, 373–80
constitutional writ, 370–72
habeas corpus, 384–91
mandamus, 355–57
prohibition, 358–62
quo warranto, 362–69

Z

ZONING LAWS, 317–20